CAMBRIDGE
UNIVERSITY PRESS

Cambridge IGCSE™
International
Mathematics

COURSEBOOK

Peter Blythe, Emma Low, Andrew Manning,
Karen Morrison, Raju Taniparti & Jasmine S. M. Teo

CAMBRIDGE
UNIVERSITY PRESS

Shaftesbury Road, Cambridge CB2 8EA, United Kingdom

One Liberty Plaza, 20th Floor, New York, NY 10006, USA

477 Williamstown Road, Port Melbourne, VIC 3207, Australia

314–321, 3rd Floor, Plot 3, Splendor Forum, Jasola District Centre, New Delhi – 110025, India

103 Penang Road, #05–06/07, Visioncrest Commercial, Singapore 238467

Cambridge University Press is part of the University of Cambridge.

It furthers the University's mission by disseminating knowledge in the pursuit of education, learning and research at the highest international levels of excellence.

www.cambridge.org
Information on this title: www.cambridge.org/9781009377676

© Cambridge University Press & Assessment 2023

First published 2023

20 19 18 17 16 15 14 13 12 11 10 9 8 7 6 5 4 3 2 1

Printed in Dubai by Oriental Press

A catalogue record for this publication is available from the British Library

ISBN 978-1-009-37767-6 Paperback with Digital Access (2 Year Access)

ISBN 978-1-009-29595-6 Coursebook eBook

ISBN 978-1-009-29598-7 Cambridge IGCSE™ International Mathematics Cambridge Online Mathematics Course

Additional resources for this publication at www.cambridge.org/go

....

2023 CAMBRIDGE DEDICATED TEACHER AWARDS

Teachers play an important part in shaping futures.
Our Dedicated Teacher Awards recognise the hard work that teachers put in every day.

ank you to everyone who nominated this year; we have been inspired and moved by all of your stories. Well done to all of our nominees for your dedication to learning and for inspiring the next generation of thinkers, leaders and innovators.

CONGRATULATIONS TO OUR INCREDIBLE WINNERS!

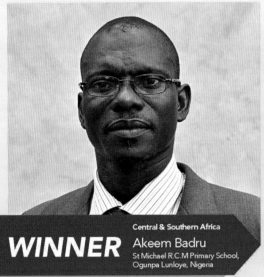

WINNER
Central & Southern Africa
Akeem Badru
St Michael R.C.M Primary School, Ogunpa Lunloye, Nigeria

Regional Winner: East & South Asia
Gaurav Sharma
FirstSteps School, India

Regional Winner: North & South America
Nathalie Roy
Glasgow Middle School, United States

Regional Winner: Australia, New Zealand & South-East Asia
Goh Kok Ming
SJKC Hua Lian 1, Malaysia

Regional Winner: Middle East & North Africa
Uzma Siraj
Future World School, Pakistan

Regional Winner: Europe
Selçuk Yusuf Arslan
Ataturk MTAL, Turkey

or more information about our dedicated teachers and their stories, go to **dedicatedteacher.cambridge.org**

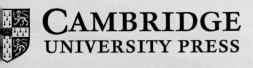

CAMBRIDGE
UNIVERSITY PRESS

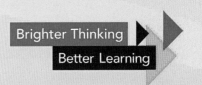

Brighter Thinking
Better Learning

Endorsement statement

Endorsement indicates that a resource has passed Cambridge International's rigorous quality-assurance process and is suitable to support the delivery of a Cambridge International syllabus. However, endorsed resources are not the only suitable materials available to support teaching and learning, and are not essential to be used to achieve the qualification. Resource lists found on the Cambridge International website will include this resource and other endorsed resources.

Any example answers to questions taken from past question papers, practice questions, accompanying marks and mark schemes included in this resource have been written by the authors and are for guidance only. They do not replicate examination papers. In examinations the way marks are awarded may be different. Any references to assessment and/or assessment preparation are the publisher's interpretation of the syllabus requirements. Examiners will not use endorsed resources as a source of material for any assessment set by Cambridge International.

While the publishers have made every attempt to ensure that advice on the qualification and its assessment is accurate, the official syllabus, specimen assessment materials and any associated assessment guidance materials produced by the awarding body are the only authoritative source of information and should always be referred to for definitive guidance. Cambridge International recommends that teachers consider using a range of teaching and learning resources based on their own professional judgement of their students' needs.

Cambridge International has not paid for the production of this resource, nor does Cambridge International receive any royalties from its sale. For more information about the endorsement process, please visit www.cambridgeinternational.org/endorsed-resources

Cambridge International copyright material in this publication is reproduced under licence and remains the intellectual property of Cambridge Assessment International Education.

Third-party websites and resources referred to in this publication have not been endorsed by Cambridge Assessment International Education.

❯ Contents

Introduction   viii
How to use this series   ix
How to use this book   x
Using a graphic display calculator   xii
Carrying out mathematical
investigations   xiv

1 Number   1
1.1   Types of number   2
1.2   Other types of number   9
1.3   Products of prime factors   14
1.4   Highest common factors (HCF) and
      lowest common multiples (LCM)   17
1.5   Square roots and cube roots   20
1.6   Estimating and rounding   24
1.7   Accuracy and estimating   29
Past paper questions   35

2 Operations with numbers   37
2.1   Working with decimals   38
2.2   Equivalent fractions   43
2.3   Calculating with fractions   46
2.4   Fractions, decimals and percentages   49
2.5   Using negative numbers   52
2.6   The order of operations   55
Past paper questions   58

3 Using number   59
3.1   Using ratio   60
3.2   Time and rates   63
3.3   Percentages   69
3.4   Percentage change   72
3.5   Further applications of percentages   75
3.6   Interest   77
3.7   Exponential growth and decay   80
Past paper questions   83

4 Angles and bearings   85
4.1   Introduction to geometry   86
4.2   Angle properties   92
4.3   Lines   94
4.4   Bearings   99
Past paper questions   107

**5 Triangles, quadrilaterals and
   polygons   109**
5.1   Properties of triangles   110
5.2   Properties of quadrilaterals   116
5.3   Polygons   120
Past paper questions   128

6 Indices, standard form and surds   130
6.1   Indices I   131
6.2   Fractional indices   136
6.3   Standard form   138
6.4   Calculations with standard form
      without a calculator   143
6.5   Simplifying surds   145
6.6   Adding and subtracting with surds   147
6.7   Multiplying and dividing with surds   150
6.8   Rationalising the denominator   153
Past paper questions   155

7 Introduction to algebra   156
7.1   Forming algebraic expressions   157
7.2   Substituting in algebraic expressions
      and formulas   160
7.3   Collecting like terms   163
7.4   Expanding single brackets and
      expanding two brackets with one
      variable   164
7.5   Expanding two or more brackets   167
7.6   Factorising   170
7.7   Factorising quadratic expressions   175

7.8	Algebraic fractions	180
7.9	Solving linear equations with one variable	184
7.10	Constructing linear equations	186
7.11	Solving quadratic equations by factorisation	188
7.12	Solving fractional equations	189
7.13	Indices II	192
Past paper questions		197

8 Simultaneous linear equations — **198**

8.1	Changing the subject of a formula	199
8.2	Solving simultaneous linear equations	201
8.3	Representing linear inequalities on a number line	206
8.4	Representing linear inequalities graphically	207
8.5	Proportion	212
Past paper questions		216

9 Symmetry, congruency and similarity — **218**

9.1	Line and rotational symmetry	219
9.2	Congruency	228
9.3	Similarity	231
9.4	Area and volume of similar shapes	238
Past paper questions		246

10 Pythagoras' theorem — **248**

10.1	Pythagoras' theorem in two dimensions	249
10.2	Applications of Pythagoras' theorem	254
10.3	Pythagoras' theorem in three dimensions	259
Past paper questions		262

11 Coordinate geometry — **264**

11.1	The coordinate system	265
11.2	Calculating the distance between two points	268
11.3	Angles and directions, slopes and gradients	271
11.4	Straight lines	275
11.5	Parallel and non-parallel lines	285
Past paper questions		292

12 Mensuration — **294**

12.1	Units of measure	295
12.2	Area and perimeter of rectangles and triangles	298
12.3	Area and perimeter of parallelograms and trapeziums	302
12.4	Circles	305
12.5	Areas and perimeters of compound shapes	313
12.6	Volume and surface area of prisms and cylinders	315
12.7	Volume and surface area of pyramids and cones	324
12.8	Surface area and volume of spheres	334
12.9	Surface area and volume of compound shapes	337
Past paper questions		339

13 Quadratic equations — **341**

13.1	Graphs of quadratic equations	342
13.2	Solving quadratic equations by using a formula	345
13.3	Maximum and minimum values of quadratic equations	346
13.4	Solving equations involving quadratic expressions on a GDC	347
Past paper questions		353

14 Functions 1 — **355**

14.1	Using function notation	356
14.2	Tables and mapping diagrams	358
14.3	Graphs	361
14.4	Graphical display calculators and recognising function types by the shape of their graph	363
14.5	The domain and the range	370
14.6	Inverse functions	371
14.7	Composite functions	373
Past paper questions		375

15 Trigonometry — 377

15.1 The trigonometric ratios — 378
15.2 Solving problems using the trigonometric ratios and Pythagoras' theorem — 386
15.3 Angles of elevation and depression — 389
15.4 Solving problems in three dimensions — 393
15.5 The sine, cosine and tangent ratios as functions — 395
15.6 Area of a triangle — 406
15.7 The sine and cosine rules — 410
Past paper questions — 419

16 Circle properties — 421

16.1 Basic definitions — 422
16.2 Length of a chord — 425
16.3 Angle properties of circles — 436
16.4 More angle properties of circles — 438
16.5 Cyclic quadrilaterals — 445
16.6 Alternate segment theorem — 450
Past paper questions — 453

17 Vectors and transformations — 460

17.1 Transformations — 462
17.2 Further transformations — 486
17.3 Vectors — 490
Past paper questions — 502

18 Sets — 504

18.1 Introduction to sets — 505
18.2 Using diagrams to represent sets — 511
18.3 Venn diagrams involving two sets — 516
18.4 Three sets on a Venn diagram — 523
Past paper questions — 531

19 Descriptive statistics — 533

19.1 Classifying and tabulating data — 535
19.2 Averages, the range and quartiles — 537
19.3 Quartiles, interquartile range and using a graphical display calculator — 539
19.4 Graphs, charts and diagrams — 546
Past paper questions — 556

20 Cumulative frequency diagrams and linear regression — 558

20.1 Draw and interpret scatter diagrams — 559
20.2 Correlation and line of best fit — 562
20.3 Cumulative frequency tables and diagrams — 571
Past paper questions — 576

21 Probability — 579

21.1 Introduction to probability — 580
21.2 Relative and expected frequencies — 587
21.3 Combining probabilities — 589
Past paper questions — 609

22 Sequences — 611

22.1 Patterns and number sequences — 613
22.2 Finding a general rule — 618
22.3 More about quadratic and cubic sequences — 622
22.4 Exponential sequences and combined sequences — 625
Past paper questions — 629

23 Functions 2 — 630

23.1 Recognising and exploring graphs of functions — 631
23.2 Quadratic functions — 637
23.3 Asymptotes — 639
23.4 Logarithmic functions — 641
23.5 Transforming graphs of functions — 645
Past paper questions — 650

24 Modelling — 651

24.1 What is mathematical modelling? — 653
24.2 Modelling with sequences and patterns — 657
24.3 Modelling with diagrams — 660
24.4 Modelling with functions and graphs — 663
Past paper questions — 668

Glossary — 670

Index — 675

Acknowledgements — 680

> Introduction

This coursebook is specially written to support the Cambridge IGCSE™ International Mathematics syllabus (0607) for examination from 2025.

As the future of education shifts to a more learner-centred approach and 'Making Thinking Visible', we have incorporated investigations, self-reflections, self or peer assessment and discussion in each chapter. These features can be student-led or facilitated by teachers. Either way, there are many opportunities for you to engage in your learning, to analyse and think critically. Some discussions also encourage you to research beyond the syllabus such as Discussion 2 on the different types of prime numbers in Chapter 1. The investigations in each chapter aim to train you to look for patterns and structures in Mathematics through the topics you learn.

One specific requirement of the Cambridge IGCSE™ International Mathematics syllabus (0607) is the use of the graphic display calculator. This book makes provision for you to pick up graphic display calculator skills to enhance your readiness for the course.

The recent happenings around the world have taught us not to take face-to-face learning for granted. The worked examples come with detailed explanations and tips to facilitate self-learning where necessary.

As usual, you can expect exercises for you to practice solving problems at the end of each sub-topic in the chapters. Examples of past paper questions have also been added at the end of each chapter to help you prepare for the assessment of the syllabus.

We hope you will enjoy learning with this book and that you will find the materials interesting and valuable as you journey through the syllabus.

> How to use this series

This suite of resources supports students and teachers following the Cambridge IGCSE™ International Mathematics syllabus (0607) for examination from 2025. Up-to-date metacognition techniques have been incorporated throughout the resources.. The course is structured in such a way that the subject is taught to students so that they develop a holistic understanding of the subject. The components in the series are designed to work together.

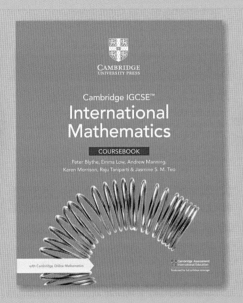

The coursebook is designed for students to use in class with guidance from the teacher. There are 24 chapters. A modelling chapter has been included to support the updated syllabus. There are a series of investigations throughout the chapters. These help to develop problem-solving skills and to meet syllabus requirements. A variety of metacognition techniques have been used such as discussion activities and reflection features to encourage students to deepen their mathematical approach. Mathematics in context has been introduced to help students understand the real use cases of mathematics in everyday life. The Mathematical connections feature links topics in the coursebook to create holistic view of mathematics for learners. Access to Cambridge Online Mathematics is provided to access the coursebook digitally. A teacher account can be set up and online classes can be created.

The digital Teacher's Resource is succinct and offers lesson ideas such as starters, main activities and plenaries for teachers. How to identify and address common misconceptions is provided as well as language support to ensure that teachers and learners are well-supported in the classroom. Differentiation ideas are also provided from helping learners who need more support to challenging students. The Teacher's Resource is in line with the coursebook and covers the same topics. Answers for the Teacher's Resource and coursebook are provided on the Cambridge GO platform.

> How to use this book

Throughout this book, you will notice lots of different features that will help your learning. These are explained below.

IN THIS CHAPTER YOU WILL

These set the scene for each chapter, help with navigation through the coursebook and indicate the important concepts in each topic.

Extended content

Where content is intended for students who are studying the Extended subject content of the syllabus as well as the Core, this is indicated using the arrow and the bar, as on the left here.

GETTING STARTED

This contains questions and activities on subject knowledge you will need before starting this chapter.

KEY WORDS

The key vocabulary appears in a box at the start of each chapter, and is highlighted in the text when it is first introduced. You will also find definitions of these words in the Glossary at the back of this book.

TIP

The information in this feature will help you complete the exercises, and give you support in areas that you might find difficult.

Exercises

Appearing throughout the text, exercises give you a chance to check that you have understood the topic you have just read about and practice the mathematical skills you have learnt. You can find the answers to these questions in the digital version of the Coursebook on Cambridge GO.

INVESTIGATION/DISCUSSION

These boxes contain questions and activities that will allow you to extend your learning by investigating a problem, or by discussing it with classmates.

WORKED EXAMPLES

These boxes show you the step-by-step process to work through an example question or problem, giving you the skills to work through questions yourself.

MATHEMATICS IN CONTEXT

This feature presents real-world examples and applications of the content in a chapter, encouraging you to look further into topics.

REFLECTION

These activities ask you to think about the approach that you take to your work, and how you might improve this in the future.

 This icon shows you where you should complete a question in an exercise or a whole exercise without using your calculator.

Past paper questions

Past paper questions allow you to practice your exam skills. Answers are available on Cambridge GO.

MATHEMATICAL CONNECTIONS

This feature will help you to link content in the chapter to what you have already learnt, and highlights where you will use your understanding again in the course.

SUMMARY

There is a summary of key points at the end of each chapter.

Are you able to... ?
recognise function types from the shape of their graphs
describe the range and domain of a function

SELF/PEER ASSESSMENT

At the end of some exercises you will find opportunities to help you assess your own work, or that of your classmates, and consider how you can improve the way you learn.

> Using a graphic display calculator

A graphic display calculator (GDC) is a type of calculator that allows you to plot graphs, produce tables of values and perform complex operations. As part of your course, you will need to be able to use a graphic display calculator to carry out particular tasks.

Getting to know your graphic display calculator

There are many different models of graphic display calculator. You do not have to use a specific model, but it must have certain features.

Get to know your own calculator. As well as the manual that comes with your calculator, you can also find lots of instruction videos on the internet that will show you how to use it.

> **TIP**
>
> Practice using your graphic display calculator throughout the course, not just as part of your exam preparation!

> **TIP**
>
> There are specific requirements for the calculator that you are allowed to use in the assessment. Ask your teacher for more information about these to ensure that you have the correct calculator.

Display

Navigation keys – these allow you to move around the display screen.

Basic calculator keys – you will be familiar with these keys from using a basic calculator.

Menu/Mode – usually provides a list of modes to select from. Each mode allows you to carry out different operations. For example, the graph mode allows you to draw graphs of functions. Most calculations should be made when the calculator is set to degrees (indicated at the top of the screen by 'Deg'). Trigonometric graphs where axes scales are in terms of pi should be drawn with the calculator in Radians mode (indicated at the top of the screen by 'Rad'). To change Degree mode to Radians mode press <SHIFT> and then <MENU> and scroll down to 'Angle'. Degrees is selected by pressing F1 and Radians is selected by pressing F2.

Image of CASIO fx-CG50 calculator model

Selecting functions

Many of the calculator keys are used for more than one function, so you need to press a second key in order to select which of the functions you want. This second key is usually colour-coded to match the colour of the function that it selects. For example:

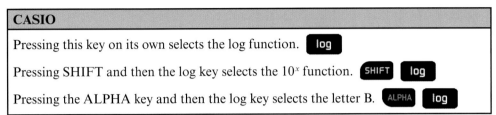

CASIO
Pressing this key on its own selects the log function.
Pressing SHIFT and then the log key selects the 10^x function.
Pressing the ALPHA key and then the log key selects the letter B.

Storing answers in memory

Graphic display calculators allow you to store the results of calculations to use in subsequent calculations. This minimises errors due to the rounding of answers during multi-step calculations. Use your calculator manual or look online to find out how to store answers in your calculator.

MATHEMATICAL CONNECTIONS

You will find instructions for carrying out specific tasks in the related chapters:

- sketch a graph – see Chapters 11, 13 and 14

- find zeros and local maxima or minima of function – see Chapter 13

- find the intersection point of two graphs – see Chapter 13

- produce a table of values for a function – see Chapter 14

- find mean, median, quartiles – see Chapter 19

- find the linear regression equation – see Chapter 20.

> Carrying out mathematical investigations

The Cambridge IGCSE™ International Mathematics syllabus (0607) includes two very interesting aspects: Investigation and Modelling. Students are presented with open-ended problems to use their newly acquired skills to investigate and solve them.

This is not a simple task – it requires skills and techniques that you must acquire during the course. Most of all, it needs you to have an open mind and to be curious about and interested in mathematics.

If you approach your learning in the right way, this is the most exciting aspect of the course.

Why investigate?

Mathematics is continually expanding as a subject; more mathematics is being discovered now than at any time in the past. (Try searching on the internet for how many new mathematics theorems are discovered each year.) The important word is 'discovered' – people who use mathematics are not simply 'told' results as you may have been and if you want to succeed in the 21st century you have to be able to think for yourself. Investigations help you develop an independent and confident way of thinking that transcends the subject.

Think about Pythagoras' theorem: perhaps you were simply told to learn the formula $a^2 + b^2 = c^2$.

But consider:

1   **When** can you use this formula?

2   **What happens** if the triangle is not right-angled? Can this formula be amended and extended to other triangles? Or to quadrilaterals? In three dimensions?

3   **How** was this formula discovered in the first place?

> **TIP**
>
> This is the nature of an investigation – asking questions and then formulating a plan.

Techniques needed in investigations

There is no definitive list of techniques that applies to all situations, however having **sound algebraic skills** is an important part of your toolkit since in many cases the end result is to discover an over-arching formula that can be applied in many situations.

Similarly, **being systematic** is vital in simplifying complex problems. For example, if you are asked to find a formula for the number of diagonals of any convex polygon it makes no sense to start with a hexagon, for example, then move to an octagon and then a square. **Start with the simplest case** (triangle) and **proceed step by step** (quadrilateral, then pentagon, and so on).

Be organised in your work – **tabulate** your systematic results (and look at it in detail, you might spot something).

Polygon	Triangle	Quadrilateral	Pentagon	Hexagon	Heptagon	Octagon
Diagonals	0	2	5	?	??	???

Look for **common factors**. (There are none in this case – but do remember to look!)

Look to **factorise the tabulated values**. (Again, there is nothing in this example, but it is helpful to check.)

In *growth* situations like this one try dividing by n. Use **improper fractions**.

Polygon	Triangle	Quadrilateral	Pentagon	Hexagon	Heptagon	Octagon
Sides (n)	3	4	5	6	7	8
Diagonals	0	2	5	9	14	20
$\dfrac{\text{Diagonals}}{n}$	0	$\dfrac{1}{2}$	1	$\dfrac{3}{2}$	2	$\dfrac{5}{2}$

Then **multiply to remove fractions**. (In this example, it means multiplying by 2.)

Sides (n)	3	4	5	6	7	8
$\dfrac{\text{Diagonals}}{n}$	0	$\dfrac{1}{2}$	1	$\dfrac{3}{2}$	2	$\dfrac{5}{2}$
$\dfrac{\text{Diagonals}}{n} \times 2$	0	1	2	3	4	5

Eventually, you simply have to **spot a pattern**. Perhaps **rewriting the table vertically** will help.

$$3 \rightarrow 0$$
$$4 \rightarrow 1$$
$$5 \rightarrow 2$$
$$6 \rightarrow 3$$
$$7 \rightarrow 4$$
$$8 \rightarrow 5$$

You should now be able to determine the formula for red numbers → blue numbers

The above mapping for $\dfrac{\text{Diagonals}}{n} \times 2$ can be represented by the mapping $n \rightarrow n - 3$

So that $\dfrac{\text{Diagonals}}{n} \times 2 = n - 3$

Now your **algebraic techniques** are needed. Rearranging a formula here.

$\times 2$ is reversed by dividing by 2 $\quad \dfrac{\text{Diagonals}}{n} = \dfrac{n-3}{2}$

$\div n$ is reversed by multiplying by n $\quad \text{Diagonals} = \dfrac{n(n-3)}{2}$

Further ideas

Using **your graphic display calculator** (or **graphing software** in day-to-day use) is an important tool in investigations. It gives a picture of a situation. Learn how to use **'sliders'** as these can be used to animate a still picture (graph) to enhance insight.

Draw diagrams where these are appropriate (diagrams could have been used in the polygon example to obtain the numerical results). Make these large and clear.

In the polygon example, a clear diagram explains **why** the formula for the number of diagonals is as it is. Looking at **one vertex** of the heptagon ($n = 7$) you can see that there are four diagonals. Moving to the next vertex there are again four diagonals and so on for all seven vertices.

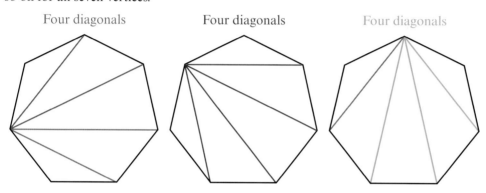

Four diagonals   Four diagonals   Four diagonals

But look at the diagram on the right – one of the four diagonals has already been counted.

If you continue drawing the diagrams, you will see that eventually **all of the diagonals are counted twice** – because each diagonal has two endpoints.

So, n vertices; each vertex forms $n - 3$ diagonals: hence $n(n - 3)$

But each diagonal has two endpoints and so has been counted twice: hence $\dfrac{n(n - 3)}{2}$

You have gathered all this information from a diagram!

Chapter 1
Number

IN THIS CHAPTER YOU WILL:

- convert between numbers and words

- identify natural numbers, integers, prime numbers, square numbers, cube numbers, triangle numbers, prime factors and rational and irrational numbers

- find the reciprocal of a number

- find the lowest common multiple (LCM) and highest common factor (HCF) of two numbers

- calculate with squares, square roots, cubes and cube roots of numbers and with other powers and roots of numbers

- round values to specific numbers of decimal places or significant figures

- estimate calculations by rounding numbers to significant figures.

GETTING STARTED

1   Write down the whole numbers:
   a   between 10 and 20
   b   greater than 25 but less than or equal to 30.

2   In the list of numbers:

$$25, \quad \frac{1}{2}, \quad 0.125$$

   write down a:
   a   decimal   b   fraction   c   whole number.

3   List the factors of:
   a   12   b   30   c   42

4   Write down the first five multiples of:
   a   3   b   5   c   11

KEY WORDS

cube number

highest common factor (HCF)

integer

irrational number

lowest common multiple (LCM)

natural numbers

prime number

reciprocal

root

square number

triangle or triangular number

1.1 Types of number

Being able to identify different types of number will help you to understand how number operations work and to evaluate problems involving numbers.

Natural numbers

The **natural numbers** are: 0, 1, 2, 3, 4, 5, 6, …

Natural numbers have no decimal or fractional parts.

Converting between numbers and words

Natural numbers have different place values. These place values allow you to convert natural numbers into words.

This table summarises the place values for the number 1 234 567 890.

TIP

Some books define the natural numbers starting from 1, but in this course the natural numbers start from zero.

Digit	Place value
1 234 567 8**90**	ones
1 234 567 8**9**0	tens
1 234 567 **8**90	hundreds
1 234 **567** 890	thousands
1 234 **5**67 890	ten thousands
1 234 **5**67 890	hundred thousands
1 2**34** 567 890	millions
1 2**3**4 567 890	ten millions
1 **2**34 567 890	hundred millions
1 234 567 890	billions

You write 1 234 567 890 in words as one billion, two hundred and thirty-four million, five hundred and sixty-seven thousand, eight hundred and ninety.

WORKED EXAMPLE 1

1 Write the following numbers in words.

    a 20 316

    b 7 000 000 009

2 Write the following in numbers.

    a One hundred and twenty-four thousand

    b Fifteen million and seventy-eight

Answers

1 **a** First look at the place value of each digit in the number 20 316.

Digit	Place value
20 3**16**	six ones
20 3**1**6	one ten
20 **3**16	three hundreds
2**0** 316	zero thousands
20 316	twenty thousands

Starting from the highest place value, you have twenty thousand, three hundred and sixteen.

    b In the number 7 000 000 009, only the digits 7 and 9 are non-zero.

Digit	Place value
7 000 000 00**9**	nine ones
7 000 000 009	seven billions

Starting from the highest place value, you have seven billion and nine.

2 **a** Consider the place value of the numbers in words.

Words	Numbers	Remarks
One hundred and twenty-four **thousand**	100 000	A thousand is 3 zeros, so a hundred thousand is 100 with 3 zeros.
One hundred and **twenty-four thousand**	24 000	Twenty-four thousand is 24 with 3 zeros.

Add up the numbers: 100 000 + 24 000 = 124 000

So, one hundred and twenty-four thousand in numbers is 124 000.

TIP

When expressing a number in words, omit any place value with a zero digit.

CONTINUED

b Consider the place value of the numbers in words.

Words	Numbers	Remarks
Fifteen million and seventy-eight	15 000 000	A million has 6 zeros, so fifteen million is 15 with 6 zeros.
Fifteen million and **seventy-eight**	78	

Add up the numbers: 15 000 000 + 78 = 15 000 078

So fifteen million and seventy-eight in numbers is 15 000 078.

Categorising natural numbers

There are many different ways to categorise natural numbers. For example, natural numbers can be even or odd.

Even numbers are divisible by two.

The even numbers are: 0, 2, 4, 6, 8, 10, …

In general, the last digit of an even number is a multiple of 2.

Numbers that are not even are odd numbers.

The odd numbers are: 1, 3, 5, 7, 9, 11, …

Odd numbers are **not** divisible by two.

In general, the last digit of an odd number is 1, 3, 5, 7, or 9.

DISCUSSION 1

1 Work with a partner to determine if the following statements are true or false.

a The sum of two even numbers is always even.

b The sum of two odd numbers is always odd.

c The sum of an even and an odd number is always odd.

d The product of two even numbers is always even.

e The product of two odd numbers is always odd.

f The product of an even and an odd number is always even.

CONTINUED

You can also classify natural numbers using their factors.

2   Copy and complete this table. Write down all the factors of the given numbers. The factors of 12 have been written for you.

Number	Factors	Working
1		
2		
3		
4		
5		
6		
7		
8		
9		
10		
11		
12	1, 2, 3, 4, 6, 12	$12 = 1 \times 12$ $= 2 \times 6$ $= 3 \times 4$
13		
14		

3   Copy and complete this table. Sort the numbers from the table in question 2 into the following groups:

Group	Number of different factors	Numbers
I	Number(s) with exactly one factor	
II	Number(s) with exactly two different factors	

The numbers in group II are known as prime numbers.

Zero and one are not prime numbers.

REFLECTION

Why are zero and one not prime numbers?

Prime numbers

A **prime number** is a natural number that has exactly two different factors, one and itself.

INVESTIGATION 1

Sieve of Eratosthenes

The Sieve of Eratosthenes is a method to find prime numbers.

In this investigation, you will use the Sieve of Eratosthenes to find all the prime numbers from 2 to 100.

	2	3	4	5	6	7	8	9	10
11	12	13	14	15	16	17	18	19	20
21	22	23	24	25	26	27	28	29	30
31	32	33	34	35	36	37	38	39	40
41	42	43	44	45	46	47	48	49	50
51	52	53	54	55	56	57	58	59	60
61	62	63	64	65	66	67	68	69	70
71	72	73	74	75	76	77	78	79	80
81	82	83	84	85	86	87	88	89	90
91	92	93	94	95	96	97	98	99	100

Start from 2 because 2 is the smallest prime number.

Follow the given instructions.

Step 1: circle 2, the smallest prime number, and cross out all the multiples of 2 less than or equal to 100.

Step 2: circle the next smallest number that is not crossed out, in this case 3. Cross out all the multiples of 3 less than or equal to 100.

Step 3: circle the next smallest number that is not crossed out, in this case 5. Cross out all the multiples of 5 less than or equal to 100.

Step 4: circle the next smallest number that is not crossed out and cross out all multiples of that number less than or equal to 100.

Step 5: repeat the same process until all the numbers are either crossed out or circled.

Answer the following.

1   Write down all the numbers you circled. These numbers are prime numbers less than 100.

2   How many prime numbers less than 100 are there?

3   How many **even** prime numbers less than 100 are there?

4   How many **odd** prime numbers less than 100 are there?

You can use the same process to find prime numbers less than any number.

A number is prime if it is not divisible by any of the prime numbers less than or equal to the square *root* of the number.

You can use this result to determine whether a given number is a prime number.

WORKED EXAMPLE 2

Determine whether the following numbers are prime numbers.

a   291   **b**   269

Answers

a   **Step 1:** use a calculator to find the square root of 291: $\sqrt{291} = 17.05872\ldots$

Step 2: identify all the prime numbers less than or equal to the square root of 291.

The prime numbers less than or equal to $17.05872\ldots$ are:
2, 3, 5, 7, 11, 13, 17.

Step 3: try dividing 291 by these prime numbers. If 291 is not divisible by any of the prime numbers identified in step 2, then it is a prime number.

Consider 2: Since 291 is not even, it is not divisible by 2.

Try 3: $291 \div 3 = 97$, so 291 is divisible by 3.

Since 291 is divisible by 3, it is not a prime number.

b $\sqrt{269} = 16.40121\ldots$

The prime numbers less than or equal to $\sqrt{269} = 16.40121\ldots$ are:
2, 3, 5, 7, 11, 13.

Consider 2: 269 is odd, so it is not divisible by 2.	Only even numbers are divisible by 2.
Try 3: $269 \div 3 = 89.6666\ldots$, so 269 is not divisible by 3.	A number is divisible by 3 if the sum of the digits of the number is divisible by 3. The digits of 269 are 2, 6 and 9. $2 + 6 + 9 = 17$, which is not divisible by 3, so 269 is not divisible by 3.
Try 5: The last digit of 269 is 9, which is neither 0 nor 5, so 269 is not divisible by 5.	Only numbers with a last digit of 0 or 5 are divisible by 5.
Try 7: $269 \div 7 = 38.42857\ldots$, so 269 is not divisible by 7.	A number is divisible by 7 if twice the last digit of the number subtracted from the remaining number is divisible by 7. The last digit of 269 is 9. $9 \times 2 = 18$. The remaining number is 26. $26 - 18 = 8$. Since 8 is not divisible by 7, 269 is also not divisible by 7.

CONTINUED

Try 11: $269 \div 11 = 24.454\,5\ldots$, so 269 is not divisible by 11.	A number is divisible by 11 if the alternating sum of the digits (alternate sum and difference) is divisible by 11. For 269, the alternating sum is $2 - 6 + 9 = 5$. Since 5 is not divisible by 11, 269 is not divisible by 11.
Try 13: $269 \div 13 = 20.692\,3\ldots$, so 269 is not divisible by 13.	A number is divisible by 13 if the difference between four times the last digit of the number and the remaining number is divisible by 13. The last digit of 269 is 9. $9 \times 4 = 36$. The remaining number is 26. $36 - 26 = 10$. Since 10 is not divisible by 13, 269 is also not divisible by 13.

Since 269 is not divisible by 2, 3, 5, 7, 11, or 13, which are all the primes less than or equal to $\sqrt{269} = 16.401\,21\ldots$, then 269 must be a prime number.

WORKED EXAMPLE 3

If a and b are natural numbers such that $a \times b = 19$, find the value of $a + b$.

Answer

Since 19 is a prime number, the only factors of 19 are 1 and 19.

So a and b must be 1 and 19 in whichever order. Then $a + b = 1 + 19 = 20$

Integers (positive, negative and zero)

The natural numbers are part of the **integers**. Integers are numbers that do not have fractional or decimal parts. Integers can be positive or negative or zero.

The positive integers are: 1, 2, 3, 4, 5, …, 100, …

The negative integers are: −1, −2, −3, …, −45, …

0 is an integer but it is neither positive nor negative.

> **MATHEMATICAL CONNECTIONS**
>
> You will learn about the four operations for calculations with integers in Chapter 2.

Exercise 1.1

1 Write the following numbers in words.

    a   540 018   **b**   9 000 342   **c**   41 020 679

    d   3 000 000 853   **e**   9 000 231 038   **f**   60 582

    g   6 500 453 684

2   Write the following in numbers.

    a   Two million, six hundred and eighteen thousand, four hundred and twenty-two.

    b   Five billion, four hundred and sixty-one.

    c   Seven hundred and four thousand and thirty-seven.

    d   Eighteen million, one hundred and fifty-three thousand and six.

3   Write down all the prime numbers that are less than 100.

4   Determine if each of these numbers is a prime number.

    a   173   **b**   129   **c**   237   **d**   281   **e**   383

5   If a and b are natural numbers such that $a \times b = 23$, find the value of $a + b$.

6   If a and b are natural numbers such that $a \times b = 89$, find the value of $a + b$.

1.2 Other types of number

Index notation, square numbers and cube numbers

Index notation is a way of writing numbers when you multiply a number by itself one or more times.

For example, you can write 3×3 as 3^2.

You read 3^2 as 'three to the power of two', where the number three is the base and the number two is the power or exponent.

The base represents the number that you multiplied by itself. The power is the number of times you multiplied the base by itself. So:

$2 \times 2 \times 2 \times 2 \times 2 = 2^5$ reads as 'two to the power of five'

$3 \times 3 \times 3 \times 3 = 3^4$ reads as 'three to the power of four'

$5 \times 5 \times 5 = 5^3$ reads as 'five to the power of three'.

When the power is two, you can also say that the base is 'squared'.

For example, you read 3^2 as 'three squared'.

Numbers with the power of two are called **square numbers**.

Examples of square numbers are:

$2^2 = 2 \times 2 = 4$ $3^2 = 3 \times 3 = 9$ $4^2 = 4 \times 4 = 16$ $5^2 = 5 \times 5 = 25$

When the power is three, you can also say that the base is 'cubed'.

For example, you read 5^3 as 'five cubed'.

Numbers with the power of three are called **cube numbers**.

Examples of cube numbers are:

$2^3 = 2 \times 2 \times 2 = 8$ $3^3 = 3 \times 3 \times 3 = 27$ $4^3 = 4 \times 4 \times 4 = 64$

> **MATHEMATICAL CONNECTIONS**
>
> Indices are discussed further in Chapter 6.

WORKED EXAMPLE 4

Write the following in index notation.

a $2 \times 2 \times 2 \times 2 \times 2 \times 2 \times 2$ **b** $a \times a \times a \times a \times a$

Answers

a $2 \times 2 \times 2 \times 2 \times 2 \times 2 \times 2 = 2^7$ The number two is multiplied by itself, so the base is two. The base two is multiplied by itself seven times, so the power is seven.

b $a \times a \times a \times a \times a = a^5$ The number a is multiplied by itself, so the base is a. The base a is multiplied by itself five times, so the power is five.

WORKED EXAMPLE 5

Evaluate.

a 17^2 **b** 6^3 **c** 11^4

Answers

a $17^2 = 17 \times 17 = 289$ You can use a calculator to evaluate the product of such a big number.
To evaluate a square number, key in:

[1] [7] [x^2] [EXE]

b $6^3 = 6 \times 6 \times 6 = 216$ To use your calculator to evaluate 6^3, key in:

[6] [∧] [3] [EXE]

c $11^4 = 11 \times 11 \times 11 \times 11 = 14641$ To use your calculator to evaluate 11^4, key in:

[1] [1] [∧] [4] [EXE]

Rational numbers and irrational numbers

A rational number is a number that can be expressed in the form $\frac{a}{b}$ where a and b are natural numbers and $b \neq 0$.

Examples of rational numbers are: $2, 3, \frac{1}{2}, -4\frac{2}{5}, -2.5$

All natural numbers and fractions are rational. Some decimals are rational.

An **irrational number** is a number that **cannot** be expressed in the form $\frac{a}{b}$ where a and b are natural numbers and $b \neq 0$.

Examples of irrational numbers are: $\sqrt{2}, \sqrt{5}, \sqrt[3]{7}, \pi$

In general, square roots and cube roots that are not exact are irrational.

> **MATHEMATICAL CONNECTIONS**
>
> You will look closer at square roots and cube roots in Section 1.5.

WORKED EXAMPLE 6

$0.13, \frac{3}{7}, \sqrt{3}, \pi, 8, 13, 16, 41, 64$

From this list of numbers, write down:

a   the square numbers

b   the prime numbers

c   the cube numbers

d   the irrational numbers.

Answers

You need to categorise the numbers.

You can express 0.13 in fractional form: $0.13 = \frac{13}{100}$, which is rational.

$\frac{3}{7}$ is itself a rational number.

$\sqrt{3}$ does not give you an exact value, so it is an irrational number.

The value of π is 3.14159265... It is not exact and cannot be expressed as a fraction. Therefore, it is irrational.

$8 = 2 \times 2 \times 2 = 2^3$, hence it is a cube number.

13 only has two distinct factors, 1 and 13, hence it is a prime number.

$16 = 4 \times 4 = 4^2$, so it is a square number.

41 only has two distinct factors, 1 and 41, hence it is a prime number.

64 is a rather special number. $64 = 8 \times 8 = 8^2$ which makes it a square number, but $64 = 4 \times 4 \times 4 = 4^3$, so 64 is also a cube number.

a   The square numbers are 16 and 64.

b   The prime numbers are 13 and 41.

c   The cube numbers are 8 and 64.

d   The irrational numbers are $\sqrt{3}$ and π.

Reciprocals

A **reciprocal** is a multiplicative inverse such that the product of a number and its reciprocal will produce 1. To put it simply, the reciprocal of a number a is $\frac{1}{a}$.

For example:

The reciprocal of 8 is $\frac{1}{8}$ $\left(8 \times \frac{1}{8} = 1\right)$

The reciprocal of $\frac{1}{3}$ is 3 $\left(\frac{1}{3} \times 3 = 1\right)$

The reciprocal of $\frac{3}{7}$ is $\frac{7}{3}$ $\left(\frac{3}{7} \times \frac{7}{3} = 1\right)$

The reciprocal of 2.5 is $\frac{1}{2.5} = 0.4$ $(2.5 \times 0.4 = 1)$

Triangle numbers

Investigation 2 explores the **triangle numbers**.

<table>
<tr><td>

INVESTIGATION 2

Triangle numbers
Look at this sequence of patterns of dots.

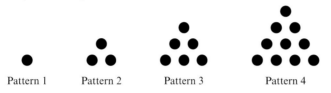

| Pattern 1 | Pattern 2 | Pattern 3 | Pattern 4 |

1   Copy and complete the following sentence: The dots in each pattern form the shape of a ....

2   Draw Pattern 5 and Pattern 6.

3   Copy and complete this table.

Pattern, n	Number of dots along one side of the shape	Total number of dots in the shape	Observation about the total number of dots	$n(n + 1)$
1	1	1	1	$1 \times 2 = 2$
2	2	3	$1 + 2$	$2 \times 3 = 6$
3	3	6		$3 \times 4 =$
4				
5				
6				

4   Without drawing the diagram for Pattern 10, write down the:

    a   number of dots along one side of the shape

    b   total number of dots in the shape

    c   observation about the total number of dots.

5   What is the relationship between the total number of dots in the shape and the last column, $n(n + 1)$?

6   Which pattern will have a total number of 496 dots? Explain how you get your answer.

The total number of dots are known as triangle numbers.

</td><td>

MATHEMATICAL CONNECTIONS

You will study sequences in Chapter 22.

</td></tr>
</table>

Triangle or triangular numbers are numbers that can make equilateral triangle patterns.

Examples of triangle numbers are: 1, 3, 6, 10 and 15.

List all the:

a   square numbers

b   cube numbers

c   triangle numbers

between 0 and 100.

Exercise 1.2

1   Express the following in index notation.

   a $4 \times 4 \times 4$

   b $7 \times 7 \times 7 \times 7 \times 7 \times 7$

   c $2 \times 2 \times 2 \times 3 \times 3 \times 3 \times 3$

   d $5 \times 5 \times 7 \times 7 \times 7 \times 11 \times 11$

   d $2 \times 5 \times 3 \times 2 \times 3 \times 3 \times 2 \times 5 \times 13 \times 13$

2   $0.35, \dfrac{1}{2}, \sqrt{5}, \dfrac{\pi}{3}, 27, 36, 43, 51, 81$

   From this list of numbers, write down:

   a   the square numbers

   b   the prime number

   c   the cube number

   d   the irrational numbers

   e   the triangle number.

3   $-5, \dfrac{22}{7}, 0, \sqrt{9}, \sqrt{11}, 17, 25, 37, 125$

   From this list of numbers, write down:

   a   the negative integer

   b   the square number

   c   the prime numbers

   d   the cube number

   e   the irrational number.

> **TIP**
>
> For Questions **2** and **3**, you might not use all of the numbers in the list.

4   Write down the reciprocal of each number.

   a   5   **b**   20   **c** $\dfrac{1}{4}$ **d** $\dfrac{2}{5}$

1.3 Products of prime factors

You can express each integer greater than one as a product of prime factors.

Worked example 7 demonstrates three methods you can use.

WORKED EXAMPLE 7

Express 60 as a product of prime factors.

Answers

Method 1: Factor tree

$60 = 2 \times 2 \times 3 \times 5$
$\quad = 2^2 \times 3 \times 5$

Step 1: first, split 60 into the product of two factors. You can use any two factors.

Step 2: check if each of the two factors are prime. If both factors are prime, you can stop.

If both factors are **not** prime, split each non-prime factor further into the product of two factors.

Repeat Step 2 until all the factors are prime.

The number is now expressed as a product of prime factors.

If any of the prime numbers appear more than once in the product, use index notation. In this example $2 \times 2 = 2^2$

Method 2: Repeated division

2	60
2	30
3	15
5	5
	1

$60 = 2 \times 2 \times 3 \times 5$
$\quad = 2^2 \times 3 \times 5$

Step 1: divide 60 by its smallest prime factor. In this case two.

Step 2: write the result of the division in the right column. Continue to divide the number in the right column by the same factor if possible. Write the result on the right column.

Step 3: repeat Step 2. If the number in the right column is **not** divisible by the same factor, divide this number by the next biggest prime factor.

Repeat Steps 2 and 3 until the number is reduced to one.

Multiply the numbers in the left column to express the original number as a product of prime factors.

Again, use index notation for any repeated prime factors.

CONTINUED

Method 3: Using the 'FACT' key on your calculator

Some calculators have the 'FACT' key which can do prime factorisation for you.

The 'FACT' key is located on the SHIFT key of the time button.

To use the 'FACT' key, press

The calculator will show you the prime factors.

Display:
```
60
        2²×3×5
```

You can only use Method 3 when you are working on a calculator paper.

DISCUSSION 2

In groups of 3 or 4, research and discuss the differences between these types of prime number:

1 twin primes and cousin primes
2 Fermat primes
3 Sophie Germain primes
4 palindromes and palindromic primes
5 coprime
6 importance and application of prime numbers in real life.

Exercise 1.3

1 Express each number as a product of prime factors.

    a   120   b   252   c   600   d   728   e   1980

2 Copy and complete these factor trees.

    a   b   c

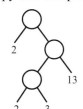
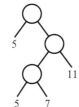
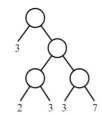

3 Written as a product of prime factors, $9504 = 2^x \times 3^y \times 11$.
Find the values of x and y.

4 Written as a product of prime factors, $3024 = 2^x \times 3^y \times 7^z$.
Find the values of x, y and z.

5 Written as a product of prime factors, $8712 = p^3 \times 3^2 \times q^2$.
Find the values of p and q.

6 The whole number p is such that $p \times (p + 22)$ is a prime number. Find:
   a p **b**   the prime number.

7 The whole number p is such that $p \times (p + 106)$ is a prime number. Find:
   a p **b**   the prime number.

INVESTIGATION 3

The total number of distinct positive factors of any natural number.

1   **a**   What are factors?

      b   List all the factors of 24.

      c   How many distinct positive factors does 24 have in total?

2   Alternative method to finding the number of distinct positive factors of a natural number, X.

    Step 1: express X as a product of prime factors.

         $X = p^a \times q^b \times r^c$

    Step 2: add one to all the powers.

         $a + 1, b + 1, c + 1$

    Step 3: the product of the results in Step 2 will give the total number of distinct positive factors of X.

    Total number of distinct positive factors of $X = (a + 1)(b + 1)(c + 1)$

    Verify that this alternative method works to find the total number of distinct positive factors of 24.

3   Consider the number 60. Use both methods from Questions **1** and **2** to verify the total number of distinct positive factors of 60.

4   Consider three different natural numbers.

    Use both methods from Questions **1** and **2** to find the total number of distinct positive factors of these numbers.

    Of your three numbers:

    a   one number must be prime

    b   one number must contain three prime factors when expressed as a product of prime factors

    c   the other number must have at least one power in the product of prime factors that is greater than one.

5   Explain why the alternative method works using the number 24.

6   Find the total number of distinct positive factors of 229 320.

1.4 Highest common factors (HCF) and lowest common multiples (LCM)

Highest common factors (HCF)

You can use a listing method to find the **highest common factor (HCF)** of small numbers.

For example:

The factors of 12 are: 1, 2, 3, 4, 6 and 12.

The factors of 40 are: 1, 2, 4, 5, 8, 10, 20 and 40.

The common factors of 12 and 40 are 1, 2, and 4.

4 is the HCF of 12 and 40.

Worked example 8 demonstrates two more efficient methods to find the HCF of two numbers.

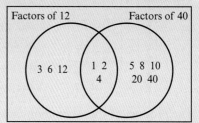

MATHEMATICAL CONNECTIONS

The list can be represented visually using a Venn diagram.

You will learn about Venn diagrams in Chapter 18.

WORKED EXAMPLE 8

Find the HCF of 84 and 378.

Answers

Method 1: Repeated division by common prime factors

2	84, 378
	42, 189

Since 84 and 378 are even, they are both divisible by 2.

Divide both numbers by 2.

2	84, 378
3	42, 189
	14, 63

42 is even but 189 is odd, so they are **not** both divisible by 2.

Try 3.

2	84, 378
3	42, 189
7	14, 63
	2, 9

14 is **not** divisible by 3, so try the next prime number.

Both 14 and 63 are **not** divisible by 5, so try 7.

Both 14 and 63 are divisible by 7, so divide both numbers by 7.

2 is a prime number so it can only be divided by itself. You already used 2 as the common factor at the beginning of this method, so there is no common factor of 2 and 9.

The division stops here.

2	84, 378
3	42, 189
7	14, 63
	2, 9

The product of the prime factors on the left gives the HCF of 84 and 378.

The HCF of 84 and 378 is $2 \times 3 \times 7 = 42$

CONTINUED

Method 2: Using products of prime factors

$84 = 2^2 \times 3 \times 7$

$378 = 2 \times 3^3 \times 7$

By using any one of the methods from Worked example 7, express both numbers individually as a product of prime factors.

$84 = \boxed{2^2} \times \boxed{3} \times \boxed{7}$

$378 = \boxed{2} \times \boxed{3^3} \times \boxed{7}$

Identify the common bases.

The common bases are 2, 3 and 7.

$84 = \boxed{2^2} \times \boxed{3} \times \boxed{7}$

$378 = \boxed{2} \times \boxed{3^3} \times \boxed{7}$

$\downarrow \quad \downarrow \quad \downarrow$

$2 \times 3 \times 7$

For the common bases, choose the smallest power of each base.

$84 = (2) \times 2 \times (3) \times (7)$

$378 = (2) \times (3) \times 3 \times 3 \times (7)$

The product of these common factors gives the HCF.

The HCF of 84 and 378 = $2 \times 3 \times 7 = 42$

> **TIP**
>
> You choose the smallest power for each base because the power indicates the number of times the base appears. To find the common prime factors, you need to consider the number of times the base is multiplied.

Lowest common multiples (LCM)

You can use a listing method to find the **lowest common multiple (LCM)** of two small numbers.

For example:

Multiples of 3: 3, 6, 9, 12, (15,) 18, 21, 24, 27, (30,) …

Multiples of 5: 5, 10, (15,) 20, 25, (30,) …

The common multiples of 3 and 5 are 15, 30, …

15 is the LCM of 3 and 5.

Worked example 9 demonstrates two more efficient methods to find the LCM of two numbers.

WORKED EXAMPLE 9

Find the LCM of 12 and 56.

Answers

Method 1: Repeated division

$$\begin{array}{c|cc} 2 & 12, & 56 \\ \hline & 6, & 28 \end{array}$$

Since 12 and 56 are both even, you can divide both numbers by 2.

$$\begin{array}{c|cc} 2 & 12, & 56 \\ 2 & 6, & 28 \\ \hline & 3, & 14 \end{array}$$

Both 6 and 28 are even. Continue to divide both numbers by 2.

CONTINUED

2	12, 56
2	6, 28
2	3, 14
	3, 7

3 is a prime number. There are no longer any common prime factors of 3 and 14. Instead of stopping here, continue to divide the numbers by prime factors until they are reduced to 1. Deal with one number at a time.

Since 14 is even, you can continue to divide 14 by 2. Leave 3 alone when you divide 14.

2	12, 56
2	6, 28
2	3, 14
3	3, 7
	1, 7

Both 3 and 7 are prime numbers. Divide 3 and 7 individually by 3 and 7 to reduce them to 1.

2	12, 56
2	6, 28
2	3, 14
3	3, 7
7	1, 7
	1, 1

When both numbers are reduced to 1, the product of the prime factors on the left will give you the lowest common multiple of 12 and 56.

The LCM of 12 and 56 is $2^3 \times 3 \times 7 = 168$

Method 2: Using products of prime factors

$12 = 2^2 \times 3$

$56 = 2^3 \times 7$

By using any one of the methods from Worked example 7, express both numbers individually as a product of prime factors.

$12 = \boxed{2^2} \times \boxed{3}$

$56 = \boxed{2^3} \times \boxed{7}$

Identify **all** the bases, common or not.

The bases are 2, 3 and 7.

$12 = \boxed{2^2} \times \boxed{3}$

$56 = \boxed{2^3} \times \boxed{7}$

$2^3 \times 3 \times 7$

If there are common bases, choose the biggest power of the common base.

$12 = 2 \times 2 \quad \times 3$

$56 = 2 \times 2 \times 2 \quad \times 7$

The product of these factors gives the LCM.

The LCM of 12 and 56 $= 2^3 \times 3 \times 7 = 168$

TIP

You choose the biggest power because you are looking for common multiples, so you need to take the maximum number of times the base appears.

Exercise 1.4

1 Find the HCF of:

a	24 and 60	b	75 and 125	c	72 and 120	d	108 and 360
e	120 and 225	f	240 and 288	g	192 and 320	h	294 and 420

2 Find the LCM of:

    a   15 and 24   b   28 and 32   c   36 and 54   d   65 and 91

    e   42 and 60   f   66 and 72   g   32 and 81   h   48 and 108

3 Find the HCF and LCM of the following pairs of numbers. Leave your answers as products of prime factors in index notation.

    a $2^2 \times 3^3 \times 11$ and $2^3 \times 3 \times 5^2$

    b $2^4 \times 3^3 \times 5 \times 11^2$ and $2^2 \times 5^2 \times 7^3 \times 11^4$

    c $2^3 \times 5^3 \times 7 \times 13$ and $2^2 \times 3^4 \times 5^3 \times 11^2$

    d $2^5 \times 3^4 \times 7^2 \times 19$ and $2^3 \times 3^2 \times 5^2 \times 7 \times 19^3$

4 120 expressed as a product of prime factors is $2^3 \times 3 \times 5$.

    a   Express 504 as a product of prime factors.

    b   Hence find:

        i   the highest common factor of 120 and 504

        ii   the lowest common multiple of 120 and 504.

5 There are 45 sweets and 72 chocolates in a bag. The sweets and chocolates are packed into gift bags such that each bag has the same number of sweets and chocolates. Find the largest number of gift bags that can be made.

6 Find the HCF and LCM of:

    a   60, 75 and 90   b   48, 84 and 132   c   70, 210, 350

7 Bus services A, B and C pass a particular bus stop every day. Bus service A passes the bus stop at 15 minute intervals, bus service B passes the bus stop at 20 minute intervals and bus service C passes the bus stop at 45 minute intervals. If all three buses are at the bus stop at 09:00, what is the next time that the three buses will all be at the bus stop?

8 When written as a products of prime factors

    $A = 2^3 \times 3^3 \times 7$

    $B = 2^2 \times 3 \times 5 \times 7$

    $C = 2 \times 5^2 \times 7^3$

    Find:

    a   the HCF of A and C   b   the LCM of B and C

    c   the HCF of A, B and C   d   the LCM of A, B and C.

    Leave your answers in index notation.

1.5 Square roots and cube roots

Square roots

The square root of a number is a number that when multiplied by itself gives that number.

For example, the square of three is $3^2 = 3 \times 3 = 9$, so the square root of nine is $\sqrt{9} = \sqrt{3^2} = 3$

Notice that the power of 3^2 is divided by two when the square root is applied.

The square root of a natural number n^2 is $\sqrt{n^2} = \sqrt{n \times n} = n$

Worked example 10 demonstrates how to use a product of prime factors to find the square root of a square number.

WORKED EXAMPLE 10

Find the square root of 144.

Answer

$144 = 2^4 \times 3^2$ — Express 144 as a product of prime factors.

$\sqrt{144} = \sqrt{2^4 \times 3^2}$ — To find the square root of 144, take the power of each base and divide each power by 2. Then multiply these numbers.

$= 2^{4 \div 2} \times 3^{2 \div 2}$

$= 2^2 \times 3^1$ — So the square root of 144 is $2^2 \times 3 = 12$

$= 12$

> **TIP**
>
> A square number will definitely have even powers in the product when expressed as the product of prime factors.

Cube roots

The cube root of a number is a number that when multiplied by itself twice gives that number.

For example eight is a cube number since $8 = 2 \times 2 \times 2 = 2^3$. The cube root of eight is $\sqrt[3]{8} = \sqrt[3]{2^3} = 2$

Notice that the powers of two is divided by three when the cube root is applied.

In general, $\sqrt[3]{n^3} = \sqrt[3]{n \times n \times n} = n$

Worked example 11 demonstrates how to use a product of prime factors to find the cube root of a cube number.

WORKED EXAMPLE 11

Find the cube root of 5832.

Answer

$5832 = 2^3 \times 3^6$ — Express 5832 as a product of prime factors.

$\sqrt{5832} = \sqrt[3]{2^3 \times 3^6}$ — To find the cube root of 5832, take the power of each base and divide each power by 3. Then multiply these numbers.

$= 2^{3 \div 3} \times 3^{6 \div 3}$

$= 2^1 \times 3^2$ — So the cube root of 5832 is $2 \times 3^2 = 18$

$= 18$

> **TIP**
>
> A cube number will have powers that are multiples of three when expressed as the product of prime factors.

You are expected to remember the squares of numbers from 1 to 15 as well as their corresponding square roots. You should also remember the cubes of numbers from one to seven and their corresponding cube roots. You may even be asked to find other roots without the use of a calculator.

WORKED EXAMPLE 12

Evaluate the following without the use of a calculator.

a 7^2 **b** $\sqrt{169}$ **c** 2^3 **d** $\sqrt[3]{64}$ **e** $\sqrt[5]{32}$

Answer

These are numbers you need to recall from memory.

a $7^2 = 7 \times 7 = 49$

b You need to know that $13^2 = 169$ so $\sqrt{169} = 13$

c $2^3 = 2 \times 2 \times 2 = 8$

d Since $4 \times 4 \times 4 = 64$, $\sqrt[3]{64} = 4$

e $2^5 = 2 \times 2 \times 2 \times 2 \times 2 = 32$. Hence, $\sqrt[5]{32} = 2$

WORKED EXAMPLE 13

a Express 108 as a product of prime factors.

b Given that h is a natural number and $h \neq 0$, find h if $108 \times h$ is a square number.

c Given that k is a natural number and $k \neq 0$, find k if $108 \times k$ is a cube number.

Answer

a $108 = 2^2 \times 3^3$

Use one of the methods from Worked example 7.

b $108 \times h = 2^2 \times 3^3 \times 3$

so that $108 \times h = 2^2 \times 3^4$

$\therefore h = 3$

From the tip in Worked example 10, a square number will have even powers when it is expressed as a product of prime factors.

Base 2: 2^2 has an even power.

Base 3: 3^3 has an odd power.

For $108 \times h$ to be a square number, the power of each prime base must be even, so you need to multiply 108 by 3 to make the power of base 3 even.

c $108 \times k = 2^2 \times 3^3 \times 2$

so that $108 \times k = 2^3 \times 3^3$

$\therefore k = 2$

From the tip in Worked example 11, a cube number will have powers that are multiples of 3 when it is expressed as a product of prime factors.

Base 2: 2^2 has a power of 2. To make the power a multiple of 3, you must multiply it by 2.

Base 3: 3^3 has a power of 3.

For $108 \times k$ to be a cube number, each power of its prime base must be a multiple of 3, so you need to multiply 108 by 2 to make the power of base 2 a 3.

Exercise 1.5

1   Without the use of a calculator, evaluate:

a 8^2 b 11^2 c $\sqrt{100}$ d $\sqrt{225}$

e 6^3 f 3^4 g 7^3 h 2^6

i $\sqrt[3]{125}$ j $\sqrt[4]{625}$ k $\sqrt[3]{1000}$ l $\sqrt[6]{1000000}$

m 1^2 n 5^2 o 6^2

2   Find the value of:

a $\sqrt{196}$ b $\sqrt{256}$ c $\sqrt{324}$ d $\sqrt{576}$

e $\sqrt{1296}$ f $\sqrt{16}$ g $\sqrt{4}$ h $\sqrt{81}$

3   Find the cube root of:

a   216 b   512 c   729 d   1728

e   3375 f   27 g   1

4   Without using a calculator, find the square root of each number. Leave your answers in index notation.

a $2^4 \times 13^2 \times 19^6$ b $2^6 \times 3^4 \times 11^2$ c $5^8 \times 11^{10} \times 13^6$

5   Without using a calculator, find the cube root of each number. Leave your answers in index notation.

a $2^9 \times 5^3 \times 11^6$ b $2^6 \times 3^{12} \times 7^3$ c $3^9 \times 11^{12} \times 17^{15}$

6   Without using a calculator, and leaving your answers in index form where appropriate, work out:

a $3^2 \times \sqrt[3]{27}$ b $4^2 \times 2 \times \sqrt{2^2}$ c $9^2 \times \sqrt[5]{32}$

7   The square root of x is $2^2 \times 7$. Find the value of x.

8   The cube root of y is $3^2 \times 5^2$. Find y. Leave your answer in index notation.

9   Without using a calculator, and leaving your answer in index form, work out $4^2 \times 2 \times \sqrt{2}$.

10   The numbers 252 and 1512, written as products of prime factors, are:

$252 = 2^2 \times 3^2 \times 7$

$1512 = 2^3 \times 3^3 \times 7$

Find:

a   the smallest positive integer value of h such that $252 \times h$ is a square number

b   the smallest integer value of k such that $1512 \times k$ is a cube number.

1.6 Estimating and rounding

In this section, you will learn how to round and how to make estimations.

Rounding whole numbers

Worked example 14 demonstrates rounding numbers to the nearest tens, hundreds or thousands.

WORKED EXAMPLE 14

Round 23 759 to the nearest:

a ten   **b** hundred   **c** thousand   **d** ten thousand.

Answer

Find the number in the column you are rounding to. If the digit to the right of it is zero, one, two, three or four, replace this digit with a zero as a place holder and leave the digit in the column unchanged.

If the digit to the right of it is five, six, seven, eight or nine, replace this digit with a zero as a place holder and increase the digit in the column by one.

a

2	3	7	5	9
ten thousands	thousands	hundreds	tens	ones
			Step 1: identify the digit in the tens place.	Step 2: examine the digit to the right of the tens place.

So 23 759 ≈ 23 760

Use the approximate equal to sign '≈' to show that you are approximating the original value of 23 759 to 23 760.

Another way to indicate the approximation is to indicate the degree of accuracy you are rounding the number to:

23 759 = 23 760 (to the nearest ten).

> You are rounding up the digit in the tens place by one.

b

2	3	7	5	9
ten thousands	thousands	hundreds	tens	ones
		Step 1: identify the digit in the hundreds place.	**Step 2:** examine the digit to the right of the hundreds place using the same rule as in part **a**.	Replace all digits to the right with a zero as a place holder.

> You are rounding up the digit in the hundreds place by one.

So 23 759 = 23 800 (to the nearest hundred).

c

2	3	7	5	9
ten thousands	thousands	hundreds	tens	ones
	Step 1: identify the digit in the thousands place.	**Step 2:** examine the digit to the right of the thousands place using the same rule as in part **a**.	Replace all digits to the right with a zero as a place holder.	

> You are rounding up the digit in the thousands place by 1.

So 23 759 = 24 000 (to the nearest thousand).

d

2	3	7	5	9
ten thousands	thousands	hundreds	tens	ones
Step 1: identify the digit in the ten thousands place.	**Step 2:** examine the digit to the right of the ten thousands place using the same rule as in part **a**.	Replace all digits to the right with a zero as a place holder.		

> You are rounding up the digit in the ten thousands place by 1.

So 23 759 = 20 000 (to the nearest ten thousand).

Rounding to decimal places

You can round a decimal to different numbers of decimal places. The method of rounding numbers to a specific number of decimal places is similar to the method shown for rounding whole numbers in Worked example 14.

For example: the place values in the number 1.234 5 are:

1	.	2	3	4	5
ones	decimal point	$\frac{1}{10}$s in the first decimal place	$\frac{1}{100}$s in the second decimal place	$\frac{1}{1000}$s in the third decimal place	$\frac{1}{10000}$s in the fourth decimal place

To round a number to a specific number of decimal places, look at the digit immediately to the right of the required decimal place.

If the digit to the right is five or more, round up the previous digit and remove all other digits after the specified decimal place.

If the digit to the right is four or less, remove the digits after the specified decimal place.

WORKED EXAMPLE 15

Round 3.456 12 to:

a three decimal places **b** two decimal places **c** one decimal place.

Answers

a To round 3.456 12 to three decimal places, look at the digit in the 4th decimal place.

3	.	4	5	6	1	2
		1st decimal place	2nd decimal place	3rd decimal place	4th decimal place	
				No rounding up required. Retain digits up to this decimal place.	One is less than five, so remove all digits from here to the right.	

3.456 12 = 3.456 (to 3 dp).

Or 3.456 12 = 3.456 (to 3 dp).

CONTINUED

b To round 3.456 12 to two decimal places, look at the digit in the 3rd decimal place.

3	.	4	5	6	1	2
		1st decimal place	2nd decimal place	3rd decimal place		
			Round up to six	Six is more than five, so round up the digit in the 2nd decimal place and remove all digits from here to the right.		

3.456 12 = 3.46 (to 2 dp).

Or 3.456 12 = 3.46 (to 2 dp).

c To round 3.456 12 to one decimal place, look at the digit in the 2nd decimal place.

3	.	4	5	6	1	2
		1st decimal place	2nd decimal place			
		Round up to five	Five is equal to or more than five, so round up the digit in the 1st decimal place and remove all digits from here to the right.			

3.456 12 = 3.5 (to 1 dp).

Or 3.456 12 = 3.5 (to 1 dp).

Sometimes you will need to consider the context of a problem to decide which degree of accuracy to round the answer to.

For example, when rounding money, you would usually round the answer to two decimal places.

WORKED EXAMPLE 16

A website recorded 2300 views in the month of August. How many people visited the website each day?

Answers

There are 31 days in the month of August. To find the number of people who visited the website in a day, divide 2300 by 31.

$2300 \div 31 = 74.193\,548\,39...$

You need to round the answer to a reasonable degree of accuracy. Since the number of people visiting a website must be an integer, round the answer to the nearest whole number.

$2300 \div 31 \approx 74$

You can say that approximately 74 people visited the website each day.

WORKED EXAMPLE 17

Alice buys 15 eggs for $4.70. How much does one egg cost?

Answers

To find the cost of one egg, divide $4.70 by 15.

$4.70 ÷ 15 = $0.3133333333...

Since dollars are made of cents, round the amount to the nearest cents (two decimal places).

$4.70 ÷ 15 ≈ $0.31

You can say that one egg cost approximately 31 cents.

Exercise 1.6

 1 Round each number to the nearest whole number.

    a   23.5   **b**   7.1   **c**   569.89   **d**   50.09.

 2 Round each number to the nearest 10.

    a   3452   **b**   4478   **c**   899   **d**   1035.

 3 Round each number to the nearest 100.

    a   1344   **b**   3288   **c**   78999   **d**   5072.

 4 Round each number to the number of decimal places specified in the brackets.

    a   101.03 (1 dp)   **b**   0.198 323 (2 dp)

    c   4.996 8 (2 dp)   **d**   0.001 906 (3 dp)

 5 The length of a plant is 44.306 741 cm when measured with a precise instrument. Express this length rounded to:

    a   four decimal places

    b   two decimal places.

 6 The height of a fence is 2.774 1 metres. Express the height rounded to:

    a   the nearest metre

    b   the nearest 0.1 metres

    c   the nearest 0.01 metres.

7 A group of 138 students are going on a trip to the zoo. The school requires that there is one teacher for every 16 students.

    a   How many teachers are required to go on the trip with the students?

    b   If one bus can take a total of 30 students, how many buses are needed for the trip?

8 A painter needs to paint 26 doors in a building. It takes approximately 120 ml for one coat of paint for a door. The painter needs to put two coats of paint on each door.

One tin holds 500 ml of paint. How many tins of paint must the painter buy?

1.7 Accuracy and estimating

Rounding to significant figures

As well as rounding numbers to decimal places, you can also round numbers to a specified number of significant figures.

MATHEMATICS IN CONTEXT

Consider these situations:

An engineer measured the width of a road to be 723.581 cm or 7.235 81 metres. The engineer must give all measurements rounded to one decimal place. Should the engineer give the measurement as 723.6 cm or 7.2 metres? Which measurement will be more accurate? Does accuracy depend on the number of decimal places or the number of digits?

This example shows that the degree of accuracy does **not** depend on the number of decimal places or digits. The degree of accuracy depends on the number of important or **significant** digits.

For example, 723.6 has four significant figures, but 7.2 has only two significant figures.

> **TIP**
>
> Significant figures are digits in a number that contribute to its accuracy. A number is more accurate when it has more significant figures.

In general, there are five rules to identify significant figures in numbers.

A   The first non-zero digit starting from the left is the first significant figure in a number.

B   All non-zero digits are significant.

C   All zeros between non-zero digits are significant.

D   In decimals numbers, the zeros at the end are significant.

E   In natural numbers, the zeros at the end are generally not counted as significant.

For example:

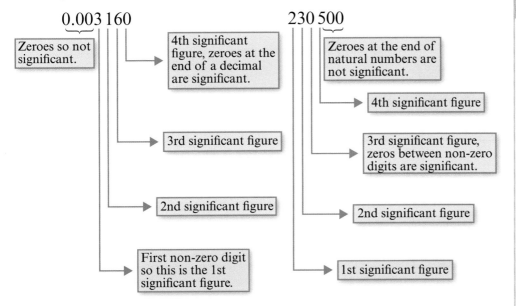

> **TIP**
>
> There may be exceptions to rule E. If a number has been rounded, the zeros at the end of the natural number may be significant depending on how many significant figures the number has been rounded to. For example, 4000 could be given to one significant figure, or two significant figures or three significant figures.

WORKED EXAMPLE 18

How many significant figures does each number have?

a   0.044 79   **b**   3.036   **c**   20.0   **d**   25 000

Answers

Use the five given rules to identify the number of significant figures for each number.

a	0.044 79 → 4th significant figure → 3rd significant figure → 2nd significant figure → 1st significant figure Four significant figures.	Rule A states that the first non-zero digit starting from the left is the first significant figure. Rule B states that all non-zero digits are significant.
b	3.036 → 4th significant figure → 3rd significant figure → 2nd significant figure → 1st significant figure Four significant figures.	Rule C states that all zeros between non-zero digits are significant.
c	20.0 → 3rd significant figure → 2nd significant figure → 1st significant figure Three significant figures.	According to rule D, the zeros at the end of a decimal are significant.
d	25 000 → 2nd significant figure → 1st significant figure Two significant figures.	According to rule E, the zeros at the end of natural numbers are generally not counted as significant unless the number is a rounded off value. 25 000 is the given value so you can take the value as it is.

WORKED EXAMPLE 19

1 Round the number 0.006 045 to:
    a three significant figures   **b** two significant figures.

2 Round the number 125 304 to:
    a three significant figures   **b** two significant figures.

TIP

The method for rounding a natural number to a specific number of significant figures is similar to the method for rounding whole numbers. You need to use the digit zero as a place holder to maintain the value of each digit.

Answers

1 **a**

0.006 045

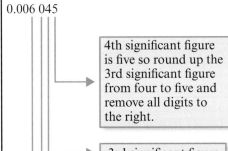

4th significant figure is five so round up the 3rd significant figure from four to five and remove all digits to the right.

3rd significant figure

2nd significant figure

1st significant figure.

0.006 045 = 0.006 05 (to three significant figures)
or 0.006 045 = 0.006 05 (to 3 sf)

To round a decimal to three significant figures, look at the fourth significant figure.
If the fourth significant figure is five or above, round up the third significant figure up by one and **remove** all other digits from the fourth significant figure to the right.
If the fourth significant figure is four or less, remove all digits to the right of the third significant figure.

b

0.006 045

4th significant figure

3rd significant figure is four. Do not round up the previous digit. Remove all digits from here to the right.

2nd significant figure

1st significant figure

0.006 045 = 0.006 0 (to two significant figures)
or 0.006 045 = 0.006 0 (to 2 sf)

To round a decimal to two significant figures, look at the third significant figure. If the third significant figure is five or above, round up the second significant figure by one and **remove** all other digits from the third significant figure to the right.
If the third significant figure is four or less, remove all digits to the right of the second significant figure.

CONTINUED

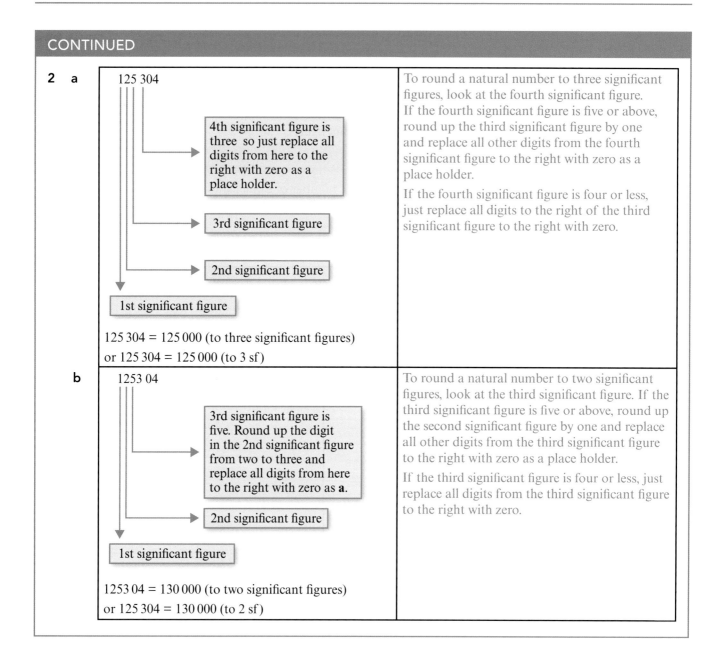

2 a 125 304

4th significant figure is three so just replace all digits from here to the right with zero as a place holder.

3rd significant figure

2nd significant figure

1st significant figure

125 304 = 125 000 (to three significant figures)
or 125 304 = 125 000 (to 3 sf)

To round a natural number to three significant figures, look at the fourth significant figure. If the fourth significant figure is five or above, round up the third significant figure by one and replace all other digits from the fourth significant figure to the right with zero as a place holder.

If the fourth significant figure is four or less, just replace all digits to the right of the third significant figure to the right with zero.

b 1253 04

3rd significant figure is five. Round up the digit in the 2nd significant figure from two to three and replace all digits from here to the right with zero as **a**.

2nd significant figure

1st significant figure

1253 04 = 130 000 (to two significant figures)
or 125 304 = 130 000 (to 2 sf)

To round a natural number to two significant figures, look at the third significant figure. If the third significant figure is five or above, round up the second significant figure by one and replace all other digits from the third significant figure to the right with zero as a place holder.

If the third significant figure is four or less, just replace all digits from the third significant figure to the right with zero.

Estimating

Rounding numbers enables you to estimate the answers to calculations. In general, you should not round values within a calculation and only round the final answer. However, if the question requires an estimation to n significant figures, round the numbers in the calculation to $(n + 1)$ significant figures to estimate the answer. When estimating, you always need one significant figure more than the specified accuracy.

For example, if the question requires an estimation to one significant figure, round the numbers in the calculation to two significant figures to estimate the answer to the calculation.

WORKED EXAMPLE 20

Estimate the value of $\sqrt{38}$.

Answer

To estimate the square root of a number, round the number in the square root to the nearest square number you recognise. In this case, the nearest square number is 36, so $\sqrt{38} \approx \sqrt{36} = 6$

$\therefore \sqrt{38} \approx 6$

WORKED EXAMPLE 21

Estimate the value of $\dfrac{8.995 \times 10.09}{1.958}$ correct to one significant figure.

Answer

To estimate the value of $\dfrac{8.995 \times 10.09}{1.958}$ to one significant figure, you need to round all numbers to two significant figures.

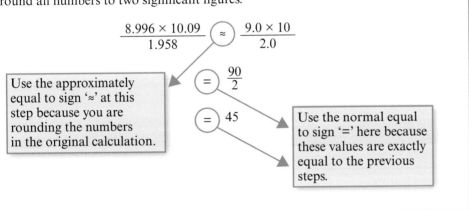

$$\dfrac{8.996 \times 10.09}{1.958} \approx \dfrac{9.0 \times 10}{2.0}$$

$$= \dfrac{90}{2}$$

$$= 45$$

Use the approximately equal to sign '≈' at this step because you are rounding the numbers in the original calculation.

Use the normal equal to sign '=' here because these values are exactly equal to the previous steps.

Exercise 1.7

1 State the number of significant figures in each number.

   a 0.2276   b 2.0304   c 30.0   d 0.000709

   e 0.000010   f 500   g 69010   h 21400

   i 200001   j 30000

2 Round each number to one significant figure.

   a 29   b 361   c 0.523   d 998

   e 0.96   f 0.00012

3 Round each number to two significant figures.

   a 57.3   b 10.5   c 0.427   d 401

   e 2189   f 0.00695

4 Round each number, measurement or quantity to three significant figures.

    a 423.1   **b** 0.982 45   **c** 0.780 5

    d 12 345   **e** 249 788 metres   **f** 99 998 kg

5 Round each number, measurement or quantity to four significant figures.

    a 2.812 5   **b** 0.012 345 6   **c** 120 586 ml

    d 6.999 5   **e** 434 901 apples   **f** 99 999

6 Round 3 418 726.5 to the nearest:

    a three significant figures   **b** whole number   **c** million.

7 Estimate the answers to each calculation correct to one significant figure.

    a $\dfrac{401.32}{13.79 - 2.09^2}$ **a** $\dfrac{\sqrt{401} + 10.1}{14.99}$ **c** $\dfrac{63.51}{10.005 \times 0.798}$

8 Rishi wants to sew a pair of curtains and needs fabric that is 3.43 metres long and 1.65 metres wide. Using estimation, calculate:

    a the total area of fabric needed for the curtains to one decimal place

    b the total price of fabric needed if the cost is \$8 per whole metre and the length is rounded to one decimal place

    c the area of leftover fabric to two significant figures if the fabric Rishi buys is 2 metres wide.

SUMMARY

Are you able to... ?
find the reciprocal of a number
express numbers as a product of prime factors
find the LCM and HCF of two numbers
round values to specific numbers of decimal places or significant figures
estimate calculations by rounding numbers to a reasonable degree of accuracy
convert between numbers and words
identify natural numbers, integers, prime numbers, square numbers, cube numbers, triangle numbers and rational and irrational numbers
calculate with squares, square roots, cubes and cube roots of numbers
calculate with other powers and roots of numbers.

Past paper questions

1   Students in a college carry out a science experiment.

   a   When the results were posted online, there were 1279 views in the first day. Write 1279 correct to the nearest 10.   [1]

   b   By the end of the week, there had been 15503 views. Write 15503 in words.   [1]

   Cambridge IGCSE International Mathematics 0607 Paper 32 Q3 c, d(i) March 2022

2   a   Write 5249.6 correct to two significant figures.   [1]

   b   Write 0.0030626 correct to three decimal places.   [1]

   Cambridge IGCSE International Mathematics 0607 Paper 21 Q2 June 2021

3   Write the number 25.0467

   a   correct to 1 decimal place,   [1]

   b   correct to 3 significant figures,   [1]

   c   correct to the nearest 10,   [1]

   d   correct to the nearest 0.001.   [1]

   Cambridge IGCSE International Mathematics 0607 Paper 41 Q2a part (i) to (iv) November 2020

4   a   Write 260512 correct to 3 significant figures.   [1]

   b   Calculate $\sqrt{27^2 - 6 \times 31^{0.3}}$. Give your answer correct to 1 decimal place.   [2]

   Cambridge IGCSE International Mathematics 0607 Paper 42 Q2 a,c March 2021

5   a   Write sixty thousand and three in figures.   [1]

   b   Work out $\sqrt{729}$.   [1]

   c   Write down all the factors of 10.   [2]

   d   Write 965.384 correct to

   i   1 decimal place,   [1]

   ii   3 significant figures,   [1]

   iii   the nearest ten.   [1]

   Cambridge IGCSE International Mathematics 0607 Paper 31 Q1 a,b,d & e November 2021

6   Here is a list of numbers.

   $$-2 \qquad \sqrt{3} \qquad 0.24 \qquad 9 \qquad -\frac{1}{3}$$

   Write down **one** of the numbers from the list to complete each statement. You must use a different number in each statement.

   .... is a natural number ($\mathbb{N}$).

   .... is an integer ($\mathbb{Z}$).

   .... is a rational number ($\mathbb{Q}$).   [3]

   Cambridge IGCSE International Mathematics 0607 Paper 31 Q2b November 2021

7   21   22   23   24   25   26   27

From the list of numbers, write down

a   the cube number,   [1]

b   the triangle number.   [1]

Cambridge IGCSE International Mathematics 0607 Paper 11 Q6 June 2021

8   Find the highest common factor (HCF) of 84 and 72.   [1]

Cambridge IGCSE International Mathematics 0607 Paper 22 Q3 March 2021

9   27   32   35   36   39   42

From the list, write down the square number.   [1]

Cambridge IGCSE International Mathematics 0607 Paper 12 Q2 November 2020

10 Written as the product of its prime factors, $540 = 2^2 \times 3^3 \times 5$.

a   Write 360 as a product of its prime factors.   [2]

b   Find the highest common factor (HCF) of 540 and 360.   [1]

c $540n$ is a cube number. Find the smallest possible value of n.   [1]

Cambridge IGCSE International Mathematics 0607 Paper 22 Q8 November 2020

11 Write down a cube number between 10 and 100.   [1]

Cambridge IGCSE International Mathematics 0607 Paper 22 Q1 March 2022

12 Write down the second triangle number.   [1]

Cambridge IGCSE International Mathematics 0607 Paper 12 Q3 March 2022

13 Write down the two rational numbers from this list.

$\dfrac{2}{3}$ $\sqrt{3}$ 2 π [1]

Cambridge IGCSE International Mathematics 0607 Paper 12 Q19 March 2022

14 By rounding each number to one significant figure, estimate the value of 3.17×4.8.   [2]

Cambridge IGCSE International Mathematics 0607 Paper 12 Q2 June 2018

> Chapter 2
Operations with numbers

IN THIS CHAPTER YOU WILL:

- put numbers in order of size, including fractions, decimals and negative numbers

- use the mathematical symbols =, ≠, <, >, ≤, ≥

- add, subtract, multiply and divide integers, fractions and decimals

- use the correct order of operations and brackets when carrying out calculations

- convert between improper fractions and mixed numbers

- recognise equivalence and convert between fractions, decimals and percentages.

GETTING STARTED

1 What fraction of each shape is shaded?

a 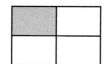   b   c

2 Use the wall shown to answer the questions.

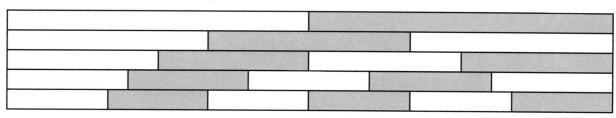

a Which is greater, $\frac{2}{3}$ or $\frac{3}{5}$?   b Which is greater, $\frac{3}{4}$ or $\frac{4}{5}$?

c Put these fractions in order of size, starting with the smallest:

$$\frac{2}{5} \quad \frac{5}{6} \quad \frac{3}{4} \quad \frac{1}{2} \quad \frac{1}{3}$$

3 a Write $\frac{3}{10}$ as a decimal.   b Write 0.07 as a fraction.   c Which is greater, 0.4 or 0.37?

2.1 Working with decimals

The **decimal** system is a number system based on 10s.

The place values are:

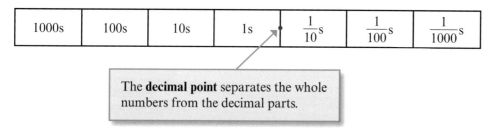

The **decimal point** separates the whole numbers from the decimal parts.

KEY WORDS

decimal

denominator

equivalent fractions

improper fraction

mixed number

numerator

product

proper fraction

recurring decimal

simplest form

sum

terminating decimal

WORKED EXAMPLE 1

Write these numbers in order of size, starting with the smallest:

2.6   2.47   13   0.79   2.567

Answer

First, line the numbers up by place value:

10s	1s	$\frac{1}{10}$s	$\frac{1}{100}$s	$\frac{1}{1000}$s
	2	6		
	2	4	7	
1	3			
	0	7	9	
	2	5	6	7

13 is the only number with any 10s, so it is the largest.

2.6, 2.47 and 2.567 all have two 1s. 2.6 is the largest of these numbers as it has six $\frac{1}{10}$s, followed by 2.567 as it has five $\frac{1}{10}$s, and 2.47 is the smallest of these numbers with four $\frac{1}{10}$s.

0.79 is the smallest number as it is the only number with no 1s.

In order of size, the numbers are: 0.78, 2.47, 2.567, 2.6, 13

To add and subtract decimals, line up the digits by place value.

WORKED EXAMPLE 2

Calculate.

a 6.8 + 5.67   **b** 4.2 − 2.8   **c** 4.28 − 1.7   **d** 5 − 2.67

Answers

a
```
    6 • 8 0
  + 5 • 6 7
  ─────────
  1 2 • 4 7
      1
```

b
```
  ⁴3 • ¹2
  − 2 • 8
  ───────
  1 • 4
```

c
```
  ⁴3 • ¹2 8
  − 1 • 7 0
  ─────────
  2 • 5 8
```

d
```
  5⁴ • ¹0⁹ ¹0
  − 2 • 6 7
  ─────────
  2 • 3 3
```

To multiply decimals, first remove the decimal points and multiply.
Then position the decimal point by estimating the answer.

TIP

It helps to fill in any spaces with zeros.

WORKED EXAMPLE 3

Multiply 6.24×3.1

Answer

Multiply 624×31 by whichever method you prefer. Two methods are shown here.

Method 1

×	**600**	**20**	**4**
30	18 000	600	120
1	600	20	4

18 000
600
120
600
20
+   4
19 344

Method 2

```
      6 2 4
    ×  3 1
      6 2 4
  + 1 8 7 2 0
    1 9 3 4 4
```

An estimate for 6.24×3.1 is $6 \times 3 = 18$, so the answer is close to 18.

$6.24 \times 3.1 = 19.344$

To divide by a decimal, multiply both numbers by 10 repeatedly until the number you are dividing by is an integer. The new question has the same answer as the original question.

DISCUSSION 1

In pairs, discuss why multiplying both numbers by 10 does not change the answer.

Does it change the answer if you double both numbers, or divide both numbers by 2, or add 10 to both numbers?

WORKED EXAMPLE 4

Calculate.

a $3.72 \div 1.2$ **b** $3.6 \div 0.08$

Answers

a $3.72 \div 1.2$

Multiply both numbers by 10:

$37.2 \div 12$

$$12\overline{)37.2}^{\;3.1}$$

CONTINUED

b $3.6 \div 0.08$

Multiply both numbers by 10:

$36 \div 0.8$

The number you are dividing by is still a decimal, so multiply both numbers by 10 again:

$360 \div 8$

$$8\overline{)360}^{\,45}$$

MATHEMATICS IN CONTEXT

The metric system of measures (length, mass, capacity, area, volume) is based on the decimal system. You can convert between units by multiplying or dividing by powers of 10.

For example: 10 mm = 1 cm, 10 mg = 1 cg, 10 millilitres = 1 centilitre, 100 cm = 1 m, 100 cg = 1 g, 100 centilitre = 1 litre, 1000 m = 1 km, 1000 g = 1 kg, 1000 litres = 1 kilolitre

DISCUSSION 2

In pairs, discuss how many mm² make 1 cm², and how many cm³ make 1 m³.

> **MATHEMATICAL CONNECTIONS**
>
> You will learn more about converting between units of measure in Chapter 12.

Some decimals, known as **recurring decimals**, have a number or sequence of numbers that repeats forever.

From the main menu on your Casio fx-CG50, select **Run-Matrix**.

Use the fraction key on your calculator, [▢/▢], to enter the fraction $\frac{1}{3}$.

Use the [**S↔D**] key to change the fraction to a decimal. Your calculator shows $\frac{1}{3}$ as a decimal, 0.333 333 333 3, although the actual answer recurs forever.

Some decimals have more than one recurring digit.

For example, $\frac{3}{11} = 0.2\dot{7}$ or $0.272\,727\,272\,7\ldots$, and $\frac{5}{13} = 0.\dot{3}846\,1\dot{5}$.

TIP

When a dot is placed above more than one digit, the position of the first dot is the beginning of the repeating sequence and the position of the second dot is the end of the repeating sequence.

INVESTIGATION 1

With a partner, find the recurring decimals that are equal to $\frac{1}{7}, \frac{2}{7}, \frac{3}{7}, \frac{4}{7}, \frac{5}{7}$ and $\frac{6}{7}$.

What do you notice?

Exercise 2.1

 1 Write these numbers in order of size, starting with the smallest.

   a 5.6   5.08   4.98   5.2

   b 0.6   0.14   0.03   0.028

   c 3.8   2.98   3   0.98

 2 James says that $5.2 + 3.16 = 8.36$

   Millie says that $5.2 + 3.16 = 8.18$

   Who is correct?

 3 Calculate.

   a $4.72 + 12.4$ b $14.2 + 5.9 + 12$ c $13.1 - 6.7$ d $9.48 - 3.2$

   e $9.1 - 3.56$ f 3.2×4.6 g 13.2×6.7 h 0.24×0.7

   i $12.4 \div 0.4$ j $43.2 \div 0.6$ k $65.4 \div 0.12$ l $0.756 \div 0.9$

 4 a Nasreen has $50.00. She spends $23.60. How much has she left?

   b Josep saves $3.25 every week. How much money will Josep save in one year?

   c Harry saves $1.20 every week. How long will it take Harry to save $32.40?

 5 Keon is eating in a Vietnamese restaurant.

   He chooses these dishes:

Grapefruit salad	$7.20
Grilled fish	$13.60
Sauteed banana	$5.40

   He pays with $30. How much change should he receive?

 6 $467 \times 24 = 11\,208$

   Use this information to write down the answer to:

   a 4.67×2.4

   b $112.08 \div 46.7$

7 Concert tickets cost $8.50 per adult and $5.75 per child.

   A family ticket costs $25.00 for two adults and two children.

   a How much can a family of two adults and two children save with a family ticket?

   b Calculate the cheapest cost of tickets for a family of three adults and three children.

8 Mary is making necklaces. Each necklace uses 0.85 m of chain. She sells the necklaces for $1.40 each.

Mary buys the chain in lengths of 25 m for $17.00.

If she throws away the leftover chain, how much profit does she make on each 25 m length?

INVESTIGATION 2

Imagine you have three bricks with dimensions as shown.

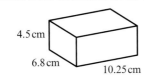

4.5 cm
6.8 cm
10.25 cm

Your task is to make a tower.

For your tower, you can:

– use one, two or three bricks

– turn your bricks around.

An example tower is shown.

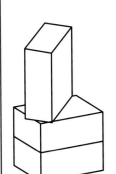

What different heights can you make?

2.2 Equivalent fractions

A fraction is a way of writing a part of something.

A fraction has a **numerator** and **denominator**.

> The numerator tells you how many parts are shaded.

In this shape, the shaded fraction is $\dfrac{3}{4}$

> The denominator tells you the number of equal parts the shape is divided into.

The three diagrams all have the same fraction shaded.

So $\dfrac{3}{4} = \dfrac{6}{8} = \dfrac{9}{12}$

Fractions that are equal are called **equivalent fractions**.

You can find equivalent fractions by multiplying the numerator and denominator by the same number:

$$\overset{\times 2}{\underset{\times 2}{\frac{3}{4} = \frac{6}{8}}} \qquad \overset{\times 3}{\underset{\times 3}{\frac{3}{4} = \frac{9}{12}}}$$

You can use equivalent fractions to compare the size of fractions.

> **MATHEMATICAL CONNECTIONS**
>
> Equivalent fractions are very useful when adding and subtracting fractions. You will discover this in Section 2.3.

> **MATHEMATICAL CONNECTIONS**
>
> You discovered lowest common multiples and highest common factors in Chapter 1.

WORKED EXAMPLE 5

Which is greater $\frac{5}{8}$ or $\frac{2}{3}$?

Answer

Find the lowest common multiple of the denominators, 8 and 3.

The lowest common multiple of 8 and 3 is 24.

Find equivalent fractions for $\frac{5}{8}$ and $\frac{2}{3}$ with denominators of 24.

$$\overset{\times 3}{\underset{\times 3}{\frac{5}{8} = \frac{15}{24}}} \qquad \overset{\times 8}{\underset{\times 8}{\frac{2}{3} = \frac{16}{24}}}$$

$\frac{2}{3}$ is greater than $\frac{5}{8}$

You can **simplify** fractions by dividing the numerator and denominator by the same number:

A fraction that cannot be simplified further is in its **simplest form**, sometimes called its lowest terms.

$$\overset{\div 5}{\underset{\div 5}{\frac{10}{15} = \frac{2}{3}}}$$

WORKED EXAMPLE 6

Write $\frac{12}{30}$ as a fraction in its simplest form.

Answer

To fully simplify a fraction, divide the numerator and denominator by their highest common factor.

The highest common factor of 12 and 30 is 6.

$$\overset{\div 6}{\underset{\div 6}{\frac{12}{30} = \frac{2}{5}}}$$

Your calculator will automatically write fractions in their simplest form.

Check this by inputting $\frac{12}{30}$. When you type EXE or = it shows the fraction as $\frac{2}{5}$.

A **proper fraction** is a fraction that is less than 1.

$\frac{2}{3}$ is a proper fraction.

Numbers greater than 1 can be written as **mixed numbers**.

A mixed number has a whole number part and a proper fraction part.

$2\frac{5}{6}$

Numbers greater than 1 can also be written as **improper fractions**. The fraction shown can also be written as an improper fraction as $\frac{17}{6}$.

In the diagram, each whole one contains six-sixths, so altogether $2\frac{5}{6}$ contains 17-sixths.

WORKED EXAMPLE 7

a Write $4\frac{3}{5}$ as an improper fraction.

b Write $\frac{26}{7}$ as a mixed number.

Answers

a To change $4\frac{3}{5}$ into fifths, split each whole one into five-fifths.

So, the 4 whole ones are equal to 20-fifths.

Altogether $4\frac{3}{5} = \frac{20 + 3}{5} = \frac{23}{5}$

b In the improper fraction $\frac{26}{7}$, every seven-sevenths makes a whole one.

$26 \div 7 = 3$ with 5 remaining.

So, $\frac{26}{7} = 3\frac{5}{7}$

Exercise 2.2

1 Copy and complete these equivalent fractions.

a $\frac{2}{3} = \frac{}{6}$ **b** $\frac{4}{5} = \frac{}{20}$ **c** $\frac{4}{7} = \frac{12}{}$ **d** $\frac{8}{12} = \frac{2}{}$ **e** $\frac{18}{30} = \frac{}{5}$

2 Write each fraction in its simplest form.

a $\frac{14}{20}$ **b** $\frac{12}{21}$ **c** $\frac{16}{24}$ **d** $\frac{36}{48}$ **e** $\frac{56}{80}$

> **TIP**
>
> Check that your answer cannot be simplified any further.

3 Write these mixed numbers as improper fractions.

a $2\frac{1}{3}$ b $3\frac{3}{4}$ c $4\frac{1}{7}$ d $6\frac{2}{3}$ e $33\frac{1}{3}$

 4 Write these improper fractions as mixed numbers.

a $\frac{7}{4}$ b $\frac{15}{8}$ c $\frac{23}{5}$ d $\frac{48}{11}$ e $\frac{55}{8}$

 5 Write these as mixed numbers in their lowest terms.

a $\frac{10}{4}$ b $\frac{42}{9}$ c $\frac{40}{12}$ d $\frac{48}{18}$ e $\frac{57}{24}$

 6 Write each group of fractions in order of size, starting with the smallest.

a $\frac{2}{5}, \frac{1}{4}$ b $\frac{5}{8}, \frac{2}{3}$ c $\frac{1}{3}, \frac{2}{7}$ d $\frac{3}{4}, \frac{5}{6}, \frac{5}{8}$

e $\frac{2}{5}, \frac{1}{3}, \frac{4}{15}, \frac{3}{10}$

INVESTIGATION 3

Marion is comparing two fractions, $\frac{3}{8}$ and $\frac{2}{5}$.

She says that $\frac{3}{8} < \frac{2}{5}$.

She adds the numerators together and the denominators together, which gives $\frac{3+2}{8+5} = \frac{5}{13}$.

She says that the answer lies between the two starting fractions, so that $\frac{3}{8} < \frac{5}{13} < \frac{2}{5}$.

She says that if you add the numerators and add the denominators of any two fractions, the answer lies between the two starting fractions.
Is she correct?

Work with a partner to investigate!

TIP

Remember that $<$ means 'is less than' and $>$ means 'is greater than'.

$5 < 7$ means '5 is less than 7'.

2.3 Calculating with fractions

Adding and subtracting with fractions

You can only add or subtract fractions if they have the same denominator.

If the denominators are different, you can use equivalent fractions with the same denominator.

WORKED EXAMPLE 8

Calculate.

a $\dfrac{3}{4}+\dfrac{1}{6}$ **b** $2\dfrac{2}{3}+1\dfrac{1}{2}$ **c** $\dfrac{5}{9}-\dfrac{1}{6}$ **d** $4\dfrac{2}{5}-1\dfrac{2}{3}$

Answers

a $\dfrac{3}{4}+\dfrac{1}{6}$

The lowest common multiple of 4 and 6 is 12, so use 12 as the denominator.

$\dfrac{9}{12}+\dfrac{2}{12}=\dfrac{11}{12}$

b $2\dfrac{2}{3}+1\dfrac{1}{2}$

Add the whole ones and use a denominator of 6 for the fraction parts.

$3\dfrac{4}{6}+\dfrac{3}{6}=3\dfrac{7}{6}$

$\dfrac{7}{6}$ is an improper fraction, equal to $1\dfrac{1}{6}$.

$=4\dfrac{1}{6}$

c $\dfrac{5}{9}-\dfrac{1}{6}=\dfrac{10}{18}-\dfrac{3}{18}=\dfrac{7}{18}$

d $4\dfrac{2}{5}-1\dfrac{2}{3}=3\dfrac{6}{15}-\dfrac{10}{15}$

Split one of the three whole ones into $\dfrac{15}{15}$.

$=2\dfrac{21}{15}-\dfrac{10}{15}=2\dfrac{11}{15}$

Use your calculator to check that it shows the same answer.
If you enter it correctly it will show the answer as an improper fraction, $\dfrac{41}{15}$.
Use shift with the fraction key to turn it into a mixed number, $2\dfrac{11}{15}$.

Multiplying and dividing with fractions

To multiply fractions, multiply the numerators and multiply the denominators.

To multiply mixed numbers, write them as improper fractions first.

When working with mixed fractions, always change the answer back into a mixed number and simplify the fraction to its simplest form.

WORKED EXAMPLE 9

Calculate.

a $\dfrac{3}{4}\times\dfrac{1}{6}$ **b** $2\dfrac{2}{3}\times1\dfrac{1}{2}$ **c** $3\dfrac{1}{5}\times1\dfrac{3}{4}$

Answers

a $\dfrac{3}{4}\times\dfrac{1}{6}=\dfrac{3\times1}{4\times6}=\dfrac{3}{24}=\dfrac{1}{8}$ **b** $2\dfrac{2}{3}\times1\dfrac{1}{2}=\dfrac{8}{3}\times\dfrac{3}{2}=\dfrac{24}{6}=4$

c $3\dfrac{1}{5}\times1\dfrac{3}{4}=\dfrac{16}{5}\times\dfrac{7}{4}=\dfrac{112}{20}=5\dfrac{12}{20}=5\dfrac{3}{5}$

Use your calculator to check that it shows the same answer. If you enter it correctly it will show the answer as an improper fraction, $\dfrac{41}{15}$. Use shift with the fraction key to turn it into a mixed number, $2\dfrac{11}{15}$.

To divide by a fraction, you multiply by its **reciprocal**.

To find the reciprocal, turn the fraction upside down.

WORKED EXAMPLE 10

Calculate.

a $\dfrac{3}{4} \div \dfrac{1}{6}$ **b** $2\dfrac{2}{3} \div 1\dfrac{3}{5}$ **c** $1\dfrac{1}{5} \div 2\dfrac{2}{3}$

Answers

a $\dfrac{3}{4} \div \dfrac{1}{6} = \dfrac{3}{4} \times \dfrac{6}{1} = \dfrac{18}{4} = 4\dfrac{2}{4} = 4\dfrac{1}{2}$

b $2\dfrac{2}{3} \div 1\dfrac{3}{5} = \dfrac{8}{3} \div \dfrac{8}{5} = \dfrac{8}{3} \times \dfrac{5}{8} = \dfrac{40}{24} = 1\dfrac{16}{24} = 1\dfrac{2}{3}$

c $1\dfrac{1}{5} \div 2\dfrac{2}{3} = \dfrac{6}{5} \div \dfrac{8}{3} = \dfrac{6}{5} \times \dfrac{3}{8} = \dfrac{18}{40} = \dfrac{9}{20}$

Exercise 2.3

 1 Calculate.

     a $\dfrac{2}{5} + \dfrac{1}{4}$ **b** $2\dfrac{5}{6} + 1\dfrac{1}{2}$ **c** $\dfrac{7}{8} - \dfrac{1}{6}$ **d** $3\dfrac{5}{9} - 1\dfrac{1}{6}$

     e $4\dfrac{1}{4} - 2\dfrac{5}{6}$ **f** $\dfrac{4}{5} \times \dfrac{1}{2}$ **g** $2\dfrac{1}{5} \times 1\dfrac{2}{3}$ **h** $4\dfrac{1}{2} \times 3\dfrac{1}{3}$

     i $\dfrac{5}{6} \div \dfrac{2}{3}$ **j** $2\dfrac{2}{5} \div 1\dfrac{1}{3}$ **k** $1\dfrac{3}{4} \div 2\dfrac{1}{3}$ **l** $2\dfrac{1}{2} + \dfrac{3}{5} - 1\dfrac{1}{4}$

     m $\dfrac{3}{4} \times 1\dfrac{2}{3} \times \dfrac{4}{5}$

 2 Keith spent $\dfrac{2}{5}$ of his wages on rent and $\dfrac{1}{4}$ of his wages on food.

     What fraction of his wages does he have left?

 3 Fang makes a drink by mixing $1\dfrac{1}{2}$ litres of fruit juice with $2\dfrac{2}{3}$ litres of soda water.

     She pours the drink into glasses that each hold $\dfrac{5}{12}$ of a litre.

     How many glasses can she fill?

 4 Copy and complete this table so that every row and every column has a **sum** of 1.

		$\dfrac{1}{6}$
	$\dfrac{19}{60}$	$\dfrac{7}{12}$
$\dfrac{2}{5}$		

5 Paula is investigating $\frac{3}{5}$ and $\frac{1}{2}$.

She calculates $\frac{3}{5} + \frac{1}{2}$, $\frac{3}{5} - \frac{1}{2}$, $\frac{3}{5} \times \frac{1}{2}$, and $\frac{3}{5} \div \frac{1}{2}$.

  a   Estimate which calculation you think will have the greatest answer.

  b   Estimate which calculation you think will have the smallest answer.

  c   Carry out the calculations. Were your estimates in parts **a** and **b** correct?

  d   Repeat the calculations using a calculator to check your answers.

6 Match these calculations into pairs with the same answer.

  a $1\frac{2}{3} \times 2\frac{4}{5}$ **b** $3\frac{1}{4} - 1\frac{3}{5}$ **c** $2\frac{1}{4} \div 1\frac{1}{2}$ **d** $1\frac{3}{5} \div 2\frac{2}{3}$ **e** $1\frac{1}{12} + \frac{2}{3}$ **f** $\frac{2}{5} - \frac{1}{15}$

  g $2\frac{1}{10} - 1\frac{1}{2}$ **h** $\frac{7}{20} + \frac{5}{8}$ **i** $3 - 1\frac{2}{3}$ **j** $1\frac{3}{10} \div 1\frac{1}{3}$ **k** $5\frac{1}{6} - \frac{1}{2}$ **l** $\frac{5}{6} \times 3$

  m $\frac{9}{10} + 1\frac{3}{5}$ **n** $\frac{5}{8} \times 2\frac{4}{5}$ **o** $2\frac{1}{5} \times \frac{3}{4}$ **p** $\frac{7}{12} \div 1\frac{3}{4}$ **q** $1\frac{1}{6} \times 1\frac{1}{7}$ **r** $\frac{5}{6} + \frac{2}{3}$

7 Marlon is making some wooden shelves.

Each shelf has a length of $2\frac{3}{8}$ metres.

He is making 6 shelves.

What is the total length of wood needed?

8 How much greater is $2\frac{1}{2} + \frac{2}{3}$ than $2\frac{1}{2} \times \frac{2}{3}$?

Now check all your answers to Exercise 2.3 by using a calculator. If you get a different answer, check both methods to see which is correct.

INVESTIGATION 4

Investigate this pattern of calculations.

$\frac{1}{2} \times \frac{2}{3} =$

$\frac{1}{2} \times \frac{2}{3} \times \frac{3}{4} =$

$\frac{1}{2} \times \frac{2}{3} \times \frac{3}{4} \times \frac{4}{5} =$

Continue the sequence.

MATHEMATICAL CONNECTIONS

You will look at sequences more closely in Chapter 22.

2.4 Fractions, decimals and percentages

Fractions, decimals and percentages are all ways of describing part of a whole.

$\frac{1}{2}$, 0.5 and 50% are equivalent as they all represent one half of a whole.

To find equivalent fractions, decimals and percentages, these facts are useful:

A fraction represents a division, for example, $\frac{3}{5} = 3 \div 5$.

A decimal has place values of $\frac{1}{10}$s, $\frac{1}{100}$s, $\frac{1}{1000}$s, and so on.

A percentage is part of 100 whereas fractions and decimals are parts of 1.

This diagram shows how to convert from one form into another.

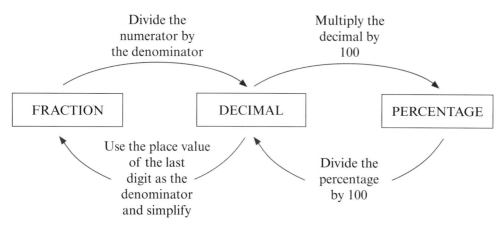

WORKED EXAMPLE 11

a Write $\dfrac{5}{8}$ as a decimal and as a percentage.

b Write 37.5% as a decimal and as a fraction.

c Write $\dfrac{5}{11}$ as a recurring decimal.

Answers

a $\dfrac{5}{8} = 5 \div 8$

$$8\overline{)5.^{5}0^{2}0^{4}0}$$
$$0.\ 6\ 2\ 5$$

$0.625 \times 100 = 62.5\%$

b $37.5\% = 37.5 \div 100 = 0.375$

In 0.375, the last digit is 5 thousandths.

So $0.375 = \dfrac{375}{1000} = \dfrac{3}{8}$

Your calculator automatically changes percentages to fractions. Input 37.5%.

Type EXE or = to change the display to $\dfrac{3}{8}$.

c $\dfrac{5}{11} = 5 \div 11$

$$11\overline{)5.^{5}0^{6}0^{5}0^{6}0}$$
$$0.\ 4\ 5\ 4\ 5$$

So $\dfrac{5}{11} = 0.\dot{4}\dot{5}$

Now check all your answers to Exercise 2.3 by using a calculator. If you get a different answer, check both methods to see which is correct.

TIP

Write the numerator with as many zeros after the decimal point as required.

Exercise 2.4

1 a Write $\frac{3}{4}$ as a decimal. b Write $\frac{3}{4}$ as a percentage.

2 a Write 0.48 as a fraction. b Write 0.48 as a percentage.

3 a Write 24% as a decimal. b Write 24% as a fraction.

4 Copy and complete this table so that each row gives equivalent fractions, decimals and percentages.

Fraction	Decimal	Percentage
$\frac{2}{5}$		
	0.85	
		60%
$\frac{1}{8}$		
	0.44	
		35%
$\frac{1}{6}$		

5 Barbara and David are trying to put these numbers in order of size.

$\frac{7}{8}$ 0.85   72% $\frac{9}{10}$ 77.5% $\frac{3}{4}$

a Barbara thinks the best way is to change them all into decimals.
Change them all into decimals and then write them in order of size, starting with the smallest.

b David thinks it would be easier to change them all into fractions.
Is he correct?

INVESTIGATION 5

Some fractions give a recurring decimal.

For example, $\frac{1}{11} = 0.090\,909\,09 \ldots = 0.\dot{0}\dot{9}$

Some fractions give a terminating decimal. For example, $\frac{1}{16} = 0.0625$

Investigate which fractions give a recurring decimal and which fractions give a terminating decimal.

2.5 Using negative numbers

Negative numbers

Here is part of a number line:

Numbers greater than zero are positive numbers, but usually you write positive numbers without the + sign.

Numbers less than zero are negative numbers. You write negative numbers with a − sign.

Zero is neither positive nor negative.

The numbers get larger as you move to the right.

So, 4 is greater than 2, 1 is greater than −3, −1 is greater than −4.

The symbol > means 'is greater than'.

So, $4 > 2$, $1 > -3$, $-1 > -4$.

The symbol < means 'is less than'.

So $-3 < -1 < 0 < 2 < 5$ This says that −3 is less than −1, −1 is less than 0, 0 is less than 2, and 2 is less than 5.

The symbol ⩽ means 'is less than or equal to'.

The symbol ⩾ means 'is greater than or equal to'.

WORKED EXAMPLE 12

1 Write these numbers in order of size, starting with the smallest:

   a   4   −2   6   −3   1

   b   1.2   −2   0   −1.1   2

   c   −1.4   1.6   1.46   −1.38   −1.5

2 Here is a list of integers:

    −5   −4   −3   −2   −1   0   1   2   3   4   5

   a   From the list, write down the integers that are:

      i > 2

      ii $⩽ -2$

      iii $⩾ 3$

      iv $⩽ 1$ and also > -2

   b   Your answers to parts **i** and **iii** should be the same. However, explain why > 2 and $⩾ 3$ do not mean **exactly** the same.

Answers

1 **a**   −3, −2, 1, 4, 6

    b   −2, −1.1, 0, 1.2, 2

    c   −1.5, −1.4, −1.38, 1.46, 1.6

TIP

Use a number line if it helps.

> **CONTINUED**
>
> **2** **a** **i** 3, 4 and 5 as these are to the right of 2 on the number line.
>
>   **ii** −5, −4, −3 and −2. The first three of these are less than −2, and the fourth is equal to −2.
>
>   **iii** 3, 4 and 5.
>
>   **iv** −1, 0 and 1.
>
> **b** >2 includes all numbers greater than 2. Some of these (for example, 2.5, 2.9, 2.01) are not ⩾3.

Calculating with negative numbers

You know that $5 + 2 = 2 + 5$, and $7 + 1 = 1 + 7$.

$-2 + 5 = 3$, as you start at −2 and move forwards 5.

What does that tell you about the value of $5 + -2$?

Adding −2 has the same effect as subtracting 2.

Subtracting −2 has the same effect as adding 2.

> **WORKED EXAMPLE 13**
>
> Calculate.
>
> **a** $6 - 8$ **b** $-2 + -5$ **c** $-4 - 3$ **d** $-2 - -7$
>
> **Answers**
>
> **a** $6 - 8 = -2$ starting at 6 and counting back 8
>
> **b** $-2 + -5 = -2 - 5 = -7$ starting at −2 and counting back 5
>
> **c** $-4 - 3 = -7$ starting at −4 and counting back 3
>
> **d** $-2 - -7 = -2 + 7 = 5$ starting at −2 and counting forwards 7

When multiplying and dividing, a negative number changes the sign of the answer.

$2 \times 3 = 6$, so $-2 \times 3 = -6$

A second negative number changes the sign back again.

$15 \div 5 = 3$, so $-15 \div 5 = -3$, and $-15 \div -5 = 3$

WORKED EXAMPLE 14

Calculate.

a 4×-2 **b** $-20 \div -5$ **c** $-18 \div 6$ **d** $-2 \times -7 \times -3$

Answers

a $4 \times -2 = -8$ as $4 \times 2 = 8$, so $4 \times -2 = -8$

b $-20 \div -5 = 4$ as $20 \div 5 = 4$, so $-20 \div 5 = -4$ and so $-20 \div -5 = 4$

c $-18 \div 6 = -3$ as $18 \div 6 = 3$

d $-2 \times -7 \times -3 = 14 \times -3 = -42$

Exercise 2.5

 1 Say whether these statements are true or false.

    a $-4 > -2$ **b** $-3 < 1$ **c** $4 + -2 > 3$

    d $-2 \times -3 = 2 \times 3$ **e** $6 \div -2 > 2$

 2 The temperature in London at 7 a.m. was $-3\,°C$.

    a By 12 noon, the temperature was 7 degrees higher. What was the temperature at 12 noon?

    b Between 12 noon and 10 p.m., the temperature dropped by 9 degrees. What was the temperature at 10 p.m.?

 3 Calculate.

    a $4 + -2$ **b** $-4 - -5$ **c** 12×-4

    d $-24 \div -6$ **e** $-7 - 4 + -3$ **f** $-4 \times -2 + 7$

    g $-4 + 20 - -4$ **h** $3 \times -4 \div -2$ **i** $-1 + 2 - -3$

    j $-4 - -4$

 4 Write down two numbers with a sum of -2 and a **product** of -24.

 5 Copy and complete these walls so that the numbers in two adjacent bricks add up to the answer in the brick below.

    a 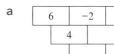   **b**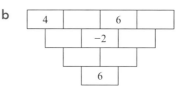

 6 Copy and complete these walls so that the numbers in two adjacent bricks multiply to the answer in the brick below.

    a    **b**

INVESTIGATION 6

Four numbers, when added in pairs, give sums of −3, 1, 2, 2, 3 and 7.

Find the four numbers.

Create your own puzzle similar to this puzzle and ask a partner to solve it.

Try creating a puzzle with five starting numbers.

2.6 The order of operations

DISCUSSION 3

Oliver asked his brother Ed, 'What is half of eight plus twelve?'

Ed said 'Sixteen'.

Oliver said, 'No, I make it ten.'

Discuss their answers with a partner.

In mathematics, there is a specific order of operations to use when carrying out multiple stage calculations.

Carry out operations in **brackets** first.

Then any **indices** or powers.

After that, **division** and **multiplication** in the order they appear.

Finally, the **addition** and **subtraction** in the order they appear.

WORKED EXAMPLE 15

Calculate.

1 $3 + 5 \times 2^3 - 12 \div (4 - 1)$

2 $6 + 0.3 \times 5 - (2 + 4)^2 \div 1.2$

3 $2\dfrac{1}{2} + \dfrac{3}{4} \div \left(1\dfrac{1}{8} - \dfrac{7}{12}\right)$

Answers

1	$3 + 5 \times 2^3 - 12 \div (4 - 1) = 3 + 5 \times 2^3 - 12 \div (4 - 1)$	Brackets first
	$= 3 + 5 \times 2^3 - 12 \div 3$	Indices
	$= 3 + 5 \times 8 - 12 \div 3$	Division and multiplication as they appear
	$= 3 + 40 - 4$	Addition and subtraction as they appear
	$= 39$	

CONTINUED

2 $6 + 0.3 \times 5 - (2 + 4)^2 \div 1.2 = 6 + 0.3 \times 5 - (2 + 4)^2 \div 1.2$ Brackets first

$= 6 + 0.3 \times 5 - 6^2 \div 1.2$ Indices

$= 6 + 0.3 \times 5 - 36 \div 1.2$ Division and multiplication as they appear

$= 6 + 1.5 - 30$ Addition and subtraction as they appear

$= -23.5$

3 $2\frac{1}{2} + \frac{3}{4} \div \left(1\frac{1}{8} - \frac{7}{12}\right) = 2\frac{1}{2} + \frac{3}{4} \div \left(1\frac{3}{24} - \frac{14}{24}\right)$ Brackets first

$= 2\frac{1}{2} + \frac{3}{4} \div \left(\frac{27}{24} - \frac{14}{24}\right)$

$= 2\frac{1}{2} + \frac{3}{4} \div \frac{13}{24}$ Division next

$= 2\frac{1}{2} + \frac{3}{4} \times \frac{24}{13}$

$= 2\frac{1}{2} + \frac{72}{52}$

$= 2\frac{1}{2} + 1\frac{5}{13}$ Then addition

$= 3\frac{13}{26} + \frac{10}{26}$

$= 3\frac{23}{26}$

Exercise 2.6

1   Choose one of these symbols to make each statement correct.

$<$ $=$ $>$

a 0.6 .... $\frac{2}{3}$

b 1.2×0.4 .... $1.2 - 0.4$

c $8 - -3$ .... -4×-3

 2   Calculate.

a $3 + 2 \times 5$ b $(3 + 2) \times 5$ c $6 - (12 \div 2)$

d $4 + 5 \times (2 + 3)$ e $4 - (3 \times 5)$ f $(13 + 2) \div 5 - 2$

g $(13 + 2) \div (5 - 2)$ h $-2 + -4 \times -3 - -1$ i $-4 - 3 \times -2 + -1$

3   Copy these calculations and insert brackets to make the answers correct.

   a $4 + 3 \times 2 = 14$ b $6 + 2 \times 5 - 1 = 14$ c $24 + 8 \div 4 - 2 = 28$

   d $3 - 1 \times 6 + 4 = 16$ e $5 - 2 \times 3 + 2 = -5$ f $4 \times 6 - 3 \div 2 = 6$

   g $3 \times 5 - 2 + 7 = 16$ h $18 \div 6 - 4 \times 2 = 18$ i $9 - 3 \times 4 + 1 = 30$

4   Calculate.

   a $2.4 + 3.2 \times 3$ b $3 \div (1.8 - 0.3)$ c $\dfrac{5}{12} + \dfrac{3}{8}$

   d $1\dfrac{3}{8} - \dfrac{5}{6}$ e $2\dfrac{1}{3} \div 1\dfrac{2}{5} - \dfrac{5}{6}$ f $\dfrac{2}{3} - \dfrac{4}{5} \times \dfrac{5}{8}$

   g $2\dfrac{1}{4} \times 1\dfrac{1}{3} - \dfrac{5}{6} \div \dfrac{5}{9}$ h $(1.4 - 0.3)^2 + 1.4 \times 0.3$ i $4\dfrac{3}{8} - \left(\dfrac{3}{4} + \dfrac{1}{2}\right)^2$

5   Jerome and Francois are doing some homework.

   Here are their answers to the question: What is $3.2 - 1.5 \times 2.4 + 0.6$?

Jerome's answer:	Francois's answer:
$3.2 - 1.5 = 1.7$	$1.5 \times 2.4 = 3.6$
$1.7 \times 2.4 = 4.08$	$3.6 + 0.6 = 4.2$
$4.08 - 0.6 = 3.48$	$3.2 - 4.2 = -1$

   Explain their mistakes and calculate the correct answer.

SUMMARY

Are you able to... ?
put numbers in order of size, including fractions, decimals and negative numbers
use the mathematical symbols $=$, $\neq$, $<$, $>$, $\leqslant$ and $\geqslant$
use the correct order of operations and brackets when carrying out calculations
convert between improper fractions and mixed numbers
add, subtract, multiply and divide: •   integers •   fractions •   decimals
recognise equivalence and convert between fractions, decimals and percentages.

Past paper questions

1   Write $\dfrac{1}{6}$, 17% and 0.16 in order of size, starting with the smallest.

................., ..., ... [1]
smallest

Cambridge IGCSE International Mathematics 0607 Paper 32 Q3 c June 2021

2   a   Work out.

    i $16.4 - 23.8$

.... [1]

    ii $5.2 - 3 \times 4.1$

.... [1]

Cambridge IGCSE International Mathematics 0607 Paper 31 Q1 a i & ii June 2018

3   a   Work out.

    Give each answer as a fraction in its simplest form.

    i $\dfrac{2}{5} + \dfrac{1}{3}$

.... [1]

    ii $\dfrac{5}{8} - \dfrac{1}{4}$

.... [1]

    iii $3\dfrac{3}{10} \times \dfrac{5}{6}$

.... [1]

Cambridge IGCSE International Mathematics 0607 Paper 31 Q2 e i, ii & iii June 2020

4   a   Insert one pair of brackets to make this calculation correct.

    $3 \quad \times \quad 6 \quad + \quad 5 \quad - \quad 4 \quad = \quad 29$

[1]

    b   Work out.

    $\dfrac{25.2}{6.1 + 3.8}$

    Write your answer correct to two decimal places.

.... [2]

Cambridge IGCSE International Mathematics 0607 Paper 33 Q4 d & e November 2017

Chapter 3

Using number

IN THIS CHAPTER YOU WILL:

- use ratio

- calculate using rate and proportion

- use percentages

- calculate percentage increase and decrease

- understand and calculate simple interest and compound interest

- use a calculator efficiently

- solve problems involving time and money

> use reverse percentages

> understand and use exponential growth and decay.

GETTING STARTED

1   Calculate.
   a $50 ÷ 4   b $30 ÷ 12   c $4 ÷ 50

2   Write these percentages as fractions and decimals.
   a   45%   b   70%   c   4%   d   12.5%

3   Write these fractions as percentages.
   a $\frac{1}{5}$ b $\frac{7}{8}$ c $\frac{11}{20}$

4   Copy and compete these statements.
   a   3 weeks = ... days
   b $3\frac{1}{2}$ hours = ... minutes
   c   84 hours = ... days
   d $2\frac{3}{4}$ minutes = ... seconds
   e   2 days = ... minutes = ... seconds

3.1 Using ratio

A **ratio** compares two or more quantities.
This necklace has 12 black beads and 8 white beads.

The ratio of black beads to white beads is 12 : 8.

You can simplify ratios by multiplying or dividing both numbers by the same amount.

4 is the highest common factor of 12 and 8.

Dividing by 4 gives the simplest ratio of 3 : 2.

Dividing by the highest common factor always gives the ratio in its simplest form.

This means that for every 3 black beads there are 2 white beads.

MATHEMATICAL CONNECTIONS

You learnt how to convert between percentages, fractions and decimals in Chapter 2.

MATHEMATICAL CONNECTIONS

You learnt about highest common factors in Chapter 1.

WORKED EXAMPLE 1

a   A bus had 65 passengers. Ten passengers were standing and the rest were seated. Find the ratio of standing passengers to seated passengers in its simplest form.

b   On another bus, the ratio of standing passengers to seating passengers was 2 : 13. If 8 passengers were standing, how many passengers were seated?

c   The next bus had 72 passengers. The ratio of standing passengers to seated passengers was 2 : 7. How many passengers were seated?

CONTINUED

Answers

a   Ten passengers were standing, so 55 passengers were seated. Ratio of standing to seated is 10 : 55. Dividing by 5, the ratio in its simplest form is 2 : 11.

b   The passengers can be split into 15 equal parts. 2 parts are standing, 13 parts are seated.

The 8 standing passengers make up 2 parts, so each part is made up of 4 passengers.

There are 13 parts of seated passengers.

13 × 4 = 52 seated passengers

c   There are 9 equal parts, 2 parts are standing and 7 parts are seated.

Each part = 72 ÷ 9 = 8 passengers

The 7 seated parts = 7 × 8 = 56 seated passengers

Map scales are often written as ratios.

A map scale of 1 : 1000 means that 1 cm on the map represents 1000 cm in reality, and 1 mm on the map represents 1000 mm in reality.

WORKED EXAMPLE 2

A map has a scale of 1 : 50 000.

a   On the map, the distance between two villages is 15.2 cm. How many km apart are the villages in the real world?

b   Jane walks 4.2 km. She looks at her route on the map. Her route will be shown by how many cm on the map?

Answers

a   The real world is 50 000 times larger than the map.
    The real distance is 15.2 × 50 000 cm = 760 000 cm = 7600 m = 7.6 km

b   4.2 km = 4200 m = 420 000 cm
    On the map, this is represented by 420 000 ÷ 50 000 = 8.4 cm

MATHEMATICS IN CONTEXT

Reading and understanding map scales is an important skill so that you can interpret a map and understand the real distances the map represents.

Exercise 3.1

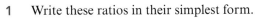

1   Write these ratios in their simplest form.

   a   6 : 18   b   12 : 20   c   15 : 18   d   20 : 15   e   8 : 20 : 12

2   Mona is making a fruit juice drink.

   She mixes orange juice and pineapple juice in the ratio 3 : 2.

   She uses 12 litres of orange juice.

   How much pineapple juice does she use?

3   Michael and Sara share some money in the ratio 5 : 6.

   Sara receives $90.

   How much money in total do they share?

4   A fish pie recipe uses 300 g fish, 400 g potato and 50 g butter.

   a   Write the ratio of fish, potato and butter in its simplest form.

   b   Marjory has only 240 g of fish. How much butter and potato should she use?

5   For her birthday, Jasmine received $450.

   She saved four times as much as she spent.

   How much money did she save?

6   A farm has horses, chickens and sheep.

   The ratio of horses to chickens is $3 : 2$.

   The ratio of chickens to sheep is $3 : 5$.

   a   What is the ratio of horses to sheep?

   b   If there are 45 horses, how many animals are there on the farm in total?

7   A class of 28 students has 4 more right-handed students than left-handed students.

   What is the ratio of right-handed students to left-handed students in its simplest form?

8   The ratio of adults to children in a café is $4 : 5$.

   An adult and two children come in. The ratio of adults to children is now $7 : 9$.

   How many customers are there now altogether?

9   Macha is drawing a map of her village. She uses a scale of $1 : 2000$.

   a   On her map, the main street is 12.4 cm long. How long is the main street in real life?

   b   From east to west, the village is 1.2 km long. What will this distance be shown as on the map?

10   A distance of 4.5 km is shown as 7.5 cm on a map.

   What is the scale of the map? Give your answer in the form $1 : n$.

11   A vegetarian stew recipe for four people has these ingredients:

> 360 g butternut squash
> 250 g sweet peppers
> 400 g cannellini beans
> 400 g chickpeas
> 400 g tomatoes
> 75 g pine nuts
> 1 onion

Maria wants to make the stew for 15 people.

   a   Write the quantities of each ingredient that she needs.

   b   Shop A sells 500 g of cannellini beans for $1.20, and 400 g of chickpeas for $1.45.

      Shop B sells 750 g of cannellini beans for $1.75 and 650 g of chickpeas for $2.30.

      Which shop offers the best value for each ingredient?

Do you think ratios are important when adapting recipes?

Are you confident that you could adapt a recipe in real life?

INVESTIGATION 1

Arthur, Beatrice and Clarissa are going to share some money in the ratio $5:4:3$.

Arthur adds 1 to each share and suggests that instead they should share the money in the ratio $6:5:4$.

They all agree, as they think their share will be bigger using this new ratio.

Who gains and who loses using the new ratio?

Investigate for different starting ratios.

SELF ASSESSMENT

Can you think of three other ratios that mean the same as $3:2$?

3.2 Time and rates

Time

You need to know that:

1 year = 365 days or 12 months

1 week = 7 days

1 day = 24 hours

1 hour = 60 minutes

1 minute = 60 seconds

Time is not metric. Take care when using a calculator.

On your Casio fx-CG50, select **Run-Matrix** from the main menu.

To input 2 hours 20 minutes and 30 seconds into the calculator, use the time key, which is found by entering the following sequence:

 OPTN (F6) ($\triangleright$) (F5) ($°\,'\,''$) (F4) ($°\,'\,''$)

(Note that this function might appear as a key on your calculator $\boxed{'\,''}$.)

Then enter 2 OPTN (F6) ($\triangleright$) (F5) (ANGLE) (F4) ($°\,'\,''$) 20 (F4) ($°\,'\,''$) 30 (F4) ($°\,'\,''$)

This is displayed as $2°20'30''$ and can then be used in calculations.

Using the (F5) ($°\,'\,''$) key after an answer of 3.25 will change the display from 3.25 hours to 3 hours 15 minutes.

> **TIP**
>
> There are 60 minutes in an hour, so $\frac{1}{4}$ of an hour is 15 minutes, so 0.25 hours = 15 minutes
>
> There are 60 seconds in a minute, so $\frac{1}{2}$ of a minute is 30 seconds, so 0.5 minutes = 30 seconds

The 24-hour clock

Timetables usually use the 24-hour clock.

In the 24-hour clock, 06:45 means 6.45 a.m., 18:45 means 6.45 p.m.

WORKED EXAMPLE 3

A train leaves at 12:43 and arrives at its destination at 15:27.
Calculate the duration of the journey.

Answer

Without a calculator:

12:43 to 13:00 = 17 minutes

13:00 to 15:00 = 2 hours

15:00 to 15:27 = 27 minutes

Total time = 2 hours 44 minutes

With a calculator:

15 ⌊ ′ ″ ⌋ 27 ⌊ ′ ″ ⌋ −12 ⌊ ′ ″ ⌋ 43 ⌊ ′ ″ ⌋ = 2°44′0″, or 2 hours 44 minutes

---

Time zones

You need to consider time zones when using flight timetables.

WORKED EXAMPLE 4

Bahrain is one hour ahead of Cairo.

a   A flight leaves Bahrain Airport at 9.40 a.m. and lands at Cairo Airport 3 hours and 20 minutes later. What is the local time in Cairo when the plane arrives?

b   A return flight leaves Cairo at 13:45 and arrives at Bahrain at 17:15. How long does this journey take?

Answers

a   3 hours and 20 minutes after 9.40 a.m. is 1 p.m. in Bahrain time. Cairo is one hour behind, so the time in Cairo is 12 noon.

b   17:15 in Bahrain is 16:15 in Cairo. So, in Cairo time, the flight is from 13:45 to 16:15, which is 2 hours 30 minutes.

Rates

There are many uses of **rates** in mathematics.

For example:

Speed is a measure of distance travelled per unit of time, for example, how many metres travelled in 1 second.

Density is a measure of the mass per unit volume of a material, for example, how many grams in 1 cm^3.

Currency exchange rates tell how much of one currency is worth 1 unit of another currency.

> ### MATHEMATICS IN CONTEXT
>
> As the world takes 24 hours to turn on its axis, the world is divided into different time zones. For example, Bahrain is one hour ahead of Cairo.

> ### MATHEMATICS IN CONTEXT
>
> Travelling across time zones can make journey times appear shorter or longer than they really are!

Speed

The speed that something travels at is the distance travelled in a unit of time.

For example, if an athlete's speed is 10 metres per second (m/s), this means on average they run 10 metres every second.

To calculate a speed, divide the distance travelled by the time taken.

$$\text{Speed} = \frac{\text{distance}}{\text{time}}$$

A useful way to remember this formula is in a triangle:

To calculate a speed, cover the S and the formula is $\frac{D}{T}$.

Similarly, time $= \frac{D}{S}$ and distance $= S \times T$

WORKED EXAMPLE 5

a Amaya cycles to work, a distance of 16 km. She cycles at 12 km/h.
   How long does the journey take?

b Amaya is paid $18 per hour. She works for 7 hours and 45 minutes.
   How much will she be paid?

c In her job, Amaya is making steel ball bearings. She makes 961 ball bearings during the day.
   How many ball bearings does she make per hour?

d Amaya cycles home in 40 minutes. What is her average speed on the journey home?

e Amaya drives a distance of 72 km, and uses 9.6 litres of fuel.
   Calculate her fuel consumption in km/litre.

Answers

a $\text{Time} = \dfrac{\text{distance}}{\text{speed}}$

$\qquad = \dfrac{16}{12}$

$\qquad = 1\frac{1}{3}$ hours

> **TIP**
>
> Pressing the time key on your calculator, (′ ″),
> will change this into hours minutes and seconds:
> 1°20′0″.

b Amaya is paid $18 per hour so she will be paid $18 × 7.75 = $139.50

> **TIP**
>
> Remember to use two decimal places when giving answers involving money.

> **TIP**
>
> You can input the time using the time key.
>
> You should press 18 × 7 (′ ″) 45 (′ ″) = 139°30′0″.
>
> Press the **S↔D** key to change this to $\dfrac{279}{2} = \$139.50$

DISCUSSION 1

When two quantities increase (become larger) or decrease (become smaller) at the same rate, they are in proportion. The amount that Amaya is paid is in proportion to the time she works. Is the number of ball bearings Amaya makes necessarily in proportion to the time she works? Discuss with a partner.

CONTINUED

c   Amaya makes 961 ball bearings in 7 hours 45 minutes.

   So on average she makes $\dfrac{961}{7.75} = 124$ ball bearings per hour.

   Alternatively, input 7 hours 45 minutes using the time key.

   The display should show $\dfrac{961}{7°45°}$

d   Speed $= \dfrac{\text{distance}}{\text{time}} = \dfrac{16}{0°40°} = 24 \, \text{km/h}$

e   Amaya uses 9.6 litres to travel 72 km. So she uses 1 litre for every $\dfrac{72}{9.6} = 7.5 \, \text{km}$.
   Her fuel consumption is 7.5 km/litre.

WORKED EXAMPLE 6

a   The density of gold is 19.3 g/cm³.
   The density of silver is 10.5 g/cm³.
   What volume of silver will have the same mass as 63 cm³ of gold?

b   On a particular day, the exchange rates between the US dollar and the Australian dollar and Nigerian naira are:

   1 US dollar = 1.41 Australian dollars

   1 US dollar = 416 Nigerian naira

   Chester changes 5000 Australian dollars into US dollars, and then changes half the US dollars into Nigerian naira.

   How much of each currency does he have?

Answers

a   Every cm³ of gold has a mass of 19.3 g, so 63 cm³ of gold has a mass of:
   $19.3 \times 63 = 1215.9 \, \text{g}$
   Every 10.5 g of silver has a volume of 1 cm³, so 1215.9 g of silver has a volume of:
   $1215.9 \div 10.5 = 115.8 \, \text{cm}^3$

b   Every 1.41 Australian dollars are worth 1 US dollar, so 5000 Australian dollars are worth $5000 \div 1.41 = 3546.10$ US dollars.
   Half of 3546.10 US dollars is 1773.05 US dollars.
   Every US dollar is worth 416 Nigerian naira.
   So 1773.05 US dollars $= 1773.05 \times 416 = 737\,588.80$ Nigerian naira
   Chester has 1773.05 US dollars and 737 588.80 Nigerian naira.

Exercise 3.2

1   Write these times in minutes.

   a   2 hours   b   3 hours 15 minutes   c   90 seconds   d   165 seconds

2   Mo gets paid on the 15th of every month. If today is the 16th of March, how many days does Mo have to wait until he gets paid again?

3 a Morris drives 210 km to visit his mother. The journey takes 3 hours. Calculate his average speed.

b Morris uses 17.5 litres of fuel. Calculate his fuel consumption in km/litre.

c Morris drives home at an average speed of 60 km/h. How long does the journey home take him?

d On his return home, his fuel consumption is 15 km/litre. How many litres of fuel does he use?

4 A hosepipe fills a 120-litre tank in 7 minutes and 30 seconds.

How many litres per minute pass through the hosepipe?

5 Mabel earns $9.50 per hour.

She works 8 hours every day from Monday to Friday, and 4 hours on Saturday.

How much does she earn for the week?

6 The exchange rate for Hong Kong dollars (HKD) and US dollars (USD) is 1 USD = 7.85 HKD.

a A traveller to Hong Kong exchanges 650 US dollars. How many Hong Kong dollars does she receive?

b On her return she changes back 942 HKD to USD. How much does she receive?

7 A truck driver fills her fuel tank. She drives 400 km.

It takes 120 litres to fill the tank again. How many km does she travel for each litre of fuel?

8 A scrap metal dealer pays $1.24 per kg of metal.

a How much does he pay for 350 kg of scrap metal?

b He paid $303.80 for some scrap metal. How much scrap metal did he buy?

9 I cycle to visit a friend at an average speed of 12 km/h. The journey takes 10 minutes.

I walk home at an average speed of 8 km/h.

Calculate:

a the distance I cycle

b the time taken to walk home

c my average speed over the two journeys.

10 A bus leaves at 25 minutes past 11 o'clock and arrives at its destination, 84 km away, on the same day at 10 minutes past one.

a Calculate the average speed of the bus.

b The bus has a fuel consumption of 3.5 km / litre. How much fuel does the bus use on the journey.

11 Mary runs 200 m in 23 seconds.

Suzie runs 120 m in 12.8 seconds.

Jasmine runs 250 m in 26.1 seconds.

Who is the fastest runner?

TIP

You will learn how to calculate the mean average in Chapter 19. Average speed is the total distance travelled divided by the total amount of time taken.

12 Brass is made by combining zinc and copper in the ratio 1 : 2 by volume.

The density of zinc is 7.1 g/cm³.

The density of copper is 8.9 g/cm³.

In a 300 cm³ block of brass, calculate:

a the mass of the zinc in grams

b the mass of the copper in grams

c the density of the brass.

13 I leave home at half past seven in the morning and walk to the bus stop 4 km away. The bus leaves at 10 minutes past 8 o'clock for the railway station, travelling 18 km at an average speed of 45 km/h.

a At what time do I arrive at the railway station?

b Calculate the total distance I have travelled from home to the station, and the number of minutes that it has taken me to get there.

c What is my average speed on the journey from home to the station?

14 Here is part of a train timetable:

Tamien	07:12	09:05	10:05	11:05	–
Lawrence	07:31	09:24	10:24	11:24	12:24
Mountain View	07:42	09:36	10:36	11:36	12:36
California Avenue	07:48	09:42	10:42	11:42	12:42
Menlo Park	07:55	09:50	10:50	11:50	12:50
Belmont	08:09	10:04	11:04	12:04	13:04
Hillsdale	08:12	10:08	11:08	12:08	13:08
Hayward Park	08:15	10:11	11:11	12:11	13:11

Amy Lives at Mountain View. She wants to arrive at Hayward Park by 11:30.

a What time train from Mountain View should she take?

b The train travels at an average speed of 72 km/h.

Calculate the distance from Mountain View to Hayward Park.

15 Rohit is travelling from Mumbai to New York. He has to take two flights, the first flight from Mumbai to Doha, and then the second flight from Doha to New York.

Mumbai is 2 hours ahead of Doha, and Doha is 8 hours ahead of New York.

Here is the timetable for his outward journey and his return journey.

Outward		Return	
Mumbai	04:45	New York	21:55
Arrive Doha	06:10	Arrive Doha	17:30 next day
Depart Doha	09:30	Depart Doha	20:35
New York	16:10	Mumbai	02:45 next day

a How long is the outward flight from Mumbai to Doha?

b How long is the outward flight from Doha to New York?

c How long after leaving Mumbai will Rohit arrive in New York?

d How long is the return flight from New York to Doha?

e How long is the return flight from Doha to Mumbai?

f How long after leaving New York will Rohit arrive in Mumbai?

DISCUSSION 2

Clara and Mandisa live 8 km apart.

They decide to meet. Clara walks towards Mandisa's house at an average speed of 6 km/h.

Mandisa leaves her home at the same time as Clara leaves her home and cycles towards Clara's house at an average speed of 14 km/h.

How far from Clara's house will they be when they meet?

Discuss with a partner.

3.3 Percentages

To use percentages in calculations, it often helps to remember the connection between percentages, decimals and fractions.

To find a percentage of a quantity, you can write the percentage as a decimal or a fraction.

MATHEMATICAL CONNECTIONS

You learnt how to convert between percentages, decimals and fractions in Chapter 2.

WORKED EXAMPLE 7

Juan has \$165.

He saves 30% and spends the rest.

How much does he save?

Answer

He saves 30% of \$165.

Using fractions: Using decimals: Using a calculator:

30% of \$165   30% of \$165   30% of \$165

$$= \frac{30}{100} \times 165 \qquad = 0.3 \times 165$$

$$= \boxed{3}\ \boxed{0}\ \boxed{\div}\ \boxed{1}\ \boxed{0}\ \boxed{0}\ \boxed{\text{EXE}}$$

$$\boxed{\times}\ \boxed{1}\ \boxed{6}\ \boxed{5}\ \boxed{\text{EXE}}$$

$$= \frac{3}{10} \times \frac{165}{1} \qquad = 49.5 = \$49.50 \qquad = 49.5 = \$49.50$$

$$= \frac{495}{10} = 49.5 = \$49.50$$

TIP

When using fractions, decimals or percentages, 'of' means multiply.

TIP

Remember to include the \$ sign and to write money with two decimal places.

To write one quantity as a percentage of another, write it as a fraction, and then change it to a percentage.

WORKED EXAMPLE 8

In a school of 650 students, 208 students wear glasses.

What percentage of the students in the school wear glasses?

Answer

As a fraction, $\frac{208}{650}$ wear glasses.

To change to a decimal, divide $208 \div 650 = 0.32$

Then change it to a percentage: $0.32 \times 100 = 32\%$

Exercise 3.3

 1 Shirley earns $240.

She gives 40% to her mother.

How much money does she give to her mother?

 2 A school has 72 students who are at least 1.7 m tall and 48 students who are shorter than 1.7 m.

What percentage of the students are shorter than 1.7 m?

 3 In a box of 325 apples, 4% of the apples are rotten.

How many rotten apples are there in the box?

 4 In one season, a football team wins 15 matches, draws 6 matches and loses 9 matches.

   a What percentage of its matches does the team lose?

   b What percentage of its matches does the team draw?

   c What percentage of its matches does the team win?

SELF ASSESSMENT

What should your answers to parts **a**, **b** and **c** of Question **4** add up to?

Check that your answers do add up to this value.

---

5 The table shows information about the number of workers in a factory.

	Left-handed	Right-handed	Total
Under 50 years old	12	60	72
50 years old and over	6	42	48
Total	18	102	120

   a What percentage of the workers are under 50 years old?

   b What percentage of the workers are right-handed?

   c What percentage of the workers under 50 years old are left-handed?

6 An ice cream seller sells 45 chocolate ice creams, 69 vanilla ice creams and 36 mint ice creams.

Calculate the percentage of each flavour that she sells.

7 In an exam, students are awarded one of six grades according to their mark:

Percentage, $x\%$	Grade
$x \geqslant 80$	A
$70 \leqslant x < 80$	B
$55 \leqslant x < 70$	C
$40 \leqslant x < 55$	D
$30 \leqslant x < 40$	E
$x < 30$	F

Calculate the grades for these students:

Alice scored 35 out of 40

Brian scored 52 out 80

Cathy scored 14 out of 25

David scored 27 out of 60

Erica scored 57 out of 120

Fergus scored 17 out of 40

8   Match these numbers into pairs with the same answer.

20% of 140	60% of 50	20% of 165	4% of 450
11% of 300	21% of 40	56% of 50	14% of 150
35% of 60	15% of 120	12.5% of 240	8% of 105

9   An electronics manufacturer makes three types of computer chip.

In one week, they manufacture 40 000 of type A, of which 720 are faulty.
In the same week they manufacture 25 000 of type B, of which 390 are faulty.

They also manufacture 5000 of type C, of which 80 are faulty.

a   Calculate the percentage of each type that are faulty.

b   Calculate the overall percentage of computer chips that are faulty.

10 Copy and complete these statements using each of the numbers in the box once.

| 10 | 15 | 20 | 25 | 40 | 45 | 50 | 60 | 75 | 80 | 125 | 150 |

a   ☐ % of ☐ = ☐

b   ☐ % of ☐ = ☐

c   ☐ % of ☐ = ☐

d   ☐ % of ☐ = ☐

DISCUSSION 3

Before a cricket match between City and Town, both teams had played the same number of matches.

City had won 80% of their matches. Town had won 60% of their matches.

After the match, City had won 75% of their matches and Town had won 62.5% of their matches.

Who won, and how many matches have they each played now?

Discuss with a partner.

3.4 Percentage change

Percentage increase and decrease

When an amount changes over time, you can calculate the percentage increase or percentage decrease in the amount. A percentage increase or decrease is the difference between the initial amount and the final amount written as a percentage. Percentage decrease is sometimes called depreciation.

The original amount is always 100%.

So, if a population increases by 5%, it is now 105% of the original population.

If an antique depreciates by 15%, its value is now 85% of the original value.

WORKED EXAMPLE 9

Caitlin buys a watch for $120.

a   During the next year, the value of the watch increases by 15%.
     How much is the watch worth now?

b   Over the next year, the value of the watch depreciates by 12%.
     How much is the watch worth now?

Answers

a   The value increases from 100% to 115%.

     115% of $\$120 = \dfrac{115}{100} \times 120 = 1.15 \times 120 = \$138$

b   The value depreciates from 100% to 88%.

     88% of $\$138 = \dfrac{88}{100} \times 138 = 0.88 \times 138 = \$121.44$

To calculate the percentage change, always calculate the new amount as a percentage of the original amount.

Then calculate the change from 100%.

WORKED EXAMPLE 10

At the start of the year, there are 60 fish in a pond.

a   By the end of the year, the number of fish has increased to 75.
     What is the percentage increase?

b   Another pond contains 75 fish at the start of the year but only has 60 fish at the end of the year.
     Calculate the percentage decrease.

CONTINUED

Answers

a   The new amount as a fraction of the original is $\frac{75}{60}$.

As a percentage, that is $\frac{75}{60} \times 100 = 125\%$

The number of fish has increased by 25%.

b   At the start of the year, the original amount was 75.

So, the percentage left is $\frac{60}{75} \times 100 = 80\%$

The percentage decrease is 20%.

> **TIP**
>
> The original amount will always be the denominator.

DISCUSSION 4

In the first pond, the number of fish increased from 60 to 75. This was a 25% increase.

In the second pond, the number of fish dropped from 75 to 60. This was only a 20% decrease.

Why are the percentage increase and percentage decrease not equal?

Discuss with a partner.

Reverse percentages

Sometimes you know the new amount and the percentage change, but you do not know the original amount.

Suppose an item increases in value by 5%.

Then the original price × 1.05 = the new price

To work back, the new price ÷ 1.05 = the original price

WORKED EXAMPLE 11

One month, after 20% tax has been deducted, Cherise's earnings are $2400.

She calculates how much she earned before tax was deducted as shown:

20% of $2400 = 0.2 × $2400 = $480

I earned $2400 + $480 = $2880 before tax was deducted.

a   What mistake has Cherise made?

b   Calculate Cherise's earnings before tax was deducted.

Answers

a   She has calculated 20% of the new amount, but the deduction was 20% of the original amount.

b   After 20% tax, Cherise received the remaining 80%.

Original earnings × 0.8 = earnings after tax

Earnings after tax ÷ 0.8 = original earnings

Original earnings = $2400 ÷ 0.8 = $3000

> **TIP**
>
> When working with percentage change, always decide whether you are working forwards from the original amount to the new amount or working backwards from the new amount to the original amount.

Exercise 3.4

1   Ann bought an antique clock for $360.
    A year later it has increased in value by 15%.
    Calculate the new value of the clock.

2   The population of a village decreased from 320 residents to 288 residents.
    Calculate the percentage decrease.

3   Chris bought a second-hand car for $6500.
    A year later, the car was worth 15% less.
    How much was the car worth then?

4   A website had 1360 views in the first week of the year. It had 1836 views in the
    second week of the year.
    Calculate the percentage increase in views.

5   In a sale, a shirt originally priced at $40.50 is reduced by 30%.
    Calculate the sale price.

6   a   A shop sold 4650 Chocco chocolate bars in 2020. In 2021, they sold 4464 Chocco
        chocolate bars.
        Calculate the percentage decrease in the number of Chocco chocolate bars sold.

    b   In 2021, the price of a Chocco chocolate bar had increased by 4%.
        In which year did the shop take more money for Chocco chocolate bar sales?
        Explain how you know.

7   On 1 March, Jenny had 80 photographs of her favourite singer.
    a   By 1 April she had 96 photographs. What is the percentage increase in the
        number of photographs?

    b   By 1 May, Jenny had 50% more photographs than she had on 1 March.
        How many photographs did she have on 1 May?

    c   What is the percentage increase in the number of photographs between 1 April
        and 1 May?

8   Bharath is an antiques dealer.
    He buys a clock and a desk for $400 each.
    In the first year, the clock depreciates by 20% and the desk increases in value by 20%.
    In the second year, the clock increases in value by 20% and the desk depreciates by 20%.
    How much is each item worth now?

9   Edina's hourly pay rate increases by 5% to $12.18 per hour.
    How much was the pay per hour before the increase?

10 Marta visits a restaurant. The cost is $74.75 including a 15% service charge.
    What was the cost without the service charge?

3.5 Further applications of percentages

Profit and loss

If you sell something for more than you paid for it, you make a **profit**.

If you sell something for less than you paid for it, you make a **loss**.

The percentage profit or loss is always a percentage of the **cost price**, how much you paid for an item.

WORKED EXAMPLE 12

Neil buys three shirts, one blue, one green and one pink.

a   He buys the blue shirt for $25 and sells it for a profit of 30%.
     Calculate how much he sold the blue shirt for.

b   He buys the green shirt for $32 and sells it for $28.
     Calculate his percentage loss.

c   He sells the pink shirt for $42, making a profit of 20%.
     Calculate how much he paid for the pink shirt.

Answers

a   He sells the blue shirt for 130% of the cost price.
     $1.3 \times \$25 = \$32.50$

b   His loss is $4 out of a cost price of $32.
     $\frac{4}{32} \times 100 = 12.5\%$

c   He sells the pink shirt for 120% of the cost price.
     Selling price = $1.2 \times$ cost price
     $\$42 = 1.2 \times$ cost price
     Cost price = $\$42 \div 1.2 = \$35$

Discounts and paying in instalments

When an item is expensive, you can often pay for the item over a period of time.

This means you pay a **deposit**, which is usually a percentage of the price, and then pay the rest of the money in monthly **instalments**.

Although this is a convenient way to buy, it often works out more expensive overall.

If you pay the whole amount at the beginning, you can sometimes negotiate a **discount**, which is a percentage off the actual price.

WORKED EXAMPLE 13

Rodrigo wants to buy a sofa. The cost is $1600.

a The store owner offers him a 5% discount if he buys it immediately.

How much would it cost Rodrigo to buy the sofa immediately?

b Alternatively, Rodrigo can buy the sofa in instalments by paying a 25% deposit followed by 24 monthly payments of $55.

How much will it cost Rodrigo in total to buy the sofa in instalments?

Answers

a After a 5% discount, Rodrigo would pay 95%.
$0.95 \times \$1600 = \$1520$

b 25% of $\$1600 = 0.25 \times \$1600 = \$400$
$24 \times \$55 = \$1320$
Total $= \$400 + \$1320 = \$1720$

> **MATHEMATICS IN CONTEXT**
>
> Paying in instalments usually costs more than paying in full at the beginning.

Exercise 3.5

1 Magnar buys a coat for $135.

He sells the coat for $162.

Calculate his percentage profit.

2 A bicycle costs $245.

You can buy the bicycle in instalments with a 20% deposit followed by 12 monthly payments of $18.50.

Calculate the total cost if you buy the bike in instalments.

3 Three shops are selling the same item.

Shop A is selling the item for $675.

Shop B usually sells the item for $720 but is offering a $7\frac{1}{2}\%$ discount.

Shop C sells the item for a deposit of $220 followed by 12 monthly payments of $37.
Which shop has the cheapest price?

4 A train ticket normally costs $37.50, but today the ticket is on offer for $33.

Calculate the percentage discount.

5 An item usually costs $2440.

The seller agrees to sell the item in instalments but adds 10% to the price.

He asks for a deposit of $320 followed by 24 monthly instalments.

Calculate the amount of each monthly instalment.

6 An antique dealer buys a table for $460.

He prices the table to make a 20% profit.

However, he does not sell the table, so he reduces the price by 20% in a sale.

What is the sale price?

7   Mr Smith has an electrical shop. He adds 25% profit
to his purchase price to get his selling price.
He then has a sale and reduces his prices by 15%.

   a   Calculate the original selling price of each item.

   b   Calculate how much Mr Smith paid for each item.

   c   Mr Smith says, 'I added 25% on to the cost price,
then took 15% off in the sale, so I have still
made a 10% profit.'

   Mr Smith is incorrect.
   Find his actual percentage profit.

8   A dealer offers a 5% discount for cash payments.

   a   What is the discounted price of an item with a
normal price of $33?

   b   I buy an item that costs $40.85 after the discount has been taken off.
What was the original price?

9   Mike sells a car for $2940, making a profit of 40%.
How much did he buy it for?

10   Kevin sells two items for $240 each.
He made a 20% profit on one item, and a 20% loss on the other item.
Calculate his overall percentage profit or loss.

DISCUSSION 5

An antique dealer sells two items.
He sells one item for $64, making a 20% loss.
He makes a 20% profit on the other item.
Overall, he has made a $5 profit.
How much did he sell the second item for?
Discuss with a partner.

3.6 Interest

Simple interest

When you invest money in a bank, they usually pay you interest every year.

The interest is a percentage of the money you invest. The actual percentage is the
rate of interest.

The money you invest is the principal.

With simple interest, the money is often paid directly to you.

For example, if you invested $6000 for 2 years at 7% interest, you would receive $\frac{7}{100} \times \$6000$ every year, or $2 \times \frac{7}{100} \times \$6000$ altogether, so you would receive a total of $840 interest.

The formula for simple interest is:

The interest paid, $I = \frac{PRT}{100}$, where P is the principal, R is the rate of interest per annum (per year) and T is the time in years that it is invested.

WORKED EXAMPLE 14

a   Helen invests $750 for 4 years and is paid 3% simple interest. How much interest does she receive?

b   Bo invests a sum for 5 years at 3% simple interest and receives $63.75 interest. How much did he invest?

Answers

a $P = 750$, $T = 4$, R $= 3$

$$I = \frac{PRT}{100} = \frac{750 \times 3 \times 4}{100} = \$90$$

b $T = 5$, $R = 3$, $I = 63.75$

$$I = \frac{PRT}{100}$$

$$63.75 = \frac{P \times 3 \times 5}{100}$$

$$63.75 = 0.15P$$

$$P = \frac{63.75}{0.15} = \$425$$

> **TIP**
>
> If $P \times 0.15 = 63.75$, then $63.75 \div 0.15 = P$

Compound interest

Most banks pay compound interest.

At the end of the year, the interest is added to your principal, so you have more money for the second year.

If you invested $6000 for 2 years at 7% compound interest, the 7% increase after the first year means you have $1.07 \times \$6000$.

This is the principal for the second year. So in the second year you get an additional 7% of that amount, so after the second year you have $1.07 \times 1.07 \times \$6000 = \$6869.40$

You can use the compound interest formula:

The final amount, A, is given by $A = P\left(1 + \frac{R}{100}\right)^T$, where P is the principal, R is the rate of interest per annum (per year) and T is the time in years that it is invested.

> **TIP**
>
> Note that the simple interest formula calculates the interest, but the compound interest formula calculates the final amount.

WORKED EXAMPLE 15

a   Jonathan invests $2400 for 5 years and is paid 4% compound interest. How much does he receive?

b   Monica invests a sum at 5% compound interest. After 3 years she has $13 891.50. How much did she invest?

Answers

a $P = 2400$, $T = 5$, $R = 4$

$A = P\left(1 + \dfrac{R}{100}\right)^{T} = 2400\left(1 + \dfrac{4}{100}\right)^{5} = 2400 \times 1.04^{5} = \$2919.97$ to the nearest cent.

b $T = 3$, $R = 5$, $A = 13\,891.50$

$A = P\left(1 + \dfrac{R}{100}\right)^{T}$

$13\,891.50 = P\left(1 + \dfrac{5}{100}\right)^{3}$

$13\,891.50 = P \times 1.05^{3}$

$P = 13\,891.50 \div 1.05^{3}$

$P = \$12\,000$

> **TIP**
>
> Remember the order of operations. Brackets first (1.04), then indices (1.04^5), then multiply by 2400.

> **MATHEMATICAL CONNECTIONS**
>
> You met the order of operations in Chapter 2.

Exercise 3.6

1   Biljana invests $540 at 4% simple interest.
Calculate the value of Biljana's investment after 3 years.

2   Khama invests $2400 at 5% compound interest.
Calculate the value of his investment after 3 years.

3   Kofi invests $5000 and is paid simple interest. After 4 years he has received $700 interest.
Calculate the rate of interest he received.

4   Aron borrows $8500 for 6 years.
He can either pay simple interest at 4% or compound interest at 3.5%.
Which method charges him the least interest?
Explain your answer.

5   Lian invests some money at 6% compound interest.
After 3 years her investment is worth $5955.08
What was the value of the initial investment?

6   Tino bought a vase for $7000.
Every year, the value increased in value by 12% of its value at the start of the year.
How much was the vase worth after 4 years?

7   Kasper invests $700 at 4% compound interest.
How many years will it take for him to have $800?

> **MATHEMATICAL CONNECTIONS**
>
> Indices are discussed further in Chapter 6.

8   Magda wants to invest $3000. She can choose Bank A or Bank B.

Bank A pays 5% simple interest.

Bank B pays 4.7% compound interest.

Which bank should she choose if she wants to invest her money for:

a   3 years

b   4 years

c   5 years?

Explain your answers.

9   Rudo wants to have $10 000 in 5 years' time.

a   She could invest $7250, $7500 or $7750 at 6% simple interest.
    Which of the three amounts will give her $10 000 after 5 years?

b   She could invest $7250, $7500 or $7750 at 6% compound interest.
    Which of the three amounts will give her $10 000 after 5 years.

Explain your answers.

SELF ASSESSMENT

Do you understand the difference between simple interest and compound interest?

INVESTIGATION 2

Marcus has $20 000.

He invests this money at 4% compound interest. At the end of the year, it has earned $800, but he then withdraws $1000.

If he does this every year how long will the investment last?

3.7 Exponential growth and decay

When a value such as a population increases repeatedly by the same percentage year after year, it is called **exponential growth**.

When a value such as a population decreases repeatedly by the same percentage year after year, it is called **exponential decay**.

The calculations are very similar to compound interest, as a quantity is increasing or decreasing by the same percentage repeatedly.

WORKED EXAMPLE 16

Marwa has $12 000.

He spends $6000 on an antique that appreciates by 5% every year.

He spends another $6000 on a motorbike that depreciates by 5% every year.

Are his investments worth more or worth less than $12 000 after 6 years?

CONTINUED

Answer

The antique increases in value by 5% every year, so at the end of each year it is worth 105% of its original value.

So after 1 year it is worth $\$(6000 \times 1.05)$

After 2 years it is worth $\$(6000 \times 1.05 \times 1.05)$

After 6 years it is worth $\$(6000 \times 1.05 \times 1.05 \times 1.05 \times 1.05 \times 1.05 \times 1.05)$
$= \$6000 \times 1.05^6 = \$8040.57$

The motorbike is worth 95% of its starting value every year.

So after 6 years it is worth $\$(6000 \times 0.95^6) = \$4410.55$

His investments are worth $\$8040.57 + \$4410.55 = \$12\,451.12$

His investments are worth more than $\$12\,000$ after 6 years.

DISCUSSION 6

One investment increases by 5%. The other investment falls by 5%. Discuss with a partner why the investment has increased overall.

WORKED EXAMPLE 17

The number of fish in a pond increases by 7% each year.

After 4 years, there are 345 fish in the pond.

How many fish were there in the pond originally?

Answer

If the original number is of fish is f, then after 5 years there are

$f \times 1.07^4 = 345$

$f \times 1.31079601 = 345$

$f = 345 \div 1.31079601 = 263.20$, or 263 fish

Exercise 3.7

1 At the start of 2016 the population of a village was 2456.

   Every year, the population increases by 4% of its value at the start of the year.

   What was the population of the village at **the end** of 2020?

2 A pond contains 4500 litres of water.

   During a dry period, the pond loses 6% of its water every month.

   To the nearest litre, how much water is left in the pond after a 4-month dry period?

3 On Monday morning there are 3200 cells in a sample of bacteria. The number of cells increases by 12% every day.

   How many cells are there on Friday morning?

4 A car depreciates by 17% of its value every year.

   Brian bought a car for $\$18\,000$ three years ago.

   What is the value of the car now?

5   A town had a population of 34 000 last year.

This year the town has a population of 31 280.

a   By what percentage of last year's figure has the population fallen?

b   Assuming the population of the town has been falling by this percentage every year, what was the population 5 years ago?

6   In one country, 192 000 people had a particular disease on 1 January 2021.

The number of people with the disease decreased by 8% every month for 7 months, until 1 August 2021.

The number of people with the disease then increased by 8% for the next 5 months, to 1 January 2022.

How many people had the disease on 1 January 2022?

7   Millie is a singer.

One of Millie's songs is streamed 4500 times one week.

Over the next 5 weeks, the number of streams increased by 18% per week.

How many times was her song streamed in the last week?

8   A company buys a machine for $60 000.

Every year, the value of the machine depreciates by 16%.

The company saves $5000 every year towards a replacement.

a   How much has the company saved after 10 years?

b   By how much has the machine depreciated in 10 years?

9   A club starts with 120 members. The club aims to increase its number of members by 15% every year.

a   How many members does the club aim to have after 5 years?

b   How many years will it take the club to have 300 members?

10 Kasinda has a choice of two options for her pension.

Option A: Kasinda receives $25 000 per annum.

Option B: Kasinda receives $23 500 in the first year, and a 2% increase every year.

a   How many years will it take for Kasinda's annual pension under option B to be greater than her annual pension under option A?

b   How many years will it be before the **total** amount received under option B is greater than the total amount received under option A?

DISCUSSION 7

A lily pad in a pond doubles in size every month.

After 30 months, the pond is completely covered by the lily pad.

After how many months was half the pond covered?

After how many months was just 1% of the pond covered?

Discuss with a partner.

SUMMARY

Are you able to... ?
calculate using rate and proportion
calculate percentage increase and decrease
understand and calculate simple interest and compound interest
use ratio
use percentages
use a calculator efficiently
solve problems involving time and money
understand and use exponential growth and decay
use reverse percentages.

Past paper questions

1   a   Increase 4.5 kg by 16%.

.... kg   [2]

    b   Find the percentage profit when the cost price of a book is \$8.50 and the selling price is \$11.05.

.... %   [3]

    c   The price of a loaf of bread increases by \$0.06.
This is a 5% increase.
Find the original price of this loaf of bread.

\$..   [2]

Cambridge IGCSE International Mathematics 0607 Paper 41 Q2 November 2019

2   a   A train takes 1 hour 30 minutes to travel from Cambridge to London.
        i   The train leaves Cambridge at 07:25.
            Find the time that this train arrives in London.

....   [1]

        ii   The distance from Cambridge to London is 105 km.
            Work out the average speed of this train.

.... km/h   [2]

    b   There are 104 trains travelling from Cambridge to London each day.
        i   3% of these trains arrive late in London.
            Work out how many of the trains arrive late in London.

....   [2]

   ii   Trains from Cambridge are either express trains or local trains.

The ratio   express trains : local trains = 5 : 3.

How many of the 104 trains are local trains?

.... [2]

Cambridge IGCSE International Mathematics 0607 Paper 33 Q5 November 2017

3   The number of fish in a lake decreases by 4% each year.
In January 2018 there are 30 000 fish in the lake.

   a   Calculate the number of fish in the lake in

      i   January 2019,

.... [2]

      ii   January 2029,

.... [3]

      iii   January 2017.

.... [3]

   b   Find the last year in which there were at least 50 000 fish in the lake.

.... [4]

Cambridge IGCSE International Mathematics 0607 Paper 41 Q5 November 2018

> Chapter 4
Angles and bearings

GETTING STARTED

1   On separate diagrams, draw the following line segments with the given measurements.
    a   Line AB, length 5 cm
    b   Line PQ, length 6.5 cm
    c   Line XY, length 10.2 cm

2   Without using a calculator work out these additions and subtractions.
    a $25 + 70 + 52$ b $180 - 121$
    c $180 - 68 - 34$ d $360 - 105 - 70 - 98$

3   a   100 sweets are divided between Amy and Bob in the ratio of $3 : 2$. Find the number of sweets that Amy has.
    b   Divide 180 in the ratio $2 : 3 : 4$.
    c   Find the angle moved by the minute hand of a clock from 08:25 hours to 08:50 hours.

4.1 Introduction to goemetry

Basic geometrical terms

Angles are a very important part of geometry. Before studying angles, you need to be familiar with some basic vocabulary and some drawing and measuring skills.

This is a **point** labelled as A.   This is a **line segment** connecting the points A and B.

In mathematics you usually label points using upper case letters. Connecting two points creates a line segment.

An angle is formed when two lines or line segments intersect at a point. You label angles using three letters.

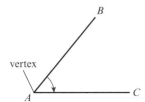

This is angle BAC This is angle BPD

Angle BAC is formed by two line segments meeting at a common point, A.
A point where two or more line segments meet is called a **vertex**.

> **TIP**
>
> A line segment has two endpoints. A **line** continues endlessly in both directions.

Angle *BPD* is formed when the line segments *AB* and *CD* intersect at a point, *P*.

You measure angles using degrees. The symbol for degrees is °. For example, you write an angle of 30 degrees as 30°.

You can use a protractor to measure and draw angles, as shown in Worked examples 1 and 2.

WORKED EXAMPLE 1

Measure and write down the size of:

a   angle *ABC*

b   angle *PQR*.

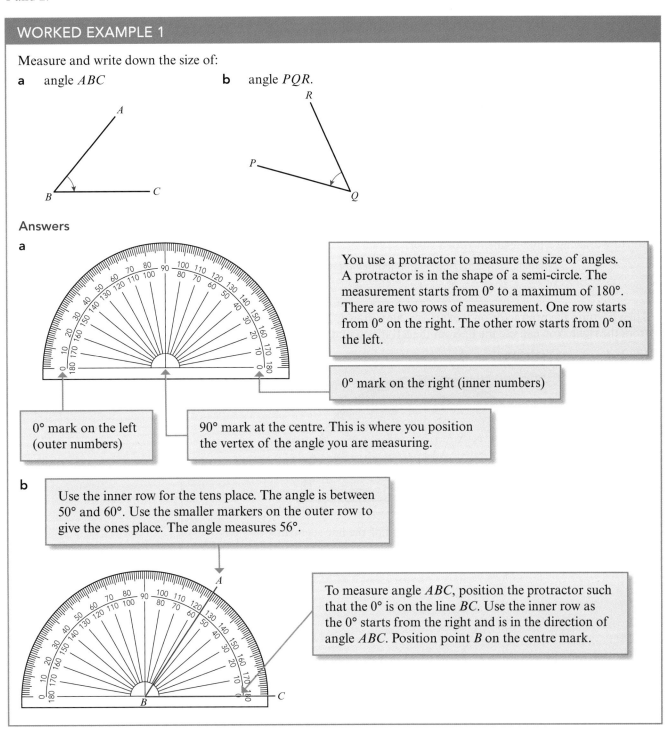

Answers

a

You use a protractor to measure the size of angles. A protractor is in the shape of a semi-circle. The measurement starts from 0° to a maximum of 180°. There are two rows of measurement. One row starts from 0° on the right. The other row starts from 0° on the left.

0° mark on the right (inner numbers)

0° mark on the left (outer numbers)

90° mark at the centre. This is where you position the vertex of the angle you are measuring.

b

Use the inner row for the tens place. The angle is between 50° and 60°. Use the smaller markers on the outer row to give the ones place. The angle measures 56°.

To measure angle *ABC*, position the protractor such that the 0° is on the line *BC*. Use the inner row as the 0° starts from the right and is in the direction of angle *ABC*. Position point *B* on the centre mark.

CONTINUED

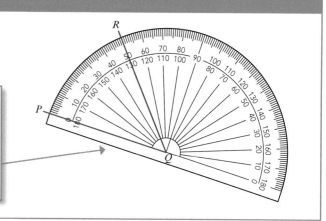

To measure angle *PQR*, position the protractor such that the 0° is on the line *PQ*. Use the outer row as the 0° starts from the left and is in the direction of angle *PQR*. Position the point *Q* on the centre mark. The point R lies exactly on the 50° mark, so angle *PQR* = 50°.

WORKED EXAMPLE 2

Draw an angle that measures 120°.

Answer

Start by drawing a line segment with a ruler:

Then position the protractor on the line you have drawn. This solution uses the 0° from the right. You can use the 0° from the left if you find it easier.

Mark the position at 120°:

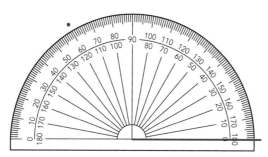

Then draw a line to connect the point to the end of the line segment:

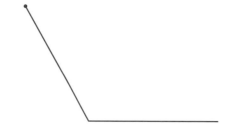

CONTINUED

Check your angle using the protractor:

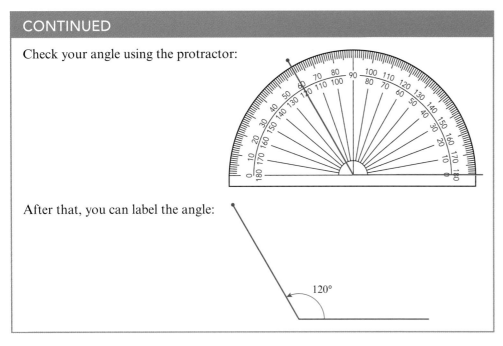

After that, you can label the angle:

120°

Types of angles

You can generally classify angles into one of the four types.

1    An **acute angle** is greater than 0° but less than 90°.

2    A **right angle** is exactly 90°.

3 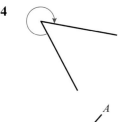   An **obtuse angle** is greater than 90° but less than 180°.

4 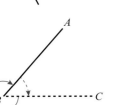   A **reflex angle** is greater than 180° but less than 360°.

Notice that there is also an acute angle at the vertex.

TIP

When referring to the acute angle, you write 'angle *ABC*'.

When referring to the reflex angle, you write 'reflex angle *ABC*'.

Exercise 4.1

1 Read off the angle in each diagram.

a

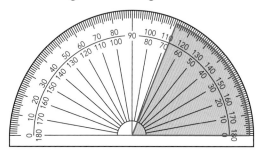

b

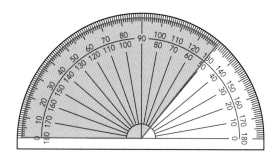

c

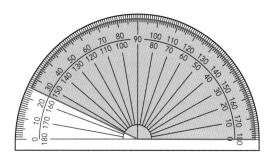

2 In the diagram shown, identify:

   a   a vertex

   b   a right angle

   c   an acute angle

   d   an obtuse angle.

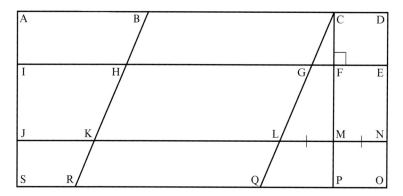

3 Measure these angles.

   a

   b

   c

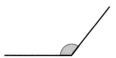

   d

4   Use a ruler and protractor to draw these angles.

    a   35°   b   110°   c   146°   d   82°   e   200°

5   Match each angle to the correct classification.

A 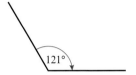   **i**   Acute angle

B   **ii**   Reflex angle

C   **iii**   Obtuse angle

D   **iv**   Right angle

MATHEMATICS IN CONTEXT

You see angles in objects in real life. These diagrams show some examples of real-life objects with angles.

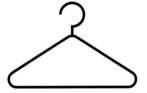 

Can you find more objects around you that show different angles?

PEER ASSESSMENT

Take a photograph of a building or a corner of your school and show it to a partner. Ask your partner to identify as many of these types of angles as possible.

acute angle   obtuse angle   right angle   reflex angle

4.2 Angle properties

Angles on a straight line

A straight line has an angle of 180°.

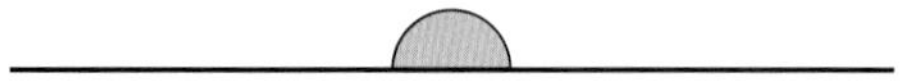

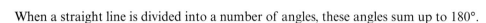

When a straight line is divided into a number of angles, these angles sum up to 180°.

Sum of angles at a point on a straight line = 180°

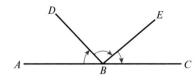

Angle ABD + angle DBE + angle EBC = 180°

You can use this property to solve problems and to find unknown angles.

WORKED EXAMPLE 3

In the diagram, PQR is a straight line. Angle XQY is a right angle and angle $YQR = 35°$. Find angle XQP. Give a reason for your answer.

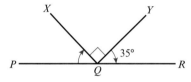

Answer

Since angle XQY is a right angle, it is equal to 90°.

PQR is a straight line, so the angles sum to 180°.

Angle $XQP = 180° - 90° - 35°$ (sum of angles at a point on a straight line = 180°)

$\qquad = 55°$

> **TIP**
>
> You can write the reason in brackets next to your working.

Angles at a point

When you turn through a full circle about a point you turn through 360°.

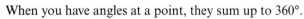

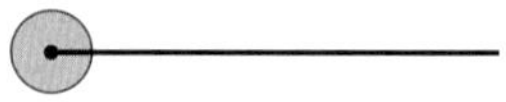

When you have angles at a point, they sum up to 360°.

Sum of angles at a point = 360°

In the diagram, the angles *AOB*, *BOC* and *AOC* are angles at a point.

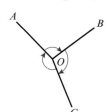

Angle *AOB* + angle *BOC* + angle *AOC* = 360°

You can apply this property to find unknown angles.

WORKED EXAMPLE 4

Find angle *AOD*, giving a reason for your answer.

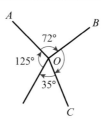

Answer

The diagram shows four angles at a point *O* (angle *AOB*, angle *BOC*, angle *COD* and angle *AOD*), so their sum is 360°.

Angle *AOD* = 360° − 125° − 35° − 72° (sum of angles at a point = 360°)

= 128°

TIP

Remember to include the reason for your answer.

Exercise 4.2

1 In each of the following, *PQR* is a on a straight line. Find the value of *x*.

a
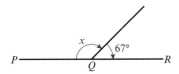

b
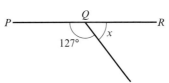

c
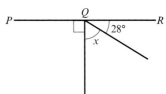

d
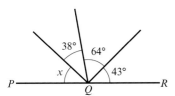

e
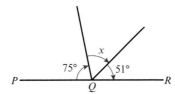

f
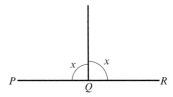

g
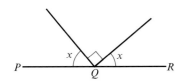

h
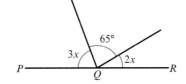

2 Find the value of x in each diagram.

a

b

c

d

TIP

Use ratio/proportion.

4.3 Lines

Definitions

Straight lines can interact with each other in different ways.

Parallel lines are always equidistant from each other and never meet.

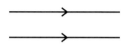

You indicate parallel lines using an arrowhead as shown.

Perpendicular lines meet or intersect each other at a right angle.

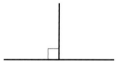

You indicate perpendicular lines using the right-angle marker as shown.

A line cutting two or more other lines is called a **transversal line**.

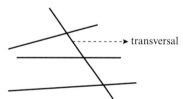

Suppose AB is a line segment with mid-point M. If the line segment CD cuts AB at a right angle at its midpoint M, then CD is called the **perpendicular bisector** of AB.

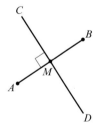

A **plane** is a flat surface.

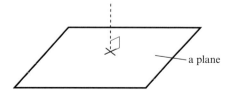

Angles on transversal lines

Many angles are formed when a transversal line cuts two parallel lines. You will now look at some important properties of these angles. You will need to use these properties to explain your working when calculating unknown angles.

Corresponding angles are equal: Angles between the transversal and two parallel lines that are on the same side of the parallel lines are equal.

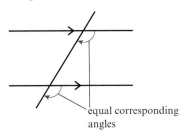

equal corresponding angles

Corresponding angles are commonly known as the angles inside the letter 'F'.

There are four pairs of corresponding angles in the diagram. The letter F can also be backwards and upside down.

> **TIP**
>
> Try to see the letter 'F'.

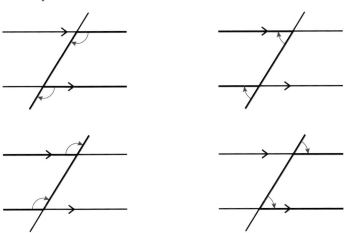

Alternate angles are equal: Angles on opposite sides of the transversal and between two parallel lines are equal.

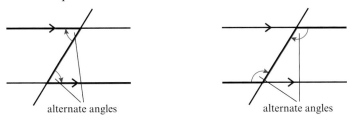

alternate angles   alternate angles

Alternate angles are commonly known as the angles inside the letter 'Z'.

> **TIP**
>
> Try to see the letter 'Z'.

Co-interior (supplementary) angles sum to 180°: Angles that lie on the same side of the transversal and between two parallel lines sum to 180°.

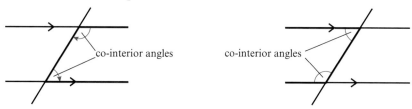

Co-interior angles are commonly known as the angles inside the letter 'C' or 'U' depending on the orientation.

The next angle property looks at angles on two intersecting lines.

Vertically opposite angles are equal: When two straight lines intersect, the pair of angles vertically opposite to each other are equal.

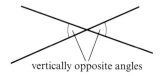 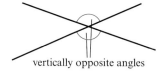

TIP
Try to see the letter 'C' or 'U'.

DISCUSSION 1

Can you prove that vertically opposite angles are equal? Discuss in pairs and present your proof to the class.

WORKED EXAMPLE 5

Find the value of x and y.
Give a reason for your working.

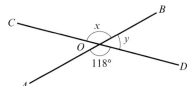

Answers

Since COD and AOB intersect at O, angle COB and angle AOD are vertically opposite to each other.

$x° = 118°$ (vertically opposite angles are equal)

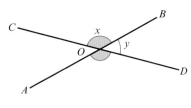

Angle AOD and angle BOD are angles at a point on the straight line along AOB, so these two angles sum to 180°.

$y° = 180° - 118°$ (sum of angles at a point on a straight line)
$\quad = 62°$

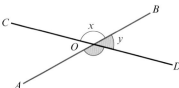

WORKED EXAMPLE 6

AB is parallel to CD. Find the angles x, y and z.

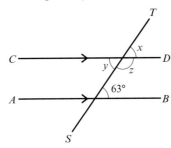

Answer

Look at the letter 'F' in the diagram.
The angle labelled x is corresponding
to the 63° angle.

$x = 63°$ (corresponding angles are equal)

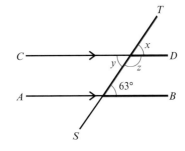

To find the angle y, look for the 'Z' shape
in the diagram.

$y = 63°$ (alternate angles are equal)

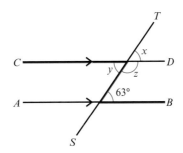

There are three ways to find angle z.

One way is to see co-interior angles that
add up to 180° (the letter 'C').

$z = 180° - 63°$ (co-interior angles sum to 180°)

　$= 117°$

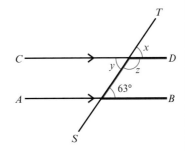

CONTINUED

The other two ways use the property
'sum of angles at a point on a straight line'.

$x + z = 180°$

or

$y + z = 180°$

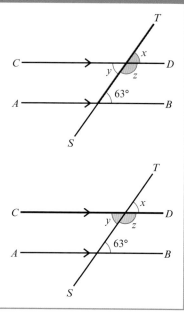

TIP

The two methods using the property 'sum of angles at a point on a straight line' require the use of the value of x or y which you calculated earlier. If you had made an error in your calculations of x or y, your value of z would also be incorrect.

Where possible, use a given value to find the unknown rather than using another value that you have calculated.

Exercise 4.3

1 Find the value of the unknown angles. Give the angle property you have used to find each angle.

a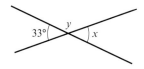

b

c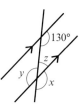

d

e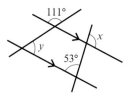

f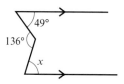

TIP

Draw a line parallel to an existing line segment.

g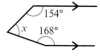

h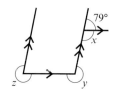

2   In the given diagram, name:
   a   a pair of parallel lines
   b   a pair of perpendicular lines
   c   a pair of alternate angles
   d   a pair of corresponding angles
   e   a pair of co-interior angles
   f   a pair of vertically opposite angles
   g   a perpendicular bisector (name the perpendicular bisector and the line segment it bisects).

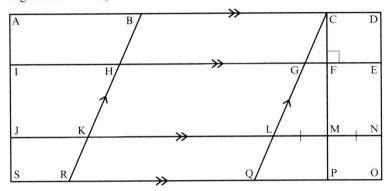

3   Use the diagram from Question **2**.
   ADOS is a rectangle. *IHGFE, JKLMN, BHKR, CGLQ* and *CFMP* are straight lines. Angle *KHG* = 130°. Find:
   a   angle *IHB*   b   angle *ABH*   c   angle *HKL*
   d   angle *GLK*   e   angle *RQL*   f   angle *LQP*.

4.4 Bearings

Bearings are angles measured clockwise from the north. You generally use the compass symbol to identify the north.

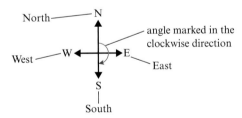

The north–south line is perpendicular to the east–west line. The angles between north and east, east and south, south and west, and west and north are each 90°.

The following are descriptions of points using the directions north, south, east and west:

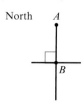

Point A is due north of point B.

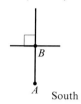

Point A is due south of point B.

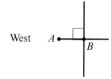

Point A is due west of point B.

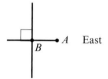

Point A is due east of point B.

To measure a bearing, you need two points: a start point where the bearing is measured **from** and an end point where the bearing is measured **to**.

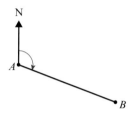

If a bearing is measured from point A **to** point B, draw a line to connect A and B. The angle is then measured from the north at point A in the clockwise direction as shown. This is the bearing of point B **from** point A.

If a bearing is measured from point B **to** point A, draw a line to connect A and B. The angle is then measured from the north at point B in the clockwise direction as shown. This is the bearing of point A **from** point B.

This diagram shows the bearing of three points: A, B and C.

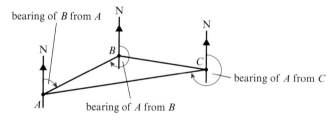

You write a bearing using three figures. For example, you write a bearing of 20° as 020°. You write a bearing of 145° as it is because it already has three figures.

WORKED EXAMPLE 7

The diagram shows point A. Point B is on a bearing of 125° from point A and the length of AB is 5 cm. Copy the diagram and mark the position of point B on your diagram.

Answer

Use a protractor to measure an angle of 125° from the north line at point A as shown.

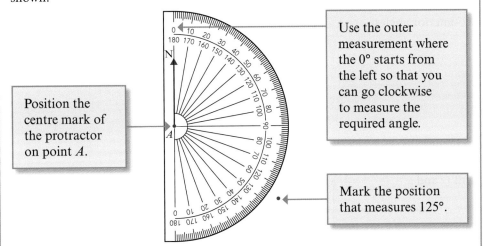

Position the centre mark of the protractor on point A.

Use the outer measurement where the 0° starts from the left so that you can go clockwise to measure the required angle.

Mark the position that measures 125°.

Then use a ruler to join point A to the marking at 125°. Draw a 5 cm line.

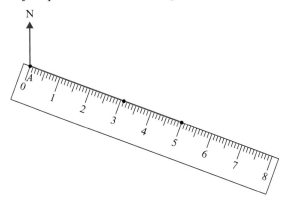

Mark the point as B.

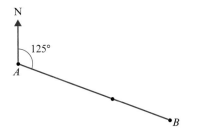

WORKED EXAMPLE 8

The diagram shows two points P and Q.
The bearing of point Q from point P is 077°.
Find the bearing of point P from point Q.

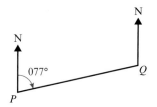

Answers

The two north lines are parallel to each other.
PQ is a transversal line. Look for the 'U' shape in the diagram. There is a pair of co-interior angles that sum up to 180°.

Label the angle at Q as $x°$.

$77° + x = 180°$

$x = 180° - 77°$

$\quad = 103°$

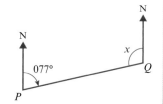

Draw the bearing of point P from point Q in the diagram.

The bearing of point P from point Q and $x°$ are angles at the point Q.

The sum of these angles is 360°.

The bearing of P from $Q = 360° - 103°$

$\qquad\qquad\qquad = 257°$

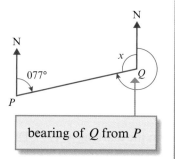

bearing of Q from P

WORKED EXAMPLE 9

The diagram shows the points A, B and C, connected to form a triangle.
The bearing of point C from point A is 070°. The bearing of point C from point B is 142°.

Calculate the bearing of:

a   point B from point A

b   point A from point C.

Answers

The bearing of point C from point A is 070°.
The bearing of point C from point A means you start from the north line at A.
Draw an angle in the clockwise direction from the north line at A to the line joining AC.

Copy the diagram and label this angle.

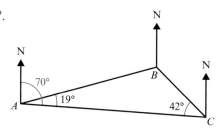

The bearing of point C from point B is 142°.

The bearing of point C from point B means you start from the north line at B. Draw an angle in the clockwise direction from the north line at B to the line joining BC.

Label this angle on your diagram.

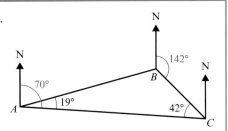

a   To find the bearing of B from A, start from the north line at A and draw an angle in the clockwise direction to the line AB.

The bearing is marked in the diagram.

This bearing is adjacent to angle BAC.

The bearing of B from A = 70° − 19°

= 51°

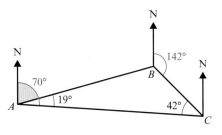

b   To find the bearing of A from C, start from the north line at C and draw an angle in the clockwise direction to the line AC.

The bearing is marked in the diagram.

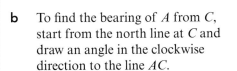

The north lines at B and C are parallel to each other. BC is a transversal line. Look for the 'U' shape between points B and C.

There is a pair of co-interior angles at B and C which sum up to 180°.

Label the angle at C as y°.

$142° + y = 180°$

$y = 180° − 142°$

= 38°

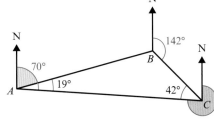

The bearing of A from C (the angle marked in the diagram) is one of the angles at the point C. The other two angles at this point are 42° and 38°. These three angles sum to 360°.

The bearing of A from $C = 360° − 42° − 38°$

= 280°

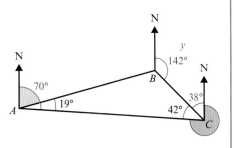

Exercise 4.4

1   The diagram shows the point A. Point B is on a bearing of 050° from point A and the length of AB is 4 cm. On a copy of the diagram, show position of point B.

2   The diagram shows the point P. Point Q is on a bearing of 154° from point P. On a copy of the diagram, mark a possible position of point Q.

3   The diagram shows the point P. Point X is on a bearing of 220° from point P. On a copy of the diagram, mark a possible position of point X.

4   These diagrams show two points P and Q. The bearing of point Q from point P is given. Find the bearing of point P from point Q.

a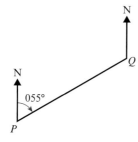

b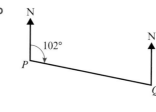

c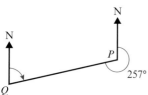

d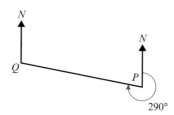

5   The diagram shows the points A, B, C and D. The labels N, S, E and W represent the north, south, east and west of the point O respectively.

Write down the bearing of:

a B from O

b C from O

c D from O

d A from O.

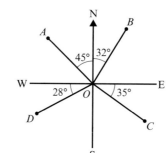

6   The diagram shows the position of points P, Q, R
    and T. The labels N, S, E and W represent
    the north, south, east and west of the
    point P respectively.

    Find the bearing of:

    a R from P

    b T from P

    c Q from P

    d P from T

    e P from R

    f P from Q.

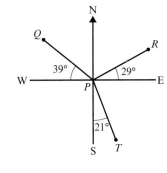

7   The diagram shows the positions of
    three towns: A, B and C.

    Find the bearing of:

    a B from A

    b C from A

    c A from B

    d A from C.

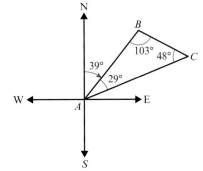

8   The diagram shows the position of four
    train stations: W, X, Y and Z.

    a   Copy and complete the statement:

        'Z is due _____ of X'

    b   Find the bearing of:

        i W from X

        ii Y from X

        iii W from Z

        iv Y from Z.

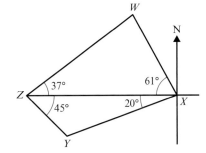

9   The diagram shows the position of three ships
    A, B and C at sea.

    Find the bearing of:

    a B from A

    b C from A

    c A from B

    d A from C.

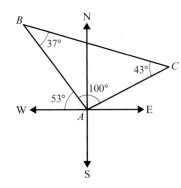

INVESTIGATION 1

You will need a ruler and a protractor for this investigation.

You need to get ingredients for a cake from Joan's grocery store and while you are out you also need to take some clothes to the laundry.

Using the map given, plan your route to the grocery store and take the clothes to the laundry, from your house (My home) and back again, using the shortest route possible.

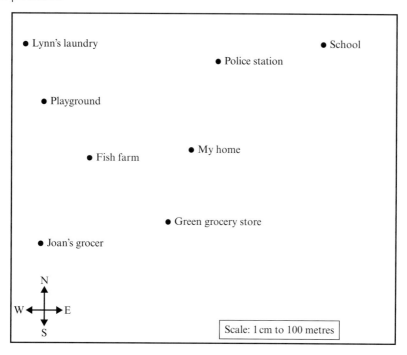

Assuming you walk to the shops and back to your home, write down a set of walking instructions using only bearings and distances.

For example: walk X m on a bearing of $ABC°$ from the butchers to the grocery store.

SUMMARY

Are you able to... ?
calculate unknown angles formed with parallel lines
calculate unknown angles using geometrical properties
understand how bearings are measured
use and interpret geometrical terms to describe angles
measure and draw lines and angles
calculate bearings from one point to another.

Past paper questions

1   a

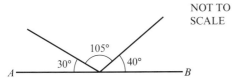

NOT TO SCALE

Explain why line AB cannot be a straight line.

.... [1]

   b

NOT TO SCALE

Complete the statement.

c = ... because ....…………….. [2]

Cambridge IGCSE International Mathematics 0607 Paper 12 Q11 November 2020

2

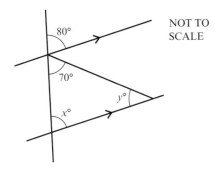

NOT TO SCALE

Find the values of x and y.

x = ...

y = ... [2]

Cambridge IGCSE International Mathematics 0607 Paper 12 Q12 June 2018

3

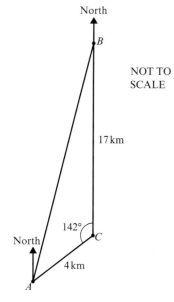

Rani sails in a boat race around a triangular course.
She sails from *A* to *B* to *C* and then directly back to *A*.
B is due north of *C*.

Find the bearing Rani sails on from *C* to *A*.

.... [1]

Cambridge IGCSE International Mathematics 0607 Paper 42 Q8 a March 2021

> Chapter 5
Triangles, quadrilaterals and polygons

IN THIS CHAPTER YOU WILL:

- calculate unknown angles in triangles

- understand and use the properties of quadrilaterals to find angles

- know and use angle properties of polygons

- calculate the interior and exterior angles of regular polygons

> calculate the interior and exterior angles of irregular polygons.

GETTING STARTED

1 In the diagram, *AB* is parallel to *CD*, and *PQ* is parallel to *RS*. Classify the following pairs of angles.

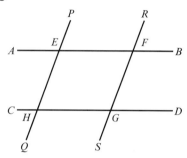

a Angle *AEP* and angle *CHE*

b Angle *EFG* and angle *FGD*

c Angle *EFG* and angle *HGF*

d Angle *HGF* and angle *DGF*

2 Find the unknown angles.

a

b

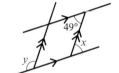

c

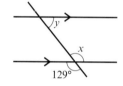

KEY WORDS

decagon

diagonal

exterior angle

heptagon

hexagon

interior angle

irregular polygon

kite

nonagon

octagon

parallelogram

pentagon

quadrilateral

rectangle

regular polygon

rhombus

square

trapezium

MATHEMATICAL CONNECTIONS

You learnt about angles on transversal lines in Chapter 4.

5.1 Properties of triangles

A triangle is a closed figure with three sides. This diagram shows triangle *PQR*. This triangle has three sides: *PQ*, *QR* and *PR*. Points *P*, *Q* and *R* are the vertices of the triangle.

TIP

'Vertices' is the plural of 'vertex'.

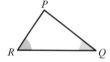

Angles *PQR*, *RPQ* and *QRP* are called the interior angles of the triangle.

The sum of the interior angles in a triangle is 180°.

Triangles can either be classified by their **angles** or by their **sides**.

Classification of triangles

Classification of triangles by angles

Acute-angled triangle A triangle in which all three angles are acute (between 0° and 90°).	
Right-angled triangle A triangle in which one of the angles is 90° (a right angle).	
Obtuse-angled triangle A triangle in which one of the angles is obtuse (between 90° and 180°).	

Classification of triangles by sides

Scalene triangle A triangle in which all three sides are of different length. All the angles in a scalene triangle are different.	
Isosceles triangle A triangle in which two of the sides are equal in length. You can indicate the equal sides by marking the two equal sides. The two base angles of an isosceles triangle are equal.	Base angles are equal
Equilateral triangle A triangle in which all three sides are equal in length. You indicate the equal sides by marking all three sides. All the angles of an equilateral triangle are equal to 60°. An equilateral triangle is a special isosceles triangle.	60° 60° 60°

DISCUSSION 1

Can you explain why each of the interior angles of an equilateral triangle is equal to 60°?

Discuss with a partner.

Exterior angles of a triangle

The **exterior angle** of a triangle is the angle on a straight line when the sides are extended outside the triangle.

Correct position of exterior angles

TIP

The exterior angle of a triangle is **not** the reflex angle outside the interior angle.

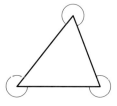

Misconception about exterior angles

Property of exterior angles of a triangle

An exterior angle of a triangle is equal to the sum of the two interior opposite angles.

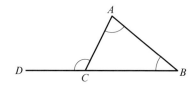

Angle ACD = angle CAB + angle ABC

DISCUSSION 2

Can you prove this property about the exterior angles of a triangle?
Discuss with a partner.

WORKED EXAMPLE 1

In the diagram, $BC = BD$, and AB is parallel to CD. Find the angles x, y and z.

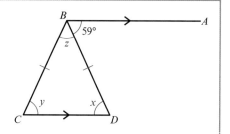

MATHEMATICAL CONNECTIONS

You learnt the properties of angles on transversal lines in Chapter 4.

Answer

AB is parallel to *CD*. *BD* is a transversal
line that cuts the lines *AB* and *CD*.
The angle properties of transversal lines
apply here.

Look for the 'Z' shape in reverse.

Angle *CDB* and angle *ABD* are
alternate angles which are equal.

x = angle *CBD* = 59°

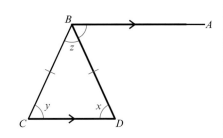

BC is equal to *BD*. Hence triangle *BCD*
is an isosceles triangle.

Angles *BCD* and *BDC* are the base angles
of the isosceles triangle and are equal.

So $y = x = 59°$

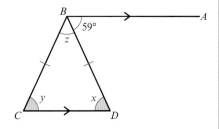

There are two methods to calculate z.

**Method 1: Use the sum of the interior angles
of a triangle**

Since *BCD* is a triangle, the sum of the
interior angles is 180°.

$x + y + z = 180°$

$z = 180° - x - y$ (sum of interior angles
of a triangle)

$z° = 180° - 59° - 59°$

$z = 62°$

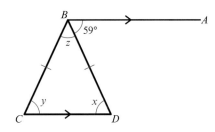

**Method 2: Use the property that co-interior
angles add up to 180°**

Look for the letter 'C'.

Angles *ABC* and *BCD* are co-interior
angles which add to 180°.

Angle *ABC* = $z + 59°$

Angle *BCD* = y

Adding them, $z + 59° + y = 180°$

$y = 59°$

$z + 59° + 59° = 180°$

$z = 180° - 59° - 59°$

$= 62°$

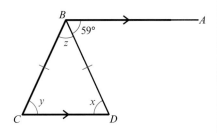

WORKED EXAMPLE 2

In the diagram, PQR is a line segment.
Find angle PQS.

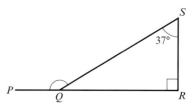

Answer

There are two methods to answer this question. The first method is shorter and uses the property of exterior angles of a triangle.

The second method is longer, but it may be more familiar to you.

Method 1

Angle PQS is an exterior angle of triangle QRS.
Angle QSR and angle QRS are the interior opposite angles in triangle QSR.

Use the property of exterior angles of a triangle:

an **exterior angle** of a triangle is equal to the sum of the two interior opposite angles.

Angle PQS = angle QSR + angle QRS
Angle PQS = 37° + 90°
$\quad\quad$ = 127°

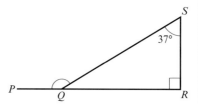

Method 2

Triangle QSR is a right-angled triangle with angle QRS = 90°.

The sum of the interior angles in a triangle is 180°.

Angle SQR + angle QSR + angle QRS = 180°

Angle SQR + 37° + 90° = 180°

Angle SQR = 180° − 90° − 37°
$\quad\quad$ = 53°

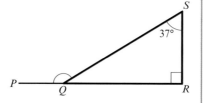

Angle PQS and angle SQR are angles on the straight line PQR. Angle PQS and Angle SQR sum to 180°.

Angle PQS = 180° − 53°
$\quad\quad$ = 127°

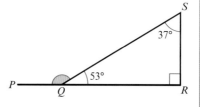

MATHEMATICAL CONNECTIONS

You learnt about angles on a straight line in Chapter 4.

MATHEMATICS IN CONTEXT

Some road signs are in the shape of an equilateral triangle. The next time you are travelling on the road, look out for them!

Exercise 5.1

1   Classify these triangles according to their **sides**.

a   b   c   d

2   Classify these triangles according to their **angles**.

a

b

c

d

3   Find the value of the unknown angle x in each triangle.

a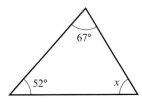

b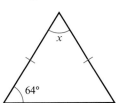

c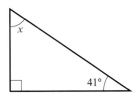

d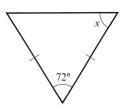

4   Find the value of the unknown angle y in each diagram.

a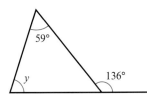

b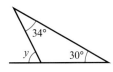

c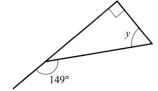

d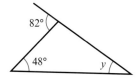

5 Find the value of the unknown angles x and y in each diagram.

a
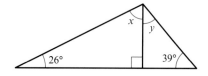

b
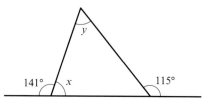

c
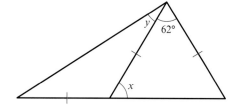

d
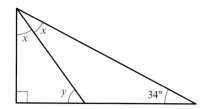

5.2 Properties of quadrilaterals

A closed figure with four sides is called a **quadrilateral**.

This diagram shows a quadrilateral $ABCD$.

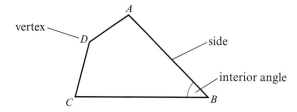

A, B, C and D are the vertices of the quadrilateral. The four sides are AB, BC, CD and AD.
A quadrilateral has four interior angles.

The line segments AC and BD are called the **diagonals** of the quadrilateral.
A quadrilateral has two diagonals.

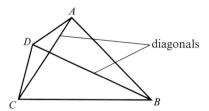

This table gives the properties of some quadrilaterals.

Quadrilaterals	Properties
Square	Four equal sides
	Opposite sides are parallel
	Four right angles
	Diagonals are perpendicular
	The diagonals have a common mid-point at M (diagonals bisect each other at a right angle)
Rhombus	Four equal sides
	Opposite sides are parallel
	Diagonals are perpendicular
	The diagonals have a common mid-point at M (diagonals bisect each other at a right angle)
Rectangle	Opposite sides are equal and parallel
	Four right angles
	The two diagonals are equal in length
	The diagonals have a common mid-point at M (diagonals bisect each other but **not** at a right angle)
Parallelogram	Opposite sides are equal and parallel
	Opposite angles are equal
	Angle DAB = angle DCB
	Angle ADC = angle ABC
	The diagonals are **not** equal (AC is **not** equal to BD)
	The diagonals have a common mid-point at M (diagonals bisect each other but **not** at a right angle)
Trapezium	One pair of parallel sides
Kite	Two long sides are equal and adjacent ($AD = AB$)
	Two short sides are equal and adjacent ($DC = BC$)
	Diagonals are perpendicular but **not** equal in length (AC is longer than BD)
	The longer diagonal bisects the shorter diagonal (AC bisects BD)

SELF ASSESSMENT

Answer these questions to assess your knowledge of quadrilaterals.

Is a square a rectangle?

Is a square a parallelogram?

Is a trapezium a parallelogram?

Which shapes can be categorised as parallelograms?

WORKED EXAMPLE 3

$ABCD$ is a kite. $AB = BC$ and $AD = DC$.
Angle $BCD = 120°$ and angle $ADC = 45°$. Find:

a   angle ABC

b   angle BAD.

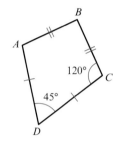

Answers

a   In a kite, the longer diagonal divides the kite into two equal halves, so BD bisects angle ADC and angle ABC.

Angle $CDB = \dfrac{45°}{2} = 22.5°$

The sum of the interior angles of a triangle is 180°.

Angle $CBD = 180° - 120° - 22.5° = 37.5°$

Since BD bisects angle ABC, angle ABC = angle $CBD \times 2$

Angle $ABC = 37.5° \times 2 = 75°$

b   As BD divides the kite into two equal halves, triangle ABD is identical to triangle CBD.

Angle BAD = angle $BCD = 120°$

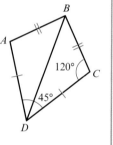

MATHEMATICAL CONNECTIONS

You will learn more about congruent and similar triangles in Chapter 9.

WORKED EXAMPLE 4

The diagram shows parallelogram $ABCD$.
Find the value of x, y and z.

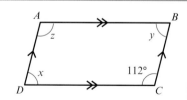

CONTINUED

Answers

Opposite angles of a parallelogram are equal.

Angle DAB = angle DCB, so angle z = 112° and angle ADC = angle ABC, so $x = y$

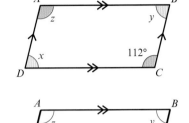

Opposite sides of the parallelogram are parallel.

Since AD is parallel to BC, angles ADC and BCD are co-interior angles which add up to 180°.

$x = 180° - 112°$

$\quad = 68°$

since $x = y$, $y = 68°$

> **MATHEMATICAL CONNECTIONS**
>
> You learnt angle properties on transversal lines in Chapter 4.

Exercise 5.2

1 Identify if each quadrilateral is a square, rhombus, kite, parallelogram, rectangle or trapezium.

a

b

c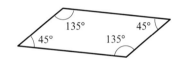

d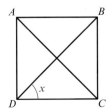

e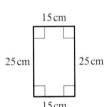

f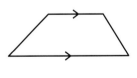

2 Find the value of the unknown angle(s) in each quadrilateral.

a $ABCD$ is a square.

b $PQRS$ is a rectangle.

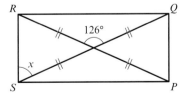

c   *WXYZ* is a kite.

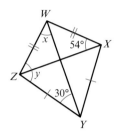

d   *EFGH* is a trapezium.

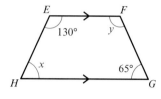

e   *EFGH* is a trapezium.

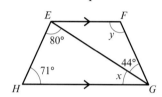

f   *WXYZ* is a kite.

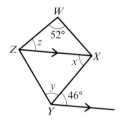

g   *KLMN* is a rhombus.

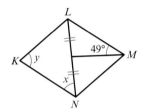

h   *KLMN* and *OPQL* are rhombuses.

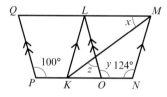

5.3 Polygons

A **polygon** is a closed figure made of **only straight line segments**. A polygon must have a minimum of three sides. Triangles and quadrilaterals are examples of polygons.
Here are some more examples of polygons:

   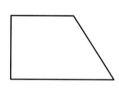

DISCUSSION 3

Explain why the following are **not** polygons.
Discuss with a partner.

a   b   c   d

A polygon can be categorised as regular or irregular. A **regular polygon** has all sides the same length and all interior angles equal. An **irregular polygon** has at least two different sides and at least two different interior angles.

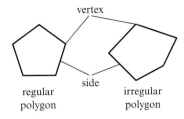

regular polygon   side   irregular polygon

Interior and exterior angles of a polygon

The diagram shows a five-sided polygon known as a **pentagon**. Recall from Section 5.1 that the exterior angle is the angle adjacent to the interior angle at the vertex on a straight line.

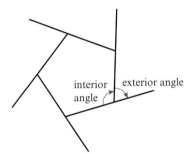

A pentagon has five sides, five vertices, five interior angles and five exterior angles.

In general, an n-sided polygon has n vertices, n interior angles and n exterior angles.

There are special names for polygons with different numbers of sides. This table summarises some of the names for these polygons.

Types of polygons

Number of sides	Name of polygon	Number of vertices	Number of interior angles	Number of exterior angles	Regular polygon
3	Triangle	3	3	3	equilateral triangle
4	Quadrilateral	4	4	4	square
5	Pentagon	5	5	5	

(Continued)

Number of sides	Name of polygon	Number of vertices	Number of interior angles	Number of exterior angles	Regular polygon
6	Hexagon	6	6	6	
7	Heptagon	7	7	7	
8	Octagon	8	8	8	
9	Nonagon	9	9	9	
10	Decagon	10	10	10	

Angle properties of polygons

INVESTIGATION 1 – FINDING THE SUM OF THE INTERIOR ANGLE OF POLYGONS

a	What is the sum of the interior angles of a triangle?	
b	A quadrilateral can be divided into two triangles by drawing a diagonal as shown. What is the sum of the interior angles of a quadrilateral?	
c	A pentagon can be divided into three triangles by drawing two diagonals as shown. What is the sum of the interior angles of a pentagon?	

(Continued)

CONTINUED

d	Consider a hexagon. Draw diagonals to divide the hexagon into triangles. What is the least number of triangles you can form? What is the sum of the interior angles of a hexagon?	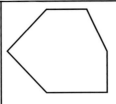

e By drawing your own polygons, copy and complete this table:

Polygon	n, number of sides	Least number of triangles formed	Sum of the interior angles
Triangle	3	1	$1 \times 180° = 180°$
Quadrilateral	4	2	
Pentagon	5	3	
Hexagon	6		
	7		
	8		
	9		
	10		

f From your table in part **e**, what can you say about the least number of triangles formed by a polygon with n sides?

g What is the general formula for the sum of the interior angles of a polygon with n sides?

> **TIP**
>
> The letter n is often used to represent the number of sides when it is unknown or can change.

Observation from Investigation 1:

Sum of the interior angles *of* **any** n-sided polygon $= (n - 2) \times 180°$

Since a regular polygon has equal sides and equal interior angles, a **regular n-sided polygon** will have n number of equal sides and n equal interior angles.

- One interior angle of a regular n-sided polygon $= \dfrac{(n - 2) \times 180°}{n}$

- One interior angle + one exterior angle $= 180°$

- Sum of the exterior angles of any n-sided polygon $= 360°$

- One exterior angle of a regular n-sided polygon $= \dfrac{360°}{n}$

DISCUSSION 4

Can you show that the sum of the exterior angles of **any** n-sided polygon $= 360°$? Discuss with a partner.

WORKED EXAMPLE 5

a Find one interior angle of a regular 15-sided polygon.

b Find one exterior angle of a regular 20-sided polygon.

Answers

a While this looks like a simple example, there are two methods to solve this question.

Method 1: Using the interior angle formula

Sum of interior angles = $(15 - 2) \times 180° = 13 \times 180° = 2340°$

One interior angle = $\dfrac{2340}{15} = 156°$

Method 2: Using the exterior angle formula

One exterior angle = $\dfrac{360}{15} = 24°$

One interior angle = $180° - 24° = 156°$

b It doesn't make sense to use the interior angle formula here since the question is asking for the size of an exterior angle.

One exterior angle = $\dfrac{360}{20} = 18°$

> **TIP**
>
> Even though the question is asking for the size of one interior angle, it is easier to use the exterior angle formula to calculate one interior angle.

WORKED EXAMPLE 6

A regular polygon has an interior angle of 165°. Find the number of sides of the polygon.

Answer

Similar to Worked example 5, there are two methods to solve this question.

Method 1: Using the interior angle formula

$\dfrac{(n - 2) \times 180°}{n} = 165$

$180n - 360 = 165n$

$180n - 165n = 360$

$15n = 360$

$n = \dfrac{360}{15} = 24$ sides

Method 2: Using the exterior angle formula

One exterior angle = $180° - 165° = 15°$

Number of sides, $n = \dfrac{360°}{15°} = 24$ sides

> **MATHEMATICAL CONNECTIONS**
>
> Method 1 requires the knowledge of algebra covered in Chapter 7, hence it is more complicated.

REFLECTION

It is easier to solve both Worked examples 5 and 6 using the formula for exterior angles. Why?

WORKED EXAMPLE 7

ABCDE are five of the vertices of a regular *n*-sided polygon. Given that angle *BAC* = 10°, find:

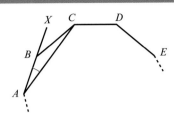

a   angle *XBC*

b   angle *ACD*

c   *n*, the number of sides of the polygon.

Answers

a   Since *ABCDE*… is a regular polygon, *AB* = *BC*.

   ABC is an isosceles triangle, with *AB* = *BC* and angles *BAC* and *BCA* are equal.

   Angle *XBC* = 2 × 10° = 20°

b   Recognise that angle *XBC* is the exterior angle of the polygon.

   The sum of one interior angle and one exterior angle is 180°.

   One interior angle = 180° − 20° = 160°

   Angle *ACD* = 160° − 10° = 150°

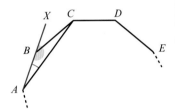

c   The exterior angles of a regular polygon are equal and the sum of the exterior angles is always 360°.

   $n = \dfrac{360°}{20°} = 18$

Interior angles and exterior angles of irregular polygons

You can also find interior angles and exterior angles of irregular polygons.

WORKED EXAMPLE 8

Find the value of *x*.

Answer

This is an irregular quadrilateral.

The sum of the interior angles of a quadrilateral = (4 − 2) × 180° = 360°

$3x + 2x = 360° − 85° − 70°$

$5x = 205°$

$x = \dfrac{205°}{5}$

$x = 41°$

> **TIP**
>
> Remember that in an irregular polygon the sides are **not** all equal length and the angles are **not** all equal.

WORKED EXAMPLE 9

Find the value of x.

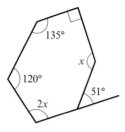

Answer

This is a six-sided irregular polygon.

The sum of the interior angles = $(6 - 2) \times 180° = 720°$

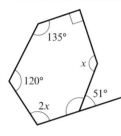

The value of the unknown interior angle marked is
$180° - 51° = 129°$

$2x + x = 720° -$ (sum of the other four known interior angles)

$= 720° - (129° + 120° + 135° + 90°)$

$= 720° - 474°$

$= 246°$

$3x = 246°$

$x = 246° \div 3$

$= 82°$

Exercise 5.3

1   Find the sum of the interior angles of each of these polygons.

    a   heptagon   b   decagon

    c   11-sided polygon   d   18-sided polygon

2   Find the size of one exterior angle of a regular:

    a   heptagon   b   decagon

    c   12-sided polygon   d   30-sided polygon.

3   Find the size of one interior angle of a regular:

    a   octagon   b   nonagon

    c   15-sided polygon   d   20-sided polygon.

4   *CDEFG* shows a regular pentagon.

    a   Find:

        i   angle *CGF*

        ii   angle *CFG*

        iii   angle *CDF*.

    b   Determine if *CG* is parallel to *DF*.

        Give a reason for your answer.

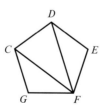

5   Given that each interior angle of a regular polygon is five times the size of its exterior angle, find the number of sides of the polygon.

6   In an *n*-sided regular polygon, the ratio of one interior angle to one exterior angle is given by $7:2$. Find *n*.

7   A regular polygon has an exterior angle of 22.5°. Find the sum of the interior angles of the polygon.

8   The diagram is made up of a regular octagon and a regular hexagon. Find the value of *x*, *y* and *z*.

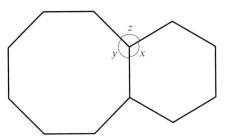

9   *PQRS* are four vertices of a regular polygon. Find:

   a   the size of one exterior angle of the polygon

   b   the number of sides of the polygon

   c   angle *PQS*.

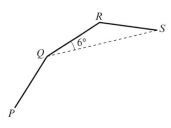

10 In each polygon, find the value of the unknown angle marked *x*.

a
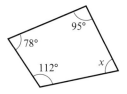

b
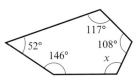

c
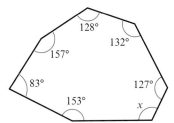

d
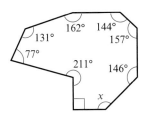

11 For each diagram, find the value of x.

a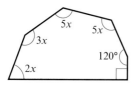

b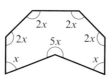

> **MATHEMATICAL CONNECTIONS**
>
> This question links to the work on algebra in Chapter 7, but you can also solve it using ratio and proportion.

c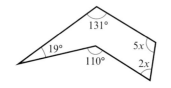

d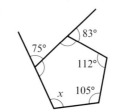

12 A polygon has n sides. Three of its exterior angles are 50°, 60° and 70°.
The remaining $(n - 3)$ exterior angles are each 12°. Calculate the value of n.

13 A polygon has n sides. Four of its interior angles are 98°, 104°, 112° and 146°.
The remaining $(n - 4)$ exterior angles are each 10°. Calculate the value of n.

SUMMARY

Are you able to... ?
use angle properties of polygons
calculate the interior and exterior angles of regular polygons
calculate unknown angles in triangles
understand and use the properties of quadrilaterals to find angles
calculate the interior and exterior angles of irregular polygons.

Past paper questions

1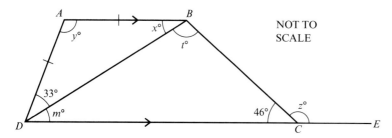

NOT TO SCALE

$ABCD$ is a trapezium with angle $ADB = 33°$ and angle $BCD = 46°$.
AB is parallel to DC and $AD = AB$. DCE is a straight line.

a Write down the mathematical name for triangle ABD. [1]

b Find the value of each of x, y, z, m and t. [5]

Cambridge IGCSE International Mathematics 0607 Paper 31 Q6 November 2021

2

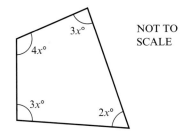

NOT TO
SCALE

Work out the value of x. [2]

Cambridge IGCSE International Mathematics 0607 Paper 12 Q20 March 2021

3

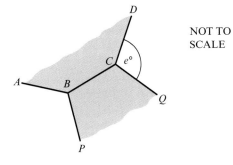

NOT TO
SCALE

$ABCD$ is part of a regular octagon. $PBCQ$ is part of a regular hexagon.

Find the value of e. [4]

Cambridge IGCSE International Mathematics 0607 Paper 32 Q7 d March 2022

> **Chapter 6**
Indices, standard form and surds

IN THIS CHAPTER YOU WILL:

- understand and use indices (positive, zero and negative integers)
- use the rules of indices
- understand and use standard form
- convert numbers into and out of standard form
- calculate values with standard form with a calculator

> understand and use fractional indices

> calculate values in standard form without a calculator

> understand and use surds, including simplifying expressions

> rationalise the denominator.

GETTING STARTED

1   Simplify and express the following using index notation.

   a $2 \times 2 \times 2 \times 2 \times 2$ b $3 \times 3 \times 3 \times 5 \times 5$

   c $\dfrac{7 \times 7 \times 7 \times 7 \times 7}{7 \times 7}$

2   Express each number as a product of its prime factors.

   a   8   b   147   c   243

3   Evaluate the following without the use of a calculator.

   a $3 - \dfrac{1}{4} + 8$ b $11 + (-6)$ c $-5 + 12$

   d $22 - (-13)$ e $(-6) \times 8$ f $48 \div (-12)$

   g $(-4)^2$ h $(-4)^3$

KEY WORDS

conjugate surds

counter example

index (plural indices)

rationalise the denominator

rules of indices

standard form

surds

6.1 Indices I

You learnt in Chapter 1 that when you multiply a number by itself you can use **index** notation to represent the result:

$$a^n = \underbrace{a \times a \times a \times \cdots \times a}_{n \text{ number of } a} \quad (n \text{ is a positive integer})$$

Index notation:

base → a^n ← index (plural indices)

MATHEMATICAL CONNECTIONS

You met index notation and learnt how to express numbers as products of their prime factors in Chapter 1.

INVESTIGATION 1

The objective of this investigation is for you to recognise patterns in the multiplication and division of numbers written in index notation.

Copy and complete the tables and observe any patterns in the multiplication and division of these numbers.

Multiplying numbers in index notation

Write out the expanded form of the multiplications. Then write the final answers in index notation. The first row has been done for you.

	Product	Expanded form	Answer
1	$3^2 \times 3^3$	$(3 \times 3) \times (3 \times 3 \times 3)$	3^5
2	$5^4 \times 5^2$		
3	$2^3 \times 2^4 \times 2^2$		
4	$a^4 \times a^5$		

CONTINUED

What do you observe about the index of the answer when you multiply numbers of the same base?

Copy and complete: In general, $a^n \times a^m =$ _____.

Does the rule apply if the numbers have different bases?

Dividing numbers in index notation

Work out the divisions of the numbers using fractions. Write the final answers in index notation. The first row has been done for you.

	Division	Expanded form written in fractions	Answer
1	$3^5 \div 3^3$	$\dfrac{3 \times 3 \times 3 \times 3 \times 3}{3 \times 3 \times 3} = \dfrac{\cancel{3} \times \cancel{3} \times \cancel{3} \times 3 \times 3}{\cancel{3} \times \cancel{3} \times \cancel{3}} = \dfrac{3 \times 3}{1}$	3^2
2	$5^7 \div 5^6$		
3	$a^9 \div a^5$		

What do you observe about the index of the answer when you divide numbers of the same base?

Copy and complete: In general, $a^n \div a^m =$ _____.

At this point, you are only looking at cases when $n > m$

Does the rule apply if the numbers have different bases?

Investigation 1 leads to the first two **rules of indices**:

$a^n \times a^m = a^{n+m}$

$a^n \div a^m = a^{n-m}$

WORKED EXAMPLE 1

Simplify the following. Write your answers in index notation.

a $\quad 2^5 \times 2^4$ **b** $\quad 5^{10} \div 5^6$

Answers

a $\quad 2^5 \times 2^4 = 2^{5+4}$ You saw in Investigation 1 that when you multiply
$\qquad\qquad\quad = 2^9$ numbers of the same base, you add the indices.

                           The question requires you to leave your answers in index notation, so leave your answer as 2^9.

b $\quad 5^{10} \div 5^6 = 5^{10-6}$ When you divide numbers of the same base, you subtract
$\qquad\qquad\qquad = 5^4$ the indices.

WORKED EXAMPLE 2

Simplify the following. Write your answers in index notation.

a $3^{-2} \times 3^3$ **b** $4^2 \div 4^{-1}$

Answers

a $3^{-2} \times 3^3 = 3^{-2+3}$
$\phantom{3^{-2} \times 3^3} = 3^1$
$\phantom{3^{-2} \times 3^3} = 3$

When you multiply numbers of the same base, you add the indices, regardless of whether the index is a positive or negative integer.

b $4^2 \div 4^{-1} = 4^{2-(-1)}$
$\phantom{4^2 \div 4^{-1}} = 4^{2+1}$
$\phantom{4^2 \div 4^{-1}} = 4^3$
$\phantom{4^2 \div 4^{-1}} = 4 \times 4 \times 4$
$\phantom{4^2 \div 4^{-1}} = 64$

When you divide numbers of the same base, you subtract the indices.

Here you are subtracting a negative number.

MATHEMATICAL CONNECTIONS

From Chapter 2, you know that subtracting negative 1 has the same effect as adding positive 1.

TIP

You have not yet calculated with a negative integer index. You will look at the meaning of negative integer indices in the next investigation. For now, focus on evaluating these products using the rules you derived in Investigation 1.

INVESTIGATION 2

This investigation looks at the bracket rule, zero index and negative integer indices.

Bracket rule

Copy and complete the table and observe the patterns in the index.

	Bracket	Expanded form using the rule $a^n \times a^m = a^{n+m}$	Answer
1	$(3^2)^4$	$3^2 \times 3^2 \times 3^2 \times 3^2 =$	
2	$(5^4)^3$		
3	$(2^5)^4$		
4	$(a^3)^5$		

What do you observe about the index of the number when you raise it to a second index?

Copy and complete: In general, $(a^n)^m =$ _____.

CONTINUED

Extension to division of indices:

Zero index

Copy and complete the following table.

	Expanded form written in fractions	Applying the rule $a^n \div a^m = a^{n-m}$	Answer
$7^4 \div 7^4$			
$a^7 \div a^7$			

What can you conclude about the value of a^0?

Negative integer indices

Copy and complete the following table.

	Expanded form written in fractions	Applying the rule $a^n \div a^m = a^{n-m}$	Answer
$2^5 \div 2^6$			
$4^3 \div 4^5$			
$a^4 \div a^7$			

What do you observe about negative integer indices?

Copy and complete: In general, $a^{-n} = $ _____.

Investigation 2 leads to three more rules of indices:

$(a^n)^m = a^{n \times m}$

$a^0 = 1$

$a^{-n} = \dfrac{1}{a^n}$

WORKED EXAMPLE 3

Evaluate.

a 11^0 **b** $(2^3)^2$ **c** 3^{-2}

TIP

Evaluate means to calculate the numerical answer.

CONTINUED

Answers

a $11^0 = 1$ Regardless of the base, $a^0 = 1$.

b $(2^3)^2 = 2^6$ Using $(a^n)^m = a^{n \times m}$, first multiply the indices
$\quad\quad = 2 \times 2 \times 2 \times 2 \times 2 \times 2$ to get 2^6.
$\quad\quad = 64$

c $3^{-2} = \dfrac{1}{3^2}$ Using the rule $a^{-n} = \dfrac{1}{a^n}$, move the base 3

$\quad\quad = \dfrac{1}{9}$ to the denominator: $3^{-2} = \dfrac{1}{3^2}$.

Then evaluate $3^2 = 9$.

Exercise 6.1

1   Simplify the following, expressing your answers in index notation.

    a $2^5 \times 2^6$ **b** $3^7 \times 3^6$ **c** $7^2 \times 7^7$

    d $5^4 \times 5^3 \times 5^2$ **e** $11^5 \times 11^4 \times 11^6$ **f** $2^9 \div 2^5$

    g $7^{10} \div 7^4$ **h** $13^{14} \div 13^7$ **i** $3^{17} \div 3^5 \div 3^6$

    j $(17^3)^5$ **k** $(10^4)^2$ **l** $(5^6)^3$

2   Evaluate the following without using a calculator.

    a 10^0 **b** 13^0 **c** 100^0

    d 3^{-1} **e** 5^{-3} **f** 9^{-2}

    g $3^{-2} + 5^0$ **h** $17^0 + 7^{-1} - 2^{-3}$ **i** $5^{-7} \times 5^6$

    j $4^{-3} \times 4^5$ **k** $2^{-1} \div 2^2$ **l** $10^7 \div 10^8$

3   Evaluate the following without using a calculator.

    a $(2^4)^2$ **b** $(7^4)^0$ **c** $(5^2)^{-1}$

    d $(3^{-2})^2$ **e** $(4^{-2})^{-1}$ **f** $(5^5)^2 \div 5^8$

    g $(6^3)^{-2} \times 6^7$ **h** $(7^4)^{-2} \times (7^3)^3$ **i** $(2^5)^{-4} \times (2^9)^2$

6.2 Fractional indices

So far you have looked at integer and zero indices. What happens if the index is a fraction? What does it mean for a number to have a fractional index?

INVESTIGATION 3

In this investigation you will attempt to find the meaning of fractional indices.

Recall from Chapter 1, $\sqrt{a \times a} = a$ and $\sqrt[3]{a \times a \times a} = a$, so you can deduce

that $\sqrt[n]{\underbrace{a \times a \times a \times \cdots \times a}_{n\text{-terms}}} = a$

Copy and complete this table. The first row has been done for you.

	$a^{\frac{1}{n}}$	Multiplying to get a	Taking n root on both sides
1	Consider $a^{\frac{1}{2}}$	$a^{\frac{1}{2}} \times a^{\frac{1}{2}} = a$	Take the square root on both sides: $R a^{\frac{1}{2}} \times a^{1/2} = \sqrt{a}$ Since $\sqrt{a \times a} = a$ LHS $= \sqrt{a^{\frac{1}{2}} \times a^{\frac{1}{2}}} = a^{\frac{1}{2}}$, hence $a^{\frac{1}{2}} = \sqrt{a}$
2	Consider $a^{\frac{1}{3}}$	$a^{\frac{1}{3}} \times a^{\frac{1}{3}} \times a^{\frac{1}{3}} = $ ____	Take the cube root on both sides: $\sqrt[3]{a^{\frac{1}{3}} \times a^{\frac{1}{3}} \times a^{\frac{1}{3}}} = $ _____ Since $\sqrt[3]{a \times a \times a} = a$ LHS $= $ _____
3	Consider $a^{\frac{1}{4}}$	$a^{\frac{1}{4}} \times a^{\frac{1}{4}} \times a^{\frac{1}{4}} \times a^{\frac{1}{4}}$ $= $ _____	Taking the _____ root on both sides:
4	Consider $a^{\frac{1}{5}}$	_____ _____	_____ _____
5	Consider $a^{\frac{1}{n}}$	_____ _____	_____ _____

What can you conclude about fractional indices?

Copy and complete: $a^{\frac{1}{n}} = $ _____, then $\left(a^{\frac{1}{n}}\right)^m = $ _____.

Investigation 3 leads to two more rules of indices:

$a^{\frac{1}{n}} = \sqrt[n]{a}$

$u^{\frac{m}{n}} = \left(\sqrt[n]{a}\right)^m = \sqrt[n]{a^m}$

WORKED EXAMPLE 4

Evaluate the following without using a calculator.

a $\sqrt{3}$ b $\sqrt[4]{5}$ c $\sqrt[5]{2^3}$

Answers

a Since $a^{\frac{1}{n}} = \sqrt[n]{a}$, $\sqrt{3} = 3^{\frac{1}{2}}$ (square root means $n = 2$)

b $n = 4$, hence this is the fourth root, $\sqrt[4]{5} = 5^{\frac{1}{4}}$

c $n = 5$, this is the fifth root, so $\sqrt[5]{2^3} = (2^3)^{\frac{1}{5}}$

  Using the rule $(a^n)^m = a^{n \times m}$, $(2^3)^{\frac{1}{5}} = 2^{3 \times \frac{1}{5}} = 2^{\frac{3}{5}}$

  $\therefore \sqrt[5]{2^3} = 2^{\frac{3}{5}}$

WORKED EXAMPLE 5

Express the following in index notation.

a $8^{\frac{1}{3}}$ b $32^{\frac{1}{5}}$ c $27^{\frac{2}{3}}$

Answers

There are two methods to evaluate these numbers. One method is to use roots, the other method is to use indices.

Method 1: Using roots

You need to be familiar with the square roots or cube roots of specific numbers.

a $8^{\frac{1}{3}} = \sqrt[3]{8} = 2$

b $32^{\frac{1}{5}} = \sqrt[5]{32} = 2$

c $27^{\frac{2}{3}} = \sqrt[3]{27^2} = \left(\sqrt[3]{27}\right)^2$

  $\sqrt[3]{27} = 3$, so $27^{\frac{2}{3}} = \left(\sqrt[3]{27}\right)^2 = 3^2 = 9$

Method 2: Using the rules of indices

Step 1: Rewrite the base in index notation with a smaller base.

Step 2: Use $(a^n)^m = a^{n \times m}$ to simplify the power.

Rewrite 8 in index notation: $8 = 2^3$

Then $8^{\frac{1}{3}} = (2^3)^{\frac{1}{3}} = 2^{3 \times \frac{1}{3}} = 2^1$

Rewrite 32 in index notation:
$32 = 2^5$

$\Rightarrow 32^{\frac{1}{5}} = (2^5)^{\frac{1}{5}} = 2^{5 \times \frac{1}{5}} = 2$

Rewrite 27 in index notation:
$27 = 3^3$

$\Rightarrow 27^{\frac{2}{3}} = (3^3)^{\frac{2}{3}} = 3^{3 \times \frac{2}{3}} = 3^2 = 9$

Exercise 6.2

1 Evaluate the following without using a calculator.

a $64^{\frac{1}{2}}$ b $16^{\frac{1}{4}}$ c $9^{\frac{3}{2}}$ d $125^{\frac{2}{3}}$

e $49^{\frac{3}{2}}$ f $32^{\frac{3}{5}}$ g $144^{0.5}$ h $64^{\frac{1}{6}}$

2   Evaluate the following without using a calculator.

a $\sqrt{121}$ b $\sqrt[3]{125}$ c $\sqrt[4]{16}$ d $\sqrt[4]{81}$

e $\sqrt[6]{64}$ f $\sqrt[3]{216}$ g $(\sqrt{16})^3$ h $\sqrt[3]{\dfrac{1}{8}}$

6.3 Standard form

Introduction to standard form

When you have a very big number such as 23 000 000 000 or a very small number such as 0.000 012 3, it can be very difficult to write down the number. **Standard form** allows you to express these big or small numbers in a more compact way.

A number in standard form is written as $A \times 10^n$, where $1 \leqslant A < 10$ and n is a positive or negative integer.

WORKED EXAMPLE 6

Convert these numbers in standard form to ordinary numbers.

a 2×10^5 b 5.6×10^4 c 5×10^{-3} d 1.23×10^{-7}

Answers

a $2 \times 10^5 = 2 \times 100\,000$

   $\qquad\quad = 200\,000$

Recall from Section 6.1:

$10^5 = 10 \times 10 \times 10 \times 10 \times 10 = 100\,000$

So 2×10^5 is the same as $2 \times 100\,000$

Note that this is equivalent to moving the decimal point 5 places to the right 2 0 0 0 0 0

So the positive number tells you the direction to move the decimal point while the number 5 indicates the number of places to move the decimal point.

b $5.6 \times 10^4 = 56\,000$

You can see this as $5.6 \times 10\,000$ or move the decimal point 4 places to the right 5 6 0 0 0 as the index is a positive 4.

c $5 \times 10^{-3} = 5 \times \dfrac{1}{10^3}$

   $\qquad\quad = 5 \times \dfrac{1}{1000}$

   $\qquad\quad = \dfrac{5}{1000}$

   $\qquad\quad = 0.005$

Recall from Section 6.1:

$10^{-3} = \dfrac{1}{10^3}$. Since $10^3 = 1000$, $10^{-3} = \dfrac{1}{10^3} = \dfrac{1}{1000}$

and $5 \times \dfrac{1}{1000} = \dfrac{5}{1} \times \dfrac{1}{1000} = \dfrac{5}{1000}$

This is equivalent to moving the decimal point 3 places to the left 0 . 0 0 5

Here the power is negative, so you move the decimal point to the left. The number 3 tells you the number of places to move the decimal point.

CONTINUED

d $1.23 \times 10^{-7} =$
    $0.000\,000\,123$

Using a similar method to part c, when the power is -7 you move the decimal point 7 places to the left.

$0\,.\,0\,0\,0\,0\,0\,0\,1\,2\,3$

In general, for $A \times 10^n$:

If the value of n is	Ordinary notation is	To change to ordinary notation
Positive	A large number	Move the decimal point n places to the right.
Negative	A decimal	Move the decimal point n places to the left.

WORKED EXAMPLE 7

Write these numbers in standard form.

a   6 500 000   **b**   0.000 22

Answers

a $6\,5\,0\,0\,0\,0\,0\,.$

   $6\,.\,5\,0\,0\,0\,0\,0$

The decimal point moved 6 places to the left, so $n = 6$

$6\,500\,000 = 6.5 \times 10^6$

6 500 000 is a very large number. The power n should be positive.

To find the value of n, put a decimal point after the last digit in the number, then move the decimal until you get a number $1 \leqslant A < 10$.

The number n is equal to the number of places you moved the decimal point.

b $0\,.\,0\,0\,0\,2\,2$

The decimal point moved 4 places to the right, so $n = -4$

$0.000\,22 = 2.2 \times 10^{-4}$

0.000 22 is a small number, so n must be negative.

Move the decimal point to the right until you get a number $1 \leqslant A < 10$.

Count the number of decimal places you moved the decimal point.

Calculations with standard form with a calculator

You may see problems involving large or small numbers in science or other subjects, so being able to use your calculator to compute operations with standard form is a useful skill.

WORKED EXAMPLE 8

Evaluate the following using a calculator. Leave your answers in standard form.

a $4.18 \times 10^8 + 1.4 \times 10^7$

b $2.4 \times 10^{-7} + 5.12 \times 10^{-8}$

c $2 \times 10^{-5} - 4.5 \times 10^{-6}$

d $(7.81 \times 10^5) \div (3.6 \times 10^{-9})$

Answers

a $4.18 \times 10^8 + 1.4 \times 10^7$

$= 432\,000\,000$

Move the decimal place 8 places to the left:

$= 4.32 \times 10^8$

To key in standard form in your calculator, use the button that says 10^x. Using a Casio fx-CG50, the button is **log**.

The command for 10^x is in yellow, so you need to press **SHIFT** then **log**.

For example, to key in 4.18×10^8, press

Then use the navigation arrows to move the cursor to the right and press the following keys:

The screen will display:

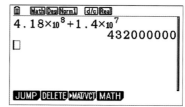

You will need to change the answer to standard form using the method in Worked example 7.

An alternative way to key in 4.18×10^8 is:

or

4 • 1 8 × ×10^x 8

CONTINUED

b $2.4 \times 10^{-7} + 5.12 \times 10^{-8}$

   $= 2.912 \times 10^{-7}$

Sometimes, the calculator will automatically provide the answers in standard form, as shown:

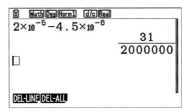

```
Math Deg Norm1  d/c Real
2.4×10⁻⁷+5.12×10⁻⁸
                    2.912×10⁰ ⁷
□

JUMP DELETE ▶MAT/VCT MATH
```

In this case, you can directly write the answer provided:

c $2 \times 10^{-5} - 4.5 \times 10^{-6}$

   $= 1.55 \times 10^{-5}$

```
Math Deg Norm1  d/c Real
2×10⁻⁵−4.5×10⁻⁶
                      31
                   ‾‾‾‾‾‾‾‾
                   2000000
□

DEL-LINE DEL-ALL
```

If the calculator gives a fraction, you can press the `S↔D` button to convert the fraction to a decimal.

```
Math Deg Norm1  d/c Real
2×10⁻⁵−4.5×10⁻⁶
                 1.55×10⁰ ⁵
□

DEL-LINE DEL-ALL
```

d $(7.18 \times 10^5) \div (3.6 \times 10^{-9})$

   $= 1.99 \times 10^{14}$ (correct to 3 sf)

When doing division, use a pair of brackets for each number in standard form:

```
Math Deg Norm1  d/c Real
(7.18×10⁵)÷(3.6×10⁻⁹)
              1.994444444×10¹ ⁴
□

JUMP DELETE ▶MAT/VCT MATH
```

When the final answer is not exact, round to three significant figures.

MATHEMATICS IN CONTEXT

Standard form also has its applications in real life. You may see standard form in other subjects such as science, economics or business studies. For example, the speed of light is approximately 3×10^8 m/s.

You can solve word problems involving standard form, as demonstrated in Worked example 9.

WORKED EXAMPLE 9

In the year 2022, the population on planet Zeus is 5.7×10^6. It is estimated that there were 1.2×10^5 deaths and 9.6×10^4 births in that year. Find the population of Zeus at the end of 2022, leaving your answer in standard form.

Answer

Deaths decrease the population while births increase the population.

To calculate the population of Zeus, subtract the number of deaths and add number of births to the original population.

$(5.7 \times 10^6) - (1.2 \times 10^5) + (9.6 \times 10^4)$

Using a calculator:

```
Math Deg Norm1 d/c Real
5.7×10⁶−1.2×10⁵+9.6×10⁴
                    5676000
□


JUMP DELETE ▶MAT/VCT MATH
```

You need to convert to standard form.

$(5.7 \times 10^6) - (1.2 \times 10^5) + (9.6 \times 10^4) = 5.676 \times 10^6$

Exercise 6.3

 1 Convert these numbers to ordinary numbers.

a 7×10^5	**b** 1.3×10^7	**c** 5.8×10^3
d 8.94×10^9	**e** 4×10^{-2}	**f** 6.1×10^{-4}
g 1.05×10^{-6}	**h** 9.55×10^{-10}	**i** 6.13×10^{-9}

 2 Express the following numbers in standard form.

a 230	**b** 140 000	**c** 35 100 000
d 469 000 000 000	**e** 0.012	**f** 0.005 06
g 0.000 0037	**h** 0.000 000 0009	**i** 0.000 000 000 000 0011

3 Use a calculator to evaluate the following. Give your answers in standard form.

a $2.4 \times 10^4 + 5.3 \times 10^5$	**b** $1.4 \times 10^{-10} + 7 \times 10^{-8}$
c $3 \times 10^6 - 8.1 \times 10^5$	**d** $6.5 \times 10^{-12} - 7.2 \times 10^{-13}$
e $(4 \times 10^6) \times (3 \times 10^9)$	**f** $(2 \times 10^{-11}) \times (1.8 \times 10^7)$
g $(3 \times 10^{-3}) \div (6 \times 10^{-7})$	**h** $(5.1 \times 10^{-5}) \div (1.7 \times 10^4)$
i $(2.6 \times 10^{-6})^2$	**j** $(1.9 \times 10^{11})^3$

Use a calculator to answer the following questions.

4   In the year 2024, the population of Soda City is estimated to be 9.8×10^5. If the average amount of soft drink each person consumed was 0.3 litres per day, how many litres of soft drink were consumed in a single day in Soda City in 2024? Give your answer in standard form.

5   A water catchment contains $8.25 \times 10^6 \, \text{m}^3$ of water. If $1 \, \text{m}^3$ of water has a mass of $1000 \, \text{kg}$, find the total mass of water in the water catchment. Give your answer in standard form.

6   The number of atoms in 12 g of Carbon-12 element is 6.022×10^{23}. What is the mass of one atom of Carbon-12 element? Give your answer in standard form, correct to three significant figures.

6.4 Calculations with standard form without a calculator

In this section you will learn how to calculate with standard form without the use of calculator.

WORKED EXAMPLE 10

Work out the following without the use of a calculator.

a $2.4 \times 10^8 + 1.6 \times 10^7$ b $5 \times 10^{-7} + 6 \times 10^{-8}$

c $2 \times 10^{10} - 4.5 \times 10^9$ d $6.4 \times 10^{-5} - 7 \times 10^{-6}$

Answers

a $2.4 \times 10^8 + 1.6 \times 10^7$ Split 10^7 into $10^8 \times 10^{-1}$.

$$10^8 \times 10^{-1}$$

Then take out the common factor 10^8.

Evaluate the sum left inside the bracket.

$$= 10^8(2.4 + 1.6 \times 10^{-1})$$

$$= 10^8(2.4 + 0.16)$$

$$= 10^8(2.56)$$

$$= 2.56 \times 10^8$$

b $5 \times 10^{-7} + 6 \times 10^{-8}$ Split 10^{-8} into $10^{-7} \times 10^{-1}$.

$$10^{-7} \times 10^{-1}$$

Then take out the common factor 10^{-7}.

Evaluate the sum left inside the bracket.

$$= 10^{-7}(5 + 6 \times 10^{-1})$$

$1 < 5.6 < 10$, so it satisfies the restrictions for the A in $A \times 10^n$.

$$= 10^{-7}(5 + 0.6)$$

$$= 5.6 \times 10^{-7}$$

TIP

From part **a**, you see that in a sum that contains positive powers of 10^a and 10^b, where $a > b$, you split 10^b into $10^a \times 10^{-(a-b)}$. You write the number with base 10 with the **smaller index** as a product of two numbers with base 10. You then take out the base 10 with the **bigger index** as a common factor.

From part **b**, when you add standard form that contains negative powers of 10^{-a} and 10^{-b}, where both a and b are positive and $a > b$ so $-a < -b$, you split 10^{-a} into $10^{-b} \times 10^{-(a-b)}$. You write the number with base 10 with the **smaller index** as a product of two numbers with base 10. You then take out the base 10 with the **smaller index** as a common factor.

CONTINUED

c $2 \times 10^{10} - 4.5 \times 10^{9}$

$10^{10} \times 10^{-1}$

Follow the same rule in subtraction. Split the number with base 10 with the smaller index, so split 10^9 into $10^{10} \times 10^{-(10-9)}$

$\Rightarrow 10^9 = 10^{10} \times 10^{-1}$

$= 10^{10}(2 - 4.5 \times 10^{-1})$

$= 10^{10}(2 - 0.45)$

$= 1.55 \times 10^{10}$

Take out the number with base 10 with the bigger index as a common factor, so take out 10^{10}.

d $6.4 \times 10^{-5} - 7 \times 10^{-6}$

$10^{-5} \times 10^{-1}$

Split the number with base 10 with the smaller index, so split 10^{-6} into $10^{-5} \times 10^{-(6-5)}$

$\Rightarrow 10^{-6} = 10^{-5} \times 10^{-1}$

$= 10^{-5}(6.4 - 7 \times 10^{-1})$

$= 10^{-5}(6.4 - 0.7)$

$= 5.7 \times 10^{-5}$

Take out the number with base 10 with the smaller index as a common factor, so take out 10^{-5}.

Worked example 10 looked at addition and subtraction with standard form.
Worked example 11 looks at multiplication and division with standard form.

WORKED EXAMPLE 11

Work out the following without the use of a calculator.

a $(4 \times 10^8) \times (1.2 \times 10^9)$

b $(5 \times 10^{-10}) \times (6 \times 10^{-9})$

c $(2 \times 10^{11}) \div (8 \times 10^7)$

d $(5 \times 10^{-13}) \div (2 \times 10^{-7})$

Answers

a $(4 \times 10^8) \times (1.2 \times 10^9)$

$4 \times 1.2 = 4.8 \qquad 10^8 \times 10^9 = 10^{8+9} = 10^{17}$

$= 4.8 \times 10^{17}$

When multiplying standard form, multiply the like terms with each other:

Number times number

Number with index times number with index

b $(5 \times 10^{-10}) \times (6 \times 10^{-9})$

$5 \times 6 = 30$

$10^{-10} \times 10^{-9} = 10^{-10+(-9)} = 10^{-19}$

$= 30 \times 10^{-19}$

$= 3 \times 10^1 \times 10^{-19}$

$= 3 \times 10^{-18}$

Take number times number and number with index times number with index.

The answer is not in standard form as $1 \leq A < 10$ in $A \times 10^n$ and 30 is bigger than 10.

Change 30 to standard form: 3×10^1

Then simplify the numbers with base 10.

CONTINUED

c $(2 \times 10^{11}) \div (8 \times 10^7)$

$2 \div 8 = 0.25$

$10^{11} \div 10^7 = 10^{11-7} = 10^4$

$= 0.25 \times 10^4$

$= 2.5 \times 10^{-1} \times 10^4$

$= 2.5 \times 10^3$

d $(5 \times 10^{-13}) \div (2 \times 10^{-7})$

$5 \div 2 = 2.5$

$10^{-13} \div 10^{-7} = 10^{-13-(-7)} = 10^{-6}$

$= 2.5 \times 10^{-6}$

Use a similar method when dividing standard forms. Take:

Number divided by number

Number with index divided by number with index

0.25 cannot be A as $1 \leqslant A < 10$ in $A \times 10^n$.

Change 0.25 to standard form: $0.25 = 2.5 \times 10^{-1}$

The final answer is in standard form.

Using the same method as part **c**:

Number divided by number

Number with index divided by number with index

The answer is already in standard form. No further simplification is required.

Exercise 6.4

1   Evaluate the following. Express your answers in standard form.

   a $5.3 \times 10^3 + 6 \times 10^4$

   b $7 \times 10^{15} + 3.5 \times 10^{17}$

   c $4.8 \times 10^{-5} + 2.1 \times 10^{-4}$

   d $9.3 \times 10^{-10} + 4 \times 10^{-8}$

   e $1.5 \times 10^7 - 4 \times 10^6$

   f $3.2 \times 10^{10} - 5 \times 10^8$

   g $2.2 \times 10^{-3} - 1.9 \times 10^{-4}$

   h $3.7 \times 10^{-9} - 9 \times 10^{-10}$

2   Evaluate the following. Express your answers in standard form.

   a $2(4.1 \times 10^7)$

   b $3 \times 10^8 \times 3.5 \times 10^9$

   c $4 \times 10^{-15} \times 7 \times 10^{-13}$

   d $8 \times 10^{-12} \times 1.1 \times 10^{18}$

   e $1.5 \times 10^{17} \div 3 \times 10^6$

   f $6 \times 10^{-5} \div 1.2 \times 10^{-3}$

   g $7.2 \times 10^{18} \div 2.4 \times 10^{-6}$

   h $2.8 \times 10^{-20} \div 7 \times 10^{15}$

6.5 Simplifying surds

The roots of some numbers can be written as whole numbers or fractions.

For example: $\sqrt{4} = 2, \sqrt{\dfrac{9}{4}} = \dfrac{3}{2}, \sqrt[3]{8} = 2, \sqrt[5]{243} = 3$. These roots are rational numbers.

Roots of numbers that cannot be written as whole numbers or fractions are known as **surds** (or radicals).

For example: $\sqrt{2} = 1.414\,213\,562..., \sqrt[3]{5} = 1.709\,975\,947....$ These roots are irrational numbers. Surds can only be approximated to a required number of significant figures or written in square root form.

In this section, you will look at simplifying surds and calculating with surds.

> **TIP**
>
> The calculations and examples in this section focus on square roots, but you can apply the same rules when working with other surds.

INVESTIGATION 4

This investigation looks at the expansion of $(ab)^n$ and $\left(\dfrac{a}{b}\right)^n$.

1 Copy and complete this table:

Product	Rewrite in expanded form	Like terms grouped and express in index notation
$(2 \times 3)^2$	$(2 \times 3) \times (2 \times 3)$	$2 \times 2 \times 3 \times 3 = 2^2 \times 3^2$
$(5 \times 6)^3$		
$(a \times b)^4$		
$(ab)^5$		

What can you generalise about $(ab)^n$?

2 Copy and complete this table:

Product	Rewrite in expanded form	Express in index notation
$\left(\dfrac{3}{4}\right)^2$	$\dfrac{3}{4} \times \dfrac{3}{4}$	$\dfrac{3 \times 3}{4 \times 4} = \dfrac{3^2}{4^2}$
$\left(\dfrac{5}{6}\right)^3$		
$\left(\dfrac{a}{b}\right)^4$		
$\left(\dfrac{a}{b}\right)^6$		

What can you generalise about $\left(\dfrac{a}{b}\right)^n$?

Investigation 4 leads to the following rules:

$(ab)^n = a^n b^n$

$\left(\dfrac{a}{b}\right)^n = \dfrac{a^n}{b^n}$

Also, recall that $a^{\frac{1}{2}} = \sqrt{a}$.

Hence, $\sqrt{2}$ is the same as $2^{\frac{1}{2}}$, and $\sqrt{8}$ is the same as $8^{\frac{1}{2}}$.

But $8 = 4 \times 2$, so

$$
\begin{aligned}
\sqrt{8} &= 8^{\frac{1}{2}} \\
&= (4 \times 2)^{\frac{1}{2}} \\
&= 4^{\frac{1}{2}} \times 2^{\frac{1}{2}} \\
&= \sqrt{4} \times \sqrt{2} \\
&= 2 \times \sqrt{2} \\
&= 2\sqrt{2}
\end{aligned}
$$

TIP

Note that 4 is a square number.

In general, you can simplify $\sqrt{a}$ if a can be expressed as the product of a square number and a non-square number.

WORKED EXAMPLE 12

Simplify these surds.

a $\sqrt{12}$ **b** $\sqrt{80}$ **c** $\sqrt{147}$

Answers

a $\sqrt{12} = \sqrt{4 \times 3}$ $12 = 4 \times 3$

     $= \sqrt{4} \times \sqrt{3}$ 4 is a square number while 3 is a non-square number.

     $= 2\sqrt{3}$

b $\sqrt{80} = \sqrt{16 \times 5}$ There are two pairs of factors for 80 which contain a square number and a non-square number.

     $= \sqrt{16} \times \sqrt{5}$ $80 = 4 \times 20$ or $80 = 16 \times 5$

     $= 4\sqrt{5}$ But you can simplify 20 further: $20 = 4 \times 5$, where 4 is a square number, so $80 = 4 \times 4 \times 5 = 16 \times 5$

     To simplify fully, you must use the largest possible square number.

c $\sqrt{147} = \sqrt{49 \times 3}$ $147 = 49 \times 3$, where 49 is the square number.

     $= \sqrt{49} \times \sqrt{3}$ $\sqrt{49} = 7$

     $= 7\sqrt{3}$

MATHEMATICAL CONNECTIONS

You learnt how to express a number as a product of prime factors in Chapter 1. This is a similar process except that you express the number as a product of a prime number and a square number.

Exercise 6.5

1 Simplify these surds.

     a $\sqrt{18}$ **b** $\sqrt{27}$ **c** $\sqrt{50}$

     d $\sqrt{72}$ **e** $\sqrt{112}$ **f** $\sqrt{243}$

     g $2\sqrt{175}$ **h** $5\sqrt{180}$ **i** $7\sqrt{363}$

6.6 Adding and subtracting with surds

Adding and subtracting surds is similar to adding and subtracting algebraic terms. When adding algebraic expressions, you can only add or subtract like terms. Similarly, you can only add or subtract surds of the same base.

For example:

You can add or subtract surds with the same base:

$2\sqrt{3} + 5\sqrt{3} = 7\sqrt{3}$

$2\sqrt{3} - 5\sqrt{3} = -3\sqrt{3}$

But you cannot add or subtract surds with different bases:

$\sqrt{3} + \sqrt{5}$

$3\sqrt{2} - \sqrt{3}$

MATHEMATICAL CONNECTIONS

You will study adding and subtracting algebraic terms in Chapter 7.
You work with a surd in a similar way as you work with an algebraic variable, x.
To add or subtract surds, you add or subtract the coefficients.

In algebra, you can add or subtract like terms:

$2x + 5x = 7x$

$2x - 5x = -3x$

But you cannot add or subtract unlike terms:

$x + y$

$2p - q$

WORKED EXAMPLE 13

Find the exact value of:

a $14\sqrt{2} + 3\sqrt{3} - 5\sqrt{2} + 8\sqrt{3}$ **b** $7\sqrt{5} - 4\sqrt{3} + 6\sqrt{5} + 8$

Answers

a $14\sqrt{2} + 3\sqrt{3} - 5\sqrt{2} + 8\sqrt{3}$ Group all the surds with the same base together.

like terms

like terms

Add/subtract the coefficients of the terms with the same base.

$= 14\sqrt{2} \;\; -5\sqrt{2} \;\; +3\sqrt{3} \;\; +8\sqrt{3}$

$= 9\sqrt{2} \;\;\; + \;\;\; 11\sqrt{3}$

b $7\sqrt{5} - 4\sqrt{3} + 6\sqrt{5} + 8$ Here only the $\sqrt{5}$ terms have the same base.

$= 7\sqrt{5} \;\; +6\sqrt{5} - 4\sqrt{3} + 8$

Add the coefficients of $\sqrt{5}$ together. The other terms are unchanged.

$= 13\sqrt{5} - 4\sqrt{3} + 8$

WORKED EXAMPLE 14

Find the exact value of:

a $\sqrt{12} + \sqrt{48}$ **b** $\sqrt{80} - \sqrt{20}$ **c** $3\sqrt{125} - 2\sqrt{45}$

Answers

When you first see these expressions, it looks as if the bases of the surds are different. However, you can simplify these surds before adding or subtracting.

TIP

Always simplify surds before adding or subtracting if you can.

CONTINUED

a $\sqrt{12} + \sqrt{48}$ Simplify the surds.

$= 2\sqrt{3} + 4\sqrt{3}$ From Worked example 12, $\sqrt{12} = 2\sqrt{3}$

$= 6\sqrt{3}$ Using the same method:

$$\sqrt{48} = \sqrt{16 \times 3}$$
$$= \sqrt{16} \times \sqrt{3}$$
$$= 4\sqrt{3}$$

b $\sqrt{80} - \sqrt{20}$ Simplify $\sqrt{80}$ and $\sqrt{20}$

$= 4\sqrt{5} - 2\sqrt{5}$ From Worked example 12 part b, $\sqrt{80} = 4\sqrt{5}$

$= 2\sqrt{5}$ $\sqrt{20} = \sqrt{4 \times 5}$

$$= \sqrt{4} \times \sqrt{5}$$
$$= 2\sqrt{5}$$

c $3\sqrt{125} - 2\sqrt{45}$ Simplify $\sqrt{125}$ and $\sqrt{45}$

$= 3(5\sqrt{5}) - 2(3\sqrt{5})$ $\sqrt{125} = \sqrt{25 \times 5}$ $\sqrt{45} = \sqrt{9 \times 5}$

$= 15\sqrt{5} - 6\sqrt{5}$ $= \sqrt{25} \times \sqrt{5}$ and $= \sqrt{9} \times \sqrt{5}$

$= 9\sqrt{5}$ $= 5\sqrt{5}$ $= 3\sqrt{5}$

Exercise 6.6

1   Simplify.

   a $3\sqrt{5} + 4\sqrt{5}$ **b** $6\sqrt{2} + 11\sqrt{2}$

   c $10\sqrt{11} + 13\sqrt{11} + 4\sqrt{11}$ **d** $2\sqrt{7} + \sqrt{63}$

   e $\sqrt{48} + 7\sqrt{3}$ **f** $10\sqrt{2} + \sqrt{50}$

   g $\sqrt{18} + \sqrt{72}$ **h** $\sqrt{27} + \sqrt{108}$

   i $\sqrt{45} + \sqrt{125}$ **j** $\sqrt{98} + \sqrt{128}$

   k $11\sqrt{2} + 3\sqrt{32} + 2\sqrt{8}$ **l** $\sqrt{125} + \sqrt{80} + \sqrt{20}$

2   Simplify.

   a $8\sqrt{3} - 6\sqrt{3}$ **b** $12\sqrt{5} - 7\sqrt{5}$

   c $\sqrt{13} - 4\sqrt{13}$ **d** $3\sqrt{11} - 13\sqrt{11}$

   e $3\sqrt{7} + 8\sqrt{7} - 2\sqrt{7}$ **f** $15\sqrt{5} - \sqrt{20}$

   g $20\sqrt{3} - \sqrt{75}$ **h** $\sqrt{28} - 5\sqrt{7}$

   i $\sqrt{32} - \sqrt{8}$ **j** $\sqrt{175} - \sqrt{63}$

   k $\sqrt{294} - \sqrt{24}$ **l** $4\sqrt{12} - 3\sqrt{75}$

   m $2\sqrt{32} - 3\sqrt{50}$ **n** $\sqrt{180} - \sqrt{80} - \sqrt{45}$

6.7 Multiplying and dividing with surds

Multiplying with surds

You will now learn how to multiply with surds.

Recall that $(ab)^n = a^n b^n$

Since $\sqrt{a} = a^{\frac{1}{2}}$,

$$\sqrt{a} \times \sqrt{b} = a^{\frac{1}{2}} \times b^{\frac{1}{2}}$$

$$= (ab)^{\frac{1}{2}}$$

$$= \sqrt{ab}$$

You can multiply surds with the same root by multiplying their bases.

WORKED EXAMPLE 15

Find the exact value of:

a $\sqrt{2} \times \sqrt{2}$ **b** $\sqrt{3} \times \sqrt{5}$ **c** $2\sqrt{6} \times 3\sqrt{2}$ **d** $2\sqrt{3}(4\sqrt{2} - 1)$

Answers

a $\sqrt{2} \times \sqrt{2} = \sqrt{2 \times 2}$ Observe that $\sqrt{2} \times \sqrt{2} = 2$, hence $\sqrt{a} \times \sqrt{a} = a$.

        $= \sqrt{4}$

        $= 2$

b $\sqrt{3} \times \sqrt{5} = \sqrt{3 \times 5}$ Use the rule $\sqrt{a} \times \sqrt{b} = \sqrt{ab}$

        $= \sqrt{15}$

c $2\sqrt{6} \times 3\sqrt{2} = 2 \times 3 \times \sqrt{6 \times 2}$ Multiply the number by the number and multiply $\sqrt{6}$ by $\sqrt{2}$.

        $= 6\sqrt{12}$ Then simplify $\sqrt{12}$.

        $= 6(2\sqrt{3})$

        $= 12\sqrt{3}$

d $2\sqrt{3}(4\sqrt{2} - 1) = (2\sqrt{3} \times 4\sqrt{2})$ Expand the product by multiplying $2\sqrt{3}$ by each of the terms inside the bracket, one term at a time.

          $- (2\sqrt{3} \times 1)$

        $= 8\sqrt{6} - 2\sqrt{3}$

> **TIP**
>
> The result in part **a** can be shown using rules of indices:
>
> $\sqrt{a} \times \sqrt{a} = (\sqrt{a})^2$
>
> $= \left(a^{\frac{1}{2}}\right)^2$
>
> $= a^{\frac{1}{2} \times 2}$
>
> $= a$

WORKED EXAMPLE 16

Find the exact value of:

a $\left(3\sqrt{2} + 1\right)^2$ **b** $\left(\sqrt{3} - \sqrt{5}\right)^2$

c $(5\sqrt{2} + 3)(5\sqrt{2} - 3)$ **d** $(4\sqrt{3} + 1)(\sqrt{3} + 2)$

CONTINUED

Answers

This question requires the use of the three quadratic expansion formulas.

You can evaluate parts **a** to **c** by using the formulas.

$(a + b)^2 = a^2 + 2ab + b^2$

$(a - b)^2 = a^2 - 2ab + b^2$

$(a + b)(a - b) = a^2 - b^2$

> **MATHEMATICAL CONNECTIONS**
>
> You will learn how to expand brackets in algebra in Chapter 13.

a $(3\sqrt{2} + 1)^2 = (3\sqrt{2})^2 - 2(3\sqrt{2})(1) + (1)^2$

$\qquad = 9(2) - 6\sqrt{2} + 1$

$\qquad = 19 - 6\sqrt{2}$

Use the expansion $(a + b)^2 = a^2 + 2ab + b^2$, where $a = 3\sqrt{2}$ and $b = 1$

b $(\sqrt{3} - \sqrt{5})^2 = (\sqrt{3})^2 - 2(\sqrt{3})(\sqrt{5}) + (\sqrt{5})^2$

$\qquad = 3 - 2\sqrt{15} + 5$

$\qquad = 8 - 2\sqrt{15}$

Use the expansion $(a - b)^2 = a^2 - 2ab + b^2$, where $a = \sqrt{3}$ and $b = \sqrt{5}$

c $(5\sqrt{2} + 3)(5\sqrt{2} - 3) = (5\sqrt{2})^2 - (3)^2$

$\qquad = 25(2) - 9$

$\qquad = 41$

Use the expansion $(a + b)(a - b) = a^2 - b^2$, where $a = 5\sqrt{2}$ and $b = 3$

The surds $(5\sqrt{2} + 3)$ and $(5\sqrt{2} - 3)$ are known as **conjugate surds** or complementary surds.

d $(4\sqrt{3} + 1)(\sqrt{3} + 2) = (4\sqrt{3})(\sqrt{3} + 2) + (1)(\sqrt{3} + 2)$

$\qquad = 12 + 8\sqrt{3} + \sqrt{3} + 2$

$\qquad = 14 + 9\sqrt{3}$

Expand the product term by term by multiplying $4\sqrt{3}$ by each term in $(\sqrt{3} + 2)$ and then multiplying 1 by each term in $(\sqrt{3} + 2)$.

Expand the two products and add the like terms.

SELF ASSESSMENT

Decide if the following statements are true or false.

If a statement is false, give a **counter example** to disprove it.

If a statement is true, prove it using algebraic manipulation of the general form.

a   The product of two conjugate surds is always a rational number.

b   The product of two surds is always a surd.

Dividing with surds

You can also divide surds.

Consider the rule $\left(\dfrac{a}{b}\right)^n = \dfrac{a^n}{b^n}$,

$$\sqrt{\dfrac{a}{b}} = \left(\dfrac{a}{b}\right)^{\frac{1}{2}}$$

$$= \dfrac{a^{\frac{1}{2}}}{b^{\frac{1}{2}}}$$

$$= \dfrac{\sqrt{a}}{\sqrt{b}}$$

You can split a fractional surd into individual surds in the numerator and denominator of the fraction.

WORKED EXAMPLE 17

Evaluate.

a $\sqrt{98} \div \sqrt{2}$ **b** $\sqrt{48} \div \sqrt{6}$

Answers

a $\sqrt{98} \div \sqrt{2} = \sqrt{\dfrac{98}{2}}$

             $= \sqrt{49}$

             $= 7$

You can write the division as a fraction:

$\sqrt{98} \div \sqrt{2} = \dfrac{\sqrt{98}}{\sqrt{2}}$

You can combine $\dfrac{\sqrt{98}}{\sqrt{2}}$ into a single surd containing

a fraction: $\dfrac{\sqrt{a}}{\sqrt{b}} = \sqrt{\dfrac{a}{b}}$

> **TIP**
>
> The solution to the division of surds can be an integer!

b $\sqrt{48} \div \sqrt{6} = \sqrt{\dfrac{48}{6}}$

             $= \sqrt{8}$

             $= 2\sqrt{2}$

Apply the same method as in part **a**.

> **TIP**
>
> If the solution is a surd, make sure that you simplify fully.

Exercise 6.7

1 Evaluate the following products.

    a $\sqrt{11} \times \sqrt{11}$ **b** $\sqrt{5} \times \sqrt{7}$

    c $\sqrt{6} \times \sqrt{8}$ **d** $2\sqrt{3} \times 4\sqrt{3}$

    e $3\sqrt{7} \times 2\sqrt{6}$ **f** $\sqrt{7}(1 + \sqrt{2})$

    g $4\sqrt{5}(3 - 2\sqrt{5})$ **h** $3\sqrt{2}(5\sqrt{2} + 7\sqrt{3})$

    i $(1 + \sqrt{2})^2$ **j** $(1 + 3\sqrt{3})^2$

    k $(3 + \sqrt{5})^2$ **l** $(\sqrt{3} + 3\sqrt{2})^2$

    m $(2 - \sqrt{5})^2$ **n** $(1 - 4\sqrt{2})^2$

o $(5 - 2\sqrt{6})^2$ p $(2\sqrt{3} - 3\sqrt{2})^2$

q $(3 + \sqrt{5})(3 - \sqrt{5})$ r $(\sqrt{7} + 3)(\sqrt{7} - 3)$

s $(2 + 3\sqrt{2})(2 - 3\sqrt{2})$ t $(2\sqrt{5} - 3\sqrt{2})(2\sqrt{5} + 3\sqrt{2})$

u $(2 + \sqrt{3})(3 - \sqrt{3})$ v $(1 + 4\sqrt{5})(3 + \sqrt{5})$

2   Evaluate the following. Give your answers in simplest form.

a $\sqrt{8} \div \sqrt{2}$ b $\sqrt{27} \div \sqrt{3}$

c $\sqrt{32} \div \sqrt{2}$ d $4\sqrt{12} \div 2\sqrt{3}$

e $\sqrt{14} \div \sqrt{2}$ f $10\sqrt{9} \div 5\sqrt{3}$

g $\sqrt{102} \div \sqrt{17}$ h $24\sqrt{18} \div 6\sqrt{3}$

6.8 Rationalising the denominator

Some fractions have surds in their denominator. For example: $\dfrac{2}{\sqrt{3}}$ or $\dfrac{1}{3 - \sqrt{3}}$

You can **rationalise the denominator** to eliminate the root from the denominator.

Rationalising the denominator uses this important result:

The product of two conjugate surds is always a rational number.

> **DISCUSS**
>
> In Worked Example 18b, there's no need to multiply the numerator and denominator by $4\sqrt{2}$. You can multiply by just $\sqrt{2}$.
>
> Why? Discuss with a partner.

WORKED EXAMPLE 18

Rationalise.

a $\dfrac{2}{\sqrt{3}}$ b $\dfrac{5}{4\sqrt{2}}$ c $\dfrac{1}{3 - \sqrt{3}}$

Answers

For parts **a** and **b**, the denominator consists of a single surd term.
You can use the rule $\sqrt{n} \times \sqrt{n} = n$ to eliminate the surd from the denominator.

a $\dfrac{2}{\sqrt{3}} = \dfrac{2}{\sqrt{3}} \times \dfrac{\sqrt{3}}{\sqrt{3}}$ Use the idea of equivalent fractions to multiply both numerator and denominator by the same number.

$= \dfrac{2\sqrt{3}}{3}$

b $\dfrac{5}{4\sqrt{2}} = \dfrac{5}{4\sqrt{2}} \times \dfrac{\sqrt{2}}{\sqrt{2}}$

$= \dfrac{5\sqrt{2}}{8}$

CONTINUED

c $\quad \dfrac{1}{3-\sqrt{3}} = \dfrac{1}{3-\sqrt{3}} \times \dfrac{3+\sqrt{3}}{3+\sqrt{3}}$

Multiply both the numerator and the denominator by $3 + \sqrt{5}$.

$\qquad = \dfrac{3+\sqrt{3}}{3^2 - (\sqrt{3})^2}$

You can simplify the denominator using the algebraic rule $(a+b)(a-b) = a^2 - b^2$ where $a = 3$ and $b = \sqrt{3}$.

$\qquad = \dfrac{3+\sqrt{3}}{9-3}$

The desired form has an integer in the denominator.

$\qquad = \dfrac{3+\sqrt{3}}{6}$

TIP

To rationalise the denominator in part **c**, use the fact that the product of two conjugate surds is rational. You need to multiply both the numerator and the denominator by the conjugate of the denominator to eliminate the root from the denominator.

Exercise 6.8

1 Rationalise the denominator in each fraction.

   a $\dfrac{3}{\sqrt{2}}$ **b** $\dfrac{5}{\sqrt{11}}$ **c** $\dfrac{4}{3\sqrt{2}}$ **d** $\dfrac{6}{\sqrt{12}}$

   e $\dfrac{1}{1+\sqrt{2}}$ **f** $\dfrac{2}{\sqrt{5}-3}$ **g** $\dfrac{5}{2+\sqrt{7}}$ **h** $\dfrac{5}{4-\sqrt{6}}$

   i $\dfrac{1}{4\sqrt{2}-3}$ **j** $\dfrac{5}{2-3\sqrt{2}}$ **k** $\dfrac{1}{\sqrt{5}-\sqrt{2}}$ **l** $\dfrac{2}{\sqrt{6}+2\sqrt{3}}$

   m $\dfrac{\sqrt{2}-4}{\sqrt{2}-1}$ **n** $\dfrac{\sqrt{5}-3}{3\sqrt{5}+2}$

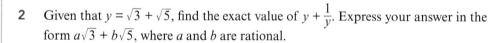

2 Given that $y = \sqrt{3} + \sqrt{5}$, find the exact value of $y + \dfrac{1}{y}$. Express your answer in the form $a\sqrt{3} + b\sqrt{5}$, where a and b are rational.

3 The area of a rectangle is $(2\sqrt{3} + 3\sqrt{2})$ cm². If the rectangle has a length of $(\sqrt{3} + \sqrt{2})$ cm, find the width of the rectangle.

4 A triangle has base $(5 + 2\sqrt{2})$ cm and height $(2 + 4\sqrt{2})$ cm. Find the area of the triangle.

5 **a** Express the following in the form $\sqrt{a} - \sqrt{b}$, where a and b are integers.

     i $\dfrac{1}{\sqrt{1}+\sqrt{2}}$ **ii** $\dfrac{1}{\sqrt{2}+\sqrt{3}}$ **iii** $\dfrac{1}{\sqrt{3}+\sqrt{4}}$

   b By recognising a pattern in part **a**, express $\dfrac{1}{\sqrt{n}+\sqrt{n+1}}$ in the form $\sqrt{a} - \sqrt{b}$.

   c Hence, evaluate $\dfrac{1}{\sqrt{1}+\sqrt{2}} + \dfrac{1}{\sqrt{2}+\sqrt{3}} + \dfrac{1}{\sqrt{3}+\sqrt{4}} + \cdots + \dfrac{1}{\sqrt{99}+\sqrt{100}}$

SUMMARY

Are you able to... ?
use the rules of indices
convert numbers into and out of standard form
calculate values with standard form with a calculator
understand and use indices (positive, zero and negative integers)
understand and use standard form
calculate values in standard form without a calculator
rationalise the denominator
understand and use fractional indices
understand and use surds, including simplifying expressions.

Past paper questions

1 Find the value of

    a 64^0,   [1]

    b $64^{\frac{1}{3}}$.   [1]

Cambridge IGCSE International Mathematics 0607 Paper 21 Q5 June 2021

2 Work out $(4 \times 10^{-3}) \times (3 \times 10^{-5})$. Give your answer in standard form.   [2]

Cambridge IGCSE International Mathematics 0607 Paper 12 Q23 March 2022

3 In this calculation, the three numbers are written in standard form.

$$(4 \times 10^p) \times (n \times 10^{p+2}) = 3.2 \times 10^t$$

n, p and t are integers.

    a   Find the value of n.   [1]

    b   Find t in terms of p.   [1]

Cambridge IGCSE International Mathematics 0607 Paper 22 Q14 March 2022

4 Rationalise the denominator and simplify.

$$\frac{2}{\sqrt{5} + 1}$$

    [3]

Cambridge IGCSE International Mathematics 0607 Paper 22 Q13 March 2021

> Chapter 7

Introduction to algebra

IN THIS CHAPTER YOU WILL:

- form algebraic expressions

- find the value of expressions by substitution

- simplify algebraic expressions by collecting like terms

- expand and simplify expressions involving one or two brackets

- factorise algebraic expressions

- simplify algebraic fractions

- understand and use the rules of indices

- construct and solve linear equations in one unknown

CONTINUED

> expand and simplify expressions involving more than two brackets

> factorise more complicated expressions

> manipulate and factorise algebraic fractions

> use and interpret fractional indices

> solve quadratic equations by factorisation

> solve fractional equations with numerical and linear algebraic denominators.

GETTING STARTED

1   The length of a rectangle is 3 cm longer than its breadth. If the breadth is 5 cm, find:

   a   the length of the rectangle

   b   the perimeter of the rectangle.

2   In the following expressions, find the value of Δ.

   a $\Delta + 3 = 15$ b $\Delta - 10 = 15$

   c $5 \times \Delta = 15$ d $\Delta \div 4 = 15$

3   a   Anna is 7 years old. Find Anna's age:

     i   two years ago   ii   after three years   iii   after n years.

   b   John is x years old. Find John's age:

     i   two years ago   ii   after three years   iii   after n years.

KEY WORDS

algebraic expression

algebraic fraction

coefficient

constant

expand

factorise

like terms

linear equation

quadratic expression

rational expressions

term

variable

7.1 Forming algebraic expressions

In Getting started Question **2**, the symbol Δ represents different numbers. You can use symbols or letters to represent numbers.

WORKED EXAMPLE 1

The cost of one apple is $\$x$. What is the cost of four apples?

Answer

$4 \times x = 4x$

The cost of four apples is $\$4x$.

In Worked example 1, x is an unknown value, or a **variable**.

The number 4 in $4x$ is called the **coefficient** of the variable x. It is the number the variable is multiplied by, which in the expression $4x$ is 4.

WORKED EXAMPLE 2

Write an **algebraic expression** for the number that is:

a   9 more than x **b**   3 less than x **c**   five times x

Answers

a $x + 9$

b $x - 3$

c $5x$ Take 5 to multiply x, 5 becomes the coefficient of the variable x.

TIP

The phrase 'more than' means add, so add 9 to x.

TIP

A number less than x means subtract the number from x.

SELF ASSESSMENT

Write each statement as an algebraic expression. The first row is done for you.

Operation	Statements	Algebraic expressions
Addition	Add a to b Sum of a and b	$a + b$
	Subtract a from b Take away a from b	
	Multiply a to b Product of a and b	
	Divide a by b, $b \neq 0$ Quotient of a divided by b, $b \neq 0$	

DISCUSSION 1

Is the statement 'the difference between a and b' the same as 'subtract a from b'?

An **algebraic expression** is a collection of known numbers and unknown variables.

For example, $2x + 3$, $1 - 5y$ and $x + 2y - 1$ are expressions.

You can use expressions to represent real-life situations.

WORKED EXAMPLE 3

Sofia is y years old. Davide is four years younger than Sofia. Giulia is twice as old as Sofia.

Write expressions in terms of y for:

a   Davide's age   **b**   Giulia's age.

Answers

a $y - 4$ years old   Subtract 4 from Sofia's age.

b $2y$ years old   Twice means two times.

WORKED EXAMPLE 4

Anagha had an operation in hospital. The cost of the operation was $200. The cost of care per day during her stay in hospital was $98. She was in the hospital for x days.

Write an expression in terms of x for the total cost of Anagha's stay in hospital.

Answer

Cost of care for x days = $98 \times x = 98x$

Total cost = cost of care + cost of operation

Total cost = $98x + 200$

An expression in terms of x for the total cost of her stay in hospital is $98x + 200$ dollars.

An expression can involve more than one variable.

WORKED EXAMPLE 5

A box of chocolates contains m milk chocolates and d dark chocolates.

Write an expression to find the total number of chocolates:

a in one box   **b** in 3 boxes.

Answers

a $m + d$ Total number of chocolates = number of milk chocolates + number of dark chocolates

b $3(m + d)$ The answer in part **a** gives the total number of chocolates in one box, to find the total number of chocolates in 3 boxes, take the answer from a to multiply by 3.

SELF ASSESSMENT

Write an algebraic expression for:

a an even number

b an odd number

c two consecutive numbers

d two consecutive even numbers

e two consecutive odd numbers.

Is there more than one way to write the above expressions?

MATHEMATICAL CONNECTIONS

You learnt about even and odd numbers in Chapter 1.

Exercise 7.1

1   Form an algebraic expression for each of the given statements.

   a   3 more than a number x

   b   9 less a number x

   c   4 times a number x

   d   Half of a number w

   e   3 times a number x minus 4 times a number y

   f   10 times a number x minus 7

2 Write an algebraic expression for the product of:

    a number and itself

    b two consecutive numbers

    c two consecutive even numbers.

3 One shirt cost $10. How much do the following cost?

    a 3 shirts   **b** n shirts

4 There are 20 biscuits in one packet. How many biscuits are there in the following?

    a 4 packets   **b** x packets

5 An apple cost $\$x$ and a pear cost $\$y$. Find the cost of:

    a 5 apples   **b** 6 pears   **c** 5 apples and 6 pears.

6 Risha bought p pencils for $2 each and q pens for $3 each. What is the total cost?

7 Sam is paid $\$z$. If he then spends $\$x$ on food and $\$y$ on clothes, how much money does he have left?

7.2 Substituting in algebraic expressions and formulas

You can replace a letter with a number to evaluate an expression.

This is called substitution.

WORKED EXAMPLE 6

Given that $a = 3$, find the value of the following expressions.

a $4a$ **b** $a + 4$ **c** $5a - 3$ **d** $\dfrac{a+1}{5}$ **e** $3 - 2a^2$

Answers

Substitute the letter a with the number 3 for each expression and work out the value:

a $4a = 4 \times a$

    $= 4 \times 3$

    $= 12$

b $a + 4 = 3 + 4$

    $= 7$

c $5a - 3 = (5 \times a) - 3$

    $= (5 \times 3) - 3$

    $= 15 - 3$

    $= 12$

> **TIP**
>
> $4a$ means 4 multiplied by a.

> **TIP**
>
> You need to evaluate $5a$ before subtracting 3.

CONTINUED

d $\dfrac{a+1}{5} = \dfrac{3+1}{5}$ In a fraction, evaluate the numerator before dividing by the denominator.

$\qquad\quad = \dfrac{4}{5}$

e $3 - 2a^2 = 3 - 2(a \times a)$

$\qquad\qquad = 3 - 2(3 \times 3)$

$\qquad\qquad = 3 - 2(9)$

$\qquad\qquad = 3 - 18$

$\qquad\qquad = -15$

> **MATHEMATICAL CONNECTIONS**
>
> You learnt the four operations of numbers in Chapter 2.

WORKED EXAMPLE 7

If $x = 3$ and $y = -1$, evaluate:

a $x + y$ $\qquad$ **b** $2x - y$ $\qquad$ **c** x^2

Answers

Substitute $x = 3$ and $y = -1$:

a $x + y = 3 + (-1)$

$\qquad\quad = 3 - 1$

$\qquad\quad = 2$

b $2x - y = 2(3) - (-1)$

$\qquad\qquad = 6 + 1$

$\qquad\qquad = 7$

c $x^2 = (3)^2 = 9$

> **TIP**
>
> Use your knowledge of the four operations of numbers to evaluate these types of questions manually. These are usually non-calculator questions.

You can substitute numbers into more complicated expressions. Remember to use the correct order of operations.

WORKED EXAMPLE 8

Find the value of the expression $2x^2y + 1$ when:

a $x = 2$ and $y = 3$

b $x = -1$ and $y = 2$

Answers

a   Substitute the values $x = 2$ and $y = 3$:

$\qquad 2 \times (2)^2 \times 3 + 1 = 25$

b   Substitute the values $x = -1$ and $y = 2$:

$\qquad 2 \times (-1)^2 \times 2 + 1 = 5$

WORKED EXAMPLE 9

Find the value of the expression $4y^2x - 8$ when:

a $x = -1$ and $y = 2$

b $x = -4$ and $y = -2$

Answers

a   Substitute the values $x = -1$ and $y = 2$:

$4 \times (2)^2 \times (-1) - 8 = -24$

b   Substitute the values $x = -4$ and $y = -2$:

$4 \times (-2)^2 \times (-4) - 8 = -72$

MATHEMATICS IN CONTEXT

You can also substitute numbers into **formulas**. Some real-life problems can be presented in a mathematical formula, such as the formula to convert temperature from degrees Fahrenheit to degrees Celsius or the formula to calculate a person's BMI (body mass index).

WORKED EXAMPLE 10

An electrician calculates the cost of a job, in $, using the formula $T = 100 + 50h$ where h is the number of hours the job takes.

What is the cost of a job that takes three hours?

Answer

Substitute $h = 3$ into the formula:

$T = 100 + 50 \times 3 = 100 + 150 = 250$

The cost of the job is $250.

Exercise 7.2

 1   Find the value of $3x + 2$ when:

    a $x = 5$ **b** $x = -1$ **c** $x = \dfrac{1}{2}$

 2   Find the value of $15 - 4y$ when:

    a $y = 2$ **b** $y = -3$ **c** $y = \dfrac{1}{4}$

 3   If $x = 3$ and $y = -1$, evaluate:

    a $2x + 3y$ **b** $4x - 2y$ **d** $x^2 + y^2$

    4   Evaluate each expression when $a = 2$, $b = -1$ and $c = 3$.

    a $a^2bc - 2b$ **b** $\dfrac{a^2}{b} + \dfrac{b^2}{c}$ **c** $(abc)^2$ **d** $\dfrac{2a^2}{b^3} + c$

5   The formula to convert temperature from $f\,°\mathrm{F}$ (Fahrenheit) to $T\,°\mathrm{C}$ (Celsius) is given by $T = \dfrac{5}{9}(f - 32)$. Find T when $f = 100$.

6   The body mass index of a person is given by the formula $I = \dfrac{m}{h^2}$, where m is the mass in kilograms and h is the height in metres. Find I if $m = 66\,\mathrm{kg}$ and $h = 1.72\,\mathrm{m}$.

7.3 Collecting like terms

Like terms are terms of the same variable(s) with the same powers.

For example, $6xy$ and $3xy$ are like terms, but $3x^2y$ and $2xy^2$ are not like terms.

In an expression you can **collect** like terms by adding or subtracting.

WORKED EXAMPLE 11

Simplify $6a + 5b - 3a + 4b$.

Answer

In the expression $6a + 5b - 3a + 4b$, $6a$ and $-3a$ are like terms and so are $5b$ and $4b$.

$6a + 5b - 3a + 4b = 6a - 3a + 5b + 4b$ 　　Put all like terms together:
$ = 3a + 9b$ 　　　　　$6a - 3a = 3a$
 　　　　　$5b + 4b = 9b$

WORKED EXAMPLE 12

Simplify $4x^2 + 3x - x^2 + x - 5$.

Answer

$4x^2 + 3x - x^2 + x - 5$ 　　　　$4x^2$ and x^2 are like terms.
　　　　　　　　　　　　　　$3x$ and x are like terms.

Collecting like terms: 　　　　Remember to subtract the x^2.
$3x^2 + 4x - 5$ 　　　　　　　Include the -5.

Exercise 7.3

Simplify the following expressions by collecting like terms.

1    $6a + 2b - 3a - 8b$

2    $x - 7y + 6x + 5y$

3    $2a + b - c + 3a - 4b - 5c$

4    $11w - 5u + 3 - 2w + 10u$

5    $gh + 5jk - 2gh + 7jk$

6    $7cd - 8dc + 3cd$

7    $4ab + 7bc - 2ab - cd$

8    $3ba - ab + 3ab - 8ab$

9    $2p^2 - 5p^2 + 2p - 4p$

10   $x^5 - 5x^3 + 2 - 2x^3 + 2x^5$

11   $h^3 + 5h - 3 - 4h^2 - 2h + 7 + 5h^2$

12   $2x^2y - x^2y + 6xy^2 - y^2x$

13 $3a^2b - 2ab + 4a^2b - ba$

14 $23z^2 + 17k^2 - 3z^2 + 8 + 4k^2$

15 $4x^2y^2 - 2x^2y + 3x^2y^2 + 2xy^2$

16 $x^5 + x^5 + x^5 + x^5$

17 $x^2 + 5x + 4 - x^2 + 6x - 3$

18 $2 + 3x^2 + x^4 - 3x^2 + 1$

7.4 Expanding single brackets and expanding two brackets with one variable

You can **expand** a single bracket by multiplying the **term** outside the bracket with each and every term inside the bracket.

WORKED EXAMPLE 13

Expand and simplify.

a $x(2x - 3y)$ **b** $8x - 2(3x + 5)$

Answers

a Multiply the x outside the bracket with the $2x$ and with the $-3y$ inside the bracket:

$x(2x - 3y) = 2x^2 - 3xy$

b $8x - 2(3x + 5)$

$= 8x - 6x - 10$

Simplify by collecting all like terms:

$8x - 6x - 10 = 2x - 10$

> **TIP**
>
> $2 \times x \times x = 2x^2$

To expand two brackets with one variable, you multiply each term in the first bracket with each term in the second bracket. This method of expanding is sometimes called the 'rainbow method' because when you multiply the terms in the first bracket to all the terms in the second bracket, it's like drawing a rainbow.

WORKED EXAMPLE 14

Expand $(3 + 2y)(4y - 6)$

Answer

$(3 + 2y)(4y - 6)$

$= 3(4y - 6) + 2y(4y - 6)$ Remember to take the terms with the sign.

Remove both the brackets:

$12y - 18 + 8y^2 - 12y$ $12y - 12y = 0$

Simplify like terms:

$= 8y^2 - 18$

Exercise 7.4

Expand and simplify.

1 $4(2x + 3)$

2 $3x(2x - 5)$

3 $2x(7x + 5y)$

4 $-y(3x + y)$

5 $5a(9x - 3y)$

6 $5 + 3(2x + 3) - 3x$

7 $3x - 4(2x - 5)$

8 $x(2x + 1) + x(x - 5)$

9 $7a(b + 2) - b(2a - 1)$

10 $3(p - 3) - (p - 4)$

11 $(x + 1)(x + 3)$

12 $(y + 4)(y + 5)$

13 $(x - 2)(x + 6)$

14 $(x + 5)(x - 2)$

15 $(x - 3)(x - 2)$

REFLECTION

- Is ab the same as ba?

- Is $(ab)c$ the same as $a(bc)$ or abc?

- Is $a(b + c)$ the same as $ab + ac$ or $(b + c)a$?

Explain your reasoning.

INVESTIGATION 1

In Worked example 13, the expansion $x(2x - 3y)$ from part **a** can be represented using a multiplication frame:

×	2x	−3y
x		

The yellow squares will give you the solution to the expansion. To find the expressions in the yellow square:

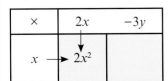

Multiply each of the row and column values.
$x \times 2x = 2x^2$

Repeat the multiplication for the other yellow square:

×	2x	−3y
x	2x²	−3xy

$x \times (-3y) = -3xy$

×	2x	−3y
x	2x²	−3xy

Hence, $x(2x - 3y) = 2x^2 - 3xy$

CONTINUED

In Worked example 14, the expansion $(3 + 2y)(4y - 6)$ can also be made using the multiplication frame. In this case, we try to arrange the terms consistently by putting the y terms first and then the **constant**: $(2y + 3)(4y - 6)$

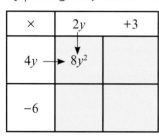   Take $2y \times 4y = 8y^2$

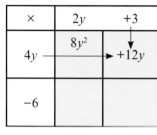   Take $+3 \times 4y = +12y$

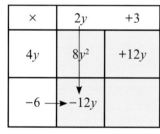   Take $2y \times (-6) = -12y$

×	2y	+3
4y	$8y^2$	$+12y$
−6	$-12y$	-18

Take $+3 \times (-6) = -18$

Hence, $(2y + 3)(4y - 6) = 8y^2 + 12y - 12y - 18 = 8y^2 - 18$

Use the multiplication frame to expand the following.

a $(a + b)(a + b)$

b $(a - b)(a - b)$

c $(a + b)(a - b)$

TIP

> The reason for rearranging the terms is so that you can use the multiplication frame to help you see the reverse process (factorisation) in Section 7.6. This method is also known as the grid method.

REFLECTION

Will the answer change if we use $(3 + 2y)(4y - 6)$ on the multiplication frame?

7.5 Expanding two or more brackets

From Investigation 1, you would have deduced the general identity for the quadratic expansion:

$(a + b)^2 = a^2 + 2ab + b^2$

$(a - b)^2 = a^2 - 2ab + b^2$

$(a + b)(a - b) = a^2 - b^2$

We will look at how you can use these identities or the multiplication frame to expand two or more brackets in the next two examples.

WORKED EXAMPLE 15

Expand the following.

a $(4x + 5)^2$ **b** $(2x - 3)^2$ **c** $(5x + 7)(5x - 7)$

Answers

a **Method 1: Using the multiplication frame**

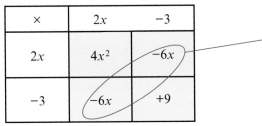

×	4x	+5
4x	16x²	+20x
+5	+20x	+25

Put $(4x + 5)^2$ in a multiplication frame and find the product in each of the yellow cells.

Hence, $(4x + 5)^2 = 16x^2 + 20x + 20x + 25$

$= 16x^2 + 40x + 25$

Method 2: Using the quadratic identity

$(a + b)^2 = a^2 + 2ab + b^2$

$(4x + 5)^2 = (4x)^2 + 2(4x)(5+) + (5)^2$

$= 16x^2 + 40x + 25$

In $(4x + 5)^2$, substitute $a = 4x$ and $b = 5$ into the identity $(a + b)^2 = a^2 + 2ab + b^2$

b **Method 1: Using the multiplication frame**

×	2x	−3
2x	4x²	−6x
−3	−6x	+9

Similarly, put $(2x - 3)^2$ in a multiplication frame and find the product in the yellow cells.

Do you realise that you can directly add the x terms from the multiplication frame?

$-6x - 6x = -12x$

You can omit this step and present your final answer to the expansion:

$(2x - 3)^2 = 4x^2 - 12x + 9$

Hence, $(2x - 3)^2 = 4x^2 - 6x - 6x + 9$

$= 4x^2 - 12x + 9$

Method 2: Using the quadratic identity

$(a - b)^2 = a^2 - 2ab + b^2$

$(2x - 3)^2 = (2x)^2 - 2(2x)(3) + (3)^2$

$= 4x^2 - 12x + 9$

In $(2x - 3)^2$, substitute $a = 2x$ and $b = 3$ into the identity $(a - b)^2 = a^2 - 2ab + b^2$.

Note that $b \neq -3$. The negative sign has already been accounted for in the identity.

CONTINUED

c Method 1: Using the multiplication frame

×	$5x$	$+7$
$5x$	$25x^2$	$+35x$
-7	$-35x$	-49

Hence, $(5x + 7)(5x - 7) = 25x^2 - 49$

Method 2: Using the quadratic identity
$(a + b)(a - b) = a^2 - b^2$

$(5x + 7)(5x - 7) = (5x)^2 - (7)^2$
$\qquad\qquad\qquad\quad = 25x^2 - 49$

Noticed that the x terms in the bottom left and top right diagonal is the same except their signs are opposite.

They will cancel each other and the resultant value is zero:

$35x - 35x = 0$

This identity is also known as the **difference of two squares** because of $a^2 - b^2$.

Substitute $a = 5x$ and $b = 7$

REFLECTION

Which method did you think was easier? Expansion using the identity $(a + b)(a - b) = a^2 - b^2$ or expansion using a multiplication frame?

WORKED EXAMPLE 16

Expand the following.

a $(2x - 3y)(x + 5y)$ **b** $(2x + 1)(x + 5)(x - 2)$

Answers

We will be using the multiplication frame in this worked example.

a

×	$2x$	$-3x$
x	$2x^2$	$-3xy$
$+5x$	$+10xy$	$-15y^2$

We can still simplify the xy terms in the diagonal:
$+10xy - 3xy = +7xy$

REFLECTION

Does it matter if you swap the position of the two brackets?

Hence, $(2x - 3y)(x + 5y) = 2x^2 + 7xy - 15y^2$

CONTINUED

b Find the product of any two brackets first. In this case, we will find $(2x + 1)(x + 5)$

×	$2x$	$+1$
x	$2x^2$	$+x$
$+5$	$+10x$	$+5$

$(2x + 1)(x + 5) = 2x^2 + 11x + 5$

Then take $(2x^2 + 11x + 5)(x - 2)$

×	$2x^2$	$+11x$	$+5$
x	$2x^3$	$+11x^2$	$+5x$
-2	$-4x^2$	$-22x$	-10

Hence, $(2x + 1)(x + 5)(x - 2)$

$= (2x^2 + 11x + 5)(x - 2)$

$= 2x^3 + 7x^2 - 17x - 10$

You can either find $(2x + 1)(x + 5)$ then take the result and multiply by $(x - 2)$ OR find $(x + 5)(x - 2)$ then take the result and multiply by $(2x + 1)$.

The diagonal in red gives

$+10x + x = +11x$

The diagonals in the red and blue ovals are like terms that can be simplified.

$-4x^2 + 11x^2 = +7x^2$

$-22x + 5x = -17x$

Exercise 7.5

Expand and simplify.

1 $(x + 4)^2$

2 $(2x + y)^2$

3 $(3x - 5)^2$

4 $(4a - 3b)^2$

5 $(2y - 3z)(2y + 3z)$

6 $(4px - 5qy)(4px + 5qy)$

7 $(3x + y)(x + 2y)$

8 $(5x - y)(3y - x)$

9 $2x(2x - 1)(2x + 1)$

10 $(x + 7)^2 + (2x + 3)^2$

11 $(4 + 2x)^2 - (x + 1)^2$

12 $(2g - 6)^2 - (g + 1)^2$

13 $(x - 4)(x + 1)(2x + 3)$

14 $(2x - 1)(x + 3)(x - 1)$

15 $(2x - 3)(x + 5)(3x - 2)$

7.6 Factorising

Factorising by extracting common factors

Factorising is the inverse process of expanding brackets.

Factorising can be an alternative to collecting like terms when the expression is in a recognisable format. For example, to **factorise** $4x + 7x + 12y + 21y$ notice that the 3rd coefficient is 3 times the 1st and that the 4th coefficient is 3 times the 2nd coefficient. This equation is of the type $ax + bx + kay + kby = (a + b)(x + ky)$ and so $4x + 7x + 12y + 21y = (4 + 7)(x + 3y) = 11(x + 3y)$

You can factorise an expression by extracting the common factor(s).

To factorise completely, you should extract the highest common factor.

MATHEMATICAL CONNECTIONS

You learnt how to find the highest common factor of two natural numbers in Chapter 1. Finding the highest common factor of algebraic terms is similar, but you must consider both the coefficient(s) and the variable(s).

WORKED EXAMPLE 17

Factorise $6x^2 + 14xy$.

Answer

Take out the highest common factor [HCF] of the two terms:

$6x^2 + 14xy$

$= ② \times 3 \times ⓧ \times x + ② \times 7 \times ⓧ \times y$ HCF $= 2x$

Write $2x$ outside the bracket and the remaining terms inside the bracket:

$= 2x(3x + 7y)$

TIP

You can expand your bracket(s) to check that this gives the original expression:

$2x(3x + 7y)$

$2x \times 3x + 2x \times 7y$

$6x^2 + 14xy$

You can also factorise an expression by grouping or by using the multiplication frame.

WORKED EXAMPLE 18

Factorise $x^2 - xy - 2x + 2y$.

Answer

Apply simple factorisation to the groups separately:

$x^2 - xy - 2x + 2y$

$= x(x - y) - 2(x - y)$ $(x - y)$ is common to both terms.

$= (x - y)(x - 2)$ Take out the factor $(x - y)$

TIP

In this example grouping will give an even number of terms.

Factorising by quadratic identities

Recall from Section 7.5, Worked example 15 part **c** that expressions of the form $a^2 - b^2$ are called difference of two squares.

From the identity $(a + b)(a - b) = a^2 - b^2$, you can factorise expressions of the form $a^2x^2 - b^2y^2$ using $a^2x^2 - b^2y^2 = (ax + by)(ax - by)$.

WORKED EXAMPLE 19

Factorise $25y^2 - 144x^2$.

Answer

Using the difference of two squares identity:

$25y^2 - 144x^2 = 5^2y^2 - 12^2x^2$

$\qquad\qquad\quad = (5y + 12x)(5y - 12x)$

Recall the identities from the previous section:

$(a + b)^2 = a^2 + 2ab + b^2$

$(a - b)^2 = a^2 - 2ab + b^2$

The reverse is true and can be used for factorising:

$a^2 + 2ab + b^2 = (a + b)^2$

$a^2 - 2ab + b^2 = (a - b)^2$

WORKED EXAMPLE 20

Factorise.

a $x^2 - 6x + 9$ **b** $4x^2 + 4xy + y^2$

TIP

A perfect square is when the number or expression is equal to the square of another element. 9 is a perfect square because it is equal to 3×3, and x^2 is a perfect square as it is x times x.

Answers

a   **Method 1: Using the identity $a^2 - 2ab + b^2 = (a - b)^2$**

$x^2 - 6x + 9 = (x)^2 - 2(x)(3) + (3)^2$

$\qquad\qquad\quad = (x - 3)^2$

Both x^2 and 9 are perfect squares.

TIP

To identify an expression that can be factorised using the identities:

$a^2 + 2ab + b^2 = (a + b)^2$

$a^2 - 2ab + b^2 = (a - b)^2$

look out for two squared terms in the expression.

Method 2: Using the multiplication frame

×		
	x^2	
		$+9$

The multiplication frame can also be used to factorise.

We first place the x^2 term and the constant in the diagonal as shown.

CONTINUED

Find the factors of $x^2 : x \times x$:

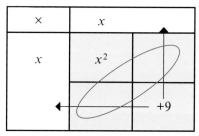

Find the possible factors of $+9$:

The factors of $+9$ will affect the terms in the red oval.

Consider $(-3) \times (-3) = +9$ and $(-3) + (-3) = -6$.

Hence,

The terms in the red oval should add up to $-6x$.

and

The multiplication frame can also be used to factorise.

We first place the x^2 term and the constant in the diagonal as shown.

$(-3x) + (-3x) = -6x$

CONTINUED

The factors are:

×	x	-3
x	x^2	$-3x$
-3	$-3x$	$+9$

$x^2 - 6x + 9 = (x - 3)^2$

b **Method 1: Using the identity $a^2 + 2ab + b^2 = (a + b)^2$**

$4x^2 + 4xy + y^2 = (2x)^2 + 2(2x)(y) + (y)^2$
$ = (2x + y)^2$

Both $4x^2$ and y^2 are perfect squares.

> **TIP**
>
> $4x^2$ is a perfect square because it is equal to $2x$ times $2x$.

Method 2: Using the multiplication frame

×		
	$4x^2$	
		$+y^2$

Put $4x^2$ and y^2 in the diagonals shown.

$x \times 4x = 4x^2$

$2x \times 2x = 4x^2$

Select the factors of the second equation so that the diagonals add to $+4xy$.

$y \times y = y^2$

Find the factors of $4x^2$:

×	$2x$	
$2x$	$4x^2$	
		$+y^2$

Find the factors of y^2:

×	$2x$	$+y$
$2x$	$4x^2$	
$+y$		$+y^2$

CONTINUED

Make sure the diagonals add to $+4xy$:

$\times$	$2x$	$+y$
$2x$	$4x^2$	$+2xy$
$+y$	$+2xy$	$+y^2$

Then,

$\times$	$2x$	$+y$
$2x$	$4x^2$	$+2xy$
$+y$	$+2xy$	$+y^2$

$$4x^2 + 4xy + y^2 = (2x + y)^2$$

Exercise 7.6

1   Factorise completely.

   a $12x^2 + 8x$
   b $35y^2 + 21xy$
   c $-20ab^2 - 15b$
   d $18by^2 - 12ay^2$
   e $42z^2 - 49xz$
   f $9y^2 - 6xy + 27y$
   g $12w^2 - 4wx - 6wz$

2   Factorise completely.

   a $3m + 3n + mx + nx$
   b $6x + xy + 6z + yz$
   c $rs - 2ts + rt - 2t^2$
   d $ab - 4bc + ac - 4c^2$
   e $mn - 2mr - 3rn + 6r^2$
   f $2ax - 2ay - bx + by$
   g $ms + 2mt^2 - ns - 2nt^2$

3   Factorise completely.

   a $144x^2 - 1$
   b $\dfrac{9}{16}a^2 - 25$
   c $x^2 - 16y^2$
   d $8a^2 - 2b^2$
   e $18m^3 - 8mn^2$
   f $m^2n^2 - 9p^2$
   g $9x^2y^2 - 4w^2$
   h $4a^4 - 16b^2$

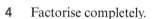

4   Factorise completely.

   a $x^2 + 2x + 1$
   b $x^2 + 10x + 25$
   c $4y^2 - 8y + 4$
   d $9x^2 - 12x + 4$
   e $x^3 - 6x^2 + 9x$
   f $a^2 + 8ab + 16b^2$
   g $36w^2 - 36wz + 9z^2$

7.7 Factorising quadratic expressions

The expression $x^2 - 6x + 9$ in Worked example 20 is called a **quadratic expression**. In a quadratic expression, the highest power of the variable is 2. A quadratic expression with one variable x is of the form $ax^2 + bx + c$, where $a \neq 0$. In this section, we will learn to factorise quadratic expressions. Before we look at the worked examples, let's observe some patterns in the expansion of two brackets in Investigation 2.

INVESTIGATION 2

1 Factors of the form $(x + p)(x + q)$. Copy and complete the table.

$(x + p)(x + q)$	Are the signs of p and q the same?	pq	$p + q$	Expansion of $x + px + q$ to $x^2 + bx + c$
$(x + 2)(x + 3)$	same	$2 \times 3 = 6$	$2 + 3 =$	$x^2 + 5x + 6$
$(x + 2)(x - 3)$	different	$2 \times (-3) =$	$2 + (-3) =$	
$(x - 2)(x + 3)$				
$(x - 2)(x - 3)$				

   a How does pq contribute to the expanded form $x^2 + bx + c$?

   b How does $p + q$ contribute to the expanded form $x^2 + bx + c$?

   c What is the coefficient of x^2?

   d How does the signs of p and q affect how you get the coefficient of x in $x^2 + bx + c$?

   e Write down a few more examples of your own to check if your observation is correct.

2 Factors of the form $(sx + p)(tx + q)$. Copy and complete the table.

$(sx + p)(tx + q)$	Expansion of $(sx + p)(tx + q)$ to $ax^2 + bx + c$	st	pq	$stpq$	Possible factors of $stpq$	Sum of the factors circled in red
$(3x + 2)(2x + 5)$						
$(3x + 2)(2x - 5)$	$6x^2 - 11x - 10$	$3 \times 2 = 6$	$2 \times (-5) = -10$	-60	$(-6) \times 10$ $6 \times (-10)$ $(-4) \times 15$ $\boxed{4 \times (-15)}$	
$(3x - 2)(2x + 5)$						
$(3x - 2)(2x - 5)$						

   a How does st contribute to the expanded form $ax^2 + bx + c$?

   b How does pq contribute to the expanded form $ax^2 + bx + c$?

   c Explain how the product $stpq$ help you to find the coefficient of x in $ax^2 + bx + c$.

   d Write down a few more examples to test out your observations.

From Question **1** of Investigation 2, quadratic expressions of the form $x^2 + bx + c$ have factors of the form $(x + p)(x + q)$, and so $pq = c$ AND $p + q = b$.

WORKED EXAMPLE 21

Factorise the following.

a $x^2 + 7x + 12$ **b** $x^2 - 3x - 10$ **c** $x^2 - 16x + 15$

Answer

a In $x^2 + 7x + 12$, $b = +7$ and $c = +12$.

By looking at the possible factors of $+12$, $3 \times 4 = +12$ and $3 + 4 = 7$.

Hence, $p = 3$, $q = 4$

$x^2 + 7x + 12 = (x + 3)(x + 4)$

Possible values of p and q

p	q	pq	$p + q$
2	6	+12	8
−2	−6	+12	−8
3	4	+12	7
−3	−4	+12	−7

> **TIP**
>
> You can expand the factors to check they match with $x^2 + 7x + 12$.

b In $x^2 - 3x - 10$, $b = -3$ and $c = -10$.

By looking at the possible factors of -10, $2 \times (-5) = -10$ and $2 + (-5) = -3$.

Hence, $p = 2$, $q = -5$

$x^2 - 3x - 10 = (x + 2)(x - 5)$

Possible values of p and q

p	q	pq	$p + q$
−1	10	−10	9
1	−10	−10	−9
−2	5	−10	3
2	−5	−10	−3

c In $x^2 - 16x + 15$, $b = -16$ and $c = +15$.

By looking at the possible factors of $+15$, $(-1) \times (-15) = +15$ and $(-1) + (-15) = -16$.

Hence, $p = -1$, $q = -15$

$x^2 - 16x + 15 = (x - 1)(x - 15)$

Possible values of p and q

p	q	pq	$p + q$
1	15	+15	16
−1	−15	+15	−16
3	5	+15	8
−3	−5	+15	−8

From Question **2** of Investigation 2, quadratic expressions of the form $ax^2 + bx + c$ have factors of the form $(sx + p)(tx + q)$ and so $st = a$, $pq = c$ and the sum of the factors $stpq$ gives b, the coefficient of x.

WORKED EXAMPLE 22

Factorise the following.

a $3x^2 - 21x + 30$ **b** $10x^2 + 9x + 2$ **c** $12x^3 + 13x^2 - 14x$

Answer

Method 1: Using the multiplication frame to help us organise the factors

a **Step 1:** Put $3x^2$ and $+30$ in the multiplication frame as shown.

×	
$3x^2$	
	$+30$

CONTINUED

Step 2: Check if any of $3x^2$ or $+30$ consists of prime numbers.

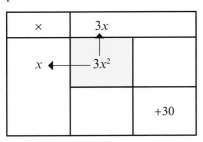

The term $3x^2$ has a prime coefficient, we can put the factors for $3x^2$ in the multiplication frame first.

Step 3: Recall that the factors of $stpq$ gives b.

$stpq = a \times c = 3 \times 30 = 90$

$b = -21$

$(-15x) + (-6x) = -21x$

Put $-15x$ and $-6x$ in the other diagonals highlighted:

Possible factors of 90 that could sum to 21

Product	Sum
$15 \times 6 = 90$	$15 + 6 = +21$
$(-15) \times (-6) = 90$	$(-15) + (-6) = -21$

×	$3x$	
x	$3x^2$	$-6x$
	$-15x$	$+30$

Step 4: Fill in the factors that will give you $-15x$ and $-6x$:

×	$3x$	-6
x	$3x^2$	$-6x$
-5	$-15x$	$+30$

Step 5: Check that the new factors you have filled in gives a product of $+30$.

Hence, $3x^2 - 21x + 30 = (3x - 6)(x - 5)$

> **TIP**
>
> If the product of the new factors does not give $+30$, switch their position and repeat step 4.

Method 2: Using factorisation by grouping

We can factorise quadratic expressions by grouping if we split the x term into the sum of two terms. We will use the factors of $stpq$ to split the x term.

From Step 3 of Method 1, we see that $(-15x) + (-6x) = -21x$

CONTINUED

Rewrite the quadratic expression into four terms:

$$3x^2 - 21x + 30 = 3x^2 - 15x - 6x + 30$$
$$= 3x(x - 5) - 6(x - 5)$$
$$= (x - 5)(3x - 6)$$

Split $-21x$ into $-15x - 6x$
Then do factorisation by grouping.
Take out the common factor $(x - 5)$.

We will use only one method for parts **b** and **c**.

b **Method 1: Using the multiplication frame**

×		+2
x	$10x^2$	
+1		+2

Put $10x^2$ and $+2$ in the multiplication frame. Since $+2$ is prime, we can directly write down the factor of $+2$.

Possible factors of 20 that could sum to 9:

Product	Sum
$5 \times 4 = 20$	$5 + 4 = +9$
$(-5) \times (-4) = 20$	$(-5) + (-4) = -9$

Now consider:

$stpq = a \times c = 10 \times 2 = 20$

$b = +9$

$5 \times 4 = 20$ and $5x + 4x = +9x$

Place $+5x$ and $+4x$ in the shaded diagonal:

×		+2
x	$10x^2$	$+4x$
+1	$+5x$	$+2$

Write down the factors that gives $+5x$ and $+4x$:

Now, we need to check if the new factors multiply to $10x^2$.

Since $2x \times 5x = 10x^2$, we have:

$$10x^2 + 9x + 2 = (5x + 2)(2x + 1)$$

REFLECTION

What happens if you switch the positions of $+5x$ and $+4x$?

SELF ASSESSMENT

Try using Method 2 to factorise this expression.

CONTINUED

c   **Method 2: Using factorisation by grouping**

The expression $12x^3 + 13x^2 - 14x$ is of the form $ax^3 + bx^2 + cx$ and has a common factor x. You **must** take out the common factor first.

$12x^3 + 13x^2 - 14x = x(12x^2 + 13x - 14)$

Then use Method 2 to factorise $12x^2 + 13x - 14$.

Consider

$stpq = a \times c = 12 \times (-14) = -168$

$b = +13$

Since

$(-8) \times 21 = -168$ and $(-8x) + 21x = +13x$,

split $+13x$ into $-8x + 21x$.

We rewrite $12x^2 + 13x - 14$ into:

$$12x^2 + 13x - 14 = 12x^2 - 8x + 21x - 14$$
$$= 4x(3x - 2) + 7(3x - 2)$$
$$= (3x - 2)(4x + 7)$$

Hence, $12x^3 + 13x^2 - 14x = x(3x - 2)(4x + 7)$

TIP

1   Factorise in the question **always** means factorise fully.

2   Make sure you check for common factors in the expression before trying Method 1 or 2.

Possible factors of -168 that could sum to $+13$:

Product	Sum
$8 \times (-21) = -168$	$8 + (-21) = -13$
$(-8) \times 21 = -168$	$(-8) + 21 = +13$

Do factorisation by grouping.

Remember to put the factors back with the original expression.

SELF ASSESSMENT

Try using Method 1 to factorise this expression.

We have looked at the factorisation of one variable quadratic expressions of the form $ax^2 + bx + c$ where $a \neq 0$. What about quadratic expressions involving two variables, such as $ax^2 + bxy + cy^2$?

WORKED EXAMPLE 23

Factorise $6x^2 - 7xy - 5y^2$.

Answer

In $6x^2 - 7xy - 5y^2$, $a = 6$, $b = -7$ and $c = -5$.

We will use Method 2 in this example. Similar to the previous example, we find the product of ac and try to split b into the sum of the product of ac.

We shall split the xy term into the sum of two terms.

Take the product of the coefficients of the x^2 and y^2 terms:

$6 \times -5 = -30$

Find the factors of -30 that sum to -7:

$3 \times (-10) = -30$ and $3 + (-10) = -7$

CONTINUED

Rewrite $-7xy$ as $+3xy - 10xy$. Let's rewrite the quadratic expression:

$$6x^2 - 7xy - 5y^2 = 6x^2 + 3xy - 10xy - 5y^2$$
$$= 3x(2x + y) - 5y(2x + y)$$
$$= (2x + y)(3x - 5y)$$

SELF ASSESSMENT

Try using Method 1 to factorise this expression.

Exercise 7.7

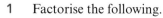

1 Factorise the following.

a $x^2 - 7x + 6$ b $y^2 - 7y - 8$

c $p^2 + 10p + 21$ d $w^2 - 12w + 35$

e $-x^2 + 4x + 32$ f $x^3 - x^2 - 12x$

g $y^3 - 6y^2 + 5y$ h $-w^3 - 5w^2 + 14w$

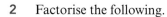

2 Factorise the following.

a $2x^2 + 7x + 5$ b $3y^2 - y - 24$

c $6p^2 - 7p - 5$ d $12w^2 + 29w + 14$

e $2x^3 + 7x^2 + 6x$ f $6x^3 - 11x^2 + 4x$

g $-2y^3 - 13y^2 + 7y$ h $-3w^3 - 10w^2 - 7w$

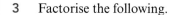

3 Factorise the following.

a $x^2 + 7xy + 6y^2$ b $x^2 + 2xy - 15y^2$

c $3a^2 + ab - 14b^2$ d $-a^2 + 2ab + 35b^2$

e $4x^2 + 10xy + 4y^2$ f $8x^2 + 4xy - 60y^2$

7.8 Algebraic fractions

An **algebraic fraction** is a fraction with letters as well as numbers.

You can simplify algebraic fractions by cancelling common factors.

WORKED EXAMPLE 24

Simplify $\dfrac{4}{6x}$.

Answer

$\dfrac{4}{6x} = \dfrac{2}{3x}$ 2 is a common factor for the numerator and denominator.

        $\dfrac{4}{6}$ can be reduced to $\dfrac{2}{3}$. Keep x in the denominator.

WORKED EXAMPLE 25

Simplify $\dfrac{x^2}{3x}$.

Answer

$\dfrac{x^2}{3x} = \dfrac{x}{3}$ x is a common factor for the numerator and denominator.
Cancel one x from the numerator and denominator.

You can also manipulate algebraic fractions using the four operations.

WORKED EXAMPLE 26

Simplify.

a $\dfrac{5x}{8} + \dfrac{x}{4}$ **b** $\dfrac{2}{x^3} + \dfrac{3}{x^2}$

Answers

a   To perform the addition, make the denominators the same:

$$\dfrac{5x}{8} + \dfrac{x}{4} = \dfrac{5x}{8} + \dfrac{x}{4} \times \dfrac{2}{2}$$

$$= \dfrac{5x + 2x}{8}$$

$$= \dfrac{7x}{8}$$

> **TIP**
>
> When the denominators are different, you first need to make the denominators the same.
>
> Using the lowest common multiple of the two denominators means that no further simplification is necessary.

> **MATHEMATICAL CONNECTIONS**
>
> You learnt how to find the lowest common multiple of two natural numbers in Chapter 1. Finding the lowest common multiple of algebraic terms is similar, but you must consider both the coefficient(s) and the variable(s).

b   The LCM of x^3 and x^2 is x^3 so make both denominators x^3:   Multiply the top and bottom of the second fraction by x.

$$\dfrac{2}{x^3} + \dfrac{3}{x^2} = \dfrac{2}{x^3} + \dfrac{3x}{x^3}$$

The denominators are now the same, so add the numerators:

$$\dfrac{2}{x^3} + \dfrac{3x}{x^3} = \dfrac{2 + 3x}{x^3}$$

> **TIP**
>
> You could also use this method in part **b**. However, to simplify completely you then need to simplify the final fraction:
>
> $$\dfrac{2}{x^3} + \dfrac{3}{x^2} = \dfrac{2}{x^3} \times \dfrac{x^2}{x^2} + \dfrac{3}{x^2} \times \dfrac{x^3}{x^3} = \dfrac{2x^2}{x^5} + \dfrac{3x^3}{x^5} = \dfrac{2x^2 + 3x^3}{x^5}$$
>
> Cancel through by x^2:
>
> $$= \dfrac{2 + 3x}{x^3}$$

To find a common denominator in more complicated algebraic fractions, multiply the top and bottom of each fraction by the denominator of the other fraction.

WORKED EXAMPLE 27

Simplify.

a $\dfrac{3}{x} - \dfrac{5}{x+2}$ **b** $\dfrac{x-1}{x+3} + \dfrac{2}{x+5}$

Answers

a First make the denominators the same:

$$\frac{3}{x} - \frac{5}{x+2} = \frac{3}{x} \times \frac{x+2}{x+2} - \frac{5}{x+2} \times \frac{x}{x}$$

$$= \frac{3(x+2)}{x(x+2)} - \frac{5x}{x(x+2)}$$

$$= \frac{3(x+2) - 5x}{x(x+2)}$$

Now that the denominators are the same, expand and simplify the numerators.

$$= \frac{3x + 6 - 5x}{x(x+2)}$$

$$= \frac{-2x + 6}{x(x+2)}$$

> **TIP**
>
> We usually keep the denominator in the factorised form.

b $\dfrac{x-1}{x+3} + \dfrac{2}{x+5} = \dfrac{x-1}{x+3} \times \left(\dfrac{x+5}{x+5}\right) + \dfrac{2}{x+5} \times \left(\dfrac{x+3}{x+3}\right)$

The LCM of $(x+3)$ and $(x+5)$ is $(x+3)(x+5)$.

$$= \frac{(x-1)(x+5)}{(x+3)(x+5)} + \frac{2(x+3)}{(x+3)(x+5)}$$

$$= \frac{x^2 + 4x - 5}{(x+3)(x+5)} + \frac{2x+6}{(x+3)(x+5)}$$

$$= \frac{x^2 + 4x - 5 + 2x + 6}{(x+3)(x+5)}$$

$$= \frac{x^2 + 6x + 1}{(x+3)(x+5)}$$

WORKED EXAMPLE 28

Simplify the following.

a $\dfrac{2ab}{25c} \times \dfrac{5ac}{3}$ **b** $\dfrac{ab}{4c} \div \dfrac{5ac}{2}$

CONTINUED

Answers

a   Check for common factor(s) that can be crossed out:

$$\frac{2ab}{25c} \times \frac{5ac}{3} = \frac{2ab}{\underset{5}{25\cancel{c}}} \times \frac{\overset{1}{\cancel{5}a\cancel{c}}}{3}$$

$$= \frac{2ab}{5} \times \frac{a}{3}$$

$$= \frac{2a^2b}{15}$$

5 is a common factor.

Multiply the remaining fraction: take numerator times numerator and denominator times denominator.

> **TIP**
>
> Only common factors in the numerator and denominator can be crossed out. You can cross out in the top and bottom direction or diagonally.

b $$\frac{ab}{4c} \div \frac{5ac}{2} = \frac{\cancel{a}b}{\underset{2}{\cancel{4}c}} \times \frac{\overset{1}{\cancel{2}}}{5\cancel{a}c}$$

$$= \frac{b}{2c} \times \frac{1}{5c}$$

$$= \frac{b}{10c^2}$$

When dividing fractions, change ÷ to × and reverse the fraction on the right of the division sign.

Then cross out common factor(s).

Fractions with algebra in the numerator and denominator are also known as **rational expressions**.

You can factorise and simplify rational expressions.

WORKED EXAMPLE 29

Simplify.

a $\dfrac{x^2 + 10x + 21}{x^2 - x - 12}$ **b** $\dfrac{a^3 + 2a^2c}{ab + 2ad + 2bc + 4cd}$

Answers

a $$\frac{x^2 + 10x + 21}{x^2 - x - 12} = \frac{(x+3)(x+7)}{(x+3)(x-4)}$$

$$= \frac{(x+3)(x+7)}{(x+3)(x-4)}$$

$$= \frac{x+7}{x-4}$$

To simplify rational expression, you must ensure both numerator and denominator are fully factorised.

Check if any of the factors are common. In this case $(x + 3)$ is common, so you can cancel them out from the numerator and denominator.

b $$\frac{a^3 + 2a^2c}{ab + 2ad + 2bc + 4cd}$$

$$= \frac{a^2(a + 2c)}{a(b + 2d) + 2c(b + 2d)}$$

$$= \frac{a^2(a + 2c)}{(b + 2d)(a + 2c)}$$

$$= \frac{a^2}{(b + 2d)}$$

Factorise the numerator by taking out any common factors.

The denominator consists of four terms and so can be factorised by grouping.

$(a + 2c)$ is a common factor that can be cancelled out.

Exercise 7.8

1   Simplify the following.

a $\dfrac{5}{15x}$ b $\dfrac{6x}{15}$ c $\dfrac{10}{12y}$ d $\dfrac{x}{x^2}$ e $\dfrac{2x^2}{8x}$

2   Simplify the following.

a $\dfrac{3x}{12x}$ b $\dfrac{6x}{15x}$ c $\dfrac{6x}{18x^2}$ d $\dfrac{9x^2}{12x}$ e $\dfrac{2xy}{8x^2}$

3   Write as a single fraction in its simplest form.

a $\dfrac{2x}{3} + \dfrac{x+1}{4}$ b $\dfrac{x}{3} - \dfrac{x-3}{5}$ c $\dfrac{x-1}{7} + \dfrac{x+2}{3}$

d $\dfrac{4x+1}{2} - \dfrac{x+3}{8}$ e $\dfrac{2(x-1)}{8} + \dfrac{x}{3}$ f $\dfrac{x-4}{7} - \dfrac{3(x+2)}{5}$

g $\dfrac{1}{x-1} + \dfrac{2}{x+3}$ h $\dfrac{3}{x-2} - \dfrac{1}{x+7}$ i $\dfrac{3}{x-1} + \dfrac{x+1}{x-3}$

j $\dfrac{2}{x+2} - \dfrac{x-1}{x-5}$ k $\dfrac{x-3}{x-1} + \dfrac{x+1}{x-3}$ l $\dfrac{x-2}{x+1} - \dfrac{x-3}{x-6}$

4   Simplify the following.

a $\dfrac{5x}{3} \times \dfrac{4x}{7}$ b $\dfrac{5x}{3} \div \dfrac{4x}{7}$ c $\dfrac{3xy}{4} \times \dfrac{9x}{8y}$

d $\dfrac{3xy}{4} \div \dfrac{9x}{8y}$ e $\dfrac{2xy}{7} \times \dfrac{3x}{8y^2}$ f $\dfrac{2xy}{7} \div \dfrac{3x}{8y^2}$

g $\dfrac{10xy}{6a} \times \dfrac{3ay}{8x}$ h $\dfrac{10xy}{6a} \div \dfrac{3ay}{8x}$

5   Simplify the following.

a $\dfrac{9x^2 - 3x}{15x^2 - 5x}$ b $\dfrac{x^2 + x - 2}{x^2 - x}$ c $\dfrac{2x - 1}{2x^2 + 5x - 3}$

d $\dfrac{x^2 - y^2}{x^2 + 2xy + y^2}$ e $\dfrac{x^2 - x - 2}{x^2 - 4}$ f $\dfrac{x^2 - 3xy + 2xz - 6yz}{xz^2 + 2z^3}$

7.9 Solving linear equations with one variable

A **linear equation** contains variables and numbers. The variables have highest power 1.

For example, $2 + x = 5$ is a linear equation.

You can **solve** a linear equation by finding the value of the variable that makes the left-hand side of the equation equal to right-hand side of the equation.

For example, $x = 3$ is the solution to $2 + x = 5$ because substituting $x = 3$ into $2 + x$ gives $2 + 3 = 5$. While this example can be solved by observation, not all linear equations can be solved this way.

To solve more complicated linear equations, we will have to perform some operations to the equation to isolate the variable x.

WORKED EXAMPLE 30

Solve $2x - 10 = 14$.

Answer

To isolate x, we first remove -10 from the LHS.

Since $-10 + 10 = 0$, to remove -10, we must add 10 to the left. However, the equation will not be balanced if you only add 10 on one side, so you must add 10 to the other side too.

$2x - 10 = 14$

Add 10 on both sides:

$2x - 10 + 10 = 14 + 10$

$\qquad 2x = 24$

We must remove the 2 on the left to isolate the x. If we take $\dfrac{2x}{2}$ we will get x, so divide by 2 on both sides:

$\dfrac{2x}{2} = \dfrac{24}{2}$

$\quad x = 12$

> **TIP**
>
> You can check your solution by substituting this value into each side of the original equation and checking that the two sides are equal.
>
> Substituting $x = 12$ into the left-hand side: $2(12) - 10 = 24 - 10 = 14$
>
> The left-hand side equals the right-hand side, so the solution is correct.

> **TIP**
>
> You must perform the same operation on both sides of the equation to balance the equation.

Sometimes the variable is on both sides of the equation and you need to rearrange before solving.

WORKED EXAMPLE 31

Solve $4(x - 5) = 2x + 6$.

Answer

Expand the brackets to get a linear equation:

$4x - 20 = 2x + 6$

To isolate the variable, put all like terms together on one side (all the variables on one side and the constants on the other side) and simplify.

Add 20 on both sides: $-20 + 20 = 0$

$4x - 20 + 20 = 2x + 6 + 20$ Get rid of -20 on the left.

$\qquad 4x = 2x + 26$

CONTINUED

Subtract $2x$ on both sides:

$4x - 2x = 2x + 26 - 2x$

$\qquad 2x = 26$

Divide both sides by 2:

$\dfrac{2x}{2} = \dfrac{26}{2}$

$\qquad x = 13$

$2x - 2x = 0$

Get rid of $2x$ on the right.

Get rid of the coefficient 2 from $2x$.

Exercise 7.9

1   Solve the equations.

    a $2x + 5 = 19$ **b** $3x + 11 = 20$ **c** $2x - 8 = 36$

    d $5x - 15 = 30$ **e** $2(x - 3) = 3x + 7$ **f** $5x - 4 = 7(3 - x)$

    g $3 - 2x = 4(x + 12)$ **h** $5(x - 3) = 2(3x - 7)$ **i** $6(7y - 1) = 3(4 - 13y)$

SELF ASSESSMENT

Raghav attempted to solve this equation as shown. His answer is incorrect. Identify and correct the errors in Raghav's working to give the correct solution.

$-4(x - 3) + 3x(x - 3) = x(3x + 3)$

$-4x - 12 + 3x^2 - 9x = 3x^2 + 3x$

$\qquad -13x - 12 = 3x$

$\qquad\qquad 16x = -12$

$\qquad\qquad\quad x = \dfrac{-3}{4}$

7.10 Constructing linear equations

You can construct an equation to represent and solve word problems.

WORKED EXAMPLE 32

Kaushal has \$5. He buys 4 pens that cost \$$x$ each. He has \$$C$ left.

a   Write an equation connecting C to x.

b   If $C = 3$, find x.

CONTINUED

Answers

a The equation can be written as $C = 5 - 4x$

b To find x, first substitute the value of C.

$C = 3$

$3 = 5 - 4x$

Subtract 5 from both sides:

$3 - 5 = 5 - 4x - 5$

$-2 = -4x$

Divide both sides by -4:

$\dfrac{-2}{-4} = \dfrac{-4x}{-4}$

Flip the equation around:

$x = \dfrac{1}{2}$

Since x represents the cost of one pen, we rewrite into decimal form:

$x = \$0.50$

WORKED EXAMPLE 33

Mia is x years old, Rayyan's age is twice Mia's age and Bekha is 5 years older than Rayyan. Their total age is 55.

a Write expressions for Rayyan's age and Bekha's age in terms of x.

b Formulate an equation and solve it to find Mia's age.

Answers

a Rayyan's age $= 2x$

Bekha's age $= 2x + 5$

b Adding the three ages to give a total of 55:

Rayyan's age + Mia's age + Bekha's age $= 55$

$2x + x + 2x + 5 = 55$

$5x + 5 = 55$

Isolate x to solve it.

Subtracting 5 from both sides:

$5x + 5 - 5 = 55 - 5$

$5x = 50$

Dividing both sides by 5:

$x = 10$

Hence Mia is 10 years old.

Exercise 7.10

 1 Paul is x years old. Ali is 6 years younger than Paul. Sara is 7 years younger than Ali.

    a Write down an expression for Ali and Sara's ages in terms of x.

    b If their total age is 44 years, what is the age of each person?

 2 Sam has five times as many marbles as John.

    a Write down two algebraic expressions in x for the number of marbles that each child has.

    b If Sam gave 16 marbles to John, they would have the same number. Form an equation and find the number of marbles that each have.

 3 I think of two numbers. The bigger number is 4 more than 3 times the smaller number.

    a If the smaller number is x, write down an expression for the bigger number in terms of x.

    b Given that the sum of the two numbers is 120, find the two numbers.

 4 Given that AB is a straight line, find x.

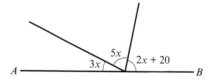

MATHEMATICAL CONNECTIONS

In Chapter 3 you learnt that the sum of the angles on a straight line add to 180°.

 5 If the perimeter of this triangle is 23 cm. Find the length of the longest side.

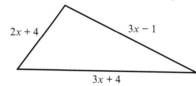

 6 The sum of three consecutive numbers is 102. Find the numbers.

 7 The sum of three consecutive odd numbers is 171. Find the numbers.

 8 When a number is doubled and then added to 15, the result is 53. Find the number.

 9 When 11 is subtracted from three times a certain number, the result is 49. What is the number?

7.11 Solving quadratic equations by factorisation

In Section 7.7, you learnt to factorise a quadratic expression of the form $ax^2 + bx + c$.

In this section, we will learn to solve a quadratic equation of the form $ax^2 + bx + c = 0$ by factorisation.

To solve a quadratic equation by factorisation, we need to ensure all the terms are on one side while the other side is a zero, i.e. $ax^2 + bx + c = 0$.

We will then factorise the algebraic side to get the form $(sx + p)(tx + q) = 0$.

We can represent the two factors in the form $A \times B = 0$. When two factors multiply to get zero, either one or both the factors can be zero. Hence, when $A \times B = 0$, we can say either $A = 0$ or $B = 0$.

Similarly, when $(sx + p)(tx + q) = 0$, we say $sx + p = 0$ or $tx + q = 0$.

We get two linear equations that we can solve easily.

WORKED EXAMPLE 34

Solve $8x^2 + 2x = 15$.

Answer

Step 1: Check that the equation is of the form $ax^2 + bx + c = 0$. If it isn't, rearrange the terms to the correct form.

$8x^2 + 2x = 15$

We need to get rid of 15 from the right-hand side of the equation, which we can do by subtracting 15 from both sides:

$8x^2 + 2x - 15 = 15 - 15$

$8x^2 + 2x - 15 = 0$

Step 2: Factorise the LHS.

$(2x + 3)(4x - 5) = 0$

Step 3: Equate each factor to zero and solve.

$2x + 3 = 0 \quad$ or $\quad 4x - 5 = 0$

$2x = -3 \qquad\qquad 4x = 5$

$x = -\dfrac{3}{2} \qquad\qquad x = \dfrac{5}{4}$

The solution to the equation $8x^2 + 2x = 15$ is $x = -\dfrac{3}{2}$ or $x = \dfrac{5}{4}$.

REFLECTION

How can you check if your solution is correct?

Exercise 7.11

1 Solve the following equations.

a $\quad x^2 - x - 12 = 0$

b $\quad x^2 + 11x - 12 = 0$

c $\quad 2x^2 + x - 1 = 0$

d $\quad 3x^2 - 22x + 7 = 0$

e $\quad 2x^2 + 7x = 4$

f $\quad 4x^2 + 14x = x^2 + 5$

g $\quad 2x^2 + 1 = 3(4x - 5)$

h $\quad 2x(4x + 1) = 15$

7.12 Solving fractional equations

In this section, you will learn how to solve fractional equations. Depending on how complicated the fractional equation is, you will need to make use of a combination of what you have learnt in the previous sections of this chapter.

You will need to simplify the fractional equation into a form where there are no more fractional expressions in the equation. A useful way to achieve this is to multiply both sides of the equation by the LCM of all the denominators.

WORKED EXAMPLE 35

Solve $\dfrac{2x-5}{7} - \dfrac{x+3}{3} = 2$.

Answer

Method 1: Multiply both sides by the LCM of the denominator

The LCM of 7 and 3 is 21.

Multiply both sides by 21:

Multiply every fraction by 21 then cancel common factors.

$$\dfrac{2x-5}{{}_1 7} \times {}^3 21 - \dfrac{x+3}{{}_1 3} \times {}^7 21 = 2 \times 21$$

$3(2x-5) - 7(x+3) = 42$ Expand the brackets and solve.

$6x - 15 - 7x - 21 = 42$

$-x - 36 = 42$

$-x = 42 + 36$

$-x = 78$

$x = -78$

Method 2: Combine the fractions into one

In Section 7.8, you learnt to combine the sum or difference of two fractions into one.

$$\dfrac{2x-5}{7} - \dfrac{x+3}{3} = 2$$ Make the denominators of the left-hand side the same.

$$\dfrac{2x-5}{7} \times \dfrac{3}{3} - \dfrac{x+3}{3} \times \dfrac{7}{7} = 2$$

$$\dfrac{3(2x-5)}{21} - \dfrac{7(x+3)}{21} = 2$$

$$\dfrac{3(2x-5) - 7(x+3)}{21} = 2$$ Combine the left-hand side into a single fraction.

$$\dfrac{6x - 15 - 7x - 21}{21} = 2$$ Simplify the numerator.

$$\dfrac{-x - 36}{21} = 2$$

$-x - 36 = 42$ Add 36 to both sides of the equation.

$-x = 42 + 36$

$-x = 78$ Multiply both sides by -1.

$x = -78$

WORKED EXAMPLE 36

Solve the following equations.

a $\dfrac{3x}{x-1} = 6$ **b** $\dfrac{3}{x+6} = \dfrac{x}{x-6}$ **c** $\dfrac{3}{2x-5} - \dfrac{2}{x-3} = -1$

Answers

We will only use Method 1 to solve Worked example 36.

a   Multiply both sides by $(x-1)$:

$$\dfrac{3x}{\cancel{x-1}} \times (\cancel{x-1}) = 6 \times (x-1)$$

> Cancel any common factors you see on the same side of the equation.

The resultant equation will not contain any more fractions.

> This is a linear equation. Expand the right-hand side and solve the equation.

$$3x = 6(x-1)$$
$$3x = 6x - 6$$
$$3x - 6x = -6$$
$$-3x = -6$$
$$x = 2$$

b   This equation is a special case where there is only one fraction on each side of the equation. A convenient way to get rid of the fractional expression is to 'cross-multiply' the fractions:

> To 'cross-multiply', multiply 3 by $(x-6)$ and multiply x by $(x+6)$.

$$\dfrac{3}{x+6} \diagdown\!\!\!\!\diagup \dfrac{x}{x-6}$$

$$3(x-6) = x(x+6)$$
$$3x - 18 = x^2 + 6x$$

> Expand the brackets.

This is a quadratic equation.

You need to move all the terms to one side while the other side is zero:

$$0 = x^2 + 6x - 3x + 18$$
$$0 = x^2 + 3x + 18$$

Rewrite the equation so that zero is on the right:

$$x^2 + 3x + 18 = 0$$

Factorise and solve:

$$(x+6)(x-3) = 0$$
$$x + 6 = 0 \quad \text{or} \quad x - 3 = 0$$
$$x = -6 \qquad\qquad x = 3$$

> **TIP**
>
> Try to move all the terms to the side where the coefficient of x^2 will be positive.

CONTINUED

c   The LCM of $(2x - 5)$ and $(x - 3)$ is $(2x - 5)(x - 3)$.

Multiply both sides by $(2x - 5)(x - 3)$:

$$\frac{3}{2x - 5} \times (2x - 5)(x - 3) - \frac{2}{x - 3} \times (2x - 5)(x - 3)$$

Cancel common factors in the fraction.

$$= -1 \times (2x - 5)(x - 3)$$

$$3(x - 3) - 2(2x - 5) = -(2x - 5)(x - 3)$$

Expand the brackets, bring all the terms to one side and factorise.

$$3x - 9 - 4x + 10 = -2x^2 + 11x - 15$$

$$-x + 1 = -2x^2 + 11x - 15$$

$$2x^2 - 11x + 15 - x + 1 = 0$$

$$2x^2 - 12x + 16 = 0$$

$$2(x^2 - 6x + 8) = 0$$

$$2(x - 4)(x - 2) = 0$$

$2 \neq 0$, hence only the factors $(x - 4)$ or $(x - 2)$ can be zero.

$$x - 4 = 0 \quad \text{or} \quad x - 2 = 0$$
$$x = 4 \qquad\qquad x = 2$$

Can you use Method 2 to solve Worked example 36?

TIP

You can substitute the answers into the equation to check!

Exercise 7.12

1   Solve the following equations.

a $\dfrac{x + 4}{3} + \dfrac{2x + 3}{2} = 5$ b $\dfrac{2x + 1}{6} - \dfrac{3x - 2}{4} = 1$ c $\dfrac{5x}{2x - 1} = 2$

d $\dfrac{15x}{4x + 7} = 3$ e $\dfrac{2}{x + 1} = \dfrac{x}{5 - x}$ f $\dfrac{4}{x + 2} = \dfrac{x}{2x - 2}$

g $\dfrac{3}{x + 3} + \dfrac{2}{x + 2} = 2$ h $\dfrac{1}{x - 1} + \dfrac{4}{x + 2} = 2$ i $\dfrac{x}{3x - 4} - \dfrac{4}{2x - 1} = 1$

7.13 Indices II

In Chapter 6, you learnt the rules of indices.

Rules of indices

$a^n \times a^m = a^{n+m}$

$a^n \div a^m = a^{n-m}$

$(a^n)^m = a^{n \times m}$

$a^0 = 1$

$a^{-n} = \dfrac{1}{a^n}$

$a^{\frac{1}{n}} = \sqrt[n]{a}$

$a^{\frac{m}{n}} = (\sqrt[n]{a})^m = \sqrt[n]{a^m}$

In Indices II, we will apply these rules to solve equations and simplify algebraic expressions.

In general,

$(ab)^n = a^n b^n$

$\left(\dfrac{a}{b}\right)^n = \dfrac{a^n}{b^n}$

if $a^n = a^m \Rightarrow n = m$, where the base a is the same.

WORKED EXAMPLE 37

Solve $3^x = 27$.

Answer

We rewrite 27 in powers of base 3: $\qquad 27 = 3^3$

$3^x = 3^3$ $\qquad\qquad\qquad\qquad$ If $a^n = a^m \Rightarrow n = m$

Hence, $x = 3$

WORKED EXAMPLE 38

Simplify the following expressions.

a $\quad 4a^2 b^9 \times 3a^5 b^{-4}$ $\qquad$ **b** $\quad 12a^{10}b^{-2} \div 3a^2 b^{-7}$ $\qquad$ **c** $\quad (4x^5)^2$ $\qquad$ **d** $\quad (5x^{-3})^2$

Answers

a $\quad$ Multiply like terms:

$4a^2 b^9 \times 3a^5 b^{-4} = (4 \times 3) \times (a^2 \times a^5) \times (b^9 \times b^{-4})$ $\qquad$ $a^n \times a^m = a^{n+m}$

$\qquad\qquad\qquad\qquad = 12 \times a^{2+5} \times b^{9+(-4)}$

$\qquad\qquad\qquad\qquad = 12a^7 b^5$

> **TIP**
>
> Multiply the number then the variables.

b $\quad$ **Method 1: Divide like terms:**

$12a^{10}b^{-2} \div 3a^2 b^{-7} = (12 \div 3) \times (a^{10} \div a^2) \times (b^{-2} \div b^{-7})$

$\qquad\qquad\qquad\qquad = 4 \times a^{10-2} \times b^{-2-(-7)}$ $\qquad$ $a^n \div a^m = a^{n-m}$

$\qquad\qquad\qquad\qquad = 4a^8 b^5$

Method 2: Change to algebraic fractions and simplify:

$12a^{10}b^{-2} \div 3a^2 b^{-7} = \dfrac{12a^{10}}{b^2} \div \dfrac{3a^2}{b^7}$

Recall $a^{-n} = \dfrac{1}{a^n}$

Change division to multiplication and reverse the fraction on the right. Then cancel any common factors.

$\qquad\qquad\qquad\qquad = \dfrac{^4\cancel{12}a^{\cancel{10}8}}{^1 b^2} \times \dfrac{b^{\cancel{7}5}}{^1\cancel{3}\cancel{a^2}_1}$

$\qquad\qquad\qquad\qquad = \dfrac{4a^8}{1} \times \dfrac{b^5}{1}$

$\qquad\qquad\qquad\qquad = 4a^8 b^5$

CONTINUED

c $(4x^5)^2 = 4^2 \times (x^5)^2$

$\qquad = 16x^{5 \times 2}$

$\qquad = 16x^{10}$

$(ab)^n = a^n \times b^n$

Recall $(a^n)^m = a^{n \times m}$

d **Method 1**

$(5x^{-3})^2 = 5^2 \times (x^{-3})^2$

$\qquad = 25 \times x^{-6} = \dfrac{25}{x^6}$

Use $(ab)^n = a^n \times b^n$ and $(a^n)^m = a^{n \times m}$

$a^{-n} = \dfrac{1}{a^n}$

Method 2

$(5x^{-3})^2 = \left(\dfrac{5}{x^3}\right)^2$

$\qquad = \dfrac{5^2}{(x^3)^2} = \dfrac{25}{x^6}$

$a^{-n} = \dfrac{1}{a^n}$

$\left(\dfrac{a}{b}\right)^n = \dfrac{a^n}{b^n}$

WORKED EXAMPLE 39

Solve.

a $7^{2x+1} = \dfrac{1}{49}$ **b** $125^{x-1} = 25^x$

Answers

a $7^{2x+1} = \dfrac{1}{49}$

$\dfrac{1}{49} = \dfrac{1}{7^2} = 7^{-2}$

Try to make the base the same:

$7^{2x+1} = 7^{-2}$

Equate the power:

$2x + 1 = -2$

Solve the linear equation:

$2x = -2 - 1$

$2x = -3$

$x = \dfrac{-3}{2}$

b Make the base on both sides the same:

$(5^3)^{x-1} = (5^2)^x$

$5^{3(x-1)} = 5^{2x}$

Equate the power:

$3(x - 1) = 2x$

Solve the linear equation:

$3x - 3 = 2x$

$3x - 2x = 3$

$x = 3$

$125 = 5^3$

$25 = 5^2$

$a^n = a^m \Rightarrow n = m$

WORKED EXAMPLE 40

Simplify.

a $\frac{3}{4}x^{-5} \times 2x^{\frac{1}{2}}$ b $\frac{3}{4}x^{\frac{1}{2}} \div 3x^{-4}$ c $\left(\frac{3a^5}{b^2}\right)^3$

Answers

a Multiply like terms:

$$\frac{3}{4}x^{-5} \times 2x^{\frac{1}{2}} = \left(\frac{3}{4} \times 2\right) \times \left(x^{-5} \times x^{\frac{1}{2}}\right)$$

$$= \frac{3}{2} \times x^{-5+\frac{1}{2}}$$

$$= \frac{3}{2}x^{-\frac{9}{2}}$$

$a^n \times a^m = a^{n+m}$

You can leave the index in negative fractional form unless the question says otherwise.

b When dividing by $3x^{-4}$, it might be easier to express $3x^{-4}$ as $\frac{3}{x^4}$ since we need to reverse the fraction on the right:

$$\frac{3}{4}x^{\frac{1}{2}} \div 3x^{-4} = \frac{3}{4}x^{\frac{1}{2}} \div \frac{3}{x^4}$$

Change ÷ to ×, then reverse the fraction on the right:

$$= \frac{{}^1\cancel{3}x^{\frac{1}{2}}}{4} \times \frac{x^4}{\cancel{3}_1}$$

$$= \frac{x^{\frac{1}{2}}}{4} \times \frac{x^4}{1}$$

$$= \frac{x^{\frac{1}{2}+4}}{4}$$

$$= \frac{x^{\frac{9}{2}}}{4}$$

$\frac{3}{4}x^{\frac{1}{2}} = \frac{3x^{\frac{1}{2}}}{4}$

Cancel common factor 3.

Multiply the remaining fraction.

c $$\left(\frac{3a^5}{b^2}\right)^3 = \frac{3^3(a^5)^3}{(b^2)^3}$$

$$= \frac{27a^{5 \times 3}}{b^{2 \times 3}}$$

$$= \frac{27a^{15}}{b^6}$$

Use $\left(\frac{a}{b}\right)^n = \frac{a^n}{b^n}$ and $(a^n)^m = a^{n \times m}$

Exercise 7.13

1 Solve.

a $2^x = 64$ b $81^x = 3$ c $7^x = \frac{1}{7}$ d $100^x = 1000$

2 Simplify.

   a $2a^{11}b^7 \times 3a^{-5}b^2$ **b** $4a^5b^4 \times 5a^{-7}b^8$ **c** $16a^{10} \div 4a^6$

   d $36b^{12} \div 6b^{-7}$ **e** $(4x^0)^2$ **f** $(11x^3)^0$

   g $(2x^5)^4$ **h** $(7x^{-6})^2$

3 Solve.

   a $5^x = \dfrac{1}{25}$ **b** $12^x = 1$ **c** $x^{-2} = \dfrac{1}{9}$

   d $6^x = \dfrac{1}{216}$ **e** $x^{-4} = \dfrac{1}{16}$

4 Solve.

   a $4^{x+2} = 64$ **b** $27^x = 3^{2x-5}$ **c** $25^{x+2} = \dfrac{1}{125}$

   d $8^{x-2} = 16^{x+1}$ **e** $4^x \times 2^{x+1} = 16$ **f** $9^x = 81 \times 3^{x+1}$

   g $4^x \div 2^{x-1} = 32$ **h** $81^x \div 3^{x+1} = 9$

5 Simplify.

   a $\dfrac{2}{3}a^5b^{\frac{2}{5}} \times 9a^{-2}b^2$ **b** $4a^6b^{-5} \times \dfrac{1}{5}a^{-\frac{1}{3}}b^8$ **c** $16a^{-4} \div \dfrac{1}{4}a^{\frac{2}{3}}$

   d $\dfrac{4}{5}b^6 \div 6b^{-\frac{5}{2}}$ **e** $\left(\dfrac{2t^2}{5s^3u^0}\right)^2$ **f** $\left(\dfrac{a}{b^2}\right)^{-1}$

   g $\left(\dfrac{4p^2}{6q^3}\right)^{-2}$ **h** $\left(\dfrac{4}{p^6}\right)^{\frac{3}{2}}$ **i** $\left(\dfrac{8f^9g^6}{27h^{12}}\right)^{-\frac{2}{3}}$

   j $\dfrac{(6x^2y^4)^2 \times (2xy)^3}{12x^6y^8}$ **k** $\dfrac{(6x^2y^4)^0 \times (2x^5y)^3}{12x^0y^8}$

SUMMARY

Are you able to... ?
form algebraic expressions
find the value of expressions by substitution
simplify algebraic expressions by collecting like terms
understand and use the rules of indices
expand and simplify expressions involving one or two brackets
factorise algebraic expressions
simplify algebraic fractions
construct and solve linear equations in one unknown

CONTINUED

expand and simplify expressions involving more than two brackets
factorise more complicated expressions
manipulate and factorise algebraic fractions
use and interpret fractional indices
solve quadratic equations by factorising
solve fractional equations with numerical and linear algebraic denominators.

Past paper questions

1   Expand. $k^2(k - 6)$ [2]

Cambridge IGCSE International Mathematics 0607 Paper 11 Q15 November 2021

2   A taxi company charges a fixed amount of $3 and then $1.50 for each
    kilometre travelled.

   i   Write a formula for the cost, C, for travelling n kilometres. [2]

   ii   Menno travels 15 kilometres in a taxi from this company.
         Work out the cost of Menno's taxi journey. [2]

   iii   Weston pays $37.50 for a taxi journey with this company.
         Work out how many kilometres the taxi travels. [2]

Cambridge IGCSE International Mathematics 0607 Paper 31 Q5a November 2021

3   Solve. $2(4x - 1) = 3(2x + 1)$ [3]

Cambridge IGCSE International Mathematics 0607 Paper 21 Q5 November 2021

Chapter 8

Simultaneous linear equations

IN THIS CHAPTER YOU WILL:

- construct equations and formulae

- construct and solve simultaneous linear equations

- change the subject of formulae

- represent, solve and interpret linear inequalities

> construct linear inequalities

> solve inequalities using a graphic display calculator

> represent linear inequalities in two variables graphically

> list inequalities that define a given region

> express direct and inverse proportion in algebraic terms

> identify the best variation model for given data.

GETTING STARTED

1   Copy and complete each calculation to make the answer correct.

   a $2 \times \sqrt{\square} = 10$

   b $\dfrac{\square}{2} = -6$

   c $\square^2 + 3 = 28$

2   Rahul had lunch in a hotel and paid his bill of \$33, which included a tip of \$5. How much did he pay for just the lunch?

8.1 Changing the subject of a formula

Consider the formula $F = \dfrac{9}{5}C + 32$.

Written in this way, F is the **subject** of the formula because it is on its own on one side of the equals symbol.

You can rearrange the formula to make C the subject.

DISCUSSION 1

Why would you want to rearrange the subject to make C the subject of this formula?

MATHEMATICS IN CONTEXT

This is the **formula** to convert a temperature in degrees Fahrenheit into the equivalent temperature in degrees Celsius.

WORKED EXAMPLE 1

Rearrange $F = \dfrac{9}{5}C + 32$ to make C the subject.

Answer

$F - 32 = \dfrac{9}{5}C$ Subtract 32 from each side to isolate the term involving C.

$\dfrac{5}{9}(F - 32) = C$ Divide both sides by $\dfrac{9}{5}$ so that C is now the subject of the formula.

TIP

Remember that dividing by $\dfrac{9}{5}$ is the same as multiplying by $\dfrac{5}{9}$.

WORKED EXAMPLE 2

Make a the subject of the formula $3(a + x) = 1$.

Answer

$3(a + x) = 1$ Expand the brackets.

$3a = 1 - 3x$ Isolate $3a$.

$a = \dfrac{1 - 3x}{3}$ Divide each side by 3 to make a the subject.

MATHEMATICAL CONNECTIONS

You learnt how to expand brackets in Chapter 7.

The same rules apply to rearranging formulae where the subject appears more than once or if there is a power or a root involved.

WORKED EXAMPLE 3

Rearrange the formula $a = x^2 + c$ so that x is the subject of the formula.

Answer

$a = x^2 + c$	Subtract c from both sides.
$a - c = x^2$	Square root both sides.
$x = \sqrt{(a - c)}$	x is the subject of the equation.

WORKED EXAMPLE 4

A formula used in science is $s = ut + \dfrac{1}{2}at^2$.

Rearrange the formula so that a is the subject of the formula.

Answer

$s = ut + \dfrac{1}{2}at^2$	Subtract the expression ut from both sides.
$s - ut = \dfrac{1}{2}at^2$	Multiply both sides by 2.
$2(s - ut) = at^2$	Divide both sides by t^2.
$a = \dfrac{2(s - ut)}{t^2}$	Make a the subject.

Exercise 8.1

1 Rearrange each formula to make x the subject.

a $3x = 7$ b $Ax = C$ c $9x = T + Q$

d $x + B = T$ e $N = x + D$ f $N^2 + x = P + Q$

g $x - A = E + K$ h $F = A - x$

i $ax = cx + b$ j $Y = x^2 - 6$

2 Make a the subject of each formula.

a $\dfrac{a}{D} = C$ b $\dfrac{a - A}{B} = T$ c $g = \dfrac{a - RT}{D}$

d $\dfrac{za - B}{D} = B$ e $n = \dfrac{ea - f}{h}$ f $\dfrac{M(a - B)}{P} = T$

g $\dfrac{r}{a} = A$ h $\dfrac{p}{a} \times q = M$

INVESTIGATION 1

The following three formulae are known as SUVAT equations by scientists.

$v = u + at$

$v^2 = u^2 + 2as$

$s = ut + \dfrac{1}{2}at^2$

a   Find out what SUVAT stands for.

b   Try rearranging each of the formulae so that a is the subject.

c   Compare your work with a partner and check that your new formulae are correct.

3   Make x the subject of each formula.

   a $x^2 = B$ **b** $x^2 + A = B$ **c** $b = a + x^2$

   d $C - x^2 = m$ **e** $mx^2 = n$ **f** $ax^2 - t = m$

   g $\dfrac{m}{x^2} = a + b$ **h** $\dfrac{x^2}{a} + b = c$ **i** $xt = b + xc$

   j $x = xc + bd$ **k** $v = \sqrt{x}$ **l** $as = \sqrt[3]{x}$

   m $a = \dfrac{bc}{\sqrt{x}}$ **n** $b = \dfrac{\sqrt[3]{x}}{n}$

8.2 Solving simultaneous linear equations

You have already solved **linear equations** with one unknown variable.

When there are two unknown variables, you need two linear equations. You can then solve these equations simultaneously to find the unknown values.

You can solve **simultaneous equations** either by the elimination method or the substitution method.

> **MATHEMATICAL CONNECTIONS**
>
> Look back at Chapter 7 if you need a reminder on how to solve linear equations with one unknown.

WORKED EXAMPLE 5

Solve these simultaneous equations to find the values of x and y.

$x + y = 6$

$x - y = 2$

Answer

Method 1: Elimination method

In the elimination method, you eliminate one of the variables to make a single linear equation in one variable which you can then solve.

You then substitute this value into one of the original equations to find the other variable.

> **MATHEMATICAL CONNECTIONS**
>
> You learnt how to substitute values into equations in Chapter 7.

CONTINUED

$x + y = 6$ (1) $x - y = 2$ (2)	Label the equations.
Equation (1) has $+y$ and equation (2) has $-y$ so you can eliminate y by adding the equations: (1) + (2): $2x = 8$	While adding the equations, make sure you add terms on the same side of the equation.

Hence, $x = \dfrac{8}{2} = 4$

Substitute $x = 4$ into either equation (1) or equation (2) to find the value of y.

Substituting $x = 4$ into equation (1):

$4 + y = 6$

$\quad\; y = 2$

You now have the full solution:

$x = 4, y = 2$

Check your answer by substituting these values into both the equations: (1): $4 + 2 = 6$ ✓ (2): $4 - 2 = 2$ ✓	It is always a good idea to check your solution.

Method 2: Substitution method

In the substitution method, you make one of the variables the subject of one of the equations and substitute it into the other equation. This gives a single equation in one variable which you can solve to find the value of the variable.

You then substitute this value into the other equation to find the value of the other variable.

$x + y = 6$ (1) $x - y = 2$ (2)	As in the elimination method, label the equations.
Rearranging equation (1) to make x the subject: $x = 6 - y$	You can rearrange either equation. Choose the equation that seems easiest to rearrange.

Substituting $x = 6 - y$ into equation (2):

$6 - y - y = 2$

Rearranging to solve for y:

$4 = 2y$

$2 = y$

CONTINUED

Substituting this value for y into equation (1) to find the value of x:

$x + 2 = 6$

$x = 4$

You now have the full solution:

$x = 4, y = 2$

As expected, using either the elimination method or the substitution method gives the same solution.

Check your answer by substituting these values into both the equations:

(1): $4 + 2 = 6$ ✓

(2): $4 - 2 = 2$ ✓

As with the elimination method, it is always a good idea to check your solution.

If the question does not specify which method to use to solve a pair of simultaneous equations, use the method you feel more confident with.

Always remember to check your solutions by substituting back into the original equations.

WORKED EXAMPLE 6

Solve these simultaneous equations.

$x + 2y = 8$

$2x + 3y = 14$

Answer

Label the equations:

$x + 2y = 8$ (1)

$2x + 3y = 14$ (2)

Here the variables have different coefficients in the different equations so you need to do some work to eliminate one of the variables.

Step 1:

Multiplying equation (1) by 2:

$(x + 2y = 8) \times 2$

$2x + 4y = 16$

Focus on the coefficients of one variable. You need to make these coefficients the same in both the equations.

Label the new equation:

$2x + 4y = 16$ (3)

Equations (2) and (3) now have the same coefficients of x.

$2x + 4y = 16$ (3)

$2x + 3y = 14$ (2)

CONTINUED

Since there is a $+2x$ in both equations, you can eliminate x by subtracting one equation from the other equation.

Subtracting equation (2) from equation (3):

$y = 2$

Substituting this value for y into equation (1):

$x + 2y = 8$

$x + 4 = 8$

$x = 4$

You now have the full solution:

$x = 4$, and $y = 2$

$4 + (2 \times 2) = 8$ ✓

$(2 \times 4) + (3 \times 2) = 14$ ✓

You can substitute into either equation (1) or (2). Choose the equation that is simplest to work with.

Remember to check your solution by substituting back into both of the original equations (1) and (2).

TIP

This solution to Worked example 6 uses the elimination method. Solve these simultaneous equations using the substitution method and check that you get the same solution.

Think carefully first about which equation you will choose to rearrange.

Sometimes you will be given a word problem with two unknowns. You need to use the given information to construct simultaneous equations and then solve them to find the unknown values.

WORKED EXAMPLE 7

Find two numbers with a sum of 14 and a difference of 2.

Answer

Two numbers (let's call them x and y) add up to 14.

So $x + y = 14$

The same two numbers have a difference of 2.

So $x - y = 2$

We now have a pair of simultaneous equations, which we label:

$x + y = 14$ (1)

$x - y = 2$ (2)

Solving by elimination (1) + (2):

$2x = 16$

Therefore $x = 8$

Substitute $x = 8$ into either equation:

$8 + y = 14$

Therefore $y = 6$

Exercise 8.2

In Questions **1** to **19**, solve each pair of simultaneous equations using the method of your choice. Remember to check your solutions.

1
$$2x + y = 12$$
$$2x - y = 8$$

2
$$3x + 2y = 13$$
$$4x = 2y + 8$$

3
$$9x + 3y = 24$$
$$x - 3y = -14$$

4
$$2x + y = 14$$
$$x + y = 9$$

5
$$x + y = 10$$
$$3x = -y + 22$$

6
$$5x - 3y = 9$$
$$2x + 3y = 19$$

7
$$2x + y = 7$$
$$3x + 2y = 12$$

8
$$2x - 3y = -3$$
$$3x + 2y = 15$$

9
$$5x + 4y = 21$$
$$x + 2y = 9$$

10
$$4x = 4y + 8$$
$$x + 3y = 10$$

11
$$x + 5y = 11$$
$$2x - 2y = 10$$

12
$$4x + 2y = 5$$
$$3x + 6y = 6$$

13
$$-2y = 0.5 - 2x$$
$$6x + 3y = 6$$

14
$$4x + y = 14$$
$$6x - 3y = 3$$

15
$$x + 3y = 6$$
$$2x - 9y = 7$$

16
$$10x - y = -2$$
$$-15x + 3y = 9$$

17
$$5x - 3y = -0.5$$
$$3x + 2y = 3.5$$

18
$$2x - 2y = 6$$
$$x - 5y = -5$$

19
$$x + y = 5$$
$$3x - 2y + 5 = 0$$

For each word problem in Questions **20** to **27**, use the information to construct a pair of simultaneous equations and then solve to find the unknown values.

20 Twice of a number added to three times another number gives 21. Find the numbers if the difference between the numbers is 3.

21 A snake can lay either white or brown eggs. Three white eggs and two brown eggs have a mass of 13 grams, while five white eggs and four brown eggs have a mass of 24 grams. Find the mass of a brown egg and of a white egg.

22 Thirty tickets were sold for a concert. Some tickets cost 60 cents each and the other tickets cost $1 each. If the total cost of all the tickets sold was $22, how many of the cheaper tickets were sold?

23 In three years' time a pet mouse will be as old as his owner was four years ago. Their present ages total 13 years. Find the ages of both the mouse and the owner now.

24 A wallet containing $40 has three times as many $1 notes as $5 notes. Find the number of each note in the wallet.

25 A man is currently four times as old as his son. Six years ago, the man was ten times as old as his son. Find their current ages.

26 Magazines cost $\$m$ each and newspapers cost $\$n$ each. One magazine costs $\$2.55$ more than one newspaper. The cost of two magazines is the same as the cost of five newspapers.

    a Write down two equations in m and n to show this information.

    b Find the values of m and n.

DISCUSSION 2

Is every pair of linear equations simultaneous?

How could you tell?

---

27 Solve each pair of simultaneous equations using the method of your choice. Remember to check your solutions.

    a $2x^2 + 3y = 8$, $x - y = 7$

    b $x^2 + 4y = 7$, $2x + 3y = -6$

    c $2x^2 + y = 12$, $2x - y = 8$

    d $3x^2 + 6y = 6$, $2x - 2y = \dfrac{1}{2}$

8.3 Representing linear inequalities on a number line

A **linear inequality** uses an inequality symbol to compare two (or more) linear expressions.

For example, $2x < 12$ means '$2x$ is less than 12'.

You can represent linear inequalities with one variable on a number line.

You use open circles to represent strict inequalities.

$<$ $\longleftarrow\!\circ$

$>$ $\circ\!\longrightarrow$

You use closed circles to represent inclusive inequalities.

$\leqslant$ $\longleftarrow\!\bullet$

$\geqslant$ $\bullet\!\longrightarrow$

> **MATHEMATICAL CONNECTIONS**
>
> You used the inequality symbols in Chapter 2.

WORKED EXAMPLE 8

Represent $-4 \leqslant x < 1$ on a number line.

Answer

The inequality $-4 \leqslant x < 1$ means that 'x is greater than or equal to -4 and x is also less than 1'.

Use a closed circle to represent the left inclusive inequality.

Use an open circle to represent the right strict inequality.

You can also interpret inequalities that are represented on a number line.

WORKED EXAMPLE 9

Represent $x \leqslant 3$ on a number line.

Answer

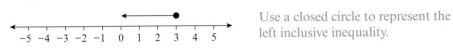

Use a closed circle to represent the left inclusive inequality.

Exercise 8.3

1   Represent the following inequalities on number lines.

  a $x < 1$ b $x > -4$ c $x \leqslant 2$

  d $x \geqslant 7$ e $-1 < x \leqslant 6$ f $-2 \geqslant x \geqslant -3$

  g $x > -2$ h $2 < x \leqslant 5$

2   Write down the inequality represented by each number line.

  a
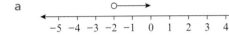

  b

  c

  d

  e

3   Determine which of the inequalities from Question **1** would contain the point $x = -1$.

8.4 Representing inequalities graphically

In Section 8.3, you represented linear inequalities with one variable on a number line.

You can represent inequalities in two variables graphically.

You use broken lines for strict inequalities ($<$ and $>$).

You use solid lines for inclusive inequalities ($\leqslant$ and $\geqslant$).

In this course you will be expected to shade unwanted regions.

TIP

In some other books, you may see unwanted regions left unshaded.

MATHEMATICAL CONNECTIONS

You will learn more about graphing equations in Chapters 11 and 14.

WORKED EXAMPLE 10

On the same pair of axes, plot the following inequalities and leave unshaded the region that satisfies all of these inequalities simultaneously.

$y \leqslant 4x$, $y \geqslant 3$, $x + y < 5$

Answer

Draw the lines:

$y = 4x$	Use a solid line because the inequality $y \leqslant 4x$ is an inclusive inequality.
$y = 3$	Use a solid line because the inequality $y \geqslant 3$ is an inclusive inequality.
$x + y = 5$	Use a broken line because the inequality $x + y < 5$ is a strict inequality.

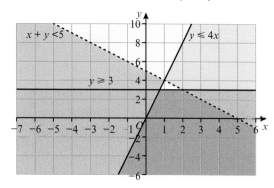

Remember to leave the required region unshaded.

You can also list inequalities that define a given region.

WORKED EXAMPLE 11

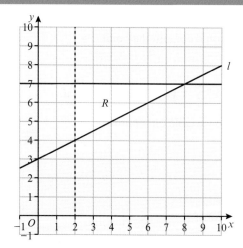

a Find the equation of the line l shown on the graph.

b Write down three inequalities that define the region R.

CONTINUED

Answers

a The line *l* intersects the *y*-axis at 3 and has a gradient $\frac{1}{2}$.

So the equation of *l* is $y = \frac{1}{2}x + 3$

b The required region in the diagram is above the line *l*.

The line *l* is drawn with a solid line, so it is an inclusive inequality.

The inequality represented by the line *l* is $y \geqslant \frac{1}{2}x + 3$

The required region is to the right of the vertical line with equation $x = 2$.
This is a broken line, so it represents a strict inequality.
The inequality represented by this line is $x > 2$.
The required region is below the horizontal line with equation $y = 7$.
This is a solid line, so it represents an inclusive inequality.
The inequality represented by this line is $y \leqslant 7$.
The complete list of inequalities represented by the unshaded region is:

$y \geqslant \frac{1}{2}x + 3, \; x > 2, \; y \leqslant 7$

MATHEMATICAL CONNECTIONS

You will learn how to find the equation of a straight line in Chapter 14.

MATHEMATICS IN CONTEXT

Inequalities can be used to solve 'optimisation problems', which is when you are looking for the best solution to a problem. These occur in areas such as agriculture and manufacturing where variables such as cost can be minimised to produce the most profit.

Representing inequalities on a graphic display calculator

You can also use your graphic display calculator to solve inequalities. Notice that the area required is the shaded area when using a graphic display calculator.

WORKED EXAMPLE 12

Use your graphic display calculator to find the area represented graphically by $3x < 2x + 7$.

Answer

1 Select **Graph** from the main menu. The graph function is highlighted in the following image.

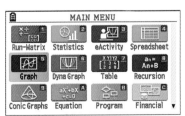

CONTINUED

The following screen opens.

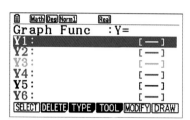

2 Press **F3** and then **F6** to select the inequality sign required for each graph and then enter the equations.

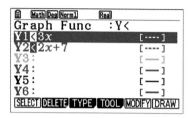

3 Press **SHIFT** **MENU** to change the setup to **Intersect**, which will show only the area where all inequalities are satisfied.

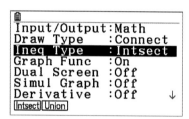

4 Press **EXIT** and then **F6** to draw the graph.

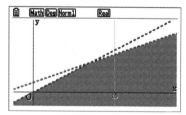

The area required is shaded in blue.

WORKED EXAMPLE 13

Use your graphic display calculator to find the area represented graphically by $3 < 3x - 8 < 14$.

Answer

1   Select **Graph** from the main menu. The graph function is highlighted in the following image.

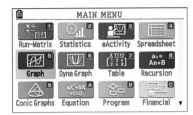

The following screen opens.

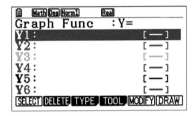

2   Press **F3** and then **F6** to select the inequality sign required for each graph and then enter the equations.

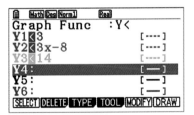

3   Press SHIFT MENU to change the setup to **Intersect**, which will show only the area where all inequalities are satisfied.

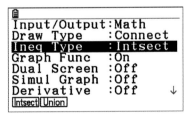

CONTINUED

4   Press **EXIT** and then **F6** to draw the graph.

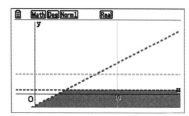

The area required is shaded in blue.

Exercise 8.4

1   Represent each set of inequalities graphically. Leave the required region unshaded.

   a $y > 3x + 2$, $x + y < 6$, $x < 0$

   b $y < x + 2$, $2x - y > 1$, $y \geqslant 3$

   c $y < -x + 3$, $x < -1$, $y \geqslant -1$

2   List the inequalities that describe the region left unshaded in each diagram.

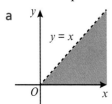 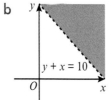 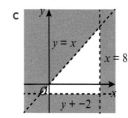 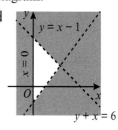

   Check your answers using your graphic display calculator.

3   Give examples of points, for each of the diagrams, that lie in the unshaded regions.

8.5 Proportion

Direct proportion

Two quantities x and y are in **direct proportion** if, as one quantity increases or decreases, the other quantity increases or decreases in the same ratio.

You say that 'y is directly proportional to x'.

You can use the mathematical symbol to write this as $y \propto x$

You can replace the symbol '$\propto$' with '$= k$' where k is called the constant of proportionality.

So, you can write $y = kx$

You can then use given information to find the value of k so that you can write a relationship linking the two variables.

Direct proportionality occurs in many real-life situations.

WORKED EXAMPLE 14

Distance travelled by a car is directly proportional to fuel consumption. A person who travels 15 km by car daily from their office to their home has a consumption of around 2 litres of gas.

Find the constant of proportionality.

Answer

$d \propto c$	Write the statement of proportionality using the symbol $\propto$. The question tells you that d is proportional to the c.
$d = kc$	Replace the symbol $\propto$ with $= k$.
$15 = k \times 2$	Substitute the values $x = 16$ and $y = 3$ to find the value of k.
$k = 7.5$	

Proportion is not always linear.

Sometimes one quantity is in direct proportion with, for example, the square, or square root, or cube of another quantity.

WORKED EXAMPLE 15

y is proportional to the square root of x.

a Given that $y = 3$ when x is 16, write a relationship linking y to x.

b Use your relationship from part **a** to find the value of y when $x = 4$.

Answers

a

$y \propto \sqrt{x}$	Write the statement of proportionality using the symbol $\propto$. The question tells you that y is proportional to the square root of x.
$y = k\sqrt{x}$	Replace the symbol $\propto$ with $= k$.
$3 = k\sqrt{16}$	Substitute the values $x = 16$ and $y = 3$ to find the value of k.
$k = \dfrac{3}{4}$	

Substitute the value of k to give the relationship linking y to x:

$$y = \frac{3}{4}\sqrt{x}$$

b To find the value of y when $x = 4$, substitute $x = 4$ into your equation:

$$y = \frac{3}{4}\sqrt{4}$$

$$y = \frac{3}{2} = 1.5$$

Inverse proportion

Inverse proportion is when one quantity increases while the other quantity decreases in the same ratio.

You say that 'y is inversely proportional to x' or 'y and x are in inverse proportion'.

You can use the mathematical symbol to write this as $y \propto \dfrac{1}{x}$

You can replace the symbol '$\propto$' with '$= k$' where k is called the constant of proportionality.

So, you can write $y = \dfrac{k}{x}$

You can then use given information to find the value of k so that you can write a relationship linking the two variables.

WORKED EXAMPLE 16

It takes 12 workers 4 days to build a wall.

How long would it take 8 workers?

Answer

The relationship is inversely proportional as fewer workers will take longer to build the wall.

Take y to be the number or workers and x to be the number of days.

You can write $12 = \dfrac{k}{4}$

The value of $k = 12 \times 4 = 48$

When the number of workers is 8, you can write $8 = \dfrac{48}{x}$

$x = 6$, so it will take 6 days to build the wall.

WORKED EXAMPLE 17

y is inversely proportional to x^3 and when x is 4, $y = 3$.
Find the value of y when $x = 5$.

Answer

$y \propto \dfrac{1}{x^3}$ means that $y = \dfrac{k}{x^3}$

When $y = 3$, $x = 4$

$3 = \dfrac{k}{64}$

$k = 192$

When $x = 5$, $y = \dfrac{192}{5}$

$y = 38.4$

Direct and inverse proportion are variation models. To determine whether you should use direct or inverse proportion to solve a problem, consider whether one quantity required is increasing or decreasing in relation to the other.

Exercise 8.5

1 Rewrite each statement in words.

  a $S \propto R$ b $X \propto s^2$ c $y \propto \sqrt{x}$

  d $Q \propto 3a^3$ e $s \propto \dfrac{1}{t^2}$ f $t \propto \dfrac{1}{\sqrt{q}}$

2 Rewrite each statement using a constant of proportionality k instead of $\propto$.

  a $S \propto R$ b $X \propto s^2$ c $y \propto \sqrt{x}$

  d $Q \propto 3a^3$ e $s \propto \dfrac{1}{t^2}$ f $t \propto \dfrac{1}{\sqrt{q}}$

3 State the type of proportionality and solve the following problems.

  a If 6 workers take 3 days to build a wall, how long will 1 worker take?

  b The distance between towns A and B is three times the distance between towns B and C. If the distance between B and C is 16 miles, what is the distance between towns A and B?

4 y is directly proportional to t. If $y = 5$ when $t = 2$, calculate:

  a the value of y when $t = 1$

  b the value of t when $y = 3$.

5 A is directly proportional to r^2. If $A = 12$ when $r = 2$, calculate:

  a the value of A when $r = 5$

  b the value of r when $A = 48$.

6 e is inversely proportional to $-(y +2)$. If $e = 12$ when $y = 4$, find:

  a e when $y = 6$

  b y when $e = 0.5$.

7 a is directly proportional to $-(x - 3)$. If $a= 10$ when $x = 6$, find:

  a a when $x = 9$

  b x when $a = 0.5$.

8 The volume V of a given mass of gas varies inversely as the pressure P. When $V = 5\,m^3$, $P = 500\,N/m^2$.

  a Find the volume when the pressure is $100\,N/m^2$.

  b Find the pressure when the volume is $20\,m^3$.

9 The volume of a gas varies inversely as the pressure. If the volume is $120\,cm^3$ under pressure of $15\,kg/cm^2$, what is the required pressure to have a volume of $270\,cm^3$?

PEER ASSESSMENT

Explain to a partner the difference between inverse and direct proportion.

REFLECTION

Think about the work you have done on inequalities in this chapter. What is the same and what is different about working with equations and inequalities?

SUMMARY

Are you able to... ?
construct equations and formulae
construct and solve simultaneous linear equations
represent, solve and interpret linear inequalities
change the subject of formulae
construct linear inequalities
solve inequalities using a graphic display calculator
represent linear inequalities in two variables graphically
list inequalities that define a given region
express direct and inverse proportion in algebraic terms
identify the best variation model for given data.

Past paper questions

1   This formula can be used to change a temperature in degrees Celsius, C, to a temperature in degrees Fahrenheit, F.

$$F = 2C + 30$$

a   Find the value of F when

i $C = 0$,

.... [1]

ii $C = 120$.

.... [1]

b   Find the value of C when $F = 350$.

.... [2]

c   Find the value of C when $F = C$.

.... [2]

d   Rearrange the formula to make C the subject.
$$F = 2C + 30$$

$C =$ .... [2]

Cambridge IGCSE International Mathematics 0607 Paper 31 Q4 June 2019

2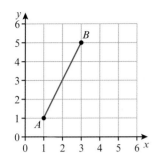

The diagram shows two points, A and B, plotted on a 1 cm² grid.

a   Write down the co-ordinates of point A and the co-ordinates of point B.

A (........................, ...….............)

B (........................, ...)   [2]

b   Calculate the length of AB.

.... cm   [2]

c   Find the co-ordinates of the midpoint of AB.

(........................, ...)   [1]

d   Find the gradient of AB.

....   [2]

e   Write down the equation of the line parallel to AB passing through $(0, 3)$.

y = ...   [2]

Cambridge IGCSE International Mathematics 0607 Paper 31 Q4 November 2019

3   Solve the simultaneous equations.

$3x + 2y = 4$

$2x - 3y = 7$

x = ...

y = ...   [4]

Cambridge IGCSE International Mathematics 0607 Paper 21 Q14 November 2018

> Chapter 9

Symmetry, congruency and similarity

IN THIS CHAPTER YOU WILL:

- recognise line symmetry in two dimensions
- recognise order of rotational symmetry in two dimensions
- use and interpret the terms similar and congruent
- calculate lengths of similar shapes

> recognise symmetry properties of prisms, cylinders, pyramids and cones

> use the relationship between lengths and areas of similar shapes

> use the relationship between lengths, surface areas and volumes of similar solids

> solve problems involving similarity.

GETTING STARTED

1 Evaluate x.

a $\dfrac{x}{4} = \dfrac{2}{3}$ b $\left(\dfrac{2}{5}\right)^2 = \dfrac{x}{4}$ c $\left(\dfrac{x}{5}\right)^2 = \dfrac{1}{4}$

2 Find the unknown angles x and y.

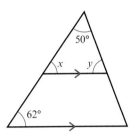

MATHEMATICAL CONNECTIONS

You studied angles on parallel lines and in triangles in Chapters 4 and 5.

9.1 Line and rotational symmetry

Symmetry plays an important role in real life. You can observe symmetry everywhere you go, in architecture, art and nature.

Line symmetry in two dimensions

You can test the **line symmetry** of a shape about a line by folding the shape along that line. If the shape is symmetrical about that line, the part to one side of the line will fit exactly onto the part to the other side of the line and vice versa. You can also see line symmetry as a reflection. For example, in the diagram, you can reflect the left side of the tree along the dotted line onto the right side.

 =  +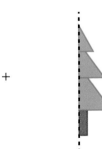

A **line of symmetry** is a straight line that divides a shape into two identical halves. The two halves are reflections of each other in the line of symmetry.

A shape may have more than one line of symmetry.

For example, in this diagram the square has four lines of symmetry, the rectangle has two lines of symmetry and the star has five lines of symmetry.

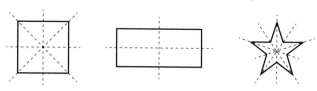

WORKED EXAMPLE 1

How many lines of symmetry does each shape have?

a   b   c

Answers

To find the lines of symmetry, look for lines of reflection. This is a line in which one half of the shape looks like a reflection of the other half of the shape.

a   This shape has two lines of symmetry.

b   This shape has four lines of symmetry.

CONTINUED

c This shape
   has eight lines
   of symmetry.

DISCUSSION 1

How many lines of symmetry does a parallelogram have?
What about a trapezium?

Discuss with a partner.

WORKED EXAMPLE 2

Copy the diagrams. Make each of your diagrams symmetrical about the dotted line(s).

a

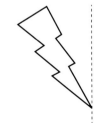

b

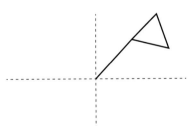

CONTINUED

Answers

a   Reflect the shape onto the other side of the dotted line.

Combine the two halves.

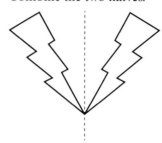

b   There are two lines of symmetry in this diagram. Look at one line of symmetry at a time.

Start with the vertical line of symmetry.

Reflect the shape onto the left side of the dotted line.

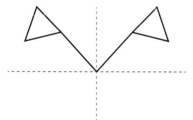

Then look at the horizontal line of symmetry.

Reflect the top image onto the underside of the horizontal line.

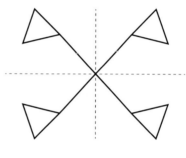

Rotational symmetry in two dimensions

A shape that can be rotated about a point at its centre (centre of rotation) through an angle other than 360° and look exactly the same (no change in size, shape and orientation) has rotational symmetry about that point.

The order of rotational symmetry of a shape is the number of times you see the same shape as it is rotated through 360°.

If you only see the same shape after it has been fully rotated through 360°, the order of rotational symmetry is 1 and the shape has no rotational symmetry.

TIP

Every shape has an order of rotational symmetry of at least 1.

WORKED EXAMPLE 3

What is the order of rotational symmetry of each shape when rotated about the centre of the shape?

a    b Z   c STOP

Answers

a

This is the starting point. Put a dot on one of the vertices and observe what happens to this dot as you rotate the shape. Do not count the starting position.

This is the shape after rotating through 120°. You see the same shape once.

This is the shape after rotating through 240°. You see the same shape a second time.

The shape returns to its starting position after rotating through 360°. This is the third time you see the shape.

You see the same shape three times as you rotate through 360°.

Hence, the shape has order of rotational symmetry 3.

b

This is the starting point. Put a dot on the top of the letter Z and observe what happens to this dot as you rotate it. Do not count the starting position.

This is the shape after rotating through 180°. You see the same shape once.

This is the shape after rotating through 360°. You see the same shape a second time.

Hence, the shape has order of rotational symmetry 2.

CONTINUED

c

This is the starting point. Put a dot on the top of the shape and observe what happens to this dot as you rotate the shape. Do not count the starting position.

This is the shape after rotating through 180°. You do **not** see the same shape here because the letters are now upside down.

This is the shape after rotating through 360°. You see the same shape once.

Hence the shape has order of rotational symmetry 1.

From Worked example 3, notice that the angle you rotate through to see the same shape is equal to $\dfrac{360°}{\text{order of rotational symmetry}}$

You will use this result in Worked example 4.

WORKED EXAMPLE 4

The diagram shows a regular hexagon inside a circle.

On separate copies of the diagram:

a   Shade three segments of the circle so that the shaded diagram has rotational symmetry of order 3.

b   Shade two segments of the circle so that the shaded diagram has rotational symmetry of order 2.

MATHEMATICAL CONNECTIONS

You will learn about the different parts of a circle in Chapter 16.

Answers

a   To have rotational symmetry of order 3, you should see the same shape when you rotate through every $\dfrac{360°}{3} = 120°$.

The hexagon is made up of six equilateral triangles. Each equilateral triangle has an angle of 60°.

Rotating through 120° means rotating through two equilateral triangles.

MATHEMATICAL CONNECTIONS

You learnt that an equilateral triangle has interior angles of 60° in Chapter 5.

CONTINUED

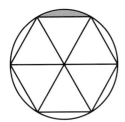

Start by marking the starting position. Shade the first segment on the top.

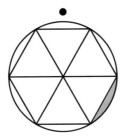

Rotate through 120° about the centre of the hexagon.

The black dot marks the position where the shaded segment was in the previous diagram.

Note where the shaded segment is now.

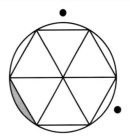

Rotate through another 120° (240° in total).

Note where the shaded segment has moved to now.

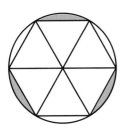

Shade the three segments together to get this diagram with rotational symmetry of order 3.

b To have rotational symmetry of order 2, you should see the same shape when you rotate through every $\dfrac{360°}{2} = 180°$.

Repeat the steps in part **a** with a rotation of 180°.

Start by marking the starting position. Shade the first segment on the top.

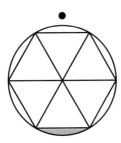

Rotate through 180°.

The black dot marks the position where the shaded segment was in the previous diagram. Note where the shaded segment is now.

This is the final diagram which has rotational symmetry of order 2.

SELF ASSESSMENT

In Worked example 4, how many lines of symmetry do the resultant diagrams in parts **a** and **b** have?

You will now investigate the symmetry of regular polygons.

MATHEMATICAL CONNECTIONS

You learnt about properties of polygons in Chapter 5.

INVESTIGATION 1

Copy and complete this table. Find the number of lines of symmetry and the order of rotational symmetry for these regular polygons.

Polygon	n, number of sides	Number of lines of symmetry	Order of rotational symmetry	Smallest angle of rotational symmetry
Triangle	3			
Square	4			
Pentagon	5			
Hexagon	6			
	7			
	8			
	9			
	10			

What can you conclude about the number of lines of symmetry and the order of rotational symmetry of a regular polygon?

A regular polygon of n sides, has n lines of symmetry and a rotational symmetry of order n.

The smallest angle of rotational symmetry is $\dfrac{360°}{n}$.

Exercise 9.1

1   For each diagram, state the number of lines of symmetry and the order of rotational symmetry.

a   b      c

d   e   f MOW

g 800   h    i

2   Copy the diagram three times. On your separate
    diagrams, shade parts so that the resulting
    diagram has rotational symmetry of:

    a   order 2

    b   order 3

    c   order 6.

3   Copy the diagram twice. On your separate
    diagrams, add one square to the diagram
    so that the resulting diagram has:

    a   one line of symmetry

    b   rotational symmetry of order 2.

4   In the diagram, *AB = BC*. Copy and
    complete the diagram to make a quadrilateral
    ABCD with two lines of symmetry and a
    rotational symmetry of order 4.
    Name the quadrilateral *ABCD*.

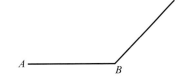

5   Copy and complete the diagram to
    make a quadrilateral *PQRS* which
    has *PR* as its line of symmetry.
    Name the quadrilateral *PQRS*.

6   Copy this square grid twice.

    On your separate diagrams, shade three
    more squares so that the completed
    square grid has:

    a   two lines of symmetry

    b   rotational symmetry of order 4.

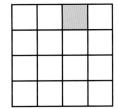

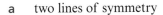

7 Copy this square grid twice.

On your separate diagrams, shade:

a one more square so that the completed square grid has one line of symmetry

b two more squares so that the completed square grid has rotational symmetry of order 2.

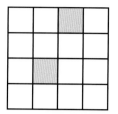

8 Copy this diagram twice.

a On one of your diagrams shade two more small squares so that the resulting diagram has exactly one line of symmetry.

b On your other diagram shade two more small squares so that the resulting diagram has rotational symmetry of order 2.

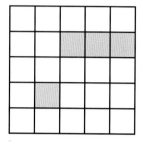

PEER ASSESSMENT

Design your own symmetry question to test a partner.

If you like, you can adapt one of the questions in Exercise 9.1.

For example, in Question **2**, what other shapes could you use other than a hexagon?

9.2 Congruency

Congruent triangles have the same shape and same size (identical).

In mathematics, you can represent congruency by using the notation '$\equiv$'.

For example, if triangles ABC and PQR are congruent, you can write the statement of congruency:

triangle $ABC \equiv$ triangle PQR

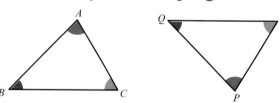

The order in which you write the statement of congruency is significant.

The statement triangle $ABC \equiv$ triangle PQR means that:

angle A = angle P

angle B = angle Q

angle C = angle R

triangle $ABC \equiv$ triangle PQR

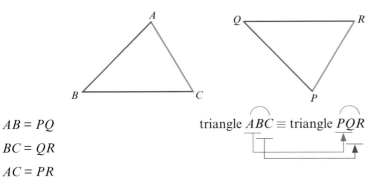

$AB = PQ$

$BC = QR$

$AC = PR$

triangle $\overset{\frown}{ABC} \equiv$ triangle $\overset{\frown}{PQR}$

When you write a statement of congruence, you must arrange the letters in the correct order to show:

1   the dimensions of their corresponding sides are **equal** and

2   each of their corresponding interior angles are **equal**.

WORKED EXAMPLE 5

In the diagram, $ABCD$ is congruent to $PQRS$.

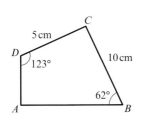
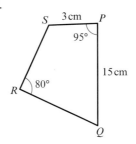

a   Write down the length of side:

   i AB ii AD iii RS iv QR.

b   Write down the size of angle:

   i BAD ii BCD iii PQR iv PSR.

Answers

a   For sides, $ABCD$ is congruent to $PQRS$

Colour coding the sides you have:

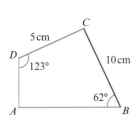
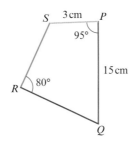

CONTINUED

    i $AB = PQ = 15\,cm$

    ii $AD = PS = 3\,cm$

    iii $RS = CD = 5\,cm$

    iv $QR = BC = 10\,cm$

b   For angles, $ABCD$ is congruent to $PQRS$

Colour coding the angles you have:

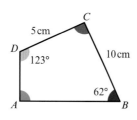
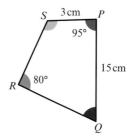

    i   angle BAD = angle $QPS = 95°$

    ii   angle BCD = angle $QRS = 80°$

    iii angle PQR = angle $ABC = 62°$

    iv angle PSR = angle $ADC = 123°$

Exercise 9.2

1   Given that $DEFGH$ is congruent to $LMNOP$, copy and complete the following statements.

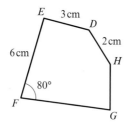
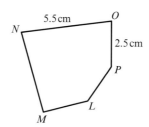

a $DE = LM = \underline{\hspace{2cm}}$ cm

b $EF = \underline{\hspace{2cm}} = \underline{\hspace{2cm}}$ cm

c $\underline{\hspace{1.5cm}} = NO = \underline{\hspace{2cm}}$ cm

d $\underline{\hspace{1.5cm}} = OP = \underline{\hspace{2cm}}$ cm

e $DH = \underline{\hspace{2cm}} = \underline{\hspace{2cm}}$ cm

f   Angle EFG = angle $\underline{\hspace{2cm}} = \underline{\hspace{2cm}}$ °

2 *ABCD* is congruent to *PQRS*. Find the values of k, u, x, y and z.

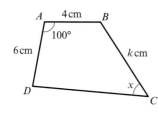
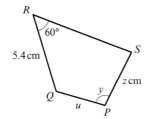

3 *ABCD* is congruent to *WXYZ*.

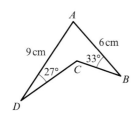
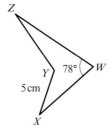

Find:
a   the length of *BC*
b   the length of *WZ*
c   angle *BAD*
d   the reflex angle *BCD*.

4 In the diagram, triangle *PQR* is congruent to triangle *SUT*.

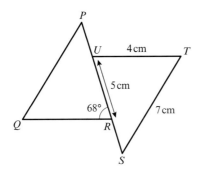

Find:
a   angle *STU*
b   length *QR*
c   length *PR*
d   length *PU*.

9.3 Similarity

In Section 9.2 you identified congruent figures that have the same shape and size.

Could you identify a pair of figures that have the same shape but different sizes?

In mathematics, figures that have the same shape but different sizes are known as similar figures. The dimensions of similar figures are proportionate to each other.

MATHEMATICS IN CONTEXT

You frequently see similar figures in everyday life. For example, a model airplane is similar to its real counterpart and a photograph is similar to the real image it captures.

Similar triangles

You can represent similar triangles by using a similarity statement, for example:

triangle ABC is similar to triangle XYZ

Since similar triangles have the same shape, for each angle in one triangle, there is an angle of equal size in the other triangle. As you saw with the statement of congruency, the order in which the triangles are labelled in the similarity statement tells you which angles are equal.

If triangle ABC is similar to triangle XYZ, then:

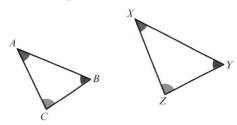

  angle A = angle X

  angle B = angle Y

  angle C = angle Z

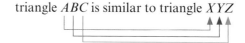

triangle ABC is similar to triangle XYZ

Unlike with congruency, similar triangles are **not** the same size, so you cannot say that the lengths of corresponding sides are equal.

However, similar objects are proportionate to each other, so the lengths of corresponding sides are in the same ratio.

For example, for the similar triangles ABC and XYZ, if triangle XYZ is twice the size of triangle ABC, then each side of triangle XYZ will be twice the size of the corresponding side in triangle ABC.

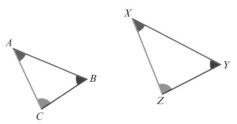

Looking at the similarity statement:

triangle ABC is similar to triangle XYZ

Observe that AB and XY correspond, BC and YZ correspond, AC and XZ correspond.

So, if triangle XYZ is twice the size of triangle ABC, then $\dfrac{XY}{AB} = \dfrac{YZ}{BC} = \dfrac{XZ}{AC} = 2$

In general:

If triangle ABC is similar to triangle XYZ such that triangle XYZ is k times the size of triangle ABC, then $\dfrac{XY}{AB} = \dfrac{YZ}{BC} = \dfrac{XZ}{AC} = k$

MATHEMATICAL CONNECTIONS

You learnt about ratio and proportion in Chapter 3. You will learn about enlargements in Chapter 17 on vectors and transformations.

DISCUSSION 2

The diagrams show three pairs of triangles.

a

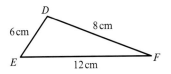 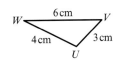

b

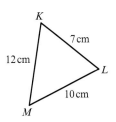 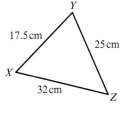

c

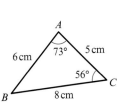 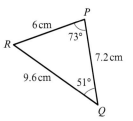

Is triangle ABC similar to triangle PQR?

Is triangle DEF similar to triangle UVW?

Is triangle KLM similar to triangle XYZ?

Discuss in pairs and explain your answers.

Similar shapes

When you name similar shapes, you must arrange the letters in the correct order to show:

1   each of their corresponding interior angles are **equal** and

2   the lengths of their corresponding sides are **in the same ratio**.

Worked example 8 shows how this rule can be generalised to all similar shapes.

WORKED EXAMPLE 6

In the diagram, *ABCDE* is similar to *PQRST*. Find:

a   angle *QRS*

b   length *PT*

c   length *BC*.

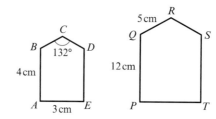

Answers

a   According to the order of the similarity statement,

ABCDE is similar to *PQRST*

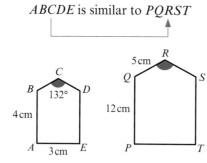

angle *QRS* = angle *BCD*

so, angle *QRS* = 132°

You need to find corresponding sides and find the ratio of their lengths to answer parts **b** and **c**.

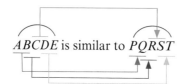

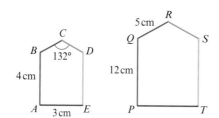

$$\frac{PQ}{AB} = \frac{QR}{BC} = \frac{RS}{CD} = \frac{ST}{DE} = \frac{PT}{AE} = k$$

The lengths of *AB* and *PQ* are given in the diagram.

$\frac{PQ}{AB} = \frac{12}{4} = 3$, hence $k = 3$

CONTINUED

b $\dfrac{PT}{AE} = 3$

$\dfrac{PT}{3} = 3$

$PT = 3 \times 3$

$\quad = 9\,\text{cm}$

c $\dfrac{QR}{BC} = 3$

$\dfrac{5}{BC} = 3$

$3BC = 5$

$BC = \dfrac{5}{3}\,\text{cm}$

You can also apply the concept of similar shapes to three-dimensional solids. You will not be given the similarity statement, but it is not difficult to recognise corresponding sides. Worked example 9 shows the application of similarity to finding missing lengths in three-dimensional solids.

WORKED EXAMPLE 7

The diagram shows two similar tables. Find the length of the unknown sides x and y.

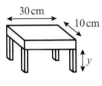
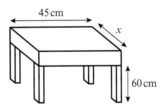

Answer

The labelled measurements give you the length, width and height of the tables:

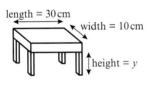
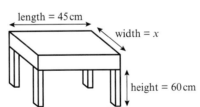

By taking the ratio of the lengths:

$$\dfrac{\text{length of bigger table}}{\text{length of smaller table}} = \dfrac{45}{30} = \dfrac{3}{2}$$

CONTINUED

This tells you that the bigger table is $\frac{3}{2}$ times the size of the smaller table. Hence,

$$\frac{\text{width of bigger table}}{\text{width of bigger table}} = \frac{3}{2}$$

$$\frac{x}{10} = \frac{3}{2}$$

$$x = \frac{3}{2} \times 10$$

$$= 15 \, \text{cm}$$

$$\frac{\text{height of bigger table}}{\text{height of bigger table}} = \frac{3}{2}$$

$$\frac{60}{y} = \frac{3}{2}$$

$$3y = 2 \times 60 = 120$$

$$y = \frac{120}{3}$$

$$= 40 \, \text{cm}$$

Exercise 9.3

1   Given that triangle ABC is similar to triangle PQR, find the value of the unknowns in each diagram.

a

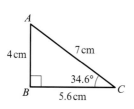

b

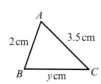

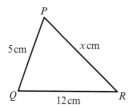

c

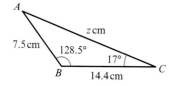

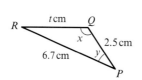

2 Given that *ABCD* is similar to *PQRS*, find the value of the unknowns in each diagram.

a

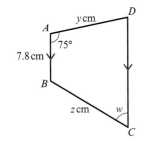

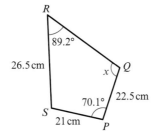

b

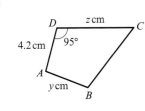

c

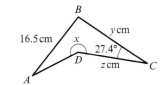

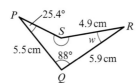

3 The two figures shown are similar. The arc length of the smaller figure is 13 cm. Find the arc length, *x*, of the bigger figure.

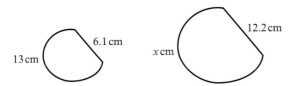

4 *ABCD* is similar to *APQR*. Find the values of *x* and of *y*.

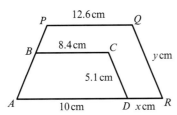

5 The two pentagons are similar. Find the value of *x*.

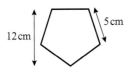

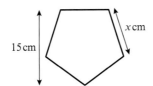

6   The diagram shows two similar cups. Find the height of the bigger cup.

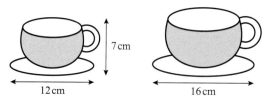

7   These two toy buses are similar. Find the length of the smaller toy bus.

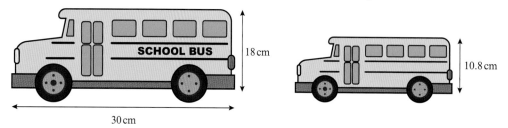

8   Two similar bottles are shown. Copy and complete the table.

Radius of the base	18 cm	15 cm
Height	60 cm	
Circumference of the cover		14 cm

REFLECTION

What are the conditions for two figures to be congruent?

What are the conditions for two figures to be similar?

What are the differences between the conditions for congruent figures and similar figures?

9.4 Area and volume of similar shapes

You have already seen that when two objects are geometrically similar their size is proportionate to each other.

You will now look at how the area and volume of similar objects relate to each other.

DISCUSSION 3

If an object is k times the size of another similar object, will the area of that object be k times the area of the object? What about the volume?

Discuss with a partner.

INVESTIGATION 2

Generalising the area of similar figures

a   In the diagram triangle ABC is similar to triangle PQR.

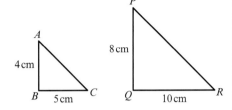

Copy and complete these ratio calculations:

$$\frac{\text{height of triangle } ABC}{\text{height of triangle } PQR} =$$

$$\frac{\text{base of triangle } ABC}{\text{base of triangle } PQR} =$$

$$\frac{\text{area of triangle } ABC}{\text{area of triangle } PQR} =$$

b   The diagram shows two similar semicircles, A and B.

 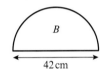

i   What is the ratio of the radius of A to the radius of B?

ii   By taking $\pi = \frac{22}{7}$, what is the ratio of the area of A to the area of B?

c   What do you observe about the ratio of the areas of similar figures? Write down your **conjecture** (a statement that is yet to be proved).

d   Test your conjecture with two other pairs of similar geometrical shapes. Copy and complete this table:

Shapes	$\dfrac{l_1}{l_2}$	$\dfrac{A_1}{A_2}$

e   Copy and complete:

If figure A is similar to figure B and the length of A is k times the length of B, then

$$\frac{\text{area of figure } A}{\text{area of figure } B} =$$

MATHEMATICAL CONNECTIONS

You will learn how to find the area of triangles and semicircles in Chapter 12. The formulas for the areas of these shapes will be very useful in Investigation 2.

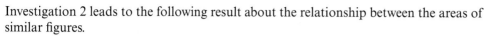

Investigation 2 leads to the following result about the relationship between the areas of similar figures.

$$\frac{\text{Area of figure 1}}{\text{Area of figure 2}} = \left(\frac{\text{length of } A}{\text{length of } B}\right)^2$$

This conclusion can be generalised as:

If two figures are similar, then $\dfrac{A_1}{A_2} = \left(\dfrac{l_1}{l_2}\right)^2$

WORKED EXAMPLE 8

In the diagram, $ABCDE$ is similar to $PQRST$.

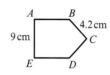 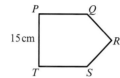

Find:

a the length of QR

b the ratio of the area of $ABCDE$ to the area of $PQRST$.

Answers

a Based on the statement $ABCDE$ is similar to $PQRST$, AE corresponds with PT and BC corresponds with QR.

The ratio of $\dfrac{QR}{BC}$ is equal to $\dfrac{PT}{AE}$, so

$$\frac{QR}{4.2} = \frac{15}{9}$$

$$QR = \frac{15}{9} \times 4.2 = 7$$

b The ratio of the area of similar figures satisfies $\dfrac{A_1}{A_2} = \left(\dfrac{l_1}{l_2}\right)^2$, so

$$\frac{\text{area of } ABCDE}{\text{area of } PQRST} = \left(\frac{9}{15}\right)^2 = \left(\frac{3}{5}\right)^2 = \frac{9}{25}$$

> **TIP**
>
> Remember that the statement of similarity tells you the order of corresponding sides.

INVESTIGATION 3

Generalising the volume of similar figures

The diagram shows two similar cubes.

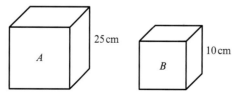

> **MATHEMATICAL CONNECTIONS**
>
> You will learn how to find the volume of prisms, pyramids and spheres in Chapter 12. The formulas for the volumes of these solids will be very useful in Investigation 3.

CONTINUED

a Write down the ratio of the length of cube A to the length of cube B.

b Find the ratio of the volume of cube A to the volume of B.

c Based on your answer to part **b**, write down a conjecture on the ratio of the volumes of similar solids.

d Test out your conjecture from part **c** using two more pairs of geometrically similar solids. (For example, cuboids, cylinders, cones, pyramids, spheres, etc.)

Copy and complete this table:

Solids	$\dfrac{l_1}{l_2}$	$\dfrac{V_1}{V_2}$

e If solid A is similar to solid B and the length of A is k times the size of B, then

$$\frac{\text{volume of solid } A}{\text{volume of solid } B} =$$

Investigation 3 leads to the following result about the relationship between the volumes of similar figures.

$$\frac{\text{Volume of figure 1}}{\text{Volume of figure 2}} = \left(\frac{\text{length of } A}{\text{length of } B}\right)^3$$

This conclusion can be generalised as:

If two solids are similar, then $\dfrac{V_1}{V_2} = \left(\dfrac{l_1}{l_2}\right)^3$

> **TIP**
>
> You can compare any length such as the base, height, radius, circumference, etc.

WORKED EXAMPLE 9

Two solid cones are geometrically similar.
The height of one cone is 2.5 times the height of the other cone.

8 cm

a Given that the height of the smaller cone is 8 cm, find the height of the larger cone.

b Write down the ratio of the total surface area of the larger cone to the total surface area of the smaller cone.

c If the total surface area of the smaller cone is 120 cm², calculate the total surface area of the larger cone.

d Without calculating the volume, find the ratio of the volume of the larger cone to the volume of the smaller cone. Express your answer as a fraction.

CONTINUED

Answers

a Since the cones are similar, their heights are proportional to each other.
Height of larger cone = 2.5 × 8 = 20 cm

b $\dfrac{A_1}{A_2} = \left(\dfrac{l_1}{l_2}\right)^2$

$\dfrac{\text{Area of large cone}}{\text{Area of smaller cone}} = \left(\dfrac{2.5}{1}\right)^2 = \left(\dfrac{5}{2}\right)^2 = \dfrac{25}{4}$

Ratio of surface area of large cone to surface area of smaller cone = 25 : 4

c Total surface area of larger cone = $120 \times \dfrac{25}{4} = 750 \text{ cm}^2$

d Using the formula for the volume ratio of similar figures: $\dfrac{V_1}{V_2} = \left(\dfrac{l_1}{l_2}\right)^3$, you have

$\dfrac{\text{volume of large cone}}{\text{volume of smaller cone}} = \left(\dfrac{2.5}{1}\right)^3 = \left(\dfrac{5}{2}\right)^3 = \dfrac{125}{8}$

TIP

From the question you know that the height of the larger cone is 2.5 times the height of the smaller cone.

TIP

The area ratio of similar figures refers to any corresponding areas. You can use the ratio to find the base area, the curved surface area or even the total surface area. As long as you are comparing the same area for two similar figures, the formula is true.

WORKED EXAMPLE 10

The diagram shows two similar statues.
The smaller statue has a volume of 25 cm³
and the larger statue has a volume of 200 cm³.

a Find the ratio of the height of the smaller statue to the height of the larger statue. Leave your answer as a fraction.

b Given that the larger statue has a surface area of 400 cm², find the surface area of the smaller statue.

$V_1 = 25 \text{ cm}^3$ $V_2 = 200 \text{ cm}^3$

Answer

a The two statues are similar, hence $\dfrac{V_1}{V_2} = \left(\dfrac{l_1}{l_2}\right)^3$

Substitute the volumes of the two statues:

$\dfrac{25}{200} = \left(\dfrac{l_1}{l_2}\right)^3$ Taking the cube root of both sides.

$\dfrac{l_1}{l_2} = \sqrt[3]{\dfrac{25}{200}}$ Cancel the fraction to its simplest form before calculating the cube root.

$= \sqrt[3]{\dfrac{1}{8}}$

$= \dfrac{1}{2}$

Therefore, $\dfrac{\text{height of the smaller statue}}{\text{height of the bigger statue}} = \dfrac{h_1}{h_2} = \dfrac{1}{2}$

CONTINUED

b The formula for the ratio of the areas of similar figures is $\frac{A_1}{A_2} = \left(\frac{l_1}{l_2}\right)^2$

Since you have the ratio of the heights, you can rewrite the formula as

$\frac{A_1}{A_2} = \left(\frac{h_1}{h_2}\right)^2$, where $\frac{h_1}{h_2} = \frac{1}{2}$ from part **a**.

The larger statue has a surface area of $400\,\text{cm}^2$, so

$\frac{A_1}{400} = \left(\frac{1}{2}\right)^2$

$\frac{A_1}{400} = \frac{1}{4}$

$A_1 = \frac{1}{4} \times 400 = 100$

The surface area of the smaller statue is $100\,\text{cm}^2$.

Exercise 9.4

1 Each pair of figures are similar. Given the lengths of one side of the figures, find the unknown area.

a

4 cm

Area = ?

B

10 cm

Area = 125 cm²

b

27 cm

Area = 648 cm²

9 cm

Area = ?

c

14 cm

Area = ?

8 cm

Area = 56 cm²

2 Each pair of figures are similar. Given the areas of the figures, find the unknown sides.

a

3.5 cm

Area = 12 cm²

? cm

Area = 48 cm²

b

5.6 cm

Area = 150 cm²

? cm

Area = 24 cm²

c

15 cm

Area = 50 cm²

? cm

Area = 72 cm²

3   Each diagram shows a pair of similar solids. Given the lengths of one side of
     the solids, find the unknown volume.

a

Volume = ?   Volume = 54 cm³

b
    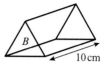

Volume = ?   Volume = 375 cm³

c

Volume = ?   Volume = 124 cm³

4   Each diagram shows a pair of similar solids. Given the volumes of the solids,
     find the unknown length.

a
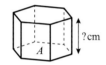

Volume = 168 cm³   Volume = 21 cm³

b
    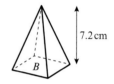

Volume = 40 cm³   Volume = 135 cm³

c

Volume = 625 cm³   Volume = 40 cm³

5   Given the surface areas of each pair of similar solids, find the unknown volume.

a

Area = 500 cm²   Area = 125 cm²
Volume = ?   Volume = 60 cm²

b
    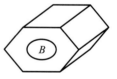

Area = 32 cm²   Area = 50 cm²
Volume = ?   Volume = 150 cm³

c

Area = 14 cm²
Volume = 51.2 cm³

6 A floorplan is drawn in the scale of 1 : 100.

 a The actual living room has a length of 3.8 m. Find the length of the living room on the floorplan in cm.

 b The bedroom has an area of 20 cm² on the floorplan. Find the actual area of the bedroom in m².

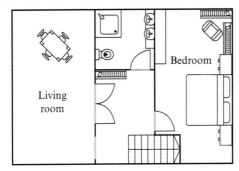

7 The two flasks shown are geometrically similar. The radii of the spherical bases of *A* and *B* are 10 cm and 25 cm respectively.

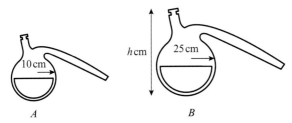

 a Given that the height of *B* is *h* cm, find the height of *A* in terms of *h*.

 b Find the ratio of the total surface area of *A* to the total surface area of *B*.

 c The flasks are filled with water. If *A* can hold 1.6 litres of water, what volume of water can *B* hold? Give your answer in litres.

8 The two conical flasks shown are geometrically similar.

 The height of the smaller flask is 13 cm and the height of the larger flask is 19.5 cm.

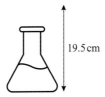

 a The diameter of the smaller flask is 5 cm. Find the diameter of the larger flask.

 b The larger flask has a volume of 270 cm³. Find the volume of the smaller flask.

9 The diagram shows three biscuit tins with circular lids. The three tins are geometrically similar. The heights of containers *A* and *C* are 12 cm and 28 cm respectively.

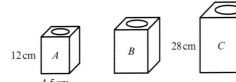

 a The width of tin *A* is 4.5 cm. Find the width of tin *C*.

 b The ratio of the area of the lid of tin *A* to the area of the lid of tin *B* is 9 : 25. Find the height of tin *B*.

 c Find the ratio of the volume of tin *B* to the volume of tin *C*.

SUMMARY

Are you able to... ?
recognise line symmetry in two dimensions
recognise order of rotational symmetry in two dimensions
how to use and interpret the terms similar and congruent
calculate lengths of similar shapes
recognise symmetry properties of prisms, cylinders, pyramids and cones
use the relationship between lengths and areas of similar shapes
use the relationship between lengths, surface areas and volumes of similar solids
solve problems involving similarity.

Past paper questions

1

Complete this statement for the parallelogram shown.

This shape has .... lines of symmetry and rotational symmetry of order .... [2]

Cambridge IGCSE International Mathematics 0607 Paper 22 Q4 June 2017

2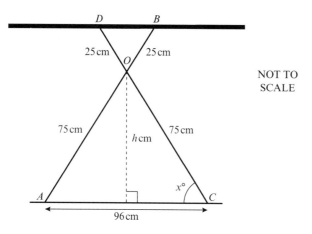

NOT TO SCALE

The diagram shows a table standing on a horizontal floor.

The table top is horizontal and is supported by two legs *AOB* and *COD*.

a   Use similar triangles to find *DB*.

DB = ... cm   [2]

b   Use Pythagoras' theorem to find the height, *h* cm, of *O* above the floor.

.... cm   [3]

Cambridge IGCSE International Mathematics 0607 Paper 32 Q11b & c March 2022

3   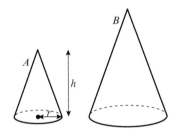 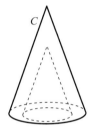   NOT TO SCALE

Cone *A* has radius *r* and perpendicular height *h*.

Cone *B* is mathematically similar to cone *A*.

Solid *C* is formed by removing cone *A* from cone *B*.

The ratio   **height of cone *A* : height of cone *B* = 2 : 3.**

Find the ratio   volume of cone *A* : volume of solid *C*.

.... : ....   [3]

Cambridge IGCSE International Mathematics 0607 Paper 42 Q10a March 2021

Chapter 10

Pythagoras' theorem

IN THIS CHAPTER YOU WILL:

- apply Pythagoras' theorem to solve problems in two dimensions

> apply Pythagoras' theorem to solve problems in three dimensions.

GETTING STARTED

1   Evaluate these calculations without using a calculator.

    a 8^2 **b** $4^2 + 5^2$ **c** $10^2 - 6^2$ **d** $\sqrt{81}$ **e** $\sqrt{4^2 - 7}$

2   Which of these triangles is a right-angled triangle?

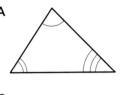

10.1 Pythagoras' theorem in two dimensions

In a right-angled triangle, the length opposite the right angle
is known as the **hypotenuse**. The hypotenuse is the longest side
of a right-angled triangle.

Investigation 1 determines the relationship
between the lengths of the sides of a right-angled triangle.

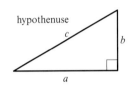

INVESTIGATION 1

Finding the relationship between the squares of the sides of a right-angled triangle

The diagram shows a geoboard with dots that are 1 cm apart.

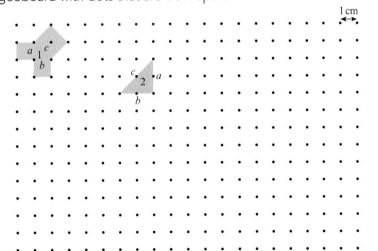

Triangle 1 has three sides labelled a, b and c where c is the hypotenuse. The first row in the table shows the
lengths of a and b and the areas of the squares formed by the lengths a, b and c.

CONTINUED

1   Copy and complete the table.

Triangle	Length of side a	Length of side b	Area of the square formed by side a	Area of the square formed by side b	Area of the square formed by side c
1	1	1	1	1	2
2	2	2			

2   For each triangle, do you observe any relationship between the areas of the squares formed by the lengths a, b and c?

3   Extend your table by drawing a few right-angled triangles of your own.

Triangle	Length of side a	Length of side b	Area of the square formed by side a	Area of the square formed by side b	Area of the square formed by side c
1	1	1	1	1	2
2	2	2			
3					
4					
5					
6					

4   Generalise an equation connecting a, b and c for any right-angled triangle.

5   How can you test out your equation in Question **4**?

MATHEMATICAL CONNECTIONS

You learnt how to write algebraic equations in Chapter 7.

Investigation 1 leads to **Pythagoras' theorem**:

$a^2 + b^2 = c^2$, where c is the hypotenuse

This theorem only applies to right-angled triangles.

The theorem can also be used to prove that a triangle is right-angled. If the square of the hypotenuse is the same as the sum of the squares of the other two sides then the triangle must be right-angled.

WORKED EXAMPLE 1

In triangle ABC, angle $BCA = 90°$, length $AC = 8\,cm$ and length $BC = 6\,cm$. Find the length of AB.

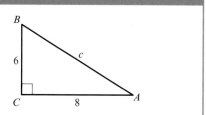

CONTINUED

Answer

AB is the hypotenuse.

Substitute the lengths of AC and BC into Pythagoras' theorem to find the value of c:

$c^2 = 6^2 + 8^2$

$c = \sqrt{36 + 64}$

$\quad = \sqrt{100}$

$\quad = 10$

The length of AB is 10 cm.

> **MATHEMATICAL CONNECTIONS**
>
> You learnt how to substitute values into algebraic expressions and equations in Chapter 7.

WORKED EXAMPLE 2

In triangle EFG, angle $EFG = 90°$, length $EG = 17$ cm and length $FG = 8$ cm. Find the length of EF.

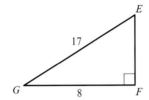

Answer

EG is the hypotenuse. You need to find the length of one of the shorter sides of the right-angled triangle, EF.

Substitute the known lengths into Pythagoras' theorem and rearrange:

$EF^2 + FG^2 = EG^2$

$EF^2 + 8^2 = 17^2$

$EF^2 = 17^2 - 8^2$

$\quad = 225$

$EF = \sqrt{225}$

$\quad = 15$

The length of EF is 15 cm.

WORKED EXAMPLE 3

In the diagram, angle $BCA = 90°$, length $AD = 24$ cm, length $BD = 15$ cm and length $AC = 10$ cm.

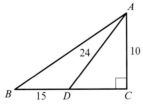

Find the length of:

a DC **b** AB.

CONTINUED

Answers

a To find the length of DC, look at right-angled triangle ACD and apply Pythagoras' theorem:

$$DC^2 + 10^2 = 24^2$$

$$DC^2 = 24^2 - 10^2$$

$$DC = \sqrt{476} = 21.81742...$$

$$DC \approx 21.8 \text{ (3 sf)}$$

The length of DC is 21.8 cm.

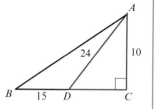

TIP

If the final answer is not exact, it is standard practice to round the value to three significant figures.

b To find the length of AB, apply Pythagoras' theorem to right-angled triangle ABC:

$$BC^2 + AC^2 = AB^2$$

$$BC = BD + DC$$

$$= 15 + 21.81742...$$

$$\approx 36.817$$

$$AB^2 = 36.817^2 + 10^2$$

$$AB \approx 38.2 \text{ (3 sf)}$$

The length of AB is 38.2 cm.

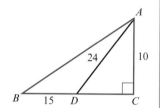

TIP

Use either the exact value for DC from your calculator or use at least one more figure than is needed in the final answer in your calculations.

WORKED EXAMPLE 4

Jamil says that she has drawn a right-angled triangle, and has measured the sides as 6 cm, 5.84 cm and 8.4 cm. Is Jamil correct?

Answer

If Jamil's triangle is right-angled, then $6^2 + 5.84^2 = 8.4^2$

$6^2 = 36$ $5.84^2 = 34.106$ $8.4^2 = 70.56$

$36 + 34.106 = 70.106 \neq 70.56$

Jamil's triangle is not right-angled.

Exercise 10.1

1 Find the value of the unknown length in each diagram.

a

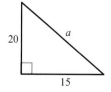

b

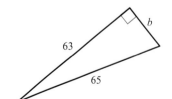

c

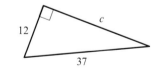

d

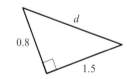

2 Find the values of the unknown lengths in these diagrams.

a
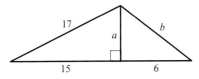

b
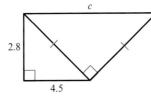

c
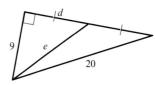

d
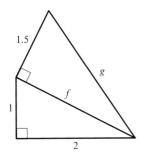

e
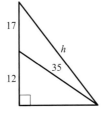

f
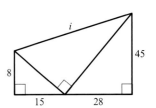

3 Use Pythagoras' theorem to determine which of the following triangles are right angled.

Triangle A
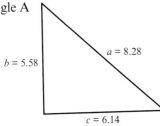

Triangle B
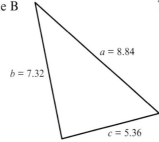

Triangle C
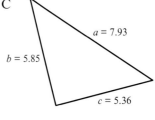

DISCUSSION 1

Pythagoras' theorem states that $a^2 + b^2 = c^2$

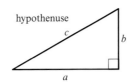

You can also show the relationship to be true using the areas of squares.

$A_1 + A_2 = A_3$

You can verify this as $A_1 = a^2$, $A_2 = b^2$ and $A_3 = c^2$.

Does this theorem also hold if you use other shapes?

For example, semicircles.

Try using other shapes such as rectangles, triangles, pentagons, etc.

Does the relationship still hold when you use other shapes?

Discuss in small groups and present your findings to other students in your class.

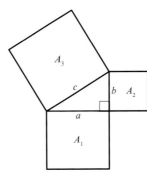

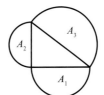

10.2 Applications of Pythagoras' theorem

You can use right-angled triangles and Pythagoras' theorem to solve problems involving points on a grid.

WORKED EXAMPLE 5

The grid shows a point A. Another point B is $\sqrt{5}$ units away from point A and lies on the intersection of two grid lines.
Mark one possible position for point B.

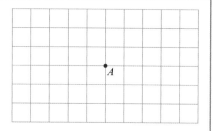

> **MATHEMATICAL CONNECTIONS**
>
> You learnt how to use surds in Chapter 6.

Answer

This problem has more than one possible solution and requires the use of Pythagoras' theorem.

Consider a right-angled triangle with a hypothenuse of $\sqrt{5}$ units.

Apply Pythagoras' theorem:
$$a^2 + b^2 = \left(\sqrt{5}\right)^2$$
$$a^2 + b^2 = 5$$

a^2 and b^2 are square numbers.

Square numbers between 1 to 10 are:
$$1^2 = 1,\ 2^2 = 4,\ 3^2 = 9$$

The only possible combination is
$$1 + 4 = 5$$
$$1^2 + 2^2 = 5$$

Either a or b can be 1.

Case 1   or   **Case 2**

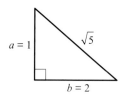   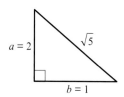

Point A can be at either end of the hypothenuse.

For Case 1:

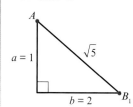   or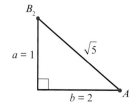

CONTINUED

Putting Case 1 on the grid, there are two possible positions for point B:

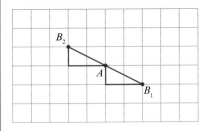

For Case 2:

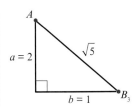 or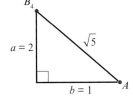

Putting Case 2 on the grid, there are two possible positions for point B:

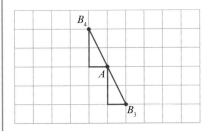

Any of these four positions of point B can be a valid answer.

You can also use Pythagoras' theorem to solve problems based on real-life situations.

WORKED EXAMPLE 6

A cat is stuck on a tree branch 2.5 m above the ground. Ingrid places a ladder against the tree to rescue the cat. If the ladder is placed 1 m from the foot of the tree, calculate the length of the ladder required to reach the cat.

Answer

Sketch a model of the situation.

Represent the tree by a vertical line perpendicular to the ground.

The ladder leaning against the tree is the hypotenuse of a right-angled triangle.

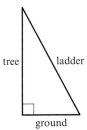

CONTINUED

Let the length of the ladder be x and use the values given in the question to find the value of x.

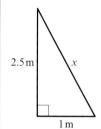

Apply Pythagoras' theorem:

$x^2 = 2.5^2 + 1^2$
$\quad = 7.27$
$x = \sqrt{7.25}$
$\quad = 2.69 \text{ m (3 sf)}$

The length of the ladder required to reach the cat is 2.69 m.

WORKED EXAMPLE 7

A children's pool is in the shape of a rectangle $ABCD$ with width x m and length $(x + 2)$ m. The length of the diagonal AC is $(x + 4)$ m.
Calculate the width of the pool.

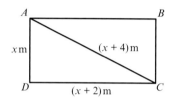

Answer

Recognise that triangle ADC is a right-angled triangle, with hypotenuse AC.

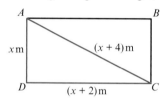

Apply Pythagoras' theorem:

$AD^2 + DC^2 = AC^2$

$x^2 + (x + 2)^2 = (x + 4)^2$ Expand the brackets and bring all the terms to one side.

$x^2 + x^2 + 4x + 4 = x^2 + 8x + 16$

$x^2 - 4x - 12 = 0$

$(x - 6)(x + 2) = 0$

$x = 6 \text{ or } x = -2 \text{ (rejected)}$ Since x is the width of the pool, it should be positive, so reject the solution -2.

The width of the pool is 6 m.

> **MATHEMATICAL CONNECTIONS**
>
> Solving quadratic equations is covered in Chapter 13.

REFLECTION

To what type of triangle can you apply Pythagoras' theorem?

Exercise 10.2

1 A ladder of length 3 m is placed against a vertical wall. The foot of the ladder is 1.2 m away from the base of the wall. How far up the wall does the ladder reach?

2 A 32-inch television has a height of 16 inches. Find the width of this TV.

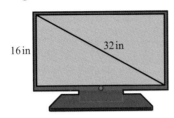

16 in   32 in

3 A farmer has a rectangular plot of land measuring 8 m by 5 m. He wants to build a fence across the diagonal of the land. What is the length of this fence?

4 Square DEFG has a diagonal that measures 30 cm. Find the length of DE.

30 cm

5 In the diagram, ABCD is the cross-section of a shed with length AB = 3 m, length BC = 3.5 m and length AD = 1.8 m. Find the length of CD.

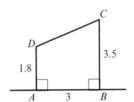

1.8   3.5   3

6 In the diagram, PQRS is a piece of land with angle PRQ = angle PSR = 90° and lengths PR = 41 m, PS = 9 m and QR = 35 m.

Find:

a the length of PQ

b the length of RS

c the area of the piece of land.

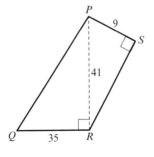

9   41   35

7 The grid shows a point A. Another point B is 5 units away from A and lies on the intersection of two grid lines. On a copy of the grid, mark three possible positions for point B.

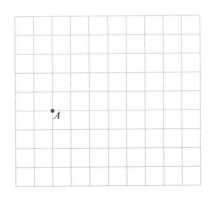

A

8   The grid shows a point P. Another point Q is $\sqrt{13}$ units away from point P and lies on the intersection of two grid lines. On a copy of the grid, mark one possible position for point Q.

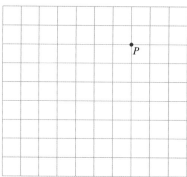

9   Point P has coordinates $(2, 3)$. Another point Q has coordinates (x, y) and is $5\sqrt{5}$ units away from point P. Find an integer value of x and the corresponding value of y.

10 A ladder AB leans against a vertical wall OT. Lengths $OA = 12\,$m and $OB = 5\,$m.
    a   Find the length of the ladder, AB.
    b   If the ladder slides down $2\,$m to a new position CD, find the distance BD.

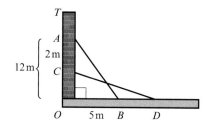

11 Ship A is $20\,$km due east of Ship B. Ship A sails north for $12\,$km then continues to sail west for $10\,$km. Ship B sails south for $15\,$km before coming to a stop. Find the new distance between the two ships.

12 A rectangular bag has dimensions given in the diagram.

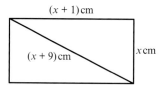

    a   Find the value of x.
    b   Can a ruler of length $30\,$cm fit into the bag? Explain your answer.

13 A right-angled triangle has length of sides given in the diagram.
    Calculate:
    a   the value of x
    b   the area of the triangle.

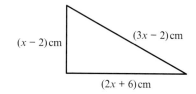

> MATHEMATICAL CONNECTIONS
>
> Solving quadratic equations is covered in Chapter 13. Finding the area of a triangle is covered in Chapter 12.

DISCUSSION 2

The lengths of the sides of triangle ABC are given in the diagram.

Aba says that triangle ABC is not a right-angled triangle because

$55 + 48 \neq 73$

Bendek says that triangle ABC is a right-angled triangle because

$55^2 + 48^2 = 5329$

$73^2 = 5329$

and since $55^2 + 48^2 = 73^2$, triangle ABC is a right-angled triangle.

Cheng says that triangle ABC is not a right-angled triangle because

$55^2 + 48^2 = 5328$ but

$73^2 = 5329 \neq 5328$

so $55^2 + 48^2 \neq 73^2$

Who is correct?

Identify the mistakes made by the other students.

Discuss with a partner.

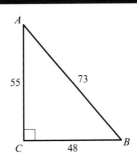

10.3 Pythagoras' theorem in three dimensions

In the previous sections, you applied Pythagoras' theorem in two dimensions. In this section, you will apply Pythagoras' theorem in three dimensions.

INVESTIGATION 2

The length of a diagonal of a cuboid

1   The diagram shows a cuboid $ABCDEFG$.

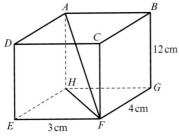

a   Find the length of HF.

b   State the angle AHF.

c   Draw a sketch of triangle AHF. Label all the known lengths on your diagram.

d   What type of triangle is AHF?

e   Find the length of AF.

CONTINUED

2 Another cuboid $PQRSTUVW$ has dimensions given in the diagram.

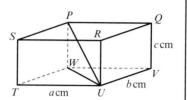

a Find an expression in terms of a and b for WU^2.

b Draw a sketch of triangle PWU. Label all the known lengths on your diagram.

c Hence, find an expression for the length of PU in terms of a, b and c.

Investigation 2 gives an expression for the length of the diagonal of a cuboid.

The length of the diagonal PQ of this cuboid is:

$\sqrt{L^2 + B^2 + H^2}$

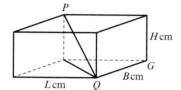

WORKED EXAMPLE 8

The diagram shows cuboid $ABCDEFG$. Find the length of AF.

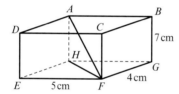

Answer

Use the formula to find the diagonal of a cuboid:

$AF = \sqrt{5^2 + 4^2 + 7^2}$

$\quad = \sqrt{90}$

$\quad = 9.49 \ (3 \ \text{sf})$

The length of AF is 9.49 cm.

You can also apply Pythagoras' theorem to other three-dimensional solids, as long as you can identify a right-angled triangle.

WORKED EXAMPLE 9

Find the length of the diagonal x in the cylinder.

CONTINUED

Answer

Identify the right-angled triangle in the diagram:

21 cm

x

20 cm

Apply Pythagoras' theorem:

$x^2 = 20^2 + 21^2$

$\quad = 841$

$x = \sqrt{841}$

$\quad = 29$ cm

The length of the diagonal x is 29 cm.

Exercise 10.3

1   In each diagram, find the length of the diagonal, x.

a

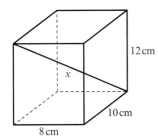

12 cm

x

10 cm

8 cm

b

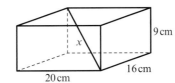

9 cm

x

16 cm

20 cm

c

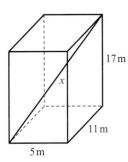

17 m

x

11 m

5 m

d

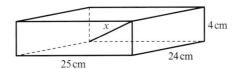

x

4 cm

25 cm

24 cm

e

x

12 cm

6 cm

f

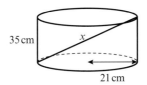

35 cm

x

21 cm

2   For the each of these pyramids, find the unknown length, x.

a

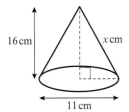

16 cm

x cm

11 cm

b

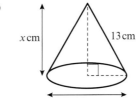

x cm

13 cm

14 cm

TIP

Identify the right-angled triangle in each diagram.

c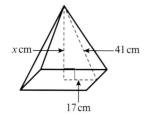

d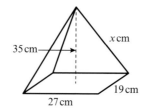

3   A cuboid drink carton measures 5 cm by 2.5 cm by 11 cm.
    A factory manufactures a straw for the drink carton
    such that it is 4 cm longer than the longest diagonal
    of the carton. Find the length of the straw to the
    nearest whole number.

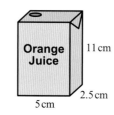

4   An ant is at A, a top corner of a rectangular room.
    There is a grain of sugar at S, the opposite
    bottom corner of the room. The floor of
    the room is 7 m by 5 m and the ceiling is
    3 m above the floor. Find the shortest
    distance the ant can crawl from A to S,
    along any wall, floor or ceiling.

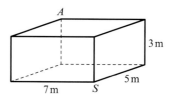

SUMMARY

Are you able to... ?

apply Pythagoras' theorem to solve problems in two dimensions

apply Pythagoras' theorem to solve problems in three dimensions.

Past paper questions

1   A rectangle has sides 6 cm and 8 cm.

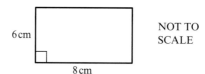

NOT TO
SCALE

    Work out the length of a diagonal of this rectangle.

.... cm   [2]

Cambridge IGCSE International Mathematics 0607 Paper 11 Q14 November 2015

2

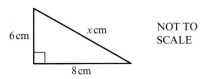

NOT TO SCALE

Work out the value of x.

$x =$ .... [2]

Cambridge IGCSE International Mathematics 0607 Paper 11 Q20 June 2020

3   In triangle ABC, $AB = \sqrt{48}$ cm, $AC = 8$ cm and angle $ABC = 90°$.
Find BC.

$BC =$ .... cm   [3]

Cambridge IGCSE International Mathematics 0607 Paper 22 Q9a November 2015

4

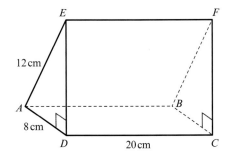

NOT TO SCALE

$ABCDEF$ is a triangular prism.
$ABCD$ is a rectangle.
Find

a AC,

$AC =$ .... cm   [2]

b ED.

$ED =$ .... cm   [2]

Cambridge IGCSE International Mathematics 0607 Paper 41 Q8a & b November 2020

> # Chapter 11
Coordinate geometry

IN THIS CHAPTER YOU WILL:

- use and interpret Cartesian coordinates in two dimensions
- find the gradient of a straight line
- calculate the distance between two points on a line segment
- find the coordinates of the midpoint of a line segment
- interpret and obtain the equation of a straight line in the form $y = mx + c$
- find the gradient and equation of a straight line parallel to a given line

> interpret and obtain the equation of a straight line graph

> find the gradient and equation of a straight line perpendicular to a given line.

GETTING STARTED

1   Draw x and y axes such that $-5 \leqslant x \leqslant 5$ and $-4 \leqslant y \leqslant 4$.
   a   Plot the points $A(1, 1)$, $B(4, 1)$, $C(4, 3)$ and $D(1, 3)$.
   b   Calculate the length of AB.
   c   Calculate the area of $ABCD$.

TIP

Shapes are described by listing the vertices in either a clockwise direction or an anticlockwise direction (this is known as cyclic order).

So, you can describe this rectangle as $ABCD$, but not as $ACBD$.

2   On the same axes plot the points $P(-4, 1)$, $Q(-1, 1)$, $R(-2, -2)$, $S(-5, -2)$.
   a   Amir thinks it is a parallelogram, but Sarah thinks it is a rhombus. Which student is correct? Explain how you know.
   b   Calculate the length of PQ.
   c   Calculate the area of $PQRS$.

DISCUSSION 1

What is the difference between a parallelogram and a rhombus?

3   Given the formula $ap + bq = r$, calculate the value of:
   a r when $a = 7$, $b = 4$, $p = 3$ and $q = 8$
   b p when $a = 2$, $b = 5$, $q = 4$ and $r = 50$
   c q when $a = -2$, $b = 4$, $p = 5$ and $r = 22$

KEY WORDS

equidistant

gradient (slope)

midpoint

parallel

perpendicular

perpendicular bisector

quadrant

MATHEMATICAL CONNECTIONS

You learnt how to substitute values into formulas in Chapter 7.

11.1 The coordinate system

To plot a point on a grid you need to know its coordinates.

The coordinates of a point are shown as a number pair written inside brackets and separated by a comma, for example, (1, 4).

The first number in the pair is the x-coordinate and measures the horizontal distance across the grid from the origin, O.

The second number in the pair is the y-coordinate and measures the vertical distance from the origin, O.

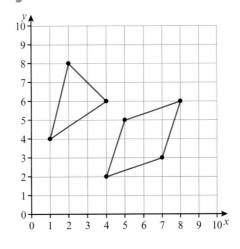

TIP

A common mistake that some students make is to get the order of the coordinates wrong. It is a mathematical convention that the x-coordinate comes first so that the point (2, 1) means the same all over the world.

The coordinates of the three vertices of the triangle are (1, 4), (4, 6) and (2, 8).

The coordinates for the vertices of the quadrilateral are (4, 2), (7, 3), (8, 6) and (5, 5).

Extending the axes – negative coordinates

Extending the axes with negative numbers creates four **quadrants** in which you can plot points.

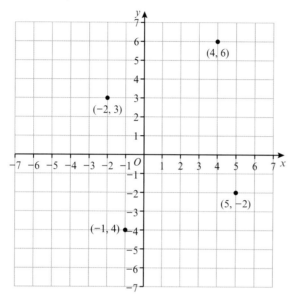

The point (4, 6) lies in the first quadrant.

The point (−2, 3) lies in the second quadrant.

The point (−1, −4) lies in the third quadrant.

The point (5, −2) lies in the fourth quadrant.

WORKED EXAMPLE 1

The three points $A(-2, -1)$, $B(5, -2)$ and $C(5, 1)$ form three vertices of a quadrilateral $ABCD$, which has rotational symmetry of order 2.

a Find the coordinates of D.

b Write down the name of $ABCD$.

Answers

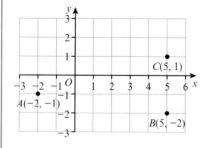

CONTINUED

a Plot the points.

The shape is labelled in cyclic order – anticlockwise in this case.

To create a shape with rotational symmetry order 2, D must be 3 units above A, parallel to the axis.

$D(-2, 2)$

b The quadrilateral has rotational symmetry order 2, and no lines of symmetry, so it is a parallelogram.

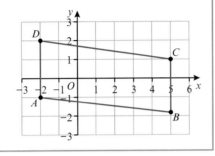

The **midpoint** of any line segment (for example, the side length of a shape) is a point that is **equidistant** from both end points.

WORKED EXAMPLE 2

The line segment AB shown has coordinates $A(2, 2)$ and $B(6, 2)$.

The midpoint is a point halfway between the two points $(2, 2)$ and $(6, 2)$.

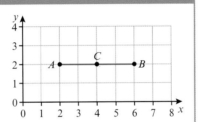

Answer

In this example the midpoint is easy to find as it lies on the horizontal line $y = 2$.

WORKED EXAMPLE 3

To find the midpoint of any line segment, calculate the mean of the sum of the x-coordinates and the mean of the sum of the y-coordinates.

Answer

Point $A(2, 1)$ and Point $B(5, 5)$.

The mean of the x-coordinates is $\dfrac{2 + 5}{2} = 3\dfrac{1}{2}$

The mean of the y-coordinates is $\dfrac{1 + 5}{2} = 3$

The coordinates of the midpoint C are $\left(3\dfrac{1}{2}, 3\right)$.

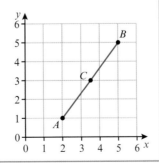

> **MATHEMATICAL CONNECTIONS**
>
> The mean is a type of average that you will meet in Chapter 19.

Exercise 11.1

 Draw a grid from −6 to 6 on each axis. The scale must be the same on each axis: 1 cm to 1 unit.

1 a   i   Plot the eight points (−4, 3), (6, 2), (0, −3), (3, 5), (−4, −3), (6, −3), (−5, 5) and (6, 5).

  ii   The points lie on the sides of a quadrilateral. Write down the name of the quadrilateral.

 b   The points (3, 5), (−4, 5) and (6, 5) lie on the top of the quadrilateral.
  i   Calculate the midpoint between (3, 5) and (6, 5).
  ii   Calculate the midpoint between (3, 5) and (−4, 5).
  ii   Calculate the midpoint between (6, 5) and (4, −4).

 c   The points (−4, −3), (−4, 5) and (−4, 3) lie on one side of the rectangle.
   Write down the coordinates of the midpoint of this side.

 2 a   Plot the points:
   (3, 2), (3, −1), (3, −4), (−4, −5), (−2, −5), (1, −5), (−5, −4), (−5, 2), (−5, 0), (2, 3), (3, −3) and (0, 3).
   Three points lie on each side of a quadrilateral. Two of its sides are horizontal and two are vertical.

 b   Draw lines on your diagram to form the quadrilateral and write down its name.

 c   Write down the coordinates of the four corners (vertices) of the quadrilateral.

 d   Calculate the coordinates of the midpoint of each of the four sides of the quadrilateral you have drawn.

 e   The centre of the square is equidistant from all four vertices. Write down its coordinates.

PEER ASSESSMENT

Check your solutions with a partner.

Have you drawn the shapes correctly?

Do you agree with all of their answers?

11.2 Calculating the distance between two points

The distance between any two points can be calculated using their coordinates.

Sometimes, like in Worked example 1, both points were on a line parallel to the axis. Here the calculation was straightforward. This will not always be the case, so you need to develop a general method for calculating the distance between two points.

Worked example 4 shows a general method for calculating the distance between two points, also known as calculating the length of a line segment.

> **TIP**
>
> Always check whether the length or height is parallel to one of the axes, as this will make your calculation easier.

WORKED EXAMPLE 4

Find the length of the line segment AB where $A(-2, 3)$ and $B(5, -1)$.

Answer

Use a grid to draw the line segment AB.

Then draw a line segment parallel to the x-axis and a line segment parallel to the y-axis.

These line segments form a right-angled triangle.

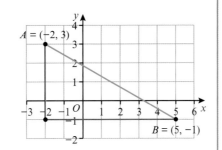

You can then use Pythagoras' theorem to calculate the length of AB.

$AB^2 = 7^2 + 4^2$

$AB^2 = 49 + 16 = 65$

$AB = \sqrt{65} = 8.06$ (correct to 3 sf)

> **TIP**
>
> Always draw a sketch. A sketch does not need to be accurate.

> **MATHEMATICAL CONNECTIONS**
>
> You learnt how to use Pythagoras' theorem in Chapter 10.

Exercise 11.2

1 Calculate the distance between each pair of points.

a (3, 10) and (7, 12)	b (4, 1) and (8, 15)	c (4, 4) and (7, 10)
d (2, 2) and (6, 10)	e (0, 3) and (5, 13)	f (5, 9) and (9, 13)
g (10, 3) and (6, 11)	h (0, 0) and (6, 8)	i (8, 12) and (0, 0)
j (9, 12) and (2, 19)	k (0, 8) and (4, 4)	l (3, 0) and (5, 0)

A formula for the distance between two points

There is a general formula for this length, which can be used to find the distance between any two points on a 2D plane and doesn't need a diagram.

To find the general formula for the length of the line segment AP, and of the midpoint of AP you need the two points.

Call the *first* point A, with coordinates $A(x_1, y_1)$.

Call the *second* point B, with coordinates $B(x_2, y_2)$.

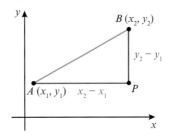

Draw a sketch showing the horizontal line segment, AP, and the vertical line segment, BP.

This gives you the right-angled triangle ABP.

You want to find an expression for AP and for BP.

Check that the coordinates of P are (x_2, y_1).

This means that BP is the difference in height $y_2 - y_1$ and AP is the horizontal difference $x_2 - x_1$.

Now apply Pythagoras' theorem:

$$AB = \sqrt{(x_2 - x_1)^2 + (y_2 - y_1)^2}$$

It is possible to calculate the coordinates of the midpoint of a line segment from the coordinates of two endpoints.

The midpoint of a line can be calculated by finding the mean of the x-coordinates and the mean of the y-coordinates.

The x-coordinate is $\dfrac{x_1 + x_2}{2}$ and the coordinate is $\dfrac{y_1 + y_2}{2}$.

WORKED EXAMPLE 5

Calculate the distance between the points $A(1, 6)$ and $B(3, 9)$ and find the coordinates of their midpoint.

Answer

Using Pythagoras' theorem:

$$AB = \sqrt{(x_2 - x_1)^2 + (y_2 - y_1)^2}$$

$$= \sqrt{(3 - 1)^2 + (9 - 6)^2}$$

$$= \sqrt{4 + 9}$$

$$= \sqrt{13}$$

$$\text{Midpoint of } AB = \left(\frac{x_1 + x_2}{2}, \frac{y_1 + y_2}{2} \right)$$

$$= \left(\frac{3 + 1}{2}, \frac{9 + 6}{2} \right)$$

$$= \left(\frac{4}{2}, \frac{15}{2} \right)$$

$$= (2, 7.5)$$

Exercise 11.3

1   Using the formula calculate the distance between each pair of points and calculate their midpoints.

    a $(3, 9)$ and $(7, 12)$ **b** $(4, -5)$ and $(-1, 7)$ **c** $(-2, -4)$ and $(4, -12)$

    d $(-2, 2)$ and $(6, 8)$ **e** $(2, 3)$ and $(10, 18)$ **f** $(-5, -11)$ and $(2, 13)$

DISCUSSION 2

You are asked to determine whether the triangle with vertices $A(4, 7)$, $B(-2, -1)$ and $C(-4, 1)$ is equilateral, isosceles or scalene, and to determine which (if any) of the angles is the smallest.

Which method would be the easiest to use?

2 Prove that the quadrilateral with vertices $A(0, 2)$, $B(-1, -1)$ $C(2, -2)$ and $D(3, 1)$ is a rhombus.

3 Show that the points $A(-2, 4)$, $B(-1, -3)$ and $C(7, 1)$ are all equidistant from point $D(2, 1)$.

A, B and C all lie on a circle. Write down the centre and radius of this circle.

4 Prove that the quadrilateral with vertices $A(2, 3)$, $B(7, 8)$, $C(10, 17)$ and $D(5, 12)$ is a parallelogram.

11.3 Angles and directions, slopes and gradients

A parallelogram is usually described as a quadrilateral with two pairs of opposite sides that are parallel.

Hence, you need to be able to determine the direction of a line segment that joins two points. You can do this by finding the **gradient** (or **slope**) of the line segment.

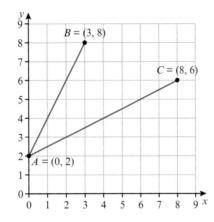

The gradient of a line measures the rate by which its 'height' increases (or decreases) compared to the distance it moves along the axis.

Looking at the diagram, both line segments start from point A at a 'height' of 2.

You can see that the height of line segment AB is increasing faster than the height of line segment AC.

Gradient measures these increases and is defined as:

$$\text{gradient} = \frac{\text{change in } y\text{-value}}{\text{change in } x\text{-value}}$$

WORKED EXAMPLE 6

Find the gradients of the following lines.

a

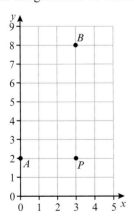

b

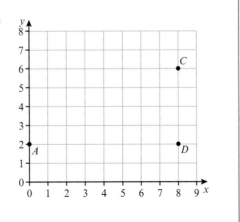

CONTINUED

c

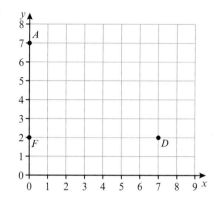

Answers

a   Consider line segment AB.

As you move from point A to point B the y-coordinate increases by 6 units from $y = 2$ to $y = 8$ and the x-coordinate increases by 3 units from $x = 0$ to $x = 3$.

The y-coordinate values are increasing at twice the rate of the x-coordinate values.

You say that the gradient of $AB = \dfrac{6}{3} = 2$

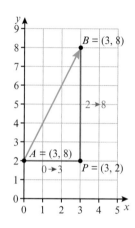

b   Now consider line segment AC.

As you move from point A to point C the y-coordinate increases by 4 units from $y = 2$ to $y = 6$ and the x-coordinate increases by 8 units from $x = 0$ to $x = 8$.

The y-coordinate values are increasing at half the rate of the x-coordinate values.

You say that the gradient of

$AC = \dfrac{4}{8} = \dfrac{1}{2}$

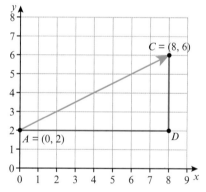

CONTINUED

c Now consider the line segment *AE*.

Here the 'height' decreases compared to the distance it moves along the axis.

The decrease (from 7 to 2) is shown as a negative value (2 − 7 = 5).

Therefore the gradient is $\dfrac{-5}{7}$.

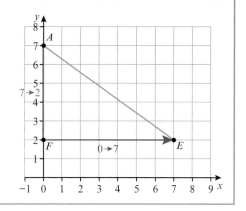

Calculating the gradient of a line segment from the coordinates of two points on the line

As an alternative to drawing a diagram, you can use a formula to calculate the gradient of a line segment.

Consider again this diagram.

Using the right-angled triangle *ABP*, you have expressions for *AP* and for *BP*:

$BP = y_2 - y_1$

$AP = x_2 - x_1$

Hence the gradient of *AB* is:

$$\text{gradient } (m) = \frac{\text{change in } y\text{-value}}{\text{change in } x\text{-value}} = \frac{y_2 - y_1}{x_2 - x_1}$$

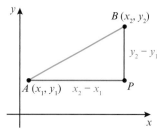

WORKED EXAMPLE 7

Calculate the gradient of line segments *AB*, *AC* and *BC*.

Answer

First note that as you move from *A* to *B* the 'height' is increasing and so the gradient of *AB* is positive.

As you move from *A* to *C* and from *B* to *C*, the 'height' is decreasing and so the gradients of both *AC* and *BC* are negative.

Using the formula:

$$\text{Gradient } (m) = \frac{(y_2 - y_1)}{(x_2 - x_1)}$$

Gradient of $AB = \dfrac{4 - 2}{1 - (-3)} = \dfrac{2}{4} = \dfrac{1}{2}$

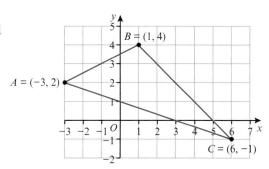

CONTINUED

Gradient of $AC = \dfrac{(-1) - 2}{6 - (-3)} = \dfrac{-3}{9} = -\dfrac{1}{3}$

Gradient of $BC = \dfrac{(-1) - 4}{6 - 1} = \dfrac{-5}{5} = -1$

TIP

The negative signs indicate that the two lines are moving downwards as you move from left to right.

Looking at the values, BC is moving downwards at three times the rate of AC.

Exercise 11.4

Calculate the gradient of the line segment with the endpoints given.

1   a   (3, 1) and (7, 2)

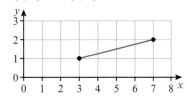

b   (4, 1) and (8, 15)

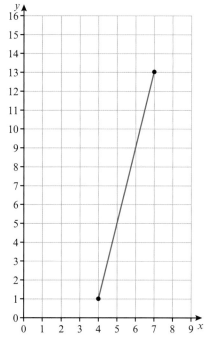

c   (4, 4) and (7, 1)

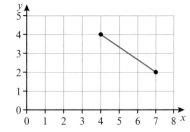

d   (2, 2) and (4, −10)

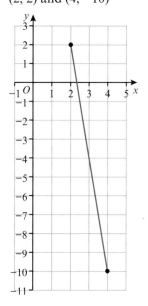

e (0, 3) and (5, 13)

f (5, 9) and (8, 6)

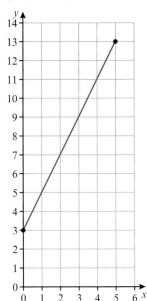

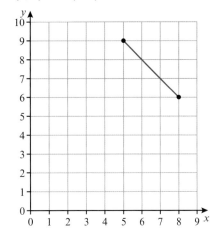

2 **a** (−3, −9) and (−7, −12)

b (3, −5) and (−1, 7)

c (−1, −4) and (4, −12)

d (−2, 2) and (6, 8)

e (−2, 3) and (10, 18)

f (−5, −11) and (2, −18)

3 Use the formula to verify the gradient of each of the line segments in Question **1**.

11.4 Straight lines

There are three types of straight lines:

1 Vertical lines   (lines that are parallel to the *y*-axis)

2 Horizontal lines   (lines that are parallel to the *x*-axis)

3 Sloping lines   (lines that are not parallel to either axis)

You must be able to recognise and find the equation of each type of line.

INVESTIGATION 1

Using your GDC, do the following.

1 Select **Graph** from the main menu. The graph function is highlighted in the following image.

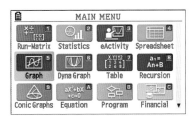

CONTINUED

The following screen opens.

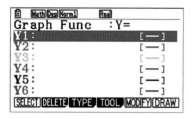

2   Press **F3** and then **F4** to change the graph type from Y= to X=.

Enter the following equations by using the keypad and pressing **EXE** after entering each value.

$x = 4$ $x = 2$ $x = -3$ $x = -1$ $x = 0$

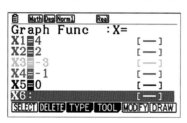

3   Press **F6** to draw the graphs.

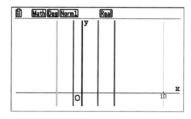

What do you notice?

Is this true of any line with equation of the form $x = k$, where k is a constant?

4   Press **EXIT** to return to the equation entry screen. Delete each of your lines using **F2** and the toggle button. This will revert the graph type back to Y=.

Enter the following equations by using the keypad and pressing **EXE** after entering each value.

$y = 5$ $y = 1$ $y = -2$ $y = -6$ $y = 0$

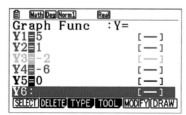

CONTINUED

5   Press **F6** to draw the graphs.

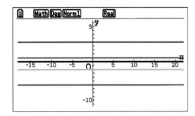

What do you notice?

Is this true of any line with equation of the form $y = k$, where k is a constant?

Draw the line with equation $y = x$. What do you notice?

What you expect the line to look like?

You know how to write down the equation of *any* horizontal or vertical straight line simply by looking at it. You should also be able to recognise the lines $y = x$ and $y = -x$.

The next stage is to be able to do this for *any* sloping line.

INVESTIGATION 2

Finding the equation of any straight line from its graph

You will need to use your GDC.

1   Draw the graph of the line $y = 2$.

a   Select **Graph** from the main menu. The graph function is highlighted in the following image.

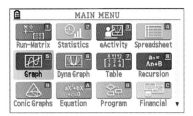

The following screen opens.

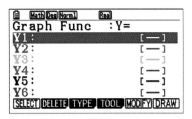

CONTINUED

b Now enter the function using the keypad.

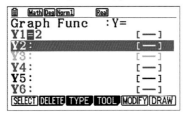

c Now press **F6** to draw the graph.

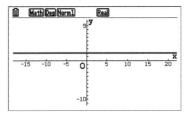

This line is horizontal and intersects the y-axis at the y-intercept – the point $(0, 2)$.

2 Press **EXIT** to return to step **1b**. Change the equation of the line to $y = 2 + 0x$.

The line should be horizontal – it is still the line $y = 2$.

3 Press **EXIT** to return to step **1b**. Change the value of the coefficient of x, m, from zero to 1, to 2, to 3, etc.

Look at what stays the same on the line and look at what changes.

The line $y = 2 + mx$ always intersects the y-axis at the y-intercept: $(0, 2)$.

The direction the line takes changes – as m changes the gradient of the line changes.

The line pivots about the y-intercept: $(0, 2)$.

When m is positive, the line moves upwards from the y-intercept: $(0, 2)$.

When m is negative, the line moves downwards from the y-intercept: $(0, 2)$.

When m is zero, the line moves horizontally.

Copy and complete the table:

Gradient	y-intercept	Equation of line
3	$(0, 2)$	$y = 2 + 3x$
2	$(0, 2)$	
1	$(0, 2)$	
0	$(0, 2)$	
−1	$(0, 2)$	
−2	$(0, 2)$	

What do you notice about the relationship between the value of and the gradient of the line?

CONTINUED

4   Press **EXIT** to return to step **1b**. Change the equation of the line to $y = 3 + 0x$.

This changes the y-intercept to the point $(0, 3)$ by entering $y = 3 + mx$.

Repeat step 3. Look at the effect of changing the value of m on the line – again the line pivots about the y-intercept: $(0, 3)$.

Copy and complete the following table. Continue this until you are sure you can write down the equation of a line just by looking at it.

y-intercept	Gradient	Equation of line
$(0, 3)$	4	
$(0, 5)$	0.5	
$(0, -1)$	1	
$(0, -2)$	-3	
$(0, 4)$	-2	
$(0, 8)$	-0.5	

In this investigation you have used the form for the equation of a straight line: $y = c + mx$

What does c represent?

What does m represent?

Remember, if the line slopes down from left to right the gradient is negative and if the line slopes up from left to right the gradient is positive.

The key to finding the equation of a diagonal line is:

1   Find the y-intercept. This is the value of c in the equation.

2   Find the gradient.

Finding the gradient and intercept of a straight line from an equation

1   The equation of a line can be expressed as $y = c + mx$.

However, the general form for the equation of a straight line is $y = mx + c$ and this is the form you will see in the rest of this chapter.

2 c represents the y-intercept of the straight line.

3 m represents the gradient of the straight line.

If m is positive, the line slopes upwards from left to right.

If m is negative, the line slopes downwards from left to right.

If m is zero, the line is horizontal.

WORKED EXAMPLE 8

Find the equation of the line.

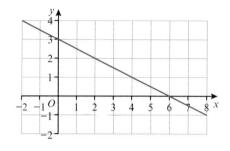

Answer

Start with $y = mx + c$

The intercept is $(0, 3)$: $c = 3$.

The line slopes down from this point: the gradient is negative.

Look at the line in more detail to find the speed of descent.

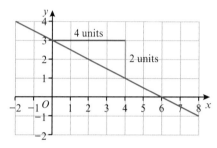

Moving across from the intercept: 4 units.

Moving back (down) to the line: 2 units.

Gradient $= m = \dfrac{-2}{4} = -\dfrac{1}{2}$

Equation: $y = -\dfrac{1}{2}x + 3$

Exercise 11.5

1 Write down the equation of each of these straight lines. They all pass through the point $(0, 4)$.

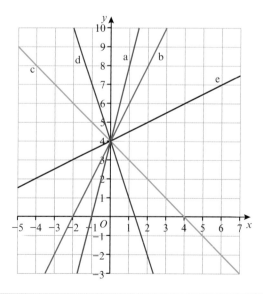

2   Write down the equation of each of these straight lines.

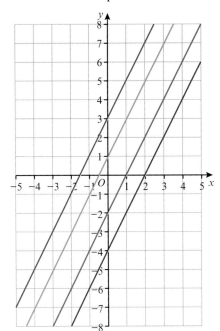 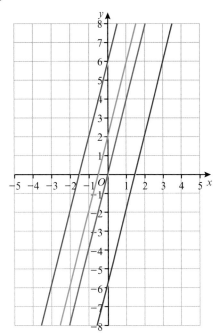

3   Write down the equation of each of these straight lines.

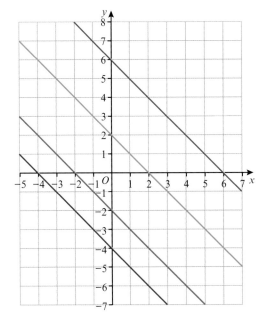 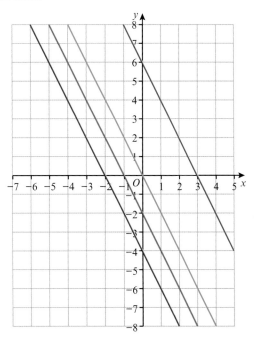

4 Write down the equation of each of these straight lines.

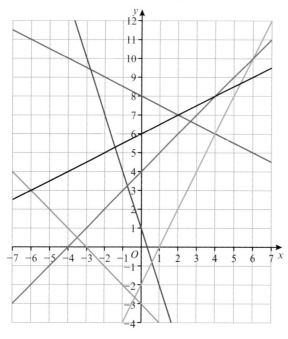

5 **a** Does the point (3, 5) lie on the line $y = 2x - 1$?

b Does the point (3, 7) lie on the line $y = 2x - 1$?

c Does the point (−2, 5) lie on the line $y = 2x - 1$?

d Does the point (8, 13) lie on the line $y = 2x - 1$?

6 Determine whether the given points lie on the given lines.

a (8, 16) on $y = 3x - 4$

b (6, 9) on $y = \dfrac{2}{3}x + 5$

c (12, 6) on $y = 10 - \dfrac{1}{2}x$

d (8, −4) on $y = 20 - 3x$

e (4, 10) on $2y = 3x - 2$

7 Write down the gradient and intercept of each of the following equations.

    a $y = 3x - 2$ **b** $y = -3x + 2$ **c** $y = \dfrac{1}{2}x - 4$ **d** $y = -\dfrac{1}{4}x + 11$

    e $x + y = 8$ **f** $x - y = 8$ **g** $x + y = -8$

> **TIP**
>
> Check your answers!
>
> This can be quickly done by choosing a point on the line and substituting the values of x and y into your equation.
>
> Your equation is only correct if the left-hand side of the equation has the same value as the right!

Drawing a straight line

If you are given the equation of a straight line, it should be easy to draw it accurately on graph paper.

WORKED EXAMPLE 9

Draw the line with equation $y = 4x - 3$.

Answer

Use the form $y = mx + c$

$y = mx - 3$	Identify the intercept: $(0, -3)$ so $c = -3$.
$y = 4x - 3$	Identify the gradient: $m = 4$.
m is positive	The line moves upwards from left to right.
$m = 4$	For every 1 unit along the axis, the line moves 4 units up the axis.

To draw the line on the axes:

1. Plot the intercept: $(0, -3)$.
2. Move one unit parallel to the axis.
3. Then move four units parallel to the axis.
4. The point reached by these moves is on the line.
5. Draw a straight line through these two points.
6. This is the line with equation $y = 4x - 3$.

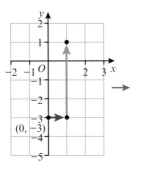 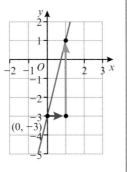

Exercise 11.6

1. Draw the following lines on graph paper with x-axis $-5 \leqslant x \leqslant 5$, y-axis $-6 \leqslant y \leqslant 12$.

   a $\quad y = 2x + 1$ b $\quad y = 4x - 4$ c $\quad y = \dfrac{1}{2}x + 2$ d $\quad y = -\dfrac{1}{2}x - 2$

2. Draw the following lines on graph paper with x-axis $-5 \leqslant x \leqslant 5$, y-axis $-6 \leqslant y \leqslant 12$. Write each equation in the form $y = mx + c$ before you draw the graph.

   MATHEMATICAL CONNECTIONS

   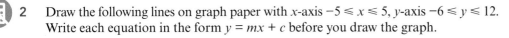

   You learnt how to change the subject of an equation in Chapter 7.

   a $\quad 2y = 6 + 4x$ b $\quad y - 3 = 4x$ c $\quad 2y + 2 = 6x$

   d $\quad y + x = 4$ e $\quad y + 4 = x$ f $\quad \dfrac{1}{2}y = x - 2$

   TIP

   Think carefully:

   if $\quad 2y = 6 + 4x$

   then $\quad y = ? + ?x$

Finding the equation of a line without drawing a graph

If two points are drawn on a piece of paper, you can use a ruler to draw a straight line through these two points. Furthermore, if you are accurate, there is only *one* straight line that you can draw through these two points.

So, if the coordinates of two points are given, there must be a way of finding the equation of the straight line that passes through these two points.

You must use the general equation of the straight line: $y = mx + c$.

WORKED EXAMPLE 10

The coordinates $A(-3, 2)$, $B(1, 4)$ and $C(6, -1)$ are the vertices of a triangle.
Find the equations of the straight lines AC and BC.

Answer

Method 1: Using the formula for the gradient of a straight line

Use $y = mx + c$

To find the line AC:

First calculate the value of m.

$$m(AC) = \frac{(-1) - 2}{6 - (-3)} = \frac{-3}{9} = -\frac{1}{3}$$

Substitute this value in $y = mx + c$.

$$y = -\frac{1}{3}x + c$$

Substitute *either* $(6, -1)$ or $(-3, 2)$ in $y = -\frac{1}{3}x + c$.

Using $(6, -1)$: $\qquad -1 = -\frac{1}{3}(6) + c$

Simplifying: $\qquad -1 = -2 + c$

Finding c: $\qquad c = -1 + 2 = 1$

Write down the equation of the line:

Since $m = -\frac{1}{3}$ and $c = 1$, $y = -\frac{1}{3}x + 1$

Method 2: Using simultaneous equations

To find the line BC:

Substitute *both* $(6, -1)$ and $(1, 4)$ in $y = mx + c$.

Using $(6, -1)$: $\qquad -1 = m(6) + c \qquad$ OR $\qquad -1 = 6m + c \quad$ (1)

Using $(1, 4)$: $\qquad 4 = m(1) + c \qquad$ OR $\qquad 4 = 1m + c \quad$ (2)

MATHEMATICAL CONNECTIONS

You learnt how to solve simultaneous equations in Chapter 8.

CONTINUED

Solve the simultaneous equations using the elimination method.

$$-1 = 6m + c \quad (1)$$
$$4 = 1m + c \quad (2)$$

Subtract: (1) − (2)
$$-5 = 5m$$
$$m = -1$$

Substitute $m = -1$ to find c:
$$4 = 1(-1)c$$
$$4 = -1 + c$$
$$c = 4 + 1 = 5$$

Write down the equation of the line: $y = -x + 5$

DISCUSSION 3

Why will you always subtract the equations when you use this method to find the equation of the line?

Exercise 11.7

1 The coordinates $A(-3, 2)$, $B(1, 4)$ and $C(6, -1)$ are the vertices of a triangle.

Verify that the equation of the line AB is $= \frac{1}{2}x + 3\frac{1}{2}$

   a   using the formula for the gradient of a straight line

   b   using simultaneous equations.

REFLECTION

Which method do you prefer?

If you prefer one method or find one method easier, then use that method.

TIP

You can use your graphic display calculator to solve simultaneous equations to check your answers.

Make sure you know how to solve simultaneous equations on your calculator as well as on paper.

---

2 Find the equation of the line that joins each of the following pairs of points.

a	(3, 10) and (7, 12)	b	(4, 1) and (8, 13)	c	(4, 4) and (7, 10)
d	(2, 2) and (6, 10)	e	(0, 3) and (5, 13)	f	(5, 9) and (9, 13)
g	(10, 3) and (6, 11)	h	(0, 0) and (6, 9)	i	(2, 12) and (10, 8)
j	(9, 12) and (2, 19)	k	(0, 8) and (4, 4)	l	(3, 4) and (5, 4)

11.5 Parallel and non-parallel lines

Parallel lines

In Questions **2** and **3** of Exercise 11.6 you found the gradients and y-intercepts of some parallel lines. You should have noticed that the gradients of the parallel lines were all the same. This is always true.

Parallel lines have equal gradients and never intersect.

When the equations of two lines are written in general form, you can immediately see if the lines are parallel or not. For example, look at these equations of straight lines:

$A: y = 3x + 8$ $B: y = 3x - 6$ $C: y = -3x + 8$

Lines A and B are parallel because they both have a gradient of 3.

Line C is not parallel to A and B because its gradient is -3.

All lines with a gradient of 3 will be parallel to lines A and C.

Sometimes you will see the equations of straight lines written in a different form and you can not always immediately see if the lines are parallel or not.

For example, the lines $y + 2x = 7$ and $3y = 18 - 6x$ are parallel, even if it does not seem so.

In order to be certain whether two lines are parallel, you must rearrange the equations.

$$y + 2x = 7 \qquad\qquad\qquad 3y = 18 - 6x$$

Subtract $2x$: $\quad y = 7 - 2x$ $\qquad$ Divide by 3: $\quad y = 6 - 2x$

It is now clear that the gradient of each line is -2 so the lines must be parallel.

You can use this fact about the gradients of parallel lines to find the equation of other lines.

WORKED EXAMPLE 11

Find the equation of the straight line that is parallel to $y = 2x - 7$ that passes through the point (5, 12).

Answer

First find the gradient of the line $y = 2x - 7$.

The equation is already in the form $y = mx + c$, so the gradient $m = 2$.

The gradient of any parallel line will also have gradient 2, so the equation will be $y = 2x + c$.

Then substitute the point (5, -3) into the equation to find the value of c.

$$12 = 2(5) + c$$
$$12 = 10 + c$$
$$ 2 = c$$

So the equation of the line parallel to $y = 2x - 7$ that passes through (5, -3) is $y = 2x + 2$.

The gradients of two non-parallel lines are not equal and the lines intersect at a point. This point is called the point of intersection of the two lines.

For example, the lines $y = 2 + 3x$ and $y = 22 - 2x$ are not parallel, hence, the lines intersect.

You can use simultaneous equations to find the point of intersection of two non-parallel lines.

$y = 2 + 3x$ $\qquad\qquad$ (1)

$y = 22 - 2x$ $\qquad\quad$ (2)

Substitute $y = 2 + 3x$ into equation (2): $\quad 2 + 3x = 22 - 2x$

Add $2x$ to both sides: $\qquad\qquad\qquad\quad 2 + 5x = 22$

Subtract 2 from both sides: $\qquad\qquad\qquad\; 5x = 20$

Divide both sides by 5: $\qquad\qquad\qquad\qquad x = 4$

> **TIP**
>
> What is the gradient of each line?

Then substitute the value of x into one of the equations to find y:

$y = 2 + 3x \quad \longrightarrow \quad y = 2 + 3(4) = 14$

The point of intersection is (4, 14).

To check your answer, substitute the value for x into the other equation:

$y = 22 - 2x \quad \longrightarrow \quad y = 22 - 2(4) = 14$

Both lines pass through the point (4, 14); this is the point of intersection of the two lines.

Exercise 11.8

1   Use the following steps to find the equation of the line that is parallel to $y = 4x - 7$ and passes through (3, 15).

   a   Write down the gradient of $y = 4x - 7$.

   b   Write down the gradient of the parallel line $y = mx + c$.

   c   Substitute m and (3, 15) in $y = mx + c$ to find the value of c.

   d   Write down equation of the line.

2   Find the equation of the line that is parallel to $y = \frac{1}{2}x - 5$ and passes through (7, 2).

3   Find the equation of the line that is parallel to $y = 12 - \frac{1}{2}x$ and passes through (−6, 8).

For Questions 4 to 9, determine whether each pair of lines are parallel. For the pairs of lines that are not parallel, find their point of intersection. Verify your answers using your graphic display calculator.

4   $y = 3x + 7$ and $y = 22 + 3x$

5   $y = 3x + 1$ and $y = 25 - 3x$

6   $y = 2 + x$ and $y = x - 4$

7   $y = 2 + 3x$ and $y = 5x + 8$

8   $2y = 4 + 8x$ and $y = 17 - 2x$

9   $y - 3x = 7$ and $y = 23 - 5x$

Perpendicular lines

INVESTIGATION 3

Consider the quadrilateral $ABCD$ as shown in the diagram.

Is $ABCD$ a kite?

A kite is constructed from two isosceles triangles (ABD and BCD) with a common base (BD).

A kite has a line of symmetry, AC in this case.

The diagonals of a kite (AC and BD) are **perpendicular**.

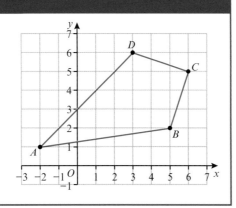

CONTINUED

1   **a**   Calculate the exact length of AB and of BC.

    b   Verify that the lengths of AD and AB are equal.

    c   Show that $ABCD$ is a kite.

2   **a**   Show that the equation of AC is $y = \dfrac{1}{2}x + 2$.

    b   Write down the gradient of AC.

    c   Show that the equation of BD is $y = 12 - 2x$.

    d   Write down the gradient of BD.

    e   Write down the product of these two gradients.

In Investigation 3, you have proved that $ABCD$ is a kite and that AC is the line of symmetry of $ABCD$. Therefore, diagonals AC and BD must be perpendicular.

The gradients of AC and BD tell you the direction of these lines.

As seen in the investigation, the product of these gradients equals -1.

This is *always* true for perpendicular lines.

The product of the gradients of two perpendicular lines $= -1$.

You may prefer to use the following formula.

If the gradient of the given line $= m$

Then the gradient of the perpendicular line $= \dfrac{-1}{m}$

WORKED EXAMPLE 12

Find the equation of the line passing through the point $(2, 5)$ that is perpendicular to the line with equation $2y = 3x - 4$.

Answer

1   Find the gradient of the given line as a fraction.

$$2y = 3x - 4$$

Divide by 2: $y = \dfrac{3}{2}x - 2$ gradient of given line $= \dfrac{3}{2}$

2   Find the gradient of the perpendicular line.

Since: $\dfrac{3}{2} \times \dfrac{-2}{3} = -1$ gradient of perpendicular line $= \dfrac{-2}{3}$

3   Use $y = mx + c$ with the perpendicular gradient $\dfrac{-2}{3}$ and the given point $(2, 5)$ to find c.

$$y = mx + c$$

$$5 = \dfrac{-2}{3} \times (2) + c$$

$$5 = \dfrac{-4}{3} + c$$

$$c = 5 + \dfrac{-4}{3} = \dfrac{11}{3}$$

The equation of the perpendicular line is $y = \dfrac{-2}{3}x + \dfrac{11}{3}$

TIP

Always follow these three steps to find the equation of the perpendicular line.

CONTINUED

Note that:

1 Improper fractions are used rather than either decimals or mixed numbers. This is more efficient and helps in the calculations.

Since, if the gradient of the given line is $\dfrac{a}{b}$ then the gradient of the perpendicular line is $\dfrac{-b}{a}$.

2 Sometimes the final answer for the equation of the line has to be given without fractions and integer values are required. In this case, then simply multiply the equation accordingly.

$$y = \frac{-2}{3}x + \frac{11}{3}$$

Multiply by 3: $3y = -2x + 11$

Exercise 11.9

1 Show that the equation of the line perpendicular to each given line passing through the given point is as shown.

   a $y = 2x + 8$ through $(2, 4)$ is $y = -\dfrac{1}{2}x + 5$

   b $y = 10 - \dfrac{1}{2}x$ through $(0, 3)$ is $y = 2x + 3$

2 Find the equation of the perpendicular line to the one given that passes through the given point:

   a $y = x + 3$ through $(-1, 7)$

   b $y = \dfrac{2}{3}x - 5$ through $(2, 4)$

   c $y = 2 - \dfrac{3}{4}x$ through $(3, 2)$

   d $2y = x + 8$ through $(4, -3)$

   e $5y = 15 - 2x$ through $(4, 13)$

   f $2x - y = 4$ through $(-8, -2)$

Finding the perpendicular bisector of a line segment

Consider the diagram of the kite $ABCD$.

The line AMC is the line of symmetry of kite. Hence it is the **perpendicular bisector** of the line segment BD.

The method of finding the equation of the perpendicular bisector of two points is summarised as follows:

1 Find the coordinates of M, the midpoint.

2 Find the gradient of BD.

3 Write down the gradient of AMC.

4 Use $y = mx + c$ for the equation of AMC.

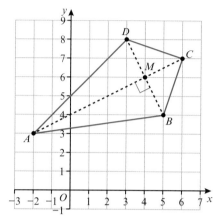

TIP

In many questions, you will be given only the coordinates of the two points, not a diagram. You may find it helpful to draw a sketch as a first step.

WORKED EXAMPLE 13

Find the equation of the perpendicular bisector of the lines segment BD where B and D have the coordinates $B(5, 4)$ and $D(3, 8)$.

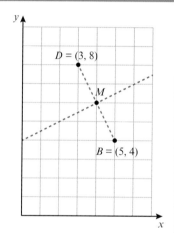

Answer

A sketch is not needed, but it is helpful. You do not need to draw your sketch to scale.

1 Coordinates of M: $\left(\dfrac{5 + 3}{2}, \dfrac{4 + 8}{2}\right) = (4, 6)$

2 Gradient of BD: $m = \dfrac{4 - 8}{5 - 3} = \dfrac{-4}{2} = -2$

3 Gradient of perpendicular: $\dfrac{-1}{m} = \dfrac{-1}{-2} = \dfrac{1}{2}$

4 Use $y = mx + c$ with $m = \dfrac{1}{2}$, $x = 4$ and $y = 6$

$6 = \dfrac{1}{2}(4) + c$ (and simplify)

$c = 4$

$\Rightarrow y = \dfrac{1}{2}x + 4$

TIP

Practise this technique.

Exercise 11.10

1 Find the equation of the perpendicular bisector of the following pairs of points.

TIP

You may find it helpful to draw a sketch in each case. You could also use graphing software to draw your sketches.

    a (7, 10) and (9, 12)   **b** (4, 11) and (8, 7)   **c** (4, 2) and (7, 8)

    d (5, 2) and (1, 10)   **e** (−3, 2) and (1, −10)   **f** (3, −5) and (−1, −7)

    g (−1, 4) and (4, 6)   **h** (2, −2) and (6,8)   **i** (2, 3) and (2, 11)

    j (5, 4) and (9, 4)

2 Consider the triangle with vertices $A(2, 1)$, $B(4, 3)$ and $C(1, 6)$.

    a Find the length of AB and of BC.

    b Find the gradient of AB and of BC.

    c Explain why ABC is a right-angled triangle.

    d Find the length of AC.

    e Find the equation of the line parallel to AB that passes through C.

    f Find the equation of the line perpendicular to AB that passes through A.

    g Find the coordinates of the point of intersection, D, of the two lines in parts **e** and **f**.

    h What is the name of the quadrilateral $ABCD$?

3 The quadrilateral $ABCD$ is a parallelogram, where $A(2, 2)$, $B(3, 5)$ and $D(0, 4)$.

    a Find the gradient of AB.

    b Find the equation of the line CD that is parallel to AB and passes through D.

    c Find the gradient of AD.

    d Find the equation of the line parallel to AD that passes through B.

    e Find the coordinates of the point of intersection, C, of these two lines found in parts **b** and **d**.

    f Calculate the distance AC.

    g Find the coordinates of the midpoint, M, of AC.

    h Find the equation of the line BD.

    i Verify that M lies on the line BD.

4 The quadrilateral $ABCD$ has vertices $A(1, 1)$, $B(4, 5)$, $C(3, 7)$ and $D(−1, 5)$.

    a Calculate the distance AB.

    b Show that AD and BC are parallel.

    c Show that AD and CD are perpendicular.

    d Calculate the area of the trapezium $ABCD$.

Past paper questions

1   A is the point $(0, 8)$ and B is the point $(6, 0)$.

The line L passes through B and is perpendicular to AB.

Find the equation of L.

.... [4]

Cambridge IGCSE International Mathematics 0607 Paper 21 Q16 Nov 2019

2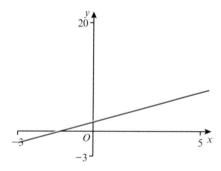

The diagram shows the graph of $y = x + 2$ for $-3 \leqslant x \leqslant 5$.

a   Find the coordinates of the y-intercept.

(...................., ...)   [1]

b   On the diagram, sketch the graph of $y = x^2 - x - 1$ for $-3 \leqslant x \leqslant 5$. [Using Past Paper Question Resource Sheet]   [2]

c   Solve this equation.

$x^2 - x - 1 = x + 2$

$x =$ .... or $x =$ ....   [2]

Cambridge IGCSE International Mathematics 0607 Paper 31 Q12 Jun 2019

3

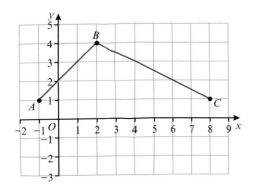

a   Write down the co-ordinates of

    i   point *B*,

(.............., ...) [1]

    ii   point *A*.

(.............., ...) [1]

b   *ABCD* is a kite.

    i   On the grid, plot the point *D* and complete the kite. [Using Past Paper Question Resource Sheet]   [1]

    ii   Write down the co-ordinates of point *D*.

(.............., ...) [1]

c   On the grid, draw the line of symmetry of the kite. [Using Past Paper Question Resource Sheet]   [1]

d   The equation of the line *BC* is $2y + x = 10$.

    i   Rearrange $2y + 10$ to make *y* the subject.

$y =$ .... [2]

    ii   Write down the gradient of the line *BC*.

.... [1]

e   The equation of the line *AB* is $y = x + 2$.

    Write down the equation of the line parallel to *AB*, passing through the point $(0, -4)$.

.... [2]

Cambridge IGCSE International Mathematics 0607 Paper 31 Q5 Nov 2018

> Chapter 12

Mensuration

IN THIS CHAPTER YOU WILL:

- use and convert between metric units of mass, length, area, volume and capacity

- calculate the perimeter and area of rectangles, parallelograms, triangles and trapezia

- calculate the circumference and area of circles

- calculate and solve problems involving the surface area and volume of cuboids, prisms, cylinders, spheres, pyramids and cones

- calculate and solve problems involving perimeters and areas of compound (or parts of) shapes

> calculate arc lengths and sector areas

> calculate and solve problems involving surface areas and volumes of compound (or parts of) solids.

KEY WORDS

arc

area

compound shape

congruent

cross-section

frustum

perimeter

prism

pyramid

right pyramid

sector

sectors (major and minor)

segment

volume (capacity)

GETTING STARTED

1 a Measure (or find on the internet) the length of the two edges of a piece of A4 paper.

  b Calculate the total length of the four edges – this is its **perimeter**. Write down the answer in **i** mm, **ii** cm and **iii** m.

  c Calculate the ratio of the longest side length divided by the shortest side length.

2 a Use Pythagoras' theorem to calculate the unknown side of each triangle labelled x.

    i

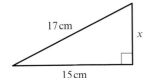

    ii

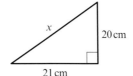

    iii

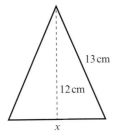

  b Calculate the perimeter of each triangle.

3 Solve each equation by finding the values of x.

  a $\quad 2x + 17 = 55$ b $\quad \dfrac{5x}{2} = 19$ c $\quad 7\pi x = 100$ d $\quad x^2 = 1225$

12.1 Units of measure

The units you use to measure something will depend on the object in question. For example, to measure the distance between two cities you would use kilometres, but to measure the size of an insect it would be more sensible to use millimetres. Similarly, if you wanted to describe the mass of an elephant it would be a good idea to use kilograms and not grams.

MATHEMATICS IN CONTEXT

The mass of a body is the amount of matter it contains, as opposed to the weight of a body, which is the force acting on it due to gravity.

An object taken to the moon will weigh less than on Earth (because of the moon's weaker gravity), but will have the same mass as on Earth.

You need to be familiar with the commonly used metric units of length, area and volume as well as mass and **capacity**. You will also need to be able to convert between different units.

MATHEMATICS IN CONTEXT

The metric system of measurement is used by most countries across the world, though there are some exceptions. The USA and the UK use imperial systems of measurement for some of their units – this means using miles instead of kilometres, feet instead of metres, pounds instead of kilograms and so on.

This is the reason why shipping containers are measured in feet – containers and container ships are an American invention, and they standardised the sizes using their system of measurement.

Interestingly, the UK and the USA imperial systems sometimes agree, but sometimes are different.

Length, mass and capacity

To convert between metric units you need to multiply or divide by powers of 10.

Some common conversions are shown here:

Length	**Mass**	**Capacity**
1 km = 1000 m	1 kg = 1000 g	1 litre = 1000 ml
1 m = 1000 mm	1 g = 1000 mg	
1 m = 100 cm		
1 cm = 10 mm		

Area and volume

The common units for area are based on the units for length. They are square kilometres (km^2), square metres (m^2), square centimetres (cm^2) and square millimetres (mm^2).

The common units for volume are cubic kilometres (km^3), cubic metres (m^3), cubic centimetres (cm^3) and cubic millimetres (mm^3).

You can work out conversion factors for area by starting with the conversion factors for length and thinking about the units themselves.

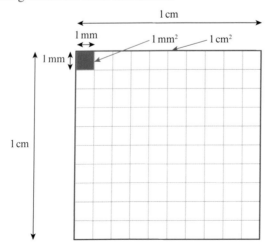

For example, starting with length: 1 cm = 10 mm

With area you square everything: $1^2 \text{cm}^2 = 10^2 \text{mm}^2$

so: $1 \text{cm}^2 = 100 \text{mm}^2$

With volume you cube everything: $1^3 \text{m}^3 = 100^3 \text{cm}^3$

so: $1 \text{m}^3 = 1\,000\,000 \text{cm}^3$

DISCUSSION 1

How can you convert between the other squared and cubed units for area and volume?

> **TIP**
>
> One m^3 is one million cm^3!
>
> The numbers with volume can become huge. Choosing the most appropriate unit in a question is an important skill.

Volume and capacity are closely related and so litres and millilitres can also be used to measure volume.

1 litre = 1000cm^3

Since $1 \text{m}^3 = 1\,000\,000 \text{cm}^3$ and 1 litre = 1000cm^3, there are 1000 litres in 1m^3.

WORKED EXAMPLE 1

a   Convert 3m^2 into   **i** cm^2 **ii** mm^2

b   Convert 17m^2 into km^2

c   Convert 385cm^3 into   **i** m^3 **ii** mm^3

d   Convert 3.5 litres into ml

e   Convert 2650 ml into l

Answers

a   In both **i** and **i** the answers will be larger: multiply.

   i   1 m = 100 cm so $1 \text{m}^2 = 100^2 \text{cm}^2 \Rightarrow 3 \text{m}^2 = 3 \times 100^2 = 30\,000 \text{cm}^2$

   ii   1 m = 1000 mm so $1 \text{mm}^2 = 1000^2 \text{cm}^2 \Rightarrow 3 \text{m}^2 = 3 \times 1000^2 = 30\,000 \text{mm}^2$

b   The answer will be smaller: divide.

   1 km = 1000 m so $1 \text{km}^2 = 1000^2 \text{m}^2 \Rightarrow 17 \text{m}^2 = 17 \div 1000^2 = 0.000017 \text{km}^2$

c   In **i** the answer will be smaller and in **ii** larger.

   i   1 m = 100 cm so $1 \text{m}^3 = 100^3 \text{cm}^3 \Rightarrow 385 \text{cm}^3 = 385 \div 100^3 = 0.000385 \text{m}^3$

   ii   1 cm = 10 mm so $1 \text{cm}^3 = 10^3 \text{mm}^3 \Rightarrow 385 \text{cm}^3 = 385 \times 10^3 = 385\,000 \text{mm}^3$

d   1 litre = 1000 ml, so 3.5 litres is $3.5 \times 1000 = 3500$ ml

e   1 litre = 1000 ml, so 2 650 ml is $2650 \div 1000 = 2.65$ litres

---

> **TIP**
>
> Before converting, think about the size of your answer. Remember that a 100 square millimetres covers the same area as 1 square centimetre. Keeping this in mind will help you to decide whether to multiply or divide by powers of ten when converting between metric units.

Exercise 12.1

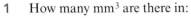

1   How many mm^3 are there in:

   a 1cm^3 **b** 5cm^3 **c** 2m^3?

2   How many cm^2 are there in:

   a 1m^2 **b** 4m^2 **c** 4000mm^2?

3 How many m^3 are there in:

    a $1\,km^3$ b $3\,km^3$ c $300\,000\,cm^3$?

 4 How many cm^3 are there in:

    a $5000\,mm^3$ b $3\,m^3$ c $0.5\,m^3$?

 5 How many m^2 are there in:

    a $5000\,cm^2$ b $2\,km^2$ c $4\,000\,000\,mm^2$?

 6 How many mm^2 are there in:

    a $1\,m^2$ b $7\,cm^2$ c $0.2\,m^2$?

 7 How many ml are there in:

    a   5.24 litres   b   10.05 litres?

 8 How many litres are there in:

    a   4251 ml   b   12450 ml?

9 A carton of milk weighs 1.8 kg and has volume 1.5 litres.

    a   Convert 1.8 kg into grams.

    b   Convert 1.5 litres into cm^3.

    c   Calculate the weight in grams of $1\,cm^3$ of milk.

    d   Calculate the volume in cm^3 of 1 g milk.

10 A wire of length 75 mm weighs 360 g and has been cut from a large reel of wire the weight of which is given as 450 kg.

    a   Convert 360 g into kg.

    b   Convert 75 mm into metres.

    c   Calculate the length of the reel of wire in metres.

11 A swimming pool holds $900\,m^3$ of water. $1\,cm^3$ of water weighs 1.1 g.

    a   Calculate the weight in kg of 1 litre of water.

    b   Calculate the volume of water in the swimming pool in litres.

    c   Calculate the weight of water in the swimming pool in kg.

    One metric tonne is equal to 1000 kg.

    d   Calculate the weight of the water in the swimming pool in metric tonnes.

> **TIP**
>
> Be careful! Check whether you are converting lengths, areas or volumes and choose the correct conversion factors.

12.2 Area and perimeter of rectangles and triangles

Area is the measured (or calculated) amount of space within a 2D shape.
You already know the formulae for the area, A, of the following shapes.

> **TIP**
>
> You will need to memorise the formulae for the areas and perimeters of different shapes.

Rectangle (square)

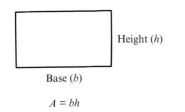

$$A = bh$$

Triangle

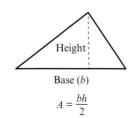

$$A = \frac{bh}{2}$$

Perimeter is the measured (or calculated) distance around the outside of a 2D shape. You can work out the perimeter of a shape by adding the lengths of all the sides together. There is no formula for the perimeter of a triangle, but if you know the base and the height of a rectangle you can find the perimeter using the formula $P = 2b + 2h$ (where b is the base and h is the height).

WORKED EXAMPLE 2

Calculate the area and the perimeter of these shapes.

a

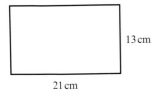

b

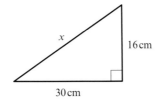

Answers

a   For a rectangle:

    Area   = base × height

          = $21 \times 13 = 273 \, \text{cm}^2$

    Perimeter = 2 × base + 2 × height

          = $2 \times 21 + 2 \times 13 = 68 \, \text{cm}$

b   For a triangle:

    Area $= \dfrac{\text{base} \times \text{height}}{2}$

          $= \dfrac{30 \times 16}{2} = 240 \, \text{cm}^2$

Before the perimeter can be calculated, x must be found using Pythagoras' theorem:

$x^2 = 16^2 + 30^2 \Rightarrow x = \sqrt{16^2 + 30^2} = 34$

Therefore, perimeter = $16 + 30 + 34 = 80 \, \text{cm}$

MATHEMATICAL CONNECTIONS

You learnt how to use Pythagoras' theorem in Chapter 10.

WORKED EXAMPLE 3

Calculate the perimeter of the rectangle.

Area = 300 cm² — 8 cm

Answer

$A = bh$ Using the area formula.

$300 = b \times 8 \Rightarrow 8b = 300$ Substituting the values.

$b = \dfrac{300}{8} = 37.5$ Solving the equation.

Therefore, perimeter = $2 \times 8 + 2 \times 37.5 = 88$ cm

Exercise 12.2

1   Calculate **i** the area and **ii** the perimeter of each shape.

Give your answers in cm or cm².

a

6.5 cm, 4 cm

b

3.2 m, 1.1 m

c

85 mm, 6 cm

d
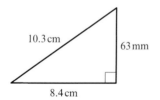
10.3 cm, 63 mm, 8.4 cm

e
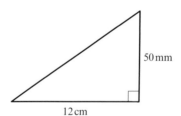
50 mm, 12 cm

f
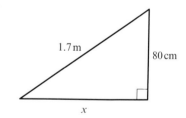
1.7 m, 80 cm, x

2   Calculate the exact area of each triangle.

a
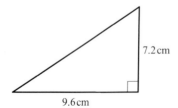
7.2 cm, 9.6 cm

b
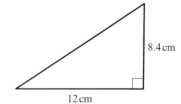
8.4 cm, 12 cm

c
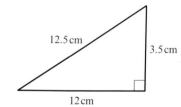
12.5 cm, 3.5 cm, 12 cm

d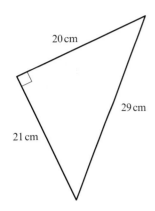

20 cm

29 cm

21 cm

e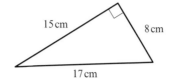

15 cm

8 cm

17 cm

f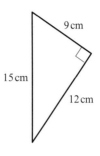

9 cm

15 cm

12 cm

3 Calculate the value of x for each triangle.

a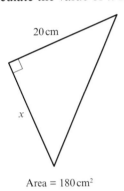

20 cm

x

Area = 180 cm²

b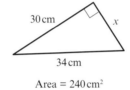

30 cm

x

34 cm

Area = 240 cm²

c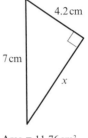

4.2 cm

7 cm

x

Area = 11.76 cm²

4 Calculate the perimeter of each shape.

a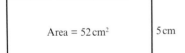

Area = 52 cm²

5 cm

b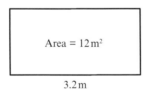

Area = 12 m²

3.2 m

c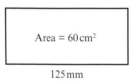

Area = 60 cm²

125 mm

d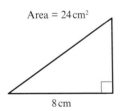

Area = 24 cm²

8 cm

e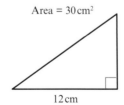

Area = 30 cm²

12 cm

f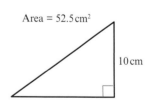

Area = 52.5 cm²

10 cm

5 Calculate the area of each shape.

a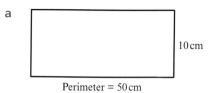
10 cm
Perimeter = 50 cm

b
60 cm
Perimeter = 28 cm

c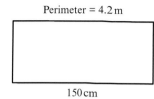
Perimeter = 4.2 m
150 cm

d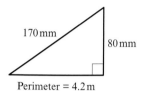
170 mm
80 mm
Perimeter = 4.2 m

e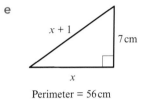
$x + 1$
7 cm
x
Perimeter = 56 cm

f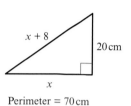
$x + 8$
20 cm
x
Perimeter = 70 cm

12.3 Area and perimeter of parallelograms and trapeziums

The area and perimeter of other quadrilaterals can also be calculated.

DISCUSSION 2

How does calculating the perimeter of a parallelogram differ from calculating the perimeter of a rectangle?

If the side lengths of the parallelogram and trapezium are known, it is a straightforward addition calculation.

> **MATHEMATICAL CONNECTIONS**
>
> You learnt about the properties of parallelograms and trapeziums in Chapter 5.

WORKED EXAMPLE 4

Find the perimeter of the parallelogram and trapezium shown.

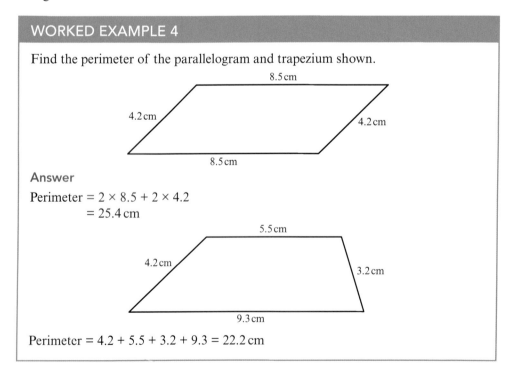

8.5 cm
4.2 cm
4.2 cm
8.5 cm

Answer

Perimeter = 2 × 8.5 + 2 × 4.2
= 25.4 cm

5.5 cm
4.2 cm
3.2 cm
9.3 cm

Perimeter = 4.2 + 5.5 + 3.2 + 9.3 = 22.2 cm

If the side lengths are not known, any question will have enough information to enable you to calculate the missing side lengths, as in Worked example 2.

To calculate the area of parallelograms and trapeziums it is helpful to consider them as compound shapes. A compound shape is a shape made up of a combination of shapes.

MATHEMATICAL CONNECTIONS

Compound shapes are discussed later in this chapter and in Chapter 24.

WORKED EXAMPLE 5

Find the area of the following parallelogram and trapezium.

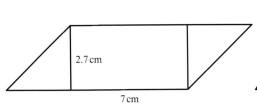 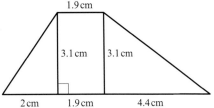

Answer

The trapezium is a combination of a rectangle and two triangles.

The perpendicular height (h) is the same for both triangles as any trapezium has a pair of parallel sides.

The area of the rectangle is $1.9 \times 3.1 = 5.89 \, \text{cm}^2$

The area of the smaller triangle is $\frac{1}{2} \times 2 \times 3.1 = 3.1 \, \text{cm}^2$

The area of the larger triangle is $\frac{1}{2} \times 4.2 \times 3.1 = 6.82 \, \text{cm}^2$

The total area is $5.89 + 3.1 + 6.82 = 15.81 \, \text{cm}^2$

The same trapezium is shown below:

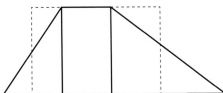

The base of each of the triangles has been halved and the perpendicular height drawn.

This has created a rectangle with the same area as the trapezium.

So another way of finding the area of the trapezium is to find the mean of the lengths of the two parallel sides and multiply them by the perpendicular height.

For this trapezium, this is $\dfrac{1.9 + 8.3}{2} \times 3.1 = 15.81 \, \text{cm}^2$

The following parallelogram can be approached in a similar way.

CONTINUED

A parallelogram has two pairs of parallel sides so the triangles at either end are identical.

This means the area can be calculated by multiplying the base length by the perpendicular height.

The area of the parallelogram is $2.7 \times 7 = 18.9\,\text{cm}^2$

Exercise 12.3

1   Find the area of the following parallelograms to one decimal place.

a

b

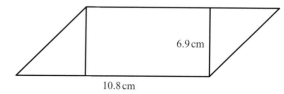

c

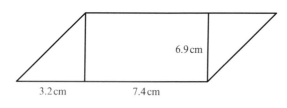

d

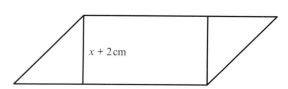

2   Find the perimeter of the following parallelograms to one decimal place.

a

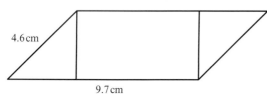

b

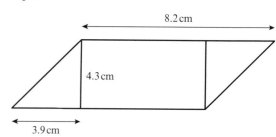

c

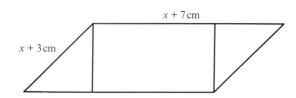

d

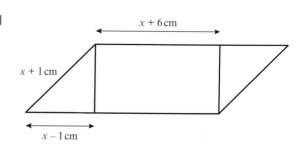

3   Calculate the area of the following trapeziums to one decimal place.

a
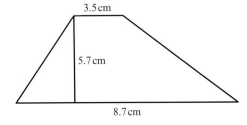
3.5 cm
5.7 cm
8.7 cm

b
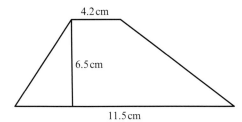
4.2 cm
6.5 cm
11.5 cm

c
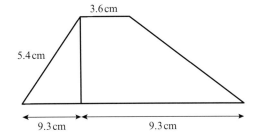
3.6 cm
5.4 cm
9.3 cm   9.3 cm

d
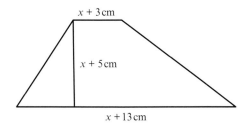
$x + 3$ cm
$x + 5$ cm
$x + 13$ cm

4   Find the perimeter of the following trapeziums to one decimal place.

a
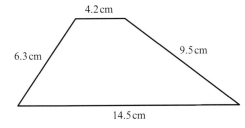
4.2 cm
6.3 cm   9.5 cm
14.5 cm

b
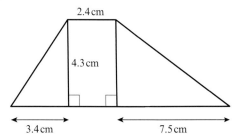
2.4 cm
4.3 cm
3.4 cm   7.5 cm

12.4 Circles

There are two formulae associated with the circle; the first for its perimeter (circumference) and the second for the area enclosed by the circle:

Circumference of a circle: $C = \pi d$

Area inside the circle: $A = \pi r^2$

There is also the link between the radius and the diameter of a circle: $d = 2r$

This link gives the alternative formula for the circumference of a circle: $C = 2\pi r$

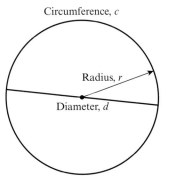
Circumference, c
Radius, r
Diameter, d

WORKED EXAMPLE 6

The diameter of a circle is 7.6 cm.

a Calculate its area.

b Calculate its circumference. Give the exact answer.

Answers

a $A = \pi r^2$ Write the formula for the area.

$d = 7.6 \Rightarrow r = \dfrac{7.6}{2} = 3.8$ You are told the diameter, so you need to divide by 2 to find the radius.

$A = \pi \times 3.8^2 = 45.36$ Substitute the values.

$\quad = 45.4 \,\text{cm}^2$ (to 3 sf)

b $C = \pi d$ Write the formula for the circumference.

$C = 7.6\pi$ Substitute the values.

> **TIP**
>
> Always check carefully whether you are being asked about the radius or the diameter.

WORKED EXAMPLE 7

The area of a circle is 80 cm². Calculate:

a its diameter

b its circumference.

Answers

a $A = \pi r^2 \Rightarrow 80 = \pi r^2$ Substitute values.

$r^2 = \dfrac{80}{\pi} \Rightarrow r = \sqrt{\dfrac{80}{\pi}} \Rightarrow r = 5.046\ldots$ Rearrange the equation.

$r = 5.05 \,\text{cm}$ (3 sf)

$d = 2r = 2(5.046\ldots) = 10.09\ldots$ Find the diameter.

$d = 10.1 \,\text{cm}$ (3 sf)

b $C = \pi r \Rightarrow C = \pi \times 10.09\ldots$ Substitute values.

$\quad\quad = 31.7 \,\text{cm}$ (3 sf)

> **TIP**
>
> Always use the full calculator display when doing further calculations. Then answers are accurate.

Exercise 12.4

1 Calculate the circumference of the circles with the given diameters, correct to three significant figures.

a

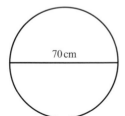

70 cm

b

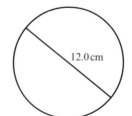

12.0 cm

c

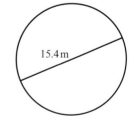

15.4 m

d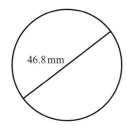

46.8 mm

e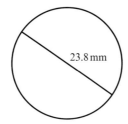

23.8 mm

2 Calculate the exact circumference of the circles with the following radii.

a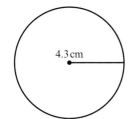

4.3 cm

b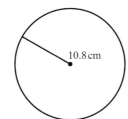

10.8 cm

c

17.3 m

d

13.6 mm

e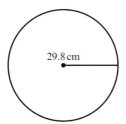

29.8 cm

3 Calculate, correct to three significant figures, the diameter of each circle, with the given circumference.

a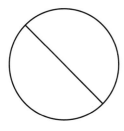

$C = 12.6$ cm

b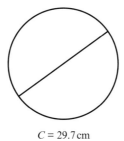

$C = 29.7$ cm

c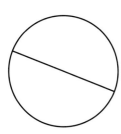

$C = 43.6$ cm

d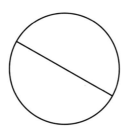

$C = 78.5$ cm

4   Calculate, exactly, **i** the radius and **ii** the area of each circle with the given circumference.

a

$C = 18.8\,cm$

b

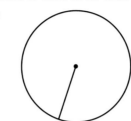

$C = 26.8\,cm$

c

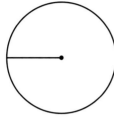

$C = 69.3\,cm$

d

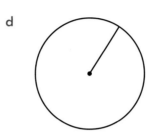

$C = 69.3\,cm$

5   A bicycle wheel has a diameter of 65 cm.
   a   Calculate the distance the bicycle travels when the wheel turns round once.
   b   How many complete revolutions does the wheel make when the bicycle travels a distance of: **i** 400 m   **ii** 2 km?

> **TIP**
>
> Remember the units! Change the distances into cm.

6   A child's bicycle has a wheel of radius 25 cm.
   a   Calculate the distance the bicycle travels when the wheel turns round once.
   b   How many complete revolutions does the wheel make when the bicycle travels a distance of: **i** 400 m   **ii** 2 km?

7   A bicycle wheel turns 45 times as it covers a distance of 100 m.
    Calculate:
   a   the circumference of the wheel
   b   the diameter of the wheel
   c   the radius of the wheel.

> **TIP**
>
> Think about the units – do you want your answer in cm or m?

8   The giant sequoia of North America is the largest tree in the world. It would take 13 people, each with an average stretch of 1.9 metres to link hands around the base of the tree, which is roughly circular.
    Calculate the approximate diameter at the base.

9   Find, correct to three significant figures, the areas of the circles with the following radii.
   a   8 cm   b   14 cm   c   9.7 cm   d   12.8 m   e   16.4 m

10 Find the exact areas of the circles with the following diameters.
   a   7 cm   b   22 cm   c   17.4 cm   d   8.6 mm   e   21.8 m

11   Find the area of the shaded ring, correct
to three significant figures, when:

a $R = 13$ cm and $r = 7$ cm

b $R = 6.3$ cm and $r = 3.7$ cm.

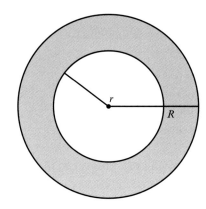

12   Calculate, correct to three significant figures, the radii of circles with the
following areas.

a   80 cm²   b   154 cm²   c   220 cm²   d   39.6 cm²   e   12 cm²

13   The area of this circle is 201 cm².
Calculate exactly:

a   its radius

b   its diameter

c   its circumference.

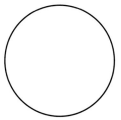

Arcs and sectors

The diagram shows some parts of a circle.

1   An **arc** of a circle is a part of its circumference.
(It is a fraction of the circumference.)

2   A **sector** of a circle is a part of the area of the
that has been formed by two radii cutting the circle.
(It is a fraction of the area of the circle.)

If the angle between the two radii is less than 180°
the sector is known as a **minor sector**, and if it is
more than 180° it is a **major sector**.
The sector shown in this circle is a minor sector.

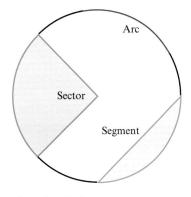

3   A **segment** is a part of the area of the circle formed by a line cutting the circle.

DISCUSSION 3

There is one special case where a segment of a circle is the same as a sector.
What is this special case?

WORKED EXAMPLE 8

The diagram shows a sector of a circle.

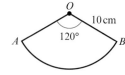

a What fraction of a circle is this sector?

b Calculate the length of the arc from A to B, giving your answer to three significant figures.

c Calculate the perimeter of the shape, giving your answer to three significant figures.

d Calculate the area of the sector, giving your answer to three significant figures.

Answers

a The fraction of the circle is $\dfrac{\text{the measured angle}}{\text{the angle in a full circle}} = \dfrac{120°}{360°} = \dfrac{1}{3}$

You need to know this to make progress with the rest of the question.

b The sector is $\dfrac{1}{3}$ of a circle, therefore the length of the arc from A to $B = \dfrac{1}{3}$ of the circumference.

$$\text{Arc length} = \frac{1}{3} \times 2\pi r = \frac{1}{3} \times 2 \times \pi \times 10$$
$$= 20.9 \,\text{cm (3 sf)}$$

c To find the perimeter, add the two radii to the arc length.

$$\text{Perimeter} = 10 + 10 + 20.9$$
$$= 40.9 \,\text{cm (3 sf)}$$

d The area of the sector $AOB = \dfrac{1}{3}$ of the area of the circle.

$$\text{Sector area} = \frac{1}{3} \times \pi \times r^2$$
$$= \frac{1}{3} \times \pi \times 100$$
$$= 115 \,\text{cm}^2 \,\text{(3 sf)}$$

WORKED EXAMPLE 9

The same sector is shown again.

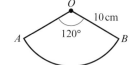

a Calculate exact values for the perimeter and the area.

b Give your answers in terms of π.

Answers

a The fraction of the circle is $\dfrac{1}{3}$.

The length of the arc from A to $B = \dfrac{1}{3}$ of the circumference.

$$\text{Arc length} = \frac{1}{3} \times 2 \times \pi \times 10 = \frac{20\pi}{3}$$

$$\text{Exact perimeter} = 10 + 10 + \frac{20\pi}{3}$$
$$= 20 + \frac{20\pi}{3}$$

TIP

Leave your answer as an improper fraction.

CONTINUED

b The area of the sector $AOB = \frac{1}{3}$ of the area of the circle.

Sector area $= \frac{1}{3} \times \pi \times 10^2 = \frac{100\pi}{3}$

The general case

The diagram shows a sector of a circle with radius, r, and angle subtended at the centre θ.

The fraction of the circle $= \frac{\theta}{360}$.

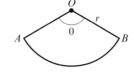

Therefore, arc length A to $B = \frac{\theta}{360} \times \pi d$

Area of sector $AOB = \frac{\theta}{360} \times \pi r^2$

If the area is given in terms of π it is possible to work out the radius and diameter of the circle by rearranging the formula.

To calculate the radius from a given area, the sector formula above would need to be rearranged in terms of r:

Area of sector $AOB = \frac{\theta}{360} \pi r^2$

$\frac{\text{Area of sector } AOB}{\pi} = \frac{\theta}{360} r^2$

$\frac{360(\text{area of sector } AOB)}{\pi \theta} = r^2$

$\sqrt{\frac{360(\text{area of sector } AOB)}{\pi \theta}} = r$

WORKED EXAMPLE 10

The area of a sector of a circle with a subtended angle of 120° is $\frac{16\pi}{3}$.

Find the radius of the circle.

CONTINUED

Answer

Substitute the area of the sector into the rearranged formula above:

$$\sqrt{\frac{360(\text{area of sector } AOB)}{\pi\theta}} = r$$

$$r = \sqrt{\frac{360 \times \frac{16\pi}{3}}{120\pi}}$$

$$r = \sqrt{\frac{1920\pi}{120\pi}}$$

$$r = \sqrt{16}$$

$$r = 4$$

Exercise 12.5

1   For each shape, calculate:

   i   the *exact* area of each sector

   ii   the *exact* perimeter of each shape.

   a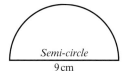
   Semi-circle
   9 cm

   b
   6 cm

2   Calculate:

   i   the area of each sector

   ii   the perimeter of each shape.

   Give answers correct to three significant figures.

   a
   60°
   10.8 cm

   b
   72°
   4.2 cm

   c
   120°
   3.7 cm

   d
   6.8 cm
   70°

   e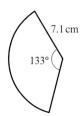
   7.1 cm
   133°

   f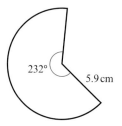
   232°
   5.9 cm

12.5 Areas and perimeters of compound shapes

Compound shapes can be formed from combinations of other shapes. Their areas and perimeters can be found by applying knowledge of their underlying shapes.

Exercise 12.6

1 *DFEC* is a parallelogram and *DCBA* is a trapezium.

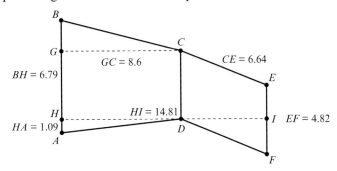

Calculate to one decimal place:

a the area of the shape *ADFECB*

b the perimeter of the shape *ADFECB*.

2 *ACDB* is a parallelogram.

Calculate to one decimal place:

a the area of *ACDB*

b the perimeter of *ACDB*

c the area of *GDFE*.

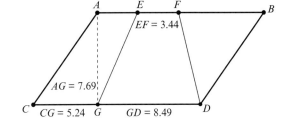

3 In the diagram, *EF*, *CD* and *AB* are parallel. *CG* and *DI* are perpendicular to *AB*.

Calculate to two decimal places:

a the perimeter of *ABDFEC*

b the area of *ABDFEC*.

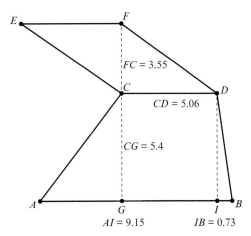

4 The decagon below has been drawn on cm² graph paper.

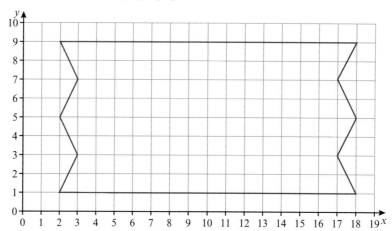

Calculate to two decimal places:

a the area and

b the perimeter of the decagon.

5 This shape is made up of half of the circumference of a circle of diameter 2 m and three straight lines.

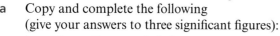

a Copy and complete the following (give your answers to three significant figures):

   i Circumference of circle   =

   ii Half the circumference   =

   iii Length of three straight lines =

   iv Perimeter of shape   =

b Calculate the area of the shape.

c Repeat parts **a** and **b** to find the exact perimeter and area of the shape

6 Calculate the perimeter of each shape, giving both **i** exact answers and **ii** answers correct to three significant figures.

a

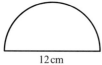

12 cm

b

8 cm

c

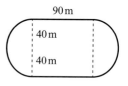

90 m

40 m

40 m

d

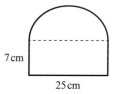

7 cm

25 cm

e

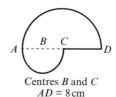

Centres B and C

$AD = 8$ cm

f

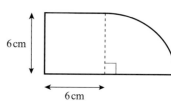

6 cm

6 cm

g

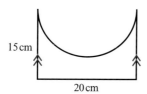

15 cm

20 cm

h

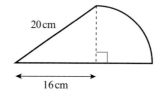

20 cm

16 cm

7 Calculate the exact area of each shape in Question 6.

DISCUSSION 4

The diagram in Question **6** part **c** represents a running track. However, the perimeter of the track needs to be 400 m. If the length of the straight remains 90 m, what must be the radius of the bend?

8 Discs of radius 4 cm are cut from a rectangular sheet of plastic that measures 26 cm by 75 cm.

    a   Calculate the number of discs that fit along the width.

    b   Calculate the number of discs that can be cut from the rectangular sheet.

    c   Calculate the area of the sheet that is wasted.

    d   Calculate the percentage wasted area.

    e   Given that 27 discs are to be cut from the rectangular sheet, what are the smallest dimensions of the sheet?

    f   What is the percentage wasted area?

9 The shapes shown are both constructed from semicircles.

    a

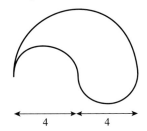

    b

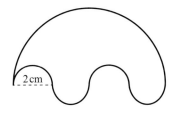

    i   Calculate their exact areas.

    ii   Calculate their exact perimeters.

12.6 Volume and surface area of prisms and cylinders

Volume of prisms and cylinders

Volume measures the amount of space a three-dimensional object takes up.

DISCUSSION 5

What is the difference between an object's volume and its capacity?

Prisms

The simplest **prism** is a cuboid.

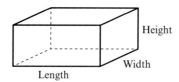

You may already know the formula:

Volume of a cuboid = length × width × height

$V = lwh$

Looking at this formula in more detail, you can see that length × width is the area of the base of the cuboid.

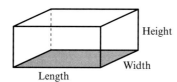

So,

Volume of a cuboid = base area × height

The base is a **cross-section** of the cuboid.

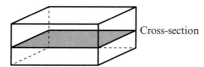

Imagine a horizontal plane slicing through the cuboid anywhere along its height. The plane creates the cross-section of the cuboid and this cross-section is exactly the same shape and size at whatever height it crosses the cuboid.

So,

Volume of a cuboid = area of cross-section × height

Any shape that has a **congruent** (exactly the same shape and size) polygon cross-section is a prism, and you can calculate its volume in a similar way using the general result:

Volume of a prism = area of cross-section × length (or height)

Rectangles and triangles are common cross-sections, but the cross-section of a prism can be any polygon provided its shape and size does not vary.

The cross-section of a triangular prism is a triangle:

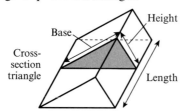

Volume of triangular prism $= \dfrac{lbh}{2}$

> **MATHEMATICAL CONNECTIONS**
>
> You learnt about congruency and similarity in Chapter 9.

> **TIP**
>
> Remember, a polygon is a 2D shape with straight edges.

The cross-section of a pentagonal prism is a pentagon:

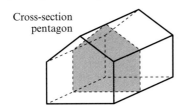

Cross-section
pentagon

Cylinders

A cylinder cannot be called a prism because it has a
circular cross-section instead of a polygon cross-section.

However, the cross-section is congruent all along
the solid, so you can calculate the volume in the
same way by multiplying the area of the
cross-section by the length.

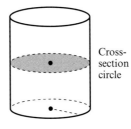

Cross-
section
circle

Volume of cylinder = $\pi r^2 h$

WORKED EXAMPLE 11

The cross-section of this prism is made up of a rectangle joined to a quarter circle
and its length is 6 cm.

Calculate the volume of the prism.

Give your answer exactly in terms of π and also approximately to three
significant figures.

Answer

The radius of the quarter circle = $12 - 7 = 5$ cm

Cross-section = rectangle + quarter circle

Area of cross-section = $7 \times 5 + \dfrac{1}{4} \times \pi \times 5^2$

$= 35 + \dfrac{25\pi}{4}$

Volume of prism = area of cross-section × length

$= \left(35 + \dfrac{25\pi}{4}\right) \times 6$

$= 210 + \dfrac{150\pi}{4}$

$= 210 + \dfrac{75\pi}{2}$ cm²

$= 328$ cm³ (correct to 3 sf)

| |
Use the diagram to work
out the radius of the
quarter circle.

Write down all the steps in
your method.

Substitute the values, but
you do not need to calculate
the cross-sectional area.

Multiply everything inside
the brackets by 6.

Write the fraction in its
simplest form. This is the
exact answer.

Use your calculator to write
the approximate answer.

Calculating unknown lengths

Sometimes you will be told the volume of a prism or cylinder and asked to work out one of the lengths, for example the height of a prism or the radius of the base of a cylinder.

In this case, you will need to use the result that the volume of a prism is the product of its base area and its height in order to write down a formula for the volume.

Once you have written the formula, substitute all given values and solve it to find the unknown length.

WORKED EXAMPLE 12

The volume of a triangular prism is $720 \, \text{cm}^3$.

The length of the prism is $12 \, \text{cm}$.

The height of triangular cross-section is $8 \, \text{cm}$.

Calculate the base of the triangle.

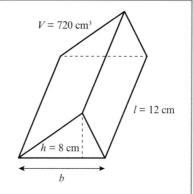

Answer

All measurements are in cm or cm³	Check the units are consistent.
Volume = area of cross-section × length	Write the formula for the volume.
$V = \dfrac{bhl}{2}$	
$720 = \dfrac{b \times 8 \times 12}{2}$	Substitute the given values.
$= 48b$	Simplify.
$\dfrac{720}{48} = b$	Divide both sides by 48 to solve.
$b = 15 \, \text{cm}$	

WORKED EXAMPLE 13

The capacity of a cylindrical can is 1 litre.

The height of the can is $18 \, \text{cm}$.

Calculate the radius of the base of the can.

Give your answer to three significant figures.

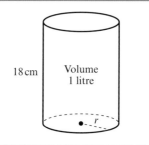

> **TIP**
>
> In this situation the capacity of the can is the same as its volume.

CONTINUED

Answer

1 litre = 1000 cm³	Start by making the units consistent.
Volume = area of cross-section × height	Write the formula for the volume
$V = \pi r^2 h$	
$1000 = \pi \times r^2 \times 18$	Substitute the given values.
$18\pi r^2 = 1000$	Simplify.
$r^2 = \dfrac{1000}{18\pi}$	Divide both sides by 18π.
$r = \sqrt{\dfrac{1000}{18\pi}}$	Take the square root of both sides.
$= 4.205...$	
$= 4.21$ cm (to 3 sf)	Write your answer to three significant figures.

Exercise 12.7

1   Calculate the volume of each of the prisms. Give your answers correct to three significant figures.

a

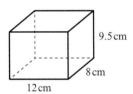
9.5 cm
8 cm
12 cm

b

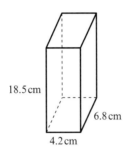
18.5 cm
6.8 cm
4.2 cm

c

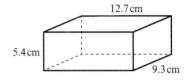
12.7 cm
5.4 cm
9.3 cm

d

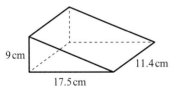
9 cm
11.4 cm
17.5 cm

e

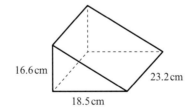
16.6 cm
23.2 cm
18.5 cm

2   Calculate the volume of each of cylinder. Give your answers exactly, in terms of π.

a

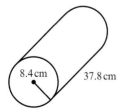
8.4 cm
37.8 cm

b

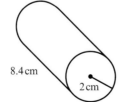
8.4 cm
2 cm

c

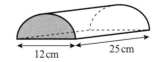
12 cm
25 cm

d

e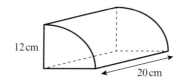

3 Calculate the volume of each of the prisms. Give your answers correct to three significant figures.

a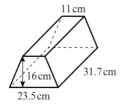

b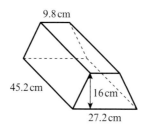

c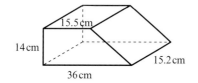

d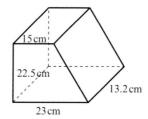

4 Copy and complete this table with the missing dimensions for each cuboid.
Give all your answers to three significant figures.

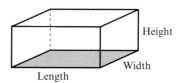

Volume	Length	Width	Height
23 cm³		3 cm	4 cm
90 cm³	10 cm	12 cm	
970 cm³	18 cm		5.8 cm
2 litres		13.5 cm	4.3 cm

5 Copy and complete this table with the missing dimensions for each triangular prism.
Give all your answers to three significant figures.

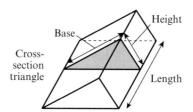

Volume	Base	Height	Length
60 cm³	8 cm	6 cm	
200 cm³	5 cm	2.5 cm	

6   Copy and complete this table with the missing
    dimensions for each cylinder.
    Give all your answers to three significant figures.

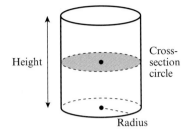

Volume	Radius	Diameter	Length
72 cm³	4 cm		
500 cm³		14 cm	
85 cm³			13 cm
4 litres			56 cm

Surface area of prisms and cylinders

Although area is a measure of a two-dimensional object, every three-dimensional
object has two-dimensional surfaces and calculating these is an important skill.

To calculate the surface area of any solid, you must be able to visualise:

- the number of surfaces a prism possesses
- the shape of each surface.

For example: a cuboid has six surfaces and all of them are rectangles; a cylinder has
three surfaces, two are circles and one is a rectangle.

DISCUSSION 6

How many surfaces does a triangular prism have and what shapes are they?

Once you know the number of surfaces and their shapes, you can calculate the value of
each surface and find the *total surface area*.

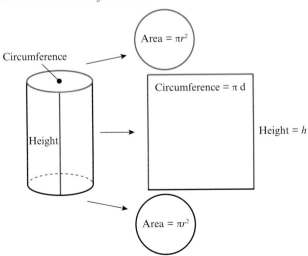

The cylinder is the trickiest to visualise.

Imagine removing the top and bottom circles to leave the curved surface area.

Then, cut along the red line and fold out the curved surface until it becomes flat. It is a rectangle.

One side length of the rectangle is equal to the height of the cylinder. The length of the other side is equal to the circumference of the circular cross-section.

WORKED EXAMPLE 14

For the cylinder shown in the diagram, calculate:

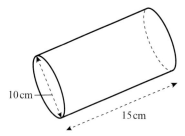

10 cm

15 cm

a the volume

b the total surface area.

Give your answers to the nearest integer.

Answers

The diameter of the circular cross-section = 10 cm
Therefore, the radius of the cross-section = 5 cm

a   Volume of cylinder = area of circular cross-section × height of cylinder
$$= \pi r^2 \times h$$
$$= \pi (5)^2 \times 15$$
$$= 1178 \text{ cm}^2 \text{ (correct to the nearest integer)}$$

b   Area of two end faces $= 2 \times \pi r^2$
$$= 2 \times 25\pi = 50\pi$$

Area of the curved surface = length × width
(the rectangle)   = circumference of cross-section × height of cylinder
$$= \pi d \times h$$
$$= 150\pi$$

Total surface area = two circles + one rectangle
$$= 50\pi + 150\pi$$
$$= 200\pi$$
$$= 628 \text{ cm}^2 \text{ (correct to the nearest integer)}$$

Exercise 12.8

1 Calculate the total surface area of each of the solid prisms correct to the nearest integer. Before you start each part, count the number of surfaces of the solid.

a
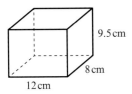
9.5 cm
8 cm
12 cm

b
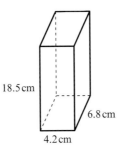
18.5 cm
6.8 cm
4.2 cm

c
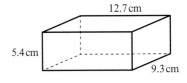
12.7 cm
5.4 cm
9.3 cm

d
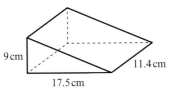
9 cm
11.4 cm
17.5 cm

e
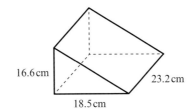
16.6 cm
23.2 cm
18.5 cm

f
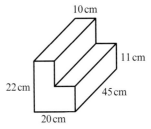
10 cm
11 cm
22 cm
45 cm
20 cm

g
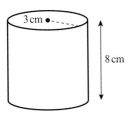
15.5 cm
14 cm
15.2 cm
36 cm

h
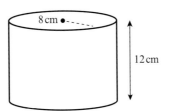
15 cm
22.5 cm
13.2 cm
25 cm

2 Calculate **i** the volume and **ii** the total surface area of each solid cylinder.

a
3 cm
8 cm

b
8 cm
12 cm

c
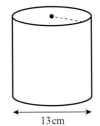
13 cm

3 This solid is formed by cutting in half a cylinder of height 14 cm and base diameter 20 cm.

   a How many surfaces does this solid have?

   b What is the shape of the cross-section?

   c Calculate its:

      i volume

      ii total surface area.

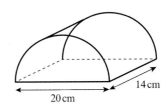
20 cm
14 cm

4 Calculate **a** the volume and **b** the total surface area of this solid.

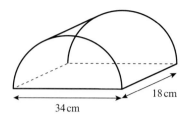

34 cm   18 cm

5 For each solid, calculate:

  i its volume   **ii** its total surface area.

a
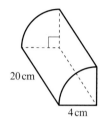
20 cm
4 cm

b
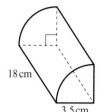
18 cm
3.5 cm

c
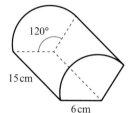
120°
15 cm
6 cm

12.7 Volume and surface area of pyramids and cones

Volume of pyramids and cones

A **pyramid** is a three-dimensional object with a flat base that rises to a point called the apex. The famous pyramids in Egypt have square bases, but the base of a pyramid can be a triangle, rectangle, hexagon … in fact it can be any polygon.

    Rectangular-based pyramid

   Square-based pyramid

    Tetrahedron

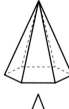   Hexagonal-based pyramid

    Cone

A three-dimensional object with a circular base that rises to a point is called a cone.

A pyramid with a triangular base is called a tetrahedron. Regular tetrahedrons, where all four faces are equilateral triangles, are often used as dice.

Pyramids with the apex above the centre of the base are called **right pyramids**.

However, the apex can be placed at any point above the base as shown here:

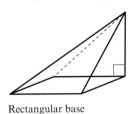

Rectangular base

The volume of a pyramid

A pyramid is different to a prism, in that the cross-section is not the same throughout the shape. The formula for the **volume** of a pyramid is linked to that of a prism, and is given as:

$$\text{Volume} = \frac{\text{base area} \times \text{height}}{3}$$

The formula for the volume of a pyramid is valid for both right and non-right pyramids.

WORKED EXAMPLE 15

Calculate the volume of this solid pyramid. Its base is a rectangle.

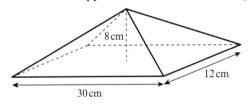

8 cm

12 cm

30 cm

Answer

$V = \dfrac{1}{3}Ah$ Use the formula for the volume of a pyramid.

$\quad = \dfrac{1}{3}lwh$ A is the base area and h is the height.

$V = \dfrac{1}{3} \times 30 \times 12 \times 8$ Substitute values.

$\quad = 960 \text{ cm}^3$

The volume of a cone

A cone, like a pyramid, does not have a uniform cross-section. The formula for the volume of a cone is linked to that of a cylinder, and is given as:

$$V(\text{cone}) = \frac{\pi r^2 h}{3}$$

DISCUSSION 7

How is the formula for the volume of a cone similar to the formula for the volume of a pyramid?

WORKED EXAMPLE 16

Calculate the volume of a (right) cone with height 10 cm and base radius 6 cm. Give your answer exactly as a multiple of π.

Answer

$V = \dfrac{1}{3}Ah$ The formula for the volume of a cone is the same as for a pyramid.

$a = \pi r^2$ The base of the cone is a circle.

$\quad = \pi \times 6^2 = 36\pi$

So, $V = \dfrac{1}{3} \times 36\pi \times 8$

$\qquad = 96\pi \text{ cm}^3$

Sometimes, the volume (or surface area) of a cone is known and you must design its shape where, for example, its height is fixed and the radius calculated.

The theory involved uses the work you have previously studied on rearranging formulae.

WORKED EXAMPLE 17

Find the height of a cone with volume = 120π and base radius = 6.

Answer

$V = \dfrac{\pi r^2 h}{3}$

$120\pi = \dfrac{\pi 6^2 h}{3}$

$120\pi = 12\pi h$

$\quad\; h = 10$

Exercise 12.9

1   Calculate the volume of each solid pyramid.

a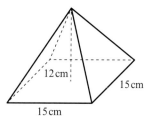

b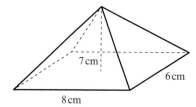

c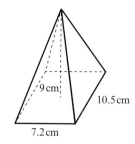

2 Calculate the volume of each solid cone.

a

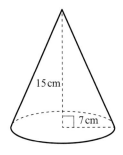

b

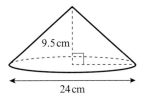

c

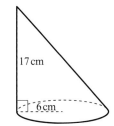

d

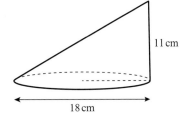

3 The area of the base of a square-based pyramid is 42.25 cm² and its volume is 169 cm³.

Calculate **a** its height and **b** the length of the edge of its base.

4 The length of the edge of the base of a square-based pyramid is 5.7 cm and its volume is 162.45 cm³.

Calculate **a** the area of its base and **b** its height.

5 The height of a square-based pyramid is 10.5 cm and its volume is 143.36 cm³.

Calculate the area of its base.

6 A pyramid has a rectangular base with edges of lengths 7.5 cm and 8.2 cm. Its volume is 123 cm³. Calculate its height.

7 A pyramid has a rectangular base with one edge of length 13.8 cm and height 20 cm. Its volume is 874 cm³. Calculate the length of the other edge of the base.

Surface area of pyramids and cones

As you did with prisms, to calculate the surface area of pyramids and cones you must identify the number and shape of the surfaces, work out their areas and add together to find the total surface area.

WORKED EXAMPLE 18

Calculate the surface area of the square-based right pyramid.

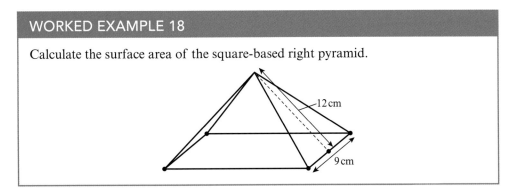

CONTINUED

Answer

The base of the pyramid is a square of area $9\,\text{cm} \times 9\,\text{cm} = 81\,\text{cm}^2$

Each of the four triangular sides have a base of $9\,\text{cm}$ and a perpendicular height of $12\,\text{cm}$.

Each triangle has an area of $\frac{1}{2} \times 9 \times 12 = 54\,\text{cm}^2$

So the surface area is $4 \times 54\,\text{cm} + 81\,\text{cm} = 297\,\text{cm}^2$

WORKED EXAMPLE 19

Calculate the surface area of the solid pyramid.

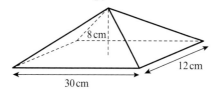

TIP

You will need to use Pythagoras' theorem to complete this example.

Answer

Plan your method:

Total surface area = area of two triangles with base $30\,\text{cm}$ + area of two triangles with base $12\,\text{cm}$ + area of the rectangle

To find the area of the triangular faces, you first need to work out the 'sloping heights'.

The height of the pyramid is not the same as the 'sloping heights' of the triangular sides. This is the challenge of working in three dimensions.

Look at the diagram in more detail.

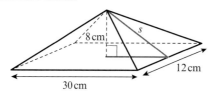

For the triangles with base $12\,\text{cm}$, the blue line (s) is the height.

The red line is parallel to the $30\,\text{cm}$ side of the rectangle and half its length.

These two lines, together with the vertical height of the pyramid form a right-angled triangle.

s is the hypotenuse and you can use Pythagoras' theorem to calculate its length.

$s^2 = 8^2 + 15^2 = 289$

$s = 17\,\text{cm}$

CONTINUED

For the triangles with base 30 cm, the blue line (x) is the height.

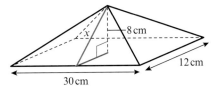

The red line is parallel to the 12 cm side of the rectangle and half this length.

Again, you can form a right-angled triangle:

$$x^2 = 8^2 + 6^2 = 100$$

$$x = 10 \text{ cm}$$

You can now find the total surface area.

Total surface area = area of two triangles with base 30 cm + area of two triangles with base 12 cm + area of the rectangle

$$= 2 \times \frac{bh}{2} + 2 \times \frac{bh}{2} + lw$$

$$= 2 \times \frac{30 \times 10}{2} + 2 \times \frac{12 \times 17}{2} + 30 \times 12$$

$$= 864 \text{ cm}^2$$

A solid cone has two surfaces – the flat bottom (that is circular in shape) and the curved surface. You will need to find the area of both surfaces in order to find the total surface area.

So, imagine you have a cone made from paper. Then imagine that you cut along the line l and flatten the curved surface, as shown.

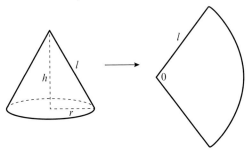

When it is flattened, the curved surface of the cone becomes the sector of a circle.

The radius of the sector is equal to the sloping edge, l of the cone.

The arc length of the sector is equal to the circumference of the circular base of the cone: $2\pi r$.

Combining the formulae for these two areas gives us a formula for the surface area of a cone:

Surface area of a cone = area of base + area of curved surface

$$= \pi r^2 + \pi r l$$

WORKED EXAMPLE 20

Calculate the surface area of the cone with the dimensions shown to three significant figures.

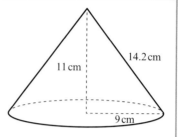

Answer

The radius r of the cone is 9 cm.

The sloping length l of the cone is 14.2 cm.

$\pi r^2 + \pi r l$	Use formula for surface area.
$\pi \times 9^2 + \pi \times 9 \times 14.2$	Substituting in the values of r and l.
$= 656$ cm^2	

WORKED EXAMPLE 21

The makers of a paper ice cream cone want it to hold 150 cm^3 of ice cream and have a height of 10 cm.

a Calculate the radius of the ice cream cone.

b Calculate the area of the paper that covers the *curved* surface of the cone.

c Calculate the area of paper needed to cover the *total* surface of the cone.

Answers

If you are not given a diagram, it might help to draw a sketch to show the information.

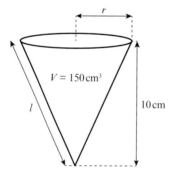

a $V = \pi r^2 h$ The volume of a cone.

    $150 = \pi r^2(10)$ Substitute and simplify.

     $15 = \pi r^2$

    $r^2 = \dfrac{15}{\pi}$ Rearrange and solve.

    $r = \sqrt{\dfrac{15}{\pi}} = 2.19$ cm (to 3 sf)

CONTINUED

b You know that $h = 10$ and $r = 2.185...$ so you can use Pythagoras' theorem to calculate l:

$l^2 = h^2 + r^2$

$\Rightarrow l^2 = 10^2 + 2.185^2$

$\Rightarrow l = 10.235... = 10.2\,\text{cm}$ (3 sf)

Calculate the area: $A = \pi r l$

$\qquad\qquad = \pi \times 2.185... \times 10.235...$

$\qquad\qquad = 70.266... = 70.3\,\text{cm}^2$ (to 3 sf)

c Total surface area = curved surface area + circular area on top

$\qquad\qquad = \pi r^2 + \pi r l$

$\qquad\qquad = \pi \times 2.185^2 + 70.266...$

$\qquad\qquad = 85.266... = 85.3\,\text{cm}^2$ (to 3 sf)

> **TIP**
>
> Use your *full* calculator display for all values to increase accuracy.

Exercise 12.10

1 For each solid pyramid, calculate the surface area.

a

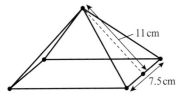

11 cm

7.5 cm

b

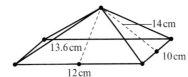

14 cm

13.6 cm

10 cm

12 cm

2 For each solid pyramid, calculate the:

i volume

ii surface area.

a

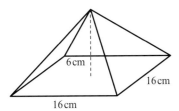

6 cm

16 cm

16 cm

b

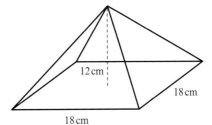

12 cm

18 cm

18 cm

c

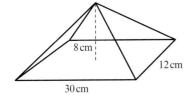

8 cm

12 cm

30 cm

3   Calculate the *total* surface area of each cone. Give your answers i as a multiple of π and then ii correct to three significant figures.

a
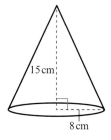

b
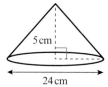

c
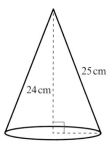

d
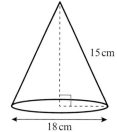

4   An object made from a two cones joined together at their common base.

The heights of the cones are 7 cm and 32 cm and the radius of the common base is 24 cm.

Calculate:

a   the exact surface area of the object

b   the exact volume of the object.

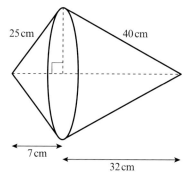

5   A solid object is made from a two cones joined together at their common base.

The heights of the cones are 8 cm and 36 cm and the radius of the common base is 15 cm.

Calculate:

a   the exact surface area of the object

b   the exact volume of:

  i   the smaller cone

  ii   the larger cone.

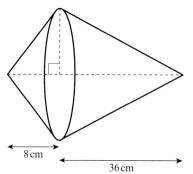

6   A solid right cone has base radius 5 cm and volume 366.5 cm³. Calculate:

a   the height of the cone

b   the length of the sloping edge of the cone

c   the total surface area of the cone.

7   A solid right cone has a base radius 5 cm and total surface area 224π cm^3.
     Calculate:

   a   the curved surface area of the cone
   b   the length of the sloping edge
   c   the height of the cone
   d   the volume of the cone.

8   An 8-metre-high conical tower with a base radius of 4 metres is built from concrete.

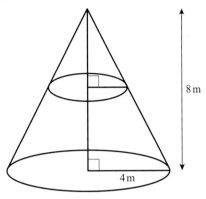

   a   Calculate its volume in m^3, correct to the nearest m^3.

   For safety reasons, the top quarter of the tower must be removed.

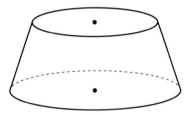

   Calculate:
   b   the height of the cone removed
   c   the base radius of the cone removed
   d   the fraction of the original tower that has been removed.

> TIP
>
> The shape that remains when a cone has had its top chopped off is called a **frustum**.

Frustums

A **frustum** is a cone or pyramid that has been cut in a plane parallel to its base.

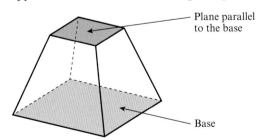

INVESTIGATION 1

Work with a partner and think about how you might find the volume and the surface area of a frustum of a pyramid like the one shown in the diagram.

What dimensions would you need to know?

What about the frustum of a cone?

What would be the same and what would be different about the formulae for the frustum of a pyramid and of a cone?

12.8 Surface area and volume of spheres

There is no easy way to derive the volume of a sphere. The first person who did this was Archimedes, arguably the greatest of the ancient Greek mathematicians.

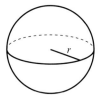

The formula for the volume of a sphere is:

The formula for the surface area, A, of a sphere is:

$$V = \frac{4\pi r^3}{3}$$

In both formulae, r is the radius of the sphere.

$$A = 4\pi r^2$$

WORKED EXAMPLE 22

A sphere has a diameter of 12 cm. Calculate its:

a exact volume   **b** exact surface area.

Answers

The formulae for the volume and surface area of a sphere are written in terms of the radius, so start by calculating r:

$$r = \frac{12}{2} = 6 \text{ cm}$$

a   Volume $= \dfrac{4\pi r^3}{3}$

$\qquad = \dfrac{4\pi(6^3)}{3}$

$\qquad = 288\pi \text{ cm}^3$

b   Surface area $= 4\pi r^2$

$\qquad = 4\pi(6^2)$

$\qquad = 144\pi \text{ cm}^2$

WORKED EXAMPLE 23

The volume of a sphere is 288π cm³. Calculate its radius.

Answer

$V = \dfrac{4\pi r^3}{3} = 288\pi$ Use the volume formula.

$r^3 = \dfrac{288\pi \times 3}{4\pi}$ Rearrange and solve.

$\Rightarrow r = \sqrt[3]{\dfrac{500 \times 3}{4}} = 6$ cm

> **TIP**
>
> The volume (or area) may be given as a multiple of π.

WORKED EXAMPLE 24

The volume of a sphere is 500 cm³. Calculate its surface area.

Answer

$V = \dfrac{4\pi r^3}{3} = 500$ Use the volume formula.

$r^3 = \dfrac{500 \times 3}{4\pi}$ Rearrange and solve to find r.

$r = \sqrt[3]{\dfrac{500 \times 3}{4\pi}}$

   $= 4.923\ldots = 4.92$ cm (to 3 sf)

$A = 4\pi r^2$ Use the area formula.

   $= 4 \times \pi \times 4.923\ldots^2$

   $= 305$ cm² (to 3 sf)

> **TIP**
>
> The key to solving questions like this one is to calculate the radius.

> **TIP**
>
> Remember to use the full calculator display for the radius.

Exercise 12.11

1   For each sphere, calculate:

   i   the volume

   ii   the surface area.

   Give your answers exactly, as multiples of π.

   a 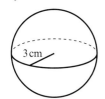   **b** 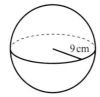   **c**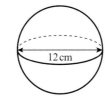

     3 cm   9 cm   12 cm

   d   Show that the ratio of the volumes of the spheres is $1 : 27 : 8$.

   e   Show that the ratio of the surfaces areas is $1 : 9 : 4$.

2   The volume of a sphere is 1200 cm³. Calculate its surface area.

3   The surface area of a sphere is $800\,cm^2$. Calculate its volume.

4   Calculate the volume of each solid hemisphere. Give your answers correct to three significant figures.

a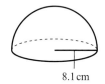

8.1 cm

b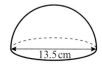

13.5 cm

5   Calculate the *total* surface area of each hemisphere in Question **4**.
    Give your answers correct to three significant figures.

6   The volume of a hemisphere is $720\,cm^3$. Calculate its total surface area.

7   The *curved* surface area of a hemisphere is $36\,5cm^2$. Calculate its volume.

8   The *total* surface area of a sphere is $500\,cm^2$. Calculate its volume.

TIP

Remember:
A hemisphere has two surfaces – the flat surface and the curved surface.

9   A hemispherical bowl is constructed from clay and is filled with water.

    It has an external radius of 10 cm and an internal radius of 9 cm.

    a   Calculate, correct to three significant figures.

        i   the volume of water that the bowl will hold.
        ii   the amount of clay needed to construct the bowl.

    The three surfaces of the bowl are coated in a glaze.

    b   Calculate, correct to three significant figures, the total surface area that must be coated by glaze.

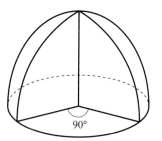

10 A hemisphere of radius 10 cm is cut into two congruent halves. Calculate:

    a   the volume of each of the two pieces
    b   the total surface area of the three surfaces of each piece.

11 A cake is made in the shape of a hemisphere with radius 20 cm.

    a   Calculate the volume of the cake.

    The curved surface of the cake is covered in a crust of icing.

    b   Calculate the area of the crust.

    A piece of the cake is cut as shown in the diagram.
    The angle of the cut piece is 90°.

    c   Calculate the volume of the cut piece of cake.
    d   Calculate the total surface area of the cut piece of cake.

    e   Calculate the total surface area of the cake left behind.

12 A hemisphere is constructed so that its volume is equal to its total surface area.
    Calculate the radius of the hemisphere.

12.9 Surface area and volume of compound shapes

Compound shapes can be formed from combinations of other shapes. Their volumes and surface areas can be found by applying knowledge of their underlying shapes.

Exercise 12.12

1   Calculate the volume of each of the prisms. Give your answers correct to three significant figures.

a

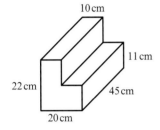

10 cm

11 cm

22 cm

45 cm

20 cm

b

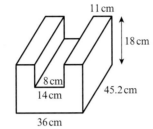

11 cm

18 cm

8 cm

14 cm

45.2 cm

36 cm

c

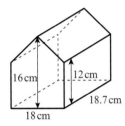

16 cm

12 cm

18.7 cm

18 cm

d

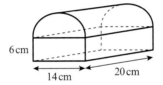

6 cm

14 cm

20 cm

2   A child's toy is made in the shape of a hemisphere of radius 4.8 cm with a cone of height 6.4 cm placed on top.

Calculate:

a   the volume of the toy

b   the surface area of the toy.

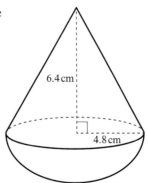

6.4 cm

4.8 cm

3 A child's toy is made from a hemisphere of radius 2.5 cm with a cylinder of height 1.5 cm and a cone of height 6 cm placed on top, as shown in the diagram.

Calculate:

a the volume of the toy

b the surface area of the toy.

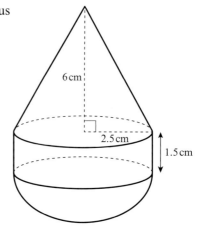

4 A cone of radius 3 cm and height 12.4 cm sits on the largest face of a cuboid that is 4.6 cm × 7.3 cm × 8.2 cm.

Calculate to one decimal place:

a the volume of the complete shape

b the surface area of the complete shape.

5 A wooden toy is made from a cylinder with an identical cone at each end. The cylinder has a radius of 7.2 cm, as do both cones. The cylinder is 14.6 cm long, as is the sum of both cones.

Calculate to one decimal place:

a the volume of the complete toy

b the surface area of the complete toy.

6 An engineering company has made a steel cuboid with dimensions 345 mm × 645 mm × 310 mm. The smallest face has a hemispherical indentation that is 112 mm deep.

Calculate to the nearest whole number:

a the volume of the complete shape

b the surface area of the complete shape.

7 A museum creates a large model of a square-based pyramid that has base length 36.4 m and perpendicular height of 32.8 m.

a Calculate to one decimal place:

   i the volume of the complete shape

   ii the surface area of the complete shape, including the base.

The pyramid is hollow, and is made of walls which are 1.5 m thick.

b Calculate to one decimal place:

   i the volume of the internal space

   ii the surface area of the internal shape.

SUMMARY

Are you able to... ?
use and convert between metric units of mass, length, area, volume and capacity
calculate the perimeter and area of rectangles, parallelograms, triangles and trapezia
calculate the circumference and area of circles
calculate and solve problems involving the surface area and volume of cuboids, prisms, cylinders, spheres, pyramids and cones
calculate arc lengths and sector areas
calculate and solve problems involving perimeters and areas of compound (or parts of) shapes
calculate and solve problems involving surface areas and volumes of compound (or parts of) solids.

Past paper questions

1   The diagram shows a pyramid with vertical height 30 cm.
    The horizontal base of the pyramid is a square with side 7 cm.
    Work out the volume of the pyramid.

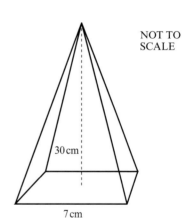

NOT TO SCALE

30 cm

7 cm

.............................cm³   [3]

Cambridge IGCSE International Mathematics 0607 Paper 11 Q19 Nov 2019

2   The diagram shows a hemisphere joined to a cone.
    The hemisphere has a radius of 3 cm.
    The cone has a radius of 3 cm and a height of 7 cm.
    The total volume of the shape is $k\pi$ cm³.
    Find the value of k.

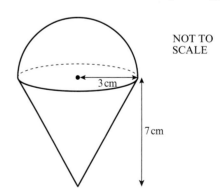

NOT TO SCALE

3 cm

7 cm

    k = ...   [3]

Cambridge IGCSE International Mathematics 0607 Paper 21 Q7 Nov 2019

3

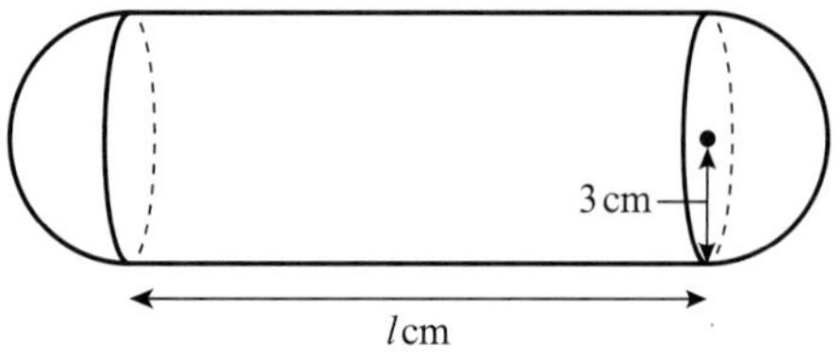

3 cm

_l_ cm

NOT TO SCALE

The diagram shows a solid made from a cylinder and two hemispheres.

The radius of the cylinder and each hemisphere is 3 cm.

The total volume of the solid is 144π cm³.

a   The length of the cylinder is _l_ cm.

Find the value of _l_.

_l_ = ... [3]

b   The solid is made of steel.

1 cm³ of steel has a mass of 7.8 g.

Calculate the mass of the solid.

Give your answer in kilograms.

.... kg   [2]

Cambridge IGCSE International Mathematics 0607 Paper 42 Q4 Jun 2019

> Chapter 13

Quadratic equations

IN THIS CHAPTER YOU WILL:

- use a graphing calculator to solve and find the vertex of quadratic equations

- factorise quadratic equations

> solve quadratic equations by factorisation

> solve quadratic equations by use of the quadratic formula.

GETTING STARTED

1 Sketch the graphs of the following equations.

   a $y = 5$ b $y = -6$ c $x = 4$ d $x = -2$

   e $y = x$ f $y = -x$ g $y = 2x + 1$ h $y = -2x - 1$

2 Write down the equation of three lines which are parallel to $y = \dfrac{x}{2}$.

3 Write down the equation of the line which is perpendicular to $y = 3x + 2$ and passes through the point $(2, -2)$.

4 Factorise the following expressions.

   a $3x + 6$ b $12 + 4x$ c $16x + 12y$

13.1 Graphs of quadratic equations

A **quadratic equation** is the mathematical name given to an equation that has at least one term with a power of 2. The equation $y = x^2 + 4x + 3$ is an example of a quadratic equation.

In Chapter 7 you factorised quadratic equations using grouping methods. In this chapter you will learn how to solve equations of the form $y = ax^2 + bx + c$ when these methods cannot be used.

Graphs of quadratic equations take one of the following forms:

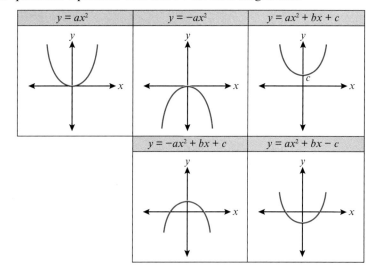

MATHEMATICS IN CONTEXT

Quadratic equations are used in a surprising number of everyday situations. The basic equation for velocity used by rocket scientists, athletes and video game programmers is a quadratic equation.

The points where the graph crosses the axis give the **roots** or **zeros** of the quadratic **expression** and correspond to the factors of the equation.

WORKED EXAMPLE 1

Draw the graph of $y = x^2 - 4x - 5$ using a graphic display calculator and hence find the solutions to the equation $x^2 - 4x - 5 = 0$.

Answer

1   Select **Graph** from the main menu. The graph function is highlighted in the following image.

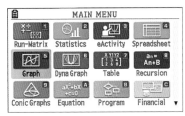

The following screen opens.

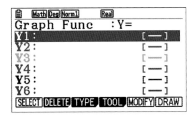

2   Now enter the function using the keypad.

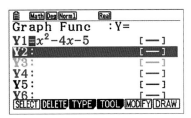

3   Press **F6** to select the **DRAW** option to draw the graph.

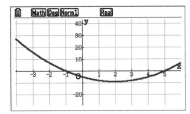

4   Press **F5** to show the options for finding points on the graph.

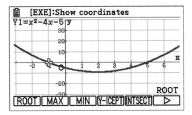

CONTINUED

5   Press **F1** to select the roots. You can toggle between them using the toggle button ◉.

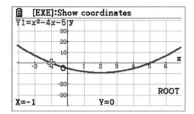 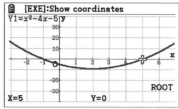

The zeros of the equation are $x = -1$ and $x = 5$.

INVESTIGATION 1

Use your graphic display calculator to investigate graphs of the form $y = ax^2 + bx + c$.

Using the equation from Worked example 1, change the value of the coefficient of x^2.

What effect does this have on the graph?

Now change the coefficient of x. What effect does this have on the graph?

Finally, explore changing the values of the constant c. What effect does this have on the graph?

Exercise 13.1

1   Draw the graph of the following equations using a graphic display calculator and hence find their solutions:

a $x^2 + 2x = 0$
b $x^2 - 1 = 0$
c $x^2 + 5x + 6 = 0$
d $x^2 + x - 12 = 0$

e $x^2 + 5x + 4 = 0$
f $x^2 + 9x + 18 = 0$
g $x^2 - 5x + 6 = 0$
h $x^2 - 5x - 14 = 0$

i $2x^2 - 4x - 6 = 0$
j $2x^2 + 10x - 28 = 0$
k $2x^2 - 9x - 18 = 0$
l $3x^2 - 2x - 1 = 0$

m $4x^2 - 1 = 0$
n $6x^2 - 10x - 24 = 0$
o $9x^2 - 24x + 16 = 0$
p $-x^2 + 5x - 4 = 0$

q $-x^2 + 7x - 6 = 0$
r $-2x^2 + 8x + 10 = 0$
s $-3x^2 + 10x + 8 = 0$

REFLECTION

In some of the questions above there is no coefficient value of (e.g. $4x^2 - 1 = 0$).
What do you notice about the solutions to graphs of these equations?
Can you explain why?

13.2 Solving quadratic equations by using a formula

Factorising is an important skill to learn when solving quadratic equations in order to find the zeros of the equation.

Some quadratic expressions can be factorised by simply removing a factor, as you would with linear expressions, but others cannot.

Quadratic equations of the form $ax^2 + bx + c = 0$ cannot always be factorised.

When this is the case they can be solved using the formula:

$$x = \frac{-b \pm \sqrt{b^2 - 4ac}}{2a}$$

The values of a, b and c can be taken from the equation and substituted into the formula.

TIP

Although the formula always works, it is always better to factorise if you can as there are less opportunities to make errors.

WORKED EXAMPLE 2

Solve $3x^2 - 8x + 2 = 0$.

Answer

Step 1

Comparing $3x^2 - 8x + 2 = 0$ with $ax^2 + bx + c = 0$, we have $a = 3$, $b = -8$ and $c = 2$.

Step 2

Substitute these values in the formula:

$$x = \frac{-b \pm \sqrt{b^2 - 4ac}}{2a}$$

$$= \frac{-(-8) \pm \sqrt{(-8)^2 - 4 \times 3 \times 2}}{2 \times 3}$$

$$= \frac{8 \pm \sqrt{64 - 24}}{6}$$

$$= \frac{8 \pm \sqrt{40}}{6} \qquad \text{The value in the root must be positive.}$$

$$= \frac{(8 + \sqrt{40})}{6} \text{ or } = \frac{(8 - \sqrt{40})}{6}$$

$x = 2.39$ or $= 0.28$

DISCUSSION 1

Why does the formula contain the sign $\pm$?

DISCUSSION 2

In Worked example 2 is it better to leave the answer in surd form?

Exercise 13.2

Use the quadratic formula to solve the following equations. Leave your answer in surd form.

a $x^2 + 5x + 3 = 0$

b $x^2 + 6x + 6 = 0$

c $x^2 + 11x + 6 = 0$

d $2x^2 + 6x - 7 = 0$

e $3x^2 - x - 9 = 0$

f $5x^2 - 3x - 7 = 0$

g $12x^2 - 5x - 12 = 0$

h $7x^2 - 3x - 6 = 0$

PEER REFLECTION

Check with a partner that you have accurately identified both solutions to each question.

13.3 Maximum and minimum values of quadratic equations

The most extreme value of a quadratic expression is either its minimum or its maximum, depending on the graph of the equation. This is called its **vertex**.

In Worked example 1, the graph has a minimum and so there are no points below this value.

WORKED EXAMPLE 3

Find the minimum point on the graph of $y = x^2 - 4x - 5$ from Worked example 1 using a graphic display calculator.

Answer

1 Draw the graph of $y = x^2 - 4x - 5$ on a graphic display calculator.

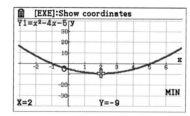

2 Press **F5** to show the options for finding points on the graph.

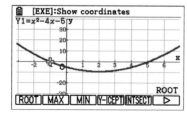

CONTINUED

3 Press **F3** to show the minimum.

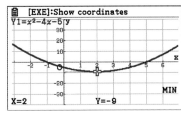

The minimum of $y = x^2 - 4x - 5$ is $(2, -9)$.

Exercise 13.3

1 Find the vertex of the following quadratic expressions using your graphic display calculator.

  a $x^2 - 6x + 5$ b $-2x^2 + 8x - 6$ c $x^2 + 2x + 1$ d $x^2 - 12x - 8$

2 Find the vertex of the following quadratic expressions using your graphic display calculator.

  a $2x^2 - 6x - 3$ b $3x^2 + 6x + 1$ c $-5x^2 + 20x - 13$ d $2x^2 - 3x - 10$

3 Solve the following quadratic equations using either the quadratic formula or your graphic display calculator. Give your answers to two decimal places.

  a $2x^2 + 11x + 5 = 0$ b $3x^2 - 7x - 20 = 0$ c $2x^2 + 6x - 1 = 0$ d $3y^2 - 2y - 5 = 0$

  e $2 - x - 6x^2 = 0$ f $12 - 5x^2 - 11x = 0$ g $5x^2 - 5x + 1 = 0$ h $2x^2 - 7x - 15 = 0$

13.4 Solving equations involving quadratic expressions on a GDC

WORKED EXAMPLE 4

Use a graphic display calculator to solve $6x^2 = 3x$.

Answer

Depending on the type of equation, you could choose to rearrange the equation to form a quadratic and solve it by finding roots. You could also solve the equation graphically or using the Equation mode on your graphic display calculator.

Method 1: Graphically

1 Select **Graph** from the main menu by pressing **5**.

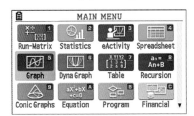

CONTINUED

Enter both sides of the equation as separate graphs. The solutions will be where they intersect.

Use the toggle button ⊕ to select **Y1** and press [6] [X,θ,T] [x²] [EXE]

and then press [3] [X,θ,T] [EXE].

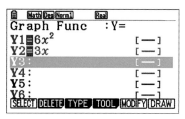

2 Press **F6** to draw the graphs.

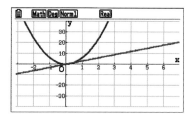

3 Press **F5** twice to see the intersection points and use the toggle button ⊕ to move between them.

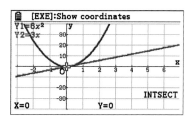 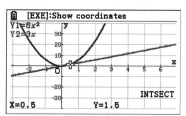

Method 2: Equation mode

1 Select **Equation** from the main menu. Press [ALPHA] and then [X,θ,T] to enter **A** and select it.

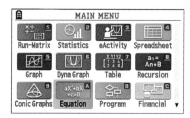

CONTINUED

2 In Equation mode you see the following menu.

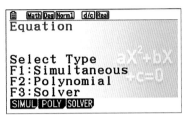

3 Press **F2** to solve a polynomial equation.

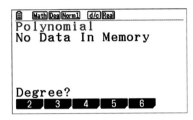

4 Enter the highest index in the equation to be solved, in this case 2 so press **F1**.

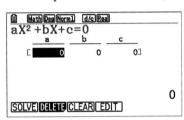

5 Enter the values of a, b and c in the equation to be solved.
Rearranging $6x^2 = 3x$ gives $6x^2 - 3x = 0$ and so $a = 6$, $b = -3$, $c = 0$.

Enter these values and press **F1** to solve.

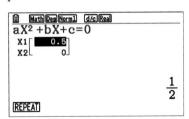

There are two values of x that are solutions. $x = \dfrac{1}{2}$, $x = 0$.

MATHEMATICAL CONNECTIONS

You rearranged equations in Chapter 8.

WORKED EXAMPLE 5

Use a graphic display calculator to solve $\dfrac{1}{6x^2} = 3x - 1$

Answer

Depending on the type of equation, you can choose to either solve the equation algebraically as before, graphically or using the Equation mode on your graphic display calculator.

Method 1: Graphically

1   Select **Graph** from the main menu by pressing **5**.

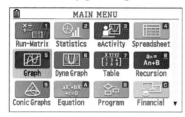

2   Enter both sides of the equation as separate graphs. The solutions will be where they intersect.

Use the toggle button ⊕ to select **Y1** and press **1** ÷ **6** **X,θ,T** **x²** **EXE** and then press **3** **X,θ,T** **−** **1** **EXE**.

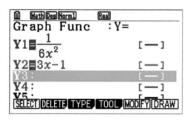

3   Press **F6** to draw the graphs.

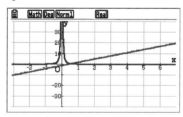

4   Press **F5** twice to see the intersection points and use the toggle button ⊕ to move between them.

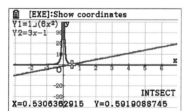

There is one solution, $x = 0.530\,636\ldots$

CONTINUED

Method 2: Equation mode

1   Select **Equation** from the main menu. Press ![ALPHA] and then ![x,θ,T] to enter **A** and select it.

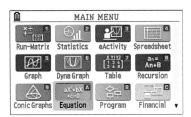

2   In Equation mode you see the following menu.

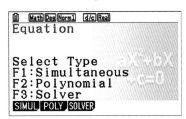

3   Press **F2** to solve a polynomial equation.

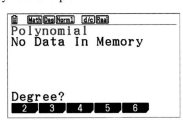

4   Enter the highest index in the equation to be solved, in this case 3, so press **F2,** as rearranging:

$$\frac{1}{6x^2} = 3x - 1 \qquad \text{gives}$$

$$\frac{1}{6x^2} = 3x - 1 = 0 \qquad \text{multiplying by } 6x^2$$

$$-1 + 18x^3 - 6x^2 = 0 \qquad \text{rearranging}$$

$$18x^3 - 6x^2 - 1 = 0$$

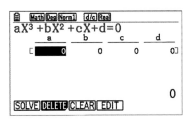

CONTINUED

5 Enter the values of a, b, c and d in the equation to be solved and so $a = 18$, $b = -6$, $c = 0$, $d = -1$. Enter these values and press **F1** to solve.

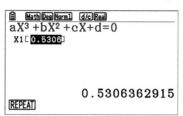

There is one solution, $x = 0.530\,636...$

Exercise 13.4

1 Solve the following equations using whichever method is appropriate.

   a $3x^2 = 4x$ **b** $2x^2 = 7x$ **c** $x^2 = -6x$

   d $3x^2 = 3x + 2$ **e** $4x^2 = x + 2$ **f** $5x^2 = 3x + 2$

   g $3x^2 = -4x + 1$ **h** $6x^2 = -3x + 9$

2 Solve the following equations using whichever method is appropriate. Give your answers to five decimal places.

   a $\dfrac{1}{4x^2} = 2x - 1$ **b** $\dfrac{1}{3x^2} = 5x + 2$ **c** $\dfrac{1}{2x^2} = 3x - 8$

   d $\dfrac{1}{x^2} = 7x - 3$ **e** $\dfrac{1}{x^2} = -3x + 7$ **f** $\dfrac{1}{3x^2} = 2x - 5$

   g $\dfrac{1}{5x^2} = 7x - 2$ **h** $\dfrac{1}{2x^2} = 11x + 3$

SUMMARY

Are you able to... ?
use a graphing calculator to solve and find the vertex of quadratic equations
factorise quadratic equations
solve quadratic equations by factorisation
solve quadratic equations by use of the quadratic formula.

Past paper questions

1

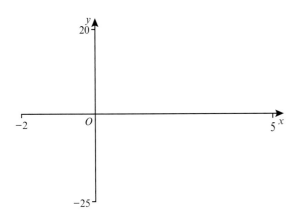

$f(x) = x^3 - 5x^2 + 2x + 8$

a   On the diagram, sketch the graph of $y = f(x)$ for $-2 \leqslant x \leqslant 5$. [Using Past Paper Question Resource Sheet] [3]

b   Write down the co-ordinates of the point where the curve crosses the y-axis.

(.........................., ...) [1]

c   Write down the co-ordinates of the three points where the curve crosses the x-axis.

(..............., ...), (..............., ...), (..............., ...) [2]

d   Find the co-ordinates of the local maximum.

(.........................., ...) [2]

e   Find the number of times that the line $y = 9$ crosses the curve $y = f(x)$.

.... [1]

Cambridge IGCSE International Mathematics 0607 Paper 31 Q10 Nov 2019

2   a   Expand and simplify.
$(2p - 7q)(p + q)$

.... [2]

b   Factorise.
$2 - t - 2a + at$

.... [2]

Cambridge IGCSE International Mathematics 0607 Paper 21 Q6 Jun 2018

3

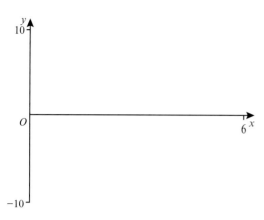

$f(x) = -2x^2 + 12x - 10$

a On the diagram, sketch the graph of $y = f(x)$ for $0 \leqslant x \leqslant 6$. [Using Past Paper Question Resource Sheet]   [2]

b Find the co-ordinates of the points where the graph crosses the x-axis.

(............. , ...) and (............. , ...)   [2]

c Find the co-ordinates of the local maximum.

(............. , ...)   [1]

d **i** On the same diagram, draw the line $y = x - 2$.   [2]

    ii Solve.

      $-2x^2 + 12x - 10 = x - 2$

$x = $ .... or $x = $ ....   [2]

Cambridge IGCSE International Mathematics 0607 Paper 31 Q11 Jun 2018

> Chapter 14
Functions 1

IN THIS CHAPTER YOU WILL:

- use function notation

- create tables for functions

- sketch graphs of functions

- use a graphic display calculator to explore functions

- recognise linear and quadratic function types from the shape of their graphs

> learn how to describe the range and domain of a function

> understand and find inverse functions

> form composite functions.

GETTING STARTED

1 C alculate the value of y in each of these equations when $x = 7$.

   a $y = 5x + 10$ **b** $y = \dfrac{4(x + 3)}{8}$

   c $y = 100 - x^2$ **d** $y = x^2 - 3x + 5$

2 **a** Copy and complete this table for the equation $y = 3x - 5$.

x	0	1	2	3
y	−5			
(x, y)	(0, −5)			

   b Copy this grid and plot the coordinates from your table onto your grid.

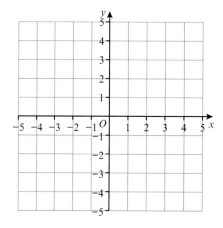

   c Join your plotted points with a ruler. They should make a straight line. Label the line $y = 3x - 5$.

3 **a** Draw and complete a table for the equation $y = 2 - x$.

   b Draw a grid and plot the points you have recorded in your table for $y = 2 - x$.

   c Draw a line through the points and label the line.

KEY WORDS

composite function

domain

function

input

inverse function

linear function

output

quadratic function

range

real number

MATHEMATICAL CONNECTIONS

In Chapter 7 you learnt about substituting values into equations. This will be very useful when you are working with functions.

14.1 Using function notation

A **function** relates an **input** to an **output**. The value that is entered into a function is called the input. The value that is returned by a function is called the output.

Algebraic equations are very useful for recording functions. However, using function notation allows you to do more with functions than the equations you have used before.

This is a function written in function notation:

$$f(x) = x^2 - 5$$

f is the name of the function. You can use any letter. f is commonly used because it is the first letter of the word 'function'. The value of $f(x)$ is the output.

x is the input.

This is what the function does to the input.

WORKED EXAMPLE 1

Consider the function $f(x) = x^2 + 2x - 1$.

a Describe what this function does in words.

b Evaluate $f(3)$.

Answers

a
$$f(x) = x^2 + 2x - 1$$

The function squares the input (x), adds the input multiplied by two, then subtracts one.

b Substitute x for 3 in the function.
$$f(3) = 3^2 + (2 \times 3) - 1$$
$$= 9 + 6 - 1$$
$$= 14$$

Exercise 14.1

1 Describe what each function does in words.

   a $f(x) = 8x$ **b** $f(x) = \dfrac{x}{10}$

   c $f(x) = 3x - 10$ **d** $f(x) = x^2 + 9$

   e $f(x) = 2x^2 - 4x + 3$

2 Write each of these functions using function notation.

   a The function multiplies the input x by 12, then subtracts four.

   b The function divides the input x by five, then adds seven.

   c The function squares the input x, then divides by two.

   d The function squares the input x, multiplies it by eight, then subtracts the original input multiplied by five.

3 Which of these functions does *not* have an output of 10 when the input is $x = -2$?

  a $f(x) = -5x$ **b** $g(x) = x + 12$ **c** $h(x) = \dfrac{x + 2}{3}$

  d $f(x) = 8 + x$ **e** $g(x) = 8 - x$ **f** $h(x) = x^2 + 10$

> **MATHEMATICS IN CONTEXT**
>
> Functions are a way of concisely describing many events that happen in real life. Functions can be used to calculate prices or predict outcomes. Question **4** asks you to use a function to calculate the cost of a boat trip. It is useful to use a function here because you can substitute x into the function to work out the total cost for any number of people.

> **TIP**
>
> Don't forget to give your answer in units based on the context of the problem. Think about what your answer represents.

4 Jo sells boat trips to groups of customers. Jo charges \$21 for each customer and there is a booking fee for the group of \$30.

  a Express the cost of a boat trip as a function where $f(x)$ is the total cost and x is the number of customers.

  b Use the function to calculate:

  i $f(10)$

  ii $f(57)$

  iii $f(129)$

> **TIP**
>
> The notation $f(10)$ is the value of $f(x)$ when $x = 10$. So, this is the total cost of a boat trip for 10 customers.

5 The mass of the biscuit box is 58 g. The mass of one biscuit is 13 g.

  a Express the total mass of the biscuit box and biscuits as a function where $g(x)$ is the total mass and x is the number of biscuits.

  b Use your function to evaluate:

  i $g(25)$

  ii $g(82)$

  iii $g(3.5)$

> **REFLECTION**
>
> What do your answers to part **b** represent?

14.2 Tables and mapping diagrams

You can record the inputs and outputs for a function in a table or with a mapping diagram. You can then use these sets of values to explore and understand what a function does.

> **WORKED EXAMPLE 2**
>
> For the function $f(x) = x + 4$, copy and complete:
>
> **a** the table of values
>
> | The input x | 1 | 2 | 3 | 4 |
> |---|---|---|---|---|
> | The output $f(x)$ | 5 | | | |

CONTINUED

b   the mapping diagram

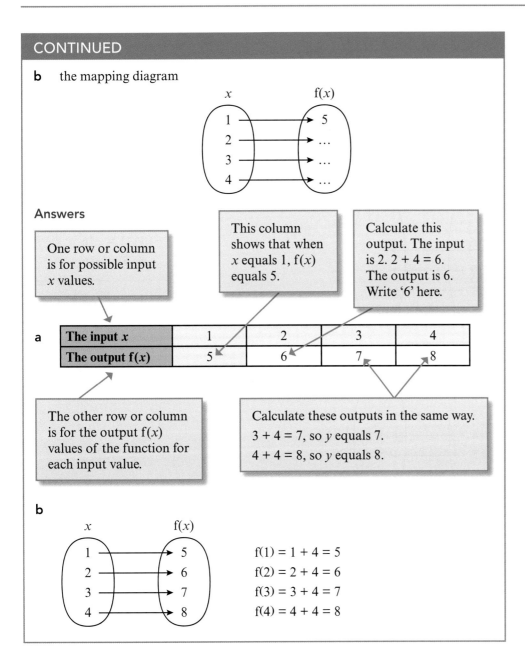

Answers

One row or column is for possible input *x* values.

This column shows that when *x* equals 1, f(*x*) equals 5.

Calculate this output. The input is 2. 2 + 4 = 6. The output is 6. Write '6' here.

a

The input *x*	1	2	3	4
The output f(*x*)	5	6	7	8

The other row or column is for the output f(*x*) values of the function for each input value.

Calculate these outputs in the same way.
3 + 4 = 7, so *y* equals 7.
4 + 4 = 8, so *y* equals 8.

b

f(1) = 1 + 4 = 5
f(2) = 2 + 4 = 6
f(3) = 3 + 4 = 7
f(4) = 4 + 4 = 8

Exercise 14.2

1   Copy and complete the table of values for the function f(*x*) = 2*x* + 3.

Input, *x*	Output, f(*x*)
1	5
2	7
3	
4	
5	
6	

The input is 1.

2 × 1 + 3 = 5

The output is 5.

2 This table shows some inputs and outputs of a function.

Input	1	2	3	4	5
Output	3	6	9	12	15

    a Describe the function in words.

    b Write the function using function notation.

3 Copy and complete the mapping diagram of values for the function $g(x) = 5x - 1$.

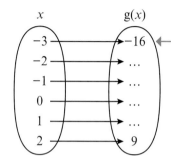

> **TIP**
>
> $x = -3$
> $-3 \times 5 = -15$
> $-15 - 1 = -16$
> $g(-3) = -16$

4 **a** Copy and complete the mapping diagram.

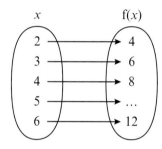

    b Express the function from part **a** using function notation.

5 Copy and complete the equation to describe the function $h(x)$.

x	1	2	3	4	5	6
$h(x)$	11	21	31	41	51	61

$h(x) = \boxed{}x + \boxed{}$

6 Copy and complete the mapping diagram of values for the function $f(x) = \dfrac{12}{x}$.

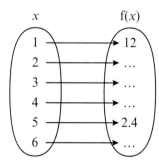

> **TIP**
>
> It is not possible to divide a number by 0, so the input for this function cannot be 0.

7   Copy and complete the table of values for the function $g(x) = x^2 - 1$.

x	-3	-2	-1	0	1	2
$g(x)$						

TIP

In this table you calculate the two parts of the function in separate rows. You then add the two parts to calculate the output values for $f(x)$.

8   Copy and complete the table of values for the function $f(x) = x^2 + 4x$.

x	-2	-1	0	1	2	3
x^2	4					
$4x$	-8					
$f(x)$	-4					

9   Copy and complete the table of values for the function $f(x) = x^2 + 7x + 10$.

x						
x^2						
$7x$						
$+10$	$+10$	$+10$	$+10$	$+10$	$+10$	$+10$
$f(x)$						

10 Draw and complete your own tables of values for these functions.

    a $f(x) = x^2 + x - 1$ **b** $g(x) = x^2 + 4x - 7$

    c $h(x) = -x^2 + 2x + 2$ **d** $f(x) = -x^2 - x + 5$

TIP

$-x^2$ means $-(x^2)$, not $(-x)^2$. Square x first, then make it negative.

INVESTIGATION 1

Investigate different integer inputs and outputs for the function $f(x) = 2x - 1$. Record your inputs and outputs in a table. Describe what property the outputs for this function have in common.

Find a function where the output will never be a negative number. Explain why your function will never produce a negative number.

14.3 Graphs

You can represent a function on a graph which helps you to see, understand and use the relationship between inputs and outputs. The input is along the horizontal axis and the output is along the vertical axis.

WORKED EXAMPLE 3

Sketch the graph of the function $f(x) = 2x - 3$.

Answer

First create a table of values for the function.

x	-1	0	1	2	3
$f(x)$	-5	-3	-1	1	3

CONTINUED

Draw a pair of axes. Make sure that all your x values fit on the horizontal axis and all of your f(x) values fit on the vertical axis.

Convert the values in your table into coordinates, (x, f(x)). Then plot the coordinates onto your grid.

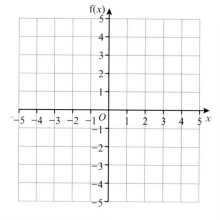

x	−1	0	1	2	3
f(x)	−5	−3	−1	1	3
(x, f(x))	(−1, −5)	(0, −3)	(1, −1)	(2, 1)	(3, 3)

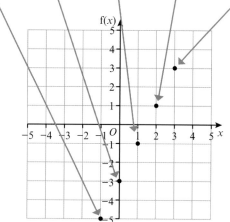

Draw a line through the plotted points. A **linear function**, in the form f(x) = ax + b, creates a straight line graph. If the points are in a straight line, use a ruler to join them. Label the line with the function.

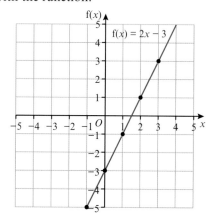

Exercise 14.3

1 a   Draw and complete a table of values for the function $f(x) = x - 2$.

   b   Draw a grid and plot the points you have recorded in your table for $y = f(x)$.

   c   Draw a line through the points and label it with the function.

2 a   Draw and complete a mapping diagram for the function $f(x) = 2 - x$.

   b   Convert the inputs and outputs recorded in your mapping diagram to coordinates $(x, f(x))$. Draw a grid and plot the points from your mapping diagram.

   c   Draw a line through the points and label it with the function.

3 a   Copy and complete the table for the function $f(x) = x^2 + 2x - 4$.

x	−2	−1	0	1	2
x^2	4	1			
$2x$	−4	−2			
−4	−4	−4			
$f(x)$	−4				

   b   Sketch the graph of $f(x)$.

TIP

The x^2 makes this a **quadratic function**. Quadratic functions have the general form

$f(x) = ax^2 + bx + c$

A graph of a quadratic function will look similar to

when a is positive   or   when a is negative

Join the points on the graph with a smooth curve, not a straight line.

14.4 Graphic display calculators and recognising function types by the shape of their graph

You can enter a function into your graphic display calculator. You can then use the function mode on your calculator to explore features of the graph of the function.

WORKED EXAMPLE 4

Draw a graph of the function $5x + 2$ using a graphic display calculator.

Answer

This example shows the Casio fx-CG50 calculator. You will need to check the steps for your particular calculator in case they are different.

1   Select **Graph** from the main menu. The Graph function is highlighted in the following image.

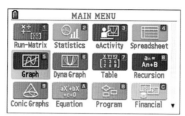

> **TIP**
>
> Familiarise yourself with the buttons that allow you to navigate between options on the screen and to select them.

The following screen opens.

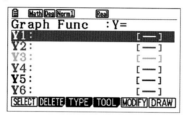

2   Now enter the function using the keypad.

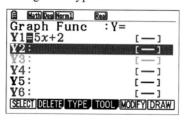

3   Press **F6** to select the **DRAW** option. This draws the graph of the function.

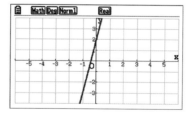

4   You can use the toggle button to move around the screen to display more of the graph.

WORKED EXAMPLE 5

Create a table of values for the function $5x + 2$. The values should be for $x = -2$ to $x = 1$, in intervals of 0.5.

Answer

1   Select **Table** from the main menu. The Table function is highlighted in the following image.

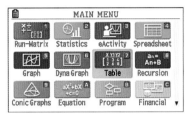

2   Now enter the function using the keypad.

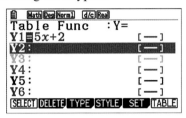

3   Press **F5** to select the **SET** option. This is where the start, end and interval values are entered.

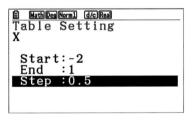

4   Press **EXIT** and then **F6** to select the **TABLE** option. This creates the table of the function.

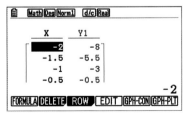

5   You can use the toggle button to move through the table entries.

Exercise 14.4

1   Select the graph function mode on your graphic display calculator.
    Use the graph menu to reveal features of these graphs.

    a   On your graphic display calculator sketch the graph of the function
        $f(x) = -x^2 + 2x + 1$

        i   Find the vertex of the graph of the function.

        ii   Find the zeros of the graph of the function.

    b   On your graphic display calculator sketch the graph of the function
        $f(x) = x^2 - 2x - 6$

        i   Find the vertex of the graph of the function.

        ii   Find the zeros of the graph of the function.

> **TIP**
>
> A quadratic function has the general form $f(x) = ax^2 + bx + c$. If a in the quadratic function is negative, the graph will have a maximum value vertex. If a in the quadratic function is positive, the graph will have a minimum value vertex.

MATHEMATICAL CONNECTIONS

You found intersections, vertices and zeros on a graph using a graphic display calculator in Chapter 13.

2   Select the table function mode on your graphic display calculator.

Enter the function $f(x) = 7x^2 - 3$

Use your calculator to create a table of values from $x = -2$ to $x = 1$, in intervals of 0.5.

Copy the table.

3   Sketch both these functions on your graphic display calculator.

$f(x) = -2x^2 + 3x - 1$

$g(x) = -x - 2$

Use your calculator to find the intersections of the functions.
Round solutions to two decimal places.

4   On your graphic display calculator sketch the graph of the function
    $f(x) = x^3 - 3x + 0.5$

Use your calculator to find the coordinates of:

    a   the local maximum where $-2 < x < 0$

    b   the local minimum where $0 < x < 2$

    c   the zeros of the graph of $f(x)$.

Give your answers correct to three significant figures where appropriate.

> **TIP**
>
> You will need to identify how to change settings to specify the values of x in the table. Check with your teacher or the calculator instructions if needed.

> **TIP**
>
> A local maximum on a graph is the point on the line that has the highest value of y in a given part of the graph. A local minimum on a graph is the point on the line that has the lowest value of y in a given part of the graph.

DISCUSSION 1

Discuss with your partner, or in a small group, what you have learnt about using your graphic display calculator to explore functions.

Quiz each other on how to:

- sketch a graph
- produce a table of values
- find the vertex of a quadratic function (maximum or minimum)
- find the coordinates of an intersection of two graphs of functions
- find the zeros, local maximum or minimum.

INVESTIGATION 2

Here are four types of function.

1 **Linear**. In the form $f(x) = ax + b$, for example $f(x) = 3x - 2$

2 **Quadratic**. In the form $f(x) = ax^2 + bx + c$, for example $f(x) = x^2 + 2x$

3 **Cubic**. In the form $f(x) = ax^3 + bx^2 + cx + d$, for example $f(x) = x^3 + 5$

4 **Reciprocal**. In the form $\frac{a}{x}$, for example $f(x) = \frac{1}{x}$

Select the graph function mode on your graphic display calculator.

Enter at least three different linear functions and look at the graphs they create.

Describe the shape of the graph made by the functions.
How are the graphs similar?

Enter at least three different quadratic functions and look at the graphs they create.

Describe the shape of the graph made by the functions.
How are the graphs similar?

Repeat with cubic and reciprocal functions.

REFLECTION

Reflect on your choices of function in Investigation 2. Did you choose a variety of different functions including:

- functions with negative and positive values
- functions with integer and decimal values
- functions with very high or very low values?

Discuss with a partner or in a small group why it might be important to choose a variety of different functions when investigating the properties of the graphs of these functions.

5   a   Which of these graphs represent a linear function?

      b   Which of these graphs represent a quadratic function?

A
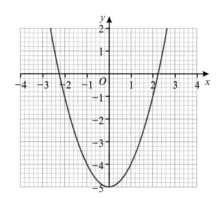

B
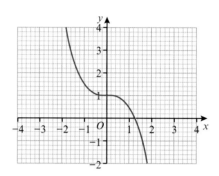

C
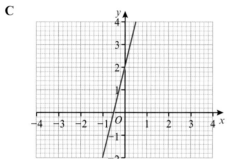

D
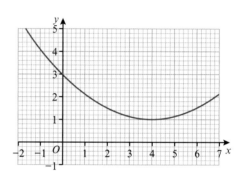

E
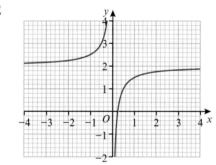

F
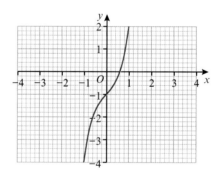

G
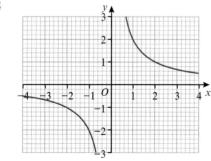

H
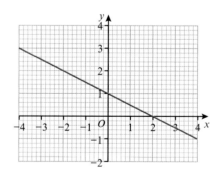

6   Look again at the graphs in Question **5**.

    a   Which graphs represent a cubic function?

    b   Which graphs represent a reciprocal function?

7   Enter each of these functions into your graphic display calculator.

    a   Copy and complete the table to show the features of each graph.

Function	Vertical axis intercept	Gradient
$f(x) = x + 1$		
$f(x) = 2x + 1$		
$f(x) = 3x + 2$		
$f(x) = 3x - 1$		
$f(x) = -2x + 3$		
$f(x) = -3x - 2$		

    b   For a linear graph in the form $f(x) = ax + b$, describe the link between the function and where the graph of the function intercepts the vertical axis.

    c   For a linear graph in the form $f(x) = ax + b$, describe the link between the function and the gradient of the graph of the function.

8   Use what you know about graphs of functions, the vertical axis intercept and the gradient of a line to match each function to its graph.

    a $f(x) = 3x + 1$ **b** $f(x) = -2x - 2$ **c** $f(x) = -x + 1$

    d $f(x) = 2x - 3$ **e** $f(x) = -3x + 2$ **f** $f(x) = 2x + 2$

A
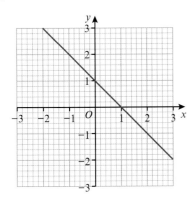

B
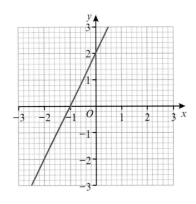

C
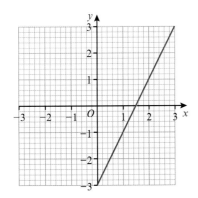

D
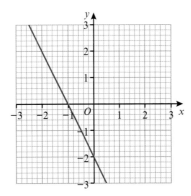

> **MATHEMATICAL CONNECTIONS**
>
> You will be able to apply what you have learnt about equations in coordinate geometry in Chapter 11 to the graphs of functions.

> **TIP**
>
> If necessary, change the minimum and maximum values of the horizontal and vertical axes so that you can see the place where the function line intercepts with the vertical axis.

E
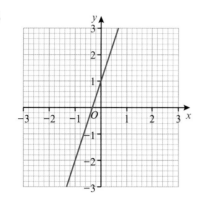

F
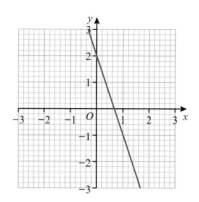

14.5 The domain and the range

The **domain** refers to the set of possible **real number** inputs that will produce a real number output when the function is applied. Many functions can have an input that is any number from $-\infty$ to ∞ and it will create an output. However, for some functions there are some input values that do not create an output value.

The **range** of the function describes the set of all the possible output values for the function. If you enter the function into a graphic display calculator it should give you an idea as to which values are possible output values of the function.

TIP

We use the '∞' to denote infinity.

WORKED EXAMPLE 6

a What is the domain of the function $f(x) = \sqrt{x + 1}$?

b What is the range of the function $f(x) = \sqrt{x + 1}$?

Answers

a Think about which values of x produce a real number output $f(x)$.

The square root of a negative number is not a real number, so $x + 1$ cannot be negative.

If x is -2, then $x + 1 = -1$. $\sqrt{-1}$ does not produce a real number output.

x cannot equal -2, so -2 is not in the domain of $f(x)$.

Any value for x less than -1 is not in the domain of $f(x)$.

The domain of $f(x)$ is $x \geqslant -1$.

b Enter the function into your graphic display calculator.

This is the graph of $f(x)$.

The vertical axis represents the output of the function.

There are no values of y less than 0 because x must be greater than or equal to -1.

The range of $f(x)$ is $f(x) \geqslant 0$.

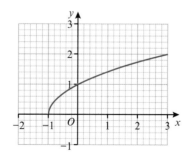

Exercise 14.5

1   **a**   For each of these functions there is a value, or values, of x that is impossible. Find the impossible value(s) of x.

   i $f(x) = \dfrac{5}{x}$ **ii** $g(x) = \dfrac{2x + 2}{x - 8}$ **iii** $h(x) = \dfrac{7x}{x^2 - 36}$

   b   Explain why the values you identified in part **a** are impossible input values for the functions.

2   For each of these functions there is a set of input values that are impossible. Copy and complete the statements to describe the set of values for x that *will* give a real number defined output for each function.

   a $f(x) = \sqrt{x}$

   The domain of $f(x)$ is ...

   b $g(x) = \sqrt{5 - x}$

   The domain of $g(x)$ is ...

   c $h(x) = \dfrac{7}{\sqrt{x - 3}}$

   The domain of $h(x)$ is ...

3   What is the range of each function?

   a $f(x) = x^2$

   b $g(x) = \dfrac{1}{x}$

   c $h(x) = \dfrac{x + 6}{3}$ when $0 \leqslant x \leqslant 9$

   d $k(x) = 3x^2 - 10$ when $-5 \leqslant x \leqslant 5$

> **TIP**
>
> For a value to be a possible input value, the output created must be a real number. For part **a**, use your knowledge of number and operations to consider what number 5 cannot be divided by.

> **TIP**
>
> Domains are specified for functions $h(x)$ and $k(x)$. A domain specified in this way is called a restricted domain. Calculate the possible outputs for the specified domain only.

14.6 Inverse functions

Here is the function $f(x) = 5x - 8$ represented as a function machine:

input $(x) \rightarrow \boxed{\times 5} \rightarrow \boxed{-8} \rightarrow$ output $(f(x))$

To calculate $f(10)$ you multiply 10 by 5 and then subtract 8.

$f(10) = 42$

An **inverse function** takes an output of the function and calculates what the input was.

You use the notation $f^{-1}(x)$ to describe the inverse function for $f(x)$.

> **WORKED EXAMPLE 7**
>
> Consider the function $f(x) = 5x - 8$.
> **a**   Find $f^{-1}(x)$.
> **b**   If $f(x) = 27$, what is the input value x?

CONTINUED

Answers

a **Method 1: Using a function machine**

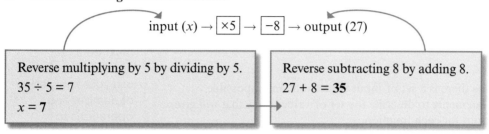

input $(x) \rightarrow \boxed{\times 5} \rightarrow \boxed{-8} \rightarrow$ output (27)

| Reverse multiplying by 5 by dividing by 5.
$35 \div 5 = 7$
$x = \mathbf{7}$ | Reverse subtracting 8 by adding 8.
$27 + 8 = \mathbf{35}$ |

Rename the output as x and write this inverse function as: $f^{-1}(x) = \dfrac{x+8}{5}$

Method 2: Using changing the subject in an equation

You can also find the inverse function by changing the subject in the original function.

Let $y = f(x)$

Rearrange to make x the subject:

$y = 5x - 8$

$y + 8 = 5x$

$\dfrac{y+8}{5} = x$

Swap x for $f^{-1}(x)$, and swap y for x:

$x = \dfrac{y+8}{5}$

$f^{-1}(x) = \dfrac{x+8}{5}$

b Substitute $x = 27$ into $f^{-1}(x)$ to find the value of x that gives $f(x) = 27$:

$f^{-1}(27) = \dfrac{27+8}{5} = 7$

$x = 7$

Exercise 14.6

1 **a** For the function $f(x) = 3x - 4$, express the inverse function in the form $f^{-1}(x) = \ldots$

b For the function $g(x) = \dfrac{x+2}{3}$, express the inverse function in the form $g^{-1}(x) = \ldots$

c For the function $h(x) = x^2 + 8$, express the inverse function in the form $h^{-1}(x) = \ldots$

d For the function $k(x) = 5 - x$, express the inverse function in the form $k^{-1}(x) = \ldots$

Look back at Worked example 7 to recap the two methods for finding the inverse of a function.

- Which method(s) did you use for the questions in this exercise? Why?
- Are there any questions that can only be solved using one of the methods?
- What are the benefits and disadvantages of each method?

2   $f(x) = 7x - 10$, $g(x) = 8 - 2x$, $h(x) = \dfrac{3}{x + 1}$

Consider your answers to the reflection questions as you find:

a $f^{-1}(x)$ b $g^{-1}(x)$ c $h^{-1}(x)$

3   a   Copy and complete the mapping diagram.

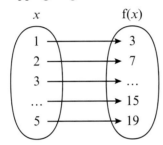

b   For the function in part **a**, use function notation to express:

i $f(x)$ ii $f^{-1}(x)$

14.7 Composite functions

Two functions can be combined into a single function called a **composite function**. In a composite function, one function is the input of the other function.

$fg(x)$

$g(x)$ is a function. In $fg(x)$, $g(x)$ is the input of function f. This means you need to carry out the function $g(x)$ first, then apply function $f(x)$ to the output of $g(x)$. Always apply the function closest to the x is first.

$f(x) = 5x - 3$ and $g(x) = \dfrac{x}{2}$

Find:

a   i $fg(x)$ ii $fg(4)$

b   i $gf(x)$ ii $gf(4)$

CONTINUED

Answers

a **i** $fg(x) = f(g(x)) = f\left(\frac{x}{2}\right) = 5\left(\frac{x}{2}\right) - 3 = \frac{5x}{2} - 3$

> $g(x)$ is the input.

ii When $x = 4$

$fg(4) = \frac{5 \times 4}{2} - 3 = 7$

b **i** $gf(x) = g(f(x)) = g(5x - 3) = \frac{5x - 3}{2}$

> $f(x)$ is the input.

ii When $x = 4$

$gf(4) = \frac{5 \times 4 - 3}{2} = 8.5$

Exercise 14.7

1 $f(x) = 2x + 1$ and $g(x) = x^2 - 3$

Find:

a **i** $fg(x)$ **ii** $fg(5)$

b **i** $gf(x)$ **ii** $gf(5)$

2 $f(x) = \frac{x}{4}$, $g(x) = 3x^2$ and $h(x) = -2x + 5$

Find:

a $fg(8)$ **b** $gh(3)$ **c** $fh(2)$ **d** $gf(-10)$

e $hg(0.8)$ **f** $hf(\pi)$ (round your answer to two decimal places)

3 $f(x) = \frac{6}{x + 1}$, $g(x) = (2x - 3)^2$ and $h(x) = \frac{x - 3}{8}$

Find:

a $gf(2)$ **b** $fg(5)$ **c** $gh(3)$

d $hg\left(\frac{1}{2}\right)$ **e** $fh(67)$ **f** $hf(-7)$

> **TIP**
>
> If your answer is a fraction, give your answer in its simplest form.

SUMMARY

Are you able to... ?
use function notation
create tables for functions
sketch graphs of functions
use a graphic display calculator to explore functions
recognise function types from the shape of their graphs
describe the range and domain of a function
understand and find inverse functions
form composite functions.

Past paper questions

1   $f(x) = \dfrac{x - 3}{2}$ for $-5 \leqslant x \leqslant 21$

Find the range of $f(x)$.

.... [2]

Cambridge IGCSE International Mathematics 0607 Paper 11 Q20 June 2021

2

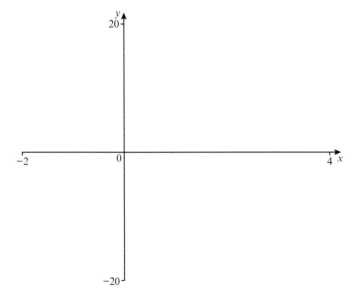

a   On the axes, sketch the graph of $y = x^3 - 3x^2$. [Using Past Paper Question Resource Sheet]   [3]

b   Write down the zeros of $y = x^3 - 3x^2$.

Answer (b) x = ... *x =* .... [1]

c   Write down the co-ordinates of any local maximum or local minimum points.

Answer (c) .... [2]

Cambridge IGCSE International Mathematics 0607 Paper 41 Q2 June 2011

3 **a**

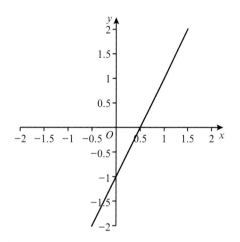

The graph shows $y = f(x)$, where $f(x) = 2x - 1$.

i   Find the inverse function, $f^{-1}(x)$.

Answer (a)(i) $f^{-1}(x) = $ .... [2]

ii   Sketch the graph of $y = f^{-1}(x)$ on the diagram above. [Using Past Paper Question Resource Sheet]   [1]

b

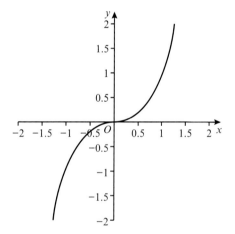

The graph shows $y = g(x)$, where $g(x) = x^3$.

i   Find the inverse function, $g(x)$.

Answer (b)(i) $g^{-1}(x) = $ .... [1]

ii   Sketch the graph of $y = g^{-1}(x)$ on the diagram above. [Using Past Paper Question Resource Sheet]   [2]

Cambridge IGCSE International Mathematics 0607 Paper 4 Q7a,bi,bii June 2009

> Chapter 15

Trigonometry

IN THIS CHAPTER YOU WILL:

- use the tangent, sine and cosine ratios to calculate side lengths and angles in right-angled triangles

- solve 2D problems using the trigonometric ratios and Pythagoras' theorem

> solve 3D problems using the trigonometric ratios and Pythagoras' theorem

> recognise, sketch and use graphs of the sine, cosine and tangent functions

> solve trigonometric equations with and without a graphic display calculator

> learn the exact values for the sine, cosine and tangent of some angles

> use the sine ratio to calculate the area of a triangle

> use the sine and cosine rules to calculate side lengths and angles in non-right-angled triangles.

GETTING STARTED

1 Use Pythagoras' theorem to calculate the side length labelled x in each triangle.

Give your answer to three significant figures.

a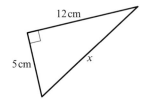

b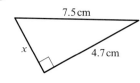

c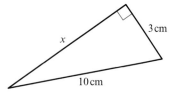

2 The diagram shows three towns at points A, B and C. C is due east of A.

Find the bearing of:

a B from A

b C from A

c C from B

d A from C

e B from C

f A from B.

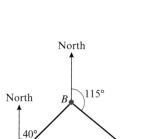

3 Solve each equation to find the value of x.

a $\dfrac{x}{7} = 2.3$　　**b** $0.81 = \dfrac{x^2}{4}$　　**c** $0.375 = \dfrac{7.5}{x}$　　**d** $0.625 = \dfrac{3}{\sqrt{x}}$

KEY WORDS

adjacent

angle of depression

angle of elevation

cosine ratio

cosine rule

hypotenuse

sine ratio

sine rule

tangent ratio

15.1 The trigonometric ratios

Trigonometry is the area of mathematics used to calculate lengths and angles in triangles.

In this section you will learn about the relationships between the angles and side lengths in right-angled triangles.

The first thing you need to learn is how to correctly label the sides in a right-angled triangle relative to the angle you are interested in.

You already know that the longest side in a right-angled triangle is called the **hypotenuse**.

MATHEMATICS IN CONTEXT

The word *trigonometry* comes from the Ancient Greek for 'triangle measure'. Surveyors use trigonometry to calculate the height of mountains, and astronomers use it to calculate how far stars and planets are from Earth.

The other two sides are labelled relative to the marked angle θ.

They are:

- the opposite side, opp(θ)
- the **adjacent** side, adj(θ).

The tangent ratio

The two right-angled triangles *ABC* and *DEF* are similar. Each side of *DEF* is twice as long as the corresponding side of *ABC* and angle α is equal to angle β.

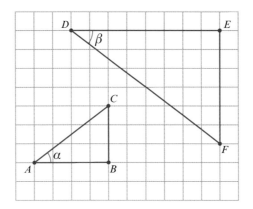

Consider triangle *ABC*:

$BC = 3$ and $AB = 4$

The ratio $\dfrac{BC}{AB} = \dfrac{3}{4} = 0.75$

Consider triangle *DEF*:

$EF = 3$ and $DE = 4$

The ratio $\dfrac{EF}{DE} = \dfrac{6}{8} = 0.75$

The ratios are equal because the triangles are similar. In fact, any other similar triangle will have the same ratio.

Notice that, relative to the angle θ, you can write both ratios as $\dfrac{\text{opposite side}}{\text{adjacent side}}$

This is called the **tangent ratio**: $\tan \theta = \dfrac{\text{opp}(\theta)}{\text{adj}(\theta)}$

> **TIP**
>
> Remember that the hypotenuse is always opposite the right angle.

> **MATHEMATICAL CONNECTIONS**
>
> You learnt about similar shapes in Chapter 9.

> **TIP**
>
> The word 'adjacent' means 'next to'.

> **TIP**
>
> Mathematicians often use the Greek letter θ (theta) to stand for an unknown or variable angle.

WORKED EXAMPLE 1

Write down the tangent ratio for angle α.

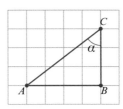

Answer

$\tan \alpha = \dfrac{\text{opp}(\alpha)}{\text{adj}(\alpha)}$ Write down the tangent ratio.

$\text{opp}(\alpha) = AB$ Side *AB* is opposite angle α.

$\text{adj}(\alpha) = BC$ Side *BC* is adjacent to angle α.

$\tan \alpha = \dfrac{AB}{BC}$

Calculating side lengths

The tangent ratio is built into your calculator. Look for the **tan** button.
You can use this to find the tangent ratio for any angle.

For example, to find the tangent of an angle of 35°, you press:

tan **3** **5** **EXE**

Your calculator should show the value 0.4738147204

You can use this function on your calculator to work out unknown side lengths in right-angled triangles.

> **TIP**
>
> You will need to make sure your calculator is set to degrees mode. If you are not sure about this, check your calculator manual.

WORKED EXAMPLE 2

Calculate the unknown length x for each triangle.
Give your answers to one decimal place.

a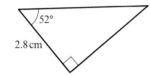

b

Answers

a
$$\tan \theta = \frac{\text{opp}(\theta)}{\text{adj}(\theta)}$$

$$\tan 52° = \frac{x}{2.8}$$ Substitute values into the ratio.

$$x = 2.8 \times \tan 52°$$ Rearrange and solve to find x.

$$= 3.6 \text{ (to 1 dp)}$$

b
$$\tan \theta = \frac{\text{opp}(\theta)}{\text{adj}(\theta)}$$

$$\tan 26° = \frac{45}{x}$$

$$x \tan 26° = 45$$

$$x = \frac{45}{\tan 26°}$$

$$x = 92.3 \text{ (to 1 dp)}$$

Exercise 15.1

Where necessary in this exercise, give side lengths to three significant figures and angles to one decimal place.

1   Write down the tangent ratio for each angle θ, marked in the triangles.

a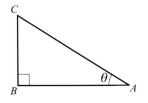

b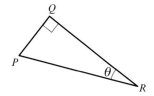

c

2   Use your calculator to write down each value.

   a $\tan 58°$ **b** $\tan 76.3°$ **c** $\tan 0.82°$ **d** $\tan 14.9°$

3   Find the length of the side marked x in each triangle.

a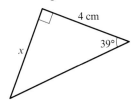

b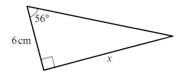

c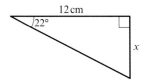

4   Find the length of the side marked y in each triangle.

a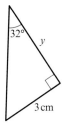

b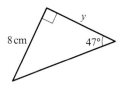

c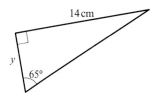

5   A flagpole of length 2.65 m is held in place by two
equal-length ropes on opposite sides of the pole.
The ropes each make an angle of 60° with the ground.
Find the distance d along the ground from the end
of one rope to the end of the other rope.

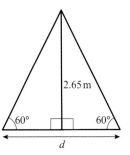

6   A ladder leans against a vertical wall at an angle of 78° to the horizontal ground.
The base of the ladder is 0.6 m from the wall. Find the height of the top of the
ladder above the ground.

> **TIP**
>
> If a diagram is not
> provided then sketch
> your own to show
> the information.

Calculating angles

Sometimes you will know the value of the tangent ratio, but not the angle.
To find the angle you will need to 'undo' the tangent ratio using the inverse tangent, or $\tan^{-1}$ function on your calculator. To find this function you may need to use the **SHIFT** button.

For example if you know that $\tan\alpha = 2.305$, to work out α you press:

Your calculator should show the value 66.54689633

So, the angle α is 66.5° (to 1 dp).

> **TIP**
>
> Make sure you know which buttons to press on *your* calculator.

WORKED EXAMPLE 3

Calculate the size of angle α.
Give your answer to three significant figures.

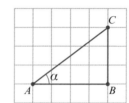

Answer

$$\tan\theta = \frac{\text{opp}(\theta)}{\text{adj}(\theta)}$$

$$\tan\alpha = \frac{BC}{AB} = \frac{3}{4}$$

$$\alpha = \tan^{-1}\left(\frac{3}{4}\right)$$

$$= 36.9° \text{ (to 3 sf)}$$

Exercise 15.2

Where necessary in this exercise, give side lengths to three significant figures and angles to one decimal place.

1   Use your calculator to write down the value of each acute angle.

   a $\tan\alpha = 17.5$ b $\tan\alpha = 0.35$ c $\tan\alpha = 5.81$ d $\tan\alpha = 2.6$

2 Calculate the size of each angle x.

a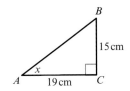

b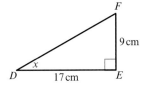

c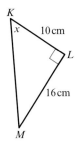

d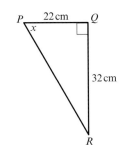

e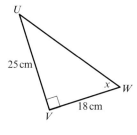

3 ABC is a right-angled triangle.
Calculate:
a the length of side x
b the angle θ.

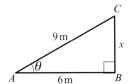

4 A ladder leans against a wall. The top of the ladder is 4.62 m above the ground and the bottom of the ladder is 1.17 m from the wall. The ground and the wall are at right angles.
Find the angle that the ladder makes with the ground.

The sine and cosine ratios

There are two other ratios that you can use to calculate sides and angles in right-angled triangles.

These are:

- the **sine ratio** $\quad \sin\theta = \dfrac{\text{opp}(\theta)}{\text{hyp}}$

- the **cosine ratio** $\quad \cos\theta = \dfrac{\text{adj}(\theta)}{\text{hyp}}$

You use these ratios in the same way as the tangent ratio and these functions are also built into your calculator – look for the **sin** and **cos** buttons.

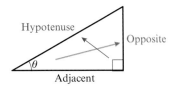

> **TIP**
>
> You will also need to use the inverse sine and cosine functions so make sure you know how to do this on **your** calculator.

To answer questions involving missing lengths or angles, you will have to decide which of the three ratios to use. You can use the acronym SOHCAHTOA to help you remember which ratio is which.

S O H
$\sin\theta = \dfrac{\text{opposite side}}{\text{hypotenuse}}$

C A H
$\cos\theta = \dfrac{\text{adjacent side}}{\text{hypotenuse}}$

T O A
$\tan\theta = \dfrac{\text{opposite side}}{\text{adjacent side}}$

WORKED EXAMPLE 4

Calculate the length of the side labelled x in each diagram.
Give your answers to three significant figures.

a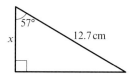

b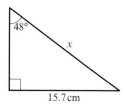

Answers

a
$$\cos \theta = \frac{\text{adj}(\theta)}{\text{hyp}}$$

$$\cos 57° = \frac{x}{12.7}$$

$$x = 12.7 \times \cos 57°$$

$$x = 6.92 \text{ cm (to 3 sf)}$$

You know the length of the hypotenuse.

The unknown length x is adjacent to the given angle.

So, use the ratio that includes H and A: the cosine ratio.

Substitute values and solve to find x.

Remember to give the units in your answer.

b
$$\sin \theta = \frac{\text{opp}(\theta)}{\text{hyp}}$$

$$\sin 48° = \frac{15.7}{x}$$

$$x \sin 48° = 15.7$$

$$x = \frac{15.7}{\sin 48°} = 21.2 \text{ cm (to 3 sf)}.$$

You know the length of the hypotenuse.

The unknown length x is opposite the given angle.

So, use the ratio that includes H and O: the sine ratio.

x is the denominator of the fraction, so be careful when you solve the equation.

WORKED EXAMPLE 5

Calculate the size of angle x.
Give your answer to one decimal place.

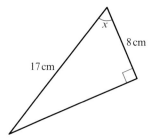

CONTINUED

Answer

17 is the hypotenuse.   Look at the information you have.

8 is the side adjacent to angle x.

Use the cosine ratio.   Decide which ratio to use.

$$\cos \theta = \frac{\text{adj}(\theta)}{\text{hyp}}$$

$$\cos x = \frac{8}{17}$$ Substitute values.

$$x = \cos^{-1}\left(\frac{8}{17}\right)$$ Use the inverse cosine function.

$$x = 61.9° \text{ (to 1 dp)}$$

Exercise 15.3

Where necessary in this exercise, give side lengths to three significant figures and angles to one decimal place.

1   Use your calculator to write down each value.

   a $\sin 55°$ **b** $\cos 60°$ **c** $\sin 15°$ **d** $\cos 90°$

   e $\sin 45°$ **f** $\cos 45°$ **g** $\sin 90°$ **h** $\cos 30°$

> **TIP**
>
> You will need to use all three trigonometric ratios in this exercise.

2   Find the length of each side length labelled with a letter.

a
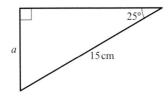

b
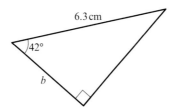

c

d
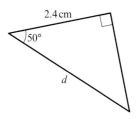

e
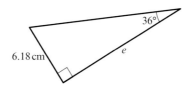

f
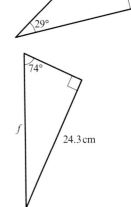

g
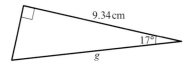

h
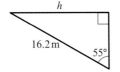

i
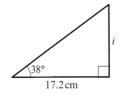

3 Calculate each labelled angle.

a

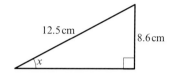

b

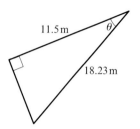

c

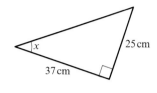

d

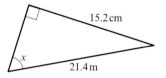

e

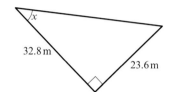

f

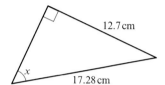

g

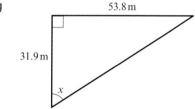

h

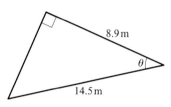

i

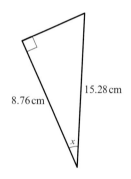

4 Calculate each value of x.

a

b

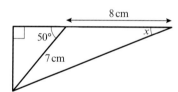

c

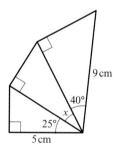

15.2 Solving problems using the trigonometric ratios and Pythagoras' theorem

When you solve problems that involve calculating unknown angles or lengths you will often need to use a combination of trigonometric ratios along with Pythagoras' theorem.

You should always start by drawing a large clear diagram and labelling all the angles and lengths that you know.

WORKED EXAMPLE 6

MATHEMATICAL CONNECTIONS

A ship leaves a port, P, and sails 35 km on bearing of 100° to point Q.

Calculate:

a how far east of the port the ship has travelled

b how far south of the port the ship has travelled.

Give your answers to three significant figures.

You learnt about three-figure bearings in Chapter 4. Remember that when you give a bearing, you always measure the angle from north and write it using three figures.

Answers

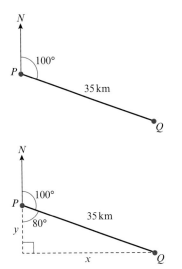

Start by drawing a diagram and labelling all the information.

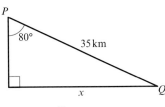

Add lines to form a right-angled triangle.

x is the distance east from port.

y is the distance south from the port.

a

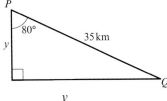

x is opposite to the angle 80°.

35 km is the hypotenuse.

So, use the sine ratio to find x.

$$\sin\theta = \frac{\text{opp}\,(\theta)}{\text{hyp}}$$

$$\sin 80° = \frac{x}{35}$$

$$x = 35 \times \sin 80°$$

$$= 34.468\ldots$$

The ship has travelled 34.5 km east.

b

y is adjacent to the angle 80°.

Use the cosine ratio.

$$\cos\theta = \frac{\text{adj}\,(\theta)}{\text{hyp}}$$

$$\cos 80° = \frac{y}{35}$$

$$y = 35 \times \cos 80°$$

$$= 6.077\ldots$$

The ship has travelled 6.08 km south.

DISCUSSION 1

What alternative method can you use to answer part **b**?

What are the advantages and disadvantages of each method?

Sometimes you will need to use Pythagoras' theorem as well as more than one trigonometric ratio in order to solve a problem.

Exercise 15.4

Where necessary in this exercise, give side lengths to three significant figures and angles to one decimal place.

1   $ABCD$ is a rectangle. $CD = 6\,\text{cm}$ and angle $BAD = 35°$.
Calculate the area of $ABCD$.

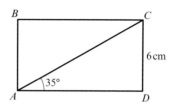

2   Town Y is 15 km due east of Town X.
Town Z is 25 km due south of Town Y.
   a   Calculate the value of θ.
   b   Find the bearing of Town X from Town Z.

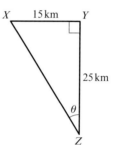

3   XYZ is an isosceles triangle. $XY = YZ = 10\,\text{cm}$ and $X = 5\,\text{cm}$.
   a   Find the perpendicular height, h.
   b   Find the sizes of the three interior angles of the triangle.

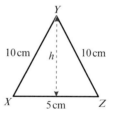

TIP

If a diagram is not provided, draw your own to show the information.

4   a   Ship A sails 35 km on a bearing of 042°.
Calculate:
   i   the distance north it has sailed
   ii   the distance east it has sailed.

   b   Ship B sails 200 km on bearing 243.7°.
Calculate:
   i   the distance south it has sailed
   ii   the distance west it has sailed.

5   A ship sails from *A* to *B* travelling 52 km on a bearing of 090°.
The ship then sails from *B* to *C* travelling 45 km on a bearing of 130°.

Find the total distance the ship has sailed:

a   east

b   south.

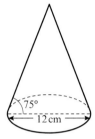

6   The diagram shows a right cone with diameter 12 cm.
The angle between the sloping side and the base is 75°.

Calculate the cone's:

a   perpendicular height

b   sloping edge length.

7   To measure the width of a straight river a conservationist marks a point, *A*, on one side of the river, directly opposite an object, *B*. She then walks 50 m along the bank from point *A* to point *C*. She measures the angle *ACB* = 34°.

Calculate the width of the river.

15.3 Angles of elevation and depression

Imagine you are looking at the top of a tree that is some distance away from you.
The angle you raise your eyes from the horizontal is called the **angle of elevation**.

Now imagine you are standing on a cliff looking at a ship out at sea. The angle you lower your eyes from the horizontal is called the **angle of depression**.

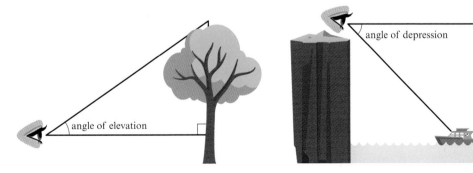

You can use what you know about angles and sides in right-angled triangles to solve problems involving angles of elevation and depression. It is very important to remember that these angles are *always* measured above or below the horizontal direction.

WORKED EXAMPLE 7

The angle of depression from the top of a cliff of height 85 m to a ship at sea is 28.6°. How far from the cliff is the ship?

Give your answer to the nearest metre.

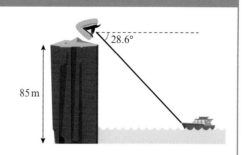

Answer

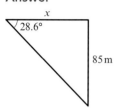

$\tan 28.6° = \dfrac{85}{x}$

$x \times \tan 28.6° = 85$

$x = \dfrac{85}{\tan 28.6°}$

$x = 155.90\ldots = 156\,\text{m}$ (to the nearest metre)

Draw a right-angled triangle to show the information.

The opposite side is 85 m and the unknown side, x, is adjacent, so use the tangent ratio.

Rearrange and solve to find x.

WORKED EXAMPLE 8

A student is looking up at the top of a tree that is a horizontal distance of 200 m away.

The angle of elevation to the top of the tree is 12.8° and the student's eyes are 1.49 m above the ground.

Calculate the height of the tree, giving your answer to three significant figures.

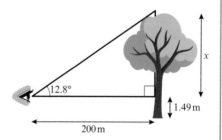

Answer

The height of the tree = $x + 1.49\,\text{m}$

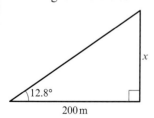

$\tan 12.8° = \dfrac{x}{200}$

$x = 200 \times \tan 12.8°$

$\quad = 45.438\ldots$

The height of the tree = $45.438\ldots + 1.49$

$\qquad\qquad\qquad\quad = 46.9\,\text{m}$ (to 3 sf)

x is the vertical distance between the student's eyes and the top of the tree.

If it helps, draw the right-angled triangle separately.

Use the tangent ratio to find x.

TIP

Be careful – the angle is measured from eye level *not* ground level – don't forget about the distance between the ground and the student's eyes.

Shortest distances

Look at triangle PQR.

If you are asked to find the distance from vertex P to side QR, what distance would you find?

You could travel along side PQ in which case the distance would be 5 cm, or you could travel along side PR in which case the distance would be 8 cm.

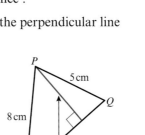

In mathematics when we talk about 'the distance' between a point and a line we almost always mean 'the shortest distance'.

The shortest distance between a point and a line is equal to the perpendicular line between the point and the line.

So, in triangle PQR, to the shortest distance from vertex P to side QR, is the line from P that meets side QR at a right angle.

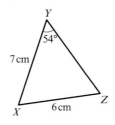

The shortest distance from P to QR

MATHEMATICAL CONNECTIONS

This is similar to the perpendicular angle between the radius of a circle and a tangent line touching the circle. You will learn more about circles and their properties in Chapter 16.

WORKED EXAMPLE 9

Calculate the shortest distance from vertex X to side YZ in triangle XYZ.
Give your answer to three significant figures.

Answer

Draw a perpendicular line to show the shortest distance, d. This has formed a right-angled triangle.

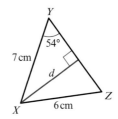

The distance d is opposite the angle 54°, so use the sine ratio to calculate the length:

$$\sin \theta = \frac{\text{opp}(\theta)}{\text{hyp}}$$

$$\sin 54° = \frac{d}{7}$$

$$d = 7 \times \sin 54°$$

$$= 5.66 \text{ cm (to 3 sf)}$$

Exercise 15.5

1   The angle of elevation of the top of a post from a point on level ground 38 m away is 33.2°. Find the height of the post.

2   A tree is 62.8 m tall and the angle of elevation from the ground to the top of the tree is 64.2°. Calculate the distance from where the angle was measured to the base of the tree.

3   A park ranger whose eyes are 1.65 metres above ground level stands 34 metres from the base of a tree. If the angle of elevation to the top of the tree is 52.8°, calculate the height of the tree.

TIP

Don't forget to include the distance between the ranger's eyes and the ground when calculating the height of the tree.

4   A cliff is 150 m high and the angle of depression from the top of the cliff to a ship is 24°. Calculate the distance from the cliff to the ship.

5   A ship is 725 m from the bottom of a cliff and the cliff is 86 m high. Find the angle of depression from the top of the cliff to the ship.

6   The diagram shows triangle ABC.
Calculate:

   a   the shortest distance from B to AC

   b   the size of angle α.

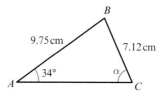

7   The diagram shows isosceles triangle ABC.
Calculate:

   a   the shortest distance from Y to XZ

   b   the area of the triangle.

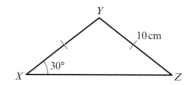

8   An equilateral triangle has side lengths 7 cm. Calculate the shortest distance from any vertex to its opposite side.

9   A ship is 152 m from the bottom of a cliff.

   The angle of elevation from the ship to the top of the cliff is 14° and the angle of elevation from the ship to the top of a lighthouse on the cliff is 19°.

   Calculate the height of the lighthouse.

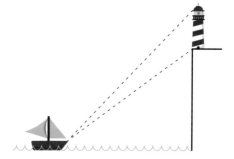

10 The angle of depression from the top of a lighthouse to a yacht is 47°.
The angle of depression from the bottom of the lighthouse to the yacht is 41°.
The cliff is 127 metres high.

   What is the height of the lighthouse?

11 The angle of depression from the top of a lighthouse to a yacht is 54°.
The angle of depression from the bottom of the lighthouse to the yacht is 49°.
The lighthouse is 44 metres high.

Calculate:

a the height of the cliff

b the distance from the yacht to the cliff.

15.4 Solving problems in three dimensions

You can use the trigonometric ratios and Pythagoras' theorem to solve problems in three dimensions.

When solving problems like this you need to identify right-angled triangles within the three-dimensional shapes. It is helpful to draw each triangle separately so you can see clearly what you need to do.

WORKED EXAMPLE 10

The diagram shows a triangular prism $ABCDEF$. The cross-section is a right-angled triangle and the face $ABCD$ is a rectangle.

Calculate the size of angle FAC.

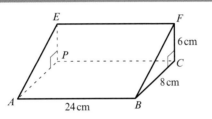

Answer

Start by identifying angle FAC. Triangle FAC is right-angled and the side $FC = 6$ cm.
To find angle FAC you need to know the length of one of the other sides.

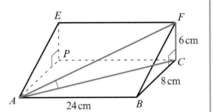

Look at the right-angled triangle ABC:
$AB = 24$ cm and $BC = 8$ cm.

So, using Pythagoras' theorem:

$AC^2 = 24^2 + 8^2 = 640$

$AC = \sqrt{640}$

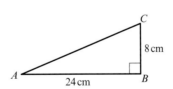

Now, you know two sides of triangle FAC:

the side opposite angle $FAC = 6$ cm

the side adjacent to angle $FAC = \sqrt{640}$ cm

So, $\tan(FAC) = \dfrac{6}{\sqrt{640}} = 0.237...$

Angle $FAC = \tan^{-1}(0.237...) = 13.3°$ (to 1 dp)

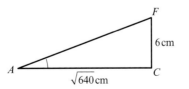

> **MATHEMATICAL CONNECTIONS**
>
> You have the opportunity to use the skills you have already learnt about shapes and their properties in Chapter 12.

Exercise 15.6

1 *ABCDEF* is a triangular prism.
   CF = 10 cm, *BC* = 24 cm and *AB* = 32 cm.
   Calculate:

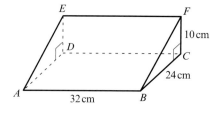

   a *BF*

   b angle *EAD*

   c *AC*

   d *AF*

   e angle *CAF*

   f the angle between *EB* and the face *ABCD*

   g the volume of the prism.

2 *ABCDEF* is a triangular prism.
   CF = 15 cm, *AB* = 20 cm and angle *CAF* =30°.
   Calculate:

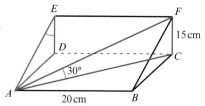

   a *AF*

   b *AC*

   c *BC*

   d angle *AED*

   e the angle between *AE* and the face *ABCD*

   f the volume of the prism.

3 *ABCDPQRS* is a cuboid.
   AB = 12 cm, *BC* = 5 cm
   and *CR* = 9 cm.
   Calculate:

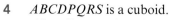

   a *AC*

   b *DR*

   c *AR*

   d angle *CAR*

   e angle *SBD*

   f angle *RDC*

   g the angle between *AR* and face *ABQP*.

4 *ABCDPQRS* is a cuboid.
   AB = 40 cm, *BC* = 72 cm
   and *CR* = 21 cm.
   Calculate:

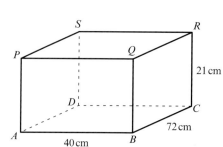

   a *BR*

   b *AR*

   c the angle between *BR* and face *ABCD*

   d the angle between *AQ* and face *ABCD*

   e the angle between *AR* and face *ABCD*

   f the angle between *AR* and face *BCRQ*.

5 *ABCDV* is a right pyramid.
The base *ABCD* is a rectangle.
M is the midpoint of *BC* and *P* is
the midpoint of *AB*. *AB* = 48 cm,
BC = 36 cm and *VN* = 7 cm.

Calculate:

a   *DB*

b   *VM*

c   *VC*

d   *AM*

e   the angle between *VM* and the base

f   the angle between *VB* and the base

g   the angle between *VP* and the base.

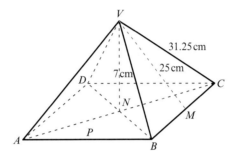

TIP

A right pyramid is one where the apex is directly above the centre of the base, so *VN* meets the base at a right angle.

6 *ABCDV* is a right pyramid.
The base *ABCD* is a rectangle.
M is the midpoint of *BC* and *P*
is the midpoint of *AB*. *VM* = 25 cm,
VC = 31.25 cm and *VN* = 7 cm.

Calculate:

a   *MC*

b   *NM*

c   *AC*

d   *PM*

e   the angle between *VC* and the base

f   the angle between *VM* and the base

g   the angle between *VP* and the base.

15.5 The sine, cosine and tangent ratios as functions

So far you have used your calculator to work out the sine, cosine or tangent of particular angles in right-angled triangles. In fact, it is possible to find these values for **any** angle and you can think of sine, cosine and tangent as functions, each with its own graph.

The sine function

If you plot the values of sine *x* against *x* you get the graph of *y* = sin *x*.

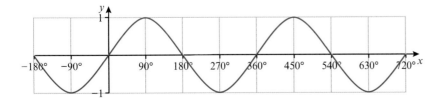

TIP

You will need to remember the shape and key features of the graph *y* = sin *x*.

Looking at the graph you should be able to see that:

- the maximum value of $\sin x$ is 1
- the minimum value of $\sin x$ is -1
- the graph repeats itself every 360°
- the curve crosses the y-axis at (0°, 0).

The graph has a line of symmetry at $x = 90°$.

This means that for $0° \leqslant x \leqslant 90°$: $\sin x = \sin(180° - x)$

You can check this by testing some values on your calculator.

DISCUSSION 2

What other symmetry can you see on the graph of $y = \sin x$?

What is the relationship between: $\sin x$, $\sin(180° + x)$ and $\sin(360° - x)$?

Amplitude and period

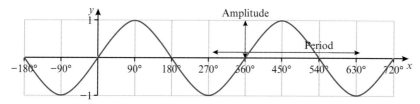

The amplitude of a curve is the maximum displacement of the curve from the central horizontal line of the curve.

So, the amplitude of $y = \sin x$ is 1.

The period (or wavelength) of a curve is how long it takes to repeat itself.

So, the period of $y = \sin x$ is 360°.

The cosine function

If you plot the values of cosine x against x you get the graph of $y = \cos x$.

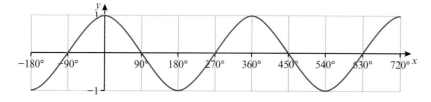

Look at the graph and make sure you can see the following features:

- the maximum value of $\cos x$ is 1
- the minimum value of $\cos x$ is -1
- the graph repeats itself every 360°
- the curve crosses the y-axis at (0°, 1).

TIP

As for $y = \sin x$, the function $y = \cos x$ has an amplitude of 1 and a period of 360°.

The graph has a line of symmetry at $x = 180°$.

This means that for $0° \leqslant x \leqslant 180°$: $\cos x = \cos(360° - x)$

You can check this by testing some values on your calculator.

The tangent function

If you plot the values of tangent x against x you get the graph of $y = \tan x$.

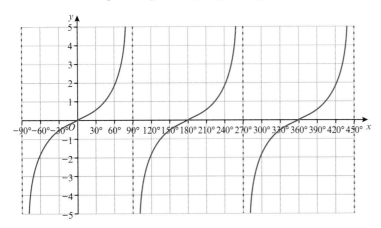

The graph of $y = \tan x$ looks quite different from the other two graphs:

- there are no maximum or minimum points
- the graph repeats itself every 180°, so $\tan x = \tan(x + 180°)$

There are breaks in the curve, indicated by dashed vertical lines at $x = -90°$, $x = 90°$, $x = 270°$, and so on.

These lines are known as asymptotes. The function gets closer and closer, but never meets them.

MATHEMATICAL CONNECTIONS

You will learn more about functions in Chapter 23.

WORKED EXAMPLE 11

Find all possible values of θ for $0° \leqslant \theta \leqslant 360°$ that satisfy:

a $\sin \theta = \sin 47°$ **b** $\sin \theta = -\sin 47°$

Answers

Start by sketching the sine curve for
$0° \leqslant \theta \leqslant 360°$

Label 47° and draw a vertical line to the curve.

Draw a horizontal line through the value $\sin 47°$.

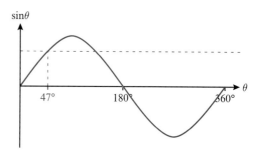

a All other places where this horizontal line meets
the curve have the same sine value.

By the symmetry of the graph:
$\sin 47° = \sin(180° - 47°) = \sin 133°$

So, $\theta = 133°$

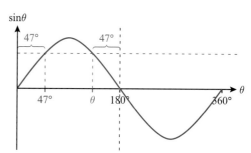

b Draw a horizontal line at $-\sin 47°$.

Use the symmetry of the graph to work out
the places where this line meets the curve.

$\theta_1 = 180° + 47° = 227°$

$\theta_2 = 360° - 47° = 313°$

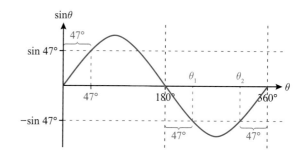

Exercise 15.7

1 Write down another angle between 0° and 360° that has the same sine value as:

    a $\sin 10°$ **b** $\sin 25°$ **c** $\sin 42°$ **d** $\sin 107°$

2 Write down another angle between 0° and 360° that has the same cosine value as:

    a $\cos 10°$ **b** $\cos 25°$ **c** $\cos 42°$ **d** $\cos 107°$

3 Write down another angle between 0° and 360° that has the same tangent value as:

    a $\tan 10°$ **b** $\tan 25°$ **c** $\tan 42°$ **d** $\tan 107°$

4 Find all possible values of θ for $0° \leqslant \theta \leqslant 360°$ that satisfy each equation.

    a $\sin 15° = -\sin \theta$ **b** $\sin 167° = -\sin \theta$

    c $\cos 38° = -\cos \theta$ **d** $\cos 150° = -\cos \theta$

TIP

The symmetry of the
sine curve shows:

$\sin \theta = -\sin(180° + \theta)$

$\sin \theta = -\sin(360° - \theta)$

Similarly, for the
cosine curve:

$\cos \theta = -\cos(180° - \theta)$

$\cos \theta = -\cos(180° + \theta)$

Solving trigonometric equations with a graphic display calculator

You have already been solving trigonometric equations earlier in this chapter.

Every time you found an angle in a triangle using a trigonometric ratio, you solved an equation.

For example, to solve find the angle x in this triangle,

you write the equation $\sin x = \dfrac{4}{5}$ or $\sin x = 0.8$.

To solve this equation you enter $\sin^{-1} 0.8$ into your calculator and get the answer $53.1°$.

However, $53.1°$ is not the only solution to the equation $\sin x = 0.8$.
There are many solutions.

You will be able to see why this is the case if you think about the graph of $y = \sin x$.

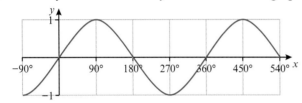

The graph is periodic (it repeats itself) so there are an infinite number points on the curve when $\sin x = 0.8$.

You do not need to find all these values, but you do need to be able to find all the solutions to trigonometric equations for $0° \leqslant x \leqslant 360°$.

WORKED EXAMPLE 12

Solve $6 - 5\sin x = 2$ for $0° \leqslant x \leqslant 360°$.

Answer

Either draw the graph of each side of the equation:

$y = 6 - 5\sin x$ and $y = 2$ and then find the points of intersection.

Or, start by rearranging the equation to the form $\sin x = \dots$.

$6 - 5\sin x = 2 \ \Rightarrow \ 5\sin x = 4$

$\qquad\qquad\ \Rightarrow \ \sin x = \dfrac{4}{5} = 0.8$

Then draw the graphs of $y = \sin x$ and $y = 0.8$ and find the points of intersection.

Next, solve the equation using your graphic display calculator, by following these steps:

1 Select **Graph** from the main menu. The Graph function is highlighted in the following image.

CONTINUED

The following screen opens.

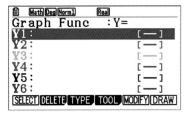

2   Now enter the functions from both sides of the equation using the keypad.

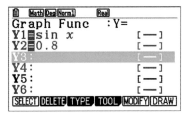

3   Press **F6** to select the **DRAW** option. This draws the graphs of the functions.

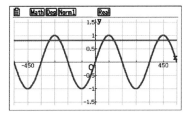

4   Then press **F3** and then **F2** to set the scales and range of the axes.

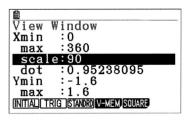

5   Press **EXE** to return to the graph.

6   Press **F5** twice to select the intersection points. You can use the toggle button to move between them.

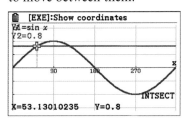   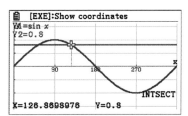

You can solve **any** trigonometric equation in this way, by drawing the graph of each side of the equation on your graphic display calculator and finding the *x*-coordinate of the points of intersection.

TIP

If your graph doesn't look like the one above, then setting these will often solve the problem.

Exercise 15.8

Solve the following equations for $0° \leq x \leq 360°$ and check your answers using your graphic display calculator. Give non-exact answers correct to three significant figures.

1 $3\cos(x) = 2$ **2** $2\tan(x) = -1$

3 $4\sin(x) + 3 = 2$ **4** $1 + 5\sin(x) = 4$

5 $6 - 4\tan(x) = 2$ **6** $5 = 2 + 3\sin(x)$

7 $4 - 2\cos(x) = 3$ **8** $10\cos(x) + 8 = 2$

9 $11 - 4\tan(x) = 8$ **10** $6 + 5\sin(x) = 3.5$

11 $\sin(x) = \dfrac{\sqrt{3}}{2}$ **12** $\cos(x) = \dfrac{\sqrt{3}}{2}$

13 $\tan(x) = \dfrac{1}{\sqrt{3}}$ **14** $\cos(x) = \dfrac{1}{\sqrt{2}}$

Exact trigonometric values

Sometimes you may have to solve trigonometric equations without using a calculator. In order to do this you will need to know the sine, cosine and tangent values of some angles.

By considering the graphs of the trigonometric functions, you should be able to remember the values in this table.

Angle (x)	0°	30°	45°	60°	90°
$\sin x$	0	$\dfrac{1}{2}$	$\dfrac{1}{\sqrt{2}} = \dfrac{\sqrt{2}}{2}$	$\dfrac{\sqrt{3}}{2}$	1
$\cos x$	1	$\dfrac{\sqrt{3}}{2}$	$\dfrac{1}{\sqrt{2}} = \dfrac{\sqrt{2}}{2}$	$\dfrac{1}{2}$	1
$\tan x$	0	$\dfrac{1}{\sqrt{3}} = \dfrac{\sqrt{3}}{3}$	1	$\sqrt{3}$	—

> **TIP**
>
> You must know these trigonometric values rather than 'try to remember'. It is a requirement to know the exact values of sin, cos: 0, 30, 45, 60 and 90 and tan: 0, 30, 45 and 60.

You also need to know the trigonometric ratios for angles of 30°, 45° and 60°. You can find these values using two special triangles.

INVESTIGATION 1

You can find the values for 45° from a right-angled isosceles triangle with two side lengths of 1 unit.

1   Use Pythagoras' theorem to write down the *exact* length of the hypotenuse as a square root.

2   Use the definitions of the trigonometric ratios to write down values for:

    a $\sin 45°$ **b** $\cos 45°$ **c** $\tan 45°$

You can find the values for 30° and 60° from an equilateral triangle with side length 2 units.

3   Draw the equilateral triangle and mark a line of symmetry on your diagram.

4   Label the sizes of the three angles in one of the two triangles formed.

5   Find the **exact** lengths of the sides of this triangle. (You will need to use Pythagoras' theorem.)

6   Use the definitions in the right-angled triangle to write down values for:

    a $\sin 30°$ **b** $\cos 30°$ **c** $\tan 30°$

    d $\sin 60°$ **e** $\cos 60°$ **f** $\tan 60°$

You should have found the values given in the table.

Test yourself or a partner to see how many you can recall.

WORKED EXAMPLE 13

The diagram shows a right-angled triangle.

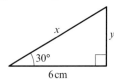

Find the exact:

a   perimeter

b   area.

CONTINUED

Answers

a $\cos 30° = \dfrac{6}{x}$

$\dfrac{\sqrt{3}}{2} = \dfrac{6}{x}$

$x = \dfrac{2 \times 6}{\sqrt{3}} = \dfrac{12}{\sqrt{3}}$

$\quad = \dfrac{12\sqrt{3}}{\sqrt{3} \times \sqrt{3}} = \dfrac{12\sqrt{3}}{3} = 4\sqrt{3}$

$\tan 30° = \dfrac{y}{6}$

$\dfrac{1}{\sqrt{3}} = \dfrac{y}{6}$

$y = \dfrac{6}{\sqrt{3}} = \dfrac{6\sqrt{3}}{3} = 2\sqrt{3}$

Perimeter $= 6 + 4\sqrt{3} + 2\sqrt{3} = 6 + 6\sqrt{3}$ cm

Use the cosine ratio to calculate x.

$\cos 30° = \dfrac{\sqrt{3}}{2}$

Multiply top and bottom by $\sqrt{3}$ to rationalise the denominator.

Use the tangent ratio to calculate y.

$\tan 30° = \dfrac{1}{\sqrt{3}}$

b Area $= \dfrac{1}{2} \times$ base $\times$ height

$\quad = \dfrac{1}{2} \times 6 \times 2\sqrt{3} = 6\sqrt{3}$ cm²

WORKED EXAMPLE 14

Acute angle θ has a sine value of $\dfrac{1}{2}$.

Write down the value of:

a $\quad \theta$ **b** $\quad \cos\theta$ **c** $\quad \sin(180° - \theta)$ **d** $\quad \cos(180° - \theta)$

Answers

a $\sin\theta = \dfrac{1}{2}$, so $\theta = 30°$

The exact value of $\sin 30° = \dfrac{1}{2}$.

b $\cos\theta = \cos 30° = \dfrac{\sqrt{3}}{2}$

Use the exact value of $\cos 30°$.

c $\sin(180° - \theta) = \sin\theta = \dfrac{1}{2}$

Use the symmetry of the sine curve.

d $\cos(180° - \theta) = -\cos\theta = -\dfrac{\sqrt{3}}{2}$

Use the symmetry of the cosine curve.

Exercise 15.9

1 Find the exact value of:

     a $\quad \cos 30° \times \sin 30°$

     b $\quad \tan 60° \times \cos 45°$

     c $\quad \sin 60° \times \tan 60°$

2   a   Write down the exact values of:

   i $\tan 30°$ ii $\tan 45°$ iii $\tan 60°$

   b   Calculate the exact values of:

   i $\dfrac{\sin 30°}{\cos 30°}$ ii $\dfrac{\sin 45°}{\cos 45°}$ iii $\dfrac{\sin 60°}{\cos 60°}$

REFLECTION

   c   What do you notice about your answers to parts **a** and **b**?
        Why do you think this is?

---

3   Find the exact value of length x in each triangle.

   a 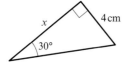   b   c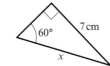

4   Find the values of a and b and the
     area of quadrilateral $PQRS$.

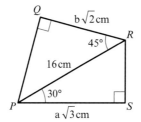

5   Calculate the exact perimeter and area of each shape.

   a 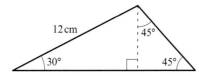   b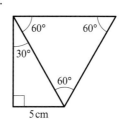

6   θ is an acute angle and $\tan \theta = \sqrt{3}$. Write down the exact value of:

   a $\sin \theta$

   b $\cos \theta$

   c $\tan (\theta + 180°)$

   d $\sin (\theta + 180°)$

   e $\cos (\theta + 180°)$

Solving trigonometric equations without a graphic display calculator

You can use the exact values in the table and the symmetries in the graphs to solve
trigonometric equations for $0° \leqslant x \leqslant 360°$ without using a calculator.

WORKED EXAMPLE 15

Solve $\tan x = \sqrt{3}$ giving all possible solutions for $0° \leqslant x \leqslant 360°$.

Answer

Use what you know about exact trigonometric values to find one value for x.

$\tan 60° = \sqrt{3}$, so $x = 60°$

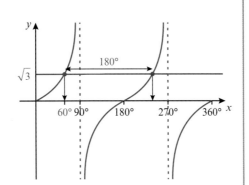

Sketch the graph of $y = \tan x$ and draw the line $y = \sqrt{3}$.

The tangent graph repeats every 180°, so the second value for
$x = 60° + 180° = 240°$

So, the solutions to $\tan x = \sqrt{3}$ for $0° \leqslant x \leqslant 360°$ are $x = 60°$ and $x = 120°$.

TIP

The line $y = \sqrt{3}$ intersects the curve in two places, so there are two solutions in $0° \leqslant x \leqslant 360°$.

TIP

Your drawing does not need to be an accurate graph. A sketch is good enough provided you can see the symmetry.

WORKED EXAMPLE 16

Solve $\sin x = -\dfrac{1}{2}$, giving all possible solutions for $0° \leqslant x \leqslant 360°$.

Answer

Start by sketching the graph of $y = \sin x$ and the line $y = -\dfrac{1}{2}$. The points of intersection are the solutions to $\sin x = -\dfrac{1}{2}$.

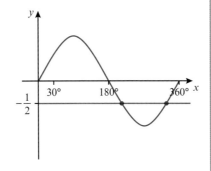

$\sin x = -\dfrac{1}{2}$ is not one of the exact trigonometric values you know, but you do know that $\sin 30° = \dfrac{1}{2}$, so draw the line $y = \dfrac{1}{2}$.

Use the symmetry of the graph to identify that the first point where $\sin x = -\dfrac{1}{2}$ is $180° + 30° = 210°$ and the second point is $360° - 30° = 330°$

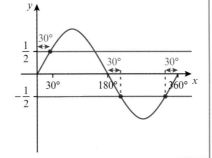

So, the solutions to $\sin x = -\dfrac{1}{2}$ for $0° \leqslant x \leqslant 360°$ are $x = 210°$ and $x = 330°$.

TIP

The line $y = -\dfrac{1}{2}$ meets the curve $y = \sin x$ twice so there are two solutions in the range $0° \leqslant x \leqslant 360°$.

When solving equations, if you cannot use the exact trigonometric values to solve for x, then use your calculator to find one solution and then use the symmetry of the graph to find the other solutions.

Exercise 15.10

1   Angle θ has a value between $0°$ and $360°$. Write down the two possible values of θ when:

a $\sin\theta = \dfrac{1}{\sqrt{2}}$

b $\sin\theta = -\dfrac{1}{\sqrt{2}}$

c $\cos\theta = \dfrac{\sqrt{3}}{2}$

d $\cos\theta = -\dfrac{\sqrt{3}}{2}$

2   Solve these equations for $0° \leqslant x \leqslant 360°$.

a $2\sin(x) + \sqrt{3} = 0$

b $2\cos(x) - 1 = 0$

c $\tan(x) = -\dfrac{1}{\sqrt{3}}$

d $\dfrac{3\tan(x)}{6} - \dfrac{3}{2\sqrt{3}} = 0$

e $2\cos(x) = \sqrt{2}$

f $\sqrt{2}\cos(x) + 1 = 0$

> **TIP**
>
> Rearrange the equation to:
> $\sin\theta =$
> $\cos\theta =$
> or $\tan\theta =$

15.6 Area of a triangle

You already know how to find the area of a triangle using the formula:

$\text{Area} = \dfrac{1}{2} \times \text{base} \times \text{perpendicular height}$

In Investigation 2 you will derive another formula for the area of a triangle using trigonometry.

First you will need to know the conventions for labelling the sides and angles of a triangle.

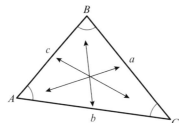

- The vertices of a triangle are labelled with upper case letters, for example A, B and C.

- The angles are labelled with the same letters as the vertices.

- The sides are labelled with lower case letters, for example a, b and c.
  Each side is labelled with the same letter as the **opposite** angle.

INVESTIGATION 2

Finding the area of a triangle

Part 1

a   Calculate the areas of these three triangles. Note that **none** of the triangles is right-angled.

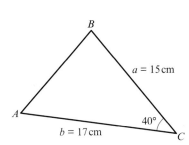 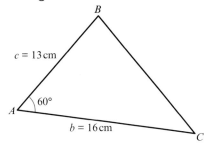 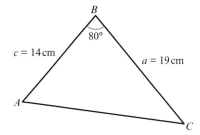

In each of these examples, you first had to split the triangle into two right-angled triangles and then use your knowledge of trigonometry.

In all three cases you will have used the same trigonometric ratio in finding the height of the triangle. Which ratio was it?

Part 2

b   Derive a formula for the area of triangle ABC. Think about the method and the trigonometric ratio you used in the **Part 1**, but this time you must work algebraically.

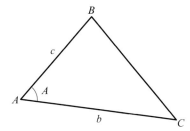

Your formula will include the angle A and sides b and c.

c   Repeat the process with these two triangles, using the two given sides and the given angle.

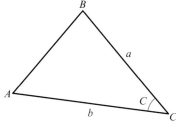 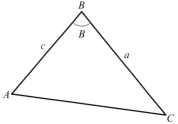

In Part 2 of the investigation you should have discovered that in each case you can find the area using the lengths of two sides and the angle **between** these two sides.

Area of triangle $= \frac{1}{2}ab\sin C = \frac{1}{2}bc\sin A = \frac{1}{2}ac\sin B$

WORKED EXAMPLE 17

Calculate the area of the triangle.

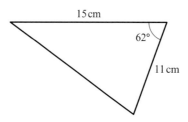

Answer

The angle lies in between the two sides.

Area of triangle = $\frac{1}{2}ab \sin C$

$= \frac{1}{2} \times 15 \times 11 \times \sin 62$

$= 72.8\text{ cm}^2$ (to 3 sf)

TIP

This triangle does not have any labels. If you find it helpful you can label the angles and sides on a copy of the diagram.

Calculating the angle given the area

If you know the area of a triangle and two side lengths, you can work backwards to find the size of the angle between the sides.

WORKED EXAMPLE 18

Triangle ABC has area 20 cm^2.
The length of AB is 6 cm and the length of BC is 7 cm.
Calculate the size of angle B.

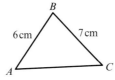

Answer

Area $= \frac{1}{2}ac \sin B$ — Use the formula for the area of a triangle.

$20 = \frac{1}{2} \times 7 \times 6 \times \sin B$ — Substitute: area $= 20\text{ cm}^2$, $a = 7\text{ cm}$ and $c = 6\text{ cm}$.

$20 = 21 \sin B$

$\sin B = \dfrac{20}{21}$ — Rearrange the equation.

$B = \sin^{-1}\left(\dfrac{20}{21}\right) = 72.2°$ — Use the inverse function to find angle B.

The angle B found here is an acute angle and this fits with the diagram shown in the question. However, there is another possible triangle with sides 6 cm and 7 cm, and area 20 cm^2.

You know from the symmetry of the sine function that $\sin x = \sin(180° - x)$.

This means that $\sin 72.2° = \sin(180° - 72.2°) = \sin(107.8°)$

So another possible value for angle B is $107.8°$.

Exercise 15.11

1 Calculate the area of each triangle.

a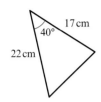

17 cm
40°
22 cm

b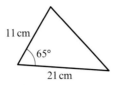

11 cm
65°
21 cm

c

34 cm
45 cm
53°

d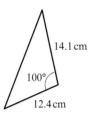

14.1 cm
100°
12.4 cm

e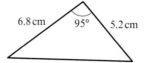

6.8 cm
95°
5.2 cm

f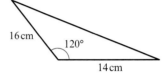

16 cm
120°
14 cm

2 Calculate the angle marked x in each triangle, where $0° \leqslant x \leqslant 90°$.

a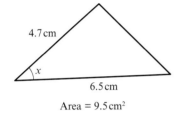

4.7 cm
x
6.5 cm
Area = 9.5 cm²

b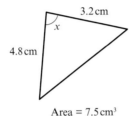

3.2 cm
x
4.8 cm
Area = 7.5 cm³

c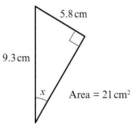

5.8 cm
9.3 cm
x
Area = 21 cm²

3 Calculate two possible values for angle B in each triangle ABC where:

a side AB is 15 cm, side BC is 14 cm and the area of ABC is 70 cm²

b side AB is 12.5 cm, side BC is 10.4 cm and the area of ABC is 56.4 cm².

DISCUSSION 4

If Question **2c** is calculated using Pythagoras' theorem the answer is different than using the sine formula. Why do you think this is?

4 Find the area of each parallelogram.

a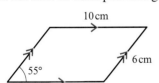

10 cm
6 cm
55°

b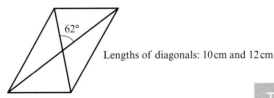

62°
Lengths of diagonals: 10 cm and 12 cm

5 Calculate the area of this regular hexagon.

18 cm

TIP

Start by finding size of the interior angles and then divide the hexagon into six triangles.

15.7 The sine and cosine rules

So far you have used the sine and cosine ratios to find angles and sides in right-angled triangles, but you can also use them in triangles that are not right-angled.
There are two formulas that are often used: the **sine rule** and the **cosine rule**.

The sine rule

In the investigation for deriving the formula for the area of a triangle, you found three different ways to find the area:

Area of triangle $= \frac{1}{2}ab \sin C = \frac{1}{2}bc \sin A = \frac{1}{2}ac \sin B$

You can use this result to derive the sine rule.

$\frac{1}{2}ab \sin C = \frac{1}{2}bc \sin A$ Equate the first two formulas.

$a \sin C = c \sin A$ Simplify by dividing both sides by $\frac{1}{2}b$.

$\frac{a \sin C}{\sin A} = c$ Divide both sides by $\sin A$.

$\frac{a}{\sin A} = \frac{c}{\sin C}$ [1]   Divide both sides by $\sin C$.

$\frac{b}{\sin B} = \frac{a}{\sin A}$ [2]   Repeating this with $\frac{1}{2}bc \sin A = \frac{1}{2}ac \sin B$.

$\frac{a}{\sin A} = \frac{b}{\sin B} = \frac{c}{\sin C}$ Combine [1] and [2] to give the sine rule.

> **TIP**
>
> You can use the sine rule if you need to find:
> - an angle and you know the opposite side and another pair of opposite sides and angles
> - a side and you know the opposite angle and another pair of opposite sides and angles.

WORKED EXAMPLE 19

In triangle ABC, angle $B = 57°$, angle $C = 44°$ and side $AC = 14.2$ cm. Calculate the length of side AB, giving your answer to three significant figures.

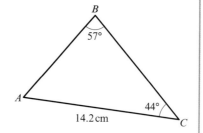

> **TIP**
>
> If it helps, copy the diagram and label the sides with the letters a, b and c.

Answer

Side AC is opposite angle B and side AB is opposite angle C, so you can use the sine rule.

$\frac{b}{\sin B} = \frac{c}{\sin C}$ Choose only the relevant part of the sine rule.

$\frac{14.2}{\sin 57°} = \frac{AB}{\sin 44°}$ Substitute values.

$AB = \frac{14.2 \times \sin 44°}{\sin 57°} = 11.761...$ Rearrange and solve to find AB.

$AB = 11.8$ cm (to 3 sf)

CONTINUED

You can also use the sine rule to calculate angles.

You can turn the formula upside down:

$$\frac{\sin A}{a} = \frac{\sin B}{b} = \frac{\sin C}{c}$$

The symmetry of the sine function means that sometimes there are two possible values for the size of an angle.

WORKED EXAMPLE 20

In triangle ABC, side $AC = 18$ cm, side $BC = 11$ cm and angle $A = 25°$.

a   Calculate the possible sizes of angle B, giving your answers to 1 decimal place.

b   Use these values to find the possible sizes of angle C.

Answers

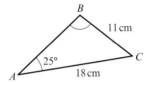

It is always helpful to draw a sketch.

a $$\frac{\sin A}{a} = \frac{\sin B}{b}$$

Use the version of the sine rule with the angles on the top.

$$\frac{\sin 25°}{11} = \frac{\sin B}{18}$$

Substitute values and rearrange.

$$\sin B = \frac{18 \times \sin 25°}{11} = 0.691\,557...$$

$B = \sin^{-1}(0.691\,557...) = 43.753...$

But, $\sin x = \sin(180° - x)$, so

$B = 180 - 43.753... = 136.246...$

So the possible values for B are:

43.8° and 136.2° (to 1 dp)

Use the inverse sine function to find the angle.

Remember to check for a second value using the symmetry of the sine graph.

b $A + B + C = 180°$

If $B = 43.8$ then

$C = 180 - 25 - 43.8 = 111.2°$

If $B = 136.2°$ then

$C = 180 - 25 - 136.2 = 18.8°$

The two possible triangles are:

Use the fact that angles in a triangle sum to 180° to work out the possible sizes of angle C.

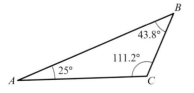

DISCUSSION 5

In triangle ABC, AB = 14.2 cm, BC = 12.7 cm and angle C = 52°.
Why is there only one possible value for angle A in this triangle?

Exercise 15.12

1 Use the sine rule to find the unknown side length or angle in each triangle.

a
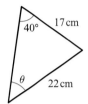

b
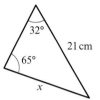

c
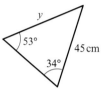

d
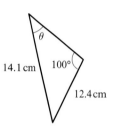

e
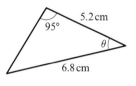

f
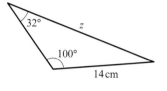

2 Calculate the value of x in each triangle.

a
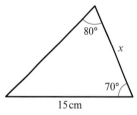

b
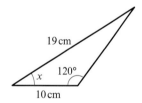

c
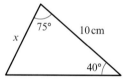

3 Find the possible values for x in each triangle.

a
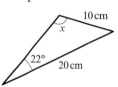

b
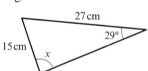

c
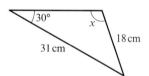

4 Calculate the value of x.

a
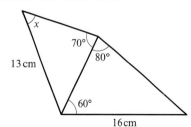

b
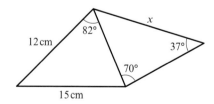

5   A conservationist wanted to measure the width of a straight stretch of river. She stands at point A on one bank and measures the angle to a tree, T, on the opposite bank. She then walks 100 m to point B and again measures the angle to the tree. The diagram shows her results.

Calculate the width of the river.

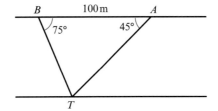

The cosine rule

To be able to use the sine rule you need to know the values for one pair of opposite sides and angles. If you do not know one angle and its opposite side length, you will not be able to use the sine rule.

In these cases you may be able to use the cosine rule instead.

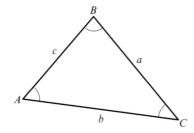

The formula for the cosine rule uses all three sides but just one angle:

$a^2 = b^2 + c^2 - 2bc \cos A$

Notice that the side length on the left-hand side of the formula (a) is opposite the angle used on the right-hand side ($\cos A$).

By rearranging the labels the formula can be written in two other ways:

$b^2 = a^2 + c^2 - 2ac \cos B$
$c^2 = a^2 + b^2 - 2ab \cos C$

This form of the cosine rule is useful if you need to find the length of a side.

If you need to find the size of an angle you can rearrange the formula:

$a^2 = b^2 + c^2 - 2bc \cos A$ Add $2bc \cos A$ to both sides.

$a^2 + 2bc \cos A = b^2 + c^2$ Subtract a^2 from both sides.

$2bc \cos A = b^2 + c^2 - a^2$ Divide both sides by $2bc$.

$\cos A = \dfrac{b^2 + c^2 - a^2}{2bc}$

Similarly, $\cos B = \dfrac{a^2 + c^2 - b^2}{2ac}$ and $\cos C = \dfrac{a^2 + b^2 - c^2}{2ab}$

> **TIP**
>
> You can use the cosine rule if you need to find:
>
> - an angle and you know all three sides
> - a side and you know the opposite angle and both the other two sides.

> **TIP**
>
> Always check whether you can use the sine rule first as it is a simpler formula.

WORKED EXAMPLE 21

In triangle ABC, $BC = 15\,cm$, $AC = 17\,cm$ and angle $C = 54°$.

Calculate the length of AB.
Give your answer to three significant figures.

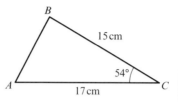

Answer

There is not a known pair of opposite sides and angles, so it is not possible to use the sine rule.

So, use the cosine rule in its form for finding lengths:

$c^2 = a^2 + b^2 - 2ab \cos C$

Substitute values into the formula:

$AB^2 = 15^2 + 17^2 - 2 \times 15 \times 17 \times \cos 54°$

$AB^2 = 214.229\ldots$

$AB = 14.6\,cm$ (to 3 sf)

WORKED EXAMPLE 22

In triangle XYZ, $XY = 13\,cm$, $YZ = 15\,cm$ and $XZ = 17\,cm$.

Calculate the size of angle Y.
Give your answer to 1 decimal place.

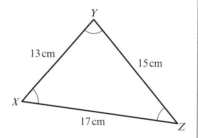

Answer

$\cos A = \dfrac{b^2 + c^2 - a^2}{2bc}$
    Three side lengths are given, so use the cosine rule to find the angle.

$\cos Y = \dfrac{13^2 + 15^2 - 17^2}{2 \times 13 \times 15}$
    Substitute values.

$\quad = 0.269\ldots$

$Y = \cos^{-1} 0.269\ldots$
    Use the inverse cosine function.

$\quad = 74.4°$ (to 1 dp)

> **TIP**
>
> You might find it helpful to redraw the triangle and label the sides and angles using the letters in the formula.

Exercise 15.13

1   Calculate the unknown side length in each triangle.

a
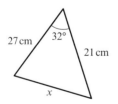

b
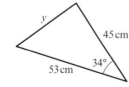

c
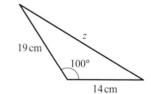

2 Calculate the angle marked θ in each triangle.

a
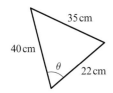

35 cm

40 cm

22 cm

θ

b
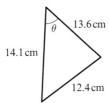

θ

13.6 cm

14.1 cm

12.4 cm

c
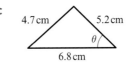

4.7 cm

5.2 cm

θ

6.8 cm

3 In triangle PQR, $PQ = 6$ cm, $QR = 7$ cm and angle $PQR = 55°$. Find PR.

4 In triangle XYZ, $XY = 5$ cm, $YZ = 7$ cm and $XZ = 9$ cm.

Find:

a the size of the largest angle

b the area of the triangle.

5 The hands of a clock are 5 cm and 12 cm in length. Calculate the distance between the tips of the hands at:

a 2 p.m.

b 5 p.m.

Solving problems using the sine and cosine rules

To solve more complex problems you will need to use a combination of the sine and cosine rules along with Pythagoras' theorem and the trigonometric ratios for right-angled triangles.

WORKED EXAMPLE 23

A ship leaves the port (A) and sails 11 km on a bearing 090° to point B.
It then sails 15 km on a bearing of 040° to point C.

a Calculate the distance from point C to the port, giving your answer to three significant figures.

b The ship now returns directly to the port sailing in a straight line from C to A.

Calculate the bearing along which the ship must sail. Give your answer to one decimal place.

Answers

Draw a diagram to show the information in the question.

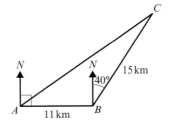

a Use the cosine rule to find distance AC.

Angle $B = 90° + 40° = 130°$

$AC^2 = 11^2 + 15^2 - 2 \times 11 \times 15 \times \cos 130°$

$ = 558.119...$

$AC = 23.624... = 23.6$ km (to 3 sf)

> **TIP**
>
> To avoid rounding errors, use accurate values in your calculations and only round at the end.

CONTINUED

b Use the sine rule to find angle C.

$$\frac{\sin C}{c} = \frac{\sin B}{b}$$

$$\sin C = 11 \times \frac{\sin 130°}{23.624...} = 0.356...$$

$C = \sin^{-1} 0.356... = 20.9°$ (to 1 dp)

The ship must sail on the bearing of A from C.

The bearing is measured from north.

Bearing of A from $C = 180° + 40° + 20.9°$

$= 240.9°$

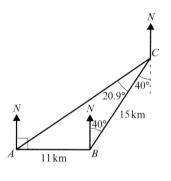

TIP

To calculate the bearing in part **b** you need to use the result that alternate angles are equal.

WORKED EXAMPLE 24

The diagram shows quadrilateral $PQRS$ divided into two triangles.

Calculate:

a the distance PR

b the shortest distance from S to PR

c the area of quadrilateral $PQRS$.

Give your answers to three significant figures.

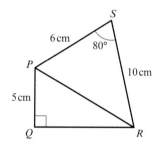

Answers

a $PR^2 = 6^2 + 10^2 - 2 \times 6 \times 10 \times \cos 80°$

$= 115.162...$

$PR = 10.731... = 10.7$ cm (to 3 sf)

Use the cosine rule:

$a^2 = b^2 + c^2 - 2bc \cos A$

b The shortest distance from S to PR is the perpendicular distance, call this d.

Before you can calculate this, you first need to find one of the other angles in triangle PRS.

Use the sine rule to calculate angle PRS.

$$\frac{\sin PRS}{6} = \frac{\sin 80}{10.731...}$$

$$\sin PRS = 6 \times \frac{\sin 80}{10.731...} = 0.550...$$

Angle $PRS = \sin^{-1} 0.550... = 33.41...°$

You can now use the sine ratio to calculate the distance d.

$$\sin 33.41... = \frac{d}{10}$$

$d = 10 \times \sin 33.41... = 5.506... = 5.51$ cm (to 3 sf).

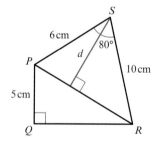

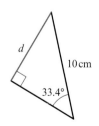

TIP

In part **b** you can calculate either angle PRS or angle RPS before working out distance d.

CONTINUED

c To find the area of *PQRS*, find the area of the two triangles and add them together.

In triangle *PRS* you know two sides and the angle between them, so:

Area of triangle $PRS = \frac{1}{2} \times 6 \times 10 \times \sin 80$

$= 29.54... \text{ cm}^2$

Triangle *RPQ* is right-angled, so use:

Area $= \frac{1}{2} \times$ base $\times$ perpendicular height

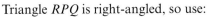

Use Pythagoras' theorem to find the length of the base, *QR*:

$QR^2 + PQ^2 = PR^2$

$QR^2 + 25 = 115.162...$

$QR^2 = 115.162... - 25 = 90.162...$

$QR = 9.459...$

So, area of triangle $RPQ = \frac{1}{2} \times 9.459... \times 5 = 23.73... \text{ cm}^2$

Area of quadrilateral $PQRS = 29.54... + 23.73... = 53.3 \text{ cm}^2$ (to 3 sf).

> **TIP**
>
> There are often several ways to solve problems like this one. Think about what you already know and what you need to find out. It is helpful to draw separate diagrams showing the information you need at each stage.

DISCUSSION 6

Can you think of another way to find the area of triangle *PRS*?

Which method do you think is better? Why?

Exercise 15.14

1 In triangle *PQR*, *PQ* = 6 cm, *QR* = 7 cm and *PR* = 8 cm. Find the size of all three angles in the triangle.

2 *ABCD* is a trapezium. *AB* = 10 cm, *BC* = 16 cm, *AD* = 13 cm and angle *BAD* = 105°.

Calculate:

a the length of *BD*

b the size of angle *DBA*

c the size of angle *DBC*

d the perimeter of the trapezium

e the area of the trapezium.

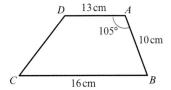

> **TIP**
>
> You will need to use the rules for angles within parallel lines for some parts of this question.

3   A ship leaves a port at *A* and sails due west for 60 km to point *B*. It then sails on a bearing of 240 for 97 km to point *C*.

   a   How far is point *C* from the port?

   b   What is the bearing of the port from point *C*?

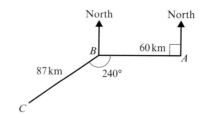

4   A helicopter leaves an airport at point *A* and flies 22 km on a bearing of 042° and then a further 30 km on bearing 090° to reach a helipad at point *H*. On the return journey the helicopter flies directly from *H* to *A*.

   Calculate:

   a   the distance from *H* to *A*

   b   the bearing along which it must fly.

5   The diagram shows the distances between three villages at *A*, *B* and *C*. The bearing of *B* from *A* is 286°. The bearing of *C* from *A* is 213°.

   Calculate:

   a   the distance between *B* and *C*

   b   the bearing of *C* from *B*

   c   the bearing of *B* from *C*.

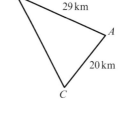

6   The quadrilateral *ABCD* is made up of isosceles triangle *ABD* and right-angled triangle *BCD*.

   a   Calculate angle *BAD*.

   b   Find the shortest distance from *A* to *BD*.

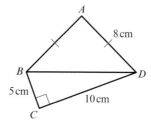

7   Calculate the area of this regular pentagon.

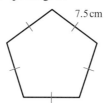

8   The diagram shows quadrilateral *ABCD*.
   Calculate:

   a   obtuse angle *BDC*

   b   the area of *ABCD*.

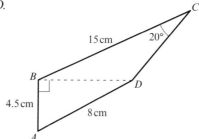

SUMMARY

Are you able to... ?
find the sine, cosine and tangent ratios of angles
calculate side lengths and angles using the sine, cosine and tangent ratios
solve problems in two dimensions using the sine, cosine and tangent ratio and Pythagoras' theorem
calculate angles of elevation and depression
find the shortest distance between a vertex and a side of a triangle
solve problems in three dimensions using the sine, cosine and tangent ratio and Pythagoras' theorem
recognise and sketch graphs of the sine, cosine and tangent functions
use graphs of the sine, cosine and tangent functions to solve trigonometric equations, finding all solutions between 0 and 360 degrees
find or recall the exact values of $\sin x$ and $\cos x$ for $x = 0, 30, 45, 60$ and 90
find or recall the exact values of $\tan x$ for $x = 0, 30, 45$ and 60
use the sine ratio to calculate the area of a triangle
use the sine rule and cosine rule to solve problems in non-right-angled triangles.

Past paper questions

1   A vertical post, 1.75 m tall, stands on horizontal ground.

One day, the post casts a shadow of length 3.28 m.

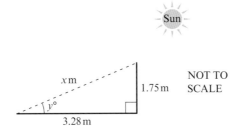

a   Find the value of x.

$x =$ .... [2]

b   Find the value of y, the angle of elevation of the Sun.

$y =$ .... [2]

Cambridge IGCSE International Mathematics 0607 Paper 31 Q11 Jun 2019

2   The diagram shows a rectangular field.

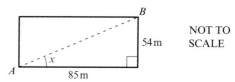

a   Find how much further it is from A to B when walking along two sides of the field rather than straight across the field.

.... m   [4]

b   Use trigonometry to calculate angle x.

$x =$ .... [2]

Cambridge IGCSE International Mathematics 0607 Paper 31 Q12 Jun 2017

3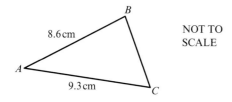

The area of triangle $ABC = 23.5\,\text{cm}^2$.

a   Show that angle $BAC = 36.0°$, correct to 1 decimal place.   [2]

b   Use the cosine rule to find BC.

$BC =$ .... cm   [3]

c   All the angles in triangle ABC are acute.

Use the sine rule to find the largest angle in the triangle ABC.

.... [3]

Cambridge IGCSE International Mathematics 0607 Paper 41 Q11 Nov 2018

> ## Chapter 16
Circle
properties

IN THIS CHAPTER YOU WILL:

- use and interpret the vocabulary of a circle
- use Pythagoras' theorem to calculate the length of a chord in a circle
- use Pythagoras' theorem to find the distance of a chord from the centre of a circle
- recognise that a tangent line is perpendicular to the radius at the point of contact and use this property to solve problems
- identify and use angles in a semicircle
- use the property that tangents from an external point of a circle are equal in length

> solve problems involving angles at the centre and angles at the circumference
> use the property that angles in the same segment are equal
> identify cyclic quadrilaterals and find unknown angles in cyclic quadrilaterals
> identify and use angles in an alternate segment
> use the property that equal chords are equidistant from the centre of a circle
> use the property that the perpendicular bisector of a chord passes through the centre of the circle.

GETTING STARTED

1   Calculate the unknown angle x in each of the following.

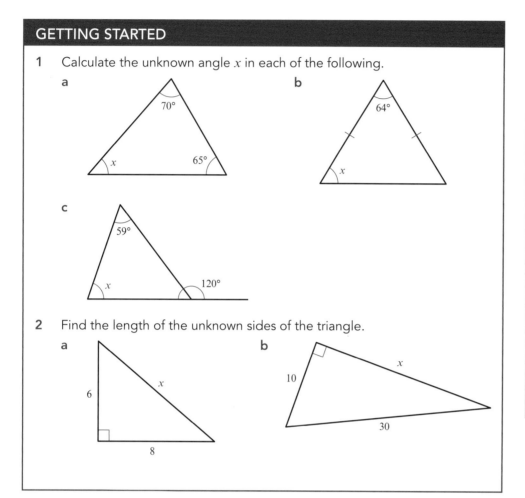

a

70°

x 65°

b

64°

x

c

59°

x 120°

2   Find the length of the unknown sides of the triangle.

a

6

x

8

b

10

x

30

KEY WORDS

arc (major and minor)

centre

chord

circumference

diameter

inscribed

radius (plural radii)

secant

sectors (major and minor)

segments (major and minor)

semicircle

tangent

16.1 Basic definitions

The circle is one of the most common shapes used on road signs, furniture, jewellery and architecture.

MATHEMATICS IN CONTEXT

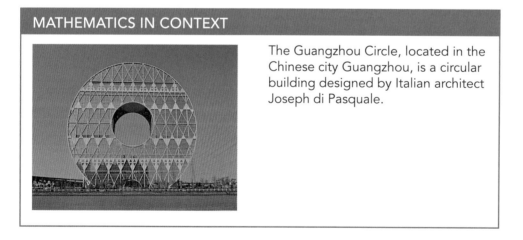

The Guangzhou Circle, located in the Chinese city Guangzhou, is a circular building designed by Italian architect Joseph di Pasquale.

Before studying circle properties, you need to understand the vocabulary of a circle.

1   The outline of a circle is called the **circumference**.

2   The point O is the **centre** of the circle.

3   The length from O to any point on the circumference is the **radius**.

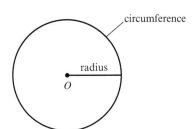

4   A line joining two points on the circumference of a circle is called a **chord**. AB is a chord.

5   The **diameter** passes through the centre of a circle and is the longest chord of the circle.

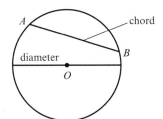

6   The diameter divides the circle into two **semicircles**.

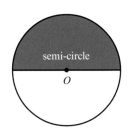

7   A chord divides a circle into **segments**: a **minor segment** and a **major segment**.

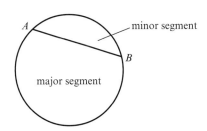

8   A radius of a circle is a straight line from the centre of the circle to its circumference. OA and OB are radii of the circle with centre O. $OAPB$ is a **minor sector** of the circle while $OAQB$ is a **major sector**.

9   A segment of the circumference is an **arc** of the circle. The arc APB is known as the **minor arc** while the arc AQB is the **major arc**.

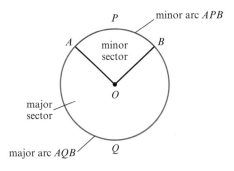

10 A straight line that cuts a circle at two distinct points is called a **secant**. If the straight line touches the circumference of a circle at one point, it is called a **tangent**.

AB is a secant while *CD* is a tangent.

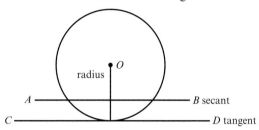

Exercise 16.1

Identify the features of these circles highlighted in red.

a

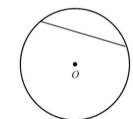

b

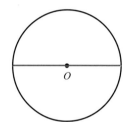

c

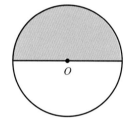

d

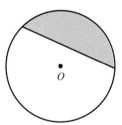

e

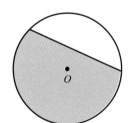

f

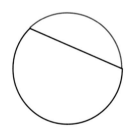

g

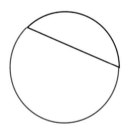

h

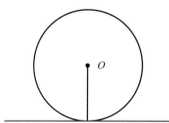

i

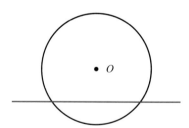

j

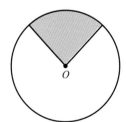

k

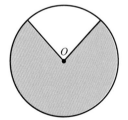

16.2 Length of a chord

A circle is a unique shape. You can draw an infinite number of chords and tangents on the circle. It is worthwhile to investigate the relationship between the radius and a chord in order to calculate the length of a chord or the distance from the centre to the chord.

INVESTIGATION 1

Using GeoGebra – Geometry online to investigate the relationship between the radius and a chord in a circle

Part 1

1   Access the geometry site for GeoGebra.

2   Click on to access the settings menu.

3   Uncheck 'Show Axes' and check 'No Grid' to remove the gridlines.

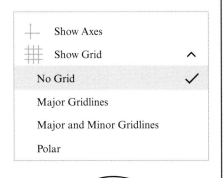

4   Select   to construct a circle as shown (click 'MORE' if you can't find the button).

    Circle with center

    When you select a tab, an instruction will appear to tell you what to do to construct what you want. When you select 'Circle with centre' the programme will automatically generate a point at the centre as well as the circumference as shown.

5   Select   *A* Point   to create another point on the circumference.

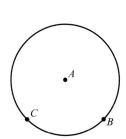

CONTINUED

6 Select [segment icon] to connect points *B* and *C*.
Segment

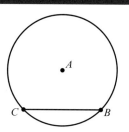

7 Select [midpoint icon] to construct the midpoint of chord *BC*.
Midpoint or Center

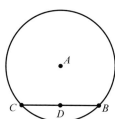

8 Repeat step 6 to connect points *A* (centre of the circle) and *D* (midpoint of *BC*).

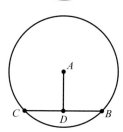

9 Select [angle icon α] to measure angle *ADB*.
Angle

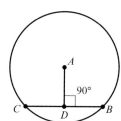

10 Select [move cursor icon] to move point *C* along the circumference.
Move

What did you notice about angle *ADB*?

Part 2

11 Select [circle with center icon] to construct another circle as shown.
Circle with center

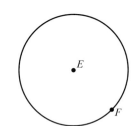

CONTINUED

11 Select [Circle with center] to construct another circle as shown.

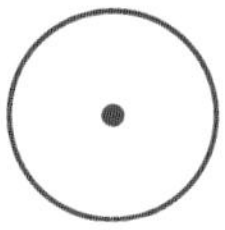

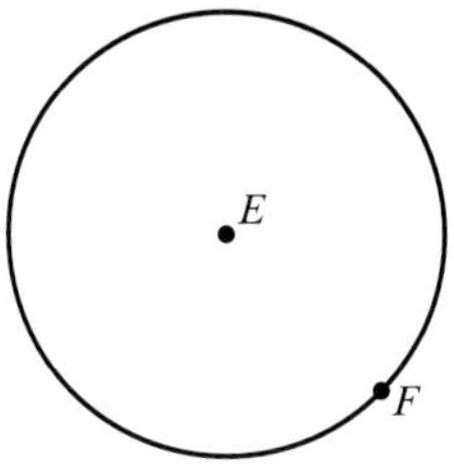

12 Select [Point A] to create another point on the circumference.

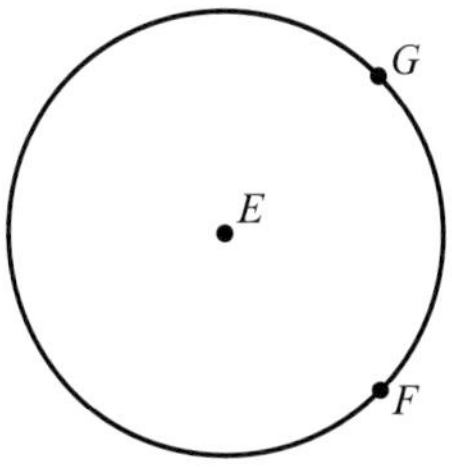

13 Select [Segment] to connect points F and G.

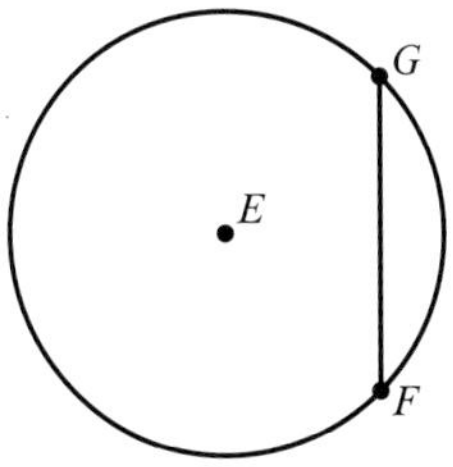

14 Select [Perpendicular Line] to construct a line perpendicular to chord FG that passes through the centre E.

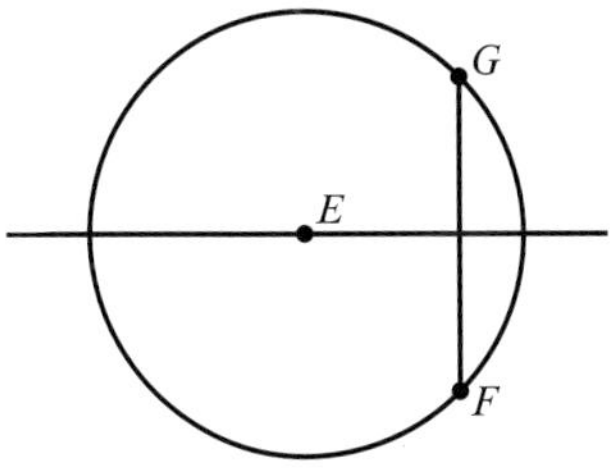

15 Select [Point A] to create a point on the intersection of chord FG and the perpendicular line.

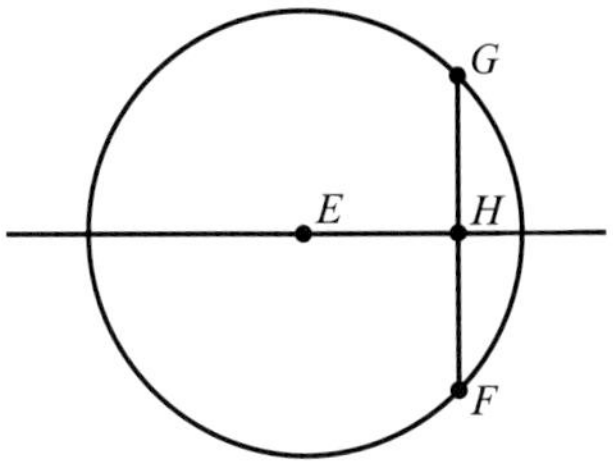

16 Select [cm Distance or Length] to measure the length of GH.

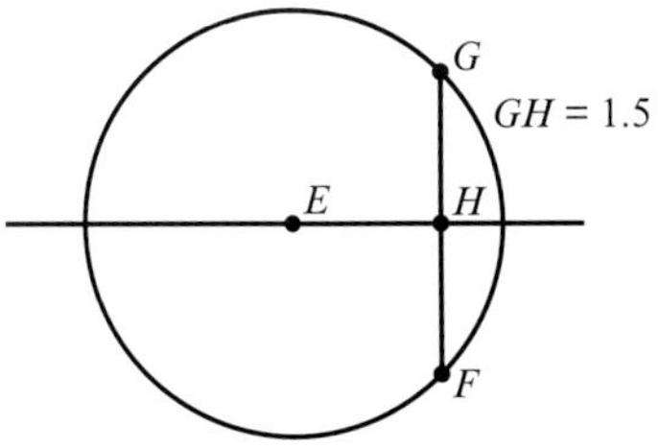

$GH = 1.5$

CONTINUED

17 Repeat step 16 to measure the length of *FH*.
What do you notice?

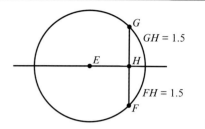

18 Select 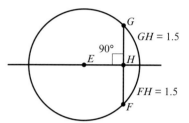 to measure angle *EHG*.

19 Select to move point *G* along the circumference.

What do you notice about the length of *GH* and *FH*?
What do you notice about angle *EHG*?
What conclusions can you make from your investigations?

Observation from Part 1 of Investigation 1:

Property 1

If a radius cuts a chord *AB* at its midpoint, *M*, then angle *OMA* = angle *OMB* = 90°.

You say that *OM* is the perpendicular bisector of the chord *AB*.

Part 2 of Investigation 1 demonstrates that the converse is also true:

If *OM* is perpendicular to *AB*, then *AM* = *MB* and *M* is the midpoint of *AB*.

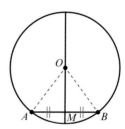

WORKED EXAMPLE 1

a The diagram shows a circle with centre *O* and radius 5 cm. Given that *OM* is perpendicular to *AB* and *OM* = 4 cm, find the length of the chord *AB*.

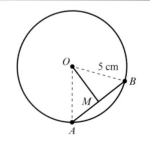

CONTINUED

b   The diagram shows a circle with centre O and radius 8 cm. The chord CD is 10 cm and N is the midpoint of CD. Find the distance ON, from the centre of the circle to the chord.

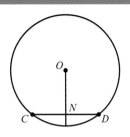

Answers

a   Recognise that triangle OMB is a right-angled triangle.

By Pythagoras' theorem:

$OM^2 + MB^2 = OB^2$

$4^2 + MB^2 = 5^2$

$MB^2 = 5^2 - 4^2$

$MB = \sqrt{25 - 16} = 3$

M is the midpoint of AB, so

$AB = 2 \times 3 = 6$ cm

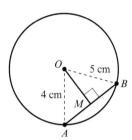

b   From Property 1, ON is perpendicular to CD and cuts CD into two equal halves.

So $CN = ND = 10 \div 2 = 5$ cm

By Pythagoras' theorem:

$ON^2 + ND^2 = OD^2$

$ON^2 + 5^2 = 8^2$

$ON^2 = 8^2 - 5^2$

$ON = \sqrt{64 - 25} = 6.24$ cm (3 sf)

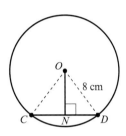

INVESTIGATION 2

Using GeoGebra online to investigate the relationship between the radius and the tangent of a circle at the point of contact

Some problems can involve a circle and a tangent. What is the relationship between the radius and a tangent of a circle?

Go to GeoGebra online. Repeat steps 1 to 3 from Part 1 of Investigation 1.

1   Select to construct a circle as shown (click 'MORE' if you can't find the button).

Circle with center

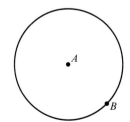

CONTINUED

2   Select 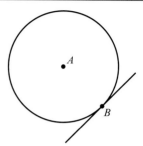 to construct a tangent on the circumference at B.
    Tangents

3   Select to connect points A and B.
    Segment

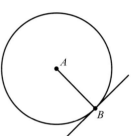

4   Select to measure the angle between the radius and the
    Angle   tangent.

    What is the angle between the radius and the tangent at the
    point of contact?

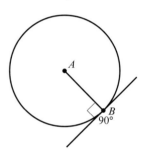

5   Select to move point B along the circumference.
    Move

    What do you notice about the angle between the radius and the
    tangent at the point of contact?

    What conclusion can you make from this investigation?

Observation from Investigation 2:

Property 2

A tangent to a circle is perpendicular to the radius drawn at the point of contact.

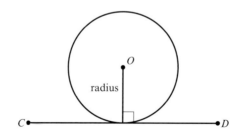

WORKED EXAMPLE 2

AB is a tangent to the circle shown with centre O. Given that $AB = 10$ cm and $OB = 13$ cm, find the radius of the circle.

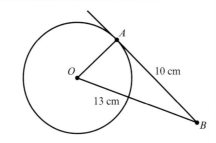

Answer

From Property 2:

OA is perpendicular to AB, OAB is a right-angled triangle, so OA = radius.

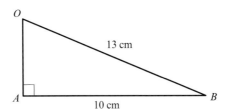

Apply Pythagoras' theorem:

$OA^2 + 10^2 = 13^2$

$OA^2 = 13^2 - 10^2$

$ = 69$

$OA = \sqrt{69}$

$ = 8.31$ (to 3 sf)

DISCUSSION 1

Tangents from an external point

A circle with centre O and two tangents PA and PB is shown.

From Property 2, you know that angle OAP = angle OBP = 90°.

OA and OB are radii of the circle.

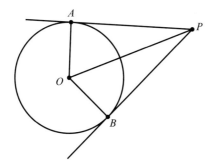

What can you say about the length of AP and BP? Why? Can you prove it?

Observation from Discussion 1:

Property 3

Two external tangents meeting at a point are equal in length, $AP = BP$.

You get two congruent triangles, where triangle $AOP \equiv$ triangle BOP.

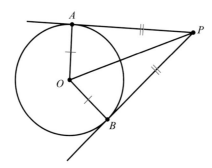

MATHEMATICAL CONNECTIONS

The symbol $\equiv$ represents congruency. You learnt about congruent figures in Chapter 9.

WORKED EXAMPLE 3

The diagram shows a circle with centre O. AT and BT are tangents to the circle at A and B respectively.

a Given that AT is 12 cm and OT is 13 cm:

   i find the radius of the circle

   ii name a triangle congruent to triangle AOT.

b What is the name of the quadrilateral $AOBT$?

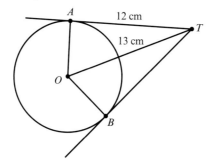

Answers

a **i** Remember that the tangent is perpendicular to the radius at the point of contact.

   By Pythagoras' theorem:

$$OA^2 = 13^2 - 12^2$$
$$OA = \sqrt{169 - 144} = 5 \, \text{cm}$$

   Radius = 5 cm

  ii $OA = OB$ = radius of the circle

   From Property 3, $AT = BT$ and triangle $AOT \equiv$ triangle BOT

b It is a kite.

WORKED EXAMPLE 4

The diagram shows a circle. AB, BC and AC are tangents to the circle at P, Q and R respectively. Given that $AB = 10\,\text{cm}$, $BC = 15\,\text{cm}$ and $AC = 12\,\text{cm}$, find the length of AP.

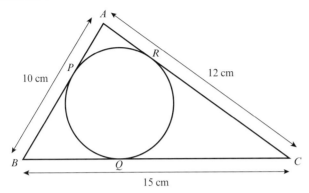

Answer

By Property 3, two external tangents meeting at a point are equal in length so $AP = AR$, $BP = BQ$ and $CQ = CR$.

Let $AP = x\,\text{cm}$, then $AR = AP = x\,\text{cm}$.

$BP = AB - AP$
$\quad = 10 - x$

$BQ = BP = 10 - x$

$CR = AC - AR$
$\quad = 12 - x$

$CQ = CR = 12 - x$

$\qquad BQ + CQ = BC$

$(10 - x) + (12 - x) = 15$

$\qquad\quad 22 - 2x = 15$

$\qquad\qquad\quad 2x = 7$

$\qquad\qquad\quad\ x = 3.5\,\text{cm}$

> **MATHEMATICAL CONNECTIONS**
>
> You learnt to solve linear equations in Chapter 7.

Exercise 16.2

1   The diagrams show a circle with centre O. AB is a chord on the circle and M is the midpoint of AB. Find the length of the chord given the radius of each circle and the length of the perpendicular line OM.

   a   Radius = 5 cm

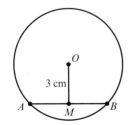

   b   Radius = 13 cm

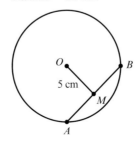

c   Radius = 27 cm

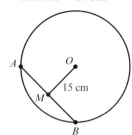

d   Radius = 44 cm

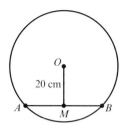

2   The diagrams show a circle with centre O. AB is a chord on the circle and M is the midpoint of AB. Find the distance of the perpendicular line OM given the radius of each circle and the length of the chord.

a   Radius = 7 cm, AB = 8 cm

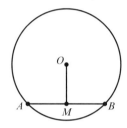

b   Radius = 24 cm, AB = 36 cm

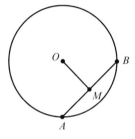

c   Radius = 50 cm, AB = 64 cm

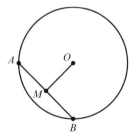

d   Radius = 8 m, AB = 10 m

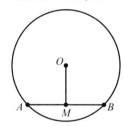

3   In the following diagrams, TA is a tangent to the circle with centre O. OBT is a straight line.

a   Given that AT = 17 cm, OT = 19 cm, find OA.

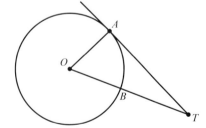

b   Given that OA = 12 cm, OT = 37 cm, find AT.

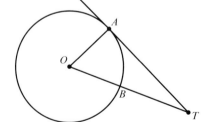

c Given that $OA = 28$ cm, $AT = 45$ cm, find OT.

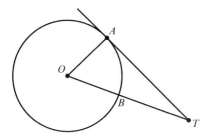

d Given that $OA = 15$ cm, $AT = 25$ cm, find BT.

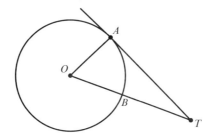

4 The diagram shows a circle of radius 10 cm, with centre O. PQ is parallel to AB. M and N are the midpoints of AB and PQ respectively. Given the length of $PQ = 18$ cm and the length of $AB = 16$ cm, find the length of MN.

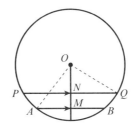

5 The diagram shows a circle with centre O and radius 7 cm. AT and BT are tangents to the circle at A and B respectively. Given that the length of OT is 25 cm, find:

a the length of AT

b the area of $BOAT$.

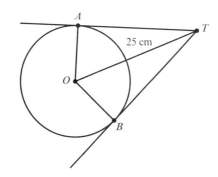

6 The diagram shows a circle with centre O. PQ is parallel to AB. M and N are the midpoints of AB and PQ respectively. The length of $PQ = 20$ cm and the length of $AB = 12$ cm. If the ratio of $ON : OM$ is $3 : 5$, find the length of MN.

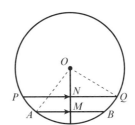

TIP

You will need to form two equations to solve Question **6**.

7 The diagram shows a circle with radius r cm, centre at O. M is the midpoint of chord PQ. $PQ = 6$ cm and $NM = 10$ cm.

a Write down the length of OM in terms of r.

b Hence, find the radius of the circle.

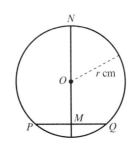

MATHEMATICAL CONNECTIONS

You learnt to solve linear equations in Chapter 7.

8 The diagram shows a circle. *AB*, *BC* and *AC* are tangents to the circle at *P*, *Q* and *R* respectively. Given that *AB* = 16 cm, *BC* = 21 cm and *AC* = 19 cm, find the length of *BP*.

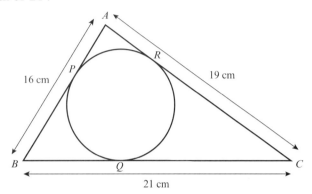

9 In the diagram, *PA* is the tangent to the circle with centre *O*. *OBP* is a straight line. Given *AP* = 22 cm, *BP* = 12 cm, find the radius of the circle.

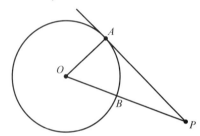

16.3 Angle properties of circles

In Section 16.2, you calculated unknown lengths in a circle. In this section, you will look at angles in a circle.

INVESTIGATION 3

Using GeoGebra – Geometry online to investigate the angle in a semicircle

1 Select ⌒ Semicircle to construct a **semicircle**.

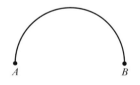

2 Select ⟋ Segment to connect points *A* and *B* and create two segments using *A* and *B* with the circumference. The point *C* will be created automatically when you select *A* and anywhere on the arc *AB*.

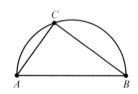

CONTINUED

3 Select 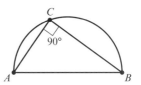 to measure the angle ACB.

Angle ACB is known as the **angle in a semicircle**.

4 Select ⌖ to move point C along the arc AB. What happens to
Move angle ACB?

Try changing the size of the semicircle, then move point C along
the arc AB. What do you notice about the angle ACB?
What conclusion can you make about the angle in a semicircle?

Observation from Investigation 3:

Angle property 1: Right angle in a semicircle

An angle **subtended** by the diameter at the
circumference is always 90°.

**When the lines AC and BC meet at point C to form
an angle ACB, you say that the angle is subtended
by the line AB.**

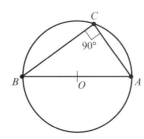

WORKED EXAMPLE 5

The diagram shows a circle with centre O.
Find the unknown angle marked x.

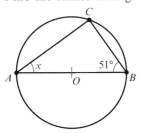

Answer

AB is the diameter of the circle, hence ACB is a semicircle.

By Angle property 1:

Angle $ACB = 90°$ (right angle in a semicircle)

The sum of the angles in a triangle is 180°, hence

$x = 180° - 90° - 51°$

$\quad = 39°$

Exercise 16.3

1   For each circle, find the unknown angle marked x.

a
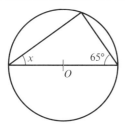

b
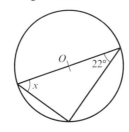

c
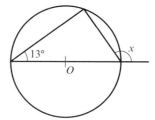

d
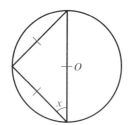

e
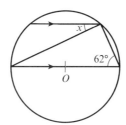

f
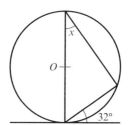

16.4 More angle properties of circles

In the diagram, the minor arc AXB is opposite angles APB and AOB.

You say that angle APB is subtended by the *minor* arc AXB at the circumference while angle AOB is subtended by the *minor* arc AXB at the centre of the circle. Observe that both angles 'face' the *minor* arc AXB.

This diagram shows angle APB subtended by the *major* arc AYB at the circumference while angle AOB is subtended by the *major* arc AYB at the centre of the circle. Observe that both angles 'face' the *major* arc AYB.

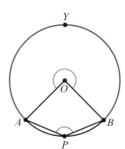

INVESTIGATION 4

Using GeoGebra – Geometry online to investigate the relationship between angles at the centre and angles in the same segment

Create the following figure using appropriate geometry tools:

CONTINUED

A is the centre of the circle. Points B, C and D lie on the circumference.

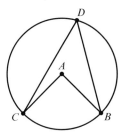

Measure angle CAB and angle CDB and copy and complete:

Angle CAB = _____   Angle CDB = _____

Use the [Move] tool to move point D along the major arc CB on the circumference.

What do you notice about angle CAB and angle CDB?

Try moving point B to vary the size of angle CAB, then move point D along the major arc on the circumference. Then record your angles using a copy of this table:

Position	Size of angle CAB	Size of angle CDB
1		
2		
3		
4		

What do you observe?

Using the fact that angle CAB is the angle at the centre subtended by the minor arc AB while angle CDB is the angle at the circumference subtended by the minor arc AB, write down your conclusion.

Move point D such that it lies on the minor arc AB as shown:

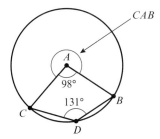

Record the size of angle CDB and the reflex angle CAB. GeoGebra does not show values of reflex angles. You will need to manually calculate the size of reflex angle CAB. Vary the position of point B and repeat your readings for a few positions of point B. Use a copy of this table to help you:

CONTINUED

Position	Size of angle *CDB*	Size of reflex angle *CAB*
1		
2		
3		
4		

What do you observe?

Using the fact that reflex angle *CAB* is the angle at the centre subtended by the major arc *AB* while angle *CDB* is the angle at the circumference subtended by the major arc *AB*, write down your conclusion.

Observation from Investigation 4:

Angle property 2: Angles at the centre

The angle at the centre of a circle is always twice the size of the angle at the circumference subtended by *the same arc*.

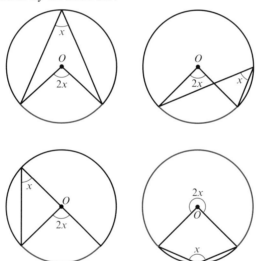

The diagram shows three angles (angle *APB*, angle *AQB* and angle *ARB*) subtended by the minor arc *AXB* at the circumference of the circle. Observe that all three angles lie in the major segment of the circle. You say that these are angles in the same segment.

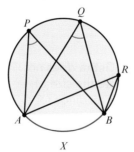

INVESTIGATION 5

Using GeoGebra – Geometry online to investigate the relationship between angles in the same segment

Create three angles in the same segment as shown:

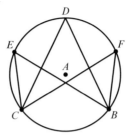

B, C, D, E and F are points on the circumference and point A is the centre of the circle.

Measure the angles CDB, CEB and CFB. Vary the position of point B and take a few readings. Use a copy of this table to help you:

	Angle *CDB*	Angle *CEB*	Angle *CFB*
1			
2			
3			
4			

What do you observe?

Write down your conclusion.

Observation from Investigation 5:

Angle property 3: Angles in the same segment

Angles in the same segment of a circle subtended by the same arc are always equal.

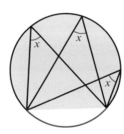

WORKED EXAMPLE 6

For each circle, find the unknown angle marked x.

a

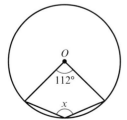

b

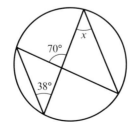

CONTINUED

Answers

a The reflex angle marked y is an angle at the centre subtended by the major arc while the angle x is an angle at the circumference subtended by the same major arc. By Angle property 2, y is twice the size of x.

$y = 360° − 112°$ (angles at a point)

$\quad = 248°$

$x = 248° ÷ 2$

$\quad = 124°$

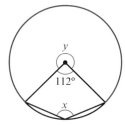

> **MATHEMATICAL CONNECTIONS**
>
> Remember angles at a point from Chapter 4.

b The angle marked y is an angle in the same segment as the angle marked 38°, subtended by the same arc highlighted in red.

To find angle x, look at the triangle in green.

$x + y = 70°$ (the sum of interior angles of a triangle add up to the exterior angle)

$y = 38°$

$x = 70° − 38°$

$\quad = 32°$

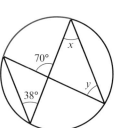

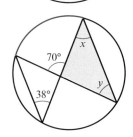

> **MATHEMATICAL CONNECTIONS**
>
> You learnt about the sum of interior angles in a triangle in Chapter 5.

WORKED EXAMPLE 7

In the figure, angle $PQT = 102°$ and angle $QSR = 58°$. Find angle QRT.

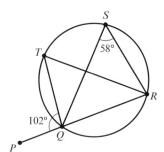

CONTINUED

Answer

Recognise that angle *QTR* and angle *QSR* are subtended by the minor arc *QR*, hence

angle *QTR* = angle *QSR* (angles in the same segment)
        = 58°

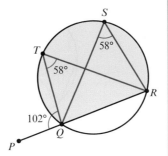

To find angle *QRT*, look at triangle *QRT*.

The sum of angles *QTR* and angle *QRT* adds up to the size of angle *PQT*, hence

angle *QRT* = 102° − 58° (exterior angle of triangle)
        = 44°

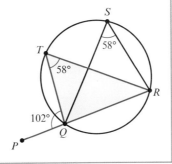

MATHEMATICAL CONNECTIONS

You learnt about the sum of interior angles in a triangle in Chapter 5.

REFLECTION

Draw a mind map to summarise the three length (radius/chord/tangent) properties and three angle properties you have learnt.

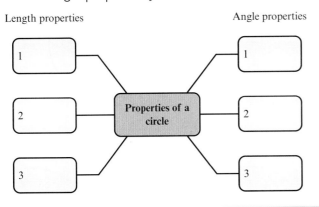

Exercise 16.4

1   For each circle, find the unknown angle marked x.

a

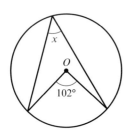

b

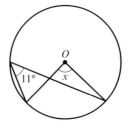

c

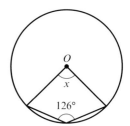

d

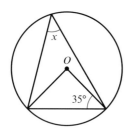

e

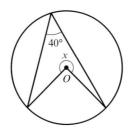

f

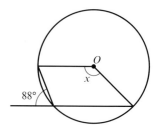

g

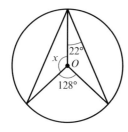

h PT and QT are tangents to
the circle at P and Q.

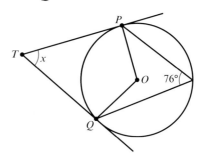

2   Find the values of the unknowns in these diagrams.

a

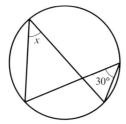

b

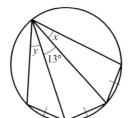

c

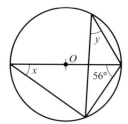

d

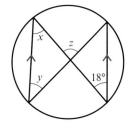

e

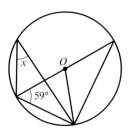

f

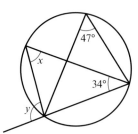

g

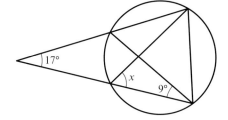

h

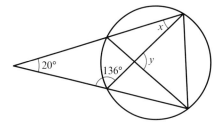

16.5 Cyclic quadrilaterals

A quadrilateral **inscribed** in a circle is known as a
cyclic quadrilateral. In the diagram, *ABCD* is a
cyclic quadrilateral. All four vertices of a cyclic
quadrilateral must lie on the circumference of
the circle.

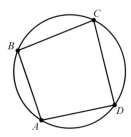

Angle properties of a cyclic quadrilateral

DISCUSSION 2

You have done a series of investigations of circle properties using GeoGebra
in the earlier sections of this chapter. Design your own investigation to find the
relationship between angle *ABC* and angle *ADC*.

Work in groups and write down a plan to investigate these angles.

Record your findings and present to your class what you have found and how
you did it.

PEER ASSESSMENT

Pay attention to your classmates' presentation. Suggest how they could improve
their investigation.

Your investigation should lead you to the following conclusion:

Angle property 4

If *ABCD* is a cyclic quadrilateral, then the opposite angles within the cyclic quadrilateral add up to 180°.

Angle *ABC* + angle *ADC* = 180°

Angle *BAD* + angle *BCD* = 180°

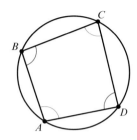

This property is also called angles in opposite segments as the angles are in different segments of the circle.

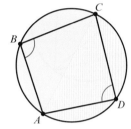
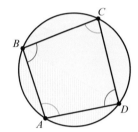

DISCUSSION 3

In the diagram, angle *CDE* is an exterior angle of the cyclic quadrilateral *ABCD*. What is the relation between angle *CDE* and the interior angle *ABC* in the cyclic quadrilateral?

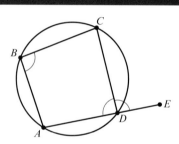

Copy and complete:

Angle *ABC* + angle *ADC* = _____° (reason:_____)

Angle *ADC* + angle *CDE* = _____° (reason:_____)

What can you conclude about angle *ABC* and angle *CDE*?

Angle property 5

The exterior angle *CDE* of a cyclic quadrilateral *ABCD* is equal to the interior opposite angle *ABC*.

Angle *ABC* = angle *CDE*

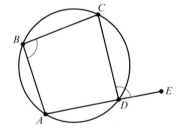

WORKED EXAMPLE 8

In the diagram, *A*, *B*, *C* and *D* are points on a circle with centre *O*. Angle *BAD* = 114° and Angle *COD* = 78°. Find:

a angle *CBD*

b angle *BCD*

c angle *BCO*.

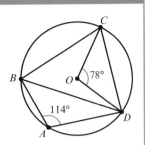

Answers

a Angle *COD* is an angle at the centre subtended by the minor arc *CD* while angle *CBD* is an angle at the circumference subtended by the same minor arc *CD*.

By Angle property 2:

angle $CBD = \dfrac{78°}{2} = 39°$

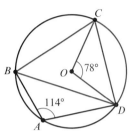

b *ABCD* is a cyclic quadrilateral

By Angle property 4:

angle *BAD* + angle *BCD* = 180°

angle *BCD* = 180° − 114° (angles in opposite segment)

= 66°

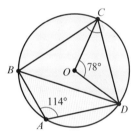

c Triangle *OCD* is an isosceles triangle since *OC* = *OD* = radius, so

angle $OCD = \dfrac{180° - 78°}{2}$ (base angle of isosecles ΔOCD)

= 51°

From part **b**: angle *BCD* = 66°, so

angle *BCO* = 66° − 51° = 15°

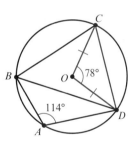

WORKED EXAMPLE 9

In the diagram, *ABC* and *AED* are straight lines. Angle *BED* = 123° and angle *CDE* = 70°. Find:

a angle *BCD*

b angle *BAE*.

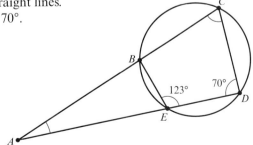

CONTINUED

Answers

a   *BCDE* is a cyclic quadrilateral.
By Angle property 4:
angle *BCD* = 180° − 123°
            = 57°

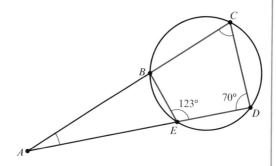

b   Remember that the sum of
angles in a triangle add to 180°.
Using triangle *ACD*:
angle *BAE* = 180° − 57° − 70°
            = 53°

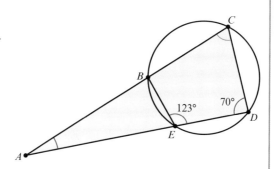

Exercise 16.5

1   For each circle, find the value(s) of the unknown angle(s).

a

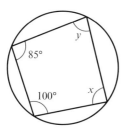

b

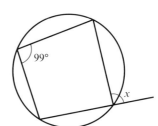

c

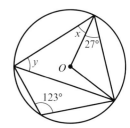

d

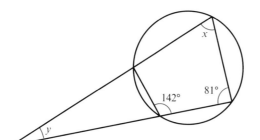

e

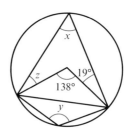

f

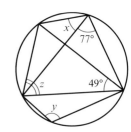

2 The diagram shows two circles with points *A*, *B*, *C*, *D* and *E* on the circumferences. *ABC* and *AED* are straight lines. Given that angle *BAE* = 19° and angle *CBE* = 107°, calculate:

    a angle *EDC*

    b angle *AEB*.

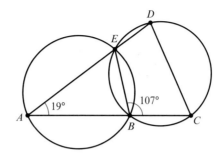

3 In the diagram, *P*, *Q* *R*, *S*, *T* and *U* are points on the circumferences of two circles. *PQR* and *STU* are straight lines. *QT* is a common chord. Given that angle *UPQ* = 91° and angle *TSR* = 80°, calculate:

    a angle *PUT*

    b angle *QRS*.

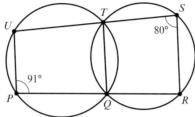

4 The diagram shows points *A*, *B*, *C*, *D* and *E* on the circumference of a circle. Given angle *ABC* = 100° and angle *CAD* = 29°, calculate:

    a angle *DBC*

    b angle *ACD*

    c angle *AED*.

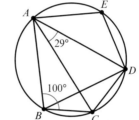

5 In the diagram points *A*, *B*, *C* and *D* lie on the circumference of the circle. *ABP*, *DCP*, *ADQ* and *BCQ* are straight lines. Given angle *ABC* = 99° and angle *APD* = 37°, calculate:

    a angle *ADC*

    b angle *PAD*

    c angle *CQD*.

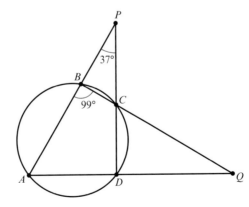

16.6 Alternate segment theorem

DISCUSSION 4

In the figure, O is the centre of the circle. Angle CAQ is between a tangent PQ and a chord AC. Angle ABC is an angle subtended by the same chord AC in a different segment. You say that angle ABC is an angle in the alternate segment. Discuss how the angle between the tangent and the chord relates to the angle subtended by the same chord in the alternate segment.

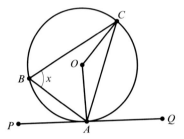

Work in pairs to copy and complete the following statements (give your angles in term of x).

Let angle $ABC = x$,

Angle $AOC = $ _____ reason: _____

Angle $OAC = $ _____ reason: _____

Angle $OAQ = $ _____ reason: _____

Angle $CAQ = $ _____ reason: _____

What can you conclude about angle ABC and angle CAQ?

Observation from Discussion 4:

Angle property 6

If PAQ is a tangent of the circle at A, then the angle between the tangent and the chord AC is equal to the angle subtended by the same chord in the alternate segment.

Angle $ABC = $ angle CAQ

Similarly:

Angle $ACB = $ angle BAP

This is known as the **alternate segment theorem** or the **tangent-chord theorem**.

WORKED EXAMPLE 10

In the figure, *ABC* is an isosceles triangle
with *BC* = *AC*. *PAQ* is a tangent to the circle
at *A*. Given that angle *ABC* = 64°, find:

a   angle *BCA*

b   angle *BAP*.

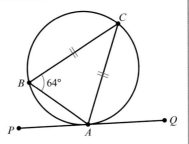

Answers

a   Given *ABC* is an isosceles triangle,

angle *BCA* = 180° − (2 × 64°)

= 52°

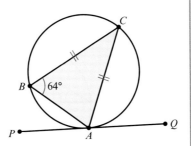

b   Angle *BAP* is between the tangent *PAQ*
and the chord *AB*. Using Angle
property 6, angle *BAP* is equal to the
angle opposite the chord *AB* in the
alternate segment, hence

angle *BAP* = angle *BCA* = 52°

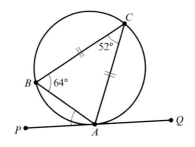

Exercise 16.6

1   In the following diagrams, *PAQ* is the tangent to the circle at *A*.
   Find the value(s) of the unknown angle(s).

a

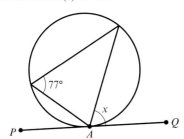

b

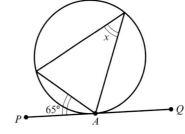

c

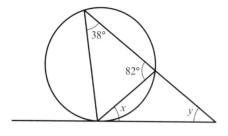

d

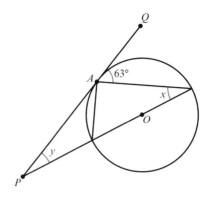

2 In the diagram, QR is the diameter of the circle and PS is the tangent to the circle at P. QRS is a straight line. Given that angle $PQR = 28°$, calculate, showing your working clearly:

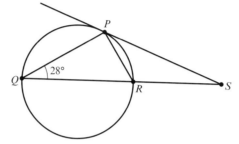

  a angle PRQ

  b angle PSR.

3 The diagram shows two circles meeting at point B. AB is the diameter of the bigger circle while BC is the diameter of the smaller circle. ABC is a straight line. CD is a tangent to the bigger circle at D. Given angle $BAD = 33°$, find:

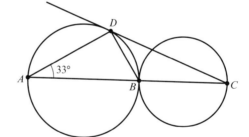

  a angle ABD

  b angle BDC

  c angle BCD.

4 In the diagram points A, B and C lie on the circumference of a circle with centre O. AT is the tangent to the circle at A and CBT is a straight line. Given angle $BAT = 39°$ and angle $BOC = 128°$, calculate:

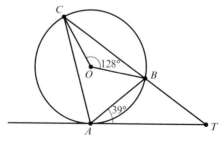

  a angle OCB

  b angle CAB

  c angle ACO

  d angle ATB.

5 In the diagram points A, B, C and D lie on the circumference of the circle with centre O. PAQ is the tangent of the circle at A.

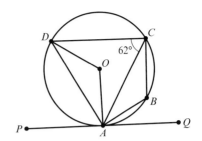

a Write down the angle OAQ.

b Given that angle $ACD = 62°$, calculate:

   i angle AOD ii angle OAC

   iii angle ADC iv angle ABC.

c What type of triangle is triangle ACD?

SUMMARY

Are you able to... ?
use and interpret the vocabulary of a circle
use Pythagoras' theorem to calculate the length of a chord in a circle
use Pythagoras' theorem to find the distance of a chord from the centre of a circle
recognise that a tangent line is perpendicular to the radius at the point of contact and use this property to solve problems
identify and use angles in a semicircle
use the property that tangents from an external point of a circle are equal in length
solve problems involving angles at the centre and angles at the circumference
use the property that angles in the same segment are equal
identify cyclic quadrilaterals and find unknown angles in cyclic quadrilaterals
identify and use angles in an alternate segment
use the property that equal chords are equidistant from the centre of a circle
use the property that the perpendicular bisector of a chord passes through the centre of the circle.

Past paper questions

1

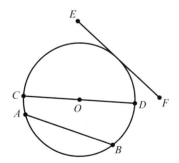

Complete the statement using letters from the diagram.

Line .... is a tangent to the circle, centre O.   [1]

Cambridge IGCSE International Mathematics 0607 Paper 11 Q3 June 2021

2   a   Shade a segment inside this circle. [Using Past Paper Question Resource Sheet]

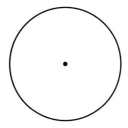

[1]

   b   Draw a radius inside this circle. [Using Past Paper Question Resource Sheet]

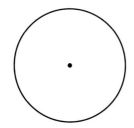

[1]

   c

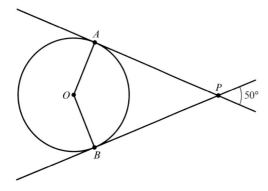

NOT TO SCALE

The diagram shows a circle, centre O.

AP and BP are tangents to the circle at A and B.

Find angle AOB.

Angle AOB = ... [3]

Cambridge IGCSE International Mathematics 0607 Paper 11 Q13 June 2017

3

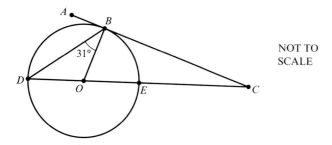

NOT TO SCALE

The diagram shows a circle, centre O.

The straight line ABC touches the circle at B.

$DOEC$ is a straight line, D and E lie on the circumference and angle $OBD = 31°$.

a Using the letters in the diagram, write down
  i   the diameter, [1]
  ii   a radius, [1]
  iii a chord, [1]
  iv the tangent. [1]

b Find
  i   angle *OBC*,

Angle *OBC* = ... [1]

  ii   angle *ABD*,

Angle *ABD* = ... [1]

  iii angle *BOD*,

Angle *BOD* = ... [2]

  iv angle *BCO*.

Angle *BCO* = ... [2]

Cambridge IGCSE International Mathematics 0607 Paper 32 Q5 November 2020

4

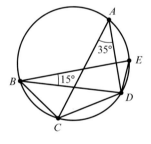

NOT TO SCALE

A, *B*, *C*, *D* and *E* are points on the circle.
Angle *CAD* = 35° and angle *EBD* = 15°.
Find

a angle *CBD*,

Angle *CBD* = ... [1]

b angle *CDE*.

Angle *CDE* = ... [1]

Cambridge IGCSE International Mathematics 0607 Paper 22 Q12 June 2017

5

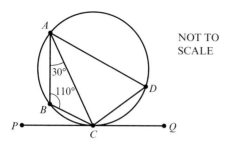

NOT TO SCALE

The points A, B, C and D lie on a circle.
PCQ is a tangent to the circle at C.
Angle $ABC = 110°$ and angle $BAC = 30°$.
Find

a   angle ADC,

Angle $ADC = $ .... [1]

b   angle ACP,

Angle $ACP = $ .... [1]

c   angle PCB.

Angle $PCB = $ .... [1]

Cambridge IGCSE International Mathematics 0607 Paper 22 Q12 November 2020

6   a

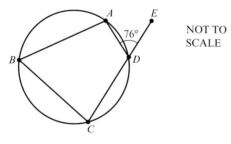

NOT TO SCALE

A, B, C, and D are points on a circle.
CDE is a straight line.
Find angle ABC.

Angle $ABC = $ .... [1]

b

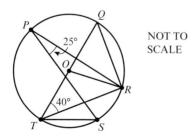

NOT TO SCALE

P, Q, R, S and T are points on the circle centre O.
TOQ is a straight line.

i   Find angle STR.

Angle STR = ... [1]

ii   Find angle QOR.

Angle QOR = ... [1]

Cambridge IGCSE International Mathematics 0607 Paper 22 Q9 March 2021

7
NOT TO SCALE

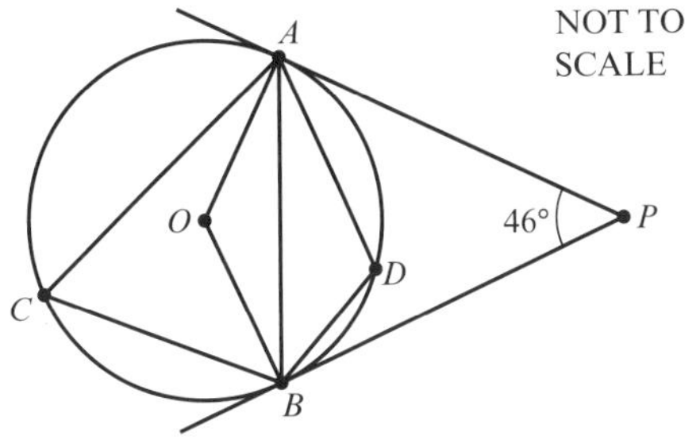

A, B, C and D lie on a circle, centre O.
AP and BP are tangents to the circle.
Angle $APB = 46°$.

a   Complete the statement.

Angle $OAP = 90°$ because .... [1]

b   Find the value of
     i   angle AOB,

Angle AOB = ... [2]

     ii   angle OAB,

Angle OAB = ... [2]

     iii angle ACB,

Angle ACB = ... [2]

     iv   angle ADB.

Angle ADB = ... [2]

c OB bisects angle ABC.
     Find angle OAC.

Angle OAC = ... [3]

Cambridge IGCSE International Mathematics 0607 Paper 41 Q5 June 2017

8

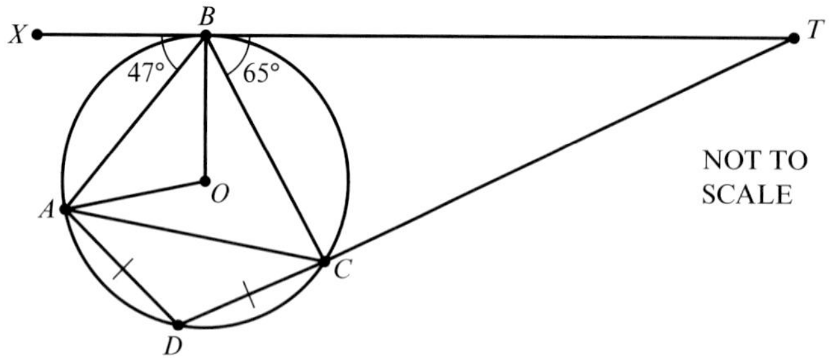

NOT TO SCALE

A, *B*, *C* and *D* lie on a circle, centre *O*.

AD = *CD* and *XBT* is a tangent to the circle at *B*.

TCD is a straight line.

Angle *XBA* = 47° and angle *TBC* = 65°.

Find the value of

a   angle *OBX*,

Angle *OBX* = ... [1]

b   angle *AOB*,

Angle *AOB* = ... [2]

c   angle *CAO*,

Angle *CAO* = ... [2]

d   angle *CDA*,

Angle *CDA* = ... [2]

e   angle *DAC*,

Angle *DAC* = ... [2]

f   angle *CTB*.

Angle *CTB* = ... [2]

Cambridge IGCSE International Mathematics 0607 Paper 41 Q5 November 2020

9

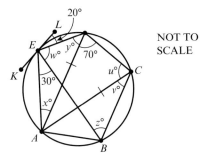

NOT TO
SCALE

A, *B*, *C*, *D* and *E* are points on the circle.

KL is a tangent to the circle at *E*.

AC = AD.

Find the values of *u*, *v*, *w*, *x*, *y* and *z*.

u = ...   x = ...

v = ...   y = ...

w = ...   z = ... [6]

Cambridge IGCSE International Mathematics 0607 Paper 42 Q4b March 2022

> Chapter 17

Vectors and transformations

IN THIS CHAPTER YOU WILL:

- recognise, describe and draw a reflection of a shape in a vertical or horizontal line

- recognise, describe and draw a rotation of a shape about the origin, vertices or midpoints of edges of the shape, through multiples of 90°

- recognise, describe and draw an enlargement of a shape from a centre by a scale factor

- recognise, describe and draw a translation of a shape by a vector $\begin{pmatrix} x \\ y \end{pmatrix}$

> describe a translation using a vector represented by $\begin{pmatrix} x \\ y \end{pmatrix}$, $\overrightarrow{AB}$ or **a**

> add and subtract vectors

> multiply a vector by a scalar

> calculate the magnitude of a vector $\begin{pmatrix} x \\ y \end{pmatrix}$ as $\sqrt{x^2 + y^2}$.

GETTING STARTED

1 Write down the equation of each of the lines shown in the diagram.

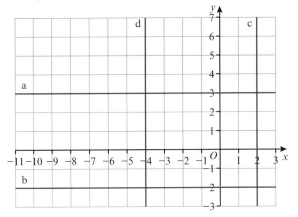

2 What is the equation of the y-axis?

3 The triangle ABC shown below has the dimensions $AB = 6$, $BC = 5$ and $CA = 7$.

The triangle DEF is similar to ABC, but bigger by a scale factor of 2.5.

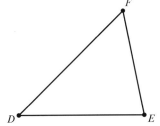

What are the lengths of the sides DE, EF and FD?

4 The triangle MNO is a right-angled triangle.

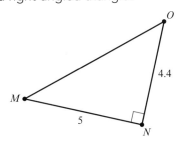

Calculate the length of the side OM to two decimal places.

KEY WORDS

centre of enlargement

centre of rotation

congruent

enlargement

magnitude

orientation

perpendicular

perpendicular bisector

reflection

rotation

scalar

scale factor

translation

vector

17.1 Transformations

A mathematical transformation is simply a movement, or mapping, of a shape from one place on a coordinate grid to another.

The four transformations that you will learn about in this chapter are:

- **translation** – where an object slides from one place to another, but stays in the same orientation
- **reflection** – where an object is flipped over a mirror line
- **rotation** – where an object turns about a point
- **enlargement** – where an object is made larger or smaller.

Translations

Translation maps an object to its image by sliding. Every point on the object moves exactly the same distance and direction.

The object and the image after a translation are exactly the same shape and size and are in the same **orientation**. The object and image are **congruent**.

You can describe a translation using a **vector**, $\begin{pmatrix} x \\ y \end{pmatrix}$, to show the distance moved parallel to the x-axis and the distance moved parallel to the y-axis.

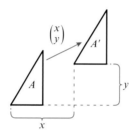

When x is positive it is a movement to the right, and a movement to the left when it is negative.

When y is positive it is a movement up, when it is negative it is a movement down.

In the graph object B is translated to image B' by the vector $\begin{pmatrix} 3 \\ -1 \end{pmatrix}$.

This means the object moves 3 units in the **positive** x-direction (to the right) and 1 unit in the **negative** y-direction (down).

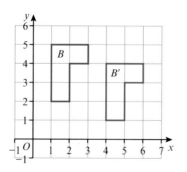

> **MATHEMATICAL CONNECTIONS**
>
> Programmers use transformations to control movements of objects and images around a computer screen when designing games and other software.

> **MATHEMATICAL CONNECTIONS**
>
> You have used the word **congruent** before in Chapter 9 to mean a shape that is exactly the same shape and size.

> **TIP**
>
> The prime notation is often used in transformations. For example, object A can be mapped to image A' or point A can be mapped to point A'.

WORKED EXAMPLE 1

a   Translate triangle A by the vector $\begin{pmatrix} -2 \\ 5 \end{pmatrix}$ and label the image B.

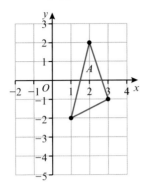

b   Translate triangle B by the vector $\begin{pmatrix} 6 \\ -7 \end{pmatrix}$ and label the image C.

c   Find the vector that translates triangle A to triangle C.

Answers

a   Translation $\begin{pmatrix} -2 \\ 5 \end{pmatrix}$ means every point in triangle A moves 2 units left and 5 units up.

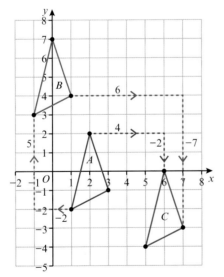

b   Translation $\begin{pmatrix} 6 \\ -7 \end{pmatrix}$ means every point in triangle B moves 6 units right and 7 units down.

c   Choose a vertex of triangle A and find the corresponding vertex on triangle C.

To get from A to C we move 4 units in the positive x-direction (right) and 2 units in the negative y-direction (down).

So the vector that translates triangle A to triangle C is $\begin{pmatrix} 4 \\ -2 \end{pmatrix}$.

Exercise 17.1

1 Identify the image triangle when:

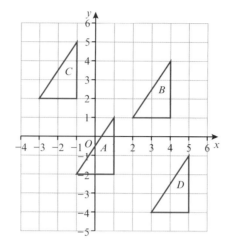

a triangle A is translated by $\begin{pmatrix} 4 \\ -2 \end{pmatrix}$

b triangle B is translated by $\begin{pmatrix} -3 \\ -3 \end{pmatrix}$

c triangle C is translated by $\begin{pmatrix} 5 \\ -1 \end{pmatrix}$

d triangle D is translated by $\begin{pmatrix} -4 \\ 2 \end{pmatrix}$

2 Write down the vectors that describe the following translations.

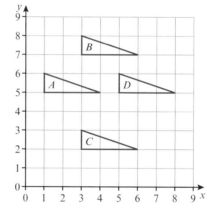

a	A to B	b	A to C
c	A to D	d	B to D
e	D to A	f	D to C
g	B to A	h	C to D

3 Copy the diagram and translate shape P by vector:

a $\begin{pmatrix} 4 \\ -2 \end{pmatrix}$ and label the image Q b $\begin{pmatrix} -1 \\ 4 \end{pmatrix}$ and label the image R

c $\begin{pmatrix} -5 \\ 0 \end{pmatrix}$ and label the image S d $\begin{pmatrix} 3 \\ 2 \end{pmatrix}$ and label the image T.

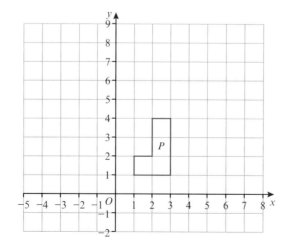

4   Triangle *ABC* has coordinates *A*(−3, 3), *B*(−2, 6) and *C*(1, 4).

The triangle is translated by vector $\begin{pmatrix} 5 \\ -7 \end{pmatrix}$.

Find the coordinates of the image *A′B′C′*.

Reflections

Reflection maps an object to its image by flipping it over a mirror line. The object and the image are congruent and are 'mirror images' of each other.

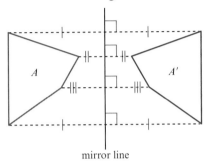

mirror line

Each point on the object is the same distance from the mirror line as the corresponding point of the image.

The distance from a point to a mirror line is always the **perpendicular** distance, so the mirror line is the **perpendicular bisector** of the lines joining corresponding points on the object and the image.

> **TIP**
>
> When you describe a reflection on a coordinate grid you must give the equation of the mirror line.

WORKED EXAMPLE 2

The diagram shows triangle *ABC*.

a   Reflect triangle *ABC* in the *y*-axis and label the image *A′B′C′*.

b   Reflect triangle *ABC* in the line *y* = −1 and label the image *A″B″C″*.

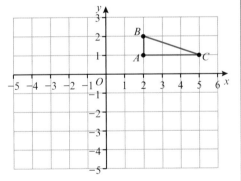

> **TIP**
>
> Remember that another way to describe the *y*-axis is the line *x* = 0.

Answers

a   *A* is 2 units from the *y*-axis, so *A′* will be 2 units from the *y*-axis on the opposite side.

Similarly, *B′* and *C′* will be the same distance on the opposite side of the *y*-axis as *B* and *C*.

Mark the vertices and join them together to show the image *A′B′C′*.

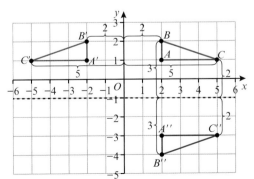

CONTINUED

b   The line $y = -1$ is the horizontal line that crosses the y-axis at -1.

A is 2 units, B is 3 units and C is 2 units from the mirror line $y = -1$.
So A', B' and C' will be 2 units, 3 units and 2 units respectively away from
the mirror line on the opposite side.

WORKED EXAMPLE 3

The diagram shows object
A and images A' and A''.

Find the mirror line that reflects:

a   object A to image A'

b   object A to image A''.

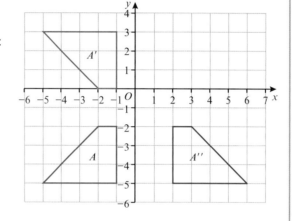

Answers

a   Find the points that are
halfway between
corresponding vertices
on A and A'.

Join these points to give
the mirror line.

The mirror line is
horizontal and intersects
the y-axis at -1, so the
equation of the mirror
line is $y = -1$.

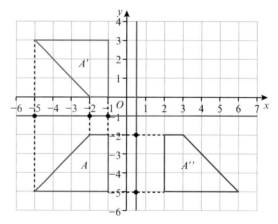

b   The line that is halfway between corresponding vertices on A and A'' is a
vertical line that crosses the x-axis at 0.5.

So, the equation of the mirror line is $x = 0.5$.

DISCUSSION 1

Do the coordinates of all the points on an object always change when it
is reflected?

Explain why or why not.

More reflections

So far you have reflected shapes through vertical or horizontal lines, but you can reflect an object through any line.

WORKED EXAMPLE 4

Reflect triangle ABC in the line $y = x$ and label the image $A'B'C'$.

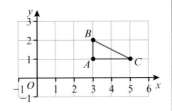

Answer

Draw the mirror line.

Work out the perpendicular distance from each vertex to the mirror line. Drawing them on the diagram can help.

Mark the point of the image the same distance away on the opposite side of the line.

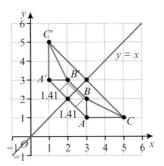

WORKED EXAMPLE 5

Reflect triangle DEF in the line $y = -x$ and label the image $D'E'F'$.

Answer

Draw the mirror line.

Work out the perpendicular distance from each vertex to the mirror line. Drawing them on the diagram can help.

Mark the point of the image the same distance away on the opposite side of the line.

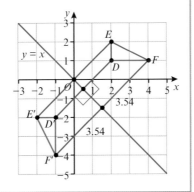

Exercise 17.2

1

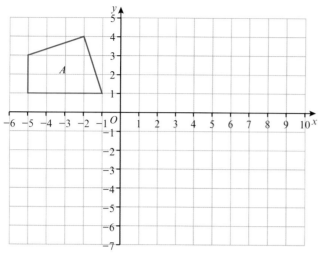

a   Copy the diagram and reflect shape A in the line $x = 2$, label the image A'.

b   Reflect shape A in the line $y = -1$, label the image A''.

2   Describe each reflection by stating the equation of the mirror line.

a

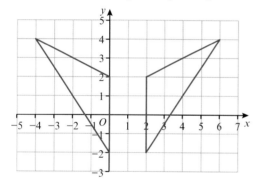

b

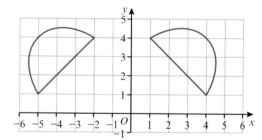

c

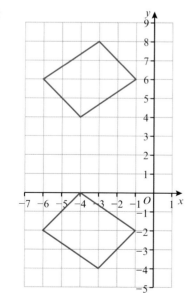

3   **a**   On a set of axes $-6 \leqslant x \leqslant 7$ and $-5 \leqslant y \leqslant 11$, draw the triangle ABC with coordinates $A(-5, -1)$, $B(-1, 1)$, $C(-2, -4)$.

     b   Reflect ABC in the line $x = 0.5$ to give the image $A'B'C'$.

     c   Reflect ABC in the line $y = 3$ to give the image $A''B''C''$.

4   Triangle PQR has coordinates $P(1, 1)$, $Q(2, 4)$, $R(5, 4)$. Answer parts **a** to **c** without drawing a diagram.

     a   Reflect PQR in the x-axis and find the coordinates of image $P'Q'R'$.

     b   Look at the coordinates of PQR and $P'Q'R'$. What do you notice?

     c   Predict the coordinates of the image $P''Q''R''$ when PQR is reflected in the y-axis.

     d   Carry out the reflection of PQR in the y-axis to check your prediction.

5   The diagram shows quadrilateral $WXYZ$.

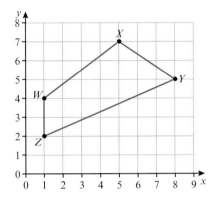

   Copy the diagram and reflect $WXYZ$ in the line $x = 4$. Label the image $W'X'Y'Z'$.

6   The quadrilateral $ABCD$ has the coordinates $A(2, 1)$, $B(6, 1)$, $C(5, 4)$, $D(3, 5)$.

     a   Reflect $ABCD$ in the line $y = x$ and write down the coordinates of the shape $A'B'C'D'$.

     b   Reflect $ABCD$ in the line $y = -x$ and write down the coordinates of the shape $A''B''C''D''$.

     c   Reflect $A'B'C'D'$ in the line $y = -x$ and write down the coordinates of the shape $A'''B'''C'''D'''$.

7   On a set of axes $-6 \leqslant x \leqslant 6$ and $-6 \leqslant y \leqslant 6$, draw the triangle ABC with coordinates $A(-4, 0)$, $B(-1, 1)$, $C(-2, -4)$.

     a   Reflect ABC in the line $y = x + 1$ to create triangle $A'B'C'$ and draw this on your diagram.

     b   Reflect the new triangle $A'B'C'$ in the line $y = -\frac{1}{2}x$ and draw this on your diagram.

8 In each diagram the triangle ABC has been reflected to produce the image $A'B'C'$.
   Write the equation of the mirror line for each reflection.

a

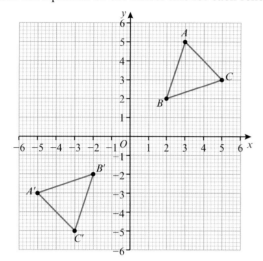

b

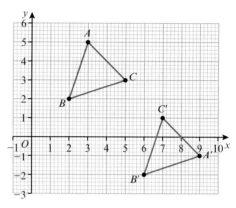

c

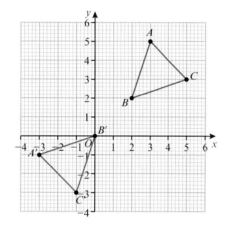

d

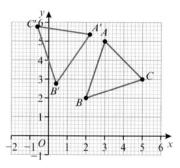

e

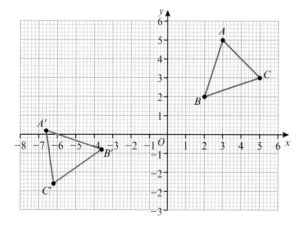

f

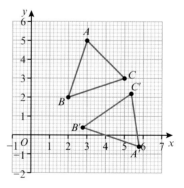

Rotations

Rotation maps an object to its image by turning it about a fixed point.

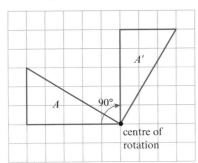

You need to know three things to carry out or describe a rotation:

* the angle of rotation – 90°, 180°, 270° or 360°

* the direction of rotation – clockwise or anticlockwise

* the **centre of rotation** – could be the origin, a vertex or the midpoint of a side, or any other point on a 2D plane.

An object and its image after a rotation are the same distance from the centre of rotation.

They are also the same shape and size, so they are congruent, but their orientations are different.

WORKED EXAMPLE 6

Rotate shape X.

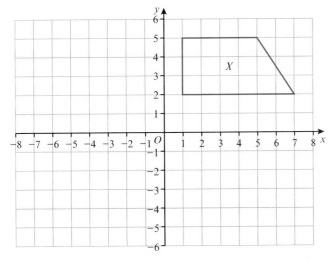

a   90° anticlockwise about centre of rotation (7, 2) and label the image Y.

b   180° about the origin, (0, 0) and label the image Z.

CONTINUED

Answers

Use tracing paper to trace image X.

Put your pencil on the centre of rotation.

Turn the tracing paper through the given rotation to find the position of the image.

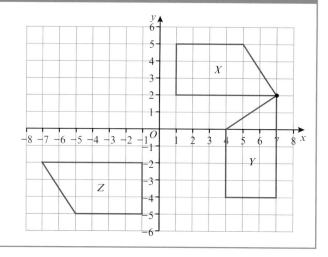

WORKED EXAMPLE 7

Fully describe the rotation from object A to image A'.

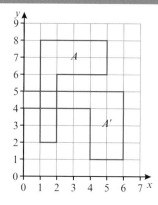

Answer

By looking at the orientation of the object and image, you can see that object A has been rotated 90° clockwise.

Use tracing paper to trace the object and try rotating it around different points until you find the centre of rotation.

Object A has been rotated 90° clockwise about centre of rotation (2, 4).

TIP

Start by trying the origin, the vertices or the midpoints of the sides when looking for the centre of rotation.

INVESTIGATION 1

Take a piece of tracing paper and a grid and make a copy of the triangle in question 1c above.

Mark each of the points with whole number co-ordinates inside the triangle or on the edge of the triangle.

Rotate the triangle 90° clockwise about the vertex B.

Mark each of your points and their image on your grid.

What can you say about each point?

Is there a rule that always seems to be true for rotations?

Hint: draw a line from each point and its image to the centre of rotation.

More rotations

The centre of rotation does not always have to be at the origin or a point on the outside of the object. It can be any point, including a point inside the object.

WORKED EXAMPLE 8

Rotate shape A through 90° clockwise about centre of rotation (−1, 1).

Label the image A'.

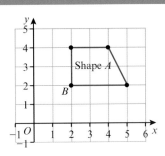

Answer

Choose a vertex of Shape A, for example the point (2, 2) (point B).

Draw a line from B to the centre of rotation.

Draw a line of the same length, rotated 90° in a clockwise direction about the centre of rotation.

This will give the location of point B'. Other vertices can be found in the same way until the shape is complete.

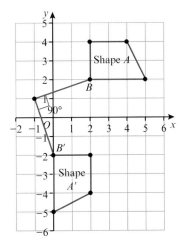

Exercise 17.3

1 Copy the diagram and carry out the rotation described for each part.

You will need to extend the coordinate grids in order to complete the rotations.

a

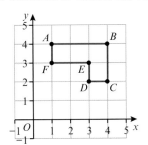

Rotate 180° about centre of rotation (0, 0).

b

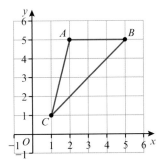

Rotate 90° clockwise about centre of rotation (1, 1).

c

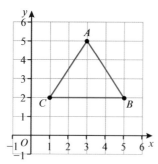

Rotate 90° anticlockwise about centre of rotation (0, 0).

d

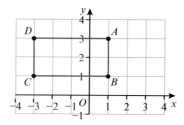

Rotate 90° anticlockwise about centre of rotation (1, 2).

2   Fully describe the rotation that maps each object onto its image.

a

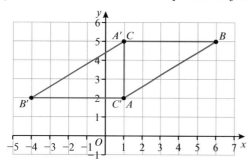

b

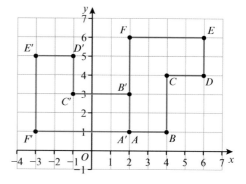

c

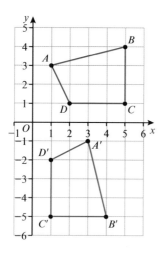

d

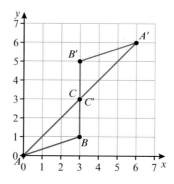

3   Copy the diagram and carry out the rotations described for each part.

You will need to extend the coordinate grids in order to complete the rotations.

a   Rotate 90° anticlockwise about centre of rotation (1,1).

b   Rotate 90° clockwise about centre of rotation (4, 1).

c   Rotate 90° anticlockwise about centre of rotation (6, 3).

d   Rotate 90° clockwise about centre of rotation (4, 4).

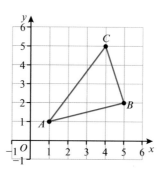

4   In each of the diagrams, describe fully the rotation that has taken place to transform the object to its image.

a
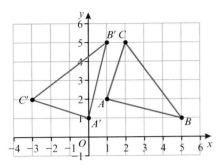

b
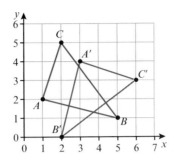

c
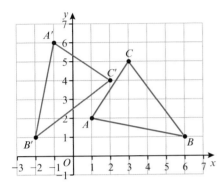

d
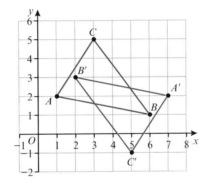

Enlargements

Enlargement changes the size of an object depending on the given **scale factor**. If the scale factor is greater than one the image is larger than the object.

If the scale factor is less than one (but greater than zero) the image is smaller than the object.

After an enlargement, the shape of the image is the same as the object, but the size is different, so the image and object are similar but **not** congruent.

To carry out an enlargement you need to know the scale factor and the **centre of enlargement**.

> **TIP**
>
> Be careful – the word 'enlargement' is used even if the image is smaller than the object.

In the diagram, the object is enlarged by scale factor **2** from centre of enlargement O. This means that:

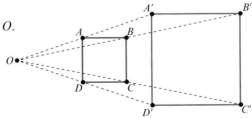

- distance $OA' = \mathbf{2} \times OA$
- distance $OB' = \mathbf{2} \times OB$
- distance $OC' = \mathbf{2} \times OC$
- distance $OD' = \mathbf{2} \times OD$
- side length $A'B' = \mathbf{2} \times AB$
- side length $B'C' = \mathbf{2} \times BC$
- side length $C'D' = \mathbf{2} \times CD$
- side length $D'A' = \mathbf{2} \times DA$

> **TIP**
>
> Each vertex on the image is on the same straight line as the line from the centre of enlargement to the corresponding vertex on the object.

WORKED EXAMPLE 9

Enlarge quadrilateral $ABCD$ by scale factor 3 and centre of enlargement $(-2, 1)$.

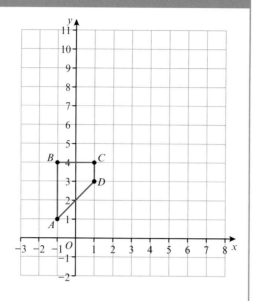

Answer

Mark the centre of enlargement at $(-2, 1)$ and label it O.

Measure the distance from O to each vertex of $ABCD$ and multiply by the scale factor to work out the distance to the vertices of $A'B'C'D'$.

OA = 1 unit right, so OA' = 3 units right.

OB = 1 right and 3 up, so OB' = 3 right and 9 up.

OC = 3 right and 2 up, so OC' = 9 right and 6 up.

OD = 3 right and 3 up, so OD' = 9 right and 9 up.

Join $A'B'C'D'$ to give the enlarged quadrilateral.

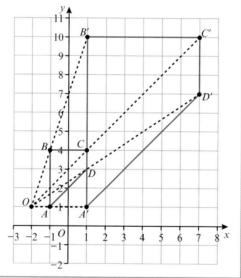

To find a side length of an enlarged image, you multiply the corresponding side length of the object by the scale factor:

Side length of image = scale factor × side length of object

You can rearrange this equation to work out the scale factor if you know the side lengths of the object and the image:

$$\text{Scale factor} = \frac{\text{side length of image}}{\text{side length of object}}$$

If you are given an object and its image, you can work out the centre of enlargement by drawing lines through the corresponding vertices. These lines will all meet at a single point, which is the centre of enlargement.

WORKED EXAMPLE 10

Fully describe the enlargement of triangle ABC to triangle $A'B'C'$.

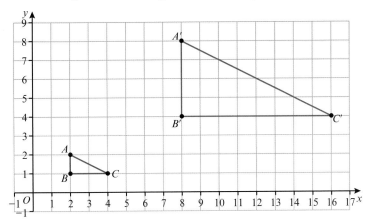

To fully describe the enlargement, we need to know:

a the centre of enlargement

b the scale factor.

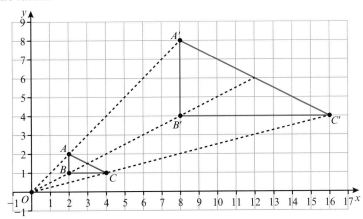

Answers

a To find the centre of enlargement, join the corresponding vertices and extend the lines until they intersect.

The lines intersect at the origin, $(0, 0)$.

b Scale factor $= \dfrac{\text{side length of image}}{\text{side length of object}}$

Side $AB = 1$ unit

Side $A'B' = 4$ units

Scale factor $= \dfrac{4}{1} = 4$

So triangle $A'B'C'$ is an enlargement of triangle ABC with scale factor 4 and centre of enlargement $(0, 0)$.

> **TIP**
>
> You can use any pair of corresponding sides to work out the scale factor. It is a good idea to check your answer using another pair of sides.

DISCUSSION 2

Instead of comparing side lengths of the object and image, how else can you work out the scale factor?

WORKED EXAMPLE 11

Fully describe the enlargement of shape $ABCDE$ to shape $A'B'C'D'E'$.

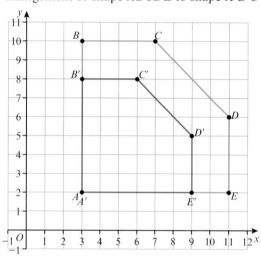

> **TIP**
>
> The image $A'B'C'D'E'$ is smaller than the object $ABCDE$, so you should expect the scale factor to be less than 1.

Answer

Scale factor

$$= \frac{\text{side length of image}}{\text{side length of object}}$$

$AB = 8$ units

$AB = 6$ units

Scale factor $= \dfrac{6}{8} = \dfrac{3}{4}$

The lines joining corresponding points intersect at vertex A, which is the point $(3, 2)$.

So, $ABCDE$ is an enlargement of $ABCDE$ with scale factor $\dfrac{3}{4}$ and centre of enlargement $(3, 2)$.

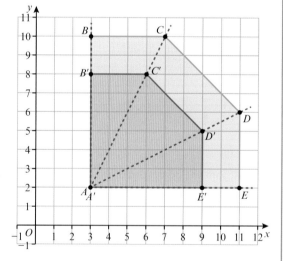

> **TIP**
>
> The centre of enlargement can be anywhere – outside the object, a vertex, a point on an edge or even a point inside the object.

More enlargement

You already know that enlarging by a scale factor greater than 1 makes the object larger and that enlarging by a scale factor less than 1 (but greater than zero) makes the object smaller, but what about when the scale factor is negative?

You follow the same method to find the position of the vertices of the image as for a positive scale factor, but the direction is changed.

WORKED EXAMPLE 12

Enlarge quadrilateral $ABCD$ by scale factor -1.5 and centre of enlargement $(3, 5)$.

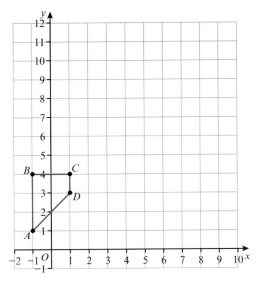

Answer

Mark the centre of enlargement and label it O.

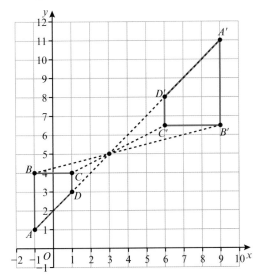

Measure the distance from O to each vertex of $ABCD$ and multiply by 1.5 to work out the distance to the vertices of $A'B'C'D'$.

$OA = 4$ units left and 4 units down, so $OA' = 6$ units right and 6 units up.

$OB = 4$ left and 1 down, so $OB' = 6$ right and 1.5 up.

$OC = 2$ left and 1 down, so $OC' = 3$ right and 1.5 up.

$OD = 2$ left and 2 down, so $OD' = 3$ right and 3 up.

Join $A'B'C'D'$ to give the enlarged quadrilateral.

WORKED EXAMPLE 13

Fully describe the enlargement of triangle ABC to triangle $A'B'C'$.

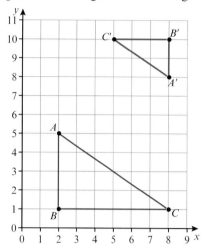

Answer

To find the centre of enlargement, join the corresponding vertices and find the point of intersection.

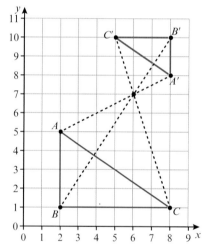

The lines meet at $(6, 7)$.

$$\text{Scale factor} = \frac{\text{side length of image}}{\text{side length of object}}$$

Side $AB = 4$ units

Side $A'B' = 2$ units

Scale factor $= \dfrac{2}{4} = \dfrac{1}{2}$

But the image is on the opposite side of the centre or enlargement,

so the scale factor $= -\dfrac{1}{2}$.

So triangle $A'B'C'$ is an enlargement of triangle ABC with scale factor $-\dfrac{1}{2}$ and centre of enlargement $(6, 7)$.

Exercise 17.4

1   Copy the diagram.

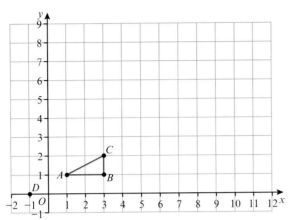

a   Enlarge the triangle ABC to show the triangle $A'B'C'$ with a scale factor of 3
and a centre of enlargement $D(-1, 0)$.

Draw the triangle EFG with points $E(4, 3)$, $F(7, 3)$ and $G(6, 5)$.

b   Enlarge the triangle EFG to show the triangle $E'F'G'$ with a scale factor of
two and a centre of enlargement $H(9, 2)$.

2   Copy the diagram and enlarge the quadrilateral $ABCD$ from the centre of
enlargement, E, by scale factor 2.5.
Label the image $A'B'C'D'$.

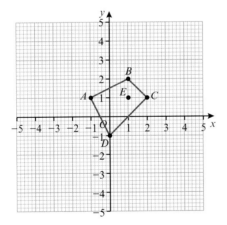

3   The quadrilateral $ABCD$ has vertices $A(-1, 1)$, $B(2, 0)$, $C(3, 1)$, $D(1, 2)$.

The quadrilateral is enlarged by a scale factor of 2 with the centre of
enlargement $E(1, 0)$.

What are the coordinates of the points A', B', C' and D'?

4 The diagram shows a triangle *ABC* and other triangles which are all enlargements of *ABC*.

For each triangle, give the scale factor and the centre of enlargement.

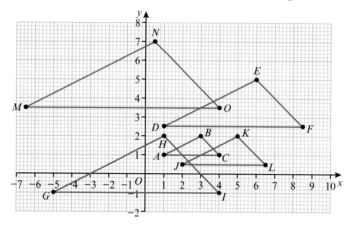

 5 Fully describe the enlargement of shape *ABCDE* to shape *A'B'C'D'E'*.

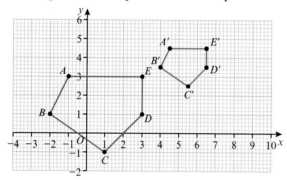

 6 The quadrilateral *ABCD* has been enlarged by a scale factor 2.5 and centre of enlargement *E*(−5, −1).

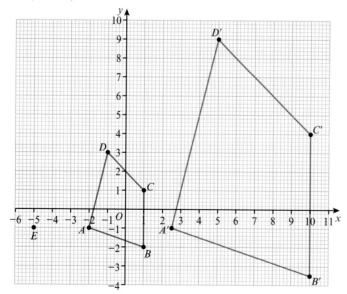

Fully describe the enlargement that would make *ABCD* the image of *A'B'C'D'*.

7   Draw a diagram to show the result of enlarging the quadrilateral $ABCD$ with
    points $A(-4, -3)$ $B(5, 0)$ $C(2, 3)$ $D(-4, 3)$, scale factor $\frac{1}{3}$ and centre of
    enlargement $(8, 6)$.
    Write down the coordinates of $A'B'C'D'$.

8   In each diagram, describe fully the enlargement that has taken place to transform
    the object to its image.

a

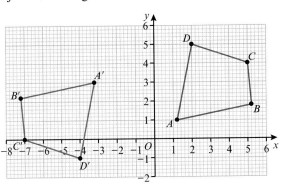

b

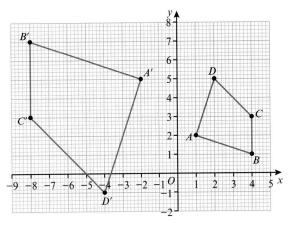

c

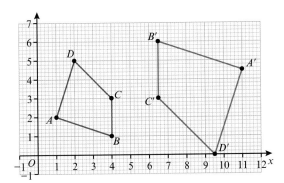

d

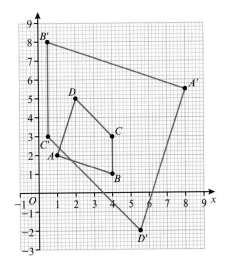

9   Draw a pair of axes such that $-10 \leqslant x \leqslant 10$ and $-10 \leqslant y \leqslant 10$ on squared or
    graph paper.

    a   Draw the quadrilateral $ABCD$ with the coordinates $A(3, 3)$, $B(7, 1)$,
        $C(8, 3)$, $D(6, 5)$.
        Enlarge $ABCD$ with a scale factor -1.5 with a centre of enlargement $(1, 2)$.

    b   Draw the quadrilateral $ABCD$ with the coordinates $A(4, 3)$, $B(6, 1)$,
        $C(7, 4)$, $D(6, 6)$.
        Enlarge $ABCD$ with a scale factor -2 with a centre of enlargement $(4, 2)$.

Exercise 17.5

This exercise reviews the work you have completed on transformations.

For Questions **1–6**, if required, draw a pair of axes such that $-10 \leqslant x \leqslant 10$ and $-10 \leqslant y \leqslant 10$ on squared or graph paper.

 1 The triangle ABC is given by $A(-1, -2)$, $B(2, -2)$, $C(2, 2)$.

     a Reflect the triangle ABC in the line $y = 3$ and write down the coordinates of $A'B'C'$.

     b Reflect the triangle ABC in the line $y = -3$ and write down the coordinates of $A''B''C''$.

 2 The triangle ABC is given by $A(1, -2)$, $B(2, -2)$, $C(1, 2)$.

     a Describe using a vector the translation that moves the triangle so that $A'(5, -1)$, $B'(6, -1)$, $C'(5, 3)$.

     b Translate the triangle ABC by the vector $\begin{pmatrix} -3 \\ -4 \end{pmatrix}$ and write down the coordinates of A'', B'' and C''.

 3 The quadrilateral $ABCD$ is given by $A(-2, -3)$, $B(2, -2)$, $C(3, 2)$, $D(-3, 2)$.

The quadrilateral has been transformed so that $A'(2, 3)$, $B'(1, 7)$, $C'(-3, 8)$, $D'(-3, 2)$.

     a Describe fully the transformation that has taken place.

     b The same quadrilateral $ABCD$ is rotated 90° clockwise about the origin to form quadrilateral $A''B''C''D''$.

       Write down the coordinates of $A''B''C''D''$.

 4 **a** A quadrilateral A has been reflected in the line $y = -2$ to give the quadrilateral A'.

       Which transformation will transform A' to A?

     b The triangle ABC has vertices $A(1, 1)$, $B(5, 2)$, $C(3, 3)$.

       The triangle $A'B'C'$ is given as $A'(1, 1)$, $B'(0, 5)$, $C'(-1, 3)$.

       Describe fully the single transformation that has taken place.

 5 The quadrilateral $ABCD$ is given as $A(0, -2)$, $B(2, -1)$, $C(1, 2)$, $D(-2, 0)$.

The quadrilateral is enlarged so that $A'(2, -3)$, $B'(6, -1)$, $C'(4, 5)$, $D'(-2, 1)$.

     a Find the scale factor and the centre of enlargement.

       The same quadrilateral $ABCD$ is enlarged by a scale factor 3 with a centre of enlargement $(2, -2)$ to form $A''B''C''D''$.

     b Write down the coordinates of A'', B'', C'', D''.

 6 The triangle ABC is given as $A(4, 1)$, $B(5, 4)$, $C(1, 0)$.

     a Reflect ABC in the line $y = x$ to give $A'B'C'$ and write down the coordinates of A', B' and C'.

     b Reflect ABC in the line $y = -x$ to give the triangle $A''B''C''$. Write down the coordinates of A'', B'', C''.

7   The diagram shows the quadrilateral $ABCD$ and its image $A'B'C'D'$.
    Describe the single transformation that has mapped $ABCD$ to $A'B'C'D'$.

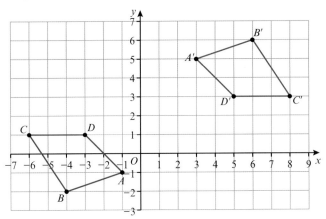

8   The quadrilateral $ABCD$ has been enlarged to create the shape $A'B'C'D'$.

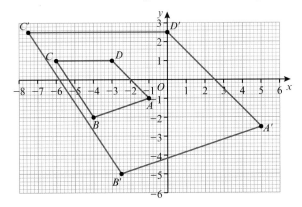

a   Write down the centre of enlargement and the scale factor that has been used
    to create $A'B'C'D''$.

b   If the centre of enlargement was moved by the vector $\begin{pmatrix} 2 \\ 0 \end{pmatrix}$ and the scale
    factor changed to 1.5, what would be the coordinates of the new
    quadrilateral $A''B''C''D''$?

17.2 Further transformations

You learnt about four types of transformations in the previous section and in this section you will learn more about reflections, rotations and enlargements, and about combining transformations.

Reversing transformations

The diagram shows an enlargement.

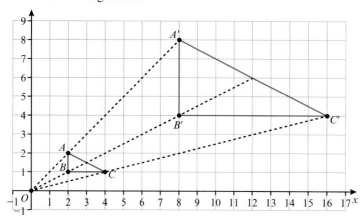

In fact, it shows **two** enlargements:

- the enlargement ABC to $A'B'C'$ with centre $(0, 0)$ and scale factor 3

- the enlargement $A'B'C'$ to ABC with centre $(0, 0)$ and scale factor $\frac{1}{3}$

These two enlargements are connected. Enlargement B reverses enlargement A and enlargement A reverses enlargement B.

MATHEMATICAL CONNECTIONS

You can also think about reverse transformations as inverse transformations because one 'undoes' the other. Enlargement A maps the object onto its image and the inverse transformation, enlargement B, maps the image back to the object.

You learnt about inverse functions in Chapter 14.

WORKED EXAMPLE 14

Triangle ABC has been rotated 90° anticlockwise about centre of rotation $(1, 0)$ to give the image $A'B'C'$.

Find the transformation that maps $A'B'C'$ back onto triangle ABC.

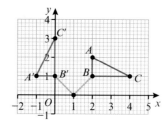

Answer

The transformation that maps triangle $A'B'C'$ back onto ABC is the reverse transformation.

To undo a rotation, turn the shape the same amount in the opposite direction about the same centre of rotation.

So, $A'B'C'$ is mapped onto ABC by a rotation of 90° clockwise about centre of rotation $(1, 0)$.

INVESTIGATION 2

1   By drawing objects and their images, find the reverse transformation for:

    a   a translation of:

      i $\begin{pmatrix} 1 \\ 0 \end{pmatrix}$ **ii** $\begin{pmatrix} 2 \\ -1 \end{pmatrix}$ **iii** $\begin{pmatrix} a \\ b \end{pmatrix}$

    b   an enlargement of:

      i   scale factor 0.5, centre (0, 0)   **ii**   scale factor −3, centre (1, 2)   **iii**   scale factor P, centre (x, y)

    c   a rotation of:

      i   120° clockwise, centre (2, 0)   **ii**   180° centre (0, 0)

    d   a reflection in:

      i   the x-axis   **ii**   the line $y = -x$.

2   **a**   What do you notice about your answers to part **d**?

    b   Will this be true for a reflection in any straight line?

Combining transformations

As well as mapping an object to an image with a single transformations, you can combine two or more transformations, one after another. For example, you can enlarge an image and then reflect it, or you can rotate it and then translate it.

Sometimes you can then work out the single transformation that is equivalent to the combination – this is the transformation that maps the original object to its final image.

We can use an arrow notation $\rightarrow$ to signify that one shape maps to another shape.

WORKED EXAMPLE 15

The diagram shows triangle ABC.

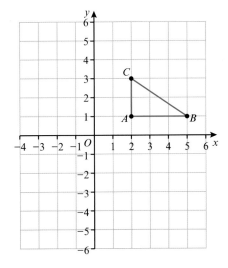

CONTINUED

a Rotate ABC 90° anticlockwise about centre $(0, 0)$. Label the image $A'B'C'$.

b Reflect $A'B'C'$ in the x-axis. Label the image $A''B''C''$.

c Find the single transformation that maps ABC directly to $A''B''C''$. ($ABC \to A''B''C''$)

d State the transformation that maps $A''B''C''$ back to the original object ABC. ($A''B''C'' \to ABC$)

Answers

a Mark the centre of rotation $(0, 0)$. Rotate the object to $A'B'C'$.

b $A''B''C''$ is the same distance from the x-axis as $A'B'C'$, but on the opposite side.

c $A''B''C''$ is a reflection of ABC. Join corresponding vertices and find the midpoints to work out the line of reflection.

$ABC \to A''B''C''$ by a reflection in the line $y = -x$

d Therefore a reflection in the line $y = -x$ will map $A''B''C''$ back to ABC.

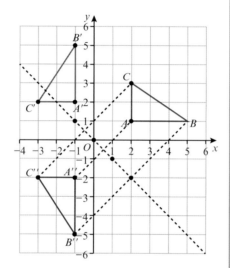

Exercise 17.6

1 Draw triangle $A(1, 2)$, $B(1, 1)$, $C(3, 1)$ on axes such that $-5 \leqslant x \leqslant 5$, $-5 \leqslant y \leqslant 5$.

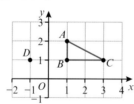

a Rotate ABC 180° about centre $D(-1, 1)$. Label the new triangle P.

b Rotate P clockwise 90° about centre D. Label the new triangle Q.

c Rotate Q 180° about centre D. Label the new triangle R.

d Describe the following transformations.

    i $R \to Q$

    ii $ABC \to Q$

    iii $P \to R$

    iv $R \to ABC$

2 Draw triangle $A(2, 3)$, $B(1, 2)$, $C(3, 1)$ on axes such that $-5 \leqslant x \leqslant 5$, $-5 \leqslant y \leqslant 5$.

    a Rotate ABC clockwise 90° about centre $D(-1, 1)$.
Label the new triangle P.

    b Rotate ABC anticlockwise 90° about centre D.
Label the new triangle Q.

    c Rotate P clockwise 90° about centre D. Label the new triangle R.

    d Describe the following transformations.

       i $R \rightarrow ABC$

       ii $Q \rightarrow ABC$

       iii $P \rightarrow ABC$

       iv $R \rightarrow P$

3 Draw a grid such that $-10 \leqslant x \leqslant 10$ and $-10 \leqslant y \leqslant 10$.

    a Draw the shape given by $(2, 1)$ $(8, 1)$ $(8, 4)$ $(4, 4)$. Label it A.

    b Reflect A in the line $y = x$ and label it B.

    c Rotate A by 90° anticlockwise centre $(0, 0)$ and label it C.

    d Rotate C by 180° centre $(0, 0)$ and label it D.

    e Rotate D by 90° clockwise centre $(0, 0)$ and label it E.

    f Reflect E in the y-axis and label it F.

    g Rotate F by 90° clockwise centre $(0, 0)$ and label it G.

    h Reflect C in the line $y = -x$ and label it H.

    i Describe the single transformations that map:

       1 $B \rightarrow D$ and $D \rightarrow B$

       2 $F \rightarrow D$ and $D \rightarrow F$

       3 $G \rightarrow A$ and $A \rightarrow G$

       4 $F \rightarrow C$ and $C \rightarrow F$

       5 $E \rightarrow A$ and $A \rightarrow E$

       6 $H \rightarrow B$ and $B \rightarrow H$

In the remaining questions use your own triangle ABC as the initial object to be transformed.

4 Reflect ABC in the x-axis $\rightarrow A'B'C'$.
Rotate $A'B'C'$ by 180° centre $(0, 0) \rightarrow A''B''C''$.
Determine the single transformation that maps $ABC \rightarrow A''B''C''$.

5 Rotate ABC by 180° centre $(0, 0) \rightarrow A'B'C'$.
Reflect $A'B'C'$ in the x-axis $\rightarrow A''B''C''$.
Determine the single transformation that maps $ABC \rightarrow A''B''C''$.

6 Reflect ABC in $y = x \rightarrow A'B'C'$.
Rotate $A'B'C'$ by 90° anticlockwise centre $(0, 0) \rightarrow A''B''C''$.
Determine the single transformation that maps $ABC \rightarrow A''B''C''$.

7 Rotate ABC by 90° anticlockwise centre $(0, 0) \rightarrow A'B'C'$.
Reflect $A'B'C'$ in $y = x \rightarrow A''B''C''$.
Determine the single transformation that maps $ABC \rightarrow A''B''C''$.

DISCUSSION 3

Does the order in which the transformations are made change the final single transformation?

DISCUSSION 4

Does changing the order of transformations matter in this case?

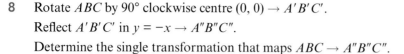

8   Rotate ABC by 90° clockwise centre $(0, 0) \rightarrow A'B'C'$.

Reflect $A'B'C'$ in $y = -x \rightarrow A''B''C''$.

Determine the single transformation that maps $ABC \rightarrow A''B''C''$.

9   Reflect ABC in $y = -x \rightarrow A'B'C'$.

Rotate $A'B'C'$ by 90° clockwise centre $(0, 0) \rightarrow A''B''C''$.

Determine the single transformation that maps $ABC \rightarrow A''B''C''$.

10   Reflect ABC in the x-axis $\rightarrow A'B'C'$.

Reflect $A'B'C'$ in the y-axis $\rightarrow A''B''C''$.

Determine the single transformation that maps $ABC \rightarrow A''B''C''$.

> **TIP**
>
> Changing the order of transformations may result in a different single transformation.

INVESTIGATION 3

Triangle A is translated by vector $\begin{pmatrix} 3 \\ -2 \end{pmatrix}$ to triangle B. Triangle B is then translated by vector $\begin{pmatrix} 1 \\ 5 \end{pmatrix}$ to triangle C.

a   Choose your own coordinates for the vertices of triangle A, carry out the translations and work out the vector that translates triangle A directly to triangle C.

b   Does it make a difference if you choose different coordinates?

c   Can you explain to someone how they can work out the vector that translates triangle A directly to triangle C without drawing a diagram?

17.3 Vectors

When you described a translation, you used a column vector $\begin{pmatrix} x \\ y \end{pmatrix}$.

The column vector tells you how far and in what direction to move the object.

For example, for the vector $\begin{pmatrix} 2 \\ -3 \end{pmatrix}$ you move 2 units in the positive x-direction and 3 units in the negative y-direction.

Quantities which are described using both a **magnitude** (size) and a direction are called vector quantities. Some examples are velocity, force and acceleration.

Quantities which are described using only a magnitude are called **scalar** quantities. Some examples are speed, time and distance.

Vector notation

You have seen how a vector can be written as a column vector using a pair of numbers, but there are also other ways of writing vectors.

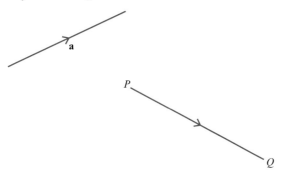

The diagram shows a directed line segment that represents vector **a**. Notice that **a** is printed in bold type when it represents a vector.

Vectors can also be represented using its start and end points, for example $\overrightarrow{PQ}$. An arrow is drawn above the letters to show it is a vector and not a side length.

The order of the letters is important: $\overrightarrow{PQ}$ represents the vector from point P to point Q, but $\overrightarrow{QP}$ represents the vector going the opposite direction from point Q to point P.

$\overrightarrow{PQ}$ and $\overrightarrow{QP}$ have the same magnitude but the opposite direction, so you can write $\overrightarrow{PQ} = -\overrightarrow{QP}$.

WORKED EXAMPLE 16

Draw these vectors on a coordinate grid.

$$\mathbf{a} = \begin{pmatrix} 2 \\ -5 \end{pmatrix} \qquad \mathbf{b} = \begin{pmatrix} 0 \\ 3 \end{pmatrix} \qquad \mathbf{c} = \begin{pmatrix} -3 \\ 4 \end{pmatrix} \qquad \mathbf{d} = \begin{pmatrix} 4 \\ 0 \end{pmatrix} \qquad \mathbf{e} = \begin{pmatrix} 5 \\ 5 \end{pmatrix}$$

Answer

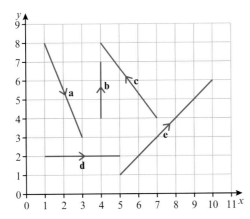

It doesn't matter where on the grid you draw the vectors.

Choose a starting point and move up, down, right or left according to the column vector to reach the end point.

Draw arrow on the vectors to show the direction and label them clearly.

Equal vectors

The diagram shows the translation of triangle ABC to triangle DEF.

Vertex A is translated to vertex D and this can be written as $\overrightarrow{AD}$. Looking at the grid, you can see that $\overrightarrow{AD} = \begin{pmatrix} 4 \\ 2 \end{pmatrix}$.

Similarly $\overrightarrow{BE} = \begin{pmatrix} 4 \\ 2 \end{pmatrix}$ and $\overrightarrow{CF} = \begin{pmatrix} 4 \\ 2 \end{pmatrix}$.

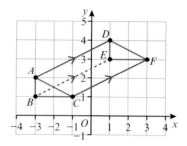

The vectors $\overrightarrow{AD}$, $\overrightarrow{BE}$ and $\overrightarrow{CF}$ are all the same length and they all go in the same direction (they are parallel).

Since both the magnitude and the direction of $\overrightarrow{AD}$, $\overrightarrow{BE}$ and $\overrightarrow{CF}$ are equal, then $\overrightarrow{AD} = \overrightarrow{BE} = \overrightarrow{CF}$.

> **TIP**
>
> Two vectors are equal if they have the same magnitude **and** direction.

WORKED EXAMPLE 17

Represent each vector using a column vector.

a $\overrightarrow{AB}$ b $\overrightarrow{BA}$

c $\overrightarrow{EF}$ d $\overrightarrow{CD}$

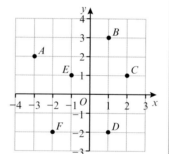

Answers

a A to B is 4 units right and 1 unit up.

$\overrightarrow{AB} = \begin{pmatrix} 4 \\ 1 \end{pmatrix}$

b B to A is 4 units left and 1 unit down.

$\overrightarrow{BA} = \begin{pmatrix} -4 \\ -1 \end{pmatrix}$

c E to F is 1 unit left and 3 units down.

$\overrightarrow{EF} = \begin{pmatrix} -1 \\ -3 \end{pmatrix}$

d C to D is 1 unit left and 3 units down.

$\overrightarrow{CD} = \begin{pmatrix} -1 \\ -3 \end{pmatrix}$

DISCUSSION 5

$\overrightarrow{EF}$ and $\overrightarrow{CD}$ have the same magnitude and the same direction, so $\overrightarrow{EF} = \overrightarrow{CD}$.
How many other pairs of equal vectors can you find in the diagram?

Multiplying a vector by a scalar

Multiplying a vector by a scalar changes the magnitude of the vector. For example, vector **a** multiplied by 2 gives vector 2**a**. This is twice as long as vector **a** in the same direction.

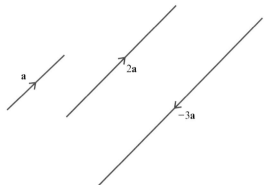

TIP

All vectors that have the same direction are parallel to each other.

In Worked example 17, $\overrightarrow{BA} = -\overrightarrow{AB}$, which means that the vectors $\overrightarrow{AB}$ and $\overrightarrow{BA}$ have the same magnitude but the opposite direction.

Multiplying by a negative scalar reverses the direction of a vector. Vector $-3\mathbf{a}$ is 3 times as long as vector **a** in the opposite direction.

To multiply a column vector $\begin{pmatrix} x \\ y \end{pmatrix}$ by a scalar, k, multiply both the x and y values by the scalar:

$$k \times \begin{pmatrix} x \\ y \end{pmatrix} = \begin{pmatrix} kx \\ ky \end{pmatrix}$$

WORKED EXAMPLE 18

If $\overrightarrow{XY} = \begin{pmatrix} 4 \\ 6 \end{pmatrix}$ and $\mathbf{z} = \begin{pmatrix} -3 \\ -9 \end{pmatrix}$, find:

a $5\overrightarrow{XY}$ b $-4\mathbf{z}$ c $1.5\overrightarrow{XY}$ d $\dfrac{1}{10}\mathbf{z}$

Answers

a $5\overrightarrow{XY} = 5 \times \begin{pmatrix} 4 \\ 6 \end{pmatrix} = \begin{pmatrix} 5 \times 4 \\ 5 \times 6 \end{pmatrix} = \begin{pmatrix} 20 \\ 30 \end{pmatrix}$

b $-4\mathbf{z} = -4 \times \begin{pmatrix} -3 \\ -9 \end{pmatrix} = \begin{pmatrix} -4 \times -3 \\ -4 \times -9 \end{pmatrix} = \begin{pmatrix} 12 \\ 36 \end{pmatrix}$

c $1.5\overrightarrow{XY} = 1.5 \times \begin{pmatrix} 4 \\ 6 \end{pmatrix} = \begin{pmatrix} 1.5 \times 4 \\ 1.5 \times 6 \end{pmatrix} = \begin{pmatrix} 6 \\ 9 \end{pmatrix}$

d $\dfrac{1}{10}\mathbf{z} = \dfrac{1}{10} \times \begin{pmatrix} -3 \\ -9 \end{pmatrix} = \begin{pmatrix} \dfrac{1}{10} \times -3 \\ \dfrac{1}{10} \times -9 \end{pmatrix} = \begin{pmatrix} -\dfrac{3}{10} \\ -\dfrac{9}{10} \end{pmatrix}$

Exercise 17.7

1 Express in terms of **a**.

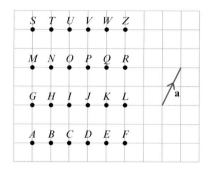

a $\overrightarrow{CQ}$

b $\overrightarrow{ZQ}$

c $\overrightarrow{BW}$

d $\overrightarrow{OA}$

e $\overrightarrow{WB}$

2 Name the end point after starting at H and applying:

a **a** b 2**a** c −**a**

3 Name the end point after starting at P and applying:

a **a** b −2**a** c −**a**

4 Draw the following vectors on a coordinate grid

a $\begin{pmatrix} 2 \\ 5 \end{pmatrix}$ b $\begin{pmatrix} -1 \\ 7 \end{pmatrix}$ c $\begin{pmatrix} 3 \\ -2 \end{pmatrix}$ d $\begin{pmatrix} -6 \\ -3 \end{pmatrix}$

5 If $\overrightarrow{AB} = \begin{pmatrix} 3 \\ -1 \end{pmatrix}$ and $\overrightarrow{CD} = \begin{pmatrix} -2 \\ -3 \end{pmatrix}$, find:

a $4\overrightarrow{AB}$ b $-3\overrightarrow{CD}$ c $\frac{1}{3}\overrightarrow{AB}$ d $-\frac{1}{2}\overrightarrow{CD}$

Adding and subtracting vectors

As well as multiplying a vector by a scalar, you can add and subtract vectors.

The diagram shows vectors **a** and **b**.

To add **a** and **b**, join them together 'nose to tail'.

   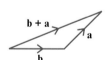

The single vector that moves from the start of **a** to the end of **b** is the vector **a + b**.

You can see from the diagram that vector **a + b** is the same as vector **b + a**.
It doesn't matter which order you add vectors: **a + b = b + a**.

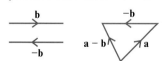

> **TIP**
>
> Be careful to position the vectors so you can follow the arrows from the start point to the end point.

> **TIP**
>
> Vector addition is commutative. This means the sum of the vectors remains the same regardless of the order in which they are added.

Subtracting a vector is the same as adding a negative version of it: $\mathbf{a} - \mathbf{b} = \mathbf{a} + (-\mathbf{b})$

Vector $-\mathbf{b}$ has the same magnitude as $\mathbf{b}$, but the opposite direction.

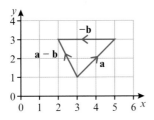

> **DISCUSSION**
>
> Is $a - b$ the same as $b - a$?

Adding and subtracting column vectors

When vectors are shown on a coordinate grid you can express them as column vectors.

You can see from the diagram that $\mathbf{a} = \begin{pmatrix} 2 \\ 2 \end{pmatrix}$ and $\mathbf{b} = \begin{pmatrix} 3 \\ 0 \end{pmatrix}$.

To add column vectors, add the x-values and add the y-values:

$$\mathbf{a} + \mathbf{b} = \begin{pmatrix} 2 + 3 \\ 2 + 0 \end{pmatrix} = \begin{pmatrix} 5 \\ 2 \end{pmatrix}$$

You can check this result by looking at the movement in the x- and y-directions for vector $\mathbf{a} + \mathbf{b}$.

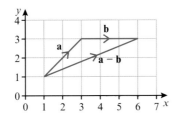

To subtract column vectors, subtract the x- and y-values:

$$\mathbf{a} - \mathbf{b} = \begin{pmatrix} 2 - 3 \\ 2 - 0 \end{pmatrix} = \begin{pmatrix} -1 \\ 2 \end{pmatrix}$$

In general:

$$\begin{pmatrix} x_1 \\ y_1 \end{pmatrix} + \begin{pmatrix} x_2 \\ y_2 \end{pmatrix} = \begin{pmatrix} x_1 + x_2 \\ y_1 + y_2 \end{pmatrix} \text{ and } \begin{pmatrix} x_1 \\ y_1 \end{pmatrix} - \begin{pmatrix} x_2 \\ y_2 \end{pmatrix} = \begin{pmatrix} x_1 - x_2 \\ y_1 - y_2 \end{pmatrix}$$

WORKED EXAMPLE 19

$\mathbf{x} = \begin{pmatrix} 3 \\ -1 \end{pmatrix}$, $\mathbf{y} = \begin{pmatrix} 5 \\ 3 \end{pmatrix}$ and $\mathbf{z} = \begin{pmatrix} 0 \\ 2 \end{pmatrix}$

Find column vectors that are equal to:

a $-2\mathbf{x}$ **b** $\mathbf{y} + \mathbf{z}$ **c** $\mathbf{x} - 3\mathbf{y} + \mathbf{z}$ **d** $\frac{1}{2}\mathbf{z} - 5\mathbf{x}$

Answers

a $-2\mathbf{x} = -2 \times \begin{pmatrix} 3 \\ -1 \end{pmatrix} = \begin{pmatrix} -2 \times 3 \\ -2 \times -1 \end{pmatrix} = \begin{pmatrix} -6 \\ 2 \end{pmatrix}$

b $\mathbf{y} + \mathbf{z} = \begin{pmatrix} 5 \\ 3 \end{pmatrix} + \begin{pmatrix} 0 \\ 2 \end{pmatrix} = \begin{pmatrix} 5 + 0 \\ 3 + 2 \end{pmatrix} = \begin{pmatrix} 5 \\ 5 \end{pmatrix}$

CONTINUED

c $\quad x - 3y + z = \begin{pmatrix} 3 \\ -1 \end{pmatrix} - 3\begin{pmatrix} 5 \\ 3 \end{pmatrix} + \begin{pmatrix} 0 \\ 2 \end{pmatrix} = \begin{pmatrix} 3 - 3 \times 5 + 0 \\ -1 - 3 \times 3 + 2 \end{pmatrix} = \begin{pmatrix} 3 - 15 + 0 \\ -1 - 9 + 2 \end{pmatrix} = \begin{pmatrix} -12 \\ -8 \end{pmatrix}$

d $\quad \frac{1}{2}z - 5x = \frac{1}{2}\begin{pmatrix} 0 \\ 2 \end{pmatrix} - 5\begin{pmatrix} 3 \\ -1 \end{pmatrix} = \begin{pmatrix} \frac{1}{2} \times 0 - 5 \times 3 \\ \frac{1}{2} \times 2 - 5 \times (-1) \end{pmatrix} = \begin{pmatrix} -15 \\ 6 \end{pmatrix}$

> **TIP**
>
> Take care when calculating with positive and negative numbers.
>
> You should write out each step of your working to avoid making mistakes.

Having only one named vector on a two-dimensional grid is very restrictive.

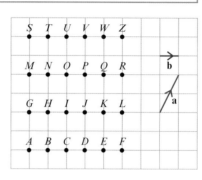

To fully describe and move around the grid a second vector, **b**, is required.

So that, for example, to move from B to K first move along $B \rightarrow I$ using **a** then along $I \rightarrow K$ using $2\mathbf{b}$.

$\overrightarrow{BK} = \mathbf{a} + 2\mathbf{b}$

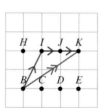

Note to move from B to K the route could first be along $B \rightarrow D$ using $2\mathbf{b}$ then along $D \rightarrow K$ using **a**

$\overrightarrow{BK} = 2\mathbf{b} + \mathbf{a}$

Hence, $B \rightarrow D$ and $\overrightarrow{BK} = 2\mathbf{b} + \mathbf{a}$

Although, the routes are different, the final vector $\overrightarrow{BK}$ is obtained.

WORKED EXAMPLE 20

Express $\overrightarrow{JP}$ in terms of **a** and **b**.

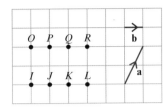

Answer

Once again, there are two efficient options:

$J \to Q$ then $Q \to P$ or $J \to I$ then $I \to P$

1 $J \to Q$ then $Q \to P$

This is equivalent to $\overrightarrow{JQ} + \overrightarrow{QP}$, where $\overrightarrow{QP} = -\mathbf{b}$

Hence, $\overrightarrow{JP} = \overrightarrow{JQ} + \overrightarrow{QP} = \mathbf{a} + (-\mathbf{b}) = \mathbf{a} - \mathbf{b}$

2 $J \to I$ then $I \to P$

This is equivalent to $\overrightarrow{JI} + \overrightarrow{IP}$, where $\overrightarrow{JI} = -\mathbf{b}$

Hence, $\overrightarrow{JP} = \overrightarrow{JI} + \overrightarrow{IP} = (-\mathbf{b}) + \mathbf{a} = \mathbf{a} - \mathbf{b}$

It is more usual to use **column vectors** when describing a problem.

Exercise 17.8

Questions **1–3** relate to the grid shown.

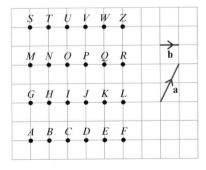

1 Express in terms of **a** and **b**.

a $\overrightarrow{BZ}$ b $\overrightarrow{AQ}$ c $\overrightarrow{VK}$ d $\overrightarrow{DN}$ e $\overrightarrow{TA}$

2 Name the end point after starting at H and applying:

    a $\mathbf{a} + 3\mathbf{b}$ **b** $2\mathbf{b} - \mathbf{a}$ **c** $-3\mathbf{b} + 2\mathbf{a}$

3 Name the end point after starting at P and applying:

    a $-\mathbf{a} - \mathbf{b}$ **b** $\mathbf{a} - 4\mathbf{b}$ **c** $\mathbf{b} - 2\mathbf{a}$

4 Given that $\mathbf{b} = \begin{pmatrix} 2 \\ 1 \end{pmatrix}$, $\mathbf{b} = \begin{pmatrix} 1 \\ -3 \end{pmatrix}$, $\mathbf{c} = \begin{pmatrix} -3 \\ -2 \end{pmatrix}$, $\mathbf{d} = \begin{pmatrix} -2 \\ 5 \end{pmatrix}$, write down the following as column vectors.

a $\mathbf{a} + \mathbf{b}$	**b** $\mathbf{a} + 2\mathbf{b}$	**c** $2\mathbf{c} + \mathbf{d}$	**d** $\mathbf{a} + \mathbf{b} + \mathbf{d}$
e $\mathbf{a} - \mathbf{b}$	**f** $2\mathbf{a} - \mathbf{c}$	**g** $3\mathbf{c} - 2\mathbf{d}$	**h** $\mathbf{c} + \mathbf{b} - \mathbf{d}$

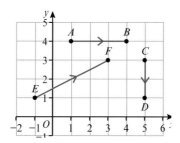

5 Find the vector, $\mathbf{x}$, as a column vector, given that:

    a $\mathbf{x} + \begin{pmatrix} 1 \\ 1 \end{pmatrix} = \begin{pmatrix} 3 \\ 5 \end{pmatrix}$ **b** $\mathbf{x} - \begin{pmatrix} 2 \\ 3 \end{pmatrix} = \begin{pmatrix} 4 \\ 2 \end{pmatrix}$ **c** $2\mathbf{x} - \begin{pmatrix} 5 \\ 3 \end{pmatrix} = \begin{pmatrix} 1 \\ 7 \end{pmatrix}$

    d $\mathbf{x} + \mathbf{a} = \begin{pmatrix} 3 \\ 5 \end{pmatrix}$ **e** $\mathbf{x} - \mathbf{d} = \begin{pmatrix} 4 \\ 2 \end{pmatrix}$ **f** $2\mathbf{c} - \mathbf{b} = \begin{pmatrix} -3 \\ 5 \end{pmatrix}$

    g $2\mathbf{x} - \mathbf{c} = 2\vec{d}$ **h** $\mathbf{c} + \mathbf{b} - \mathbf{x} = 2\mathbf{a}$ **i** $3\mathbf{x} - 2\mathbf{c} = \mathbf{a} + \mathbf{b}$

The magnitude of a vector

The magnitude of a vector is the same as its length.

You write the magnitude of a vector using modulus signs, for example $|\overrightarrow{AB}|$ or $|\mathbf{a}|$.

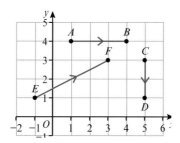

From the diagram it is easy to see that $|\overrightarrow{AB}| = 3$ (because the line segment AB is 3 units long).

Similarly, $|\overrightarrow{CD}| = 2$.

But how do you find $|\overrightarrow{EF}|$?

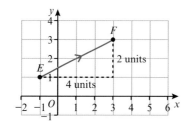

TIP

You can simply count the squares on a grid for horizontal and vertical vectors.

To calculate the length of the line segment *EF*, create a right-angled triangle and use Pythagoras' theorem:

$\overrightarrow{EF} = \begin{pmatrix} 4 \\ 2 \end{pmatrix}$ and so $|\overrightarrow{EF}| = \sqrt{4^2 + 2^2} = \sqrt{20} = 4.47$ (to 3 sf)

In general, if a vector $\mathbf{a} = \overrightarrow{AB} = \begin{pmatrix} x \\ y \end{pmatrix}$, then $|\mathbf{a}| = |\overrightarrow{AB}| = \sqrt{x^2 + y^2}$.

WORKED EXAMPLE 21

$\mathbf{x} = \begin{pmatrix} 5 \\ 2 \end{pmatrix}$ and $\overrightarrow{YZ} = \begin{pmatrix} -2 \\ 3 \end{pmatrix}$

Calculate, to three significant figures:

a $|\mathbf{x}|$ **b** $|\overrightarrow{YZ}|$

Answer

a $|\mathbf{x}| = \sqrt{5^2 + 2^2} = \sqrt{29} = 5.39$ (to 3 sf)

b $|\overrightarrow{YZ}| = \sqrt{(-2)^2 + 3^2} = \sqrt{13} = 3.61$ (to 3 sf)

Exercise 17.9

In Questions **1** to **5** let $\mathbf{a} = \begin{pmatrix} 2 \\ 1 \end{pmatrix}$, $\mathbf{b} = \begin{pmatrix} 1 \\ -3 \end{pmatrix}$, $\mathbf{c} = \begin{pmatrix} -3 \\ -2 \end{pmatrix}$, $\mathbf{d} = \begin{pmatrix} -2 \\ 5 \end{pmatrix}$.

1 Calculate $|\mathbf{a}|$, $|\mathbf{b}|$, $|\mathbf{c}|$, $|\mathbf{d}|$. Leave your answers in surd form.

2 Calculate $3\mathbf{a} + \mathbf{b}$ and write down $|3\mathbf{a} + \mathbf{b}|$.

3 Calculate $\mathbf{a} + \mathbf{d}$ and write down $|\mathbf{a} + \mathbf{d}|$.

4 **a** Calculate $\mathbf{a} + \mathbf{b}$ and write down $|\mathbf{a} + \mathbf{b}|$.

     b Determine whether $|\mathbf{a} + \mathbf{b}| = |\mathbf{a}| + |\mathbf{b}|$.

5 Determine whether $|\mathbf{a} + \mathbf{c}| = |\mathbf{a}| + |\mathbf{c}|$.

Geometric vectors

Vectors can be used to construct geometric arguments and proofs.

They can be used to identify parallel lines, find midpoints and share lines in a given ratio.

In the diagram, the vectors **a** and **b** are shown.

The vector $\overrightarrow{CD} = -\mathbf{a} + \mathbf{b}$

The vector $\overrightarrow{DC}$ is $-\mathbf{b} + \mathbf{a}$

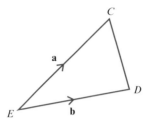

If the point M is the midpoint of CD, then $\overrightarrow{CM} = \frac{1}{2}(\mathbf{b} - \mathbf{a})$ and $\overrightarrow{DM} = \frac{1}{2}(\mathbf{a} - \mathbf{b})$.

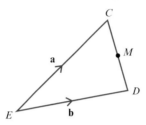

The point N is on the line EC such that the ratio of $EN:NC = 1:3$.

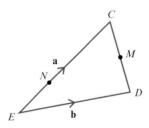

The ratio of $EN:NC = 1:3$, therefore the point N is such that $3EN = NC$.

Therefore $EN = \frac{1}{4}\mathbf{a}$.

WORKED EXAMPLE 22

The diagram shows a parallelogram $ABCD$.

M is the midpoint of CB and N is the midpoint of CD.

Prove that the MN is parallel to BD

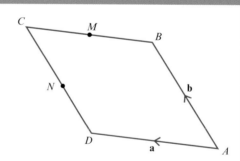

Answer

$BD = -\mathbf{b} + \mathbf{a}$

$MN = MB + BA + AD + DN$

$\quad = -\frac{1}{2}\mathbf{a} - \mathbf{b} + \mathbf{a} + \frac{1}{2}\mathbf{b}$

$\quad = \frac{1}{2}(-\mathbf{b} + \mathbf{a})$

As MN is a multiple of BD they are parallel.

Exercise 17.10

1 *ABCD* is a parallelogram.

M is the midpoint of *DC* and *N* is the midpoint of *CB*.

$AB = \mathbf{a}$

$AD = \mathbf{b}$

Find the following vectors.

a $\overrightarrow{BN}$ b $\overrightarrow{DM}$ c $\overrightarrow{AM}$

d $\overrightarrow{MB}$ e $\overrightarrow{ND}$ f $\overrightarrow{MN}$

2 The diagram shows two similar triangles *ABC* and *APQ*.

$AB = \mathbf{a}$ and $AC = \mathbf{b}$

The ratio $BP : PA = 1 : 3$.

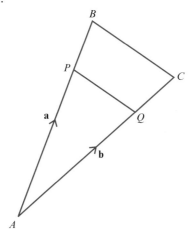

Find the vectors:

a $\overrightarrow{BC}$ b $\overrightarrow{CB}$ c $\overrightarrow{AQ}$ d $\overrightarrow{PA}$ e $\overrightarrow{PQ}$ f $\overrightarrow{QB}$

3 The diagram shows a regular hexagon *GHIJKL*, with centre *O*.

S and *T* are the midpoints of *KJ* and *JI* respectively.

$OG = \mathbf{m}$ and $OL = \mathbf{n}$

a   Find the vectors:

  i   *KL*   ii   *GH*   iii   *LI*

  iv   *IK*   v   *JT*   vi   *OS*

b   Prove that *KH* is parallel to *JI*.

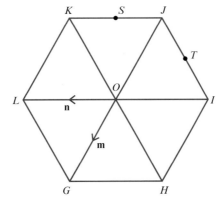

SUMMARY

Are you able to... ?
recognise, describe and draw a reflection in a horizontal or vertical line
recognise, describe and draw a rotation of a shape around the origin, vertices or midpoints of edges of the shape through a multiple of 90°
recognise, describe and draw an enlargement of a shape from a centre by a scale factor
translate a shape by a vector $\begin{pmatrix} x \\ y \end{pmatrix}$
recognise, describe and draw a reflection in a straight line
recognise, describe and draw a rotation of a shape around a point through a multiple of 90°
describe a translation using a vector represented by $\begin{pmatrix} x \\ y \end{pmatrix}$, $\overrightarrow{AB}$, or **a**
add and subtract vectors
multiply a vector by a scalar
calculate the magnitude of a vector $\begin{pmatrix} x \\ y \end{pmatrix}$ as $\sqrt{x^2 + y^2}$

Past paper questions

1

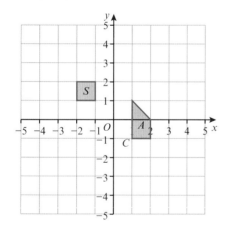

a   On the grid, draw the image of shape A after an enlargement by scale factor 2 about centre C.
[Using Past Paper Question Resource Sheet]   [2]

b   Shape S is the image of a shape **after** a translation by the vector $\begin{pmatrix} 2 \\ 3 \end{pmatrix}$.
On the grid, draw the original shape.   [2]

Cambridge IGCSE International Mathematics (0607) Paper 11 Q22, November 2019

2   $\mathbf{p} = \begin{pmatrix} 12 \\ -5 \end{pmatrix}$

Find

a $2\mathbf{p}$,   (   )   [1]

b $|\mathbf{p}|$.   .... [2]

Cambridge IGCSE International Mathematics (0607) Paper 21 Q9, November 2019

3   OAC is a triangle with $AB:BC = 1:2$ and $OD:DC = 1:2$.

The lines OB and AD intersect at X.

$\overrightarrow{OA} = 6\mathbf{a}$ and $\overrightarrow{OC} = 6\mathbf{c}$.

a   Find an expression, in terms of $\mathbf{a}$ and/or $\mathbf{c}$, for

    i $\overrightarrow{AC}$,

        $\overrightarrow{AC} = $ .... [1]

    ii $\overrightarrow{BC}$,

        $\overrightarrow{BC} = $ .... [1]

    iii $\overrightarrow{BD}$, giving your answer in its simplest form.

        $\overrightarrow{BD} = $ .... [2]

b   Use your answer to **part a iii** to explain why OA and BD are parallel.

    .... [1]

c   Explain why triangle OAX and triangle BDX are similar.

    .... [2]

d   Find an expression, in terms of $\mathbf{a}$ and $\mathbf{c}$, for

    i $\overrightarrow{AD}$,

        $\overrightarrow{AD} = $ .... [2]

    ii $\overrightarrow{XD}$, giving your answer in its simplest form.

        $\overrightarrow{XD} = $ .... [2]

e   Find the ratio area AXO : area BXD.

        .... : .... [2]

Cambridge IGCSE International Mathematics (0607) Paper 41 Q10, November 2018

Chapter 18

Sets

IN THIS CHAPTER YOU WILL:

- understand and use set language and notation to describe sets

- understand and use Venn diagrams involving two sets

> understand and use set language and notation to represent relationships between sets

> understand and use Venn diagrams involving three sets.

1 **a** List the factors of 24.

   b List the factors of 36.

   c List the common factors of 24 and 36.

2 **a** List the prime factors of 40.

   b Find the smallest integer that has exactly 3 prime factors.

3 **a** Find the value of:

   b 3^2 5^2 and 6^2 These are all square numbers.

   c $1 + 2$ $1 + 2 + 3$ $1 + 2 + 3 + 4$ These are all triangle numbers.

KEY WORDS

complement

element

empty set

intersection

set

subset

union

universal set

18.1 Introduction to sets

To understand the ideas used in set theory, you should know the following terms.

- The factor of an integer
- The prime factor of an integer
- The multiples of an integer
- The square numbers
- The triangle or triangular numbers

MATHEMATICAL CONNECTIONS

You used all of these types of numbers in Chapter 1.

square numbers

1   4   9   16   25

triangular numbers

1   3   6   10   15

A **set** is a collection of objects that share a common property. These objects are called the **elements** of the set and may be mathematical objects or not.

The numbers 1, 2, 3, 4… form a set of mathematical objects. The common property is that they are all positive integers. The number 1.5 does not share this property and is not an element of the set.

The words gate, item, four and mist share the common property that they all have four letters. They are all elements of this set.

The positive integers is an example of an infinite set. The number of elements of the set of words with four letters is very large – but not infinite.

More generally, a postage stamp collection is an example of a set. The elements of that set are the postage stamps themselves. The common property they share is that they *are* postage stamps.

The postage stamps in the collection that have been issued by Singapore also form a set. These elements share a more detailed property: *both* that they are postage stamps *and* that they have been issued by Singapore. They form a **subset** of the stamp collection. Similarly, postage stamps from Malaysia form a different subset and the postage stamps issued by European countries form yet another set.

A set can be defined by the common property, for example, the factors of six, or by listing the elements of the set, for example, 1 2 3 6.

So, the two sets, the factors of six and the integers 1 2 3 6, are in fact equal and the set has four elements.

INVESTIGATION 1

List some examples of how sets could be used in everyday life that are not related to numbers.

Could you find sets in a kitchen, or a shopping centre?

MATHEMATICS IN CONTEXT

Set theory is the foundation of many different areas of mathematics and is used extensively in computer science.

For example, let F denote the set of factors of six.

You can express a set by listing its elements inside curly brackets or braces, so in this case you can write $F = \{1, 2, 3, 6\}$.

Then you write 'the number of factors of six is 4' as $n(F) = 4$.

You can also use set builder notation to represent a set, rather than listing all of its elements.

In general, the notation is $\{x \mid$ properties of $x\}$.

The set always starts with $\{x \mid ...\}$ and then the properties of x are given.

So you can also write $F = \{x \mid x$ is a factor of six$\}$

TIP

You can save time by using set notation and by giving the set you are referring to a name.

You should always use a capital letter to refer to a set.

WORKED EXAMPLE 1

Let G be the set of factors of 16.

a Express G using set builder notation and list the elements of G.

b Write down $n(G)$.

Answer

a $G = \{x \mid x$ is a factor of 16$\}$ and $G = \{1, 2, 4, 8, 16\}$

b $n(G) = 5$

Looking at each of the sets F and G you can see that the number 3 is an element of set F but that 3 is not an element of set G. We write this as $3 \in F$ and $3 \notin G$.

The notation for 'is an element of' is $\in$ and 'is not an element of' is $\notin$.

WORKED EXAMPLE 2

Let $P = \{x \mid x \text{ is a factor of } 20\}$ and $Q = \{x \mid x \text{ is a prime factor of } 15\}$.

a Find the number of elements in each set.

b Determine whether there is an element of Q that is not an element of P.

Answers

a $P = \{1, 2, 4, 5, 10, 20\}$

Factors of 15 are 1, 3, 5, 15

Hence $Q = \{3, 5\}$

$\Rightarrow n(P) = 6$ and $n(Q) = 2$

> As your starting point, it is good technique to list the elements of each set.

b Looking at Q, it is clear that 5 is an element of Q and also that 5 is an element of P.

$5 \in Q$ and $5 \in P$

Also that 3 is an element of Q but that 3 is not an element of P.

$3 \in Q$ but $3 \notin P$

So 3 is the required answer.

Sets often involve using inequalities to define the elements of a set.

WORKED EXAMPLE 3

List the elements of the following sets.

a $A = \{x \mid x \leqslant 6, x \text{ is a positive integer}\}$

b $B = \{x \mid -2 \leqslant x < 4, x \text{ is an integer}\}$

c $C = \{x \mid -2 \leqslant x < 4\}$

d $D = \{(x, y) \mid y = 2x + 3, x \leqslant 7, x \text{ is a positive integer}\}$

> **MATHEMATICAL CONNECTIONS**
>
> You learnt how to use inequality notation in Chapter 8.

Answers

a $A = \{1, 2, 3, 4, 5, 6\}$, positive integers only.

b $B = \{-2, -1, 0, 1, 2, 3\}$ -2 is an inclusive inequality and 4 is strict, so the range of elements is from -2 to 3.

c Set C does not have the extra condition that integers only are required. Therefore, **every** number starting from (and including) -2 up to (but not including) 4 is an element of C.
Set C is an infinite set, as it contains all fractions, decimals and irrational numbers that lie within the set.

d Set D is defined as a set of coordinates, with the condition that x is a positive integer less than or equal to 7, so is $\{(1, 5), (2, 7), (3, 9), (4, 11), (5, 13), (6, 15)\}$.

WORKED EXAMPLE 4

Express in set builder notation the set $A = \{3, 4, 5, 6\}$.

Answer

First note that these are integers: this must be stated.

Then decide on inclusive or strict inequality at each end.

There are four possible solutions in this example, depending on whether you chose strict or inclusive inequalities.

Finally, decide on the variable: x

$A = \{x \mid 3 \leqslant x \leqslant 6, x \text{ is an integer}\}$ or

$A = \{x \mid 2 < x \leqslant 6, x \text{ is an integer}\}$ or

$A = \{x \mid 2 < x < 7, x \text{ is an integer}\}$ or

$A = \{x \mid 3 \leqslant x < 7, x \text{ is an integer}\}$

The universal set

DISCUSSION 1

Is the following statement true or false: 'All numbers are either odd or even'?
Discuss this with your partner.
What does the whole class think?

First, define what is meant by an odd number.
Also, define what is meant by an even number.
Is −4 odd or even?
Is 3.4 odd or even?
Is zero an even number?
What is meant by a number?
What does the whole class think?

The problem is that the statement 'all numbers are either odd or even' can be correct or false depending on the type of number that is being discussed.

1   If you are discussing the set of **integers**, then −4 is even and the statement is true.

2   If you are discussing the set of **all possible numbers**, then again −4 is even *but* the statement is *false*.

3   If you are discussing the set of **positive integers**, the statement is *true*, but −4 cannot be considered: −4 *does not exist* in the set of positive integers.

You cannot start to discuss different sets unless you first define what type of number/object you are going to consider.

You *must* define the **universal set** first.

You use the letter U to denote the universal set.

For example, if the universal set is given as U = {first ten positive integers} it can be rewritten as:

U = {1, 2, 3, 4, 5, 6, 7, 8, 9, 10}

You can also use set builder notation to represent the universal set.

Set builder notation for U in this case is U = $\{x \mid 1 \leqslant x \leqslant 10, x \text{ is an integer}\}$.

WORKED EXAMPLE 5

Define the universal set for the following.

a   Singapore postage stamps in a stamp collection.

b $T = \{5, 10, 15, 20, 25...\}$

Answers

a   In a postage stamp collection, the postage stamp collection itself is the obvious universal set.

b   There are many choices. For example:

1   U = $\{x \mid x \text{ is a positive integer}\}$

2   U = $\{x \mid x \text{ is an integer}\}$ [so, positive, negative *and* zero]

3   U = $\{x \mid x \text{ is a rational number}\}$ [integers and fractions].

TIP

In part **a** this is not the only possible universal set: U could be the set of *all* stamps issued worldwide (not just those in this collection).

WORKED EXAMPLE 6

List the elements of the following sets.

a   U = $\{x \mid x \leqslant 6, x \text{ is a positive integer}\}$

b   U = $\{x \mid -2 \leqslant x < 4, x \text{ is an integer}\}$

c   U = $\{x \mid x = y^2, y \leqslant 4, y \text{ is a positive integer}\}$

d   U = $\{x \mid x = 3z, -2 \leqslant x < 1, z \text{ is an integer}\}$

Answers

a   U = {1, 2, 3, 4, 5, 6}

b   U = {−2, −1, 0, 1, 2, 3}

c   U = $\{1^2, 2^2, 3^2, 4^2\}$ = {1, 4, 9, 16}

d   U = {3(−2), 3(−1), 3(0)} = {−6, −3, 0}

Exercise 18.1

 1 Express the set $A = \{3, 4, 5, 6\}$ in set builder notation in three different ways.

 2 Express the set $B = \{2, 4, 6, 8\}$ in set builder notation in two different ways.

> **PEER ASSESSMENT**
>
> Discuss and compare your answers with a partner.
> Is it possible to find all the possible answers?

 3 Use braces to list the elements of each set.

   a A = the first five letters of the alphabet in the English language

   b B = the different types of triangle

   c C = the odd positive integers less than 10

   d D = the even positive integers less than 10

   e E = the letters in the word MISSISSIPPI

   f F = the third, fourth and fifth triangle numbers

   g G = the square numbers greater than 100 and less than 200.

 4 Describe the following sets in words.

   a $P = \{m, a, t, h, s\}$ **b** $Q = \{1, 3, 6, 10, 15\}$

   c $R = \{x, y, z\}$ **d** $S = \{1, 2, 3, 4, 6, 12\}$

   e $T = \{5, 10, 15, 20, 25, 30\}$

 5 Use the correct notation $n(\ )$ to write down the number of elements in each of the sets in Questions **3** and **4**.

 6 List the elements of the following sets.

   a $U = \{x \mid x \leqslant 8, x \text{ is a positive integer}\}$

   b $U = \{x \mid -2 < x \leqslant 4, x \text{ is a positive integer}\}$

   c $U = \{x \mid x = y^2, 2 < y \leqslant 5, y \text{ is an integer}\}$

 7 List the elements of the following sets.

   a $G = \{(x, y) \mid y = 3x + 2, x \leqslant 6, x \text{ is a positive integer}\}$

   b $H = \{(x, y) \mid y = 3x + 2, -3 < x \leqslant 6, x \text{ is an integer}\}$

   c $I = \{(x, y) \mid y = 2x - 3, -6 \leqslant x \leqslant 1, x \text{ is an integer}\}$

   d $J = \{(x, y) \mid y = -3x - 2, x \leqslant 6, x \text{ is a positive integer}\}$

 8 Use 'is an element of' notation and the sets in Questions **3** and **4** to denote an element:

   a of set A and of set P **b** of set D and of set F

   c of set T and of set C **d** of set F but not of set D

   e of set F but not of set T **f** of set Q but not of set S.

9   State a possible universal set for the following sets.

   a A = the first five letters of the alphabet in the English language.

   b C = the odd positive integers less than 10.

   c D = the even positive integers less than 10.

   d E = the letters in the word MISSISSIPPI.

   e G = the square numbers greater than 100 and less than 200.

   f $P = \{a, e, i, o, u\}$

   g $Q = \{1, 3, 6, 10, 15\}$

   h $R = \{x, y, z\}$

   i $S = \{1, 2, 3, 4, 6, 12\}$

   j $T = \{5, 10, 15, 20, 25...\}$

> **TIP**
>
> Remember to use braces.

18.2 Using diagrams to represent sets

You can use Venn diagrams to represent sets visually.

In the diagram the universal set is *always* shown as a rectangle, labelled U.

The set or sets in question are usually shown as labelled circles within the rectangle.

For example, in a postage stamp collection:

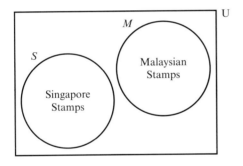

U = {stamps in the collection}

M = {Malaysian stamps (in the collection)}

S = {Singapore stamps (in the collection)}

You will first look at representing one set within the universal set on a Venn diagram.

> **TIP**
>
> Note that the two sets do not overlap since postage stamps *are not issued jointly* by both Singapore and Malaysia.

WORKED EXAMPLE 7

Let $U = \{x \mid 1 \leqslant x \leqslant 10, x \text{ is an integer}\}$ and let $A = \{x \mid x \text{ is a factor of } 12\}$.

Draw a Venn diagram to show this information.

Answer

First, list the elements of the sets:

$U = \{1, 2, 3, 4, 5, 6, 7, 8, 9, 10\}$

$A = \{1, 2, 3, 4, 6, \cancel{12}\}$ 12 is removed!

Draw the Venn diagram:

12 is a factor of 12, but 12 is *not* in the universal set.

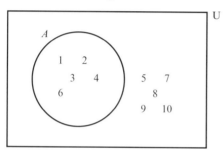

From the diagram you can see that, for example, $6 \in A$ or $5 \notin A$ and also that all ten integers are elements of the universal set.

The complement of a set

You can see from the Venn diagram in Worked example 8 that 5 is not an element of A; however, the integer 5 *is* an element of a set.

The integer 5 belongs to the set of integers that are *not* factors of 12.

You say that the integer 5 is an element of the **complement** of set A, denoted as A'.

This is an important idea: if you define a set by elements within a universal set which *all share a common property,* this automatically creates a second set − the elements within that universal set that *do not* share this property.

WORKED EXAMPLE 8

Let $U = \{\text{first ten positive integers}\}$ and let $A = \{\text{factors of } 12\}$.

List sets A and A'.

Answer

$A = \{1, 2, 3, 4, 6\}$ and $U = \{1, 2, 3, 4, 5, 6, 7, 8, 9, 10\}$

Removing the factors of 12 that lie in U, leaves $A' = \{5, 7, 8, 9, 10\}$.

Exercise 18.2

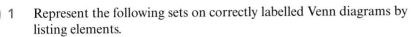

1   Represent the following sets on correctly labelled Venn diagrams by
   listing elements.

   a $M = \{x \mid x \text{ is a multiple of } 4\}$, $U = \{x \mid x \text{ is a factor of } 16\}$
   b $P = \{x \mid x \text{ is a prime number}\}$, $U = \{x \mid x \text{ is one of the first}$
       eight positive integers$\}$
   c $V = \{x \mid x \text{ is a vowel}\}$, $U = \{x \mid x \text{ is one of the first six letters of the}$
       English alphabet$\}$
   d $R = \{x \mid x \text{ is a shape that has four right angles}\}$, $U = \{x \mid x \text{ is a quadrilateral}\}$
   e $T = \{x \mid x \text{ is a triangle number}\}$, $U = \{x \mid x \text{ is one of the first seven}$
       square numbers$\}$

> **TIP**
>
> The vowels in the English language are a, e, i, o and u.

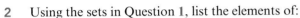

2   Using the sets in Question **1**, list the elements of:

   a M' b P' c R' d T'.

> **REFLECTION**
>
> In Worked example 6, how would you describe the complement of set
> $S = \{\text{Singapore stamps}\}$?

The empty set, $\varnothing$

Recall the idea of the complement, A', of a given set A.

> **WORKED EXAMPLE 9**
>
> Let $U = \{x \mid 4 \le x \le 10, x \text{ is an integer}\}$ $A = \{x \mid x = 2y, y \text{ is an integer}\}$
> and $B = \{x \mid x \text{ is an integer}\}$.
>
> Write down the sets A, A', B, B'.
>
> **Answer**
>
> First write out the sets by listing elements:
>
> $U = \{4, 5, 6, 7, 8, 9, 10\}$
>
> $A = \{x \mid x = 2y, y \text{ is an integer}\}$ is simply the set of even numbers within U:
>
> $A = \{4, 6, 8, 10\}$
>
> Therefore, A' is the set of odd numbers within U:
>
> $A' = \{5, 7, 9\}$
>
> However, B is the set of integers that lie within U, so that $B = \{4, 5, 6, 7, 8, 9, 10\}$.
>
> Hence there are no elements remaining to put in the complement of B:
>
> B' is empty: $B' = \{\ \}$

The set that does not contain any elements is known as the **empty set**.

You can represent the empty set in one of two ways: either as braces with a space between them { } or more usually with the symbol ∅.

INVESTIGATION 2

Consider these statements:

1 You have seen that the complement of the universal set is the empty set: $U' = \varnothing$
So, what is the complement of the empty set? $\varnothing' = ?$

2 If U = {positive integers} and A = {even integers} then what is A' ?
You now know A'.
How would you describe the complement of A'?
Now an important question: What is the complement of A'?

3 So, to be clear: $(A')' =$ $(U')' =$ $(\varnothing')' =$

DISCUSSION 2

If you can use either { } or ∅ to represent the empty set, what does {∅} represent?

Does it represent the empty set? How many elements does {∅} contain?

Subsets

Any set that has all its elements as part of another set can be described as a **subset** of that set.

WORKED EXAMPLE 10

Set A = {even numbers less than 21}

Set B = {multiples of 4 less than 21}

List the elements of A and B and decide if any subsets exist, writing appropriate notation.

Answer

The elements of A are {2, 4, 6, 8, 10, 12, 14, 16, 18, 20}.

The elements of B are {4, 8, 12, 16, 20}.

All of the elements of set B are contained within set A.

So set B is a subset of set A.

We can write this as $B \subset A$.

TIP

Note that the open side of the symbol ⊂ faces the larger set.

WORKED EXAMPLE 11

Let $U = \{x \mid 7 \leqslant x \leqslant 14, x$ is an integer$\}$, $A = \{$prime numbers$\}$ and
$B = \{$multiples of 5$\}$.

a List the three sets.

b Write down all the subsets of A and of B.

Answers

a List the sets:

    $U = \{7, 8, 9, 10, 11, 12, 13, 14\}$

    $A = \{7, 11, 13\}$

    $B = \{10\}$

> $A \subset U$ and $B \subset U$ since you are allowed to use only elements of the universal set.

b Be systematic, starting with the smallest subsets:

Subsets of A:

Subsets with zero elements: $\varnothing \subset A$

Subsets with one element: $\{7\} \subset A$
                                  $\{11\} \subset A$
                                  $\{13\} \subset A$

Subsets with two elements: $\{7, 11\} \subset A$
                                    $\{7, 13\} \subset A$
                                    $\{11, 13\} \subset A$

Subsets with three elements: $\{7, 11, 13\} \subset A$

These eight sets are known as the subsets of A, since all of them contain **fewer** elements than in the original set, A. You use the notation $\subset$ in this case when the subset contains **fewer** elements.

Subsets of B:

Subsets with zero elements: $\varnothing \subset B$

Subsets with one element: $\{10\} \subset B$

Set B is not a subset of set A and we write $B \not\subset A$.

Exercise 18.3

In the following exercise the universal set, $U = \{$non-negative integers$\}$.

1 Write down:

  a the smallest element of U

  b the smallest subset of U

  c $n(U)$.

Consider the following subsets of U.

$A = \{1, 2, 3, 4, 5\}$

$B = \{x \mid 0 \leqslant x \leqslant 5\}$

C = {Number of students absent from today's mathematics lesson}

D = $\{x \mid x + y = 5\}$

E = $\{p \mid p$ is a prime number and a multiple of $10\}$

F = $\{4, 5, 6, 7\}$

G = $\{x \mid x^2$ is less than $50\}$

H = $\{x \mid x < 200\}$

2 Calculate the following.

    a $n(B)$ **b** $n(E)$ **c** $n(D)$

    d $n(G)$ **e** $n(H)$.

3 State whether the following are true or false.

    a $5 \in D$ **b** $E = \varnothing$ **c** $B \subset A$

    d $A \subset B$ **e** $E \subset F$ **f** $\{5\} \in D$

4 State whether the following are true or false.

    a $A \not\subset B$ **b** $A \in D$ **c** $B \not\subset H$ **d** $F \not\subset G$

    e $\varnothing \notin D$ **f** $D \not\subset A$ **g** $\varnothing \in F$ **h** $F \not\subset F$

REFLECTION

There is a lot of new and unfamiliar notation to learn.

Make sure that you know when to use $\in$ and when to use $\subset$.

Finally, write down the answers to $n(\varnothing)$ and $n(\{\varnothing\})$.

18.3 Venn diagrams involving two sets

You can use Venn diagrams to consider situations where there are two sets contained within the universal set.

Depending on the elements of the sets, the diagrams might look different.

The universal set is the rectangle, and the two sets are represented by circles within the rectangle.

If the two sets share some elements, the two circles will intersect.

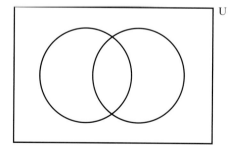

If the two sets do not share any elements, the two circles are distinct.

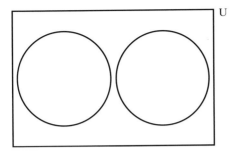

If one set is a subset of the other, one circle is contained within the other circle.

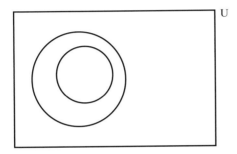

WORKED EXAMPLE 12

Universal set = {positive whole numbers less than 20}

Set A = {even numbers}

Set B = {odd numbers}

As there are no elements in common, the Venn diagram that represents this is:

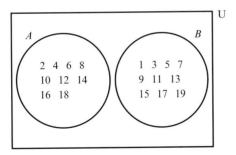

For the same universal set, write down:

set C = {multiples of 2}

set D = {multiples of 3}.

CONTINUED

Answer

Here there are some elements in common, so the Venn diagram looks like this:

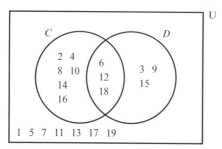

For the same universal set, set E = {multiples of 2}, set F = {multiples of 4}

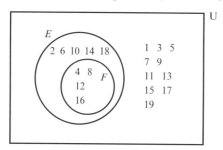

Venn diagrams with two sets can also be shaded to show relationships between them.

The **intersection** of two sets A and B is written as $A \cap B$ and is elements which are common to both sets.

This is represented on a Venn diagram as:

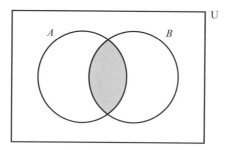

The **union** of two sets is all the elements of both sets and is written as $A \cup B$.
This could be represented as:

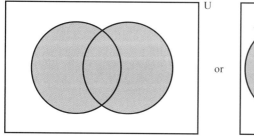 or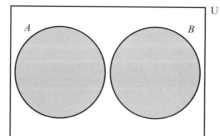

TIP

Be careful. The symbol for the **universal set** looks similar to the symbol for the union of sets.

The union symbol always appears between two sets in set notation

INVESTIGATION 3

Work with a partner to consider how Venn diagrams with two sets can be shaded to show complements of sets.

What would $(A \cap B)'$ look like?

What about $(A \cup B)'$ or $A \cap B'$ or $A \cup B'$?

If set B is a subset of set A, how would a Venn diagram be shaded to show:

$A \cap B$

$A \cup B$?

Exercise 18.4

In the following exercise use the universal set, U = {non-negative integers}

Once you have listed sets A and B, it is best to draw a Venn diagram for each question.

1   $A = $ {factors of 20} and $B = $ {factors of 30}
    List the following sets.
    A
    B
    $A \cap B$
    $A \cap B'$
    $A' \cap B$

2   $A = \{x \mid 0 < x < 10\}$ and $B = $ {factors of 15}
    List the following sets.
    A
    B
    $A \cap B$
    $A \cap B'$
    $A' \cap B$

3   $A = \{x \mid 6 \leqslant x < 11\}$ and $B = $ {first five positive multiples of 3}
    a   List the following sets.
        A
        B
        $A \cap B$
        $A \cap B'$
        $A' \cap B$
    b   True or false: $n(A) + n(B) = n(A \cap B) + n(A \cap B') + n(A' \cap B)$?

4   $A = \{x \mid 1 \leqslant x < 5\}$ and $B = \{x \mid 5 \leqslant x < 8\}$
    a   List the following sets.
        A
        B
        $A \cap B$
        $A \cap B'$
        $A' \cap B$
    b   True or false: $n(A) + n(B) = n(A \cap B) + n(A \cap B') + n(A' \cap B)$?

5   $C = \{x \mid -3 < x < 10, x \text{ is an integer}\}$

$D = \{x \mid -1 < x < 6, x \text{ is an integer}\}$

True or false, $D \subset C$?

6   List the sets:

$A \cup B$

$(A \cup B)'$

$A' \cup B$

$A \cup B'$

for each Venn diagram.

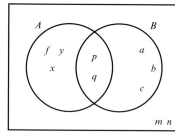 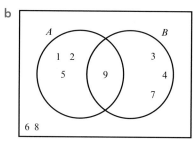 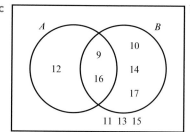

In Questions **7–11**, list the sets U, A and B and then draw a Venn diagram.

7   $U = \{x \mid 1 \leqslant x \leqslant 8\}$ $A = \{\text{factors of } 6\}$ and $B = \{\text{factors of } 8\}$

List the following sets.

$A \cup B$

$(A \cup B)'$

$A \cup B'$

8   $U = \{x \mid 1 \leqslant x \leqslant 9\}$ $A = \{x \mid 4 < x < 8\}$ and $B = \{\text{factors of } 9\}$

List the following sets.

$A \cup B$

$A' \cup B$

$A \cup B'$

9   $U = \{x \mid 3 \leqslant x < 10\}$ $A = \{x \mid x > 5\}$ and $B = \{x \mid 4 < x \leqslant 6\}$

List the following sets.

$(A \cup B)'$

$A' \cup B$

$A \cup B'$

10 $U = \{x \mid 4 \leqslant x \leqslant 10\}$ $A = \{x \mid 6 \leqslant x < 11\}$ and $B = \{\text{even numbers}\}$

List the following sets.

$(A \cup B)'$

$A' \cup B$

$A \cup B'$

11 Shade the given regions on the Venn diagrams.

a

A

B

$A \cup B$

$A \cap B$

$A \cap B'$

$A' \cap B$

$(A \cap B)'$

$(A \cup B)'$

$A \cup B'$

$A' \cup B$

$A' \cap B'$

$A' \cup B'$

b Does $A' \cup B' = (A \cap B)'$? Use the diagrams to help you.

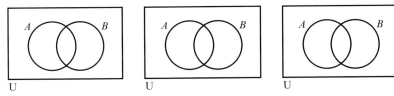

c Does $A' \cup B' = (A \cap B)'$? Use the diagrams to help you.

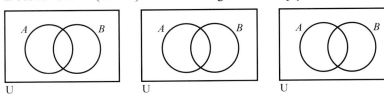

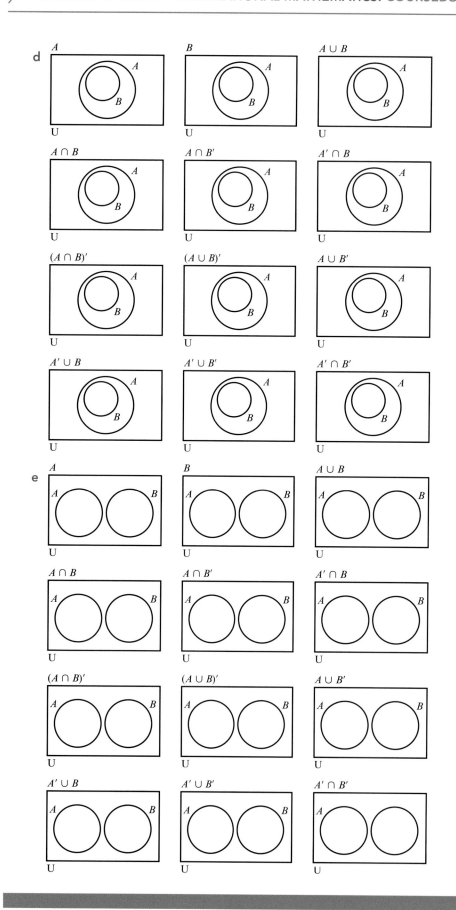

Work with a partner and provide examples that show that you understand:
* set notation
* how to draw a Venn diagram from given information
* how to interpret a Venn diagram
* how to solve problems by drawing and interpreting an adapted Venn diagram.

18.4 Three sets on a Venn diagram

Venn diagrams can also be used to represent the relationships between three sets. It might be that one of the three sets is a subset of one of the others.

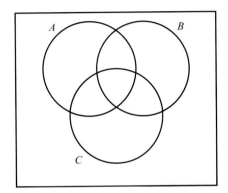

WORKED EXAMPLE 13

Universal set = {positive whole numbers less than 20}

Set A = {odd numbers}

Set B = {multiples of 3}

Set C = {square numbers}

Draw a Venn diagram to show these sets.

Answer

The Venn diagram to represent these sets would look like:

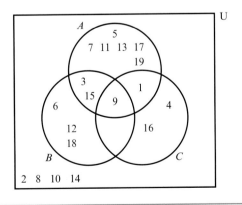

WORKED EXAMPLE 14

Universal set = {positive whole numbers less than 13}

Set A = {odd numbers}

Set B = {multiples of 3}

Set C = {multiples of 12}

Draw a Venn diagram to show these sets.

Answer

The Venn diagram to represent these sets would look like:

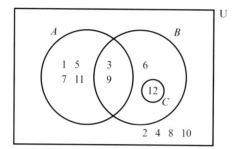

PEER ASSESSMENT

With a partner, agree and sketch Venn diagrams that show unions, intersections and complements of combinations of three sets.

What does $A \cup B \cup C$ look like?

How about $A \cap B \cap C$?

INVESTIGATION 4

Can you find three sets that would have elements in each section of the following Venn diagram?

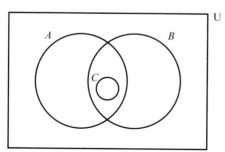

Combining intersection and union with three sets

You must use brackets when combining intersection and union in a three-set expression.

TIP

We use brackets when using set notation in the same way as we do when we are completing calculations. The brackets tell us which operation must be completed first.

WORKED EXAMPLE 15

On a Venn diagram, shade the regions:

a $(A \cap B) \cup C$

b $A \cap (B \cup C)$

TIP

Look at the two expressions. They are identical apart from the brackets.

Answers

a $(A \cap B) \cup C$

Start with the expression in brackets: $(A \cap B)$. This corresponds to regions 1 and 2, as shown in the first diagram.

Consider next, set C. This corresponds to regions 1, 3, 4, 7, as shown in the second diagram.

Since $(A \cap B)$ connects to C by **union**, $\cup$, regions 1 and 2 are added to regions 1, 3, 4, 7.

Hence $(A \cap B) \cup C$ corresponds to regions 1, 2, 3, 4, 7, as shown in the final diagram.

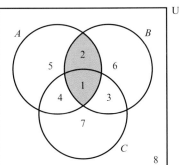 ∪ 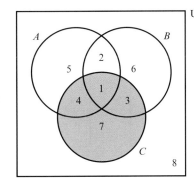  =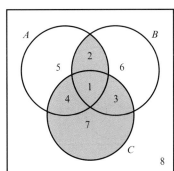

CONTINUED

b $A \cap (B \cup C)$

Start with the expression in brackets: $(B \cup C)$.

This corresponds to regions 1, 2, 3, 4, 6, 7, as shown in the first diagram.

Consider next, set A. This corresponds to regions 1, 2, 4, 5, as shown in the second diagram.

In this case, $(B \cup C)$ connects to A by intersection, $\cap$, therefore identify the regions **common to both** sets. These are regions 1, 2, 4.

Hence $A \cap (B \cup C)$ corresponds to the regions 1, 2, 4, as shown in the final diagram.

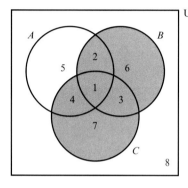 $\cap$ 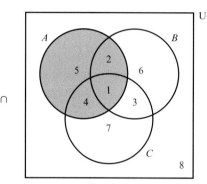 $=$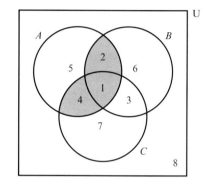

$(A \cap B) \cup C$ and $A \cap (B \cup C)$ are completely different regions on the Venn diagram.

The use of brackets is vital.

Exercise 18.5

Shade the appropriate regions on the Venn diagrams.

a i A
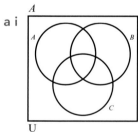

ii B
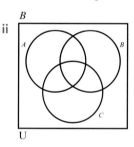

iii $A \cup B$
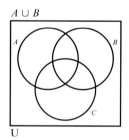

b i $A \cup C$
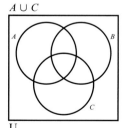

ii $B \cup C$
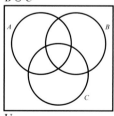

iii $A \cap B$
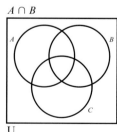

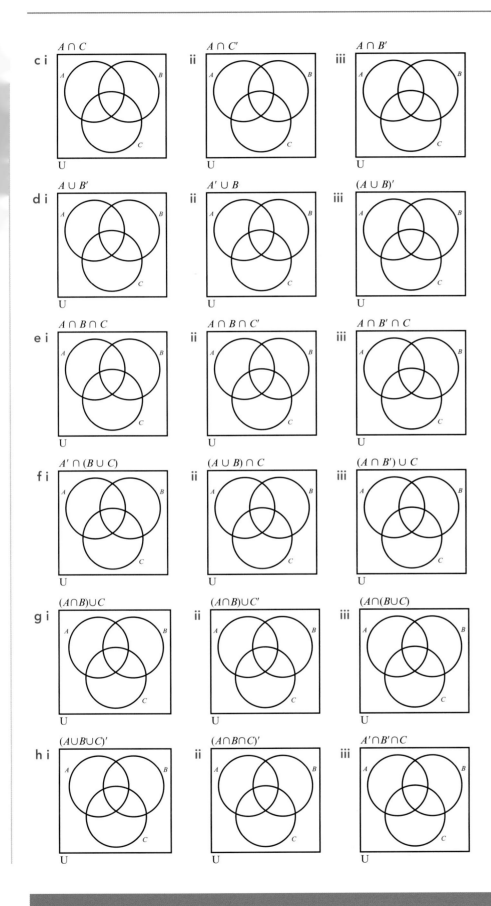

c i $A \cap C$ ii $A \cap C'$ iii $A \cap B'$

d i $A \cup B'$ ii $A' \cup B$ iii $(A \cup B)'$

e i $A \cap B \cap C$ ii $A \cap B \cap C'$ iii $A \cap B' \cap C$

f i $A' \cap (B \cup C)$ ii $(A \cup B) \cap C$ iii $(A \cap B') \cup C$

g i $(A \cap B) \cup C$ ii $(A \cap B) \cup C'$ iii $(A \cap (B \cup C)$

h i $(A \cup B \cup C)'$ ii $(A \cap B \cap C)'$ iii $A' \cap B' \cap C$

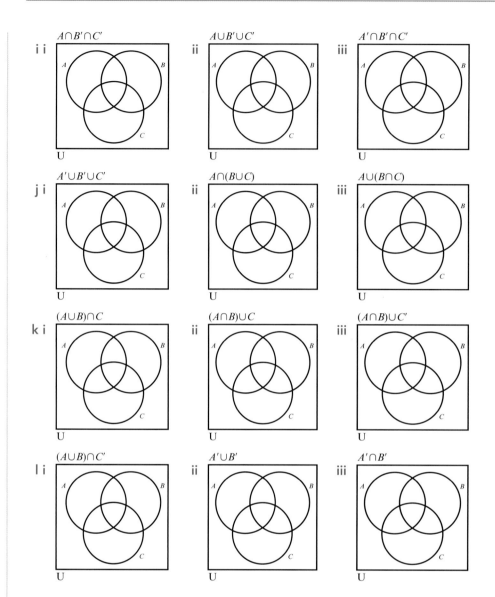

i i $A \cap B' \cap C'$ ii $A \cup B' \cup C'$ iii $A' \cap B' \cap C'$

j i $A' \cup B' \cup C'$ ii $A \cap (B \cup C)$ iii $A \cup (B \cap C)$

k i $(A \cup B) \cap C$ ii $(A \cap B) \cup C$ iii $(A \cap B) \cup C'$

l i $(A \cup B) \cap C'$ ii $A' \cup B'$ iii $A' \cap B'$

Placing elements on a Venn diagram

If the elements of three different sets are listed, you can use a Venn diagram to categorise these elements according to common properties.

WORKED EXAMPLE 16

Consider the following sets.

$U = \{x \mid 1 \leqslant x \leqslant 12, x \text{ is an integer}\}$

$A = \{\text{factors of } 12\}$, $B = \{\text{even integers}\}$, $C = \{\text{multiples of } 3\}$

List the following sets.

a $(A \cap B') \cap C$ and $A \cap (B' \cap C)$

b $(A \cap B') \cup C$

c $(A' \cup B) \cap C$

CONTINUED

Answers

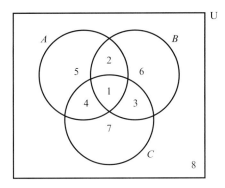

First list the three sets (and the universal set) and identify any elements common to all three sets.

$U = \{1, 2, 3, 4, 5, 6, 7, 8, 9, 10, 11, 12\}$
$A = \{1, 2, 3, 4, 6, 12\}$ 6, 12
$B = \{2, 4, 6, 8, 10, 12\}$ 6, 12
$C = \{3, 6, 9, 12\}$ 6, 12

$6, 12 \in A \cap B \cap C$ 6 and 12 go into region 1

Next, identify the elements that lie in regions 2, 3 and 4.

Region 2 is $A \cap B \cap C'$ so find the elements common to sets A and B (but ignoring 6 and 12).

$A = \{1, 2, 3, 4, 6, 12\}$ 2, 4
$B = \{2, 4, 6, 8, 10, 12\}$ $2, 4 \in A \cap B \cap C'$

Region 3 is $A' \cap B \cap C$ so find the elements common to sets B and C (and ignoring 6 and 12).

$B = \{2, 4, 6, 8, 10, 12\}$
$C = \{3, 6, 9, 12\}$ There are no common elements.

Region 4 is $A \cap B' \cap C$ so find the elements common to sets A and C (and ignoring 6 and 12).

$A = \{1, 2, 3, 4, 6, 12\}$ 3
$C = \{3, 6, 9, 12\}$ $3 \in A \cap B' \cap C$

The partially completed Venn diagram is:

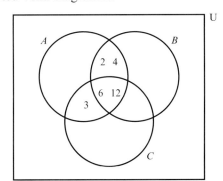

CONTINUED

To complete the Venn diagram, identify any remaining elements left in each of sets *A*, *B* and *C*.

$A = \{1, 2, 3, 4, 6, 12\}$
$B = \{2, 4, 6, 8, 10, 12\}$
$C = \{3, 6, 9, 12\}$

To complete the Venn diagram, identify any unused elements remaining in the universal set:

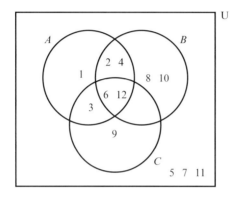

$U = \{1, 2, 3, 4, 5, 6, 7, 8, 9, 10, 11, 12\}$

Now to list the following sets.

a $(A \cap B') \cap C$ and $A \cap (B \cap C')$
b $(A \cap B') \cup C$
c $(A' \cup B) \cap C$

a $(A \cap B') \cap C = (\{1, 3\}) \cap \{3, 6, 9, 12\} = \{3\}$
   $A \cap (B' \cap C) = \{1, 2, 3, 4, 6, 12\} \cap (\{3, 9\}) = \{3\}$

b $(A \cap B') \cup C = (\{1, 3\}) \cup \{3, 6, 9, 12\} = \{1, 3, 6, 9, 12\}$

c $(A \cup B) \cap C = (\{2, 4, 5, 6, 7, 8, 9, 10, 11, 12\}) \cap \{3, 6, 9, 12\} = \{6, 9, 12\}$

TIP

In part **a** of Worked example 19, the final set is the same – even though the methods were different.

When there is no combination of union and intersection, there is no need for brackets.

Exercise 18.6

1 $U = \{x \mid 1 \leqslant x \leqslant 15, x \text{ is an integer}\}$
   $A = \{\text{factors of } 15\}$, $B = \{\text{odd integers}\}$, $C = \{\text{multiples of } 5\}$
   List the following sets.
   a $A' \cap B' \cap C$ b $(B' \cap C') \cup A$ c $(A \cup B') \cap C$

2 $U = \{x \mid 2 \leqslant x \leqslant 14, x \text{ is an integer}\}$
   $A = \{\text{factors of } 14\}$, $B = \{\text{even integers}\}$, $C = \{\text{prime numbers}\}$
   List the following sets.
   a $A' \cap B' \cap C$ b $(C \cup B') \cap A$ c $(B' \cap C') \cup A$

3 $U = \{x | 20 \leqslant x \leqslant 30, x \text{ is an integer}\}$

$A = \{\text{multiples of } 5\}$, $B = \{\text{even integers}\}$, $C = \{\text{multiples of } 3\}$

List the following sets.

a $A' \cap B \cap C$ b $(A \cap B) \cup C$ c $(B' \cup C) \cap A$

4 $U = \{x | 3 \leqslant x \leqslant 12, x \text{ is an integer}\}$

$A = \{\text{factors of } 12\}$, $B = \{\text{even integers}\}$, $C = \{\text{prime numbers}\}$

List the following sets.

a $A' \cap B' \cap C'$ b $(A \cap B') \cup C'$ c $(A \cup C') \cap B'$

SUMMARY

Are you able to... ?
understand and use set language and notation to describe sets
use Venn diagrams to describe sets
understand and use set language and notation to represent relationships between sets
use Venn diagrams to represent relationships between sets.

Past paper questions

1 20 people were asked if they liked banana milk shake, B, or chocolate milk shake, C.

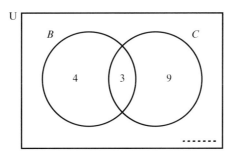

a Complete the Venn diagram. [Using Past Paper Question Resource Sheet]   [1]

b Write down $n(B \cap C)$.

.... [1]

c One of these 20 people is chosen at random.
Find the probability that this person likes

i banana milk shake,

.... [1]

    ii   chocolate milk shake but not banana milk shake.

    .... [1]

  d   On the Venn diagram, shade $C' \cap B$.   [1]

    Cambridge IGCSE International Mathematics (0607) Paper 31 Q9, November 2019

2 $U = \{1, 2, 3, 4, 5, 6\}$ $A = \{2, 4, 6\}$ $B = \{2, 3, 5, 6\}$ $C = \{2, 4\}$

    Complete the following.

  a $A \cap B$ $= \{ .... \}$ [1]

  b B' $= \{ .... \}$ 1]

  c $B \cup C$ $= \{ .... \}$ [1]

  d $n(B \cup C) = ...$ [1]

    Cambridge IGCSE International Mathematics (0607) Paper 11 Q9, November 2017

3   Shade the region indicated in each of these Venn diagrams. [Using Past Paper Question Resource Sheet]

  a   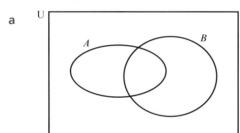 $A' \cap B'$ [1]

  b   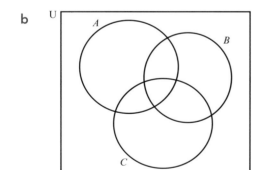 $A \cup (B \cap C)$ [1]

  c   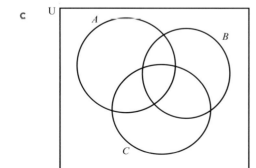 $A \cap B \cap C'$ [1]

    Cambridge IGCSE International Mathematics (0607) Paper 21 Q8, November 2017

Chapter 19

Descriptive statistics

IN THIS CHAPTER YOU WILL:

- use tables to classify statistical data

- recognise continuous and discrete data

- calculate the mean, median, mode, quartiles, range and interquartile range for discrete data

- use a graphic display calculator to calculate the mean, median and quartiles for discrete data and the mean for grouped data

- draw and interpret bar charts, pie charts, pictograms, stem-and-leaf diagrams, frequency distributions

- read, interpret and draw inferences from statistical diagrams

- compare sets of data

> calculate an estimate of the mean for grouped data

> identify the modal class from a grouped frequency distribution.

GETTING STARTED

1   A maths class record the number of letters in their first names to help them with a project in IT. They display the data in a **bar chart** so that they can compare the different lengths of name.

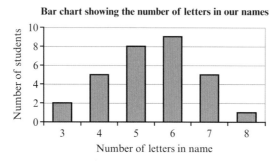

Bar chart showing the number of letters in our names

a   What is the most common number of letters in a name in the maths class?

b   How many students have names with more than four letters?

c   How many more students have names have five letters than names with three letters?

2   A group of people were asked to name their favourite fruit.

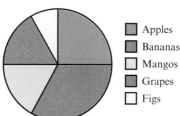

Apples
Bananas
Mangos
Grapes
Figs

a   Estimate what percentage of the group prefers apples.

b   Estimate what fraction of the group prefers bananas.

c   There were 12 people in total in the group. How many people in the group prefer grapes?

d   Who might find data about people's favourite fruits useful or interesting? What might they do with the information?

KEY WORDS

average

bar chart

bimodal

composite bar chart

continuous

discrete

dual bar chart

frequency distributions

grouped data

interquartile range

mean

median

mode

pie chart

quartiles

range

stem-and-leaf diagrams

MATHEMATICS IN CONTEXT

Organisations collect data to improve their products and services, and answer questions. Skilled collection and presentation of data organised into tables, presented in graphs, charts and diagrams can make it easier to see patterns and compare information.

19.1 Classifying and tabulating data

Two types of data are **discrete** and **continuous**.

Discrete data is information that you can count, for example the number of shoes people own. Continuous data is information that you can measure, for example the length of peoples' feet.

WORKED EXAMPLE 1

Members of a youth group were asked what day they would prefer to do an activity, and which activity they would prefer to do. Create a two-way table from this list of responses.

Name	Preferred day	Preferred activity
Abe	Thursday	Bowling
Bev	Thursday	Cinema
Cam	Friday	Cinema
Dee	Thursday	Cinema
Eli	Friday	Bowling
Fay	Thursday	Bowling
Gus	Thursday	Bowling

Answer

Draw a two-way table to organise the data. One direction of the table is 'Preferred day', the other direction is 'Preferred activity'.

Go down the list putting a tally mark in the section of the table that corresponds to the person's response.

Abe prefers Thursday and bowling. Put his tally mark where the vertical section for bowling crosses the horizontal section for Thursday.

	Bowling	Cinema	Total
Thursday	I		
Friday			
Total			

Once you have made all the tally marks, record the totals for each section. Also record the totals for each row and column.

	Bowling	Cinema	Total
Thursday	III (3)	II (2)	5
Friday	I (1)	I (1)	2
Total	4	3	7

> **TIP**
>
> Check that the row total is equal to the column total.

Exercise 19.1

 1 Write 'continuous' or 'discrete' to describe the type of data collected in each of these investigations.

a Investigation into the number of pets in different households.

b Investigation into whether there is a link between a person's height and the width of their hand span.

c Investigation into the average mass of bunches of grapes produced by a vine.

d Investigation into people's favourite pizza toppings.

e Investigation into the change of temperature in different locations over a day.

TIP
Think about whether you would count or measure the data.

 2 This data shows the number of siblings each student in a class has.

0   3   1   1   2   3   0   4   2   1   2   3   1

2   1   3   5   0   2   1   4   1   2   1   3   2

a Is this data discrete or continuous?

b Copy and complete the tally table to organise the data.

Number of siblings	Tally	Frequency
0					
1		
2		
3		
4		
5		

Use your tally table to answer the following questions.

c How many students have one sibling?

d How many students have more than three siblings?

e How many students have an odd number of siblings?

 3 A youth group completed a survey of sports activities. Their responses are shown in this two-way table.

	Football	Hockey	Total
Thursday	28	15	43
Friday	4	18	22
Total	32	33	65

a How many people play football on a Thursday?

b How many people do not play football on a Friday?

c How many people completed the survey in total?

DISCUSSION 1

Gus says that the table shows that the youth group should play hockey on Thursday.

Fay says that the table shows that they should play football on Thursday.

Discuss with a partner or in a small group how Gus and Fay could use data from the table to support what they say.

Do you agree with Gus or Fay? Explain why.

4   This list shows the results some children achieved in an examination and the class they attended.

Name	Class	Result
Hal	1	Merit
Ida	1	Pass
Jeb	1	Merit
Kim	2	Merit
Leo	2	Pass
Mae	1	Merit
Ned	2	Merit
Ola	2	Pass

Name	Class	Result
Pat	2	Merit
Ray	2	Pass
Sal	1	Pass
Tia	2	Pass
Una	1	Merit
Val	1	Merit
Wes	2	Pass
Zoe	1	Merit

a   Create a two-way table for this data.

b   How many children attended Class 2?

c   How many more children gained a Merit than a Pass result?

TIP

You could make the columns the different possible results and the rows the different possible classes. Don't forget to add a total column and row.

DISCUSSION 2

Zoe says: 'The teacher in Class 1 is better than the teacher in Class 2'. Discuss with a partner whether Zoe's statement is true, false, or whether you need more information. Explain your answer.

19.2 Averages, the range and quartiles

There are three types of **average** that can be used to represent a typical value. Condensing the data to a single representative value helps you to describe the data and compare with different data sets.

The **range** helps you to describe, understand and compare sets of data by informing you about how spread out the values are in the data. Using the range you can start to draw conclusions about how consistent the values are, whether there might be extreme values, and how typical the average might be.

WORKED EXAMPLE 2

Sam recorded the maximum temperature each day for two weeks. Here are the temperatures (°C):

2, 5, 3, 2, 6, −4, 0, −3, 1, −2, 3, 6, 3, 9

Find the range and the **mode**, **median** and **mean** averages of the temperatures.

Answer

The range is the difference between the highest and lowest values.

9 is the highest temperature recorded, −4 is the lowest temperature recorded.

The difference between 9 and −4 is 13.

The range is 13.

The mode is the most common value.

The temperature that was recorded the most times is 3 °C.

The mode is 3 °C.

The median is the middle value when the set of values is ordered by size. The set of values ordered by size is:

−4, −3, −2, 0, 1, 2, 2, 3, 3, 3, 5, 6, 6, 9

As there is an even number of values the middle falls between two temperatures.

−4, −3, −2, 0, 1, 2, 2, 3, 3, 3, 5, 6, 6, 9

↑
median

The median is halfway between 2 and 3.

Halfway between 2 and 3 is 2.5.

The median is 2.5 °C.

> **TIP**
>
> This can be calculated by finding the sum of the two values, then dividing by 2.
> $$\frac{(2 + 3)}{2} = 2.5$$

The mean is the sum of all the values in the set, divided by the number of values in the set.

$$\frac{-4 + {-3} + {-2} + 0 + 1 + 2 + 2 + 3 + 3 + 3 + 5 + 6 + 6 + 9}{14}$$

$$= \frac{31}{14} = 2.21 \text{ °C (to 2 dp)}$$

The mean is 2.21 °C (to 2 dp).

Exercise 19.2

1   Sam recorded the maximum temperatures (°C) in different locations around the world for two weeks. For each of these sets of temperatures find the range and the mode, median and mean averages.

    a   21, 23, 24, 27, 24, 25, 19, 22, 25, 27, 30, 25, 27, 26

    b   −6, −2, −2, 1, −3, −5, −3, −1, 0, −4, −5, −7, −6, −5

    c   7.5, 9, 6.7, 5.3, 5.8, 8.1, 6.2, 7.9, 4, 5.5, 8, 9.7, 7.1, 6.9

    d   18, 17, 19, 31, 34, 33, 34, 32, 29, 30, 21, 18, 20, 16

> **TIP**
>
> A set of data can have more than one mode if there is more than one equally most common value. A set of data with two modes is called **bimodal**. Also, if there is not a value that is most common then the data has no mode.

DISCUSSION 3

The three types of average have advantages and disadvantages that help you to describe a set of data in a meaningful way.

a   Discuss with a partner or in a small group which of these descriptions of advantages and disadvantages matches each of the types of average (mean, median and mode).

A

Type of average	Advantages	Disadvantages
?	This type of average uses all of the data so is usually most representative.	This average is not always a data value. The average may be distorted by extreme data values.

B

Type of average	Advantages	Disadvantages
?	This type of average is easy to find in tallied data. The average is always a data value.	Sometimes a data set might not have this type of average. It is not always a good representation of the data set.

C

Type of average	Advantages	Disadvantages
?	This type of average is not distorted by extreme data values.	The average is not always a data value.

b   Look at the averages for the sets of temperatures Sam recorded in Question **1** in Exercise 19.2. Discuss with your partner or in a small group which of the averages best and worst represent the average temperature for each location.

INVESTIGATION

Find a set of five numbers that have the same mean, median, mode and range.

Create a similar investigation to give to your partner to investigate. Make sure you know the solution.

19.3 Quartiles, interquartile range and using a graphical display calculator

You can divide an ordered set of data into sections. When you divide the ordered set into four equal sections the set is divided into quarters. The **quartiles** are at the dividing lines on the set of ordered data when it is divided into quarters.

Quartile 2 (Q2) is also the median of the data.

Quartile 1 (Q1), also called the lower quartile (LQ), is the median of the lower half of the data.

Quartile 3 (Q3), also called the upper quartile (UQ), is the median of the upper half of the data.

The **interquartile range** is a measure of spread from Q1 to Q3. The middle half of the set of data is in the interquartile range. It is useful for understanding the spread of the data without being influenced by extreme values.

Interquartile range = Q3 – Q1

WORKED EXAMPLE 3

Here are some marks scored by students in a test:

72 52 63 58 81 58 95 77 67 60 82 72 88

What is the interquartile range of the test scores? Use your GDC to check the answer and to find the mean and median.

Answer

First order the scores:

52 58 58 60 63 67 72 72 77 81 82 88 95

Find the median (Q2):

52 58 58 60 63 67 72 72 77 81 82 88 95

The median is 72.

Find the lower quartile by finding the median of the lower half of the scores:

52 58 58 60 63 67 (72 72 77 81 82 88 95)

Q1 = 59

Find the upper quartile by finding the median of the higher half of the scores:

(52 58 58 59 63 67 72) 72 77 81 82 88 95

Q3 = 81.5

Subtract Q1 from Q3:

Q3 − Q1 = 81.5 − 59 = 22.5

The interquartile range is 22.5

Check the result using your GDC.

> TIP
>
> If the median lands on a data value, ignore it and find the median of the values lower than this to find the lower quartile.

CONTINUED

Step 1: Select **Statistics** from the main menu. The Statistics function is highlighted in the following image.

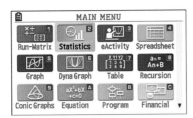

The following screen opens.

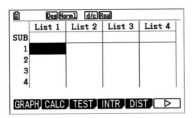

Step 2: Enter the unordered scores by inputting the values and pressing **EXE** between them.

Step 3: Press **CALC** and then **F1** to show the following screen.

```
1-Variable
x̄    =71.1538461
Σx   =925
Σx²  =67841
σx   =12.4767238
sx   =12.9861859
n    =13            ↓
```

Step 4: Scroll through the results using the toggle button to find Q1 and Q3.

```
1-Variable
minX =52            ↑
Q1   =59
Med  =72
Q3   =81.5
maxX =95
Mod  =58            ↓
```

Q3 − Q1 = 81.5 − 59 = 22.5

Median = 72

The mean is the result defined as $\bar{x} = 71.2$ (3 sf)

Grouped data

WORKED EXAMPLE 4

The children at a youth club have started collecting badges. This frequency table shows how many children have collected different numbers of badges.

Number of badges	Frequency
1–4	2
5–8	3
9–12	6
13–16	7
17–20	6

Use your GDC to:

a find an estimate of the mean of this data

b identify the modal class for this data

c find the mean of this data without using a GDC.

Answers

a As the data is grouped you cannot know exactly how many badges are collected.

For each group find the midpoint of the values.

For example, in the group 1–4 badges the midpoint is 2.5. This can be calculated by adding the two end point values and dividing by 2.
$(1 + 4) \div 2 = 2.5$

Number of badges	Midpoint	Frequency
1–4	2.5	2
5–8	6.5	3
9–12	10.5	6
13–16	14.5	7
17–20	18.5	6

To estimate the total number of badges in each category you assume that each child in a group collected the midpoint amount of badges for that group.

Number of badges	Midpoint	Frequency	Estimated total badges
1–4	2.5	2	$2.5 \times 2 = 5$
5–8	6.5	3	$6.5 \times 3 = 19.5$
9–12	10.5	6	$10.5 \times 6 = 63$
13–16	14.5	7	$14.5 \times 7 = 101.5$
17–20	18.5	6	$18.5 \times 6 = 111$
		Total number of children = 24	Sum of estimated total badges = 300

TIP

A frequency table is a table showing how many times each item occurs.

CONTINUED

You can estimate the mean by dividing the estimated total number of badges by the number of children.

$$\text{The estimated mean} = \frac{\text{Sum of estimated total badges}}{\text{Number of children}} = \frac{300}{24} = 12.5$$

The estimated mean number of badges collected was 12.5.

b   The modal class is the class with the highest frequency, which in this example is 13–16 badges.

c   You can use your GDC to enter grouped data.

Step 1:   Select **Statistics** from the main menu. The Statistics function is highlighted in the following image.

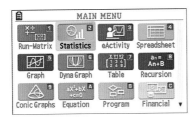

The following screen opens.

Step 2:   Enter the mid-point values of the number of badges in List 1. Enter the frequency values in List 2.

Step 3:   Press **SET** and specify List 2 as the frequency values.

CONTINUED

Step 4: Press EXIT and then F1 to show the analysis.

```
📄         Deg Norm1 d/c Real
1-Variable
x̄      =12.5
Σx     =300
Σx²    =4326
σx     =4.89897948
sx     =5.00434593
n      =24              ↓
```

The mean is the result, defined as $\bar{x} = 12.5$.

Exercise 19.3

1   These are the daily wages of employees at a small company.

$100 $90 $160 $300 $80 $100 $120 $120 $80

   a   What is the range of the wages?
   b   What is the median of the wages?
   c   What are the lower and upper quartiles of the wages?
   d   What is the interquartile range of the wages?

2   A plant grower wants to compare the growth of two different types of seeds. The plants are measured after three months growing. These are the heights in centimetres.

Seed A   43   35   31   44   50   49   52   48   37   48
Seed B   62   25   46   34   65   22   15   57   28   42

   a   Copy and complete the table for the two seed types.

	Shortest height (cm)	Tallest height (cm)	Median (cm)	Interquartile range
Seed A				
Seed B				

   b   Use the information in your table to compare the two seed types. Which type would you recommend to the plant grower and why?

3 Amy wanted to know how to arrange tables in her restaurant to seat groups of people. She recorded how many people there were in each group entering the restaurant one evening. This frequency table shows how many groups of each number of people she recorded.

Number of people in the group	Frequency
1	3
2	19
3	10
4	16
5	7
6	5
7	0
8	2

a Enter the table into your graphical display calculator.

b Use the calculator to find the:

    i total number of groups

    ii total number of people

    iii the mean number of people in a group ($\bar{x}$)

    iv the median number of people in a group

    v the lower quartile (Q1)

    vi the upper quartile (Q3).

> **TIP**
>
> Your graphical display calculator can calculate properties of a data set from a table. Set your calculator to 'statistics' mode. Use the settings to tell your calculator that the table is a frequency table. Check that the calculator is in the correct mode and settings by comparing the output of the calculator with your own estimate for one or more of the properties.

DISCUSSION 4

With a partner, explore the other properties of the data that your graphical display calculator can calculate. Discuss which properties you think would be more or less useful for Amy in choosing the arrangement of tables in her restaurant.

4 A youth club recorded how many children have collected different numbers of badges.

Number of badges	Frequency
1–10	2
11–20	6
21–30	10
31–40	5
41–50	1

a What is the modal group?

b What is the estimated mean number of badges collected?

5 These frequency tables show the ages of people using two different buses.

Bus A

Age of people on the bus (years)	Frequency
0 to 15	17
16 to 30	6
31 to 45	3
46 to 60	4
61 to 75	9
76 to 90	2

Bus B

Age of people on the bus (years)	Frequency
0 to 15	4
16 to 30	6
31 to 45	8
46 to 60	6
61 to 75	12
76 to 90	4

a Use your graphical display calculator to calculate an estimated mean age of the people on Bus A.

b Use your graphical display calculator to calculate an estimated mean age of the people on Bus B.

DISCUSSION 5

Discuss with your partner or in a small group the differences in ages between the people on the two buses. Think of reasons why the people on the two buses might be different ages. Write some questions that you would ask to find out why the people on the two buses are different ages.

19.4 Graphs, charts and diagrams

There are many different useful graphs, charts and diagrams that you can use to present and interpret data, including bar charts, pie charts, pictograms, stem-and-leaf diagrams and frequency distributions.

You can also use charts and diagrams to compare data sets.

WORKED EXAMPLE 5

Draw **one** bar chart so that the data in this table can be easily compared.

Favourite sport	Year 1	Year 2	Year 3
Cricket	9	4	11
Football	10	19	7

TIP

To use the graphical display calculator to find the estimated mean of **grouped data**, first work out the midpoint of each group and use the midpoint value for column 1 in the table on the calculator.

TIP

Frequency distributions are sometimes called frequency diagrams

TIP

Pie charts and pictograms are used in Questions **1–3** of Exercise 19.4

CONTINUED

Answer

There are two different ways to show the data in one bar chart.

A **dual bar chart** shows the data side by side.

Draw the axes so that there is space for the highest individual frequency. The highest value in the table is 19 so the vertical axis goes up to 20. Along the horizontal axis group the bars according to one of the variables. In this bar chart the years are grouped, so there is a bar for football and a bar for cricket for each year.

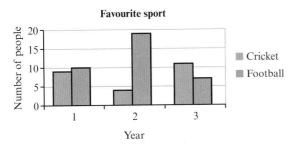

A **composite bar chart** shows the data stacked.

Draw the axes so that there is space for the highest sum of frequencies for the variable. For the variable 'years' the highest sum is for Year 2, which is 23, so the vertical axis goes up to 25. In this bar chart each year is represented by a bar, with the frequency for each sport stacked on that bar.

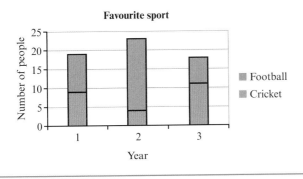

TIP

Always include a key to explain the second variable.

A **stem-and-leaf diagram** allows you to group data, without losing any of the detail of the original data. Data can be grouped according to a common stem, such as numbers in their twenties. The grouping is described using a key. The data should be ordered before analysis.

WORKED EXAMPLE 6

Ava recorded the ages of people entering a museum one afternoon. These are the ages recorded in years:

45   43   11   14   68   70   16   16   33   28   52   48   56

24   33   35   42   21   30   8   27   9   43   67   68

Create a stem-and-leaf diagram of the data.

CONTINUED

Answer

The ages are all two-digit numbers with no decimal places. Make the tens digit the stem and the ones digit the leaf.

stem	leaf
0	8 9
1	1 4 6 6
2	8 4 1 7
3	3 3 5 0
4	5 3 8 2 3
5	2 6
6	8 7 8
7	0

Add a key to explain the units for the stem and the leaf.

Key: 4 | 5 means 45 years old

Rearrange the diagram so that the data is in numerical order.

Key: 4 | 5 means 45 years old

stem	leaf
0	8 9
1	1 4 6 6
2	1 4 7 8
3	0 3 3 5
4	2 3 3 5 8
5	2 6 9
6	7 8 8
7	0

Exercise 19.4

1   A group of students recorded the number of different types of vehicle that entered the school car park one morning. These pictograms show what the students saw between 09:00 and 09:30, and again between 10:00 and 10:30.

Key : ⊚ = 8 vehicles

Number of vehicles entering the car park between 08:30 and 09:00

Type of vehicle	Frequency
Car	⊚⊚⊚⊚⊚⊚
Bicycle	⌒
Motorcycle	⊚⌒
Van	⊚⊚⊚⌒
Bus	⌒

Number of vehicles entering the car park between 09:30 and 10:00

Type of vehicle	Frequency
Car	⊚⊚⊚⊚⊚⌒
Bicycle	⌒
Motorcycle	⌒
Van	⊚⊚⊚⊚
Bus	⌒

a   How many cars entered the car park between 08:30 and 09:00?

b   How many buses entered the car park between 09:30 and 10:00?

c   During which period of time did most vans enter the car park?

d   How many more motorcycles entered the car park between 08:30 and 09:00, than between 09:30 and 10:00?

e   During which period of time was the car park busiest? Explain your answer using statistics from the pictograms. What other information would you need to answer this question more fully?

2   This table shows the number of tickets sold during a festival.

Festival day	Number of tickets sold
Thursday	87
Friday	103
Saturday	174
Sunday	172

a   Create a pictogram showing the number of tickets sold during the festival.

TIP

Choose a picture to represent a number of tickets. Choose a way to divide that picture so that it can represent smaller numbers of tickets. Don't forget to include a key.

REFLECTION

With your partner or in a small group compare and discuss the different pictograms you have drawn. Reflect on how the choice of key makes the pictogram easier or more difficult to interpret.

3   a   This table shows the different expenses Ella had on a trip.

Expense	Cost
Food and drink	$36
Entertainment	$32
Gifts	$21
Tour	$17

Present Ella's expenses in a pie chart.

b   This pie chart shows Kay's expenses on a trip.

Kay's expenses

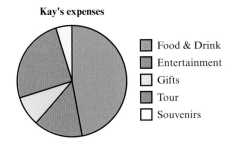

- Food & Drink
- Entertainment
- Gifts
- Tour
- Souvenirs

TIP

To draw a pie chart first calculate the sum of values in the data set (n). Each value is represented by an angle in the chart that can be calculated by multiplying the value by $\frac{360°}{n}$. Always include a title and a key with your pie chart.

For each of these statements write whether it is 'True', 'False' or you 'Need more information'.

i   Kay spent approximately 25% of their money on a tour.

ii   Kay spent over half of their money on food and drink.

TIP

A good understanding of fractions and percentages, including knowing equivalence between the forms is helpful in interpreting pie charts and other graphs.

    iii   Kay spent less money than Ella on entertainment.

    iv   Kay spent more money than Ella on souvenirs.

    v   Kay's tour was more expensive than Ella's tour.

c   Where the answers in **b** are 'Need more information', explain what other information you need to know if the statements are true or false.

4   These two bar charts show the goals scored for five teams in a tournament last year and this year.

A Dual bar chart showing the goals scored in the tournament

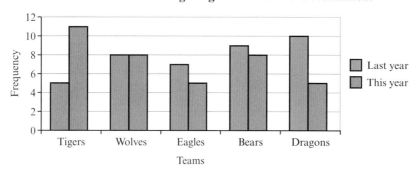

B Composite bar chart showing the goals scored in the tournament

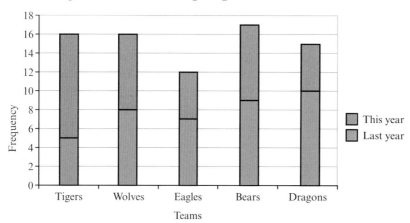

a   Which team scored the most goals in the tournament this year?
Is this information more clearly represented on chart A or chart B?

b   Which team scored the largest total number of goals over both years?
Is this information more clearly represented on chart A or chart B?

c   How many more goals did the Bears score last year than this year?
Is this information more clearly represented on chart A or chart B?

5   A café recorded how many hot and cold drinks they sold over five days to help them understand what stock they should purchase in the future.

The drinks sold are represented in this bar chart.

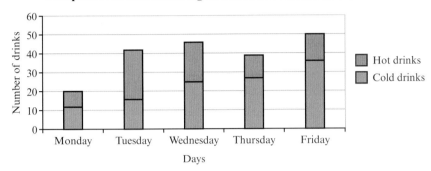

Composite bar chart showing the number of drinks sold at a café

a   How many hot drinks were sold on Friday?

b   How many drinks in total were sold on Wednesday?

c   How many more cold drinks were sold on Friday than on Tuesday?

d   Approximately how many cold drinks were sold in total over the five days?

DISCUSSION 6

Discuss with your partner or in a small group. What reasons could there be for the change in number of cold drinks sold during the week?
What other data would be useful to find the reason for the change in number of cold drinks sold?

6   This bar chart compares the interest rates at three banks.

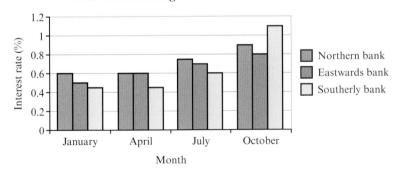

Bar chart showing interest rates at three banks

a   Which bank has the highest percentage rate in July?

b   What was the percentage rate at Southerly Bank in April?

c   What is the difference between the percentage rate at Northern Bank and the percentage rate at Eastwards Bank in October?

DISCUSSION 7

Gus says: 'The data in this bar chart would not be as usefully represented in a composite bar chart.' Discuss with your partner or in a small group whether Gus is correct.

TIP

You could sketch the graph as a composite bar chart and discuss what the bars represent.

7 This table shows the votes received for two candidates in committee elections over four years.

	Year 1	Year 2	Year 3	Year 4
Alex	38	61	21	49
Dana	20	38	59	52

a Draw a composite bar chart to represent the data in the table.

b Use your bar chart to answer these questions.

   i Which candidate received more votes in Year 1?

   ii How many people in total voted in Year 2?

   iii Approximately what fraction of the vote did Dana receive in Year 3?

   iv In which year did the most people vote?

8 A farmer records the mass of 30 strawberries to find their average size and range of sizes. This is a stem-and-leaf diagram of the mass of the strawberries recorded.

Key: 8 | 6 means 8.6 g

stem	leaf
8	6
9	3 8
10	2 7 7 8
11	0 1 5 5
12	2 2 5 5 6 9 9
13	0 1 7 7 7 9
14	3 4 4 8
15	1 3

a What is the range of the mass of the strawberries?

b What mass represents the mode?

c What is the median mass of the strawberries?

9 The farmer also records the mass of 30 potatoes to find their average size and range of sizes. Mass of potatoes in grams:

213	205	198	217	210	235	208	244	217	229
183	254	235	227	224	189	241	216	193	200
181	224	240	222	241	210	224	236	248	221

a Draw a stem-and-leaf diagram of the mass of potatoes. Use the key 22 | 1 means 221 g.

b What is the range of the data?

c What is the mode of the data?

d What is the median of the data?

10 This table shows grouped discrete data for the scores students got on a spelling test.

Score	Frequency
1–4	3
5–8	2
9–12	5
13–16	8
17–20	7

TIP

Because the data is grouped numerically you do not need to leave gaps between the columns. This type of graph is called a frequency distribution.

a Copy and complete the frequency distribution.

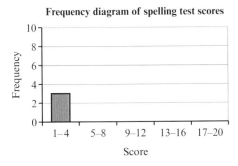

Frequency diagram of spelling test scores

b What is the modal class?

c What is the most number of students that might have scored 20 marks?

d What is the least number of students that might have scored 20 marks?

11 This frequency table of continuous data shows the heights of some students.

Height h (cm)	Frequency
$130 \leqslant h < 140$	1
$140 \leqslant h < 150$	4
$150 \leqslant h < 160$	13
$160 \leqslant h < 170$	11
$170 \leqslant h < 180$	9
$180 \leqslant h < 190$	2

a Copy and complete the frequency distribution for the data in the table.

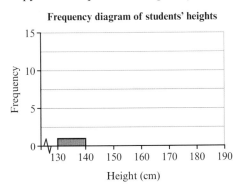

Frequency diagram of students' heights

TIP

Notice that on a frequency distribution for discrete data the horizontal axis has labelled sections. On a frequency distribution for continuous data the horizontal axis is a scale.

b   Which group of heights contains the median?

c   Lea says: 'The range of the data is 60cm, because 190 subtract 130 equals 60.' Is this true, false, or do you need more information?

d   Use your graphical display calculator to calculate the mean height of the class.

12   These are the scores some students achieved in their science test.

34   36   22   18   45   36   14   44   49   30   29   23   18

23   9   42   41   32   38   21   41   33   27   27   39   46

a   Put the scores into a frequency table. You will need to group the data.

b   Draw a frequency distribution to represent the data.

PEER ASSESSMENT

c   Write three questions about the data in your frequency distribution and give them to your partner to answer. Check their answers with your own solutions.

13   These tables show the long jump distances achieved by the students at two different clubs.

Club 1

Distance jumped, d (metres)	Frequency
$1.50 \leqslant d < 1.65$	2
$1.65 \leqslant d < 1.80$	1
$1.80 \leqslant d < 1.95$	8
$1.95 \leqslant d < 2.10$	10
$2.10 \leqslant d < 2.25$	1

Club 2

Distance jumped, d (metres)	Frequency
$1.50 \leqslant d < 1.65$	1
$1.65 \leqslant d < 1.80$	5
$1.80 \leqslant d < 1.95$	6
$1.95 \leqslant d < 2.10$	7
$2.10 \leqslant d < 2.25$	3

a   Create two frequency distribution to show the jumps from the two clubs.

PEER ASSESSMENT

b   Write three questions about the data in your frequency distributions and give them to your partner to answer. Check their answers with your own solutions.

INVESTIGATION 2

You are going to carry out statistical investigations. Consider how you would carry out each of these investigations:

*   Which sport is most popular in your class? How does that compare to another class in your school?

*   What is the most common shoe size in your classroom right now? Would there be a different result on a different day?

CONTINUED

- How many of each different plant is grown in the school grounds? How does the type of plant vary between locations in the light and in the shade?

- If you choose 50 students in your school, what percentage of students will be left-handed? Is there a difference in the percentage of students who are left-handed according to age, gender or another factor?

You could investigate a different question of your own where the data you will collect will be discrete data. Ask your teacher to check your question before you start investigating.

a   Write a sentence explaining what you think will be the result of your investigation and why.

b   Collect your data in a frequency table.

c   Choose two ways to represent your data. You could choose from a bar chart, pictogram, stem-and-leaf diagram, pie chart or frequency distribution.

d   Calculate the averages, range and interquartile range of your data.

e   Discuss your investigation and data with a partner or in a small group. Explain why you chose those two ways of representing your data. Describe any patterns you can see in your data.

f   Does your data suggest that your prediction was correct? Use the information in your table, graph and charts to answer your statistical question.

g   What other questions could you ask to help you answer your question in more detail or to find out more about the subject of your investigation?

SUMMARY

Are you able to... ?
use tables to classify statistical data
recognise continuous and discrete data
calculate the mean, median, mode, quartiles, range and interquartile range for discrete data
use a graphic display calculator to calculate the mean, median and quartiles for discrete data and the mean for grouped data
draw and interpret bar charts, pie charts, pictograms, stem-and-leaf diagrams, frequency distributions.
read, interpret and draw inferences from statistical diagrams
compare sets of data
calculate an estimate of the mean for grouped data
identify the modal class from a grouped frequency distribution.

Past paper questions

1 This table shows the ages of 20 cars.

Age (years)	Frequency
1	2
2	7
3	4
4	3
5	4

a Work out the range.

.... years [1]

b Work out the mean age of the cars.

.... years [3]

Cambridge IGCSE International Mathematics (0607) Paper 11 Q9 November 2021

2 The table shows a set of data.

x	Frequency
5	16
6	18
7	25
8	11
9	6
10	4
Total	80

a When x represents the number of emails Essa receives each day, find
  i the median,

.... [1]

  ii the range,

.... [1]

  iii the upper quartile,

.... [1]

  iv the mean.

.... [2]

b When x represents the height of a seedling, correct to the nearest centimetre, explain why you cannot work out the range of the heights.

....

.... [1]

Cambridge IGCSE International Mathematics (0607) Paper 41 Q4 November 2021

3   The table shows the percentage of students in each of three classes who study physics, chemistry and biology.

	Physics (P)	Chemistry (C)	Biology (B)
Class H	34	28	38
Class J	24	18	58
Class K	46	32	22

Complete the compound bar chart to show this information. [Using Past Paper Question Resource Sheet]

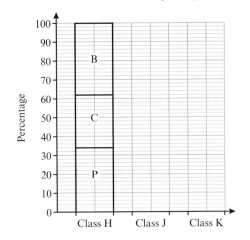

[3]

Cambridge IGCSE International Mathematics (0607) Paper 21 Q4 November 2021

Chapter 20

Cumulative frequency diagrams and linear regression

IN THIS CHAPTER YOU WILL:

- draw scatter diagrams to represent data

- interpret data using scatter diagrams

- learn about correlation

- draw a line of best fit on a scatter diagram

> use a graphic display calculator to find and use the equation of linear regression

> draw and interpret cumulative frequency tables and diagrams

> estimate and interpret the median, percentiles, quartiles and interquartile range from cumulative frequency diagrams.

GETTING STARTED

1   This table shows the shoe size and height of seven people.

Name	Shoe size (EU)	Height (cm)
Abe	37	158
Bev	40	170
Cam	41	182
Dev	38	158
Eli	38	167
Fay	42	175
Gus	40	168

a   How tall is Bev?

b   Who has shoe size 38 and a height of 167 cm?

c   Who has a height of 158 cm but not a shoe size of 37?

d   What is the shoe size of the tallest person?

e   What is the height of the person with the smallest shoe size?

f   How many people are taller than 170 cm?

2   These are the scores 13 people achieved on a computer game.

2005, 1898, 3500, 2376, 1612, 2879, 3076, 2910, 2878, 3513, 1688, 3102, 2244

a   What is the range of these scores?

b   What is the mean?

c   What is the median?

d   What is the lower quartile value?

e   What is the upper quartile value?

f   What is the interquartile range?

MATHEMATICAL CONNECTIONS

You learnt how to work out the averages, range and quartiles of a data set in Chapter 19.

20.1 Draw and interpret scatter diagrams

Scatter diagrams enable you to plot two variables against each other.

The scatter diagram shown here shows the shoe sizes and heights of seven people. Each × on the scatter diagram represents one person. The horizontal scale represents their shoe sizes. The vertical scale represents their heights in centimetres. The circled × represents Bev who has shoe size 40 and height 170 cm.

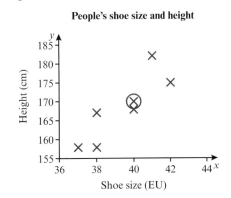

People's shoe size and height

WORKED EXAMPLE 1

This table shows the numbers of years that some children have been in a football team and how many goals they scored in a recent tournament.

Name	Years in a team	Goals scored
Hal	3	4
Ida	1	3
Jeb	2	5
Kim	3	7

Draw a scatter diagram of this data

Answer

Draw axes for your scatter diagram. The horizontal axis represents one variable and the vertical axis represents the other variable.

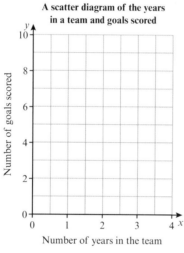

Mark the first data point onto the diagram. Hal has been on the team for 3 years and scored 4 goals in the tournament. Mark an × to represent Hal where 3 years and 4 goals cross.

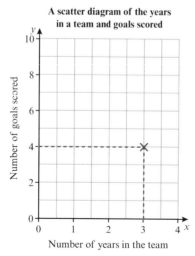

TIP

Make sure that you mark the points clearly. A small cross is a good clear marker to use.

CONTINUED

Plot the other points in the same way.

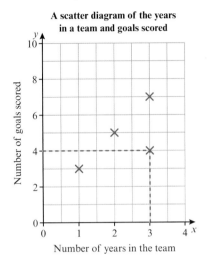

Exercise 20.1

1 a Each of the people from the table in Getting started Question 1 are represented in the scatter diagram at the start of this section. Identify each person on the diagram.

b More people's heights and shoe sizes were collected and added to the scatter diagram as shown.

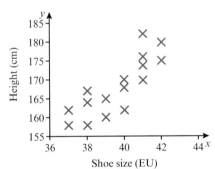

i How many people are represented in this scatter diagram?

ii How many people have a height less than 170 cm?

iii How many people have a shoe size greater than or equal to 40?

2 This is the full list of team members for the football team in Worked example 1.

Name	Years in a team	Goals scored
Hal	3	4
Ida	1	3
Jeb	2	5
Kim	3	7
Leo	0	4
Mae	1	2
Ned	3	0
Ola	0	1
Pat	2	2
Ray	2	6
Sal	3	9
Tia	1	5
Una	2	4

a Draw a scatter diagram to represent the data in the table.

b How many players joined the team this year?

c How many players scored more than 4 goals in the tournament?

3 Data was collected about young children's ages and heights.

6 years old, 108 cm   8 years old, 125 cm   7 years old, 119 cm   10 years old, 145 cm

9 years old, 138 cm   6 years old, 116 cm   10 years old, 129 cm   5 years old, 114 cm

5 years old, 102 cm   7 years old, 125 cm   10 years old, 136 cm   9 years old, 131 cm

6 years old, 120 cm   5 years old, 108 cm   7 years old, 122 cm   8 years old, 127 cm

a Draw a scatter diagram of the children's ages and heights.

b What age is the shortest child?

c How many of the children are taller than 120 cm?

20.2 Correlation and line of best fit

Sometimes when you plot a scatter diagram you can see that there appears to be a relationship between the two variables. This relationship is called **correlation**.

The beginning of this chapter used a scatter diagram of the shoe sizes and heights of seven people showing a trend that as the shoe size increases the height also tends to increase. You can describe the data using correlation.

Positive correlation: as the values on the x-axis increase, the values on the y-axis also increase.

Negative correlation: as the values on the x-axis increase, the values on the y-axis decrease.

Zero correlation: there is no upwards or downwards trend for the values on the y-axis as the x-axis values increase.

MATHEMATICS IN CONTEXT

Scientist, engineers and market researchers use correlation to make predictions in many useful areas such as population growth, strength of materials and the likelihood of products to sell to different consumers.

If there is a correlation between two variables you can draw a **line of best fit** to show the relationship and to make predictions.

This line should be a single ruled line that passes through the mean and extends across the whole data set.

The line should have the correct gradient to match the trend of the plotted points. The line doesn't necessarily need to pass through any of them.

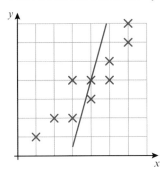 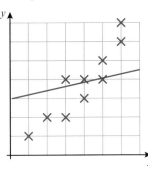 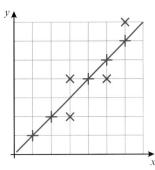

This gradient is too steep. The plotted points do not go up as quickly as this line.

This gradient is not steep enough. The plotted points go up quicker.

This gradient is correct.

The line should go through the middle of the points so that there are approximately the same number of points above the line as below the line.

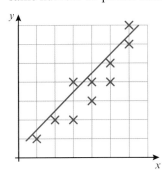 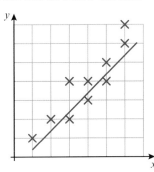 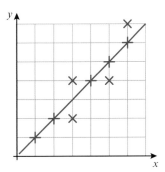

This line is too high. Almost all the points are under it.

This line is too low. Almost all the points are above it.

This line is correct.

WORKED EXAMPLE 2

a   Draw a line of best fit on the scatter diagram.

b   Use your line of best fit to predict the foot length of someone with a hand span of 19.5 cm.

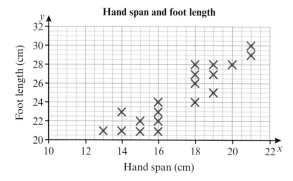

Answers

a   Calculate the mean for each variable.

The mean hand span is 17.2 cm (to 1 dp).

The mean foot length is 24.7 cm (to 1 dp).

Mark the mean point on the diagram.

Place a clear plastic ruler on the diagram so that is goes through the mean point. Rotate the ruler until the gradient matches the trend of the data points.

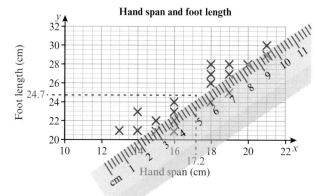

Draw the line of best fit using the ruler.

CONTINUED

b   Draw a vertical line from the point 19.5 on the *x*-axis to find the point where 19.5 cm hand span meets the line of best fit. Draw a horizontal line from this point along to the *y*-axis and read off the vertical scale at that point.

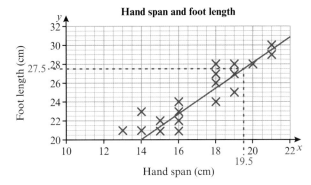

The predicted foot length for someone with a hand span of 19.5 cm will be approximately 27.5 cm.

Using a GDC for linear regression

You can use your graphic display calculator to find and use the **equation of linear regression**.

First you need to ensure that your calculator is in statistics mode.

WORKED EXAMPLE 3

Use your graphic display calculator to plot a scatter diagram of the data in the table. Draw a line of regression and use this line to predict the mark achieved on the test by a student who does 2.5 hours of revision.

Hours of revision	Mark on test
1	1
2	3
3	2
4	6
5	7
6	7

CONTINUED

Answer

Select the Statistics mode.

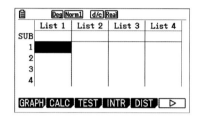

Input the data in the table as a list.
(To remind yourself how to input data as a list, refer back to Chapter 19.)

Input the data in the 'Hours of revision' column as List 1.

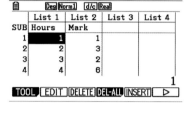

Input the data in the 'Mark on test' column as List 2.

Generate a scatter diagram.

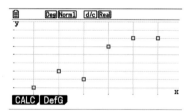

You might need to use the settings, or view, to change the scale to improve the presentation of the diagram. Refer to your calculator's user manual for instructions.

You can see from the scatter diagram that there appears to be a positive correlation between the number of hours of revision and the mark in the test. This means you can use your calculator to calculate and draw a line of best fit, or a line of regression.

Generate the line of regression $y = ax + b$

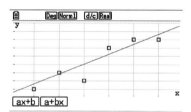

Calculate the predicted mark on the test (y) when the revision (x) = 2.5 hours.

Input the value for x:

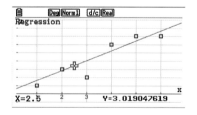

The pink cross marks the predicted value of 3.019 marks for a student who does 2.5 hours of revision. The y-value is also shown under the axis.

Exercise 20.2

1 Which type of correlation do each of these diagrams show? Compare your answers with your partner or in a small group. Discuss any difference and reach an agreement.

a
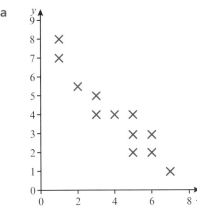

b
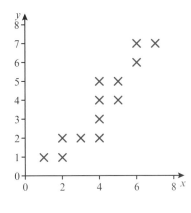

c
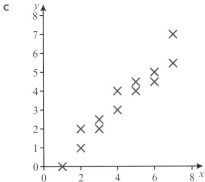

d
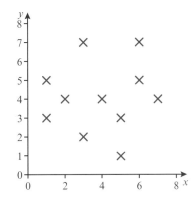

e
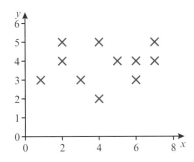

f
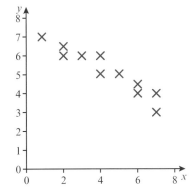

2 A group of students measured their head circumference and recorded the distance that they travelled to school.

Head circumference (cm)	55	57	55	54	56	56	58	56
Distance travelled to school (km)	0.5	1.2	3.6	2.1	1.0	2.8	1.9	1.3

a Plot the data on a scatter diagram.

b Describe the correlation between head circumference and distance travelled to school.

3 A shop records the temperature each day and the number of bags of ice they sell.

The data is represented in this scatter diagram.

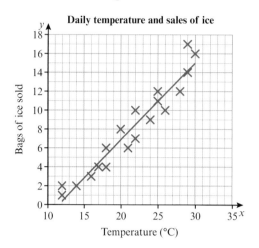

a   What was the lowest temperature recorded?

b   What was the highest number of bags of ice sold in a day?

c   How many bags of ice were sold on the day when the temperature was 24 °C?

d   Describe the correlation between temperature and bags of ice sold.

e   Use the line of best fit to predict how many bags of ice would be sold if the temperature was 19 °C.

f   Use the line of best fit to predict the temperature if 8 bags of ice were sold.

4 A shop records the temperature each day and the number of hot water bottles they sell.

The data is represented in this scatter diagram.

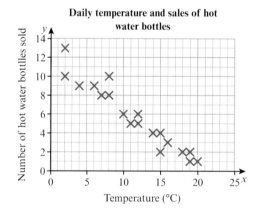

a   What was the highest temperature recorded?

b   What was the highest number of hot water bottles sold in a day?

c   How many hot water bottles were sold on the day that the temperature was 10 °C?

d   Describe the correlation between temperature and hot water bottle sales.

e   Calculate the mean of the temperatures and the mean number of hot water bottles sold. Identify the mean point on the diagram.

f   Place a clear plastic ruler on the scatter diagram where you would put the line of best fit. Ask your partner to check that your line is at the correct gradient and not too high or too low.

g   Using your ruler as the line of best fit, predict the number of hot water bottles that would be sold if the temperature was 9 °C.

5   The ages and masses of ten puppies are recorded in this table.

Puppy age (weeks)	10	8	11	10	12	8	11	8	12	11
Puppy mass (kg)	3.1	2.5	4.3	3.8	4.8	2.9	3.8	3.1	4.2	3.2

a   Plot the data from the table onto a scatter diagram.

b   Calculate the mean of the age of the puppies and the mean of their mass.

c   Draw a line of best fit.

d   Use your line of best fit to predict the mass of a 9-week-old puppy.

6   Some children at an athletics club record their ages and the time it took them to run 100 m. The ages and times are recorded in this table.

Age (years)	Time to run 100 m (seconds)
12	14.2
13	13.5
11	15.5
15	11.7
11	19.8
13	16.9
15	12.6
11	21.9
12	17.3
13	15.0

a   Plot the data from the table onto a scatter diagram.

b   Calculate the mean age and their mean time.

c   Draw a line of best fit.

d   Use your line of best fit to predict the time to run 100 m for a 14 year old.

7 Six gardeners planted a plant. A few months later they recorded the number of days since they had planted the plant and the number of flowers the plant had produced. The data is recorded in this table.

Number of days since planting	Number of flowers produced
60	6
53	2
66	13
62	5
72	15
68	13

a Enter the data from the table into your graphic display calculator. Use your calculator to create a scatter diagram of the data and to calculate the line of linear regression.

b Describe the correlation between the number of days since planting and the number of flowers.

c Use your calculator to calculate a prediction for the number of flowers on a plant planted 65 days ago.

8 A doctor recorded the number of hours of exercise done per week and the resting heart rate of some patients. The data is recorded in this table.

Number of hours of exercise per week	1	2	0	2	3	5	1	5
Resting heart rate (beats per minute)	82	79	91	85	68	68	79	62

a Enter the data from the table into your graphic display calculator. Use your calculator to create a scatter diagram of the data and to calculate the line of linear regression.

b Describe the correlation between the number of hours of exercise done per week and the resting heart rate of the patients in the study.

c Use your calculator to calculate a prediction for the resting heart rate of a patient that does 4 hours of exercise per week.

INVESTIGATION 1

Write a statistical question asking about a possible link between two variables and a group of people, such as the students in your class. Variables you could choose from include:

- height
- speed at completing a written task, such as writing their name ten times
- speed at completing an athletic task, such as completing an obstacle course
- total score in a game
- stride length
- head circumference
- number of languages spoken.

a   You could investigate a different question of your own where the data you will collect will be either discrete or continuous data. Ask your teacher to check your question before you start investigating.

b   Write a sentence explaining what you think the result of your investigation will be and why.

c   Collect your data in a table.

d   Represent your data in a scatter diagram.

e   Decide if there is a correlation between the two variables and draw a line of best fit if appropriate.

f   Discuss your investigation and data with a partner or in a small group.

g   Describe any patterns you can see in your data.

h   Does your data suggest that your prediction was correct? Use the information in your table and diagram to answer your statistical question.

i   Do you think that one of your variables causes the result in the other variable? What other questions could you ask to help you to answer your original question in more detail or to find out more about the subjects of your investigation?

20.3 Cumulative frequency tables and diagrams

A **cumulative frequency table** shows a running total of the frequencies. A **cumulative frequency diagram** reproduces this table as a graph.

To calculate the cumulative frequencies, add the frequencies together.

WORKED EXAMPLE 4

These are the marks scored on a test.

Score	Frequency	Cumulative frequency
1	1	1
2	2	3
3	2	5
4	3	8
5	7	15
6	1	16

Plot the data from the table into a cumulative frequency diagram and calculate the interquartile range of the scores.

Answer

Use the data in the table to plot the cumulative frequency as a diagram.

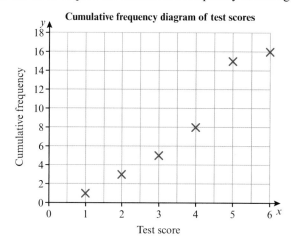

Join the points with a smooth curve, not a ruler.

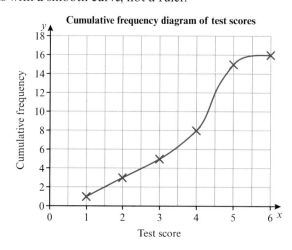

CONTINUED

The highest point represents the total number of students (16). All of the students scored 6 marks or fewer on the test.

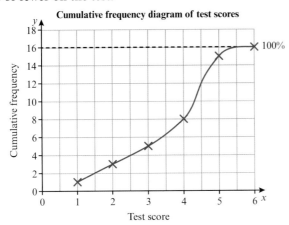

You can use the diagram to find the median score. The median is at 50% of the total frequency.

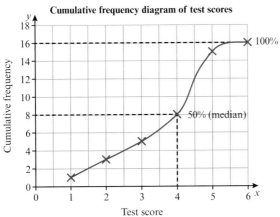

The median test score is 4 marks.

You can also use the diagram to find the upper quartile (75%) and the lower quartile (25%).

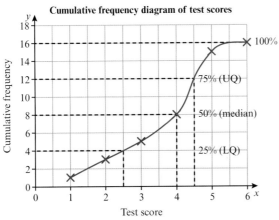

CONTINUED

The upper quartile is 4.5 marks, this means that 75% of the students scored 4.5 or fewer marks.

The lower quartile is 2.5 marks, this means that 25% of the students scored 2.5 or fewer marks.

The interquartile range is calculated by subtracting the lower quartile from the upper quartile.

$4.5 - 2.5 = 2$

The interquartile range is 2. This means that the middle 50% of students were within 2 marks of each other.

Exercise 20.3

1   A team played 30 matches. This table shows how many goals were scored.

   a   Copy and complete the cumulative frequency table

Number of goals scored in the match	Number of matches	Cumulative frequency
0	3	3
1	5	8
2	6	
3	8	
4		29
5	1	30

Add the 5 matches where there was 1 goal to the 3 matches where there were 0 goals.

Add another 6 matches.

The cumulative frequency in the final row shows the total number of matches.

   b   In how many matches were there fewer than 5 goals?

2   These are the ages of children attending a summer activity club.

   3   13   12   7   7   10   8   4   15   15   12   6   11
   8   3   5   11   5   7   9   10   14   13   9   6   3

   a   Copy and complete the cumulative frequency table for the data.

Age (years)	Number of children	Cumulative frequency
1 to 3		
4 to 6		
7 to 9		
10 to 12		
13 to 15		

TIP

You could put in an extra column to tally the children's ages in each group.

   b   How many children were from 4 to 6 years old?

   c   How many children were younger than 10 years old?

3 A delivery company recorded the mass of the parcels it delivered in a morning. These are the masses of the parcels in kilograms.

1.2, 2.3, 1.9, 3.8, 3.7, 0.8, 1.9, 2.4, 3.5, 4.9,
4.2, 0.9, 1.2, 2.6, 3.1, 4.5, 3.7, 2.0, 4.1, 1.1

Draw a cumulative frequency table of the data. You will need to choose how to group the data by mass.

4 A teacher measured the time it took students to solve a puzzle. The results were recorded in this table.

Time t (minutes)	Number of students	Cumulative frequency
$0 < t \leq 2$	1	1
$2 < t \leq 4$	2	3
$4 < t \leq 6$	5	8
$6 < t \leq 8$	8	16
$8 < t \leq 10$	9	25
$10 < t \leq 12$	6	31
$12 < t \leq 14$	1	32

a Copy and complete a cumulative frequency diagram, mark the median and quartiles on the diagram.

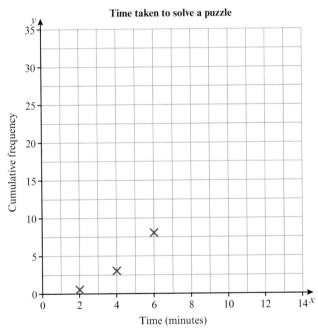

Time taken to solve a puzzle

> **TIP**
>
> Think of the cumulative frequency diagram as showing the cumulative frequency up to the next point. Plot the highest point in the range for each group with the cumulative frequency. For example, in the diagram shown the group $0 < t \leq 2$ is plotted at 2 on the x-axis.

b What is the interquartile range?

5 The mass of the pumpkins in a field is recorded in this table.

Mass of pumpkin m (kg)	Number of pumpkins	Cumulative frequency
$0 < m \leqslant 5$	9	
$5 < m \leqslant 10$	16	
$10 < m \leqslant 15$	12	
$15 < m \leqslant 20$	8	
$20 < m \leqslant 25$	2	
$25 < m \leqslant 30$	1	

  a Copy and complete the table.
  b How many pumpkins were weighed in total?
  c Using your GDC, draw a cumulative frequency diagram of the data in the table.
  d What is the median mass of the pumpkins?
  e What is the interquartile range of the pumpkins?

SUMMARY

Are you able to... ?
draw scatter diagrams to represent data
interpret data using scatter diagrams
describe correlation
draw a line of best fit on a scatter diagram
use a graphic display calculator to find and use the equation of linear regression
draw and interpret cumulative frequency table and diagrams
estimate and interpret the median, percentiles, quartiles and interquartile range from cumulative frequency diagrams.

Past paper questions

1 **a** 200 people took part in a charity walk.

They each recorded how far, d metres, they walked in one hour.
The table shows the results.

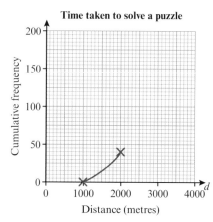

Distance (d metres)	$1000 < d \leqslant 2000$	$2000 < d \leqslant 2500$	$2500 < d \leqslant 3000$	$3000 < d \leqslant 4000$
Number of people	40	60	80	20

    i   Complete the cumulative frequency curve. [Using Past Paper Question Resource Sheet]

[3]

    ii   Use your curve to find the inter-quartile range.

.... m [2]

    iii   Use your curve to estimate the number of people who walked further than 3500 m.

.... [2]

Cambridge IGCSE International Mathematics (0607) Paper 41 Q8a November 2019

2   Pepe wants to find out if there is a correlation between the hours of sunshine, x hours, and the rainfall, y cm, in Phuket.

Pepe recorded the following results.

Month	Jan	Feb	Mar	Apr	May	Jun	Jul	Aug	Sep	Oct	Nov	Dec
Daily sunshine (x hours)	8	9.2	7.9	9.4	8	7.4	7.9	8	7.3	7.4	7.5	8
Monthly rainfall (y cm)	4	3	4	15	20	24	30	26	40	28	20	6

    a   **i**   Complete the scatter diagram. [Using Past Paper Question Resource Sheet]

              The first eight points have been plotted for you.

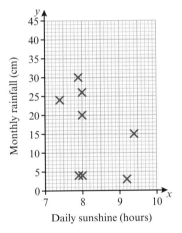

Daily sunshine (hours)

[2]

        ii   What type of correlation is shown by the scatter diagram?

.... [1]

    b   **i**   Find the mean number of hours of sunshine.

.... hours [1]

        ii   Find the mean rainfall.

.... cm [1]

    c   **i**   Find the equation of the regression line for y in terms of x.

y = ... [2]

        ii   Estimate the rainfall when the number of hours of sunshine is 7.7 .

.... cm [1]

Cambridge IGCSE International Mathematics (0607) Paper 43 Q3 November 2017

3   A farmer finds the mass, in kilograms, of each of 100 chickens. The results are shown in the table.

Mass (w kg)	Frequency
$1 < w \leqslant 1.5$	8
$1.5 < w \leqslant 2$	15
$2 < w \leqslant 2.5$	32
$2.5 < w \leqslant 3$	23
$3 < w \leqslant 3.5$	16
$3.5 < w \leqslant 4$	6

a   Write down the modal class.

.... $< w \leqslant$ .... [1]

b   Complete the cumulative frequency table for this data. [Using Past Paper Question Resource Sheet]

Mass (w kg)	Cumulative frequency
$w \leqslant 1.5$	
$w \leqslant 2$	
$w \leqslant 2.5$	
$w \leqslant 3$	
$w \leqslant 3.5$	
$w \leqslant 4$	100

[2]

c   On the grid, draw a cumulative frequency curve. [Using Past Paper Question Resource Sheet]

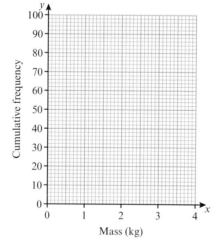

[3]

d   Use your curve to find an estimate for
   i   the median,

.... kg [1]

   ii   the interquartile range,

.... kg [2]

   iii   the number of chickens with a mass greater than 3.25 kg.

.... [2]

Cambridge IGCSE International Mathematics (0607) Paper 31 Q11 November 2021

> # Chapter 21
Probability

IN THIS CHAPTER YOU WILL:

- understand and use the probability scale from 0 to 1

- calculate the probability of a single event

- understand that the probability of an event not occurring = 1 – the probability of the event occurring

- understand relative frequency as an estimate of probability

- calculate expected frequencies

- calculate the probability of combined events with replacement using, where appropriate: sample space diagrams, tree diagrams and Venn diagrams (limited to two sets)

> understand and use probability notation

> calculate the probability of combined events without replacement using, where appropriate:
  - sample space diagrams
  - tree diagrams
  - Venn diagrams.

GETTING STARTED

1   Copy and complete the table by inserting the equivalent fraction, percentage or decimal.

Fraction	$\frac{1}{5}$				
Decimal		0.25		0.9	
Percentage			5%		12.5%

2   Evaluate the following.

a $\frac{1}{4} \times \frac{2}{5}$

b $\frac{2}{7} + \frac{3}{7}$

c $\frac{2}{7} \times \frac{3}{5} + \frac{5}{7} \times \frac{2}{5}$

d $1 - \frac{3}{8}$

e 0.5×0.7

f 0.3×0.2

g $0.4 \times 0.6 + 0.7 \times 0.9$

h $1 - 0.5 \times 0.7$

KEY WORDS

bias

combined event

event

expected frequency

experimental probability

fair

independent event

mutually exclusive

relative frequency

theoretical probability

21.1 Introduction to probability

Probability is the branch of mathematics that deals with numerical descriptions of how likely an **event** is to occur. An event is the set of outcomes from an experiment.

When all results (or outcomes) are equally likely then we can express the probability of a particular outcome as a fraction:

number of successful outcomes
─────────────────────────────
   number of total outcomes

This is defined as the **theoretical probability** that an event will occur.

An event is said to be **fair** if all outcomes are equally likely. If a dice has an equal chance of landing on any of the sides it is said to be fair. It is possible for a dice to be **biased** if it has been made in such a way that all outcomes aren't equally likely, for example, being weighted on one side.

When you toss a coin, there are only two possible outcomes, a 'head' or a 'tail', and they are both equally likely to occur.

The probability of a head is calculated as number of outcomes (a head) ÷ number of all possible outcomes (a head and a tail) $= \frac{1}{2}$.

Similarly, you know that when you roll an unbiased 6-sided dice there are six possible and equally likely outcomes: that you will roll a 1, 2, 3, 4, 5 or 6. If the successful outcome is 'a multiple of 3' then there are two possible successful outcomes, a 3 or a 6.

This means the probability of rolling a multiple of three with a fair 6-sided dice is $\frac{2}{6}$ or $\frac{1}{3}$.

The sample space is the term given to all the possible outcomes.

MATHEMATICS IN CONTEXT

Probability has many real-world applications, for example, insurance companies need to know how likely you are to make a claim so that they can charge the right price for a policy.

All probabilities lie on the probability scale between 0 and 1.

The lowest value for an event is 0, when it is impossible.

The highest value for an event is 1, when it is certain.

Tossing a coin and getting *both* heads *and* tails is an impossible event and has a probability 0.

Tossing a coin and getting *either* heads *or* tails is a certain event and has a probability 1.

Rolling an unbiased 6-sided dice labelled 1 to 6 and getting a score of 7 is an impossible event and has a probability of 0.

The closer to 1 the probability of an event is, the more likely it is to occur. The closer it is to 0, the less likely it is to occur.

Probabilities are most often expressed as fractions, but can be given using their decimal equivalents. Percentages are also sometimes used, particularly in the USA.

The probability scale below has been marked using decimals, and shows that an event with a probably of $\frac{1}{2}$ or 0.5 lies in the middle of the probability scale, and is known as an 'equally likely' event.

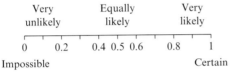

INVESTIGATION 1

Mark the following events on a probability scale:

- Tuesday will follow Wednesday
- a sheep will fly past the window
- there will be snow on the top of Mount Everest this winter
- there is a red car in the car park
- it will be your birthday tomorrow
- Thailand will win the next men's FIFA world cup
- toss a coin and get a 'head'
- someone you know will win become an astronaut and fly to Mars.

WORKED EXAMPLE 1

A fair spinner is marked with the each of the numbers from 1 to 5.

What is the probability that the spinner lands on an even number?

Answer

There are five equally likely outcomes that can occur.

There are two even numbers, 2 and 4.

So the probability of landing on an even number is $\frac{2}{5}$, 0.4 or 40%.

TIP

Identifying equally likely outcomes is key to solving probability problems. You can then count the number of possible ways in which an event can occur.

Be aware that not all outcomes are equally likely. For example, if the sector for '5' on the spinner was bigger than that for the other numbers, the outcomes would not be equally likely.

If a piece of equipment is referred to as 'fair', it means that the outcomes are equally likely.

You can use the notation P(*A*) to represent the statement 'the probability that event *A* occurs'.

In Worked example 1 you could write P(even) = $\frac{2}{5}$, P(even) = 0.4 or P(even) = 40%.

The classic definition of the probability that event *A* occurs is then:

$$P(A) = \frac{n(A)}{n(U)}$$ where U is the sample space.

MATHEMATICAL CONNECTIONS

You used the notation for the number of elements in a set in Chapter 18.

WORKED EXAMPLE 2

Roll an unbiased 6-sided dice once. Calculate the probability that:

a   a square number is rolled

b   a multiple of 3 is rolled

c   a number that is not a multiple of 3 is rolled.

CONTINUED

Answers

The sample space is $\{1, 2, 3, 4, 5, 6\}$ − there are six equally likely outcomes to the experiment.

The square numbers in the sample space are (in red) $\{1, 2, 3, 4, 5, 6\}$

The multiples of three in the sample space are (in blue) $\{1, 2, 3, 4, 5, 6\}$

a The probability that a square number is rolled $= \dfrac{2}{6} = \dfrac{1}{3} = 0.\dot{3} = 33.\dot{3}\%$.

b The probability that a multiple of 3 is rolled $= \dfrac{2}{6} = \dfrac{1}{3} = 0.\dot{3} = 33.\dot{3}\%$.

c The probability that a non-multiple of 3 is rolled $= \dfrac{4}{6} = \dfrac{2}{3} = 0.\dot{6} = 66.\dot{6}\%$.

Using probability notation:

a $P(\text{square}) = \dfrac{2}{6} = \dfrac{1}{3} = 0.\dot{3} = 33.\dot{3}\%$

b $P(\text{multiple of 3}) = \dfrac{2}{6} = \dfrac{1}{3} = 0.\dot{3} = 33.\dot{3}\%$

c $P(\text{non-multiple of 3}) = \dfrac{4}{6} = \dfrac{2}{3} = 0.\dot{6} = 66.\dot{6}\%$

Parts **b** and **c** of Worked example 2 demonstrate an important result:

The probability of an event *not* occurring = 1 − the probability of the event occurring.

Using probability notation, you write the probability that event A does *not* occur as $P(A')$.

So, if $P(A) = p$, then $P(A') = 1 - p$

INVESTIGATION 2

This task is a simulation of tossing two discs. Each disc has a red face and a green face.

The random experiment is: toss the two discs.

There are two outcomes of interest:

1 The two discs show the same colour. This is a win.

2 The two discs show different colours. This is a loss.

Before starting the simulation, make an educated guess about the probability of winning.

Is the probability of winning likely? Certain? Very unlikely?

WORKED EXAMPLE 3

In a class of 28 students, 20 of the students study French.

Draw a Venn diagram to show this information.

Answer

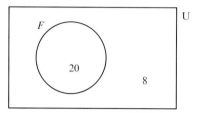

Let F be the set of students who study French.

The probability that a student studies French is $\dfrac{20}{28} = \dfrac{5}{7}$.

The probability that a student does not study French is $\dfrac{8}{28} = \dfrac{2}{7}$.

Using probability notation, $P(F) = \dfrac{20}{28} = \dfrac{5}{7}$ and $P(F) = \dfrac{8}{28} = \dfrac{2}{7}$.

MATHEMATICAL CONNECTIONS

You learnt about Venn diagrams and the universal set in Chapter 18.

Exercise 21.1

 1 A bag contains 11 discs, 5 red and 6 black. One disc is chosen at random from the bag. Find the probability that the chosen disc is:

 a red

 b not red

 c either red or black.

 Place these probabilities on a probability scale.

 2 A bag contains nine counters, four red, three blue and two black. One counter is chosen at random from the bag. Find the probability that the chosen counter is:

 a blue

 b not black

 c either red or black

 d neither black nor blue.

 Place these probabilities on a probability scale.

3 A bag contains eight socks, one red, three blue and four black. One sock is chosen at random from the bag.

 Giving your answer as a decimal to three decimal places, find:

 a the probability that the sock chosen is blue

 b the probability that the sock chosen is either red or black

 c the colour of the sock with the smallest probability of being chosen

 d the colour of the sock with an even chance of being chosen.

4 An unbiased 6-sided dice is rolled once.

Giving your answers as percentages to one decimal place, find the probability that the score on the dice is:

a 4

b more than 4

c an even number

d a prime number.

5 Eight cards, numbered from 2 to 9 inclusive, are placed in a bag. Sanya takes one card from the bag at random. Giving your answers as decimals to three decimal places, find the probability that she takes:

a the number 5

b a multiple of 3

c a factor of 6

d a square number

e a composite number.

> **TIP**
>
> A composite number is a number that is not prime.

6 The weather tomorrow will be one of the three types: sunny, stormy or foggy. Given that the probability that it will be sunny is 0.35 and the probability that it will be stormy is 0.45, determine the probability that it will be foggy.

7 Ten cards, numbered from 1 to 10 inclusive, are placed in a bag. Gunou takes one card from the bag at random. Giving your answer as a percentage, find the probability that he takes:

a a number less than 5

b a multiple of 4

c a factor of 10

d a square number

e a triangle number.

8 In a school students are placed in one of four houses, Red, Blue, Green or Yellow. The school also records whether students are left- or right-handed. The table shows the number of students in each house and which their dominant hand is.

	Red	Blue	Green	Yellow
Left	21	17	30	35
Right	250	190	240	260

a Calculate the number of:

   i left-handed students in the school

   ii right-handed students in the school

   iii students in the school.

A student is chosen at random to represent the school.

b Calculate the probability that this student is:

   i left-handed

   ii right-handed and from the Red house

   iii a member of the Blue house

> iv not in the Green house

> v either a right-handed Yellow house member or a left-handed Green house member

> vi from the house with the smallest number of left-handed students.

9 Two schools – the Franco-Malay School and Fullerton Institution – monitored their successful applications to university in 2020 and 2021. The results are shown:

	Fullerton Institution			Franco-Malay School	
	Applied	Successful		Applied	Successful
2020	48	12		411	104
2021	582	183		140	45

> a Calculate the probability that a student's university application is successful, correct to three decimal places, in 2020 for:

> i Fullerton Institution

> ii The Franco-Malay School.

> b Calculate the probability that a student's university application is successful, correct to three decimal places, in 2021 for:

> i Fullerton Institution

> ii The Franco-Malay School.

> c In which school does a student chosen at random have a better chance of being accepted to university:

> i in 2020

> ii in 2021?

10 The table shows the results of a survey carried out in a shopping mall.

Adults were asked for their age group, gender and preferred way of following current events.

Age range	Males			Females		
	Newspaper	News websites	Social media	Newspaper	News websites	Social media
18–40	12	24	72	8	32	81
41–60	25	42	56	33	48	62
Over 60	84	31	25	67	25	33

Give your answers as percentages to one decimal place.

> a Calculate the probability that a male over 60 selected at random follows current events through news websites.

> b Calculate the probability that a female over 60 selected at random follows current events through news websites.

> c All the results are anonymised and one person is chosen at random. What is the probability that it is:

> i a female between 41 and 60 who prefers social media

> ii a male between the ages of 18 and 40 who reads a newspaper

> iii a female over 60 who follows news websites?

11 Let A be the event 'a 6 is rolled on an unbiased 6-sided dice' and let B be the event 'a square number is rolled on an unbiased 6-sided dice.'

  a Write down:

    i $P(A)$ **ii** $P(B)$

  b Express in words the event:

    i A' **ii** B'

  c Write down:

    i $P(A')$ **ii** $P(B')$

  d Find $P(A \text{ or } B)$.

DISCUSSION 1

Discuss this problem with a partner.

A teacher has a bag of pens for students to use during lessons. There are four blue pens and two black pens. On Monday, Dylan and Jade each choose one pen at random from the teacher's bag. Dylan chooses first.

a Find the probability that Dylan chooses a black pen.

Now Jade chooses, but first she notices that Dylan has taken a black pen.

b Find the probability that now Jade also chooses a black pen.

On Tuesday, Dylan, Jade and Dhruv each choose one pen at random from the teacher's bag. Again, Dylan chooses first, followed by Jade. After Dylan and Jade have chosen, the teacher looks in the bag and says to Dhruv, 'You have an even chance of choosing blue or black.'

c Determine the colour of the pens that Dylan and Jade chose.

21.2 Relative and expected frequencies

All of the examples we have looked at so far are examples of theoretical probability. However, when conducting probability experiments, for example by spinning spinners or flipping coins, the results do not often match the theoretical probabilities.

In Section 21.1, we defined the theoretical probability as $\dfrac{\text{number of successful outcomes}}{\text{number of possible outcomes}}$ where all outcomes are equally likely.

INVESTIGATION 3

Find a partner and a coin.

Flip the coin ten times.

Do you get exactly five heads and five tails?

Check with other pairs in the classroom.

How often does five heads, five tails occur?

Carrying out Investigation 3 allowed you to toss the coin ten times, to try and discover the probabilities of getting a head or tail through an experiment rather than looking at the theoretical probability. This is called **experimental probability**, where you try an experiment multiple times to make an estimate of the actual probability. It is particularly useful when performing calculations where the theoretical probability would not be easy or possible.

When conducting an experiment like this, we refer to the probabilities we find as the **relative frequency**.

$$\text{Relative frequency is } \frac{\text{frequency of an event happening}}{\text{total number of trials in the experiment}}$$

Worked example 4 is an example of how relative frequency is calculated.

WORKED EXAMPLE 4

A class decided to find out the probability of a piece of toast landing butter-side down when dropped from a fixed height.

The experiment was repeated 30 times, and the toast landed butter-side down 12 times.

Answer

$$\text{The relative frequency was } \frac{\text{frequency of butter-side down}}{\text{total number of trials in the experiment}}$$

$$= \frac{12}{30} \text{ or } \frac{2}{5} = 0.4 = 40\%.$$

When conducting a probability experiment, the results do not always match the theoretical probability. If a coin is tossed ten times, theoretical probability says that there should be five heads and five tails. This is not always the case. It might be that there was one more head than expected, so 60% heads and 40% tails.

If the same coin is tossed 100 times and there was one more head than expected that would be 51% heads and 49% tails.

This shows that the more often an experiment is repeated, the more likely the relative frequency will match the theoretical probability, because each individual result is a smaller proportion of the total number of results.

The extra head from ten throws represents 10%, but the extra head from 100 throws represents 1%.

Expected frequencies

We can use theoretical probability to help us estimate an **expected frequency** of an event. The expected frequency is the amount of times an event should occur, given its probability and the number of times the experiment takes place.

WORKED EXAMPLE 5

The theoretical probability of getting a 5 when rolling a fair dice is $\frac{1}{6}$.

If I roll a dice 210 times, how many times should I get a 5?

Answer

I should get a 5 one-sixth $\left(\frac{1}{6}\right)$ of the time, so if I roll a dice 210 times I can expect to get $\frac{1}{6} \times 210 = 35$ fives.

Note that this doesn't mean I definitely would get 35 fives, but it is an estimate of the expected frequency.

Exercise 21.2

1   A fair 5-sided spinner is spun 465 times.

   a   How many 5s are likely to be spun?

   b   How many even numbers are likely to be spun?

2   The theoretical probability of winning a prize at a fairground game has been calculated as 0.15. If 290 people try the game, estimate the number of prizes that will be won.

   Explain your answer.

3   A fair 6-sided dice is rolled 700 times.

   a   What is the expected frequency that a 6 will be rolled?

   b   Justify your answer.

4   Two fair 6-sided dice are rolled and the results added together.

   If this experiment is repeated 1290 times, find the expected frequency of:

   a   a total of 5

   b   a total of 1

   c   a total of 12

   d   a total of 7.

21.3 Combining probabilities

So far we have considered finding probabilities of single events only.

Sometimes we need to find the probability of two or more events happening.

When probabilities are combined they may be **independent events**. Independent events are events where the probability of one event does not affect the probability of the other event. For example, when flipping two coins the outcome of the first flip has no impact on the outcome of the second flip.

Events are said to be **mutually exclusive** when they cannot happen at the same time. When flipping a coin once the outcome is a either a head or a tail, it cannot be both.

When you have mutually exclusive events, you can simply add the two separate probabilities to determine the probability of one event *or* the other event occurring.

So, in the case of flipping a coin:

$$P(\text{head or tail}) = \frac{1}{2} + \frac{1}{2} = 1$$

The general rule for calculating mutually exclusive events is $P(A \text{ and } B) = P(A) + P(B)$.

WORKED EXAMPLE 6

Toss an unbiased 50¢ coin together with an unbiased 20¢ coin.

Find the probability that both of the two coins show 'heads'.

Answer

Two things are happening – *both* the 50¢ coin is tossed *and* the 20¢ coin is tossed – so you need to use a two-way table to visualise the correct sample space.

		50¢ coin	
		H	T
20¢ coin	h	Hh	Th
	t	Ht	Tt

This table is a sample space diagram.

Looking at the table, you can see that there are *four* equally likely outcomes in the sample space: {*Hh, Ht, Th, Tt*} with the event you are interested in being *Hh* in which there are two heads showing.

So, the probability that both the two coins show heads $= \frac{1}{4}$ (or 0.25 or 25%).

Using probability notation, $P(Hh) = \frac{1}{4}$.

Sample space diagrams

You have already seen a sample space diagram in Worked example 6, and they are one way of finding the probability of **combined events**.

The general rule for calculating two independent events $P(A \text{ and } B)$ is given as $P(A) \times P(B)$.

When a coin is tossed twice, they are independent events as the second toss is not influenced by the first one.

So $P(2H) = \frac{1}{2} \times \frac{1}{2} = \frac{1}{4}$

WORKED EXAMPLE 7

Consider the random experiment where two unbiased 6-sided dice are rolled. One dice is coloured red and the other dice is coloured blue. The blue dice is rolled first.

Calculate the probability that:

a the total score on the two dice is 7

b the same number is shown on both dice

c the difference between the scores on the two dice is 1

d the score on the red dice is less than the score on the blue dice

e the total score on the two dice is a prime number.

Answers

There are 36 equally likely outcomes to this experiment. Listing 36 outcomes is not simple. Instead, you can use a sample space diagram to show the outcomes more clearly and to count the outcomes systematically.

The sample space diagram for this random experiment is shown with the possible outcomes listed as pairs of scores.

Score on dice	1	2	3	4	5	6
1	1,1	1,2	1,3	1,4	1,5	1,6
2	2,1	2,2	2,3	2,4	2,5	2,6
3	3,1	3,2	3,3	3,4	3,5	3,6
4	4,1	4,2	4,3	4,4	4,5	4,6
5	5,1	5,2	5,3	5,4	5,5	5,6
6	6,1	6,2	6,3	6,4	6,5	6,6

You can then use the diagram to answer any questions about the experiment.

a

Score on dice	1	2	3	4	5	6
1	1,1	1,2	1,3	1,4	1,5	1,6
2	2,1	2,2	2,3	2,4	2,5	2,6
3	3,1	3,2	3,3	3,4	3,5	3,6
4	4,1	4,2	4,3	4,4	4,5	4,6
5	5,1	5,2	5,3	5,4	5,5	5,6
6	6,1	6,2	6,3	6,4	6,5	6,6

The probability that the total score on the two dice is $7 = \dfrac{6}{36} = \dfrac{1}{6}$.

b The probability that the same number is shown on both dice $= \dfrac{6}{36} = \dfrac{1}{6}$.

c The probability that the score on the red dice is less than the score on the blue dice $= \dfrac{15}{36} = \dfrac{5}{12}$.

d The probability that the difference between the scores on the two dice is $1 = \dfrac{10}{36} = \dfrac{5}{18}$.

e The probability that the total score on the two dice is a prime number $= \dfrac{15}{36} = \dfrac{5}{12}$.

MATHEMATICAL CONNECTIONS

You could write the outcomes as coordinate pairs. So, a 4 on the red dice and a 6 on the blue dice is (4, 6) and so on. You could then represent the 36 possible outcomes as coordinate points on a grid with the scores on the red dice placed on the x-axis and the scores on the blue dice placed on the y-axis.
You met coordinate points on a grid in Chapter 13.

TIP

If there are many different parts to the question, using different coloured highlighters is a useful way of showing your working.

Exercise 21.3

1   Two tetrahedral dice, one dice blue and the other dice red, are each numbered 1 to 4.

They are rolled and the result noted.

Draw the sample space for this random experiment.

Find the probability that:

   a   the number on the red dice is equal to the number on the blue dice

   b   the difference between the numbers on the dice is 1

   c   the red dice shows an even number and the blue dice shows an odd number

   d   the sum of the numbers on the dice is 5.

TIP

A tetrahedral dice has four faces.

2   A 4-sided dice and a 6-sided dice are rolled and the results noted.

Draw the sample space diagram for this random experiment.

Find the probability that:

   a   the number on the 4-sided dice is equal to the number on the 6-sided dice

   b   the number on the 4-sided dice is *greater than* the number on the 6-sided dice

   c   the difference between the numbers on the dice is 2

   d   the sum of the numbers on the dice is 5

   e   the sum of the numbers on the dice is odd.

3   A box contains three cards numbered 2, 3 and 4. A second box contains four cards numbered 3, 4, 5 and 6. A card is chosen at random from each box.

Draw the sample space diagram for the random experiment.

Find the probability that:

   a   the cards have the same number

   b   the difference between the two numbers drawn is 3

   c   the sum of the two numbers on the cards is at least 9

   d   the product of the numbers on the cards is less than 8

   e   at least one odd number is chosen.

4   A box contains four cards numbered 2, 3, 4 and 4. A bag contains five cards numbered 3, 4, 4, 5 and 5. Two cards are chosen at random: one card from the box and one card from the bag.

Draw the sample space diagram for the random experiment.

Find the probability that:

   a   the cards have the same number

   b   the difference between the two numbers drawn is 1

   c   the sum of the two numbers on the cards is 7

   d   the product of the numbers on the cards is odd

   e   at least one even number is chosen.

TIP

Think carefully: *equally* likely outcomes must be drawn.

5   A box contains three cards numbered 3, 4 and 4. A bag contains five cards
     numbered 3, 3, 4, 5 and 5. Two cards are chosen at random: one card from the box
     and one card from the bag.
     Draw the sample space diagram for the random experiment.
     Find the probability that:
     a   the cards have the same number
     b   the difference between the two numbers drawn is 1
     c   the sum of the two numbers on the cards is 7
     d   the product of the numbers on the cards is odd
     e   at least one even number is chosen.

6   Six cards, numbered 0, 1, 2, 3, 4 and 5, are placed in a bag. One card is drawn at
     random, its number noted and then it is replaced in the bag. Then a second card
     is chosen.
     Draw the sample space diagram for the random experiment.
     Find the probability that:
     a   the cards have the same number
     b   the difference between the two numbers drawn is 4
     c   the sum of the two numbers on the cards is 7
     d   the product of the numbers on the cards is odd
     e   at least one even number is chosen.

7   Six cards, numbered 0, 1, 2, 3, 4 and 5, are placed in a bag. One card is drawn at
     random, its number noted and then it is *not* replaced in the bag. Then a second
     card is chosen.
     Draw the sample space diagram for the random experiment.
     Find:
     a   P(the cards have the same number)
     b   P(the difference between the two numbers drawn is 4)
     c   P(the sum of the two numbers on the cards is 7)
     d   P(the product of the numbers on the cards is odd)
     e   P(at least one even number is chosen)

TIP

Think about how
the card *not* being
replaced affects the
probabilities. You will
study more examples
of combined events
without replacement
using tree diagrams
later in this chapter.

8   Members of a school class are asked how many children are in their family.
     The results are shown on the graph.

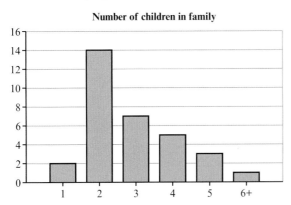

If one child is chosen at random, find:
a   P(2)   **b**   P(5)   **c**   P(3 or 4)

9 A single fair dice is rolled and the results recorded in the graph.

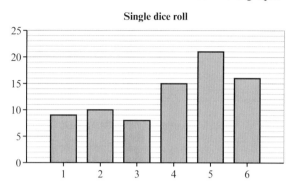

Find:

a P(2)

b P(odd number)

c P(square number)

d P(number > 3)

Venn diagrams

WORKED EXAMPLE 8

There are 27 students in a class. Fifteen of the students are Malaysian and eight of the students are Singaporean. Draw a Venn diagram to show this information.

Note that dual nationality is not permitted in either Malaysia or Singapore, so a student *cannot* be both Malaysian and Singaporean.

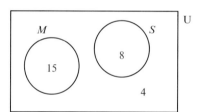

Answer

Let M be the set of Malaysian students.

Let S be the set of Singaporean students.

The probability that a student is Malaysian is $\frac{15}{27} = \frac{5}{9}$.

The probability that a student is Singaporean is $\frac{8}{27}$.

The probability that a student is Malaysian or Singaporean is $\frac{15 + 8}{27} = \frac{23}{27}$.

Using probability notation, $P(M) = \frac{15}{27} = \frac{5}{9}$ and $P(S) = \frac{8}{27}$.

Also, using the result for mutually exclusive events, $P(M \text{ or } S) = \frac{15}{27} + \frac{8}{27} = \frac{23}{27}$.

In set notation probability of being Malaysian or Singaporean in this example is the union of the two sets. This is written as $P(M \cup S)$.

When two outcomes are mutually exclusive as in this example, the intersection of the two sets is 0.

So $P(M \cap S) = 0$

| WORKED EXAMPLE 9 |

There are 25 students in a class.
Fifteen students study French and 13 students study mathematics.
Also, five students study neither French nor mathematics.
A student is chosen at random from the class.
Find the probability that the student studies *both* French *and* mathematics.

Answer

Draw a Venn diagram to visualise the situation. Let F be the set of students that study French and let M the set of students that study mathematics.

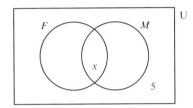

> **TIP**
>
> There are 4 separate regions on the Venn diagram and 4 pieces of information given in the problem. Therefore you have enough information to be able to solve the problem.

Let the number who study *both* French and mathematics be x. Write x in the overlap region of the two sets (the **intersection** of the two sets).

You can then write the information about the French students, the mathematics students and the other students on the Venn diagram.

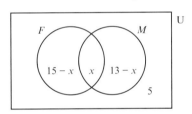

You can now construct an equation since the total number of students in the class is 25.

The equation is $5 + (15 - x) + x + (13 - x) = 25$

Solve for x:
$$33 - x = 25$$
$$x = 8$$

Update the Venn diagram:

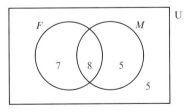

So, the probability that the randomly chosen student studies *both* French *and* mathematics is $\dfrac{8}{25}$.

In set notation, this is the intersection of French and mathematics and is written as $P(F \cap M)$.

DISCUSSION 2

Once you have drawn (and represented the equally likely events on) the Venn diagram in Worked example 8, you can determine further probabilities, for example:

The probability that a randomly chosen student studies French but not mathematics is $\dfrac{7}{25}$.

The probability that a randomly chosen student studies at least one of the two subjects is $\dfrac{20}{25}$.

Discuss with a partner to make sure you both understand how these probabilities are determined.

Exercise 21.4

1   Use the Venn diagram to find the probability that a person chosen at random:

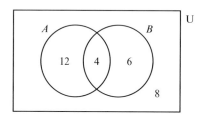

a   is in set A
b   is not in set B
c   is in neither set A nor set B
d   is in set A and set B.

2   Use the Venn diagram to find the probability that a person chosen at random:

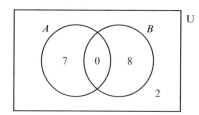

a   is in set B
b   is not in set A
c   is in set B but not in set A
d   is not in either set A or set B
e   is not in both sets A and B.

For Questions **3** and **4**, use a Venn diagram to represent each situation.

3 In a class, 20 students study physics, 17 students study biology, 10 students study both subjects and 1 student studies neither subject.

    a How many students are there in the class?

One student is chosen at random from the class.

Find the probability that this student:

    b studies physics

    c studies physics but not biology

    d studies physics or biology but not both.

4 There are 27 students in a class. Fifteen students study art and 20 students study drama. Four students study neither subject.

    a How many students study both subjects?

One student is chosen at random from the class.

Find the probability that this student:

    b studies drama and art

    c studies art but not drama

    d does not study art and does not study drama

    e studies at least one of the two subjects

    f studies exactly one of the two subjects.

5 There are 29 students in a maths class. Twenty students have studied probability, 14 students have studied set theory and 2 students have studied neither probability nor set theory. One of these maths students is chosen at random.

Find the probability that this student:

    a has studied both subjects

    b has not studied either set theory or probability

    c has studied set theory but not probability

    d has not studied set theory and not studied probability

    e has not studied probability

    f has studied exactly one of the two topics.

6 There are 25 students in a sports class. Thirteen students have practised aerobics before and 17 students have practised gymnastics before. One student has practised neither activity before. One student is chosen at random from the group.

Find the probability that this student:

    a has practised both activities before

    b has practised gymnastics but not aerobics before

    c has practised at least one of these activities before

    d has practised exactly one of these activities before

    e has not practised aerobics before.

7   There are 27 students in a sports club. Eighteen of the students play tennis, nine of the students play badminton and six of the students play both sports. One student is chosen at random from the sports club. Find the probability that this student:

   a   plays both sports

   b   plays tennis

   c   plays tennis and does not play badminton

   d   plays badminton only

   e   does not play either sport.

8   Use the Venn diagram to find the following probabilities when a person is chosen at random.

   a $P(A)$ b $P(B')$ c $P(A \cup B)'$ d $P(A \cap B)$

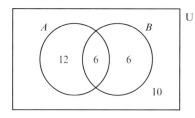

9   There are 25 students in a class. Seventeen students study French, 12 students study Spanish and 10 students study both languages. A student is chosen at random from the class. Use a Venn diagram to answer the following questions.

   Find the probability that this student:

   a $P(F \cap S')$ b $P(S \ or \ F)$ c $P(A \cup B)'$

Tree diagrams

You can use tree diagrams to analyse combined probability experiments by breaking them down into two or more simple events that occur in sequence, one event after another.

In the sample space experiment from Worked example 5 when two unbiased 6-sided dice are rolled, you can use a tree diagram to answer less general questions about the results.

WORKED EXAMPLE 10

Two unbiased 6-sided dice are rolled, one dice is coloured red and the other dice is coloured blue.

Find the probability that:

   a   two 6s are rolled   b   no 6s are rolled

   c   exactly one 6 is rolled   d   at least one 6 is rolled.

CONTINUED

Answers

You need to sequence the experiment by imagining that *first* the red dice is rolled and *then* following this, the blue dice is rolled. You can then analyse more simply these two simple experiments and represent them together in the tree diagram.

Probability that a 6 is rolled on the red dice $= \frac{1}{6}$.

Probability that not a 6 is rolled on the red dice $= \frac{5}{6}$.

Similarly:

Probability that a 6 is rolled on the blue dice $= \frac{1}{6}$.

Probability that not a 6 is rolled on the blue dice $= \frac{5}{6}$.

Write these probabilities on the branches of your tree diagram, together with the final outcomes.

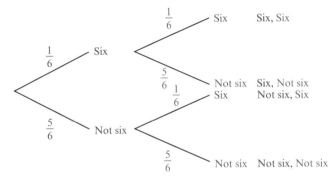

Then, to calculate the probability of each of the four final outcomes, you multiply the probability on each of the branches.

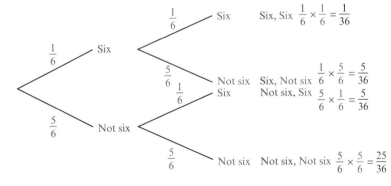

So:

Probability that a red six and a blue six are rolled $= \frac{1}{6} \times \frac{1}{6} = \frac{1}{36}$.

Probability that a red six is rolled and not a blue six is rolled $= \frac{1}{6} \times \frac{5}{6} = \frac{5}{36}$.

Probability that not a red six is rolled and a blue six is rolled $= \frac{5}{6} \times \frac{1}{6} = \frac{5}{36}$.

Probability that not a red six is rolled and not a blue six is rolled $= \frac{5}{6} \times \frac{5}{6} = \frac{25}{36}$.

CONTINUED

TIP

You can verify these four outcomes using a sample space diagram.

Probability that a red six and a blue six are rolled $= \frac{1}{36}$ (shown in white).

Probability that a red six is rolled and not a blue six is rolled $= \frac{5}{36}$ (shown in orange).

Probability that not a red six is rolled and a blue six is rolled $= \frac{5}{36}$ (shown in yellow).

Probability that not a red six is rolled and not a blue six is rolled $= \frac{25}{36}$ (shown in green).

Score on dice	1	2	3	4	5	6
1	1,1	1,2	1,3	1,4	1,5	1,6
2	2,1	2,2	2,3	2,4	2,5	2,6
3	3,1	3,2	3,3	3,4	3,5	3,6
4	4,1	4,2	4,3	4,4	4,5	4,6
5	5,1	5,2	5,3	5,4	5,5	5,6
6	6,1	6,2	6,3	6,4	6,5	6,6

Once the tree diagram is complete, you can determine the required probabilities.

a	Probability that two sixes are rolled $= \frac{1}{36}$	The *top* outcome at the end of the tree diagram.
b	Probability that no sixes are rolled $= \frac{25}{36}$	The *bottom* outcome at the end of the tree diagram.
c	Probability that exactly one six is rolled $= \frac{10}{36}$	The *middle two* outcomes of the tree diagram. Add these two probabilities.
d	Probability that at least one six is rolled $= \frac{10}{36}$	The *bottom three outcomes* of the tree diagram. Add these three probabilities.

WORKED EXAMPLE 11

A bag contains three red discs and four blue discs, identical except for colour.
A disc is chosen from the bag, its colour is noted and then the disc is replaced in
the bag. Then a second disc is chosen.

Draw the tree diagram for this random experiment and find the probability that:

a two red discs are chosen

b two different coloured discs are chosen

c a blue disc is chosen on the second choice.

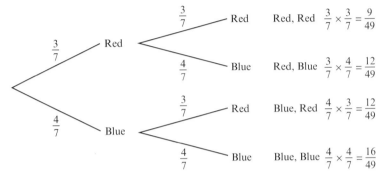

Answers

The probability that:

a	two red discs are chosen $= \dfrac{9}{49}$	There is only one possible outcome in the tree diagram: red, red.
b	two different coloured discs are chosen $= \dfrac{12}{49} + \dfrac{12}{49} = \dfrac{24}{49}$	There are two possible outcomes in the tree diagram: red, blue or blue red. Add the two probabilities.
c	a blue disc is chosen on the second choice $= \dfrac{12}{49} + \dfrac{16}{49} = \dfrac{28}{49}$	There are two possible outcomes in the tree diagram: red, blue or blue, blue. Add the two probabilities.

So far, the probabilities of combined events you have calculated have been based on the
item being replaced after being picked.

Sometimes you will be asked to calculate the probability of a second event when the
item has not been replaced.

WORKED EXAMPLE 12

A bag contains six red discs and three blue discs (all identical). Two discs are
chosen at random, *one after another without replacement.* Find:

a P(two blue discs are chosen)

b P(a blue disc is chosen on the second choice).

CONTINUED

Answers

Make sure you understand what is happening in the experiment:

First, a disc is chosen from the bag. It is *not* replaced. Then a second disc is chosen.

In this way you split the problem into a sequence of simpler events that you can analyse using the tree diagram shown.

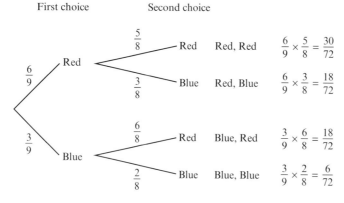

First choice   Second choice

Look at the tree diagram in detail – there are some important points that you must remember.

1 Look at the first-choice probabilities: $\frac{6}{9}$ for red and $\frac{3}{9}$ for blue.

Note that the fractions have not been cancelled and written them in lowest terms.

Never cancel the fractions in tree diagrams.

2 Look at the second-choice probabilities – these change according to the colour of the disc that was chosen on the first choice. Think carefully about this!

For example, if the first choice was a red disc, then there are now only five red discs remaining in the bag along with the three blue discs.

So, the probability that a red disc is chosen on the second choice is $\frac{5}{5+3} = \frac{5}{8}$.

Similarly, the probability that a blue disc is chosen on the second choice is $\frac{3}{5+3} = \frac{3}{8}$.

Also, if the first choice was a blue disc, then there are still six red discs remaining in the bag however there are now only two blue discs.

So, the probability that a red disc is chosen on the second choice is $\frac{6}{6+2} = \frac{6}{8}$.

Similarly, the probability that a blue disc is chosen on the second choice is $\frac{2}{6+2} = \frac{2}{8}$.

> **CONTINUED**
>
> **3** Note again, that the fractions $\frac{6}{8}$ and $\frac{2}{8}$ have not been cancelled.
>
> The final fractions have not been cancelled and these fractions all have denominator 72. This is deliberate as it shows that there are 72 equally likely possibilities that make up the sample space.
>
> Now you are ready to evaluate the required probabilities:
>
> | | |
> |---|---|
> | **a** P(two blue discs are chosen) $= \frac{6}{72} = \frac{1}{12}$ | The bottom event on the tree diagram. |
> | **b** P(a blue disc was chosen on the second choice) $= \frac{18}{72} + \frac{6}{72} = \frac{24}{72} = \frac{1}{3}$ | The second and fourth events on the tree diagram. |

Exercise 21.5

1 An unbiased 6-sided dice has two faces coloured black and four faces coloured white. The dice is rolled once and the colour of its top face is noted.

  a Find the probability that:

      i the top face is black

      ii the top face is white.

  The dice is rolled twice, and the colour of its top face is noted each time it is rolled.

  b Copy and complete the tree diagram that shows the possible outcomes.

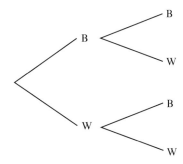

  c Find the probability that:

      i the two top faces are white

      ii at least one top face is black

      iii the top face on the second roll is black.

TIP

You can write these probabilities as fractions in lowest terms.

2   On her journey to school, a teacher must pass through two sets of traffic lights.
At the first set of lights, the probability that the light is green is $\frac{1}{3}$ and at the
second set of lights there is an even chance that the light is green or red. If she
meets a red light she must stop.

    a   Copy and complete the tree diagram that shows the possible outcomes.

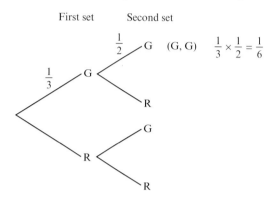

> **TIP**
>
> The events are sequenced in time by going through the first set of lights and then the second set of lights.

    b   Find the probability that the teacher:

        i   does not have to stop at any traffic lights

        ii   has to stop at exactly one set of traffic lights

        iii has to stop at at least one set of traffic lights.

3   A bag contains four red discs and six differently coloured discs (all identical).
A disc is chosen at random from the bag and its colour is noted. The disc is then
returned to the bag. A second disc is then chosen, and its colour is noted.

    a   Copy and complete the tree diagram that shows the possible outcomes.
Write down the relevant probability on each branch. Do not reduce the
probabilities to lowest terms.

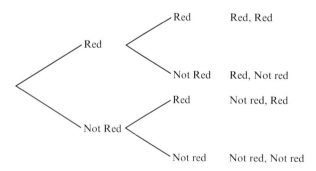

> **TIP**
>
> Think carefully about the probability that is placed on each branch.

    b   Find the probability that:

        i   two red discs are chosen

        ii   exactly one red disc is chosen

        iii at least one red disc is chosen

        iv a red disc is chosen on the second choice.

4   A student sits two examinations as part of his driving test. The first exam is a
    written test and the second exam is a practical test. He has a 90% chance of
    passing the first exam and an 80% chance of passing the second exam. To become
    a driver, he must pass both exams.

    a   Write down, as a fraction, the probability that he:

        i   fails the first (written) exam

        ii   fails the second (practical) exam.

    b   Copy and complete the tree diagram that shows his possible results.
        Write down the relevant probability as a fraction on each branch.

```
        First exam      Second exam      Outcome       Probability

                          ┌── Pass        Pass, Pass
                 ┌── Pass ┤
                 │        └── Fail        Pass, Fail
                 ┤
                 │        ┌── Pass        Fail, Pass
                 └── Fail ┤
                          └── Fail        Fail, Fail
```

    c   Use the tree diagram to find the probability that:

        i   he becomes a driver

        ii   he does not become a driver

        iii he fails one exam only

        iv   he fails the practical exam.

5   A bag contains six red counters and five blue counters. One counter is chosen
    at random, its colour is noted, and the counter is then put back in the bag.
    Then a second counter is chosen.
    By first drawing a tree diagram, find the probability that:

    a   exactly one red counter is chosen

    b   one counter of each colour is chosen

    c   at least one blue counter is chosen.

6   An unbiased five-sided spinner is marked with the numbers 1, 2, 3, 4 and 5.
    The spinner is spun twice, and it is noted each time whether or not a prime
    number is seen.
    Use a tree diagram to find the probability that in the two spins:

    a   exactly one prime number is seen

    b   at least one prime number is seen.

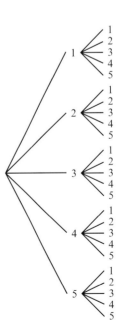

7 On my journey to work I must go through two sets of traffic lights – first at Aleph Junction and then at Beth Road. I am delayed at Aleph Junction 7 times in 10 on average and I am delayed at Beth Road 3 times in 5 on average.

Draw the tree diagram to show the possible delays on my journey to work to find the probability that:

a I am delayed once only   **b** I am not delayed at all.

8 A bag contains seven blue discs and five green discs. One disc is chosen at random. The disc is not returned to the bag. A second disc is then chosen.

By first drawing a tree diagram, find the probability that:

a two blue discs are chosen   **b** exactly one green disc is chosen

c at least one green disc is chosen.

9 A bag contains four red discs and six differently coloured (but otherwise identical) discs. A disc is chosen at random from the bag and its colour is noted. The disc is not returned to the bag. A second disc is then chosen, and its colour is noted.

a Copy and complete the tree diagram that shows the possible outcomes. Write down the relevant probability on each branch. Do not reduce the probabilities to lowest terms.

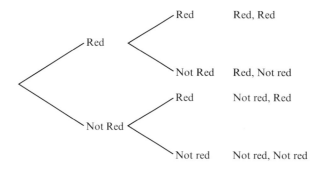

> **TIP**
>
> Again, think carefully about the probability that is placed on each branch. This problem is similar to Worked example 14.

b Find:

i P(two red discs are chosen)

ii P(exactly one red disc is chosen)

iii P(at least one red disc is chosen)

iv P(a red disc was chosen on the second choice)

10 X is playing a tennis match against Y. The probability that X wins the first set is $\frac{3}{4}$. If X wins a set, the probability that he wins the next set is $\frac{9}{10}$. If X loses a set, the probability that he wins the next set is $\frac{4}{5}$. The first player to win two sets is the winner of the match.

a Copy and complete the tree diagram that shows his possible results. Write down the relevant probability on each branch.

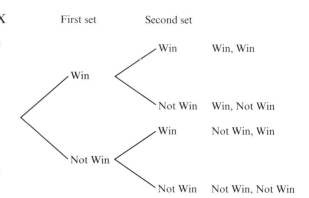

b Find the probability:

   i that X wins the match in two sets

   ii that X loses the match in two sets

   iii that the match is not won in two sets by either X or Y.

c If the match is tied at one set all, X and Y will need to play a third set to find the winner. Extend the tree diagram to include the possible outcomes of a third, and deciding, set. Use this extended tree diagram to find the probability that:

   i X wins the match in three sets

   ii X wins the match.

11 To get to school I can take one of two routes, via Chatima Road or via Nyerere Way. I take the Chatima Road route on average 3 times in a (five day) week. If I take this route, the probability that I am delayed is 0.25. If I take Nyerere Way the probability that I am delayed is 0.5.

a By drawing the tree diagram for my journey to school, find the probability that I use Chatima Road and am delayed.

b Find the probability that I go via Nyerere Way and I am not delayed.

12 The probability that it will rain on Saturday is 0.9. If it does rain on Saturday, then the probability that it will rain on Sunday is 0.7. However, if it does not rain on Saturday, then the probability that it will rain on Sunday is 0.6.

a Draw the tree diagram which shows whether it rains or not for the two days of the weekend.

b Find the probability that:

   i it doesn't rain on either day of the weekend

   ii it rains exactly one day of the weekend

   iii it rains at least one day of the weekend.

13 On a journey to school a teacher passes through two sets of traffic lights (set A and set B).

The probability that she has to stop at set A is 2 in 7, and the probability that she has to stop at set B is 1 in 3. If she stops at set A she has a delay of two minutes, and if she stops at set B she has a delay of four minutes. Without any delays, her journey to school takes 30 minutes.

a Draw the tree diagram to illustrate her journey to school and the possible delays.

b The teacher claims that she has an even chance or better of reaching school in 30 minutes. Determine whether her claim is correct.

c Find the probability that:

   i her journey to school takes more than 35 minutes

   ii the teacher has only one delay on her journey to school.

14 The probability that it rains today is $\frac{3}{5}$. If it rains today, the probability that it rains tomorrow is $\frac{4}{5}$. If it does not rain today, the probability it rains tomorrow is $\frac{7}{10}$.

    a Draw a tree diagram that shows whether it rains or not on these two days. Write down the relevant probability on each branch.

    b Find the probability that:

        i it rains on both days

        ii it rains at least one day

        iii it rains on the second day.

15 In Shangri-La the days are either rainy or fine. The probability that it will rain today is 0.2. If it rains today, the probability that it will rain tomorrow is 0.2. If it is fine today, then the probability it will be fine tomorrow is 0.9.

    Find the probability that at least today or tomorrow is fine.

SUMMARY

Are you able to... ?
understand and use a probability scale from 0 to 1
understand the probability of an event not happening is 1 − the probability of the event happening
understand relative frequency as an estimate of probability
calculate the probability of a single event
calculate expected frequencies
calculate the probability of combined events using Venn diagrams, sample space diagrams and tree diagrams
understand and use probability notation.

Past paper questions

1 Jono walks to school when the weather is fine.
   When the weather is not fine, Jono takes the bus.
   If Jono walks to school, the probability that he is late is 0.2.
   If Jono takes the bus, the probability that he is late is 0.05.
   On any day, the probability that the weather is fine is 0.7.

   a Complete the tree diagram. [Using Past Paper Question Resource Sheet]   [3]

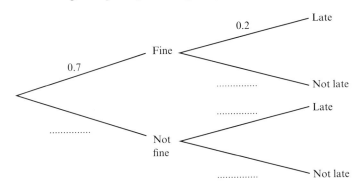

   b i Find the probability that, on any day, Jono is late.

   .... [3]

      ii Jono attends school on 200 days.
          Find the expected number of days that Jono is late.

   .... [1]

   Cambridge IGCSE International Mathematics (0607) Paper 42 Q3, June 2019

2 Angie goes to school on 5 days each week.

   On a school day, the probability that Angie gets up before 7 am is $\frac{9}{10}$.

   On a non-school day, the probability that Angie gets up before 7 am is $\frac{1}{20}$.

   a Complete the tree diagram. [Using Past Paper Question Resource Sheet]   [3]

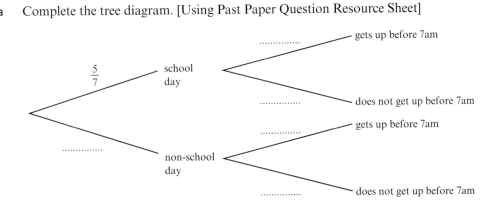

b One day of the week is chosen at random.

Find the probability that the day is a non-school day and that Angie gets up before 7 am.

.... [2]

Cambridge IGCSE International Mathematics (0607) Paper 31 Q12, November 2019

3 A bag contains black counters, white counters and red counters only.

Tam takes a counter, at random, from the bag.

He records the colour of the counter and then replaces the counter in the bag.

He does this 500 times.

The table below shows his results.

Colour of counter	Black	White	Red
Number of times	163	128	209

a Complete the relative frequency table below. [Using Past Paper Question Resource Sheet]

Give each of your answers as a decimal.

Colour of counter	Black	White	Red
Relative frequency			

[2]

b Tam chooses another counter from the bag at random.

Work out an estimate of the probability that it is either black or white.

.... [2]

c There is a total of 24 counters in the bag.

Work out an estimate of the number of red counters.

.... [2]

Cambridge IGCSE International Mathematics (0607) Paper 31 Q9, November 2018

> Chapter 22
Sequences

IN THIS CHAPTER YOU WILL:

- recognise patterns in sequences

- use patterns to continue different sequences

- find terms in a sequence when you know the rule used to generate it

- use the difference between terms to find the term-to-term rule for a sequence

- determine the value of the nth term in linear, simple quadratic and simple cubic sequences

- recognise relationships between different sequences

> use a difference method to find the nth term of quadratic, cubic and exponential sequences

> work with combinations of linear, quadratic, cubic and exponential sequences.

GETTING STARTED

1   Copy and complete the Venn diagram to classify the numbers in the box.

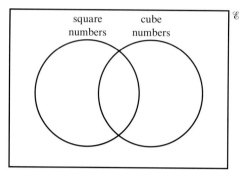

1	4	8
9	16	25
27	28	42
49	64	81
125	216	256
729	900	1000

2   This pattern is made from coloured tiles.

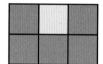 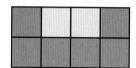 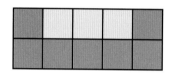

    a   Describe the pattern in words.

    b   Copy and complete this rule:

        number of pink tiles = number of yellow tiles + _____

    c   How many pink tiles would you need to build the 15th shape in the pattern?

3   List the next three numbers in each sequence. Explain your reasoning.

    a $3, 5, 7, 9 \ldots$ **b** $3, 6, 12, 24 \ldots$

    c $1000, 500, 250, 125 \ldots$ **d** $1\frac{1}{2}, 3, 4\frac{1}{2} \ldots$

    e $7, 5, 3, 1 \ldots$ **f** $1, 6, 36, 216 \ldots$

4   The rule for a number sequence is given as Term $n = n^2$.

    a   What does n represent in this rule?

    b   Write down the first three terms in this sequence.

    c   Find the value of the 80th term.

    d   Will the number 1000 be in this sequence? Give a reason for your answer.

    e   In which position in this sequence will the number 841 be?

KEY WORDS

common difference

common ratio

consecutive

cubic sequence

exponential sequence

first difference

nth term

position-to-term rule

quadratic sequence

second difference

sequence

square numbers

subscript notation

term

term-to-term rule

third difference

triangular numbers

MATHEMATICAL CONNECTIONS

You learnt how to understand and draw Venn diagrams in Chapter 18.

As you work through this chapter, you will draw on the work you did on patterns and sequences in earlier grades. The work you did on functions in Chapter 14 will be very useful in this chapter because mapping diagrams and tables can help you find the rules for more complicated sequences.

22.1 Patterns and number sequences

MATHEMATICS IN CONTEXT

Finding and recognising patterns is a key skill in mathematics. Think about learning to count. No one learns every single number off by heart. Instead, children learn to count using patterns. For example, you learnt that when a number has 9 in the units' place (12**9**) you move to the next ten (1**30**). When you decide whether a number is odd or even or when you recognise multiples of 5 or 10, you are using patterns that you already know.

A **sequence** is a set of numbers arranged in order that follow a set rule.

This pattern of dots represents the sequence of **square numbers**: 1, 4, 9, 16, 25 …

These two patterns both represent the sequence of **triangular numbers**: 1, 3, 6, 10, 15 …

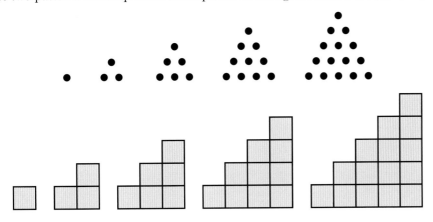

Each number (or pattern shape) in a sequence is called a **term**. The first number in the sequence is the first term. Each term has its own position (n) and we call the term in any position the **nth term**. Terms that follow each other are called **consecutive terms**.

You can use **subscript notation** to give the position of terms in a sequence. For example, the first term is T_1, the 15th term is T_{15}. T_n refers to the term in any position. This is sometimes called the general term.

TIP

Some sequences contain a specific type of number. For example: odd numbers, even numbers, the prime numbers to 100, square numbers, cube numbers and triangular numbers. If you recognise these number sequences it often makes it easier for you to work out the rule for the sequence.

Finding terms in a sequence

DISCUSSION 1

Work with a partner to answer these questions.

A bean plant is 12 cm tall when it is planted in a vegetable garden. Each week after that, the plant grows 9 cm taller.

a If the plant is 12 cm tall at the start of week one, write the first five terms of a number sequence that describes how the plant increases in height.

b Which of these graphs represents the number sequence? Justify your choice.

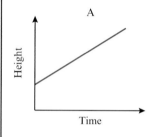
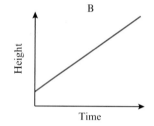
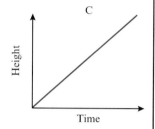

c How else could you represent this sequence? Share your ideas.

d You were given two pieces of information about the plant. What were these? How did this information help you work out the terms in the number sequence?

e What is the relationship between the number of weeks and the height of the plant?

f How could you work out the height of the plant at the start of week 10 (term 10 in the sequence) without listing all the terms?

REFLECTION

You have had many discussions about mathematics topics in this course.

- Has the way that you engage with discussions changed at all?
- Which aspects of discussing concepts have been most valuable?
- Which aspects of discussing concepts do you still need to work on? Why?

The term-to-term rule

In Discussion 1, you were given information about the first term (the height of the plant is 12 cm) and information about how the sequence continues (the plant grows 9 cm a week). Information that tells you how a sequence starts and how it continues is the **term-to-term rule**.

You might be given a rule and asked to generate a sequence or you might be given a sequence and asked to find the rule so that you can work out any missing terms.

WORKED EXAMPLE 1

The rules for two different sequences are given below. Use the rules to generate the first five terms of each sequence.

a Start with 3 and subtract 5 to get the next term.

b Start with 1 and divide by 2 to get the next term.

Answers

a You can draw a simple diagram to show the pattern:

The diagram shows that the first five terms are: $3, -2, -7, -12, -17$

b Draw a diagram:

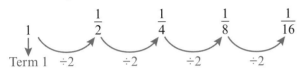

The first five terms are: $1, \dfrac{1}{2}, \dfrac{1}{4}, \dfrac{1}{8}, \dfrac{1}{16}$

WORKED EXAMPLE 2

For each sequence, list the next three terms and write the term-to-term rule you used to find them.

a 2, 8, 14, 20 ...   **b** 243, 81, 27, 3 ...   **c** 2, 6, 12, 20 ...

Answers

a You can use a diagram to work out the rule:

The term-to-term rule is 'add 6 to the previous term'. Use this to find the next terms. The next three terms are: 26, 32, 38

b Notice that the terms here do not have the same difference between them. That suggests you cannot use addition or subtraction. The terms are going down in value, so try division.

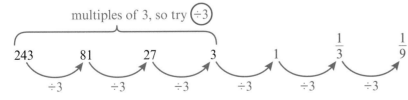

The term-to-term rule is 'divide the previous term by 3'.

The next three terms are: $1, \dfrac{1}{3}, \dfrac{1}{9}$

CONTINUED

c Using a diagram you can see that the difference between the terms increases by 2 with each term.

The term-to-term rule could be 'add the next even number to get the next term', or 'add 2 more than the previous difference to get the next term'.

The next three terms are: 30, 42, 56

TIP

There are different ways to think about the sequence in part **c** of Worked example 2. For example, you might notice that if you square the term number and add the term number to that you get the same sequence. ($1^2 + 1 = 2$, $2^2 + 2 = 6$, $3^2 + 3 = 12$). This method of thinking involves a general rule and this sequence is a quadratic sequence. You will explore these ideas further in the next sections.

WORKED EXAMPLE 3

What are the missing numbers in each sequence?

a 24, __, 16, 12, 8, __   **b** 10, 100, __, __, 100 000

Answers

a A diagram can help you find missing terms in the sequence using the terms you already know.

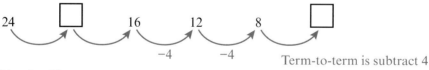

$24 - 4 = 20$
$8 - 4 = 4$

The missing terms are: 24, 20, 16, 12, 8, 4

b You should recognise that these numbers are powers of 10.

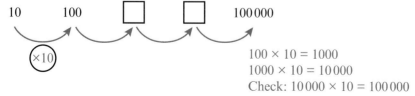

$100 \times 10 = 1000$
$1000 \times 10 = 10\,000$
Check: $10\,000 \times 10 = 100\,000$

The missing terms are: 10, 100, 1000, 10 000, 100 000

Exercise 22.1

1   Use the given rule to find the first five terms of each sequence.

   a   The first term is 200 and each term is half the previous term.

   b   The sequence starts at −8 and each term is 3 less than the previous term.

   c   Term 1 is 1.5. The difference between terms is 0.5.

2   For each sequence, give the term-to-term rule and the next three terms.

   a   1, 5, 9, 13, 17 …

   b   12, 22, 32, 42, 52 …

   c   1, 2, 4, 8, 16, …

   d $\dfrac{1}{2}, \dfrac{2}{4}, \dfrac{3}{6}, \dfrac{4}{8} \ldots$

   e   1, 4, 9, 16, 25 …

   f   2187, 729, 243, 81 …

   g   4150, 415, 41.5, 4.15 …

   h   1, 2, 6, 24, 120 …

> **TIP**
>
> There may be more than one possible rule for a sequence. Make sure you write down the rule you are using so anyone checking your work can see how you got your answers.

3   Find a rule and use it to work out the missing numbers in each sequence.

   a   24, __, 14, 9, 4

   b   1, __, 13, 19, 25

   c   16, _, 24, 28, 32

   d   0.3, __, 0.003, 0.0003

   e   4, __, __, 34, 54, 79

   f   100, 10, 1, __, __

4   Write your own rule for generating each of these sequences.

   a   The set of even numbers greater than 101.

   b   The set of negative multiples of 3.

   c   The set of descending odd numbers less than 50.

INVESTIGATION 1

The first term of a sequence is 95. The term-to-term rule for the sequence is 'subtract x'.

1   Find a value of x that will result in a sequence that meets each condition.

   a   Every second term (term 2, term 4, term 6 …) is a multiple of 10.

   b   Only every third term (term 3, term 6, term 9 …) is an integer.

   c $T_2 > T_1$

2   Make up a condition of your own. Exchange your condition with a partner. Ask your partner to find a value of x that results in a sequence that meets your condition.

22.2 Finding a general rule

The term-to-term rule is useful for finding missing terms or the next few terms in a sequence. If you want to find the 100th term or the 250th term or the nth term it is more efficient to use algebra to find a more **general rule** that allows you find the value of any term in any position.

DISCUSSION 2

Work in a small group to answer these questions.

Here are the rules for two sequences:

Rule A: The first term is 10. Find the next term by adding 2.

Rule B: Add 4 to the term number and then double the result.

a Apply the rules and find the first five terms of each sequence. What do you notice?

b Why can the second rule be called a position-to-term rule?

c What algebraic expression gives the value of the term in any position (n)?

When you work with sequences, it is useful to find a **position-to-term** rule so that you can work out the value of the nth term in the sequence without listing the previous terms.

WORKED EXAMPLE 4

Consider the sequence: 4, 10, 16, 22, 28 …

a What rule links each term to its position in this sequence?

b Write an expression for finding the term in position n.

c Use your rule to find the value of the 50th term.

Answers

a Make a table to show the term numbers and the value of each term.

Term number (n)	1	2	3	4	5
Term	4	10	16	22	28

$+6 \quad +6 \quad +6 \quad +6$

The difference between the terms is 6.

The difference tells you that the rule may involve multiples of 6.

Add a row to your table and multiply each term number by 6.

Term number (n)	1	2	3	4	5
Term	4	10	16	22	28
$n \times 6$	6	12	18	24	30

Compare the multiples of 6 with the terms.

Each term is 2 less than the multiple of 6.

The rule for finding the value of each term is 'multiply the term number by 6 and then subtract 2'.

TIP

A useful strategy for finding a position-to-term rule is to make a table of the first few terms and look for a pattern that links the term to its position in the sequence.

CONTINUED

b If the term number is n, $6 \times n = 6n$

2 less than $6n = 6n - 2$

nth term $= 6n - 2$

c Substitute 50 in place of n in your rule to find the value of the 50th term.

$6(50) - 2 = 300 - 2 = 298$

The 50th term is 298.

MATHEMATICAL CONNECTIONS

You worked with expressions and substituted values for letters in Chapter 7.

When the difference between the terms is the same, there is a **common difference**.

WORKED EXAMPLE 5

1 a Find the general rule for the nth term of this sequence:

1.5, 2, 2.5, 3, 3.5 …

b Use your rule to find the 25th term of the sequence.

c Show that the number 26 is in this sequence and work out what position it is in.

d How can you prove that a number is **not** in a sequence using the general rule?

Answers

1 a Looking at the sequence you can see that the common difference between terms is +0.5, so × 0.5 will be in the rule.

Make a table to show the position of each term. Include a row for $0.5n$.

Term number (n)	1	2	3	4	5
Term	1.5	2	2.5	3	3.5
$0.5n$	0.5	1	1.5	2	2.5

You can see from the table that each term is 1 greater than $0.5n$.

The rule for the nth term is $0.5n + 1$.

You can also write this rule as $\dfrac{n}{2} + 1$.

b You are looking for the 25th term, so $n = 25$.

Substitute $n = 25$ into the general rule.

$0.5(25) + 1 = 12.5 + 1 = 13.5$

c If the number 26 is in the sequence, then there must be a positive integer value of n for which $\dfrac{n}{2} + 1 = 26$.

Rearrange the equation to find the value of n:

$\dfrac{n}{2} + 1 = 26$

$\dfrac{n}{2} = 25$

$n = 50$

26 is the 50th term in the sequence.

TIP

Make sure you multiply the term number by 0.5 and not the actual term.

TIP

Term numbers cannot be negative and they must be integers.

CONTINUED

d Let n be the number you are checking.
Substitute this value into the rule and solve for n.

Given that n is the position of the term, the solution has to be a positive integer. If n is not a positive integer, the number is not in the sequence.

MATHEMATICAL CONNECTIONS

Can you see the connection between this work and what you learnt about changing the subject of a formula in Chapter 7?

When there is no common difference between the terms

Some sequences, such as the sequence of square numbers shown here, do not have a common difference between the terms.

The difference between terms is not the same.

The general rule for this sequence is 'square the term number' and the nth term is n^2. Sequences that involve n^2 are called **quadratic sequences**.

All quadratic sequences have a common second difference.

When there is no common difference between terms, look for other common differences.

WORKED EXAMPLE 6

Find an expression for the nth term of the sequence 0, 3, 8, 15, 24 …

Answer

Start by working out the difference between the terms. A diagram can help.

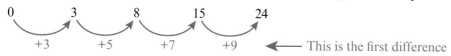

This is the first difference

This is called the **first difference**. You can see it is not the same for all terms.

Next, find the difference between each difference. This is called the **second difference**.

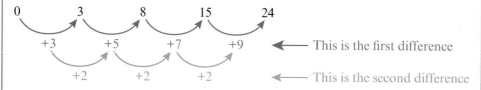

This is the first difference

This is the second difference

In this sequence the second difference is **constant**. This means that the sequence is quadratic and the rule will involve n^2.

Make a table to show the position of each term and add a row for n^2.

Position (n)	1	2	3	4	5
Term	0	3	8	15	24
n^2	1	4	9	16	25

Now you can see that each term is 1 less than the value of n^2, so the rule is $n^2 - 1$.

TIP

You can save time and work out the rule for this sequence by inspection if you recognise that the numbers are all 1 less than the sequence of square numbers. The same applies to other simple quadratic or cubic sequences.

Sequences that involve n^3 are called **cubic sequences**.

Cubic sequences all have a common **third difference**.

INVESTIGATION 2

How can you use the differences between terms to find the nth term of simple cubic sequences?

1   This diagram shows the 1st, 2nd and 3rd differences for a cubic sequence:

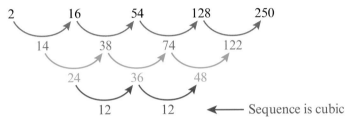

The third differences are the same, so the sequence will involve n^3.

   a   Make a table and add a row with the values of n^3 to it.

   b   What is the rule for this sequence?

2   Apply the difference method used in Worked example 6 to find the rule for this sequence:

9, 16, 35, 72, 133

REFLECTION

Think about the work in this section.

Write down:

* three things you already knew
* two things you learnt
* one question about this topic.

Exercise 22.2

1   Find a rule for each sequence and use it to find the 30th term.

   a   2, 5, 8, 11, 14 …
   b   4, 9, 14, 19, 24 …
   c   3, 8, 13, 18
   d   −3, 1, 5, 9, 13 …
   e   12, 23, 34, 45, 56 …
   f   9, 7, 5, 3, 1, …

2   Use the given rule for the nth term to write the first five terms in each sequence and calculate the value of the 25th term.

   a $2n + 5$
   b $3n - 1$
   c $4n + 7$
   d $n - 6$
   e $n^3 + 1$
   f $\dfrac{1}{n}$
   g $n^2 + 2n$
   h $n^2 + n + 1$

3   For the sequence: 2, 6, 10, 14, 18, 22 …

   a   Find the nth term.

   b   What is the value of the 32nd term?

   c   Show that the number 50 is in this sequence and determine its position.

   d   Explain why the number 105 cannot be in this sequence.

4   Use a difference method to find an expression for the nth term of each sequence.

   a   3, 12, 27, 48, 75 …   **b**   0, 3, 8, 15, 24 …

   c   0, 2, 6, 12, 20 …   **d**   −1, 6, 25, 62, 123 …

   e   0.5, 4, 13.5, 32, 62.5

DISCUSSION 3

The diagram gives you some information about a quadratic sequence.

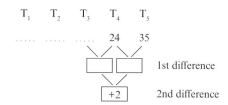

Discuss with a partner how you could use this information to work out the first three terms of the sequence.

SELF ASSESSMENT

You have worked with different types of sequences in this chapter.

- Which sequences did you find the easiest to work with? What made them easy for you?

- What was the most challenging part of this work? How did you overcome the challenge?

22.3 More about quadratic and cubic sequences

In Section 22.2, you worked only with differences to find the rules for simple quadratic and simple cubic sequences. Now you are going to learn a method that uses algebra to find the rule for any quadratic or cubic sequence.

You know that a quadratic expression takes the general form $ax^2 + bx + c$.

In a sequence, the variable is n rather than x, and the general rule for quadratic sequences is $T_n = an^2 + bn + c$.

If you substitute the term number (n) into the general rule, you get the following:

Term number (n)		1		2		3		4	
Term		$a + b + c$		$4a + 2b + c$		$9a + 3b + c$		$16a + 4b + c$	
1st difference			$3a + b$		$5a + b$		$7a + b$		
2nd difference				$2a$		$2a$			

Because you worked algebraically, you can say that:

- the first term is always $a + b + c$

- the 1st difference between the first two terms ($T_2 - T_1$) is always $3a + b$

- the 2nd difference is always $2a$.

Now you can link these expressions to actual differences and find the general rule for any quadratic sequence.

WORKED EXAMPLE 7

Find the general rule for the sequence 2, 9, 20, 35, 54, …

Answer

Start by finding the differences and linking them to the general expressions:

You have now made three equations.

$a + b + c = 2$

$3a + b = 7$

$2a = 4$

Solving these equations (from the bottom up) gives you values for a, b and c (the coefficients) that you can insert into the general form of a quadratic to find the rule for the sequence.

$2a = 4$, so $a = 2$

Substitute $a = 2$ into $3a + b = 7$: $3(2) + b = 7$, so $b = 1$

Substitute $a = 2$ and $b = 1$ into $a + b + c = 2$: $2 + 1 + c = 2$, so $c = -1$

You can now use these values for a, b and c to write the rule:

$T_n = an^2 + bn + c$

$T_n = 2n^2 + 1n + (-1)$

$T_n = 2n^2 + n - 1$

The general rule for this sequence is $T_n = 2n^2 + n - 1$

Investigation 3 looks at how you can apply this method to find the rule for a cubic sequence.

INVESTIGATION 3

The general form of a cubic sequence is $T_n = an^3 + bn^2 + cn + d$

This gives:

n	1	2	3	4
Term	$a + b + c + d$	$8a + 4b + 2c + d$	$27a + 9b + 3c + d$	$64a + 16b + 4c + d$
1st difference	$7a + 3b + c$		$19a + 5b + c$	$37a + 7b + c$
2nd difference		$12a + 2b$	$18a + 2b$	
3rd difference		$6a$		

1   Copy and complete the following statements for the form of the general rule a cubic sequence:
   a   The first term is always …
   b   The difference between the first two terms is always …
   c   The first 2nd difference is always …
   d   The 3rd difference is always …

2   Draw a diagram and find the 1st, 2nd and 3rd differences for the sequence:

   $-2, 0, 10, 34, 78 …$

3   Use the general expressions in the table to form four equations.

4   Determine the values of a, b, c and d and use these values to find the general rule for this sequence.

Exercise 22.3

1   You are given the sequence $-4, -2, 4, 14, 28, 46 …$
   a   Show that this is a quadratic sequence.
   b   Determine T_n for this sequence.
   c   Calculate T_{20}.

2   Use a difference method to find the nth term of these quadratic sequences.
   a $1, 10, 25, 46, 73 …$ b $-1, 4, 11, 20, 31 …$ c $3, 0, -1, 0, 3 …$

3   Use a difference method and the general form $an^3 + bn^2 + cn + d$ to find the nth term for each of the following sequences.
   a $4, 23, 66, 145, 272$ b $1, 14, 65, 178, 377$ c $1, 6, 19, 46, 93$

Work with a partner.

1 Write down three questions you could ask to check that someone understands the work in this exercise.

2 Work with another pair and answer each other's questions.

3 After you have listened to the responses provide some feedback to the other students. For example:

   • It seems that you understand __ very well.

   • To understand __ better you could __.

   • If you are finding __ difficult, it might help to __.

22.4 Exponential sequences and combined sequences

Exponential sequences

MATHEMATICS IN CONTEXT

Financial calculations involving compound interest and depreciation, population increase and decline and calculations involving the half-life of radioactive materials over time are all examples of **exponential sequences** in real life.

An exponent (power) tells you how many times to multiply a number.

In 2^4, the exponent (4) tells you to work out $2 \times 2 \times 2 \times 2$.

The terms in an exponential sequence increase in a **common ratio**, r.

TIP

You can find the common ratio by dividing any term by the previous term, for example calculating $\dfrac{T_2}{T_1}$ and checking that this is equal to $\dfrac{T_3}{T_2}$.

Where $\dfrac{T_2}{T_1} = \dfrac{T_3}{T_2}$, there is a common ratio.

WORKED EXAMPLE 8

The population of cane rats in a tropical area is recorded at the end of each year for 5 years. The results are shown in this table:

Year	1	2	3	4	5
Population	95	190	380	760	1520

a If the population continues to grow at this rate, what will it be at the end of year 6?

b Find an expression for T_n for this sequence.

c Use the rule to determine the population at the end of year 9.

Answers

a The population is doubling each year, so at the end of year 6 it will be $1520 \times 2 = 3040$

CONTINUED

b $\frac{190}{95} = 2$ and $\frac{380}{190} = 2$ so the common ratio is 2.

Listing each term showing how it changes from T_1 can help you find the rule:

T_1	95	
T_2	95×2	2^1
T_3	$95 \times 2 \times 2$	2^2
T_4	$95 \times 2 \times 2 \times 2$	2^3
T_5	$95 \times 2 \times 2 \times 2 \times 2$	2^4

Now look at the exponents for each term. Notice that the exponent is 1 less than the term number, or $n - 1$ (term 1 would be $95 \times 2^0 = 95 \times 1$).

The general rule is $T_n = 95 \times 2^{n-1}$

c Substitute $n = 9$ into the expression for T_n:

$T_9 = 95 \times 2^{9-1} = 95 \times 2^8 = 24\,320$

TIP

Remember that $x^0 = 1$ and $x^1 = x$.

The general rule for T_n of an exponential sequence with a common ratio is $T_1 \times r^{(n-1)}$, where r is the common ratio between the terms.

TIP

You may see this rule written as $T_n = a \times r^{(n-1)}$. In this form, a is the first term.

INVESTIGATION 4

Zora draws a growing pattern of leaves as shown:

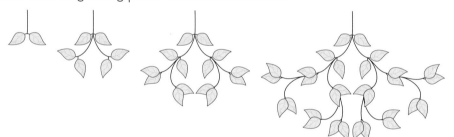

1   How does the pattern work? Describe the pattern in terms of numbers of *new* leaves in each shape.

2   Draw the next shape.

3   Zora makes a table to show the number of lines in each shape.

Shape	1	2	3	4	5	n
Number of new leaves	2	4	8	16		

She thinks this is an exponential pattern, but she cannot work out how many new leaves there would be in the nth diagram.

Use the information in the table, your own sketch and what you know about exponential sequences to find the nth term for this pattern.

Combined sequences

You can combine two or more sequences by adding or subtracting terms that are in the same position. This will give you a new sequence. You can find the rule for the new sequence by adding or subtracting the nth terms of the sequences that you combined.

WORKED EXAMPLE 9

Sequence A and B are combined to produce a new sequence C.
The first four terms of each sequence are given in the table.

Sequence	T_1	T_2	T_3	T_4	T_n
A	5	7	9	11	$2n + 3$
B	0	3	8	15	$n^2 - 1$
C	5	10	17	26	

a   How have the terms of sequences A and B been combined to get sequence C?

b   What is T_n for sequence C?

c   Use the general rule to find T_8 for Sequence C.

Answers

a   Looking at the terms in each row you can see that they have been added.

b   To find T_n, add the nth terms of Sequences A and B:

   $T_n = (2n + 3) + (n^2 - 1) = n^2 + 2n + 2$

c   Let $n = 8$:

   $T_8 = 8^2 + 2(8) + 2 = 82$

Exercise 22.4

1   Determine T_n for each sequence.

   a   1, 2, 4, 8, 16 …   b   2000, 1000, 500, 250, 125 …

   c   20 000, 16 000, 12 800, 10 240, 8192 …

2   Biologists in a lab are exploring how an insect population grows. They expect the number of insects for each of five generations to be:

   100, 150, 225, 337.5, 506.25

   a   What is T_n for this sequence?

   b   Why will the actual number of insects in each generation not be the same as the calculated values?

3   The temperature of gold being heated in a furnace increases each minute as shown:

Time in minutes	1	2	3	4	5
Temperature (°C)	5	15	45	135	405

   a   What is the rule for finding the temperature at any time?

   b   Gold melts at 1064°C. Estimate when it will reach this temperature point. Explain how you worked this out.

Use your answers to questions **1** to **3** to assess how well you understand exponential sequences.

- List the question numbers.
- Rate your work on each question using this scale:

Not there yet	On track	Excellent

4 The table gives some information about Sequences A and B.

Term	1	2	3	4	5	n
Sequence A	5	8	11	14	17	
Sequence B						$-2n^2$

  a Copy and complete the table.

  b Sequence C is formed by subtracting Sequence B from Sequence A.
     Use the information in your table to list the first five terms of Sequence C.

  c Determine T_n for sequence C.

REFLECTION

A student says: 'Finding rules for sequences is easy when you know what type of sequence you are dealing with, but it gets challenging when all the sequences are mixed up.'

What advice would you give this student to help them?

SUMMARY

Are you able to... ?
continue given number sequences and patterns
recognise sequences of square numbers, cube numbers and triangular numbers
work out and use the term-to-term rule for different sequences
find and use the nth term of linear sequences
use a difference method to find the nth term of simple quadratic sequences and simple cubic sequences
use and understand subscript notation such as T_n
find and use the nth term of quadratic sequences and cubic sequences using a difference method
recognise exponential sequences and find the nth term of exponential sequences
combine sequences and use the relationship between them to find the nth term of the resulting sequence.

Past paper questions

1 Fill in the two missing terms of the sequence.

$$-4, \boxed{}, 2, 5, 8, \boxed{}, \ldots$$

[2]

Cambridge IGCSE International Mathematics (0607) Paper 13 Q8, June 2022

2 For each sequence, write down the next two terms and find an expression for the nth term.

a 15, 11, 7, 3, −1, …

Next two terms $\boxed{}$, $\boxed{}$

n^{th} term $\boxed{}$ [3]

b 1, 2, 4, 8, 16, …

Next two terms $\boxed{}$, $\boxed{}$

n^{th} term $\boxed{}$ [3]

c 4, 10, 18, 28, 40, …

Next two terms $\boxed{}$, $\boxed{}$

n^{th} term $\boxed{}$ [3]

Cambridge IGCSE International Mathematics (0607) Paper 43 Q1, June 2020

3 Find the nth term of each sequence.

a 7, 14, 21, 28, …

$\boxed{}$ [1]

b 10, 7, 4, 1, …

$\boxed{}$ [2]

c 8, 16, 32, 64, …

$\boxed{}$ [2]

d 2, 6, 12, 20, …

$\boxed{}$ [2]

Cambridge IGCSE International Mathematics (0607) Paper 42 Q8, June 2019

Chapter 23

Functions 2

All of this chapter is extended content

IN THIS CHAPTER YOU WILL:

> use a graphic display calculator to explore functions

> recognise function types from the shape of their graphs

> recognise and explore graphs of linear, quadratic, cubic, reciprocal, exponential and trigonometric functions

> find a quadratic function from given information

> learn about asymptotes

> understand and use the logarithmic function as the inverse of the exponential function

> transform graphs for functions.

GETTING STARTED

1   From the shape of each graph, write whether the function is linear, quadratic, cubic or reciprocal.

a
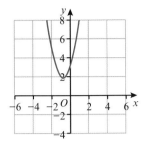

b
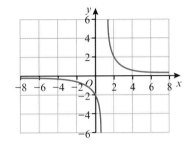

c
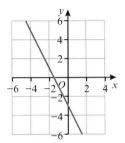

d
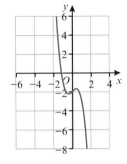

2   $f(x) = 5x - 3$, $g(x) = -x^2 + 7$ and $h(x) = \dfrac{x + 2}{3}$

a   Find:

i $f(9)$

ii $g(-2)$

iii $h(-3)$

b   i   If the domain of $f(x)$ is $-2 \leqslant x \leqslant 3$, what is the range of $f(x)$?

ii   If the domain of $g(x)$ is $-3 \leqslant x \leqslant 5$, what is the range of $g(x)$?

c   Express the inverse of the function $h(x)$ in the form $h^{-1}(x) = ...$

d   Find $hg(9)$.

KEY WORDS

amplitude

asymptote

exponential function

logarithmic function

period

trigonometric function

TIP

If you cannot remember the shape of the graphs of functions, try putting a type of function into your graphical display calculator to see what shape it makes.

TIP

Be careful to deal with the functions in the composite function in the correct order: $hg(x) = h(g(x))$, so work out function $g(x)$ first.

23.1 Recognising and exploring graphs of functions

You have already met four types of functions: linear, quadratic, cubic and reciprocal. In this chapter you will also use **exponential functions** and **trigonometric functions**.

The general form of an exponential function is $f(x) = a^x$ with $0 < a < 1$ or $a > 1$.

For example: $f(x) = 3^x$

WORKED EXAMPLE 1

Draw the graph f(x) = 3^x using your graphic display calculator.

Answer

1 Select **Graph** from the main menu.

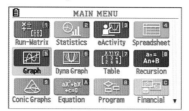

This screen opens.

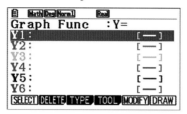

2 Now enter the function using the keypad.

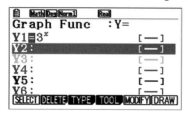

3 Press **F6** to select the **DRAW** option. This draws the graph of the function.

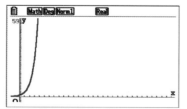

Use your graphic display calculator to explore the effect on the graph when 3 is changed to a different number or when the coefficient of the index, x, is changed.

MATHEMATICAL CONNECTIONS

You drew functions using your graphic display calculator in Chapters 13 and 14.

In this chapter you will consider trigonometric functions of the form f(x) = $a \sin (bx)$, f(x) = $a \cos (bx)$ and f(x) = $\tan x$.

For example: f(x) = $2 \cos (3x)$

INVESTIGATION 1

Use your graphical display calculator to investigate the shape of graphs of different trigonometric functions.

Choose a variety of different values for a and b in functions of the form $f(x) = a \sin(bx)$. Look at the shape of the graphs made by your chosen functions.

Describe what is similar about the graphs of all sine functions in this form.

Describe what happens to the graph as you change the values of a and b. Use both positive and negative values for a and b.

Repeat for cosine graphs of the form $f(x) = a \cos(bx)$ and tangent graphs of the form $f(x) = \tan x$.

> **TIP**
>
> The difference between the graphs of sine and cosine functions can be difficult to identify. One type of graph has a line of symmetry at $x = 0$, can you see which?

From Investigation 1, you know that the sine graph could have this shape:

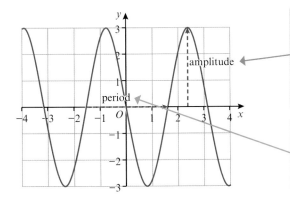

The **amplitude** is the height from the centre line to the peak (or to the valley). If it is difficult to see the centre line of the graph then you can calculate the amplitude from the distance between the valley and the peak divided by 2.
On this graph you can see that the amplitude is approximately 3.

The **period** is the length of one cycle of the wave. You can measure from peak to peak, or from any point to the next matching point.
On this graph you can see that the period is between 3 and 3.5.

The cosine graph is similar to the sine graph and looks like this:

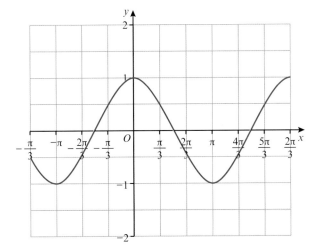

The tangent graph looks like this:

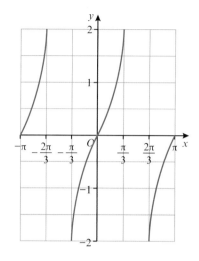

You can calculate the amplitude and period of a function.

For any sine or cosine function in the form $f(x) = a \sin (bx)$ or $f(x) = a \cos (bx)$:

Amplitude $= |a|$

Period $= \dfrac{2\pi}{b}$

WORKED EXAMPLE 1

What are the amplitude and period of the function $f(x) = -3 \sin (2x)$?

Answer

This is the graph of the function $f(x) = -3 \sin (2x)$

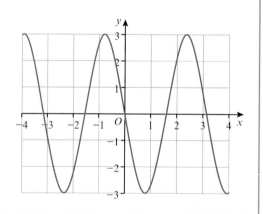

For the function $f(x) = -3 \sin (2x)$:

$a = -3$, so the amplitude is $|-3| = 3$

$b = 2$, so the period is $\dfrac{2\pi}{2} = \pi$

> **TIP**
>
> $|a|$ means the absolute value of a. That is the difference between a and zero, which in practice means to think of the number a as positive or zero. For example, $|-3| = 3$.

Exercise 23.1

1 Use the shape of each graph to identify the type of function.

    a   Which graphs represent a sine function?

    b   Which graphs represent a cosine function?

    c   Which graphs represent a tangent function?

A 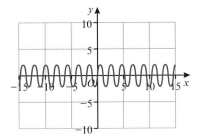   B 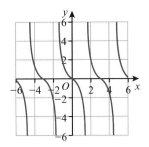   C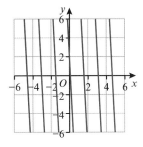

D 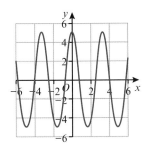   E 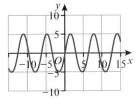   F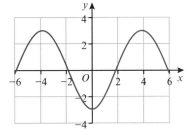

2   a Use your graphical display calculator to sketch a graph of the function
        $f(x) = -2\cos(5x)$.

    b   Use the graph on your calculator to estimate the amplitude of the function.

    c   Use the graph on your calculator to estimate the period of the function.

    d   Calculate the amplitude of the function using amplitude $= |a|$.

    e   Calculate the period of the function using period $= \dfrac{2\pi}{b}$.
        Give your answer to two decimal places.

3 This is the graph of a sine function.

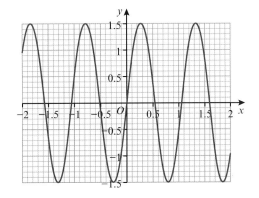

a   Estimate the amplitude shown on the graph.

b   Estimate the period shown on the graph.

c   Choose possible values for the amplitude and period of the function. Calculate a and b from your values and write the function in the form $f(x) = a \sin (bx)$.

d   Sketch your function from part **c** using your graphical display calculator. Compare the graph of your function to the graph shown. If the graphs are not the same (or very similar) try adjusting your function to improve it.

4   Write the:

    i   amplitude

    ii   period

    of each of these functions as appropriate leave answers in terms of pi, or give answers rounded to two decimal places.

    a $f(x) = 5 \sin (4x)$ **b** $g(x) = -8 \cos (7x)$ **c** $h(x) = 3.2 \sin (-2x)$

    d $f(x) = -\pi \sin (0.2x)$ **e** $g(x) = \cos (\pi x)$

5 $f(x) = 2^x$ is an exponential function.

    a   Copy and complete this table for the function $f(x) = 2^x$.

x	-3	-2	-1	0	1	2
$f(x)$						

    b   Copy this grid. Sketch the graph of $f(x) = 2^x$ for the domain $-3 \le x \le 2$, where $y = f(x)$.

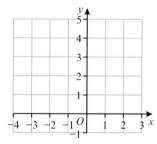

    c   On the same grid or on a separate copy, sketch the graph for the function $g(x) = -2^x$ for the domain $-3 \le x \le 2$, where $y = g(x)$.

    d   On the same grid or on a separate copy, sketch the graph for the function $h(x) = 2^{-x}$ for the domain $-2 \le x \le 3$, where $y = h(x)$.

    e   Describe how the graphs of the functions $f(x)$, $g(x)$ and $h(x)$ are similar and different.

    f   Use your graphical display calculator to explore and discover an exponential function that is a reflection of $f(x)$ in the line $x = 0$. Express the function as $k(x) = \ldots$

    g   Predict then test with your graphical display calculator which function has a graph that is a reflection of $s(x) = -5^x$ in the line $x = 0$. Express the function as $t(x) = \ldots$

    h   Predict then test with your graphical display calculator which function has a graph that is a reflection of $u(x) = \dfrac{1}{3^x}$ in the line $y = 0$. Express the function as $v(x) = \ldots$

23.2 Quadratic functions

The general form of a quadratic function is of the form:

$f(x) = ax^2 + bx + c$

You can rearrange a quadratic function to identify features of its graph.

To find a quadratic function using the coordinates of the vertex of the graph of the function and the coordinates of one other point on its graph you use the form:

$f(x) = a(x - h)^2 + k$

The vertex gives (h, k) and the values of h and k are substituted into the function:

$f(x) = a(x - h)^2 + k$

You then use the coordinates of the point given as the values of x and y to solve for a.

WORKED EXAMPLE 2

A quadratic graph has vertex $(1, 3)$. One other point on the quadratic graph is $(0, 5)$. Write the quadratic function $f(x)$ in the form $f(x) = ax^2 + bx + c$.

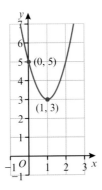

Answer

The vertex gives (h, k) in the function $f(x) = a(x - h)^2 + k$

so $f(x) = a(x - 1)^2 + 3$

The point $(0, 5)$ is where $x = 0$ and $y = 5$ on the graph. As $y = f(x)$ on the graph, you can replace x and y with these values in the function.

$5 = a(0 - 1)^2 + 3$

Solve to find the value of a:

$5 = a(-1)^2 + 3$

$5 = a + 3$

$2 = a$, or $a = 2$

You now have all the values for the function:

$f(x) = 2(x - 1)^2 + 3$

You can multiply out the brackets to find the function in the general form:

$f(x) = 2x^2 - 4x + 5$

To find a quadratic function using the coordinates of the vertex and the two places where the graph crosses the x-axis (the x-intercepts) you use the form $f(x) = a(x - p)(x - q)$.

WORKED EXAMPLE 3

A quadratic graph intercepts the x-axis at (0.5, 0) and (1, 0). One other point on the quadratic graph is (2, 3). Write the quadratic function in the general form.

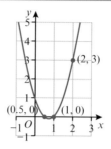

Answer

The x coordinates of the x intercepts are the values p and q in the function.

So $f(x) = a(x - 0.5)(x - 1)$

At the point (2, 3) $x = 2$ and $y = 3$. In the graph $y = f(x)$, so you can substitute these values into the function.

$3 = a(2 - 0.5)(2 - 1)$

$3 = a(1.5)(1)$

$3 = 1.5a$

$2 = a$ or $a = 2$

So the function is $f(x) = 2(x - 0.5)(x - 1)$

Multiply out the brackets to find the function in the general form:

$f(x) = 2(x^2 - 1.5x + 0.5)$

$f(x) = 2x^2 - 3x + 1$

Exercise 23.2

1 Find the quadratic function where its graph has vertex:

    a   (−1, 6) and one other point on its graph is (−2, 2)

    b   (1, −6) and one other point on its graph is (3, 6)

    c   (−1, −9) and one other point on its graph is (1, −5)

    d   (2.5, 3.5) and one other point on its graph is (4, −1)

    e   (−3, −6.5) and one other point on its graph is (0, −2)

    f   (2, 3) and one other point on its graph is (0, 2).

2 **a** Find the quadratic function where its graph intercepts the x-axis at:

      i   (−2.5, 0) and (2, 0) and one other point on its graph is (1, −7)

      ii   (1, 0) and (5, 0) and one other point on its graph is (6, 1.25)

      iii   (−0.5, 0) and (3, 0) and one other point on its graph is (4, 9)

      iv   (−0.333, 0) and (2, 0) and one other point on its graph is (1, 4).

b Check your answers for part **a** by entering your functions into your graphical display calculator to create a graph of the function where $y = f(x)$. For each function, check that the given x-intercepts match your graph and that the given point lies on your graph.

INVESTIGATION 2

Daniel says, 'When $a = 1$, I only need the vertex or the x-intercepts to work out the function. I don't need the coordinates of another point on the graph.'

Investigate whether Daniel's statement is true, and why it is or is not true for each form of the quadratic function.

23.3 Asymptotes

An **asymptote** is a straight line that a curve tends towards or approaches, as it moves towards infinity.

The curve gets closer and closer to the asymptote, but never reaches it.

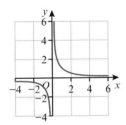

Here is the graph of $y = \dfrac{1}{x}$. The graph has a vertical asymptote at $x = 0$ and a horizontal asymptote at $y = 0$ which the function approaches as it tends to infinity. It can never meet $x = 0$, as this would result in division by zero, and it can never meet $y = 0$ either, as this would mean $1 = 0$.

> **TIP**
>
> Asymptotes can also be slanted, which occurs when the degree of the numerator is more than the degree of the denominator. These are called oblique asymptotes.

WORKED EXAMPLE 4

What is the equation of the asymptote for the graph of the function

$$f(x) = \frac{8x^2 + 1}{4x^2 - 9}?$$

Answer

Input the function $f(x)$ into a graphical display calculator to see the shape and position of the graph.

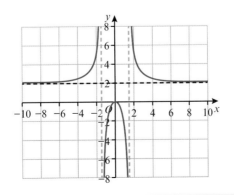

CONTINUED

You can see that the curve of the function tends towards $y = 2$, marked on the graph with a dotted black line.

Check this by substituting x with a high value that is easy to calculate with:

$$f(1000) = \frac{8 \times 1000^2 + 1}{4 \times 1000^2 - 9} = \frac{8000001}{3999991} = 2.0000047\ldots$$

You can see that for large values of x, $f(x)$ gets very close to 2.

In fact, as $x \to \infty$, $f(x)$ gets closer to 2, but the curve never crosses the line $y = 2$.

The function $f(x) = \dfrac{8x^2 + 1}{4x^2 - 9}$ has a horizontal asymptote at $y = 2$.

The curve also tends towards two vertical lines, marked on the graph by two dashed green lines.

If you enter the function into a graphical display calculator and follow the curve up and down you will see that one part tends towards -1.5 and the other part tends towards 1.5.

As $y \to \infty$ and $y \to -\infty$, x gets closer to -1.5 and 1.5.

The function $f(x) = \dfrac{8x^2 + 1}{4x^2 - 9}$ has vertical asymptotes at $x = -1.5$ and $x = 1.5$.

Exercise 23.3

1   For each of these functions sketch the graph on a graphical display calculator and work out the output of $f(1000)$. Hence write the horizontal asymptote for each function.

   a $f(x) = \dfrac{5x^2}{x^2 + 4}$ b $g(x) = \dfrac{6x^2 + 2}{-2x^2 - 4}$ c $h(x) = \dfrac{3x^2 - 12}{2x^2 - 5x - 3}$

2   a   Sketch by hand the graph of the function $f(x) = \left(\dfrac{1}{3}\right)^x + \dfrac{1}{2}$ for $-1 \leqslant x \leqslant 4$.

   b   Write the equation of the horizontal asymptote for $f(x)$.

3   a   Sketch by hand the graph of the function $g(x) = -3^x + 3$ for $-4 \leqslant x \leqslant 2$.

   b   Write the equation of the horizontal asymptote for $g(x)$.

> **TIP**
>
> Create a table of the values before drawing a grid to see the range of values needed for the y-axis.

4   This graph shows the function $f(x) = \dfrac{3}{x - 4}$

   a   What is the equation of the horizontal asymptote of $f(x)$?

   b   What is the equation of the vertical asymptote of $f(x)$?

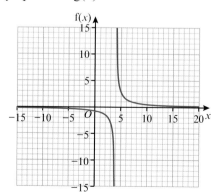

5   This graph shows the function

$g(x) = \dfrac{12x^2 + 1}{4x^2 - 16}$

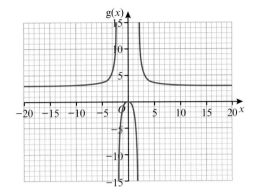

a   What is the equation of the horizontal asymptote of g(x)?

b   What are the equations of the vertical asymptotes of g(x)?

6   This is a graph of the function f(x) = tan x, where y = f(x).

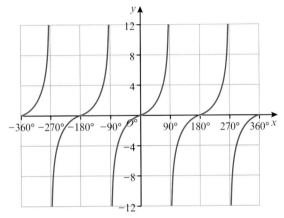

The graph shows that the function has a series of vertical asymptotes. Write the equation of each asymptote you find for −360° ≤ x ≤ 360° in the form x = __°.

23.4 Logarithmic functions

A **logarithmic function** is another way to express the relationship between values in an exponential function. The logarithmic function is the inverse of the exponential function.

You can express $a^x = b$ as $x = \log_a b$ or $x = \dfrac{\log b}{\log a}$

a is the **base**, x is the **exponent** and b is the **argument**.

The common logarithm is a logarithm with base 10. When you write a logarithm in base 10 you do not need to write the '10', so:

$\log_{10}(x) = \log(x)$

WORKED EXAMPLE 5

Rewrite the equation $4^3 = 64$ in logarithmic form.

Answer

In $4^3 = 64$, $a = 4$, $b = 64$ and $x = 3$ so $3 = \log_4 64 = \dfrac{\log 64}{\log 4}$

WORKED EXAMPLE 6

The mass in grams of a radioactive substance decays according to the formula

$m = 150 \times 3.09^{-t}$

How many years before the substance weighs 3 g? Give your answer to the nearest year.

Answer

Rewrite the equation in logarithmic form.

$\dfrac{3}{150} = 0.02 = 3.09^{-t}$

Using $x = \dfrac{\log b}{\log a}$, $-t = \log_{3.09} 0.02 = \dfrac{\log 0.02}{\log 3.09} = -3.46757\ldots$

So, $t = 3$ years.

You can also solve a logarithmic equation from a graph.

WORKED EXAMPLE 7

This is the graph of the function $g(x) = \log_b (x - a)$.

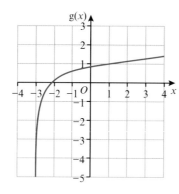

Find the equation of the logarithmic function from its graph.

CONTINUED

Answer

The logarithmic function has a vertical asymptote at $x = -3$.

This gives a in the function $g(x) = \log_b (x - a)$.

$a = -3$

Substitute this value of a into the function:

$g(x) = \log_b (x - -3)$ so $g(x) = \log_b (x + 3)$

One easily identifiable point on the graph is $(1, 1)$. This is the point where $x = 1$ and $g(x) = 1$. Substitute these values into the function:

$1 = \log_b (1 + 3)$ or

$1 = \log_b (4)$ so $b^1 = 4$ $\qquad b = 4$

The logarithmic function is $g(x) = \log_4 (x + 3)$

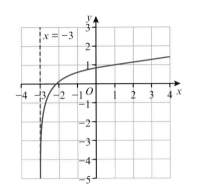

Exercise 23.4

1 Rewrite the equations in logarithmic form.

    a $3^2 = 9$ **b** $3^4 = 81$ **c** $4^{-1} = 0.25$ **d** $9^{\frac{1}{2}} = 3$

2 Rewrite the equations in exponential form.

    a $\log_4 16 = 2$ **b** $\log_5 125 = 3$ **c** $\log_{36} 6 = \dfrac{1}{2}$ **d** $\log 1000 = 3$

3 Find $f^{-1}(x)$ when $f(x) = \ldots$

    a 3^x **b** 2^{x+1} **c** $\log_5 (x)$ **d** $\log (x - 2)$

MATHEMATICAL CONNECTIONS

In Chapter 3 you learnt how to calculate compound interest using the compound interest formula:

$$A = P\left(1 + \frac{R}{100}\right)^T$$

A is final amount

P is initial balance

R is interest rate per year

T is the number of years.

4   An investment was made in dollars with compound interest applied monthly. The investment is represented by this equation where n is the number of months:

$A = 8000 (1.0075)^n$

   a   How much was the initial balance?

   b   What was the interest rate?

   c   What was the balance after two years?

   d   To the nearest year, after how many years will the investment be worth $19 600?

TIP

You can use the equation

$x = \dfrac{\log b}{\log a}$ to solve

these compound interest problems.

5   Tom saved some money in an account for 3 years at 4% compounded annually. After three years he had $5680.56.

   a   How much did Tom initially put into the account? Give your answer to the nearest whole cent.

   b   How long from the original deposit would it take Tom to have $7187.72 in the account?

6   $350 000 is invested at 2.8% per year, compounded annually. After t years the investment is worth $413 073. Find the value of t.

7   The mass in grams of a radioactive substance decays according to the formula

$m = 280 \times 1.09^{-t}$

   a   What is the mass of the substance after 5 years? Give your answer to three significant figures.

   b   How many years would it take for the substance to be reduced to 32.5 g?

8   Find the equation of each logarithmic function from its graph.

   a

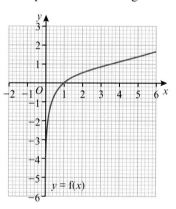

$y = f(x)$

   b

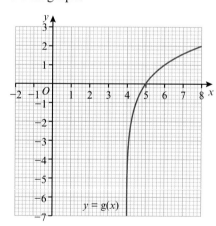

$y = g(x)$

c

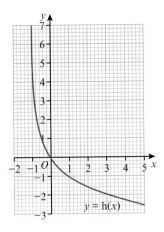

d

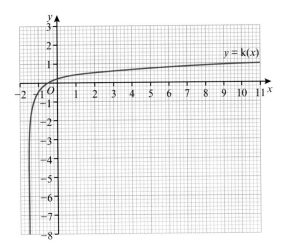

e

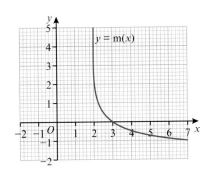

f

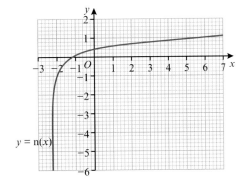

23.5 Transforming graphs of functions

MATHEMATICAL CONNECTIONS

Functions, and their graphs, can be transformed by translation in a similar way to how you translated shapes in Chapter 17. In this section you will explore and describe functions transformed by translation.

You can describe transformations that map a graph of one function on to the graph of another. One way to do this is to join points on one graph to their corresponding points on the other graph and then find the vector that describes the translation from one graph to the other.

WORKED EXAMPLE 8

The diagram shows the graph of the function $f(x) = x^2 + 2$ and the graph of $y = h(x)$.

a Describe the single transformation that maps the graph of $y = f(x)$ onto the graph of $y = h(x)$.

b Find $h(x)$ in terms of x.

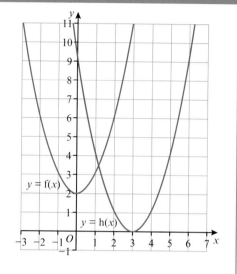

Answers

a You can join points on $y = f(x)$ to their corresponding points on $y = h(x)$. On this graph the easiest corresponding points to start with are the vertices and then places where the graph crosses easily recognisable coordinates.

The corresponding points on each graph are translated by 3 to the right and 2 down.

The graph of $y = f(x)$ maps onto $y = h(x)$ by a translation of $\begin{pmatrix} 3 \\ -2 \end{pmatrix}$.

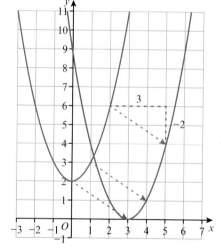

b First you can use your translation vector to express $h(x)$ in terms of $f(x)$.

$h(x) = f(x - \text{the horizontal shift}) + \text{the vertical shift}$

The horizontal shift in the translation vector is 3. The vertical shift in the translation vector is -2.

So $h(x) = f(x - 3) + -2 = f(x - 3) - 2$

You know that $f(x) = x^2 + 2$

so $h(x) = (x - 3)^2 + 2 - 2 = (x - 3)^2$

$h(x) = (x - 3)^2$

Exercise 23.5

1 Describe the single transformation that maps the graph of $y = f(x)$ onto $y = g(x)$ for each of these pairs of functions.

a $f(x) = x^2 + 4$, $g(x) = (x + 1)^2 - 1$

b $f(x) = x^3 - \dfrac{1}{2}$, $g(x) = x^3 + 6$

c $f(x) = x - \dfrac{2}{x}$, $g(x) = x - 1 - \dfrac{2}{x - 1}$

d $f(x) = |x - 3| + 2$, $g(x) = |x + 1| - 5$

> **TIP**
>
> To draw a graph with an absolute value, select **OPTN**, **F5** and then **F1** when you enter the equation in your graphic display calculator.

> **TIP**
>
> Sketch each pair of functions onto the same axes either by hand or using a graphical display calculator. If the transformation is a reflection, write the equation of the line of reflection. If the transformation is a translation write the vector.

2 In each graph $g(x)$ is a translation of $f(x)$. Express $g(x)$ in terms of x.

a $f(x) = 3x^2 + 2$ b $f(x) = -2x^3 - 1$

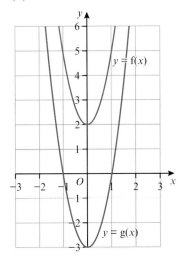

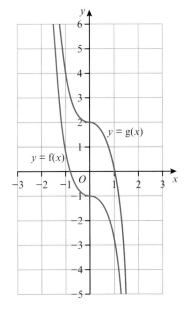

c $\quad$ f$(x) = \dfrac{3}{x + 2}$

d $\quad$ f$(x) = -x^2 + 5$

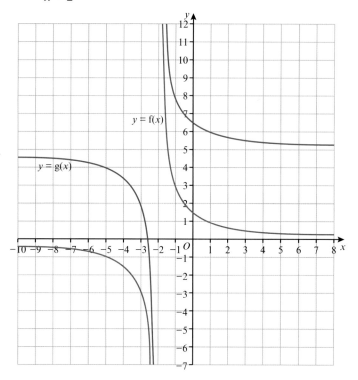

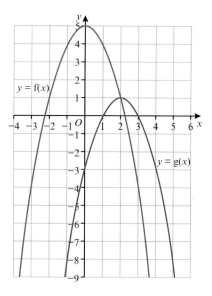

e $\quad$ f$(x) = 8^x - 2$

f $\quad$ f$(x) = \dfrac{2}{x} + 3$

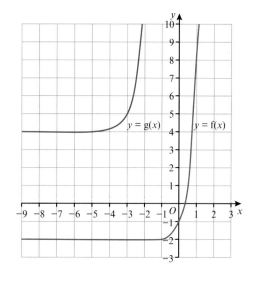

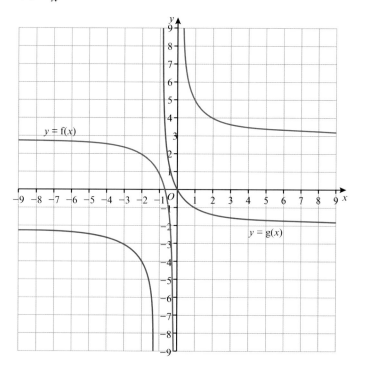

REFLECTION

Look back at this chapter and Chapter 14 and reflect on what you have learnt.

Work together with a partner or in a small group to discuss functions and create a mind map. Make sure to include:

- the different types of functions
- how to identify the graphs of different types of functions
- properties of functions
- how to use a graphical display calculator to explore or solve problems with functions
- methods used to solve problems involving functions
- the key vocabulary with examples or definitions
- anything else that you have discovered about functions.

From your mind map identify any aspects of functions that you might find more difficult to remember. Create a poster or revision cards with more information about those aspects and choose a time in the future when you will review the more difficult aspects using your poster or cards.

SUMMARY

Are you able to... ?
use a graphic display calculator to explore functions
recognise function types from the shape of their graphs
recognise and explore graphs of linear, quadratic, cubic, reciprocal, exponential and trigonometric functions
find a quadratic function from given information
describe asymptotes
understand and use the logarithmic function as the inverse of the exponential function
transform graphs for functions.

Past paper questions

1 $f(x) = x - \dfrac{4}{x}$

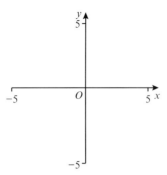

a On the diagram, sketch the graph of $y = f(x)$ for values of x between -5 and 5. [2]
[Using Past Paper Question Resource Sheet]

b Find the zeros of $f(x)$.

$x = \boxed{}$ or $x = \boxed{}$ [2]

c Solve the equation $f(x) = 2$.

$x = \boxed{}$ or $x = \boxed{}$ [2]

d $g(x) = f(x + 2)$.

   i On the same diagram, sketch the graph of $y = g(x)$ for values of x between -5 and 5. [2]

   ii Describe fully the **single** transformation that maps the graph of $y = f(x)$ onto the graph of $y = g(x)$. [2]

Cambridge IGCSE International Mathematics (0607) Paper 43 Q1, June 2021

2

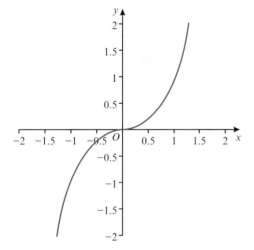

The graph shows $y = g(x)$, where $g(x) = x^3$.

a   **i** Find the inverse function, $g^{-1}(x)$.

Answer (i) $= \boxed{}$ [1]

   ii Sketch the graph of $y = g^{-1}(x)$ on the diagram above. [Using Past Paper Question Resource Sheet] [2]

   iii Describe fully the single transformation which maps the graph of $y = g(x)$ onto the graph of $y = g^{-1}(x)$.

Answer (iii) $= \boxed{}$ [2]

Cambridge IGCSE International Mathematics (0607) Paper 4 Q7b June 2009

Chapter 24

Mathematical modelling

All of this chapter is extended content

IN THIS CHAPTER YOU WILL:

> learn about and work through the steps in the modelling process

> make connections between different topics of mathematics

> use mathematical models to describe a real-life situation and draw conclusions

> analyse problems and select appropriate tools, methods and techniques

> develop solutions, consider limitations and improve models as necessary

> interpret and communicate solutions.

GETTING STARTED

1   Zara and Abi are uploading their projects to the school website. Abi's computer shows an upload speed of 13 megabytes every 4 seconds. Zara's computer is uploading at a rate of 3.9 megabytes per second.

   a   Draw a double number line to represent this situation for 3 minutes uploading time.

   b   How much more data can Abi upload per minute than Zara? Give the answer as a percentage.

   c   Zara needs to upload 400 megabytes. At this rate how many minutes will it take to upload?

   d   Abi's project took 1.2 minutes to upload at the given rate. How many megabytes did she upload?

2   These are the graphs that six students drew to **model** what happened to their kites.

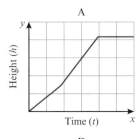
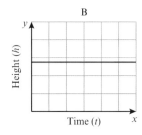
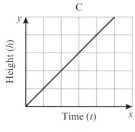

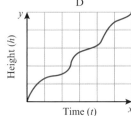
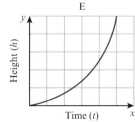
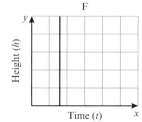

   a   Which of the graphs are not possible representations of successfully launching the kite and keeping it in the air? Explain why.

   b   One graph shows a kite rising at a steady speed with $t = h$? How can you tell which graph it is?

   c   Which of the graphs most accurately represents the launch of a kite? Why?

   d   Sketch a possible height over time graph for a launch in which the kite rises very quickly, then slowly loses height before rising again more slowly.

KEY WORDS

assumption

mathematical modelling

model

MATHEMATICAL CONNECTIONS

You learnt about calculating with rates in Chapter 3.

MATHEMATICAL CONNECTIONS

As you work through this chapter you will use a combination of skills and concepts from number, algebra, geometry, trigonometry, statistics and probability. For example, you might model the number of struts needed to build a bridge using sequences and patterns or model the height of an arch under the bridge using quadratic functions and graphs.

24.1 What is mathematical modelling?

Mathematical modelling involves using mathematics to help you represent real-life problems so that you can find solutions.

The diagram shows the steps in the modelling process.

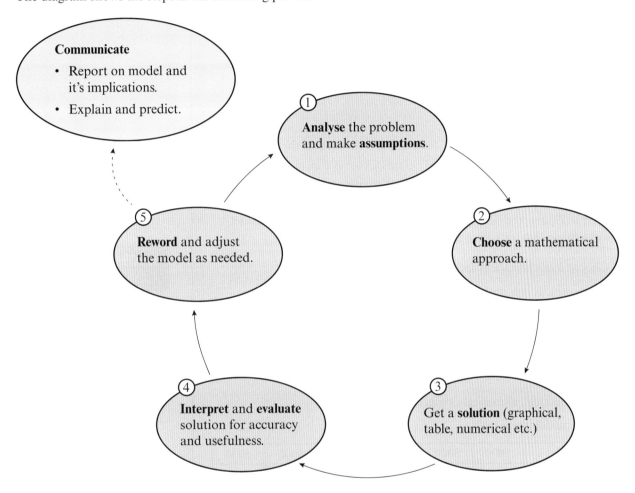

Communicate
- Report on model and it's implications.
- Explain and predict.

① **Analyse** the problem and make **assumptions**.

② **Choose** a mathematical approach.

③ Get a **solution** (graphical, table, numerical etc.)

④ **Interpret** and **evaluate** solution for accuracy and usefulness.

⑤ **Reword** and adjust the model as needed.

MATHEMATICS IN CONTEXT

New uses of mathematics are a key feature of most innovation in science, technology and engineering. These innovations often make use of models that draw on ideas from different areas of mathematics as well as computer algorithms and statistical techniques. Models can help developers optimise limited resources, such as time, money, energy requirements or space available on an electronic component. Models generally don't give perfect answers, but they do provide solutions that are good enough for decision making in real-life situations.

Worked example 1 takes you through each step in the modelling process using a familiar context to model a problem.

WORKED EXAMPLE 1

Jay wants to tile an outside table. He asks the question: 'How can I calculate how many tiles I need to cover an outdoor table of area $0.5\,\text{m}^2$?'

Step 1: Analyse the problem and make **assumptions.**

Think about this situation carefully. Consider:

a   What factors are relevant to finding a solution?

b   Which factor in this situation is constant?

c   What can you assume about the shape of the table?

d   What can you assume about the tiles?

Answers

a   The relevant factors are the area of the table and the area of the tiles.

b   The area of the table is given as $0.5\,\text{m}^2$, so this factor is constant.

c   You could assume that the table is a rectangle to make your calculations easier because most tiles are square or rectangular.

d   You need to assume the shape and dimensions of the tiles. For this model, you will assume that the tiles are square.

Step 2: Choose a mathematical approach.

How can you represent this problem mathematically?

Answer

You can find the number of tiles by dividing the area of the table by the area of one tile. As the tiles dimensions are likely to be in centimetres, you can convert the table area to cm^2 to work with. There are different ways to represent this.

Step 3: Get a graphical, numerical or algebraic solution.

For a numerical model, use a table:

Area of table (cm²)	5000	5000	5000	5000	5000	5000
Area of tile (cm²)	20	25	40	50	80	100
Number of tiles needed	250	200	125	100	62.5	50

For a symbolic model, use a formula:

Let the number of tiles be n and the area of each tile be a.

$na = 5000$

$$n = \frac{5000}{a}$$

For a graphical model, plot n against a.

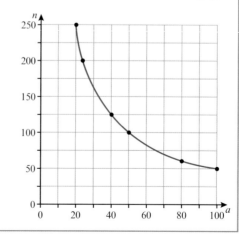

> ### MATHEMATICAL CONNECTIONS
>
> You learnt how to convert between different units of area in Chapter 12. Revise that work if you have forgotten how to do this.

CONTINUED

Step 4: Interpret and evaluate your solutions to see if they are accurate and useful in the context of the problem.

1 **a** What do these representations show?

b Jay chooses a tile that is 12 cm long and 7 cm wide. Use the graph to estimate how many tiles this size would be needed to cover the table. Is this a useful number of tiles in a real-life context?

c Why do you think this model ignores areas below 20 cm²?

2 Think about your solutions in the context of the real-life situation.

a What restrictions might affect your solution to the problem in real life?

b Why might people choose one size of tile rather than another?

Answers

1 **a** The table and graph clearly show that the value of n decreases as a increases. In other words, you need fewer tiles if you choose larger tiles.

The equation tells you that this is a reciprocal relationship that will produce a curved graph. (It should be clear to you that a cannot be 0.)

b Approximately 60 tiles. This seems a reasonable number of tiles.

c 20 cm² would be quite a small tile and anything less than that would be impractical as it would require a lot of tiles and lots of grout in between them.

2 **a** Tiles may not come in the sizes that you have used. You have assumed a square or rectangular shape for the tiles (and the table). If the tiles were hexagonal, you might need more tiles so you can cut off pieces that don't fit. And if the table was round, it would affect how many tiles you need as there would be wastage.

b Cost and design/style of tile would probably influence people's decisions. They might also choose tiles that cover the table completely with no cut tiles. People may prefer to use the biggest size possible so they have the fewest joins between the tiles.

DISCUSSION 1

Compare modelling and investigation tasks

Read these statements about modelling in mathematics.

- Modelling involves making real choices and not just following a set of steps in a given order.
- The answers to modelling problems use valid mathematical arguments but they also have to make sense in the context. There may not be a single answer.
- Modelling problems are generally practical because they deal with issues that people need to understand or decisions that have to be made.
- The process of modelling is creative and cyclical and the problems might be open-ended.
- In the real world, mathematical modelling is cooperative and people don't often work on models without input from others (or other sources).

How is modelling different from classroom exercises and problem solving?

What are the main differences between mathematical modelling and carrying out an investigation?

Exercise 24.1

1   A café owner needs to have a coffee machine repaired and serviced. There are two companies that do this. Syd's Servicing charges $45 per machine and $30 per hour. Reza's Repairs charge $60 per machine and $28 per hour. Develop a model to compare the rates and determine the number of hours for which:

   a   Syd's Servicing is cheaper

   b   the cost will be the same for both companies.

2   The table shows the volume of water in a reservoir during the dry season, recorded at the end of each week for 5 weeks.

Time (weeks)	1	2	3	4	5
Volume (litres)	35 000	27 000	26 000	21 000	14 000

   a   Draw a graphical model to represent this data and determine an equation that best fits the data.

   b   If this trend continues, estimate how much longer the water will last before it runs out.

   c   Comment on how accurate and useful your solution is.

3   The diagram shows a design for an open box made from a sheet of card 40 cm wide and 60 cm long.

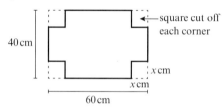

   a   What is the maximum that x could be? Why?

   b   Develop a model to determine the approximate value of x that will give you a box with the maximum possible volume.

   c   How could you get a more precise value for the volume?

DISCUSSION 2

Different models and their uses

There are different levels of mathematical models and different types of models.

1   Consider each type of problem. Suggest what type of mathematical model might be useful for each. Justify your choices.

   a   Predicting future populations of endangered species.

   b   Working out the point at which you start to make a profit from sales of handmade crafts.

   c   Deciding what dimensions to use to build a safe wheelchair ramp at school.

   d   Using the half-life of caffeine to work out how much caffeine is in your blood after drinking coffee or caffeinated drinks.

   e   Calculating how long it will take for a waterweed to cover the surface of a round pond.

   f   Working out the depth of water in a harbour given the tidal changes.

CONTINUED

2 For each of these models, suggest a real-life problem that would suit that type of modelling. Give a mathematical reason for your choice.

    a Scale diagrams   **b** Linear functions and their graphs

    c Table of numerical values   **d** 2D representation of a 3D situation

    e Computer simulations   **f** Cubic functions

24.2 Modelling with sequences and patterns

MATHEMATICAL CONNECTIONS

You worked with sequences in Chapter 22 and you worked with formulas in Chapter 7.

You can use what you know about patterns and sequences to model real-life situations.

You can often model situations where a quantity is increasing or decreasing by a fixed amount (the amount is added or subtracted) by an arithmetic sequence. If the quantity is increasing by a fixed percentage or is multiplied by a fixed amount, you can often model the situation using a geometric series.

WORKED EXAMPLE 2

The pattern along the side of this railway bridge can be isolated and modelled with beams as shown:

number of Δs	1	2	3
number of beams	3	5	7

1 **a** Continue the sequence to show the number of beams up to eight triangles.

    b What is the relationship between the number of triangles and the number of beams?

    c If n is the number of triangles and b is the number of beams, write a formula that relates the number of triangles (n) and the number of beams (b).

    d Show that your formula works.

CONTINUED

2 One side of the bridge has 100 triangular sections. Each beam must be painted and rustproofed at a cost of $123.50 per beam. Calculate the total cost.

3 One section of the bridge has 51 beams. How many triangles are in this section?

4 Why could it be useful to model the bridge structure in this way?

Answers

1 a You can use a table to do this, rather than drawing shapes.

Triangles	1	2	3	4	5	6	7	8
Beams	3	5	7	9	11	13	15	17

b The number of beams (b) is twice the number of triangles plus 1.

c $b = 2n + 1$

d Substituting values for eight triangles gives:
$b = 2(8) + 1 = 17$
This is correct based on the table.

2 First calculate how many beams will be painted:
$b = 2(100) + 1 = 201$ beams
Calculate the cost:
$123.50 \times 201 = \$24\ 823.50$

3 You are given $b = 51$, so $51 = 2n + 1$
$50 = 2n$
$25 = n$
There are 25 triangles in that section.

4 It allows you to solve problems related to the number of beams or triangles in any section of the bridge. This allows you to work out costs (as in Question **2**) and to solve related problems such as percentage of total beams that have rusted, number of bolts needed to add a triangular section and so on.

WORKED EXAMPLE 3

The table shows the relationship between time (t) and the height (h) of a projectile. Find a rule to model the relationship between t and h.

t	1	2	3	4	5
h	6	17	32	51	74

Answer

Treat the values of h as the first five terms of a sequence.

Find the difference between them.

CONTINUED

The second difference is constant, so the sequence is quadratic.

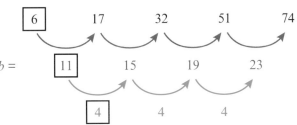

$a + b + c =$ 6   17   32   51   74

1st difference $3a + b =$ 11   15   19   23

2nd difference $2a =$ 4   4   4

Apply the general equations to find the rule:

$a + b + c = 6$

$\quad 3a + b = 11$

$\qquad 2a = 4$

$2a = 4$, so $a = 2$

$3(2) + b = 11$, so $b = 5$

$2 + 5 + c = 6$, so $c = -1$

The rule is $h = 2t^2 + 5t - 1$

> **TIP**
>
> Remember the general equation of a quadratic is $y = ax^2 + bx + c$.

Exercise 24.2

1   An alkane (saturated hydrocarbon) is a chemical compound (a molecule) that contains carbon and hydrogen atoms bonded in particular ways. Carbon atoms are bonded to other carbon atoms by a single bond and each carbon atom is bonded to at least two hydrogen atoms, also by single bonds.

This is a simple model of ethane.	This is a 3D computer model of decane.
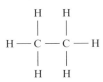	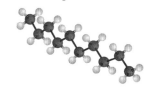

    a   Methane is the simplest alkane. A molecule of methane has one carbon atom and four hydrogen atoms. Draw a simple model of methane.

    b   Ethane is the second alkane and decane is the tenth alkane. What is the relationship between the ordinal position and the chemical structure of the molecules of alkanes?

    c   Octane is the 8th alkane. How many carbon atoms will one molecule of octane have? How many hydrogen atoms will it have?

    d   If an alkane molecule has n carbon atoms in a chain, how many hydrogen atoms will there be?

2 A family decide to set up an investment for their children. They want to know how the investment will grow if they invest $10 when their first child is 1 year old and then double the previous year's investment each year until their first child is 21 years old.

    a How could you model this mathematically?

    b How much would they need to invest at the end of year 15 if they follow this pattern of investment?

    c How much will they have put into the investment if they continue to invest in this way till the end of the 21st year?

PEER ASSESSMENT

Discuss your work with a partner.

What things did you and your partner do well?

What could you improve?

What skills did you use here that you learnt earlier or in other sections of work?

24.3 Modelling with diagrams

You can use maps, plans and other scale drawings to model real-world spaces and situations. In mathematical modelling, diagrams are often used to give you information about the situation. Drawing your own scale diagrams can help you solve modelling problems in both two- and three-dimensional situations.

WORKED EXAMPLE 4

Some satellites are carried in the cargo bay of space shuttles to launch them into orbit. A shuttle has launched and when it is 10 km from the launch site, the angle of depression is 10°.

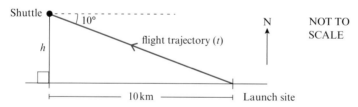

a Draw a scale diagram to determine the length of the flight trajectory and the vertical height of the shuttle at this stage.

b Show how you could calculate the measurements to a greater degree of mathematical accuracy (without using a scale diagram).

Answers

a Start by choosing a suitable scale that is easy to work with, for example 1 cm = 1 km

Note that the angle of the trajectory from the ground is alternate to the angle of depression, so it is also 10°.

Use a ruler and a protractor to construct the scale diagram.

TIP

The angle of depression is the angle between a horizontal line from the observer and the line of sight to an object below the horizontal line.

CONTINUED

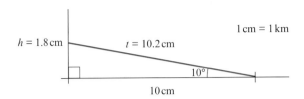

Measure the length of the trajectory and the vertical height on the diagram.

$t = 10.2\,\text{cm}$

$h = 1.8\,\text{cm}$

Convert the measurement to kilometres.

$t = 10.2\,\text{km}$

$h = 1.8\,\text{km}$

b   You can use trigonometry to solve the triangle.

Start with a rough sketch and fill in what you know:

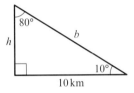

Use the correct trigonometric ratios to find the unknown sides.

$\dfrac{h}{10} = \tan 10 = 1.763\,\text{km}$

$t = \dfrac{10}{\sin 80} = 10.154\,\text{km}$

> **TIP**
>
> Use a sharp pencil. If you work on graph paper, it is easy to draw vertical lines and to check you have drawn a 10 cm long baseline.

> **TIP**
>
> Comparing the measurements from the trigonometry method shows that these measurements are more accurate and that they will round to give you the measurements you found using the scale diagram.

Exercise 24.3

1   The diagram shows the positions chosen for a light and a dimmer switch in a large room.

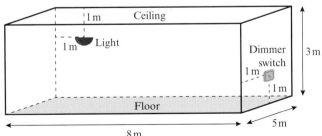

An electrician needs to install wiring to connect the light to the dimmer switch. The electrician wants to use the shortest possible length of wire.

a   Explain why the shortest distance between the light and the dimmer switch is not a practical solution for this particular problem.

b   The wire needs to go along walls and either across the floor or across the ceiling. The electrician draws this 2D diagram to model the 3D situation.

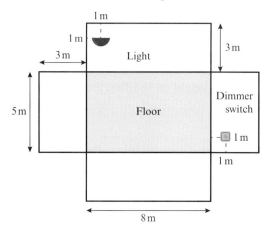

Copy the diagram and show how the electrician could use it to work out the shortest length of wire needed to connect the light and the dimmer switch if the wire goes across the floor.

c   The homeowner decides that the wire should go across the ceiling and not across the floor. Determine the shortest length of wire needed to connect the light and the switch in that way.

REFLECTION

Many mathematical modelling problems can be changed or described differently to make them simpler to solve.

How did representing the 3D room on a 2D drawing help to you to simplify and solve the problem?

In what other types of problems might this approach be useful?

2   Two villages, Dhahab and Fiddtan, are both situated north of the main metro line. Dhahab is 3 km north of the metro line and Fiddtan is 6 km north of the metro line, as shown on the diagram.

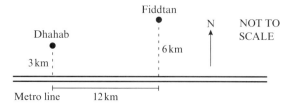

The planning department wants to build a new metro stop between the two villages. A road will be built from each village to the metro stop. The road agency wants the new roads to be straight and the total length of new road to be as short as possible.

a   What assumptions can you make about this situation?

b   What mathematics do you think will be involved in solving this problem?

c   Where should the new metro stop be built so that the total length of new road is as short as possible? Show clearly how you work this out.

d   Interpret your solution and evaluate your model based on the fact that it costs on average $2.4 million dollars to construct one kilometre of new road on level, stable ground.

REFLECTION

The metro stop problem could be modelled and solved in different ways.

- How did you model the problem? What made you choose this method?
- What strategies would you recommend for tackling other similar modelling problems? How are these strategies helpful?

24.4 Modelling with functions and graphs

You already know that functions and graphs are useful for solving problems and making predictions. Modelling often involves the process of finding a mathematical relationship or graph to fit a particular situation.

DISCUSSION 3

How do you choose a model?

Why are most door handles positioned on the edge of doors away from the hinges?

Here is some data from an experiment in which researchers measured the force needed to open a heavy wooden door by using a handle attached to the door in different positions.

Distance of handle from hinge (cm)	10	20	30	40	50	60	70	80
Force needed to open the door (N)	80	40	28	20	16	13	11	10

How would you model this situation to answer the question? Explain your choices.

WORKED EXAMPLE 5

A landscaper wants to mark out the biggest possible rectangular area using a 600 m long length of rope.

a Determine the dimensions of the rectangle.

b What is the maximum area that can be enclosed?

Answers

a Draw a sketch.

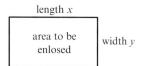

length x

area to be enlosed   width y

Let length = x and width = y

For the area of a rectangle to be a maximum, the difference between the length and width must be as small as possible. This means that the length can be at most $P \div 4$ and the width can be at its lowest $P \div 4$, where P is the perimeter.

In our case, $P = 600$

$P \div 4 = 150$

The rectangle will be 150 m long and 150 m wide.

b If $x = 150$, and $y = 150$, the area $xy = 150 \times 150$
$$= 22\,500\,\text{m}^2$$

WORKED EXAMPLE 6

The graph models the flight of a projectile that has been catapulted vertically upwards.

a Use the graph to describe the flight of the projectile.

b At what time (t) does the projectile reach a maximum height?

c If the height (h) in metres is modelled by the equation $h = 98t - 4.9t^2$, determine the maximum height reached by the projectile.

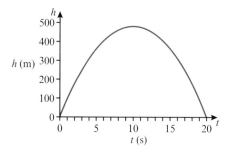

Answers

a The graph shows height in metres on the y-axis and time in seconds on the x-axis. The curve of the graph shows that the projectile's height increases from 0 m over time to a maximum and then decreases over time until it reaches 0 m again.

CONTINUED

b The turning point of the graph shows the maximum height.
   This is at 10 seconds.

c Solve the equation for $t = 10$.
   $h = 98\,(10) - 4.9\,(10^2)$
   $\quad = 980 - 490$
   $\quad = 490\,\text{m}$

DISCUSSION 4

Using a different model for the same situation

Think back to the metro stop problem in Exercise 24.3.

After public input, the road planning department agrees that the distances from Dhahab and Fiddtan to the metro stop should be equal.

One of the planners decides to model the problem on a coordinate grid as shown:

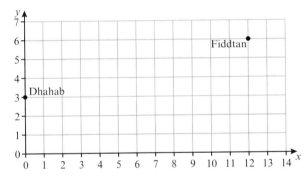

How can you use this model to decide where the metro stop should be located so that the roads from each town to the metro stop are equal in length?

REFLECTION

Think back to the original metro stop problem and the types of models that you and other students used to solve it.

Could modelling the original problem on a coordinate grid as shown in Discussion 4 be used to find the solution? How?

Exercise 24.4

1   A reservoir contains 1500 cubic metres of water. Engineers need to empty the reservoir to reline it with concrete. They have a pump that can remove water at a rate of $50\,m^3$/hour.

    a   Write down a model for the amount of water (V) left in the reservoir in terms of how long the pump has been working in hours (t).

    b   How long will it take to empty the reservoir?

2   A researcher wants to fence off an area next to a river to study the plants over time. The researcher has 20 m of fencing and wants to know the maximum area that can be enclosed.

They develop these two models to solve the problem:

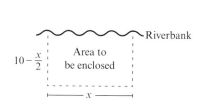 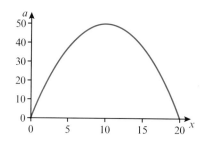

    a   Use the information in the models to show that the maximum area that can be enclosed is $50\,m^2$.

    b   What restrictions are placed on the solution by the real-life situation?

3   A cuboid-shaped open box $2x$ cm long, x cm wide and h cm high has an internal surface area of $48x - 4x^2\ cm^2$.

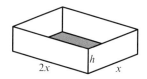

    a   Show that the height of the box is $8 - x$ cm.

    b   Write a model for the volume of the box in terms of x.

4   A conservationist notes that in a water catchment area there is an increase in the number of fast-growing water-thirsty plants. These plants impact the amount of water that flows from the rivers into the reservoirs that supply city drinking water.

They prepare this data:

Time	Present	10–20 years from present	20–40 years from present
Outflow (millions of cubic metres)	472	303	123
Cost per hectare of removing the water-thirsty plants	$200	$2000	$8000

a Design a mathematical model to describe the relationship between time and the amount of water that flows from the catchment area. State the assumptions you make and evaluate your model.

b What model best defines the relationship between time and the cost of clearing water-thirsty plants?

c Evaluate the models.

5 A simple model for the spread of an infectious disease in an isolated community of n people operates on these assumptions:

A person with the disease is infectious for 1 day (in other words, they can give other people the disease only within that day.)

After the infectious period has passed, the person who had the disease is immune and cannot get the disease again.

For the model, one person catches the disease and comes into contact with one other person during the infectious period.

The second person is infected immediately and comes into contact with one other person during their infectious period (one day).

The process continues with one contact per day until an infected person comes into contact with an immune person and the spread of the disease stops.

a Explain why this is a very basic model.

b Use a simulation model to determine how many people will be infected before the disease stops spreading if $n = 6$. Do at least five trials and calculate the mean number of infections.

c How does the number of infections vary with the size of the population (n)? Repeat your simulation model for 10, 20, 30, 40 and 50 people. Compare the results with the mean number of infections you calculated previously.

d Is the number of infections affected if there are people in the population who are immune? Use a simulation model for $n = 30$ and include another variable (p) to represent people who are immune to the disease. Use 3, 6, 9, 12 and 15 as values of p. Compare your results with your previous answers. What do you discover?

e Evaluate the model and the solutions in terms of what you know about the spread of diseases in real life.

MATHEMATICS IN CONTEXT

Scientists use fairly complex models to track and predict the spread of infectious diseases in real-world contexts.

TIP

Use what you know about probability to develop a suitable model to simulate random contact. Make sure you record your results.

SELF ASSESSMENT

Use this scale to rate your work in each of the following categories.

4 Excellent	3 Accomplished	2 Proficient	1 Still developing

- Interpreting problems and representing them mathematically.
- Level of understanding of the modelling process.
- Ability to show working clearly.
- Use of a range of mathematical processes and techniques.
- Reporting, explaining and evaluating solutions.

SUMMARY

Are you able to... ?

learn about and work through the steps in the modelling process
make connections between different topics of mathematics
use mathematical models to describe a real-life situation and draw conclusions
analyse problems and select appropriate tools, methods and techniques
develop solutions, consider limitations and improve models as necessary
interpret and communicate solutions.

Past paper questions

1   A tank has a capacity of 400 litres.

Water from Tap A flows at x litres per minute.

Water from Tap B flows at 2 litres per minute **less** than the water from tap A.

  a   Write down an expression in terms of x for the time, in minutes, for tap A to fill the tank.

[1]

  b   Tap B takes 10 minutes longer to fill the tank than tap A.

Write down an equation in terms of x and show that it simplifies to

$$x^2 - 2x - 80 = 0.$$

[4]

  c   Solve $x^2 - 2x - 80 = 0$ and find the time it takes to fill the tank when both taps are turned on. Give your answer in minutes and seconds, correct to the nearest second.

[4]

Cambridge IGCSE International Mathematics (0607) Paper 43 Q11 June 2022

2   In this question, all lengths are measured in millimetres.

A small plastic cup, A, is shown in this diagram.

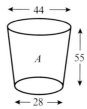

These plastic cups are stacked as shown in the diagram

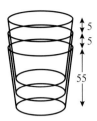

a   Find the height of a stack of 8 of these cups.

[2]

b   Find the number of these cups in a stack that has a total height of 105 mm.

[2]

c   A similar cup, B, has base diameter 42 mm.
    Find the height of this cup.

[2]

Cambridge IGCSE International Mathematics (0607) Paper 42 Q7a,b,c June 2018

3

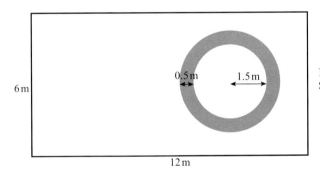

The diagram shows a rectangular garden, 6 m by 12 m. In the garden there is a circular pond with radius 1.5 m. There is a circular path of width 0.5 m around the pond.

a   The pond is 0.6 m deep.
    Work out the volume of water in the pond when it is full.

[2]

b   Work out the area of the path.

[2]

c   The rest of the garden, apart from the pond and the path, is covered by grass.
    Work out the area covered by grass.

[2]

Cambridge IGCSE International Mathematics (0607) Paper 31 Q11 November 2016

> Glossary

acute angle: an angle greater than 0 degrees but smaller than 90 degrees

adjacent: the side that forms one part of a given angle in a right-angled triangle but is not the hypotenuse

algebraic expression: a collection of letters and numbers

algebraic fractions: a fraction where the numerator and/or denominator contains algebraic expression(s)

alternate angles: a pair of angles that are on opposite sides of two parallel lines cut by another transversal line. Alternate angles are equal

amplitude: a measure of the vertical change over one cycle of a function

angle of depression: the angle below the horizontal

angle of elevation: the angle above the horizontal

arc: (major and minor) an arc is the distance between two points around the circumference of a circle: an arc bigger than that of a semicircle is a major arc, an arc smaller than the semicircle is a minor arc

arc area: the 2D space taken up by a shape

arc length: the distance between two points around the circumference of a circle

assumption: an educated guess or ideas that we accept to be true so we have a starting point, to solve or model a problem

asymptote: a line that a curve approaches, as it heads towards infinity

average: a measure used to find the middle of a data set.

bar chart: a graph using bars to show quantities or numbers

bearing: an angle in degrees measured clockwise from the north, given as three figures

bias: something that affects the chance of an event happening in favour of a particular outcome

bimodal: a data set with two modes

centre: refers to a point at the centre of a circle from which any distance from the circle is equal

centre of enlargement: the point about which a shape is enlarged

centre of rotation: a point about which when you rotate a shape through some angle other than 360°, you see the exact same shape

chord: any straight line joining two points on the circumference

circumference: the outline of the circle

coefficient: the number used to multiply a variable, it appears just before the variable. For example, $2x$ means two times the variable x

co-interior (supplementary) angles: a pair of angles that are between two parallel lines on the same side of another transversal line that cuts the two parallel lines. Co-interior angles sum to 180 degrees

combined event: two or more events occur at the same time or one after another

common difference: constant (unchanging) difference between the value of terms

common ratio: the fixed amount you multiply by to get from one term to the next in a geometric sequence

complement: objects that are not members of a given set

composite bar chart: a graph where each bar displays multiple data points stacked in a single row or column

composite function: functions combined when the output of one function becomes the input of another

compound interest: an amount payable for borrowing or investing money, which is added to the principal

compound shape: a shape made up of two or more smaller shapes

congruent: congruent objects have the same shape and the same size

conjecture: a statement that is yet to be proved

conjugate surds: the conjugate of $a + \sqrt{b}$, where a and b are integers, is $a - \sqrt{b}$ consecutive following one after the other

consecutive: following one after the other in a sequence, for example, 2, 4 and 6 are consecutive even numbers

constant: a term that always has the same value

continuous: data that is quantitative and can be measured

correlation: the strength of a relationship between two variables

corresponding angles: a pair of angles that are on the same side of two parallel lines cut by another transversal line. Corresponding angles are equal

cosine ratio: the ratio between the adjacent side and the hypotenuse in a right-angled triangle

cosine rule: a formula connecting the three sides of a triangle and one of the angles.

cost price: how much you pay for an item

counter example: an example that satisfies the required condition but leads to a different conclusion

cross-section: the shape created by the intersection of a solid by a plane

cube number: a number formed by multiplying an integer by itself twice

cubic sequence: sequence with a general term that includes $T_n = an^3 + bn^2 + cn + d$

cumulative frequency: a running total of frequencies

cumulative frequency diagram: a graph drawn by plotting the cumulative frequency against the upper class boundary

currency exchange rate: the amount of one currency that is worth 1 unit of another currency

decagon: a ten-sided polygon

decimal: reference to the decimal system, which is a number system based on tens. A decimal point is the dot separating whole ones from the decimal part of a number

decrease: to make smaller

denominator: the bottom number in a fraction, indicating how many equal parts the whole one is divided into

density: the mass of a unit of volume (e.g. $1 \, cm^3$) of a material

deposit: the amount paid at the start of a purchase

depreciation: the amount an item decreases in value

diagonal: a line segment formed in a polygon by joining two vertices that are not consecutive

diameter: a straight line joining one end of the circle to the other passing through the centre

direct proportion: two values that both increase in the same ratio

discount: an amount by which the price of an object is reduced

discrete: data that is quantitative and can be counted

domain: the set of all input values of a function

dual bar chart: graph of data using two bars besides each other. The bars can be arranged vertically or horizontally

element: a member of a given set

empty set: a set with no members

enlargement: a transformation that makes a given shape smaller or larger by a given scale factor

equidistant: the same distance away from a point or line

equivalent fractions: fractions with the same value

event: the outcomes of a probability experiment

expand: in algebra, we expand a bracket by multiplying the terms to express them as sums or difference of two or more terms. To expand algebraic terms is also to remove the brackets

expected frequency: the amount of times an event should occur

experimental probability: an estimate of a probability of an event from the results of an experiment

exponential decay: when a quantity decreases by the same percentage every year (or every day, or every month)

exponential function: a function where the base number remains constant and the exponent is a variable

exponential growth: when a quantity increases by the same percentage every year (or every day, or every month)

exponential sequence: sequence that has a constant ratio between the terms

expression: a group of numbers and letters linked by operation signs

exterior angle: an angle outside a polygon on a straight line with the interior angle

factorise: factorise is the reverse of expand, where we put back the brackets to express the algebraic expressions in product form

fair: no particular event is favoured; all outcomes are equally likely

first difference: difference between terms in a sequence

formula: a general rule or equation showing the relationship between unknown quantities

frequency distributions: data organised as an ordered list and frequencies

frustum: a cone or pyramid that has been cut in a plane parallel to its base

function: the mathematical relationship from a set of inputs to a set of outputs

gradient (slope): the rate of ascent or descent of a line

grouped data: data ordered and sorted into groups

heptagon: a seven-sided polygon

hexagon: a six-sided polygon

highest common factor (HCF): the greatest common factor that two or more numbers share

hypotenuse: the side of a right-angled triangle that is opposite the right angle. The hypotenuse is also the longest side of a right-angled triangle

hypotenuse: longest side in a right-angled triangle

improper fraction: a fraction greater than 1, where the numerator is greater than the denominator. Conversely, a proper fraction is a fraction less than 1, where the numerator is less than the denominator

increase: to make larger

independent event: an event that is unrelated to another event

index (plural indices): a small number written as a superscript. an index indicates how many times a number is multiplied by itself

input: the value (x) entered into a function f(x)

inscribed: used to describe a shape that is enclosed (fits nicely) in another figure

instalment: the amount of each monthly payment when an item is bought with a deposit

integers: numbers that do not contain fractions or decimals. Integers can be positive, negative or zero

interest: a sum of money added to an amount invested or borrowed

intersection: elements that are common to given sets

interior angle: an angle inside a polygon formed by two adjacent sides

interquartile range: a measure of spread equal to the upper quartile subtract the lower quartile in a set of data

inverse function: the reverse of an original function

inverse proportion: a relationship between two values where an increase in one leads to a decrease in the other

irrational numbers: are numbers that cannot be expressed in the form $\frac{a}{b}$

irregular polygon: a polygon where not all the sides are of the same length and not all angles are equal

kite: a four-sided polygon with two pairs of adjacent sides with equal length

like terms: terms with the same variable raised to the same power

line: a one-dimensional figure that continues endlessly in both directions

line of best fit: a trend line drawn on a scatter diagram to best represent the trend of the values

line of symmetry: a straight line that divides a shape into two identical halves. The two halves are a reflection of each other in the line of symmetry

line segment: a line connecting two endpoints

line symmetry: if a shape has line symmetry, the shape can be divided into two identical halves

linear equation: an equation in which the highest variable power is 1

linear function: a function whose graph is a straight line

linear inequalities: two linear expressions are compared by inequality symbols

linear regression: determining a line that best represents the general trend of a data set, with two or more variables

logarithmic function: an inverse function to exponentiation

loss: to sell something for less than it cost

lowest common multiple (LCM): the smallest common multiple that two or more numbers share

magnitude: the size of something

mathematical modelling: a method of using maths (numbers, shapes, graphs and equations) to represent and understand real-life situations so that we can solve problems or predict what is likely to happen

mean: the average calculated by finding the total of values in a set of data and dividing by number of values in the set

median: the average calculated by finding the middle value in an ordered set of data

midpoint: a point precisely in the middle of a line or between two specific points

mixed number: a number consisting of a whole number and a fraction

mode: the average found by identifying which value occurs most in a set of data

model: a simplified mathematical representation of a more complex situation, diagrams, graphs, functions, simulations and tables of data can all be used to model situations

mutually exclusive event: events that cannot both happen

natural numbers: the numbers 0, 1, 2, 3, …

nonagon: a nine-sided polygon

nth term: the term in any position, the general term

numerator: the top number of a fraction, indicating how many parts are included

obtuse angle: an angle greater than 90 degrees but smaller than 180 degrees

octagon: an eight-sided polygon

order of rotational symmetry: the number of times you see the exact same shape when you rotate the shape through 360°

orientation: the position of a shape relative to a grid

output: the value resulting from a function

parallel lines: lines that are equidistant to each other and never meet

parallel: lines that are side by side and have the same distance continuously between them

parallelogram: a four-sided polygon where opposite sides are parallel and of equal length

pentagon: a five-sided polygon

percentiles: dividing a data set into 100 equal parts

perimeter: the distance around the outside edge of a shape

period: the length of one complete cycle of the function

perpendicular: meeting at precisely 90°

perpendicular bisector: a straight line that cuts another line into two equal halves at right angle

perpendicular lines: lines that are at a right angle to each other

pie chart: a graph using a divided circle where each section represents a percentage of the total

plane: a flat two-dimensional surface

point: an exact location, often indicated by a dot

position-to-term rule: instruction for finding the term in any position in a sequence

prime number: a number that has only two distinct factors, 1 and itself. A prime factor is a factor which is a prime number

principal: the original size of a loan or investment

prism: a solid shape whose cross-section is constant

product: the result of multiplying numbers together

profit: to sell something for more than it cost

proper fraction: a fraction less than 1, in which the numerator is less than the denominator

proportion: two quantities are in proportion if they increase or decrease at the same rate

pyramid: a solid shape that has a flat shape at its base and triangles that meet at a point

Pythagoras' theorem: in a right-angled triangle, the square of the hypothenuse is equal to the sum of the squares of the other two sides

quadrant: the coordinate plane is divided by the axes into four quadrants

quadratic expression: an algebraic expression where the highest power of the variable is 2

quadratic function: a function containing one or more terms with a squared variable, and no variables with a power higher than 2.

quadratic sequence: sequence with a general term that includes

quadrilateral: a polygon with four sides and four angles

quartiles: a sorted data set is divided into quarters by finding the median of all the values, then finding the median of the lower and upper halves of the values

range: the difference between the lowest and highest values in a set of data

radius (plural radii): a straight line from the centre to the circumference

rate: ratio comparing two different quantities that use different units of measurement

rate of interest: the percentage used to calculate the amount of interest added to an investment or loan

ratio: a comparison of the size of two or more quantities

rational expression: a fraction where the numerator and denominator contains polynomial; a rational expression is an algebraic fraction

rational numbers: are numbers that can be expressed in the form $\frac{a}{b}$

rationalise the denominator: a method used to remove any surds from the denominator of a fraction

reciprocal: the number you would multiply a number by to get 1. The reciprocal of a is $\frac{1}{a}$; the reciprocal of the fraction $\frac{a}{b}$ is $\frac{b}{a}$

rectangle: a four-sided polygon where opposite sides are of equal length and all four angles are right angles

recurring decimal: a decimal that has a digit or a set of digits that continue repeatedly

real number: a number which can be written as a decimal

reflection: a transformation which is an exact image of a shape about a line of symmetry

reflex angle: an angle greater than 180 degrees but smaller than 360 degrees

regular polygon: a polygon where all sides are equal in length and all angles are equal

relative frequency: how often an event occurs related to all the outcomes

rhombus: a four-sided polygon where all four sides are of equal length and opposite sides are parallel

right angle: an angle that is exactly 90 degrees

right pyramid: a pyramid whose apex is directly above the centre of its base

root: a number that can be multiplied by itself a number of times to get a number, e.g. a square root is a number multiplied by itself once and a cube root is a number multiplied by itself twice

roots (zeros): the individual values of x in a quadratic equation where it intersects the x-axis

rotation: a transformation that turns an exact image of a shape around a point

rotational symmetry: if a shape has rotational symmetry, you see the exact same shape after some rotation other than 360°

rules of indices: rules to follow when calculating with indices

scalar: a numerical quantity with no direction

scale factor: the ratio between two corresponding sides of similar shapes

scatter diagram: a diagram where points are plotted to show the relationship between two variables

secant: a secant line of a circle is a straight line that intersect the circle at two points. The secant line extends outside the circle

second difference: difference between the first differences

sector: a part circle formed by two radii and an arc

sectors (major and minor): the region of a circle bounded by an arc and two radii; if the sector is bigger than a semicircle it is called a major sector, if it is smaller than the semicircle it is called the minor sector

segment (major and minor): the region bounded by a chord and an arc of a circle; a major segment is bigger than a semicircle, a minor arc is smaller than a semicircle.

selling price: how much you sell an item for

semicircle: half a circle

sequence: an ordered set of numbers that forms a pattern according to a rule

set: a collection of objects that share a common property

similar: similar objects have the same shape but a different size

simple interest: an amount payable for borrowing or investing money, usually paid at the end of a year

simplest form: a fraction that has been written such that the numerator and denominator have no common factors

simplify: to write a fraction or an algebraic expression in its simplest form

simultaneous equations: a pair of equations with two unknowns that can be solved at the same time

sine ratio: the ratio between the opposite side and the hypotenuse in a right-angled triangle

sine rule: in any triangle, the ratio of the sine of an angle to the length of the side opposite the angle is always the same

speed: the rate at which an object is moving

square: a four-sided polygon where all four sides are of equal length and all four angles are right angles

square number: a number formed by multiplying an integer by itself

square number: any number multiplied by itself

standard form: a mathematical way to express very large or very small numbers in the form $a \times 10^n$, where n is a positive or negative integer, and $1 \leqslant a < 10$

stem-and-leaf diagram: a diagram that shows groups of data arranged by place value

subject: the single variable that is expressed in terms of other variables

subscript notation: way of writing the nth term as t_n

subset: a set that is wholly contained within another set

sum: the result of adding numbers together

surds: roots that cannot be expressed as rational numbers

tangent: a straight line that touches the circle at exactly one point

tangent ratio: the ratio between the opposite and adjacent sides in a right-angled triangle

term: a single part of an expression separated by + or −, or a member of a sequence or pattern

terminating decimal: a decimal with a finite number of decimal places

term-to-term rule: instruction for finding the next term in a sequence

theoretical probability: the number of successful outcomes divided by the number of possible outcomes

third difference: difference between the second differences

trapezium: a four-sided polygon with one pair of parallel sides

triangle numbers/triangular numbers: numbers that can make equilateral triangle patterns, for example 1, 3, 6, 10 etc.

trigonometric function: a function defined using a right-angled triangle. Cosine, sine and tangent are the three main functions

union: the elements of two or more sets combined

universal set: the set of all objects that are being considered

variable: a variable in algebra refers to a letter that represents a number that varies

vector: a quantity that has both magnitude and direction

vertex: a point where two lines meet

vertex of a graph: the highest (maximum) or lowest (minimum) point on the graph

vertically opposite angles: when two straight lines intersect, the pair of angles vertically opposite to each are called vertically opposite angles

volume (capacity): the 3D space taken up by a solid shape

> Index

2-D shapes
    areas and perimeters 298–315
    similar 233–8
    symmetry in 219–28
    transformation of 461–90
3-D objects, similar 238–43

accuracy 29–33
acute-angled triangles 111
acute angles 89
addition
    algebraic fractions 181–2, 183
    fractions 46–7
    vectors 494–7
adjacent side 379
algebra 157–96
    expanding brackets 164–9
    forming expressions 157–60
    indices 192–5
    substitution 160–2
algebraic fractions 180–3
    adding and subtracting 181–2, 183
    multiplying and dividing 182–3
    simplifying 180–1
alternate angles 95
alternate segment 450
alternate segment theorem 450–1
amplitude 633
angles
    acute 89
    alternate 95
    at a point 92–3, 98
    in circles 436–43
    co-interior (supplementary) 96
    corresponding 95
    cyclic quadrilaterals 445–8
    of depression 389–90
    drawing 87–9
    of elevation 389–90
    exterior 112–14, 121–2, 125–6
    interior 110, 121–2, 125–6
    measuring 87–9
    obtuse 89
    properties 92–4
    reflex 89
    right 89
    of rotation 471
    in same segment 441–3
    in semicircle 437
    on straight line 92
    subtended 437
    supplementary 96
    on transversal lines 95–8
    types 89
    vertically opposite 96
    see also trigonometry
arcs of circles 310–11, 425
    major 423, 438
    minor 423, 438
area 298–315
    circles 305–12
    compound shape 313–15
    parallelograms 302–4
    rectangles 298–302
    similar shapes 238–43
    trapeziums 302–5
    triangles 298–302, 406–9
    units of 296
assumptions 654
asymptotes 639–40
averages 537

bar charts 534, 546–52
bearings 99–106
bias 580
bimodal data 538
bisection 94, 290, 465
brackets, expansion 164–9

calculator use, standard form
    calculation 140–2
capacity
    units of 296
    see also volume
centre of circle 423
    angle at 438–41
centre of enlargement 475
centre of rotation 222, 471
charts
    bar charts 534, 546–52
    pie charts 546, 549
    see also graphs
chords of circles 423
    length 425–9
circles
    angle properties 436–43
    arcs 310–11, 425
    area 305–12
    circumference 305–12, 423
    diameter 305, 423
    radius 305, 423
    sectors 310–12
    segments 309, 423
    tangents to 424, 429–33
circumference 305–12, 423
co-interior (supplementary) angles 96

coefficients 157
column vectors 490, 497
combined events 590–1
common difference 619
common factors 170
common ratio 625
complement of a set 512–13
composite bar charts 547
composite functions 373–4
compound interest 78–80
compound shapes 303
    area and perimeter 313–15
    surface area and volume 337–8
cones 324–5
    surface area 327, 329–31
    volume 325–6
congruency 228–31, 316, 462
conjecture 239
conjugate surds 151, 153, 154
consecutive terms 613
constant 166
    of proportionality 214
continuous data 535
conversion, metric units 296–7
coordinate system 265–8
coordinates 265
    negative 266–7
correlation 562–70
    negative 562
    positive 562
    zero 562
corresponding angles 95
cosine function 396–7
cosine graph 633
cosine ratio 383–5
cosine rule 413–14
    combining with sine rule 415–17
cost price 75
    percentage profit and loss 75
counter example 151
cross-section 316
cube numbers 9
cube roots 21–2
cubic functions 367
cubic sequences 621, 622–4
cuboids 316
cumulative frequency 571
    diagrams 571–4
    percentiles 572–4
    quartiles 572–4
    tables 571–4
currency exchange rates 64
cyclic quadrilateral 445–8

cylinders
  surface area 321–2
  volume 317–19

data
  classifying 535–7
  grouped 542–4, 546
  tabulating 535–7
decagon 122
decimals 38, 49
  and percentages 49–51
  recurring 41–2, 51
  rounding 26–8
  terminating 51
  working with 38–43
decrease 65
degrees 87
denominator 43
  rationalising 153–4
density 64
deposit 75
depreciation 72
depression, angle of 389–90
diagonals, quadrilateral 116
diagrams
  cumulative frequency 571–4
  modelling with 660–3
  sample space 590–1
  scatter 559–61
  stem-and-leaf 547–8
  tree 598–603
  Venn 511–12, 516–30, 594–6
diameter 305, 423
difference of two squares 168, 170–1
differences
  common 619
  first 620
  second 620
  third 621
direct proportion 212–13, 215
discounts 75–6
discrete data 535
distances
  between two points 268–70
  shortest 391
division
  algebraic fractions 182–3
  fractions 47–8
domain 370
dual bar charts 547

elements of a set 505
elevation, angle of 389–90
empty set 513–14
enlargement(s) 462, 475–80, 486–8
  centre of 475
  scale factor 475, 486
equal vectors 492
equations
  fractional 189–92

linear 184–7
  quadratic *see* quadratic equations
  simultaneous linear 201–6
  straight line 284–5
equidistance 267
equilateral triangles 111
equivalent fractions 43–5, 49–51
estimation 32–3
events 580
  combined 590–1
  fair 580
  independent 589
  mutually exclusive 590
  not occurring, probability 583
expansion, of brackets 164–9
expected frequency 588–9
experimental probability 588
exponential decay 80–2
exponential functions 631
exponential growth 80–2
exponential sequences 625–6
expressions, algebraic 158
  expanding brackets 164–9
  factorising 170–80
  forming 157–60
  substituting values in 160–2
  see also quadratic expressions
exterior angles
  polygons 121–2, 125–6
  triangles 112–14

factorisation 170–80
  by extracting common factors 170
  by quadratic identities 170–4
  quadratic expressions 175–80
  solving quadratic equations by 188–9
factors, prime 14–15
fair events 580
first difference 620
formulas 162
  cosine rule 413–14, 415–17
  quadratic 345
  rearranging 199–201
  sine rule 410–12, 415–17
  subject 199
fractional equations 189–92
fractional indices 136–8
fractions
  algebraic 180–3
  calculating with 46–9
  equivalent 43–5, 49–51
  and percentages 49–51
  simplifying 44
frequency
  expected 588–9
  relative 588
frequency distributions 546, 553
frequency tables 542
frustrums 333–4
function notation 356–7

functions 356–74, 631–49
  asymptotes 639–40
  composite 373–4
  cubic 367
  domain 370
  exponential 631
  graphs of 361–3
  inverse 371–3
  linear 367
  logarithmic 641–3
  modelling with 663–5
  quadratic 367, 637–9
  range 370
  reciprocal 367
  recognising types by shape of graph 363–7
  transforming graphs of 645–6
  trigonometric 631–4

general term 613
geometric vectors 499–500
gradient (slope)
  line segment 271–5
  of straight line 279–82
graphic display calculators
  in data analysis 542–5
  and linear regression 565–6
  and recognising function types 363–7
  solving trigonometric equations with 399–400
graphs
  asymptotes 639–40
  of functions 361–3
  modelling with 663–5
  quadratic equations 342–4
  scatter diagrams 559–61
  straight line 275–9
  transforming 645–6
  trigonometric 633–4
  see also charts
grouped data 542–4, 546

HCF (highest common factor) 17–18
heptagon 122
hexagon 122
highest common factor (HCF) 17–18
horizontal lines 275, 277
hypotenuse 249, 378

imperial system 296
improper fractions 45
increase 65
independent events 589
index/indices 131–5, 192–5
  fractional 136–8
  negative 133–4
  notation 9, 136–7
  rules of 132–3, 134, 192–3
  see also powers
inequalities, in one variable (linear)
  see linear inequalities

infinity 370
input 356
inscribed shapes 450
instalments 75–6
integers 8
intercepts, *y* 279
interest 77–80
    compound 78–80
    simple 77–8
interest rates 77
interior angles
    polygons 121–2, 125–6
    triangles 110
interquartile range (IQR) 540–1, 572–4
intersection, of sets 518
inverse functions 371–3
inverse proportion 214–15
investment
    compound interest 78–80
    simple interest 77–8
irrational numbers 10
irregular polygons 121, 125–6
isosceles triangles 111

kites 117, 118

LCM (lowest common multiple) 18–19
length, units of 296
like terms 163
line of best fit 563–5
line segments 86
    bisecting 94, 290
    gradient of 271–5
    midpoint of 267
line symmetry 219–22
linear equations 184–7
    simultaneous 201–6
linear functions 367
linear inequalities 206
    representing on graphic display
        calculator 209–12
    representing graphically 207–12
    representing on number line 206–7
linear regression 565–6
lines 86, 94–9
    parallel 285–7
    perpendicular 94, 287–9
    of symmetry 220
    transversal 94, 95–8
    see also straight lines
logarithmic functions 641–3
loss 75
lower quartile 540, 574
lowest common multiple (LCM) 18–19

magnitude, of vectors 490, 498–9
major arc 423, 438
major sector 309, 423
major segment 423
mapping diagrams 358–61

mass, units of 296
mathematical modelling 652–68
    description 653–7
    with diagrams 660–3
    with functions and graphs 663–5
    with sequences and patterns 657–9
    steps 653
mean 538
    grouped data 546
median 538, 540
mensuration 295–339
    units of measure 295–8
    see also area; perimeter; surface area;
        volume
metric system 296–7
midpoints 267
minor arc 423, 438
minor sector 309, 423
minor segment 423
mixed numbers 45
mode 538
models *see* mathematical modelling
multiplication
    algebraic fractions 182–3
    fractions 47–8
    of vector by scalar 493
mutually exclusive events 590

natural numbers 2–5
negative coordinates 266–7
negative correlation 562
negative indices 133–4
negative numbers 52–4
nonagon 122
notation
    function 356–7
    index 9, 136–7
    set builder 506
    subscript 613
    vector 491
*n*th term 613
numbers 1–34
    irrational 10
    order of operations 55
    powers 9
    prime factors 14–15
    prime 5–8
    rational 10
    roots 7, 20–2
    rounding 24–8
    types 2–13
numerator 43

obtuse-angled triangles 111
obtuse angles 89
octagon 122
operations, order of 55
opposite side 379
order of operations 55
order of rotational symmetry 222–4

orientation 462
outcomes, probability 580
output 356

parallel lines 285–7
parallelograms 117, 118–19
    area and perimeter 302–4
patterns 613–16
    modelling with 657–9
pentagon 121
percentage increase and decrease 72
percentage loss 75
percentage profit 75
percentages 69–77
    and decimals and fractions 49–51
    reverse 73
percentiles 572–4
perimeter
    circumference 305–12, 423
    compound shape 313–15
    parallelograms 302–4
    rectangles 298–302
    trapeziums 302–4
    triangles 298–302
period 633
perpendicular bisectors 94, 290, 465
perpendicular distance 465
perpendicular lines 94, 287–9
pie charts 546, 549
planes 94
points 86
polygons 120–8
    angle properties 122–5
    exterior angles 121–2, 125–6
    interior angles 121–2, 125–6
    irregular 121, 125–6
    regular 121
    types 121–2
position-to-term rule 618
positive correlation 562
powers 9
    see also index/indices
prime factors 14–15
prime numbers 5–8
principal 77
prisms
    surface area 321–2
    volume 316–17, 318
probability 580–608
    combined events 590–1
    definition 582
    of event not occurring 583
    experimental 588
    independent events 589
    mutually exclusive events 590
    sample space diagrams 590–1
    theoretical 580, 587
    tree diagrams in 598–603
    Venn diagrams in 594–6
probability scale 581

product 54
profit 75
proper fractions 45
proportion 65, 212–15
    direct 212–13, 215
    inverse 214–15
protractors, using 87–90, 101
pyramids 324–5
    surface area 327–9
    volume 325–6
Pythagoras' theorem 249–62
    applications of 254–9
    solving problems using 386–8, 393
    statement of 250
    in three dimensions 259–62
    in two dimensions 249–53

quadrants 266
quadratic equations 342–52
    graphs of 342–4
    maximum and minimum values
        346–7
    solving by factorisation 188–9
    solving on a graphic display
        calculator 347–52
    solving using formula 345
quadratic expressions 175
    difference of two squares 168, 170–1
    factorising 175–80
    roots (zeros) 342
quadratic formula 345
quadratic functions 367, 637–9
quadratic sequences 620, 622–3
quadrilaterals 116–20
    cyclic 445–8
    diagonals 116
quartiles 539–44, 572–4

radicals see surds
radius/radii 305, 423
    and tangent 429–33
range 537–9
    of function 370
    interquartile (IQR) 540–1, 572–4
rates 64–9
rational expressions 183
rational numbers 10
rationalising the denominator 153–4
ratios 60–3
    common 625
    and similar shapes 233–6
real number 370
reciprocal functions 367
reciprocals 11, 48
rectangles 117
    area and perimeter 298–302
recurring decimals 41–2, 51
reflections 462, 465–7, 487–8
reflex angles 89
regular polygons 121

relative frequency 588
reverse percentages 73
rhombus 117
right-angled triangles 111
    Pythagoras' theorem 249–62
right angles 89
right pyramids 325
roots 7, 20–2
    of quadratic expressions 342
rotational symmetry 222–6
    order of 222–4
rotation(s) 462, 471–3, 486–8
    angle of 471
    centre of 222, 471
rounding 24–8
    to decimal places 26–8
    to significant figures 29–32
    whole numbers 24–5
rules of indices 132–3, 134, 192–3

sample space 580
sample space diagrams 590–1
scalars 490
    multiplying vectors by 493
scale factor, of enlargement 475, 486
scalene triangles 111
scatter diagrams 559–61
secant 424
second difference 620
sectors of circles 310–12
    major and minor 309, 423
segments of a circle 309, 423
    major and minor 423
selling price 75
    percentage profit and loss 75
semicircles 423
    angles in 437
sequences 612–28
    combined 627
    cubic 621, 622–4
    exponential 625–6
    finding general rule 618–22
    finding terms in 614
    modelling with 657–9
    patterns and 613–16
    quadratic 620, 622–3
set builder notation 506
sets 505–30
    complement 512–13
    empty 513–14
    intersections 518
    set builder notation 506
    subsets 506, 514–15
    unions 518
    universal 508–9, 518
    Venn diagrams 511–12, 516–19,
        594–6
shapes
    areas and perimeters 298–315
    similar 233–8

symmetry in 219–28
    transformation of 461–90
significant figures 29
similar figures 231
similar shapes 233–8
    area 238–43
similar solids 238–43
similar triangles 232–3
similarity 231–8
simple interest 77–8
simplest form 44
simplifying algebraic fractions 180–1
simplifying fractions 44
simultaneous linear equations 201–6
sine function 395–6
sine graph 633
sine ratio 383–5
sine rule 410–12
    combining with cosine rule 415–17
slide see translations
slope see gradient
sloping lines 275, 277
solids (3-D objects), similar 238–43
speed 64, 65–6
spheres
    surface area 334–5
    volume 334–5
spread see range
square numbers 9, 613
square roots 7, 20–1
squares (power), difference of two 168,
    170–1
squares (shape) 110
standard form 138–45
    calculations with calculator 140–2
    calculations without calculator 143–5
stem-and-leaf diagrams 547–8
straight lines 275–85
    angles on 92
    drawing 283
    equations of 284–5
    gradient of 279–82
    graphs 275–9
    midpoint of segment 267
    types 275
    y-intercept 279
subject of formula 199
    changing 199–201
subscript notation 613
subsets 506, 514–15
substitution 160–2
subtended angle 437
subtraction
    algebraic fractions 181–2, 183
    fractions 46–7
    vectors 494–7
supplementary (co-interior) angles 96
surds 145–54
    adding 147–9
    conjugate 151, 153, 154

dividing 152–3
multiplying 150–1
rationalising the denominator 153–4
simplifying 145–7
subtracting 147–9
surface area
  compound shape 337–8
  cone 327, 329–31
  cylinder 321–2
  prism 321–2
  pyramid 327–9
  similar solids 242
  sphere 334–5
symmetry
  line 219–22
  lines of 220
  rotational 222–6
  in two dimensions 219–28

tables 358–61
  cumulative frequency 571–4
  frequency 542
tangent-chord theorem 450–1
tangent function 397–8
tangent graph 634
tangent ratio 379–82
tangents, to circles 424, 429–33
term-to-term rule 614–17
terminating decimals 51
terms 158, 613
  collecting like 163
  consecutive 613
  general 613
  nth 613
theoretical probability 580, 587
third difference 621
three-dimensional objects, similar 238–43
time 63–4
transformations 461–90
  combining 487–8
  enlargements 462, 475–80, 486–90
  graphs of functions 645–6
  reflections 462, 465–7, 487–8
  reversing 486–7
  rotations 462, 471–3, 486–8
  translation 462–3, 487–8, 645–6

translations 462–3, 487–8, 645–6
  described using vectors 462
transversal lines 94, 95–8
trapeziums 117
  area and perimeter 302–5
tree diagrams 598–603
triangle numbers 12
triangles 110–15
  area 298–302, 406–9
  classification 111
  equilateral 111
  exterior angles 112–14
  interior angles 110
  perimeter 298–302
  similar 232–3
  see also right-angled triangles
triangular numbers 613
trigonometric equations
  solving with graphic display
      calculator 399–400
  solving without graphic display
      calculator 404–5
trigonometric functions 631–4
trigonometric ratios 378–85
  exact values 401–3
  as functions 395–8
  solving problems using 386–8
trigonometry 378–419
  angles of elevation and depression
      389–90
  calculating angles 382, 408
  calculating area of triangle 406–9
  calculating side lengths 380
  shortest distances 391
  sine and cosine ratios 383–5
  sine and cosine rules 410–17
  solving problems using 386–8
  tangent ratio 379–82
  in three dimensions 393
two-dimensional shapes
  areas and perimeters 298–315
  similar 233–8
  symmetry in 219–28
  transformation of 461–90

union of sets 518
units
  of area 296
  of capacity 296
  imperial system 296
  of length 296
  of mass 296
  metric system 296–7
  of volume 296
units of measure 295–8
universal set 508–9, 518
upper quartile 540, 574

variables 157
vectors 490–500
  adding 494–7
  column 490, 497
  equal 492
  geometric 499–500
  magnitude 490, 498–9
  multiplying by scalar 493
  notation 491
  subtracting 494–7
  translations described using 462
Venn diagrams 511–12
  in probability 594–6
  three sets on 523–30
  two sets on 516–19
vertex/vertices 86, 346
vertical lines 275, 277
vertically opposite angles 96
vertices 86, 346
volume
  compound shape 337–8
  cone 325–6
  cylinder 317–19
  prism 316–17, 318
  pyramid 325–6
  similar solids 238–43
  sphere 334–5
  units of 296

y-intercept 279

zero correlation 562
zeros, of quadratic expressions 342

> Acknowledgements

The authors and publishers acknowledge the following sources of copyright material and are grateful for the permissions granted. While every effort has been made, it has not always been possible to identify the sources of all the material used, or to trace all copyright holders. If any omissions are brought to our notice, we will be happy to include the appropriate acknowledgements on reprinting.

Cambridge International copyright material in this publication is reproduced under licence and remains the intellectual property of Cambridge Assessment International Education.

Cambridge Assessment International Education bears no responsibility for the example answers to questions taken from its past question papers which are contained in this publication.

Thanks to the following for permission to reproduce images:

Cover FactoryTh/Getty Images; *Inside* **Unit 1** Cosmin4000/Getty Images; **Unit 2** PM Images/Getty Images; **Unit 3** Troyek/Getty Images; **Unit 4** Howard George/Getty Images; **Unit 5** Westend61/Getty Images; **Unit 6** Arctic-Images/Getty Images; **Unit 7** Fotofrog/Getty Images; **Unit 8** Llepod/Getty Images; **Unit 9** Jorg Greuel/Getty Images; **Unit 10** KTS Design/Getty Images; **Unit 11** Karl Tapales/Getty Images; **Unit 12** Gremlin/Getty Images; **Unit 13** Ivan/Getty Images; **Unit 14** Westend61/Getty Images; **Unit 15** Malorny/Getty Images; **Unit 16** Abstract Aerial Art/Getty Images; **Unit 17** Dina Belenko/Getty Images; **Unit 18** Paul Edmondson/Getty Images; **Unit 19** Matthew Ireland/Getty Images; **Unit 20** Ilona Nagy/Getty Images; **Unit 21** Xuanyu Han/Getty Images; **Unit 22** Ruhey/Getty Images; **Unit 23** Oxygen/Getty Images; **Unit 24** MirageC/Getty Images; Puttapon/Getty Images

Graphic display calculator emulator screenshots are reproduced with permission from Casio Electronics Co. Ltd.

We would like to acknowledge the work of author, Nick Asker, who contributed to reworking some material in this Coursebook.